The World of
Musical Comedy

The World of

The story of the American musical stage as

STANLEY GREEN

Musical Comedy

told through the careers of its foremost composers and lyricists

FOREWORD BY DEEMS TAYLOR

Revised and Enlarged Edition

South Brunswick and New York:
A. S. Barnes and Company
London: Thomas Yoseloff Ltd

© 1960 Ziff-Davis Publishing Company
© 1968 A. S. Barnes and Co., Inc.
Library of Congress Catalogue Card Number: 67-24246

A. S. Barnes and Co., Inc.
Cranbury, New Jersey 08512

Thomas Yoseloff Ltd
18 Charing Cross Road
London W. C. 2, England

First Edition 1960
Second Printing 1962
Third Printing 1966
Fourth Printing 1967

Revised Edition 1968

6746
Printed in the United States of America

FOR MY MOTHER AND FATHER,
WHO FIRST INTRODUCED ME TO
THE WORLD OF MUSICAL COMEDY

by Deems Taylor

STRICTLY SPEAKING, a book such as this one—like the guest of honor at a banquet—needs no introduction. Today, the American musical is admittedly without an equal anywhere in the world, although as recently as during the Gay Nineties it was the Viennese operetta that ruled the entertainment world. The evolution of this strictly American art form has taken place within the space of one lifetime—mine.

I witnessed many of the events chronicled in this book and knew many of the men who made these events possible. Victor Herbert encouraged me to study music and become a composer when he heard a college show that I had written; my first professional work was a show that was actually produced on Broadway by Charles Dillingham; I distinguished myself by delivering a tribute to the music of Jerome Kern over C.B.S. in 1941 in which I stated that I had long been a devoted "Fern can;" and not too long ago I wrote one of the ever-growing list of biographies of Richard Rodgers and Oscar Hammerstein II. Under these circumstances, I will have to leave the facts, biographical sketches, and critical estimates to the book itself and make this foreword a completely personal one.

One thing I will say before I dive into my memories, and that is that the people you are going to read about are musicians and deserve to be taken seriously as artists. The creators of musical comedy in America are a body of men (and some women) who have consistently refused to do less than the best that was in them. Anyone who works in a popular medium is constantly faced with pressures from his investors not to experiment, not to innovate; to write down, to compromise, and to be safe. If the creators of musical comedy had allowed themselves to have this sort of view of what would be successful, there would be no American musicals today—we would still be listening to Viennese operettas.

I remember an evening after World War I when I was one of a group of delighted guests at a party given by Neysa McMein, the illustrator. The reason for our delight was another guest, a young man who enjoyed the double distinction of having written some Yale football songs and of having actually joined the Foreign Legion. He played and sang some of his latest songs (one, I remember, was entitled "The Bandit Band") which received loud acclaim. We agreed that they were tuneful and absolutely charming. But many of us, myself among them, also agreed that his tunes were far too tricky and his lyrics much too sophisticated ever to have any popular success. The young guest of honor denied both accusations, and he was right. His name was Cole Porter.

There was an afternoon in the thirties when I was equally dubious and equally wrong. George Gershwin had telephoned to suggest that we have lunch together and then go to the ball game. During lunch he remarked that he was just finishing an opera about Negro life in the South.

"A *what?*" I said.

"You heard me."

So back to his house we went, and he played me all four hours of the score of *Porgy and Bess*. He was right. It *was* an opera—and we never did get to the ball game.

My acquaintance with musical comedy began long, long ago, when I used to spend part of my summer vacations with my Philadelphia cousins. Among the season's attractions were the concerts in Willow Grove Park given by Victor Herbert and his orchestra. There were four of these every day, two in the afternoon and two in the evening.

One cousin and myself were Herbert idolators, and we wanted to hear all four concerts. But the question of money reared its ugly head. Each of us was given fifty cents to cover all expenses. Trolley car fare to Willow Grove and return was thirty cents. Admission to the park was another fifteen. This left us exactly five cents for dinner, if we wanted to stay for the evening. We did, naturally, so eventually we solved the problem. We would each buy five cents' worth of the cheapest and most villainous candy we could find. This, when eaten, would render the thought of any dinner abhorrent, whereat (slightly green but smiling bravely) we would happily sit through the two evening concerts, hearing excerpts from such Herbert scores as *The Wizard of the Nile, The Idol's Eye,* and his latest, *Babes in Toyland.*

Incidentally, in after years, Victor Herbert told me that if it were physically possible, he made it a point to compose at least one tune every day. I doubt if any other composer has ever equalled that record.

One important event that this book neglects to mention is the production in 1911 of a musical comedy called *The Echo,* for which I wrote the original score. In those bad old days, it was the custom for numbers to be interpolated in musical productions at the producer's whim. *The Echo* was produced by Charles Dillingham, who promptly proceeded to hire all the dancers in the world to perform in it, all of whom brought their own music. To liven up the proceedings further, Mr. Dillingham commissioned several young song writers to write individual songs which were then scattered through the production. By the time the show opened, only three of my original numbers were left in the score (although an over-optimistic publisher had already published four).

One of the young writers who had a song in *The Echo* was Jerome Kern, who was to become one of my closest friends. On opening night, legend has it, Kern was standing nervously at the back of the theatre, where he was seen by Bruce Edwards, Dillingham's manager.

"I hope your show goes well tonight, old man," Bruce said kindly to Kern.

Fourteen men said, "Thanks."

Shortly before his death in 1945, Jerry Kern came East for the rehearsals of the revival of *Show Boat.* While he was here, he was able to attend the formal meeting of the National Institute of Arts and Letters at which he was made officially a member, and thereby became the second popular composer ever to be elected to that honorary body. The only musical comedy composer to gain that honor before him was Victor Herbert, and there has been only one since—Richard Rodgers.

But popular composers have had their fans among so-called "serious" musicians nonetheless. One of the most ardent admirers of Vincent Youmans' music was Sergei Rachmaninoff, who never tired of playing his scores. You don't have to be told that Youmans was an equally ardent admirer of Rachmaninoff's music!

He was a passionate devotee of orchestral music, and the larger the orchestra the better. He thought nothing of hiring forty musicians for one of his revues (the usual allotment is twenty-eight). On the other hand, he was deeply suspicious of librettists and lyric writers—doubtless because he had suffered so much at the hands of hack collaborators. All this led to his last folly, a revue without a book. It was a potpourri of songs, (concert) dances, and pantomimes. I played a part in it, to the extent that a four-foot dummy of myself lolled against the proscenium arch doing a sort of narration job (he finally did consent to have a book, and a holy terror it was, too).

I went down to Baltimore to attend the matinee following the opening, and arrived at the theater about halfway through the performance. The book, I discovered, had been junked overnight, but what was left was pretty awful. People were stumping indignantly up the aisles, on their way to demand their money back, to all of which Youmans paid not the slightest attention. I caught his eye, and he beckoned me to stand beside him. He was radiant. "You hear that?" he murmured. "Fifty men in the orchestra pit!"

That disaster cost his backers one hundred and ninety thousand dollars.

The ranks are thinning. Of the composers who flourished during the tens-twenties-thirties-forties, very few are left. Most of them died at ages that we would consider merely middle-aged. Of the great ones, the most untimely departure was that of George Gershwin, who died at thirty-eight. Vincent Youmans died at forty-seven, Jerome Kern at sixty, and Victor Herbert and Oscar Hammerstein II at sixty-five. As this book goes to press (1960), perhaps the oldest survivor of the formative years of musical comedy is Rudolf Friml, at eighty-one.

Friml, by the way, has a system of composing that is, I think, unique. As he described it to me, he first turns on a tape recorder; then, going to the piano, he improvises for an hour. After this he listens to the playback and jots down whatever tunes he might be able to use.

Another system of composing is attributed to Irving Berlin. He is so unbelievably prolific, both as to words and music, that a rumor was started in Tin Pan Alley by jealous composers to the effect that Berlin's songs are all written by "A little colored boy" who plays them to him. I didn't know that Irving knew this story until one day, several years ago, when I was going through the MGM studios with him. As we entered his office he waved a careless hand toward an ancient upright piano that huddled in one corner, observing, "That's where the little colored boy lives."

Irving Berlin is a man whose achievement is solidly based on an appraisal of what he does and does not know. He is anything but conceited. One of the eagerly awaited events in the musical New York of the twenties was Walter Damrosch's annual New Year's Day party, to which one and all flocked, there to imbibe wassail and other beverages. You rang the bell of the Damrosch home, the front door opened a crack, revealing a hand holding a glass, and a voice said, "Drink this." You did, the door opened, you entered, and you spent a happy afternoon. It was not, incidentally, a rowdy afternoon.

At one of these, Berlin was among the guests. I heard Damrosch say, "Irving, with your talent you ought to study music seriously."

"Doctor Damrosch," said the composer, "I have a very slender talent; and if I were to study music I might end up by despising my own stuff."

"You are quite right," said Damrosch.

I have written so much about Richard Rodgers that there is little left for me to say here about him, except that he is a dear friend. But I can't write about musical comedy without at least mentioning one of our contemporary giants. Rodgers is a compartmentalist. When he is working on a show, he works literally day and night. But otherwise, he doesn't go near the piano, and never whiles away an evening playing for friends. (In this respect he is totally unlike George Gershwin, about whom Oscar Levant once said, "An evening with Gershwin is a Gershwin evening.")

It has been a privilege for me to know, and sometimes to work with, all these men. After all, there have only been three forms of musical stage entertainment in the history of Western culture that in their day have been huge money-makers and also perfected art forms. These three are Italian grand opera, the Viennese operetta, and the American musical comedy. We can be proud that one of these belongs to us.

Preface

THE WORLD OF musical comedy covers the vast, vaguely defined area between opera and vaudeville and, at times, incorporates elements of both. "Musical comedy" is, of course, a generic term that refers to the various forms of entertainment included under the more formal designation of "American musical theatre." It covers operetta, comic opera, musical play (now frequently merely called "musical"), musical comedy itself, revue, and, in the past, spectacle or extravaganza. These forms are difficult to define precisely, as they usually overlap. However, in general, the terms operetta, comic opera, and musical play denote a greater dependence on music in the telling of a story than does musical comedy. Revue and spectacle are closest to vaudeville, as they usually consist of unrelated songs, dances, and sketches.

The growth of the American musical theatre has been in the development of all its component parts, but principally the libretto. No show can succeed today on the quality of its music and lyrics alone; they must be part of the over-all fabric of the production. And that fabric is made up of all the theatrical arts that have evolved through the years.

Because music is the one essential ingredient of the musical stage, I have chosen to tell the story of *The World of Musical Comedy* through the careers of its most significant composers and lyricists. Of all the arts that are mobilized in the creation of musical comedy, music changes the least through the years; a good song is a good song whether it was written in

xiii

1900 or in 1960. It has the power to affect people's emotions long after the particular work for which it was composed has been forgotten. Indeed, it is because of their music that shows written during the early years of this century can still be revived successfully, and even the most recent attractions are known to countless people throughout the world only through the appeal of their songs.

The cooperation of many people in the preparation of *The World of Musical Comedy* has been both heartening and indispensable. I am especially indebted to four alert and knowledgeable individuals, Charles Gaynor, Irma Hunt, Frank Jacobs, and Alfred Simon for their painstaking reading of the manuscript. In addition to the writers discussed in this book who responded willingly to my requests for assistance, information has been supplied by Edward N. Waters, Helmy Kresa, Hilda Schneider, Tom Weatherly, Irving Brown, Edward Cole, Richard Maney, Chester Kopaz, and James J. Fuld. The staff of the Theatre Collection of the New York Public Library, particularly Paul Myers and William Anderson, has also been most cooperative.

For help in obtaining photographs, I wish to thank Theresa Hart of ASCAP, John Walsh of C.B.S., Lynn Farnol, Edward Jablonski, Grace McCabe, John Springer, Jay Culver of Culver Pictures, Inc., and Harry Collins of Brown Bros.

I am also most grateful to Richard Rodgers and Oscar Hammerstein II for allowing me to reprint the lyric to their first song, "Room for One More."

Most important, to my wife, Kay, my gratitude is boundless.

STANLEY GREEN

Contents

	Foreword	vii
	Preface	xiii
ONE	Prologue	1
TWO	Victor Herbert	9
THREE	George M. Cohan	25
FOUR	Rudolf Friml, Otto Harbach	37
FIVE	Sigmund Romberg	49
SIX	Jerome Kern	63
SEVEN	Irving Berlin	85
EIGHT	George and Ira Gershwin	109
NINE	Vincent Youmans	129

TEN	*Richard Rodgers and Lorenz Hart*	141
ELEVEN	*B. G. DeSylva, Lew Brown and Ray Henderson*	165
TWELVE	*Cole Porter*	181
THIRTEEN	*Howard Dietz and Arthur Schwartz, Dorothy Fields*	203
FOURTEEN	*E. Y. Harburg, Vernon Duke, Harold Arlen, Burton Lane*	219
FIFTEEN	*Harold Rome*	241
SIXTEEN	*Kurt Weill*	251
SEVENTEEN	*Richard Rodgers and Oscar Hammerstein II*	265
EIGHTEEN	*Leonard Bernstein*	289
NINETEEN	*Alan Jay Lerner and Frederick Loewe*	297
TWENTY	*Jule Styne, Betty Comden and Adolph Green*	311
TWENTY-ONE	*Frank Loesser, Richard Adler and Jerry Ross, Meredith Willson*	329
TWENTY-TWO	*Bob Merrill, Stephen Sondheim, Jerry Bock and Sheldon Harnick, Charles Strouse and Lee Adams, Tom Jones and Harvey Schmidt*	349
TWENTY-THREE	*Cy Coleman, Carolyn Leigh, Jerry Herman, Mitch Leigh and Joe Darion, John Kander and Fred Ebb*	383
TWENTY-FOUR	*Epilogue*	407
	Appendix	412
	Index	520

The World of
Musical Comedy

CHAPTER ONE

Prologue

ALTHOUGH THERE WERE earlier attempts to present dramas on the same program with music and dancing, *The Black Crook*, in 1866, was the first successful venture in America to combine the two forms of entertainment. This distinction, however, was achieved entirely by accident. In that year a French ballet company had been signed to appear at the Academy of Music in New York City, but was left without a theatre when the Academy burned down shortly before the scheduled première. At the same time, *The Black Crook*, an incredibly ridiculous melodrama loosely based on the *Faust* legend, was scheduled to be presented at Niblo's Garden. As the play seemed to have little chance of succeeding without some added attraction to lure the public, the producer hired the ballet company (and its scenery) to perform in those sequences which could utilize the services of dancing demons and spirits. The grafting may have been crude (the opening night performance lasted from 7:45 P.M. to 1:15 A.M.), but the sight of one hundred bare-limbed dancers proved to be irresistible to post-Civil War audiences. *The Black Crook* ran for sixteen months, was revived almost continually, and toured the United States for more than forty years.

Such a phenomenal success encouraged others to present similar attractions. These early attempts, however, bore little resemblance to the

1

musical theatre as we know it today; musical interludes were either forcibly inserted into dramatic sequences or performed between scenes. Moreover, the music was usually gathered from many different sources, though *Evangeline*, in 1874, did have all of its songs composed by one man, Edward E. Rice. Many of the productions of the late 1800's relied heavily on spectacular scenic effects. The leaders in this field were the Kiralfy brothers, whose *Around the World in Eighty Days* and *Excelsior* became successful because of their dazzling settings rather than the attractiveness of their melodies. *Excelsior,* presented in 1883, was the first production to feature electric lighting, an innovation that required the personal supervision of Thomas A. Edison.

During this period, many European operettas were being imported and found a large following. At the same time, however, American writers were beginning to find new and native models for characters in their plots. In 1879, Ned Harrigan and Tony Hart introduced recent immigrant types in their series of shows about the rowdy Mulligan Guards. Soon afterward, Charles Hoyt discovered the great appeal of various regional characters. Hoyt's biggest success, *A Trip to Chinatown*, featured three remarkably durable songs, "The Bowery" and "Reuben and Cynthia" by Percy Gaunt, and "After the Ball" by Charles K. Harris.

Away from the "legitimate theatre," Tony Pastor's Music Hall, which had opened on the Bowery during the Civil War, was the nation's leading variety theatre when it moved uptown to 14th Street in 1881. Pastor's type of entertainment soon led to vaudeville and, eventually, the Broadway revue.

The twentieth century began with Victor Herbert and George M. Cohan as the leading American figures in the musical theatre. In the second decade, despite many foreign operettas imported after the success of Franz Lehár's *The Merry Widow*, Guy Bolton, P. G. Wodehouse, and Jerome Kern achieved a wide following with their intimate, well-constructed Princess Theatre musicals.

The 1920's introduced such major talents as George and Ira Gershwin, Oscar Hammerstein II, Vincent Youmans, Rodgers and Hart, and Cole Porter. Nevertheless, it was not a period distinguished by many changes in the *structure* of the musical comedy theatre. Of all the musicals written and produced during that decade, only *Show Boat* was able to offer a truly adult libretto combined with superior music and lyrics.

The Thirties were years of experimentation. *Strike Up the Band* introduced political satire. In Kern's and Otto Harbach's straightforward love story, *The Cat and the Fiddle,* the music and plot were indispensable to each other. The following year, Kern and Hammerstein accomplished the same thing with *Music in the Air.* The "folk-opera" *Porgy and Bess* was the most ambitious creation of the decade; it still remains the most universally acclaimed operatic work by an American composer. The plot of *On Your Toes* was the first to have integrated ballet sequences. *Knickerbocker Holiday* made a genuine attempt to fuse a philosophical book with songs pertinent to the play's action.

The librettos of the Forties continued to show maturity. *Cabin in the Sky* made imaginative use of Negro folklore. *Lady in the Dark* probed the subconscious with more daring than was customary even in the nonmusical theatre. An unsavory character was the hero of *Pal Joey*. The most impressive work of the decade was *Oklahoma!*, the first Rodgers and Hammerstein collaboration, which artfully blended libretto, score, and dances. Its tremendous success encouraged other writers to risk unusual themes. *Bloomer Girl* was concerned with equal rights during the Civil War period. *Street Scene* took a compassionate view of the inhabitants of a New York tenement. *Finian's Rainbow* blended Irish whimsy with the sad plight of southern sharecroppers. *Brigadoon* related a tender, evocative Scottish legend. Even the writers of more traditional musical comedies kept up with the trend. Irving Berlin's *Annie Get Your Gun* and Cole Porter's *Kiss Me, Kate* were entertaining, adult stories with music and lyrics that perfectly complemented their subject matter. The decade ended with *South Pacific*, probably the most universally popular of all Rodgers and Hammerstein's works.

In the Fifties and Sixties, there was an even greater dependence on themes of substance. Marcel Pagnol, Sidney Howard, John Steinbeck, Bernard Shaw, Voltaire, Eugene O'Neill (twice), Jane Austen, Edmond Rostand, T. H. White, Thornton Wilder, Sholom Aleichem, Clifford Odets, Cervantes, and Christopher Isherwood all turned up as progenitors of some of the decades' more ambitious musicals. This was the period that also saw the emergence of the director-librettist and the director-choreographer. George Abbott* and Joshua Logan had been staging and writing musicals for many years, but it was not until the Fifties that they became such dominant double-duty talents. Abbott's dual contributions to *The Pajama Game, Damn Yankees, New Girl in Town* and *Fiorello!*, and Logan's to *South Pacific, Wish You Were Here* and *Fanny* all helped achieve the goal of unified productions. Certainly the same is true of director-librettist Abe Burrows, whose biggest successes in the two areas have been *Can-Can, Say,*

---

* The important part George Abbott has played in the careers of young writer for the musical stage has earned him the title of "apprentice's sorcerer." Since 1941, he has been the director and frequently the author of the first—or first successful—musicals by the following composers and lyricists: Hugh Martin and Ralph Blane (*Best Foot Forward*); Leonard Bernstein, Betty Comden and Adolph Green (*On the Town*); Jule Styne and Sammy Cahn (*High Button Shoes*); Frank Loesser (*Where's Charley?*); Richard Adler and Jerry Ross (*The Pajama Game*); Bob Merrill (*New Girl in Town*); Mary Rodgers and Marshall Barer (*Once Upon a Mattress*); and Jerry Bock and Sheldon Harnick (*Fiorello!*).

Darling, and *How to Succeed in Business Without Really Trying.* And while they received no credit for writing, both George S. Kaufman, director of *Guys and Dolls,* and Moss Hart, director of *My Fair Lady* and *Camelot,* could call upon their respective experience as seasoned librettists to add greater theatrical perspective to their work.

George Balanchine and Agnes de Mille were the first modern choreographers to stage entire productions. The trend continues strongly today, based largely upon the assumption that directors schooled in the dance are better equipped to endow a production with a more pronounced homogeneity of style. Among the most successful director-choreographers have been Jerome Robbins (*Bells Are Ringing, West Side Story, Gypsy, Fiddler on the Roof*), Michael Kidd (*Li'l Abner, Destry Rides Again*), Bob Fosse (*Redhead, Sweet Charity*), Gower Champion (*Bye Bye Birdie, Carnival, Hello, Dolly!, I Do! I Do!, The Happy Time*) and Joe Layton (*No Strings, George M!*). Another modern phenomenon, the producer-director, has emerged most notably in the person of Harold Prince, with *She Loves Me* and *Cabaret.*

The importance of a close relationship between story, song, and dance has helped bring about the decline of the once high-riding revue. George Lederer offered the first collection of disconnected songs and sketches in 1894. He called his entertainment *The Passing Show,* a title which was later appropriated by the Shubert brothers. Ziegfeld began his annual *Follies* in 1907, and other producers were quick to copy the yearly pattern. In the early Twenties, the *Greenwich Village Follies,* Raymond Hitchcock's *Hitchy-Koo* revues, and *George White's Scandals* were popular annual shows. They were soon joined by such other periodic pleasures as the *Music Box Revues, Earl Carroll Vanities,* and *The Grand Street Follies.*

Most of the revues of the Twenties failed to continue beyond their first year. Yet many optimistically affixed the year of their inception to create the impression that they were inaugurating an annual series: "Broncho Billy" Anderson's *Frivolities of 1920; Broadway Brevities of 1920; Snapshots of 1921; Spice of 1922;* Charles Dillingham's *Nifties of 1923;* the Shuberts' *Topics of 1923* and *Vogues of 1924;* Dillingham's *Puzzles of 1925; Bunk of 1926; Bad Habits of 1926; Bare Facts of 1926; Nic Nax of 1926; Padlocks of 1927;* etc., etc.

The sleek, sophisticated revues of Arthur Schwartz and Howard Dietz set the pattern for the early Thirties. After the Depression came the revues of social consciousness. The best of these was *Pins and Needles.* At the other extreme—and even more popular—was Olsen and Johnson's slapstick variety show, *Hellzapoppin.* The last successful year for revues was 1948, with *Make Mine Manhattan* (Richard Lewine-Arnold Horwitt), *Inside U.S.A.*

(Schwartz-Dietz), and *Lend an Ear* (Charles Gaynor) all attracting large audiences. It was no coincidence that 1948 was also the year in which television started keeping people glued to their home screens. From then on, it became necessary for a musical to tell a coherent story in order to lure people away from the variety-type entertainment TV offered without charge. Thus, from an average of fourteen revues offered each season during the Twenties, seven during the Thirties, and six during the Forties, only three a season were shown during the Fifties. Indeed, the lone revue produced on Broadway during the season of 1958–1959 was the successful French import, *La Plume de Ma Tante*. The following season, of the four offered, the only moderate success was the two-man British import, *At the Drop of a Hat*, with Michael Flanders and Donald Swann.

Off-Broadway revues, however, continue to provide a training ground for writers and performers. Ben Bagley's two *Shoestring Revues* of the mid-1950s, *The Billy Barnes Revue*, and the more recent *Mad Show*, plus the supper club revues of Julius Monk and others have all helped develop new talent for the musical theatre. Because the revue is generally looked upon as being a step below book musicals, writers who succeed in creating scores and librettos for successful book shows seldom return to revues.

For the past four decades, the primary concern of the musical theatre has been in the strengthening of librettos and in the close integration of song and story. Good musical comedy songs accomplish this integration in three general ways: by creating the proper mood; by revealing character; and by advancing the plot. "Summertime," from *Porgy and Bess*, and "Oh, What a Beautiful Mornin'," from *Oklahoma!*, are used mainly for atmosphere. Billy Bigelow's "Soliloquy" in *Carousel* expresses his deep desires and fears. "The Rain in Spain" is performed in *My Fair Lady* at a climactic moment to provide a musical outlet essential to the story. But almost every show has at least one number, such as "Shipoopi" in *The Music Man* or "Brush Up Your Shakespeare" in *Kiss Me, Kate*, that is inserted solely as an applause-catching specialty, with little regard to its application to the story line. Frequently, too, shows dealing with musical or theatrical subjects avoid the awkwardness of having people break into song in the midst of a dramatic story by using the device of a show within a show; as in *The Cat and the Fiddle*, *Pal Joey*, *Gypsy*, *Funny Girl*, and *Cabaret*.

In achieving a skillful blend of song and story, the modern musical theatre utilizes all available arts of stagecraft. No matter how well these arts are combined, however, the plots of musicals are still frequently variations of well-tested formulas. Even the daring *West Side Story* went back to Shakespeare's *Romeo and Juliet* for inspiration. The most persistent theme of all has been the Pygmalion legend, or its almost indistinguishable parallel, the Cinderella story. The process through which a drab young girl is transformed into a glamorous star or radiant beauty is a happily identifiable metamorphosis for audiences, one that has always had great appeal. Variations on this theme have included: *Mlle. Modiste* (1905), Parisian hat shop employee to prima donna; *The Firefly* (1912), Italian street singer to prima donna; *Irene* (1919), dress-shop employee to belle of the ball; *Sally* (1920), dishwasher to Ziegfeld star; *Peggy-Ann* (1926), drudge to dreamed-of adventuress; *Lady In the Dark* (1941), austere career woman to dreamed-of woman-of-the-world; *Annie Get Your Gun* (1946), hillbilly to world-famous sureshot; *Silk Stockings* (1955), stern communist to vivacious beauty; *Gypsy* (1959), talentless vaudville trouper to burlesque headliner; *Funny Girl* (1964), ugly duckling to Ziegfeld star. That *My Fair Lady* is, in Richard Maney's phrase, the classic Cinderella story is surely an important factor in its tremendous success.

To date, *My Fair Lady*, with 2,717 Broadway performances, holds the long-run record for musicals. Before *Oklahoma!* (the previous all-time box-office champion with 2,212 performances), only two musicals, *Pins and Needles* and *Hellzapoppin*, had run over 800; since *Oklahoma!* there have been twenty-three. The increasingly lengthy tenures of musicals in New York are due to a number of reasons. In the days of Victor Herbert and George M. Cohan, a Broadway run may have indicated a certain amount of prestige, but a show had to do well on the road in order to succeed financially. The depression of the early Thirties, plus the attraction of the movies, greatly reduced the number of touring companies. Subsequently, improved means of transportation enabled more people to travel to New York to see the original production. In recent years, high operating costs have made it necessary for shows to remain on Broadway longer in order to realize a profit.

Another contributing factor to the longevity of musicals is the impact of original-cast recordings. There is no doubt that hearing songs exactly the way they are performed in the theatre contributes to a desire to see the actual performance. Decca made the first original-cast album in 1943 when it recorded most of the *Oklahoma!* score. Since then, the major record companies have become competitive bidders for the recording rights to potential hit shows. Their eagerness is understandable; because of rapidly diminishing production costs, an original-cast LP can make a greater profit than that realized from ticket sales. In 1956, the Columbia Broadcasting System was the sole investor in *My Fair Lady*, thus ensuring that Columbia Records, a division of C.B.S., would get the recording rights. Their investment paid off; *Lady* has become the largest selling original-cast album of all time.

Although the term "musical comedy" is considered somewhat old-fashioned today, it is an apt designation. The commercial musical theatre is seldom concerned with really serious themes; despite the success of *West Side Story* and others, it is still primarily the theatre of pretty costumes, gay dances, and light, witty music and lyrics. In transforming *Pygmalion* into *My Fair Lady*, it was necessary to alter the rather cold ending to make it more palatable. *Liliom* was changed into *Carousel* only after an element of hopefulness had been added to soften the tragedy. Even titles give indication of the changes. The dour *Anna Christie* becomes a bright, expectant *New Girl in Town*, while *They Knew What They Wanted* takes on an entirely different spirit as *The Most Happy Fella*. (As Irving Kolodin once pointed out, the title is an inversion of one of Tony's lines in the original play in which he refers to himself as "the most *un*happy fella.")

Nevertheless, there has been emerging a fairly definite line between what might be called "musical comedy" and "musical play." While these forms can and do overlap, musical comedy is lighter in content and looser in construction, with far more room for show-stopping numbers having only the slightest relationship to the story (i.e., the "Hello, Dolly!" number, which may have been necessary for the show, but which was unnecessary for plot development.) This is also the area in which the super stars—usually female—shine. If you want to see a Streisand, or a Channing, or a Merman, or a Verdon, or a Lansbury, it will usually be in a musical comedy. (Glaring exception to the rule: Merman in *Gypsy*). In a musical play—such as *Fiddler on the Roof*, *Man of LaMancha*, or *Cabaret*—the construction is tighter, the theme less escapist, and the musical pieces more germane to the story. And the "star" isn't all that important. At this writing, *Fiddler* is still doing well despite the fact that Zero Mostel, its original lead, has not been in it since August, 1965.

Happily, the musical theatre has enough room for any worthwhile idea. Oscar Hammerstein II concisely summed up the situation when he once wrote in *Variety*: "It is nonsense to say what a musical should or should not be. It should be anything it wants to be, and if you don't like it you don't have to go to it. There is only one absolutely indispensable element that a musical must have. It must have music. And there is only one thing that it has to be—it has to be good."

Victor Herbert.

8

Victor Herbert

THE EMERGENCE OF Victor Herbert as the first important composer of the American musical stage could not have been anticipated from his background. He was born in Dublin, educated in Germany, performed in symphony orchestras throughout Europe, and did not arrive in the United States until he was twenty-seven. Moreover, his coming to this country had nothing to do with writing musical comedies and operettas. He came here to play the cello in the orchestra of the Metropolitan Opera Company, and his Broadway career did not begin until eight years later.

Born on February 1, 1859, Victor Herbert was the son of Edward and Fanny Lover Herbert. His father died when Victor was a child of two; and during his youth, he was strongly influenced by his maternal grandfather, Samuel Lover, the celebrated Irish artist-novelist-poet-composer.

After his mother's remarriage to a German physician, the boy was taken to live in Stuttgart. Although he was expected to follow in his stepfather's career, he was far more attracted to music than to medicine, and at fifteen began to study the cello. Herbert subsequently joined touring orchestras as a member of the string section and as a soloist. In Vienna, he played for a year in the orchestra of Johann Strauss's brother, Eduard, where he quickly acquired the difficult knack of conducting Viennese waltzes with the proper authority and lilt. During his five years with the Court Orchestra of Stuttgart, Herbert studied composition under Max Seifriz, a highly regarded conductor and composer. His first work, the *Suite for Cello and Orchestra*, was published at that time.

When Herbert was twenty-six, he met Therese Förster, a young soprano who had recently become a member of the Royal Opera at Stuttgart. They soon fell in love and made plans to marry—plans which were suddenly accelerated by an unusual stroke of good luck.

The Metropolitan Opera Company of New York, having completed its first season of German operas, was anxious to recruit new singers for its Wagnerian repertory. Frank Damrosch, one of the Metropolitan's scouts, journeyed to Stuttgart to audition a young tenor. The tenor failed to impress him, but while there Damrosch decided to listen to some other singers. Fraulein Förster pleased him so much that he promptly offered her a contract. Although she was elated with the offer, she insisted, with the blind confidence of youth, that her fiancé would also have to be hired. Damrosch was a bit skeptical, but when he heard Herbert play, he signed another contract. Therese Förster and Victor Herbert were married in Vienna, and spent their honeymoon on a steamer bound for New York.

Victor Herbert upon his arrival in New York at the age of 27.

Therese sang at the Metropolitan for only one season; from then on she was content to remain in the background. For Herbert's appearances as a soloist with Theodore Thomas's and Antol Seidl's orchestras were becoming important events in the musical life of New York, and he was rapidly being recognized as one of the country's leading cellists. In addition, he was winning a limited fame as a composer of concert music and as a conductor. However, such accomplishments gave him only partial satisfaction. Herbert was a warm, gregarious, fun-loving man who enjoyed all the popular amusements of the day—bands, parades, operettas, musical comedies—and he was extremely anxious to move to the top of this world. "Is it a crime to be popular?" he once asked. "I believe that which is not popular is not of much benefit to the world."

It was, therefore, natural that when he was offered the post of director of the 22nd New York National Guard Band (succeeding the famous Patrick Gilmore), he was delighted to accept. Such a positon would not only relieve him of the monotony of playing in an orchestra, but it would also give him time to compose and perform music that could win him wider popular acclaim than he could ever receive from opera and concert audiences.

Although Herbert enjoyed his work as bandmaster, he knew that only the theatre could provide him with the perfect outlet for his composing gifts. When he first began to give serious thought to working in the popular theatre, Herbert wanted to write for a kind of "folk theatre" he equated with the earthy entertainments of Harrigan and Hart. Though his Irish heritage made this ambition understandable, he soon realized that by training and temperament he was far better suited to follow the tradition of the middle European operetta.

According to Edward N. Waters, Herbert's biographer, the composer's first comic opera was *La Vivandière*, written in 1893 especially for Lillian Russell. Little is known about it, however, because it was never produced. The following year, Herbert wrote *Prince Ananias* for The Bostonians, a well-known touring company. They opened it in New York on November 20, 1894. The score for the new work was attractive, but it was hampered by an unusually dull and awkward libretto. Nevertheless, and in spite of a lukewarm reception, the operetta remained in the company's repertory for about two years.

Herbert's second production, *The Wizard of the Nile,* in 1895, began his frequent association with librettist Harry B. Smith and established him as one of the leading light opera composers in the country. Smith wrote the book as a vehicle for Frank Daniels, a popular comedian who had won fame for his performances in Charles Hoyt's musical farces. Herbert completed the delightful Near Eastern-flavored score within a month. In addition to the song "Star Light, Star Bright," the show is best remembered today for a recurring line, "Am I a wiz?" which soon became a popular slang expression.

Having supplied Daniels with a notable Broadway debut set in Egypt, Herbert and Smith created other musicals for him with equally exotic locales—India for *The Idol's Eye,* Afghanistan for *The Ameer,* Persia for *The Tattooed Man.* None of these repeated the triumph of *The Wizard of the Nile,* though *The Idol's Eye* did give Daniels a particularly clever number about the contented wife of "The Tattooed Man" of the circus:

> "Oh, why should I go abroad," she said,
> "To Germany, France or Rome?
>   When so fine a collection
>   Awaits my inspection
> In our happy little home."

In this exciting world of nerve-racking deadlines, frantic opening nights, and temperamental stars, Victor Herbert was able to find the stimulus for his most enduring compositions. He was a desperately hard worker; he loved the challenge that each new contract presented; and he enjoyed the money his work brought him.

Aside from the pleasure he found in composing, his favorite pastime was eating and drinking the best food and wine. Indeed, as his publisher, Isidore Witmark, once related, Herbert had an ingenious way of combining his work with his fondness for drink. In the season of 1899–1900, he composed the scores for four operettas almost simultaneously, while imbibing an appropriate wine for each one to get him in the proper mood. For *Cyrano de Bergerac,* which had a French locale, he drank claret and burgundy; for *The Singing Girl,* with its Austrian setting, Rhine wine and moselle; for the Afghan-flavored *Ameer,* some special "hard stuff"; for *The Viceroy,* an operetta laid in Venice, there was chianti. All these wines were kept on ice in a washtub in his studio because Herbert jumped from one score to another as it pleased him, rather than composing one at a time.

During his career, Victor Herbert helped establish the fame of three sopranos of unusual ability—Alice Nielsen, Fritzi Scheff, and Emma Trentini. The magic worked both ways. Herbert seemed to compose his best music when he worked with, and for, an outstanding singer. Even though *The Serenade,* Herbert's first truly distinguished score, was commissioned for The Bostonians in 1897, and was not created especially for Miss Nielsen, the leading role was given to her at the composer's insistence. Only twenty years old at the time, the soprano left the company the following year to form her own Alice Nielsen Comic Opera Company. Herbert and Smith then supplied her with a second substantial hit, *The Fortune Teller,* in which Eugene Cowles sang the comforting lullaby, "Gypsy Love Song"

THE FORTUNE TELLER *(1898). A dramatic moment during the operetta. Alice Nielsen, the star, is the one in the officer's uniform about to draw her sword.*

("Slumber on, my little gypsy sweetheart"). Miss Nielsen offered the amusing "Always Do as People Say You Should," and the spirit of comic-opera gypsies was tempestuously conveyed in "Romany Life."

Despite his heavy schedule of theatre work, soon after the opening of *The Fortune Teller* Herbert became musical director of the Pittsburgh Symphony Orchestra. That Leonard Bernstein can be both the conductor of the New York Philharmonic and also the composer of musical comedy scores is accepted today as proof of his great and varied talents. At the turn of the century, however, Herbert's dual occupation subjected him to a violent attack by Marc Blumenberg, editor of *The Musical Courier*. One particularly strong editorial boldly stated: ". . . this paper . . . long since declared not only that *The Fortune Teller* has no merit whatever, but that all of Victor Herbert's 'written-to-order' comic operas were pure and simple plagiarisms . . . Everything written by Herbert is copied; there is not one original strain in anything he has done . . . How Pittsburgh intelligence could ever select this clever bandmaster as its symphony director passes

13

comprehension, unless indeed the people there never really appreciated the true significance of the artistic movement a permanent symphony orchestra represents . . . The great symphony conductors are not drafted from the ranks of the composers of the shoddy American farce operas, alias leg shows, nor are they taken from the leaders of the parading military bands. . . ."

Herbert quickly sued *The Musical Courier* for libel. Expert testimony was offered on both sides as to what, if any, plagiarism had taken place. The trial was a sensation, and when all the bombast and rhetoric had spent itself, Herbert was awarded damages by the court.

After devoting about three years almost exclusively to the Pittsburgh Symphony, Herbert returned to Broadway in 1903. Fred Hamlin and Julian Mitchell, who had produced the highly successful *Wizard of Oz* by A. Baldwin Sloane and L. Frank Baum, commissioned him and Glen Mac-Donough to write a sequel. The new work was *Babes in Toyland*. Although it lacked the sturdiness of its predecessor's libretto, *Toyland* had a score of such appeal that it gave the play a lyricism the other production lacked. In fact, whenever it is revived today, the original score is always performed, whereas *The Wizard of Oz* inevitably substitutes the songs written for the 1939 movie version by Harold Arlen and E. Y. Harburg. Among the pieces

BABES IN TOYLAND *(1903). William Norris and Mabel Barrison lead the children of Toyland in singing "I Can't Do the Sum." (Setting by John Young.)*

IT HAPPENED IN NORDLAND *(1904). The American ambassadress to Nordland, Katherine Peepfogle, is deaf to the entreaties of her long-lost brother, Hubert. Marie Cahill and Lew Fields were the stars. (Setting by John Young.)*

that still give *Babes in Toyland* its continued charm are "March of the Toys," "Toyland," and the disarming "I Can't Do the Sum," which is performed to the accompaniment of chalk tapping on slates.

In 1950, Irving Berlin's *Call Me Madam* was concerned with the misadventures of a lady ambassador to the court of a mythical country called Lichtenburg; in 1904, Victor Herbert's *It Happened in Nordland* was concerned with the misadventures of a lady ambassador to the court of a mythical country called Nordland. But there the similarity ended. The Herbert work, written with Glen MacDonough, was a rather meandering though commercially successful vehicle for two popular entertainers, Marie Cahill (as Ambassador Katherine Peepfogle) and Lew Fields (as her long-lost brother, Hubert).

Both Fields, who was appearing for the first time without Joe Weber, his regular partner, and Miss Cahill were continually adding lines and changing "business." Herbert was particularly irritated with his female star, who went so far as to interpolate some of her own vaudeville numbers. The situation between star and composer became so strained that she refused to tour in the show. When *It Happened in Nordland* returned

15

to New York, the part of the ambassadress was played by the equally undisciplined Blanche Ring, who quit after she too encountered difficulty when she insisted on adding special material. Finally, the role of Katherine Peepfogle was given to Pauline Frederick, a young actress in the company who subsequently won success in many dramatic roles on Broadway.

The score of *It Happened in Nordland* had many charming numbers, with "Absinthe Frappe" the biggest hit. "Al Fresco," originally a piano piece Herbert had written under the name of Frank Roland to test its popularity, was performed at the beginning of the second act to provide an appropriate musical setting for a gay carnival scene. Four years later, Herbert again wrote a score for a Lew Fields musical, *Old Dutch*, though it is mostly remembered today for the scene-stealing debut of a nine-year-old actress named Helen Hayes.

Writing sequels to long-running musicals and vehicles for popular entertainers was profitable, but Herbert was anxious to compose again for a truly gifted prima donna. Alice Nielsen had deserted comic opera for grand opera (only to return briefly in 1917 in Rudolf Friml's *Kitty Darlin'*), but producer Charles Dillingham had lured the vivacious, Viennese-born Fritzi Scheff from grand opera to comic opera. Although *Babette*, the first operetta Herbert composed for her, was a failure, the composer, in 1905, joined

OLD DUTCH (1909). *Though her part was small, this nine-year-old actress made an auspicious New York debut. As the critic of the New York Herald* wrote: *"Miss Helen Hayes, a wee miss, won the favor of the audience by a bit of acting that was refreshing."*

librettist Henry Martyn Blossom, Jr., to create her greatest success, *Mlle. Modiste*. In story and dialogue, the musical was far more adult than anything Herbert had previously done.

"Kiss Me Again," Herbert's most universally popular piece, was introduced in *Mlle. Modiste*. At first, Miss Scheff did not want to sing it because she felt it was too low for her voice. Blossom and Dillingham agreed with the prima donna and recommended that Herbert drop it from the score. The composer, however, was adamant, and the song remained in the show. "Kiss Me Again" was not originally sung as the sincere ballad it is accepted as today. Playing the role of Fifi, a stage-struck employee of a Paris hat shop, Fritzi Scheff offered it as part of a lengthy routine called "If I Were on the Stage." In it she attempted three different types of songs that might be suitable for her theatrical debut. As a country maid, she performed a gavotte, and as a French lady of history, a polonaise. Then, to introduce the third song, she sang:

> But best of all the parts I'd play,
> If I would only have my way,
> Would be a strong romantic role;
> Emotional and full of soul.

MLLE. MODISTE (1905). *True love conquers in the final scene at the charity bazaar. Fifi (Fritzi Scheff) is at last welcomed into the family of her beloved, Capt. Etienne de Bouvray (Walter Percival), by his uncle, the Comte de St. Mar (William Pruette). Claude Gillingwater stands between Pruette and Miss Scheff. (Setting by Homer Emens.)*

THE RED MILL (1906). "Con" Kidder and "Kid" Conner kick up their heels with two local belles beside the Red Mill Inn, in Katwyk-aan-Zee, Holland. Fred Stone, Allene Crater (Mrs. Fred Stone), David Montgomery, and Ethel Johnson.

> And I believe for such a thing
> A dreamy sensuous waltz I'd sing . . .

and immediately glided into "Sweet summer breeze, whispering trees . . ."

Herbert wrote two other operettas for Fritzi Scheff, *The Prima Donna* and *The Duchess,* but neither matched the triumph of *Mlle. Modiste.*

Much as he might have liked to write exclusively for gifted singers, Herbert could never bring himself to refuse a potentially commercial success. Therefore, in 1906, he readily agreed to collaborate with Henry Blossom on *The Red Mill,* a musical tailored to fit the talents of comedians Dave Montgomery and Fred Stone. The team had scored a great success three years earlier as the Tin Woodman and the Scarecrow in *The Wizard of Oz,* and the new vehicle turned out to be equally popular even though the stars managed to turn the show into more of a rowdy variety act than a book musical. Its run of 274 performances was the longest of any Herbert work performed during his lifetime.

The score, possibly Herbert's most deliberately commercial one, was as responsible as the stars for the show's great appeal. (Another factor that helped *The Red Mill* succeed was that it had the first moving electric sign ever erected on Broadway.) Included in its succession of attractive melodies were the delicate "Moonbeams"; the piquant hymn to self-satisfaction, "When You're Pretty and the World Is Fair" ("Why be bothered by a thought or care?"); the strutting march, "Every Day Is Ladies' Day with Me"; and "In Old New York," a rollicking paean to the city where "the peach crop's always fine."

Like *The Fortune Teller* and *Mlle. Modiste, Naughty Marietta* was created for a particular prima donna. This was the diminutive Emma Trentini who, with her rotund leading man, Orville Harrold, had been one of the featured singers of Oscar Hammerstein's Manhattan Opera Company. Mounting debts had forced the colorful Hammerstein to return to the world of lighter entertainment and in 1910 he produced *Naughty Marietta* with all the care that he customarily lavished on grand opera.

Herbert's score was equal to the high standards of performance and production. It captured the flavor of old New Orleans so fully that Earl Derr Biggers, then a critic for the Boston *Traveler,* was inspired to write: "The warmth of 'Little Paris' must have been in Mr. Herbert's very blood when he did the score of this piece. Pirates, belles, knights resplendent in haberdashery, roses, convent walls must have danced before his eyes. (Is it proper for a convent wall to dance?) No matter. Romance was in the soul of Mr. Herbert."

NAUGHTY MARIETTA *(1910). Orville Harrold, as Capt. Richard Warrington, and Emma Trentini, as Marietta d'Altena, indulge in some coquettish finger holding.*

The romance in Mr. Herbert's soul has proven to be extremely durable. The buoyant coloratura classic "Italian Street Song" ("Zing, zing, zi-zi-zi-zi-zi-zi ZING BOOM AY!"); the sweeping confession, "I'm Falling in Love with Someone"; the magnolia-drenched " 'Neath the Southern Moon"; the heroic "Tramp, Tramp, Tramp"; the intense, expansive "Ah, Sweet Mystery of Life" —all these were part of a score that, along with Sigmund Romberg's *The Desert Song,* has epitomized the word "operetta" to more people than any other American work.

Soon after the première of *Naughty Marietta,* a young actress named Christie MacDonald won acclaim in *The Spring Maid,* written by Heinrich Reinhardt and the Smith brothers, Harry Bache and Robert Bache. Just three years later, the brothers and Fred De Gresac (a young woman whose real first name was Frederique) collaborated with Victor Herbert to create the delightful *Sweethearts* for Miss MacDonald.

The new work was one of those throughout the history of the musical stage that takes place in a mythical kingdom (in this case, Zilania). Many of the songs are fondly remembered today—the fervent, but impractical title piece, "Sweethearts" ("can live on love alone"), "Game of Love," "Angelus" (developed from the ringing of the actual Angelus), and the bouncy tale of a foiled elopement, "Jeannette and Her Little Wooden Shoes":

SWEETHEARTS *(1913). The ardent Prinz Franz of Zilania (Thomas Conkey) woos the demure Sylvia (Christie Mac-Donald) not knowing that she is really a princess.*

Clip-clop-clop,
Clip-clop-clop,
Over the tiles—
Her feet
were petite,
But you heard her for miles.*

With a modernized book, *Sweethearts* was successfully revived on Broadway in 1947 with Bobby Clark as the star.

Sweethearts was also important in establishing the authority of the American Society of Composers, Authors and Publishers (ASCAP). Herbert, along with composers Silvio Hein, Gustave Kerker, Raymond Hubbell, and Louis Hirsch, librettist Glen MacDonough, publishers George Maxwell and Jay Witmark, and attorney Nathan Burkan, had organized the society in 1914 to ensure that its members would receive whatever royalties were due from public performances of their music. The Society's first test case came the following year when Herbert brought suit against Shanley's Restaurant because its orchestra had played the song "Sweethearts" without authorization. After hearing both sides, Judge Learned Hand ruled against the composer. Herbert appealed to the Circuit Court of Appeals, where the verdict again went against him. Finally the U.S. Supreme Court ruled in favor of Herbert's position, in a decision written by Justice Oliver Wendell Holmes. The power of ASCAP was at last recognized!

The rest of Victor Herbert's career never achieved the heights he reached in his earlier works. Between *The Madcap Duchess* (1913) and the posthumously produced *The Dream Girl* eleven years later, the composer wrote twelve complete scores, plus many songs interpolated in book musicals and revues. Though some of the shows attained respectable runs, they are chiefly remembered because of one or two arias from each—"I Might Be Your Once-in-a-While" from *Angel Face*, "When You're Away" from *The Only Girl*, "Neapolitan Love Song" from *The Princess Pat*, "Thine Alone" and the incongruously titled "Free Trade and a Misty Moon" from *Eileen*, and "A Kiss in the Dark" from *Orange Blossoms*.

Herbert died of a heart attack on May 24, 1924, at the age of sixty-five. None of his contemporaries, and few who succeeded him, achieved as complete a mastery of the art of composing music for the theatre. When he began to compose for the Broadway stage, the most accomplished writers were John Philip Sousa, Reginald DeKoven, and Gustave Kerker. Herbert was unquestionably their superior in melodic inspiration and versatility, yet the musical theater that he represented was not really any more ad-

---

* From *Sweethearts* (Music by Victor Herbert, Lyrics by Robert B. Smith). Copyright 1913, 1940 by G. Schirmer. Reprinted by permission.

On April 16, 1916, some members of the recently formed American Society of Composers, Authors, and Publishers took part in an Actors's Fund Benefit at the Century Theatre in New York City. Seated at the piano is Oscar Hammerstein I, producer of Naughty Marietta. Standing behind him are Jerome Kern, Louis A. Hirsch, A. Baldwin Sloane, Rudolf Friml, Alfred Robyn, Gustave Kerker, Hugo Felix, John Philip Sousa, Leslie Stuart, Raymond Hubbell, John Golden, Silvio Hein, and Irving Berlin.

Seven years later, a similar group met for a similar purpose. Standing behind Victor Herbert are Gustave Kerker, Raymond Hubbell, Harry Tierney, Louis A. Hirsch, Rudolf Friml, Robert Hood Bowers, Silvio Hein, A. Baldwin Sloane, and Irving Berlin.

vanced than theirs. His chief historical impact was that during the first two decades of the century he stood alone in raising the standards of theatre music and orchestrations. No matter how pressed he was, Herbert always turned out work that revealed great care in both composition and in the way in which the theatre orchestra might best enhance the effectiveness of a score. "Some composers think in terms of the piano," he once said, "but I pay little attention to it. I consider all the resources of orchestra and voice given me to work with. If I did not work out my own orchestrations, it would be as if a painter conceived the idea of a picture and then had someone else paint it."

Victor Herbert was part of the Old World school of sentimental ballads, swirling waltzes, and spirited marches. Within this traditional form, however, he created a richly melodious musical theatre that was so well attuned to the New World that he became the dominant composer of the early days of the American musical theatre.

George M. Cohan.

George M. Cohan

Victor Herbert and George M. Cohan were the two most important creative figures of the American musical stage during the first decade of the twentieth century. Apart from this, and the coincidence that both were of Irish descent, each man epitomized an entirely disparate form of musical theatre. Herbert, the thoroughly trained musician, sought to perpetuate the traditions of the Viennese operetta; Cohan, the untrained song-and-dance man, tried to break away from anything that suggested the Old World. For Herbert, the Broadway stage was something of a step downward from the elevated world of opera and the concert hall; for Cohan, it was a definite step upward from the world of vaudeville of which he had been a part since birth. Herbert felt that the music and the orchestrations and the singers were the most important elements, but Cohan, who created most of his tunes from four chords he could play on only the black keys of a piano, believed that the essential ingredient of a musical show was "Speed! Speed! And lots of it! That's the idea of the thing. Perpetual motion!"

In a larger sense, both men were symbols of the changes taking place in the age in which they lived. The portly, elegant, mustachioed Victor Herbert was a genuine Victorian figure whose carriage-trade entertainments kept alive the spirit of an earlier day which many people were reluctant to give up, whereas the brash, fast-talking George M. Cohan spoke and sang directly to a new world and to a new century. "Never was a plant more indigenous to a particular part of the earth than was George M. Cohan to the United States of his day," Oscar Hammerstein II once wrote in the New York *Times*. "The whole nation was confident of its superiority, its moral virtue, its happy isolation from the intrigues of the 'old country,' from which many of our fathers and grandfathers had migrated."

While these attitudes shone through most of Cohan's works, the character he himself usually portrayed was not a loud-mouthed braggart. Compared to the exaggerated antics of some of the comedians for whom Victor Herbert wrote—Frank Daniels (with his trick eyebrows), Francis Wilson, Montgomery and Stone—Cohan's characterizations were models of subtlety, frequently in contrast to the razzle-dazzle of his own entertainments. Strutting, prancing, talking a song out of the corner of his mouth in a deep nasal twang, he was the personification of the debonair man of affairs with whom audiences were happy to identify themselves.

As Cohan was the star-composer-lyricist-librettist-director-producer of most of his shows, the public image of the man was taken from his stage roles. And Cohan was delighted to encourage the impression that he was indeed the living incarnation of George Washington, Jr., The Yankee Doodle Boy, The Yankee Prince, The Little Millionaire, The Man Who Owns Broadway, and The Song and Dance Man. Conversely, many of Cohan's stage characters were based on actual people he had met or read about. In *The Governor's Son* and *Running for Office*, Cohan depicted Tammany politicians he became acquainted with at the chowder outings of Big Tim Sullivan, one of the local bosses. For his first hit, *Little Johnny Jones,* he modeled the title part to fit Tod Sloan, a famous American jockey, and for the other main character, "The Unknown," he took as his inspiration the personality of Big Tom Foley, a former New York sheriff. Kid Burns of *Forty-Five Minutes from Broadway* was copied directly from an ex-prizefighter whose name was really Kid Burns.

In his song, "The Yankee Doodle Boy," Cohan said that he was "born on the Fourth of July." This started a myth that has persisted down to today. Actually, it was on the third of July, 1878 (verified by Ward Morehouse, Cohan's biographer), that George Michael Cohan was born in Providence, Rhode Island. His parents, Jeremiah (known as "Jerry") and Helen (known as "Nellie") were vaudeville performers; Georgie first appeared in front of the footlights as an infant, when he was carried on stage during a scene in one of his father's skits, *The Two Dans*. At eight, he played the violin in the pit orchestra; the following year he spoke his first lines on the stage. He later starred in *Peck's Bad Boy*, a part for which the pugnacious youth was exceptionally well qualified. Soon he began to write material for his

The Four Cohans—Jerry, Nellie, Josie, and George.

family's act, The Four Cohans, which consisted of himself, his parents, and his sister Josephine.

Cohan's first song was published when he was sixteen. It was called "Why Did Nellie Leave Her Home?" (the girl was named after his mother), but the pleasures of its publication were greatly lessened when the young composer discovered that another writer, Walter Ford, had been called in to rewrite the lyrics. From then on, however, he wrote all of his own music and words. Some of his early successes were "Hot Tamale Alley" (a favorite of vaudeville star, May Irwin), "Venus, My Shining Love," and "I Guess I'll Have to Telegraph My Baby" ("I need the money bad, 'deed I do").

As a vaudeville act, The Four Cohans had become one of the nation's leading attractions by the turn of the century. In addition to writing all their material, George was also the business manager. He was able to demand the unusually high sum of $1,000 per week for the act in addition to specifying billing, routes, and lengths of engagements. But the uncertainties and discomforts of trouping all over the country made Cohan long for the prestige of appearing on Broadway, not as part of a variety program, but in his own musical comedy. To gain this end, he made a deal with Louis Behman of the Hyde and Behman vaudeville circuit, to have The Four Cohans tour for one season, after which they would star in a musical comedy on Broadway to be produced by Behman. Cohan had already written his Broadway script, based on his own vaudeville sketch, *The Governor's Son.* So it was that the Four Cohans (with the addition of George's new wife, Ethel Levey) toured the country, and the following season, on February 25, 1901, New Yorkers saw the first musical written and directed by George M. Cohan.

The Governor's Son had a less-than-brilliant debut. The company, unaccustomed to a New York first-night audience, showed signs of nervousness. The pacing lacked spirit and spark. To make things worse, Cohan sprained his ankle in the first scene and had to limp through the rest of the performance. In spite of the discouraging critical verdict, the twenty-two-year-old author would not accept defeat. He closed the show after a month and took it on the road for a profitable tour. The following year, Cohan tried Broadway again with *Running for Office*, another expanded vaudeville sketch. Again he found New York audiences cool to his efforts.

This show also did well on the road, but it meant little to Cohan; Broadway, as he said, was "the only bell I wanted to ring." So determined was he to win recognition in the legitimate theatre that he formed a partnership in order to have some one to handle the business end while he devoted his time to improving his writing. Through a mutual friend, he met Sam H. Harris, a one-time manager of boxer Terry McGovern, who had had some experience producing melodramas on the Bowery with Al Woods and Paddy Sullivan. After a Sunday ride on a ferryboat, Cohan and Harris shook hands on a business partnership that was to last for fifteen years. (They were also related through marriage. Following his divorce from Ethel Levey in 1907, Cohan married Agnes Nolan, a dancer; two years later, Harris married her sister, Alice.)

Cohan's first Broadway success came in 1904; *Little Johnny Jones* followed the pattern of his first two musicals by opening to generally unfavorable reviews and an apathetic public. The company beat a fast retreat to the road. With Harris now taking care of the business details, however, Cohan could do considerable rewriting while the show was touring. When he bravely brought it back to New York the same season, it suddenly caught on and ran for a respectable three and a half months.

The naïve, patriotic sentimentality of *Little Johnny Jones*, combined with its headlong pace, caught the spirit of a country just beginning to emerge as a world power. Cohan's story of an American jockey wrongly accused of throwing a race in England served as a perfect vehicle for him to project his magnetic personality and to express such honest, direct emotions as the exultant "Yankee Doodle Boy" and "Give My Regards to Broadway." The tunes were meant to be whistled; the lyrics came from the heart. New York, as well as the entire country, soon responded to the electricity of George M. Cohan.

Everything that Cohan had written before 1906 had featured only himself, his family, and the American flag. It was, therefore, an irresistible challenge when producer A. L. (Abraham Lincoln) Erlanger approached him with the idea of writing a vehicle for Fay Templeton, a popular singer and comedienne who had won fame at the Weber and Fields Music Hall.

LITTLE JOHNNY JONES *(1904)*
Johnny Jones, an American jockey in England, is slightly taken aback by the antics of his girl friend, Goldie Gates. George M. Cohan, Donald Brian, and Ethel Levey.

BROWN BROS.

"Think you could write a play without a flag?" Erlanger asked Cohan. Cohan's reply was typically flippant: "I could write a play without anything but a pencil."

Cohan and his pencil created *Forty-Five Minutes from Broadway*, an even bigger hit than *Little Johnny Jones*. Opening on January 1, 1906 (one week after Victor Herbert's *Mlle. Modiste*), it was a well-constructed amalgam of melodrama and songs, among which were "Mary's a Grand Old Name" and "So Long, Mary." The title number, an amusing piece extolling the virtues of country life in New Rochelle, called the natives "Reubens" and noted their "whiskers like hay." These aspersions caused the local Chamber of Commerce to issue a proclamation urging the townspeople to boycott the show, thus giving Cohan some gratuitous publicity. Although Miss Templeton was the star, a young actor named Victor Moore, who had never appeared in a musical comedy before, gave an equally impressive performance as the "square-sporting man," Kid Burns. (When *Forty-Five Minutes from Broadway* was revived in 1912, Cohan himself took the part.)

With *George Washington, Jr.*, Cohan returned to his family and the flag. In spite of its preposterous story which dealt with a rich young man so incensed over his father's Anglomania that he adopted the name of the father of his country, the show succeeded chiefly because of the great

29

FORTY-FIVE MINUTES FROM BROADWAY (1906). *The final scene in the play in which Mary (Fay Templeton) proves her love for Kid Burns (Victor Moore) by tearing up the will that would have made her rich.*

appeal of Cohan and his songs. "I was born in Virgin-YUH! That's the state sure to win YUH!," sang Ethel Levey to the second balcony. With his head cocked to one side, Cohan delivered the irresistible "You're a Grand Old Flag." (Ironically, the song was originally called "You're a Grand Old Rag," but the protests of patriotic organizations forced the Yankee Doodle Boy to substitute "flag" for the affectionate term "rag.")

The originality and freshness soon ran out of George M. Cohan's musicals, even though they still found a wide audience. In 1907, Cohan offered a revised version of *Running for Office* called *The Honeymooners,* and he wrote *The Talk of New York* so that Victor Moore might again portray the popular character of Kid Burns. (The song hits were "When We Are M-A-Double R-I-E-D" and "When a Fellow's on the Level with a Girl That's on the Square.") *Fifty Miles from Boston* in 1908 (in which "Harrigan" was first sung) merely put the familiar Cohan characters into a new New

GEORGE WASHINGTON, JR. (1906). George M. Cohan, in the title role, spurns the hand of his father, played by Jerry Cohan. (Setting by John Young.)

THE LITTLE MILLIONAIRE (1911). George M. Cohan makes an emphatic point to George Parsons. Note size of Cohan's heels.

I'D RATHER BE RIGHT (1937)
*George M. Cohan, as Franklin
D. Roosevelt, delivers a radio
speech in front of a portable
fireplace.*

Rochelle setting—this time North Brookfield, Massachusetts, where the author spent his summers.*

Josie Cohan, who had left the act before *Little Johnny Jones*, was reunited with her family for *The Yankee Prince* in 1908, an occasion that inspired the star to bill himself as "George M. Cohan and his Royal Family." The customary chauvinism of Cohan's plots was here expanded to include a firm stand against the then-current practice of rich American families marrying off their daughters to titled foreigners. Cohan's feelings on the subject were expressed in the song, "I'm to Marry a Nobleman" ("Quite a dutiful girl am I, Going to marry an earl am I"). Two and one-half years later Jerry and Nellie Cohan made their final appearances on the stage. This was in George's *The Little Millionaire*.

The trend toward revues accelerated in the mid-1910's. In an attempt to keep up with the change, Cohan presented *Hello, Broadway!*, "A Musical Crazy Quilt Patched and Threaded Together with Words and Music and Staged by George M. Cohan." There were also two editions of *The Cohan Revue*. Irving Berlin contributed half the score to the second one, which was described by its baseball-loving author as "A Hit and Run Play Batted out by George M. Cohan." These shows presented broad travesties on current theatrical attractions very much in the spirit of the old Weber and Fields burlesques. They always had at least one character who visited various places and entertainments to give them some semblance of a theme. In *Hello, Broadway!*, for example, Cohan (co-starring with William Collier) played "George Babbit, the Millionaire Kid," whose tour of New York took him to see such attractions as Louise Dresser as "Patsy Pygmalion, a Flower Girl" in a lampoon of the latest Bernard Shaw comedy, and Peggy Wood impersonating Elsie Ferguson in the dramatic play, *Outcast*. Miss Wood recalls that she was also in the finale, "draped in a costume of white satin decorated with red beads embroidered in stripes, a blue bodice with silver stars, and a spiked crown. I leave it to you what I was as."

Even though younger musical talents, such as Jerome Kern and Irving Berlin, were soon surpassing Cohan in the freshness, skill, and variety of their work, Cohan continued to be active in all phases of the theatre. Yet his most famous World War I song, "Over There," had nothing to do with show business. Skillfully built on the repetition of three bugle call notes and catchy enough to be whistled even after being heard but once, the song became the most popular musical expression of the war. Cohan later wrote

---

* It was during the tryout of *Fifty Miles from Boston* that Donald Brian, the leading man, received an offer to co-star in another musical then in rehearsal. Cohan agreed to release him from his contract and, as Prince Danilo in Lehár's *The Merry Widow*, the young tenor became one of the first matinee idols of the musical theatre.

GEORGE M! *(1968). Joel Grey (as George M.) strutting through "I'm a Yankee Doodle Dandy" in a scene from* Little Johnny Jones. *(Costumes by Freddy Wittop; setting by Tom John.)*

a sequel to it which enjoyed a brief vogue. It was called "When You Come Back, and You Will Come Back" ("There's a whole world waiting for you").

One of Cohan's great skills was that of play doctor. In 1919, when an old-fashioned cloak-and-dagger operetta called *The Royal Vagabond* was floundering during its out-of-town tryout, Cohan rewrote and restaged it, and turned it into a hit as a "Cohanized Opera Comique." During the run of this show, the famous strike of Actors' Equity was called to compel producers to recognize the recently formed union. Even though Cohan was both an actor and a producer, his loyalties were entirely on the side of management, and he did everything he could to crush the eventually victorious union. For the rest of his career, Cohan steadfastly refused to join Equity and always had to receive special permission to perform.

34

The irony of this dispute is that throughout the rest of his life Cohan won far greater fame as an actor than as a writer or producer. Indeed, his two most distinguished performances, Nat Miller in Eugene O'Neill's *Ah, Wilderness!* (1934), and President Roosevelt in *I'd Rather Be Right* (1937), were in plays written and produced by others. Although Cohan had already presented two musicals not written by himself (*Mary* and *The O'Brien Girl*, both by Louis Hirsch, Otto Harbach, and Frank Mandel), his impersonation of F.D.R. was his only appearance in a musical created by other talents. It was no secret that while he was happy to be reunited with the producer, Sam Harris, he felt uncomfortable singing the songs Rodgers and Hart had written for him.

George M. Cohan died on November 4, 1942, at the age of sixty-four. As a creative force in the molding of the American musical theatre, however, his influence had ended many years before. His entire appeal as a writer was based on his youthful verve, his breeziness, and his popular flag waving. No matter what he wrote during his later life (his last musical, *Billie*, was produced in 1928), Cohan never progressed beyond the simple entertainments he had created early in the first decade of the century.

Victor Herbert and George M. Cohan were separate and distinct, yet typical, products of their time. They set the pattern for the two different kinds of musicals that were to flourish in the Twenties, the romantic operettas and the fast-moving musical comedies. Even today, we still see their influence at work. *My Fair Lady* may display a dramatic and musical cohesion undreamed of by Herbert, but it does follow in the stunningly theatrical tradition that he represented. As for Cohan, surely the pace of a George Abbott show or the atmosphere and characters of *The Music Man* attest to the continued appeal of his brand of musical comedy. What's more, in 1968 theatregoers were flocking to a high-powered musical based on the life of Cohan himself. In addition to some thirty Cohan songs, *George M!* offered Joel Grey strutting through the title role with breezy, flag-waving assurance. Proof indeed that Broadway still has a soft spot for the kind of theatre that first burst upon the scene in the dynamic, sentimental, corny song-and-dance shows created by George M. Cohan.

Rudolf Friml.

Rudolf Friml
Otto Harbach

Despite THE MOVEMENT toward a genuinely native musical theatre that George M. Cohan started, there has always been a large audience for the sentimental and romantic operettas that are more a part of the Old World than the New. Victor Herbert's mantle as the leading composer of operetta in America fell on the shoulders of Rudolf Friml and Sigmund Romberg. Both Friml and Romberg were of European birth, both were thoroughly schooled in classical music, and both settled in New York in the early 1900's. Friml, the older, had his last success in 1928 with *The Three Musketeers;* Romberg, as if to confuse those who like theatrical trends to be neatly defined, had one of his greatest hits, *Up in Central Park,* as late as 1945. But the period during which both men scored their greatest triumphs was roughly from the outbreak of the First World War to the Wall Street Crash. Between them, Friml and Romberg perpetuated a musical theatre that was colorful, nostalgic, and melodious—surely as soothing to the tired business-man as a leg show.

Rudolf Friml won fame far quicker than did Sigmund Romberg, although only a year separated their initial contributions to the theatre. In 1912, Friml was suddenly called upon to substitute for Victor Herbert as composer of *The Firefly*—a task for which he seemed to have had little training or inclination. He was born in Prague, Bohemia (now Czechoslovakia), on December 7, 1879. At ten, he composed a barcarolle. Four years later, he enrolled in the Prague Conservatory of Music, where he studied composition under Antonin Dvorák. He was such an excellent student that he completed a six-year course in three years. After graduation, Friml went on a concert tour of Europe with a fellow student, the violinist Jan Kubelik; in 1901, they gave their first recital in the United States. Three years later, Friml performed his own composition, the *Piano Concerto in B-Major,* at Carnegie Hall, with Walter Damrosch conducting the New York Symphony. The response to his work was so favorable and his future seemed so assured that the young composer decided to remain in the United States.

In March, 1912, a newspaper item announced that Emma Trentini, then starring in *Naughty Marietta,* would next appear in a new work by Victor Herbert and librettist Otto Abels Hauerbach (since changed to "Harbach"), under the sponsorship of Oscar Hammerstein's son, Arthur. But these plans collapsed the following month. At a special performance of *Naughty Marietta* conducted by Herbert himself, Miss Trentini publicly insulted the composer by refusing to sing an encore of his "Italian Street Song," despite the demands of the audience. Herbert, in a rage, stormed from the orchestra pit, handed the baton to William Axt, the regular conductor, and refused to have anything further to do with the temperamental actress or her next vehicle.

A near-frantic search was then begun to find a suitable replacement for Herbert to compose the score of the forthcoming musical. Because none of the prominent song writers of the day could match Herbert's skill at writing operetta, Hammerstein felt that an unknown composer, one with a thorough background in the classics, would be best suited to take over the assignment. Friml, who had not achieved the stature he had hoped for in the world of concert music, had become interested in composing for the stage. When he heard about the search for someone to do the *Firefly* score, he felt that this might be his big chance. At the urging of Rudolph Schirmer, his publisher, and also of Max Dreyfus of Harms, Inc., Arthur Hammerstein agreed to let the thirty-three-year-old composer take over the assignment. Friml completed the score for *The Firefly* within a month, Signorina Trentini had a second hit in a row, and from then until 1934, the serious, classics-trained composer and pianist devoted himself almost exclusively to the world of Broadway musicals.

The story of *The Firefly* was constructed along familiar Cinderella lines: an Italian street singer disguises herself as a cabin boy to be near the yachtsman she loves, and somehow ends up a prima donna. Though the plot was serviceable, the music and the singing were unquestionably the chief attractions. Critic H. T. Parker, writing in the Boston *Transcript,* observed:

THE FIREFLY (1912). *A scene in the first act in which Emma Trentini (supposedly disguised as a cabin boy) exchanges harsh words with Audrey Maple. Looking on are Roy Atwell, Katherine Stewart, Ruby Norton, and Craig Campbell.*

"Mr. Friml writes for an orchestra like a musician, setting it to warm, songful, rhythmic and well-colored accompaniments and not like a Broadway jingler picking out his 'toons' with one finger on the piano and leaving the rest to an assistant and the drum sticks."

Among the best of Friml's melodies are "Giannina Mia" (another Italian street song for the diva), "Love Is Like a Firefly," "When a Maid Comes Knocking at Your Heart," and the swooping waltz, "Sympathy." ("The Donkey Serenade," without which no revival of *The Firefly* would dare be presented, was created for the 1937 film version of the operetta from a piano piece originally called "Chanson.") It should be noted, incidentally, that Emma Trentini's relationship with Rudolf Friml was far more amicable than it had been with Victor Herbert. When Friml's wife divorced him in 1915, she named the singer as corespondent.

With his first attempts for the theatre an immediate success, Friml gladly signed a contract to create additional scores for Arthur Hammerstein. His next three, *High Jinks, Katinka,* and *You're In Love,* were notable hits during the mid-1910's. *High Jinks* (the title referred to a perfume which was sprayed on the audience) contained the waltz "Love's Own Kiss," the coquettish postponement of marriage "Not Now But Later," and the insinuating piece of nonsense:

SOMETIME *(1918). Ed Wynn, as Loney Bright, is slightly dazed by the charms of Argentine dancer Mildred LeGue.*

Something seems tingle—
  ingle—
    ingle—
      ingle—
        ingle-ing

So queer,
Here in your ear,
Nearer and near . . .*

The quasi-oriental "Allah's Holiday" came from *Katinka,* as did "Rackety-Coo" (which had a flock of trained pigeons accompanying the singing), and the inevitable grandiose waltz (with a particularly grandiose title), " 'Tis the End, So Farewell." *You're in Love,* in 1917, had the distinction of being the first Broadway musical to employ a young Columbia University graduate, Oscar Hammerstein II, here serving as an assistant stage manager for his uncle's production.

Broadway continued to provide Friml with commercial successes, though many of his assignments during the late 1910's and early 1920's were

* From *High Jinks* (Music by Rudolf Friml, Lyrics by Otto Harbach). Copyright 1913, 1941 by G. Schirmer. Reprinted by permission.

40

for inferior works. Moreover, their post-war stories and settings found the composer straining to create rhythms and melodies that were contrary to his natural musical inclination. Four of his shows achieved respectable runs during this period—*Sometime* (sometimes written *Some Time*) starring Ed Wynn, with Francine Larrimore and Mae West; *Tumble In*, described as "A Comic Rhapsody in Two Raps and Four Taps"; *The Little Whopper*, featuring Vivienne Segal and David Torrence; and *The Blue Kitten*, with Joseph Cawthorn.

With the exception of *Sometime*, all of these Friml musicals were written in collaboration with lyricist-librettist Otto Harbach, with whom the composer allied himself for a total of eleven stage productions. Harbach, the son of a Danish immigrant, was born in Salt Lake City, Utah, on August 18, 1873. After earning his M.A. at Knox College in Galesburg, Illinois, he spent six years as a professor of English at Whitman College, in Walla Walla, Washington. At 29, he gave up the post to study for his Ph. D. at Columbia University. Once in New York, however, he found that teaching no longer interested him. His first job in the city was as a reporter for a short-lived newspaper; then, for a while, he became a copywriter at the George Batten advertising firm. Broadway, however, was becoming the strongest magnet. Harbach's first collaborator was composer Karl Hoschna, with whom he wrote two immensely successful musicals, *Three Twins* ("Cuddle Up a Little Closer, Lovey Mine" came out of this one) and *Madame Sherry* ("Every Little Movement Has a Meaning All Its Own"). Within a few years, Harbach found himself the most prolific writer for the stage; by the time his career was over his output, either as librettist and/or lyricist or co-librettist and/or co-lyricist, totalled 43 musical productions. Of these, ten were written in partnership with Oscar Hammerstein II, whom he had met through the younger man's Uncle Arthur.

In addition to Hoschna and Friml, other composers who worked with Harbach were Louis Hirsch (*Going Up, Mary, The O'Brien Girl*), Vincent Youmans (*Wildflower, No, No, Nanette*), Jerome Kern (*Sunny, Criss-Cross, The Cat and the Fiddle, Roberta*), George Gershwin (*Song Of the Flame*), and Sigmund Romberg (*The Desert Song*). From 1950 to 1953, Harbach served as president of the American Society of Composers, Authors and Publishers. He died in New York on January 24, 1963, at the age of 89. Paying tribute to Harbach's accomplishments, Tom Prideaux wrote in *Life*: "His words and the music were as happily mated as the lovers he wrote about."

Friml and Harbach wrote most of their early shows for Arthur Hammerstein, whose love of spectacular stage effects led to the creation of the greatest success ever scored by the three men. Early in 1924, someone

41

Otto Harbach.

had told the producer about an ice carnival held every year in Quebec which was culminated in the melting down of a huge ice palace. This struck Hammerstein as a great idea for the theatre—even though he had neither the story to go with it nor did he have any idea how the spectacle could be accomplished on stage. He quickly dispatched Harbach and nephew Oscar Hammerstein to Canada to research the project. When they arrived they found that no one had ever heard of such a celebration. Even this news did not discourage the elder Hammerstein. So determined was he to have his next musical with a Canadian locale that he told the writers to forget about the ice carnival and the ice palace and to make up their own story. He then hired Friml and Herbert Stothart to compose the score, signed Mary Ellis, Dennis King, and William Kent for the leads, and, in September, 1924, unveiled one of the decade's most enduring musicals, *Rose-Marie*.

In addition to being the first (and only) stage musical to have the Canadian Rockies as a setting, *Rose-Marie* was a pioneering effort in its use of a murder as an important part of the story and in its attempts to integrate the music with the plot. In fact, instead of listing the individual songs, the printed program carried the following message: "The musical numbers of this play are such an integral part of the action that we do not think we should list them as separate episodes. The songs which stand out, independent of their dramatic association, are 'Rose-Marie,' 'Indian Love Call,' 'Totem Tom-Tom,' and 'Why Shouldn't We?' in the first act, and 'The Door

ROSE-MARIE *(1924). The ladies of the ensemble as they performed the "Totem Tom-Tom" dance. "One of the most effective chorus numbers we have ever seen," wrote Robert Benchley in* Life. *(Costumes by Charles LeMaire.)*

ROSE-MARIE *(1924). According to Arthur Hornblow of* Theatre *Magazine, "Mary Ellis establishes herself as the peer of any musical show star in this country." This is the way she looked in the wedding scene. (Costume by Charles LeMaire.)*

of My Dreams' in the second act." The need for such a note may seem pretentious and misleading today as the play did contain many specialty numbers. Nevertheless, there was such an undeniably conscientious attempt to fit songs intelligently within the framework of a plot that Arthur Hornblow of *Theatre Magazine* considered it "head, shoulders, and waist above the customary dribble about Prohibition and Brooklyn."

A year after appearing in *Rose-Marie*, Dennis King starred in another outstanding Friml operetta, *The Vagabond King*. Faced with the competition of *No, No, Nanette*, *Dearest Enemy*, and *Sunny* all opening within the same seven-day period, *The Vagabond King* was still capable of achieving an impressive run of over 500 performances. Adapted by Brian Hooker and W. H. Post from Justin McCarthy's *If I Were King*, the story told a fanciful tale of how poet François Villon became king of France for a day. Its melodies, rich in emotion and spirit, included "Only a Rose" ("I gi-i-ve you"), "Waltz Huguette," "Some Day," and the earthy, stirring call to arms, "The Song of the Vagabonds":

THE VAGABOND KING (1925). *Dennis King, as Francois Villon, about to lead the "rabble of low degree." (Costume by James Reynolds.)*

THE THREE MUSKETEERS (1928). *Athos (Douglass Dumbrille), Aramis (Joseph Macaulay), and Porthos (Detmar Poppen) cross swords with the dashing D'Artagnan (Dennis King). Mr. King, according to Percy Hammond, had "the voice of a canary, the grace of a swallow, and the valor of an eagle." (Costumes by John Harkrider; setting by Joseph Urban.)*

Onward! Onward! Swords against the foe!
Forward! Forward! The lily banners go!*

Friml's last success, *The Three Musketeers*, was presented by Florenz Ziegfeld in 1928. For the third time, Dennis King was the dashing hero of a Friml operetta, this time appearing as D'Artagnan opposite Vivienne Segal as Lady Constance. The production's extreme length (its opening-night performance continued past midnight) prompted Alexander Woollcott's famous comment, "I did greatly enjoy the first few years of Act I." Apparently this did not disturb greedier playgoers who kept the operetta running almost a year.

Although Friml "poured melody out of his sleeve" (in Otto Harbach's phrase), after the Twenties he seemed unable either to keep up with musical and theatrical changes, or to create anything in his accustomed style that could attract the wide and loyal following he once had. There was little appeal in either *Luana* or *Music Hath Charms*; the quickly accelerating changes within the world of musical comedy during the early Thirties had made it imperative for a new work to offer more than soaring, melodic arias. Friml was aware of the change, yet he realized that the modern sophisticated musicals born of the Depression years were not for him. "When I write

46

music for the theatre," he once told an interviewer in the mid-Thirties, "I like books with charm to them. And charm suggests the old things—the finest things that were done long ago. I like a full-bodied libretto with luscious melody, rousing choruses, and romantic passions."

Rudolf Friml was probably the least assimilated composer of the American musical theatre. His European background, his classical training, and his basically Old World outlook combined to give most of his scores—even his earliest ones—a fundamentally old-fashioned quality. That they continue to have great appeal, however, there is no doubt. Though most of the musical comedies of the Twenties and Thirties can no longer be performed as originally written, the rich, emotional music of Rudolf Friml continues to provide occasions of melodic pleasure whenever his operettas are revived. Like Sigmund Romberg, he is a composer whose melodies are best appreciated when heard far from the rush of Broadway, preferably in open-air theatres on balmy, romantic summer evenings.

Sigmund Romberg.

48

Sigmund Romberg

ALTHOUGH BOTH SIGMUND ROMBERG AND RUDOLF FRIML won fame through their series of operettas, the former was a far more prolific and versatile composer. His debut in the musical theatre may have been less auspicious, but he was able to maintain his position there for a much longer period. In fact, no other theatre composer has ever matched Romberg's output: from *The Whirl of the World* in 1914 to the posthumously produced *The Girl in Pink Tights* forty years later, he was the composer of up to sixty musicals. These included operettas, musical comedies, spectacles, and revues, all in such profusion that their names are easily confused—*Maytime* and *May Wine*, *Blossom Time* and *Cherry Blossoms*; *The Whirl of the World* and *A World of Pleasure*; *Dancing Around* and *The Dancing Girl*; *The Magic Melody*, *Forbidden Melody*, and just plain *Melody*.

Sigmund Romberg was born in Nagy Kaniza, Hungary, on July 29, 1887. His first composition, "The Red Cross March," was written while he was still in elementary school. Although his early fondness for music greatly pleased his parents, they did not want him to become a musician, and so sent him off to Vienna to study engineering. There, away from the stern glances of his parents, he gave only part of his time to academic studies, putting much of his energy toward the study of composition and harmony under Victor Heuberger.

Romberg was interested in almost every kind of music, but became increasingly devoted to operettas. He spent many evenings at the local theatres, viewing the creations of Johann Strauss, Oscar Straus, Franz Lehár, and other prominent Viennese composers. In a vain attempt to dissuade him from following a musical career, Romberg's parents permitted him to take a trip to England and to the United States, hoping that this would give him sufficient time and "maturity" to become convinced of the wisdom of continuing his engineering studies. After two weeks in London, the twenty-two-year-old traveler sailed for New York. On his arrival, he immediately became caught up in the excitement and vitality of the city. Because the money his parents had given him was almost gone, Romberg took a job as a worker in a pencil factory at seven dollars a week. Soon he secured a more suitable position as a pianist in a small East Side café; later, he was hired by a larger restaurant. Determined to remain in New York, Romberg advised his parents that he would not return to Hungary and that he intended to become an American citizen.

He now had a new ambition—he wanted to compose popular songs. The ragtime craze, sparked by Irving Berlin's "Alexander's Ragtime Band," had made revolutionary changes in the kind of music performed in restaurants. As conductor of the orchestra at Bustanoby's, a popular eating place, Romberg was persuaded by music publisher Edward Marks to try to write a turkey trot in the style of a popular French tune, "Très Moutarde." Romberg deliberately copied its rhythm for his first two published songs, "Some Smoke" and "Leg of Mutton"—even adding alternate French titles, "De la Fumée" and "Le Gigot," to emphasize the relationship. They became instantly popular with the restaurant's patrons, as did another early effort, a waltz called "The Poem" ("Le Poème").

The first two numbers attracted the attention of J. J. Shubert, a steady customer at Bustanoby's. J. J. and his brother, Lee, were successful Broadway producers and theatre owners whose large organization turned out both dramatic and musical attractions with almost assembly-line precision. The brothers had built the Winter Garden Theatre as a showcase for a series of lavish musicals to be offered on a well-regulated time table—a different spectacle for the fall and spring, plus an annual revue called *The Passing Show* during the summer. Louis Achille Hirsch and Jean Schwartz had collaborated with librettist-sketchwriter-lyricist Harold Atteridge on most of the Winter Garden shows, and Hirsch was to be the composer for the next offering, *The Whirl of the World*, scheduled to open in January, 1914. But just as an argument between Victor Herbert and Emma Trentini had brought about Rudolf Friml's first Broadway score, so a disagreement between Hirsch and J. J. Shubert was responsible for winning Romberg his first assignment. However, the two commissions were completely dissimilar.

Shubert wanted Romberg to provide innocuous, pleasant tunes for his extravaganza. Never, under any circumstances, was the music to detract from the scenic splendor, the antics of the comedians, or the bevy of girls, girls, girls. Indeed, in a brochure heralding the pleasures of *The Whirl of the World*, the entertainment was enticingly described as "An Isle of Gorgeousness, Fun and Music, Entirely Surrounded by Girls. Wherever You Look—Just Girls. Whenever You Look—Just Girls." Although this advertisement named the leading members of the cast (Lillian Lorraine, Bernard Granville, Eugene and Willie Howard, Walter C. Kelly, Rozsika Dolly), there was no mention at all of the composer. Moreover, the critics paid scant attention to the music. So overcome by the isle of gorgeousness was Alan Dale of the *American* that he devoted part of his review to the mock warning: "Oh, mothers of lads, send your susceptible ones to *The Philanderer*—or, er, Forbes-Robertson, but keep them, aye, keep them from the Winter Garden!"

Romberg was young and ambitious, and though the score brought little fame or satisfaction, he became convinced that the best way for him to succeed was to accept Shubert's offer to become a staff composer. The work would be steady, he would be paid well, and he was confident that some day he would have the opportunity to show his talent.

With Atteridge as collaborator, the new cog in the Shubert theatrical wheel ground out a lengthy procession of songs for revues and spectacles, most of which have long been forgotten. But there were the occasionally compensating pleasures of working with talented performers. Marilyn Miller returned from the Lotus Club in London to make her Broadway debut singing Romberg's "Omar Khayyam" in *The Passing Show of 1914*. Al Jolson,

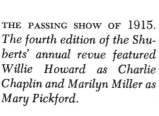

THE PASSING SHOW OF 1915. *The fourth edition of the Shuberts' annual revue featured Willie Howard as Charlie Chaplin and Marilyn Miller as Mary Pickford.*

CULVER PICTURES, INC.

THE BLUE PARADISE (1915). *Ted Lorraine and Vivienne Segal seem to be powerless to keep Teddy Webb from choking on a loaf of bread.*

who had first attracted notice in *Vera Violetta* in 1911, became a star in *Dancing Around*, though many of his specialty numbers were written by other composers.

Romberg also received assignments to add music to European importations. One of these was *The Blue Paradise*, produced in 1915. Based on a Viennese operetta for which Edmund Eysler had created the original score, it was a tender, nostalgic musical about a fleeting romance at an inn called The Blue Paradise. For the important scene in which the young girl must say a final goodbye to her lover, the composer wrote the touching waltz, "Auf Wiedersehn," which became his first successful song. (The words were by Herbert Reynolds, who had been the lyricist for Jerome Kern's first big hit, "They Didn't Believe Me," the previous year.)

The Blue Paradise was also responsible for beginning a notable theatrical career. After the leading soprano had proved unsatisfactory during the tryout, a search was made to find a suitable replacement. Because none of the professional singers auditioned seemed right for the part of the innocent and unspoiled heroine, the Shuberts decided to take a chance on an eighteen-year-old vocal student at the Curtis Institute of Music in Philadelphia. The girl was Vivienne Segal, who managed to give a memorable opening-night performance after only four days of rehearsing.

From *The Whirl of the World* to *The Passing Show of 1917*, Sigmund Romberg worked on fourteen musicals—all within twenty-six months! There was nothing about these entertainments to inspire a composer of Romberg's temperament; his melodies served the purpose for which they were written and little more. However, his next assignment, *Maytime*, made him optimistic that, at last, his hack-writing days would be over. Adapted by Rida Johnson Young from a Viennese operetta, it starred Peggy Wood and Charles Purcell in just the kind of sentimental, bittersweet romance that the composer loved, and for which he would create his most endearing music. Heralded in advertisements as "Fragrant as Flowers in May," *Maytime* was brimming full of melodic warmth, with the touching waltz "Will You Remember?" and the expressive "Road to Paradise" as its most lasting songs. The musical's immense popularity also made it unique in theatre history. Within a year after its August, 1917, première at the Shubert Theatre, a second New York company opened at the 44th Street Theatre almost directly opposite.

MAYTIME *(1917). Young Ottillie Van Zandt and Richard Wayne are a rich girl and a poor boy who have fallen in love. Peggy Wood played Ottillie and Charles Purcell was Richard. According to Miss Wood,* Maytime *was the show the boys all asked to see before they went overseas.*

The image of the new Romberg, however, could not replace the old. Shubert made him follow *Maytime* with such transient diversions as *Doing Our Bit* (with Ed Wynn, Frank Tinney, and the Duncan Sisters); *Over the Top* (the first New York musical to feature two youngsters from Nebraska, Fred and Adele Astaire); *Sinbad* (Romberg's third show for Al Jolson, but again full of interpolated numbers); and two more of the inevitable *Passing Shows* (these featuring the Astaires, Willie and Eugene Howard, Nita Naldi, Charles Winninger, and James Barton).

Enough, this time, was enough. Critics were beginning to look upon *Maytime* as an accident, and the name Sigmund Romberg was again becoming a synonym for Shubert hack. As soon as he had finished his assignment for *The Passing Show of 1919*, Romberg broke with the producers to form his own producing organization with Max R. Wilner. Although they had ambitious plans, neither of their productions, *The Magic Melody* and *Love Birds*, was successful. When the partnership was dissolved after only two years, the composer reluctantly went back to his former employers. (During this period of independence, Romberg also contributed eight songs to Lew Fields's *Poor Little Ritz Girl*, which had originally been intended as the sole product of a new song-writing team, Richard Rodgers and Lorenz Hart.)

Upon his return, Romberg was given an assignment that J. J. Shubert was sure would please him. Dorothy Donnelly had adapted *Blossom Time*

BLOSSOM TIME *(1921). Olga Cook (as Mitzi) listens as Bertram Peacock (as Franz Schubert) plays his "Song of Love."*

54

from a Viennese operetta, *Das Dreimaderlhaus,* for which Heinrich Berté had rearranged well-known themes by Franz Schubert into appropriate vocal arias. Convinced that Romberg could do a better job of organizing the songs than Berté had done, Shubert wanted the composer to scrap the previous arrangements and to create his own. Although the idea of tampering with another composer's works did not appeal to Romberg, he was greatly in need of money and reluctantly accepted the commission.

The plot of *Blossom Time,* accurately described by Romberg's biographer, Elliott Arnold, as "the old *Cyrano de Bergerac* story played somewhat in reverse," was a fictitious piece about Franz Schubert's unrequited love for a girl named Mitzi. In spite of its high sugar content, the operetta became a favorite of both critics and public. Even the usually acerbic George S. Kaufman, then a reviewer for the *Times,* wrote of the "songs of passionate longing that illuminate *Blossom Time* like pictures in a Christmas book." Four road companies set out soon after it opened on September 29, 1921, thereby beginning the celebrated cross-country association of Schubert and Shubert.

Despite Romberg's preference for tender romances, the Shubert brothers' formula of musical creation could not be altered to suit one composer. The week after *Blossom Time* opened on Broadway, *Bombo,* another Romberg vehicle for Jolson, had its première. Indeed, it was not until three years had elapsed (and ten musicals had expired) that Shubert again

BOMBO *(1921). Romberg was the nominal composer of this Al Jolson hit, but other writers were called in to contribute such songs as "Toot Toot Tootsie," "April Showers," and "My Mammy."*

THE STUDENT PRINCE IN HEI-
DELBERG (1924). Peeking out
from behind the roses are the
romantic duo, Prince Karl
(Howard Marsh) and Kathy
(Ilse Marvenga).

offered the composer a score worthy of his ability. Billed as "A Stupendous
Musical Production," *The Student Prince in Heidelberg* was in the direct
line of *The Blue Paradise* and *Maytime,* as it told of the fleeting love affair
between Prince Karl (Howard Marsh) and a waitress named Kathy (Ilse
Marvenga) in the university city of Heidelberg. The story provided the com-
poser with inspiration for some of his most dulcet melodies and robust
rhythms — "Golden Days," "To the Inn We're Marching," "The Drinking
Song" (a great favorite with Prohibition audiences), "Deep in My Heart,
Dear," and "Serenade." With a total of 608 performances in New York,
The Student Prince had the longest run of any Romberg operetta.

It had taken almost eleven years, but Sigmund Romberg had finally
achieved the eminence of a composer who could choose his own assignments
—and producers. For Ziegfeld he did the successful *Louie the 14th* (referring to a waiter named Louie, played by Leon Errol, who was hired as the
fourteenth guest at a dinner party), and for the new producing team of
Laurence Schwab and Frank Mandel, he created the music for that exotic
saga of burning dunes and lofty tunes, *The Desert Song.* Originally known as
Lady Fair, this production marked the composer's first association with Otto
Harbach and Oscar Hammerstein II, who supplied the lyrics and collabo-

56

THE DESERT SONG *(1926). A moment of high drama in French Morocco, as Margot Bon-valet (Vivienne Segal) pleads with Gen. Birabeau (Edmund Elton) to spare the life of the Red Shadow (Robert Halliday). Also deeply concerned is the native girl, Azuri (Pearl Regay). (Costumes by Vyvyan Donner and Mark Mooring; setting by Woodman Thompson.)*

rated on the book with Mandel. Its cast was headed by Robert Halliday and Vivienne Segal (as in *The Blue Paradise,* she had been called in just before the opening to replace another actress), with Eddie Buzzell as the leading comic. The score, still a great favorite, contained the smoldering title song, the muscular "Riff Song," the ardent "One Alone," and the slightly out-of-place tribute to the Elinor-Glyn-Clara Bow influence, simply called "It."

The remarkable durability of *The Desert Song* has made most people forget that it received a mixed critical reception when it opened in 1926, and that a full month elapsed before it caught on with the public. The sheik plot was so old fashioned that Richard Watts, Jr., began his *Herald Tribune* review with: "The question of how simple-minded the book of a musical comedy can be was debated last night, and the verdict arrived at was 'no end.'" But the songs, combined with an enticing locale that has always conjured up an atmosphere of mystery and grand passion, still make *The Desert Song*

ROSALIE (1928). *Jack Donahue, George Gershwin, Sigmund Romberg, Marilyn Miller, and Florenz Ziegfeld backstage during a rehearsal.*

one of the small group of musicals that summer-theatre managers can always depend on to play to packed houses.

The Shubert brothers induced Romberg back to write for a few moderately popular attractions, and one, *My Maryland* (based on Clyde Fitch's *Barbara Frietchie*), that was a decided hit. With many producers now bidding for his services, the composer agreed to undertake two commissions at almost the same time: Schwab and Mandel signed him to compose the music for *The New Moon,* and Ziegfeld hired him for *Rosalie.*

Because of the problem created by writing two scores almost simultaneously, Romberg insisted that George Gershwin be called in to share the work on *Rosalie.* The results may have been musically anachronistic, but Marilyn Miller and Jack Donahue helped make the up-to-date operetta a huge success. (The story was particularly timely, inspired as it was by the recent well-publicized visit to New York of Queen Marie of Rumania and her daughter, Princess Ileana. Also, one of the leading characters was modeled after Lindbergh.)

The New Moon could have used all of Romberg's time. With a book written by Hammerstein, Mandel, and Schwab, the show was such a disaster when it opened in Philadelphia in December, 1927, that it was quickly withdrawn for repairs. The libretto was completely rewritten, an almost entirely new score was composed, and major replacements were made in the cast. What should have been titled *The New, New Moon* reopened eight months later in Cleveland. This time all went well, and it soon began a highly profitable New York engagement. Starring Robert Halliday and Evelyn Herbert, the musical was very much in the accepted tradition of Graustarkian operetta, even though its adventuresome tale was based on an actual historical occurrence. As for the performances, according to Robert Benchley, "We haven't seen such refayned acting since the days when the Mysterious Stranger with the white plume turned out to be Prince Boris in disguise. And *then* what merry-making at the inn there was! A toast, a toast to Prince Boris!"

The score of *The New Moon* contained more hits than any other Romberg musical—"One Kiss" (echoing Vincent Youmans' "No, No, Nanette"), "Wanting You," "Stouthearted Men," "Lover, Come Back to Me" (described by critic Percy Hammond as "A hot torch psalm"), and "Softly, As in a Morning Sunrise" (which has prompted some unromantic souls to question if there is any other kind).

In addition to many motion picture assignments in the 1930's, Romberg continued to compose for the theatre, though with lessened activity and success. The moderately popular *May Wine*, written with Frank Mandel and Oscar Hammerstein II, was somewhat daring because it dealt with psycho-

THE NEW MOON *(1928). Robert Halliday, Evelyn Herbert, and William O'Neal find happiness on a peaceful island after arriving on the good ship* New Moon. (*Costumes by Charles LeMaire.*)

59

analysis and because it also eliminated the customary chorus line. Nevertheless, the story was still so basically time-worn that George Jean Nathan dismissed it as "a musical mothball laid scenically in Vienna and critically in Cain's."

Like Friml, Romberg cared little about keeping up with musical trends. For a while, when it seemed that audiences no longer appreciated his type of musical theatre, he abandoned composing to form an orchestra. It toured successfully during the early Forties, giving concerts devoted to semiclassical music, with an emphasis on his own compositions.

Romberg returned to Broadway in 1945 with *Up in Central Park*. The previous year, producer Michael Todd had read a book about the corrupt political leader, Boss Tweed, and his gang. This gave him an idea for a musical of old New York that would contrast the machinations of Tweed and Tammany Hall with the simple pastoral pleasures of Central Park. When Todd approached Herbert and Dorothy Fields to write the book, they immediately thought of Romberg for the music. The opportunity to create another period score proved irresistible, and he readily agreed to compose the music, with Miss Fields supplying the lyrics. Their songs succeeded admirably in capturing the nostalgic, Currier and Ives atmosphere of the production, most

UP IN CENTRAL PARK *(1945). Helen Tamiris' "Skating Ballet" was in the manner of an animated Currier and Ives print. (Costumes by Grace Houston and Ernest Schraps; setting by Howard Bay.)*

PHOTO BY LUCAS-PRITCHARD

notably in "The Big Back Yard," "Carousel in the Park," "April Snow," and "Close as Pages in a Book." The libretto may have been moldy, but wartime audiences found in the musical enough of the romantic charm of a bygone day to make it one of Romberg's longest-running hits.

The composer's last two theatrical ventures were also set in New York in the nineteenth century. Neither one, however, did well at the box office. *My Romance,* adapted from Edward Sheldon's play, *Romance,* was Romberg's first Shubert production in eighteen years. Other than making a star of Anne Jeffreys, however, it offered little that was noteworthy.

On November 10, 1951, at the age of sixty-four, Romberg died of a cerebral hemorrhage. The show he was working on at the time, *The Girl in Pink Tights,* was produced two and a half years later, with a score completed by Don Walker. Its historically accurate account of the first American musical comedy, *The Black Crook,* may have been fairly dull, but it did serve well enough to display the ample talents of Jeanmaire, the dynamic French dancer, making her first appearance in a Broadway musical.

Once when he was asked about musical trends, Sigmund Romberg replied, "I don't care what the form is. But a melody is still a melody. Nothing succeeds like a popular tune—a romantic tune. Romantic music will never die because deep at the roots of all people is the theme of love." Today, we might add to the Romberg observation that nothing succeeds like a Romberg operetta—particularly in the summertime. Whether they are presented in the open or under a tent; whether with amateurs, semiprofessionals, or all-Equity casts, the hardiest, most perennial summer-theatre attractions are the melodious, old-fashioned, but enduring works overflowing with sentiment, charm, and romance. Indeed, as the Jerry Bock–Sheldon Harnick song, "Summer Is," so delightfully tells us:

> Winter is gloves and homburg,
> Winter is cold cement;
> Summer is Sigmund Romberg
> In a music tent.*

* Reprinted by permission of Valando Music Corp.

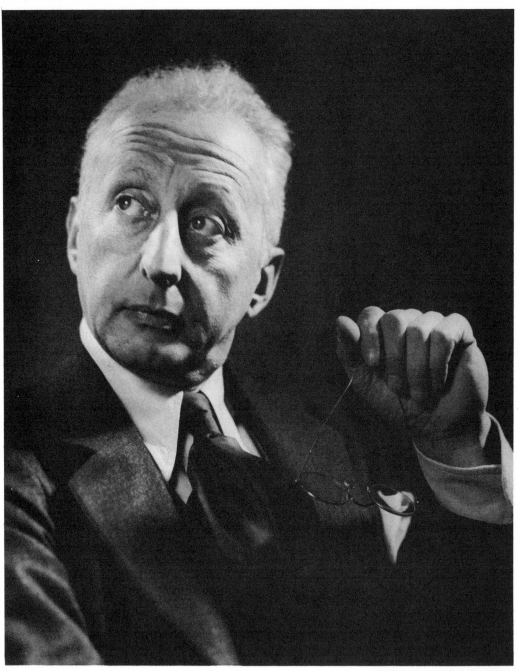

Jerome Kern.

Jerome Kern

FRANZ LEHAR's *The Merry Widow* swirled into New York at the New Amsterdam Theatre on October 21, 1907. Not only did it become the supreme musical attraction of the period, but it also inaugurated Broadway's greatest influx of European-originated or European-inspired operettas. Thereafter, for almost a decade, anything that had been shown on the banks of the Thames, the Seine, or, even better, the Danube, was imported by hopeful producers anxious to duplicate the success of the Lehár work. Of course, American writers were also creating musical entertainments. But apart from the George M. Cohan shows and the elaborate Ziegfeld and Shubert revues, the strains of the waltz heard in the Kingdom of Graustark set the musical pattern on Broadway for at least ten years.

This pattern may be detected merely from the titles of some of the leading importations. After *The Merry Widow* came *The Gay Hussars* by Emmerich Kalman, followed by Oscar Straus's *The Chocolate Soldier* and Lehár's *The Count of Luxembourg*. Female royalty of the day included *The Dollar Princess, The Slim Princess, The Balkan Princess,* and *The Merry Countess* (which was just another name for Johann Strauss's *Die Fledermaus*). Ladies of less noble birth were ardently serenaded in *The Spring Maid, The Pink Lady, The Quaker Girl, The Doll Girl,* and even *The Peasant*

Girl. Broadway also had a *Sunshine Girl* by Paul Rubens and a *Midnight Girl* by Jean Briquet, while *The Girl from Montmartre, The Maid of Athens,* and *The Girl from Brazil* used titles designed to emphasize the exotic nature of their respective locales.

Although such a grand parade of grand operettas did occasionally provide evenings that were entertaining, these productions usually proved to be just too heavy, in their original form, for American audiences. It was often necessary to call in an American composer—or, at least, one familiar with American audiences—to provide some light, bright tunes to make them more palatable. The man most often chosen for this musical grafting was a young, studious-looking song-writer named Jerome Kern. Kern had the knack of injecting a new lilt into the most soporific operettas; frequently, his would be the only songs in the scores to achieve any kind of popularity with sheet-music and record buyers.

These assignments gave Kern steady work for over ten years. Yet he was well aware that there was something wrong with a musical theatre that made such interpolations necessary, and he was determined that some day he would do what he could to rid the stage of patchwork scores and the artificial extravaganzas for which they were assembled. The Princess Theatre musicals in the mid-1910's gave him his long-desired opportunity. They were fresh, intimate, well-integrated shows, full of youth and melody, and they served better than anything else to establish Kern's reputation as a composer.

Perhaps more important than their popular acceptance, Kern's songs and musicals had an incalculable influence on future theatre composers. In 1914, a sixteen-year-old boy named George Gershwin attended his aunt's wedding at the Grand Central Hotel. After listening to the orchestra play Kern's "You're Here and I'm Here" from *The Laughing Husband,* he became so impressed with the number that he resolved to try to emulate the composer's invigorating style. Two years later, Richard Rodgers, then fourteen, saw Jerome Kern's musical, *Very Good Eddie,* at least a dozen times at the Standard Theatre at Broadway and 90th Street in order to absorb what he could of its sparkling and original music.

Years later, in recalling those days, Rodgers wrote in the New York *Times:* "Kern was typical of what was, and still is, good in our general maturity in this country in that he had his musical roots in the fertile middle European and English school of operetta writing, and amalgamated it with everything that was fresh in the American scene to give us something wonderfully new and clear in music writing."

Jerome David Kern was born in New York, on January 27, 1885. His father, Henry Kern, owned the street sprinkling concession in Manhattan; his mother, Fanny, was a gifted pianist and Jerome's first teacher. Soon after his son was born, the elder Kern sold his business to open a merchandising store in Newark, New Jersey, where "Romie" Kern attended grammar and high school. Because of his interest in music, he soon became proficient at the organ, and also composed songs for the school plays. In spite of this interest, however, his father insisted that he go into the family business. One of his first assignments was to buy two pianos from a dealer in New York. The man proved to be so persuasive that the seventeen-year-old buyer was talked into purchasing *two hundred* pianos. This experience convinced Kern's enraged father that his son was no businessman (though he eventually sold all two hundred at a profit) and he gave in to his wife's and his son's entreaties: Jerome could go to music school.

At the New York College of Music, Kern studied piano and harmony for about a year. He then persuaded his father to let him go to Europe for further studies in theory and composition. After spending some time on the Continent, he went to London, where he was able to secure a song-writing job with producer Charles Frohman. The task was rather menial, but it was good experience. In those days, English audiences always arrived fashionably late to the theatre; to accommodate this custom, unrelated songs were usually interpolated at the start of the shows to fill in the time while people were being seated. Kern created many such numbers, few of which received any notice.

Kern returned to New York in the fall of 1904 determined to find a place in the world of musical comedy. His work in London, unimportant though it was, had convinced him that only in the theatre could he write the kind of music for which he was best suited and which gave him the greatest personal satisfaction. With this goal in mind, he planned his career with considerable foresight Following a brief period as a song-plugger for the Lyceum Publishing Company (which had published his first piece, "At the Casino," even before he entered the New York College of Music), he was hired by Max Dreyfus of T. B. Harms as a salesman. Since Harms was a leading publisher of theatre scores, this enabled Kern to become friendly with many of the people associated with the musical theatre. He quickly convinced them of his talents as a pianist, and whenever the need arose for someone to serve as a rehearsal pianist, it was Jerome Kern who was most frequently in demand. Once hired, he would take every opportunity he could —usually during the lunch period or during rehearsal breaks—to play his own compositions. These tunes often sounded much fresher than anything in the original score—particularly after weeks of rehearsing the same numbers— and presently a song or two by Jerome Kern would be added to the production.

Kern's first important assignment came in 1904 when he revised the score of an English show, *Mr. Wix of Wickham*, to fit the special talents of Julian Eltinge, the celebrated female impersonator, who was making his

65

first appearance in a musical comedy. The composer's efforts won the critical approbation of the *American's* Alan Dale, who wrote: "Its music by Jerome D. Kern towers in such an Eiffel way above the hurdy-gurdy, penny-in-the-slot primitive accompaniment to the musical show that criticism is disarmed."

The next year, Kern had his first song hit, "How'd You Like to Spoon with Me?", set to a lyric by Edward Laska. Included in another English importation, *The Earl and the Girl,* the fetching invitation was posed by a bevy of six young ladies, all dressed in organdy, who sat on flower-bedecked swings that swung out over the audience.

Between *The Earl and the Girl* in 1905 and *The Red Petticoat,* Kern's first complete score five years later, the composer had songs interpolated in *The Catch of the Season, The Rich Mr. Hoggenheimer, The Dairy Maids, Fascinating Flora, Fluffy Ruffles, The Dollar Princess, The Gay Hussars, The Kiss Waltz,* and at least a dozen others. He was also co-composer of *The King of Cadonia* and *La Belle Paree.* The latter ("A Cook's Tour through Vaudeville with a Parisian Landscape"), was part of the program offered as the initial attraction of the Winter Garden Theatre. Making his Broadway debut in the show was Al Jolson, who played Erastus Sparkle, "a colored aristocrat of San Juan Hill, cutting a wide swath in Paris." *La Belle Paree* was one of the few productions Kern was associated with at the time that did not owe its origin to a work created in Europe.

The Red Petticoat was another all-American product. Adapted by Rida Johnson Young from her play *Next!,* the musical dealt with the adventures of a lady barber, Sophie Brush (played by Helen Lowell), in the silver-

LA BELLE PAREE *(1911). This "Jumble of Jollity" was the featured attraction of the first program at the Winter Garden. Among the identifiable members of the cast are Kitty Gordon (fourth from left), Mitzi Hajos (sixth from left), and Stella Mayhew and Al Jolson (seventh and eighth from right). It was Jolson's first appearance in a Broadway show.*

THE GIRL FROM UTAH (1914). *Joseph Cawthorn, Julia Sanderson, and Donald Brian.*

mining town of Lost River, Nevada. The lode was not a rich one, for the musical only ran for two months, but it did have the distinction of being the first musical comedy western.

Even after *The Red Petticoat,* Kern continued to supply additional songs for imported shows. Such an assignment was the somewhat misleadingly titled *The Girl from Utah,* an English musical with an English setting about a girl *from* Utah. Although the show had been a hit in London, producer Charles Frohman left nothing to chance. He hired Donald Brian, Julia Sanderson, and Joseph Cawthorn for the leads and commissioned Jerome Kern and Harry B. Smith to provide at least five new numbers. One of the additional songs, the soft, lovely "They Didn't Believe Me," was a contribution of Kern and M. E. (Michael Elder) Rourke, who had just begun to write lyrics under the pen name of Herbert Reynolds. As sung by Miss Sanderson and Mr. Brian, it not only became the outstanding song in the show, but it established Jerome Kern as one of the leading musical talents in the theatre.

His next endeavor, *90 in the Shade,* was a quick failure. Nevertheless, it served to begin his association with a young English librettist, Guy Regi-

67

nald Bolton. About this time (1915), F. Ray Comstock was having difficulties in presenting suitable attractions at his 299-seat Princess Theatre. He mentioned his problem to Elisabeth Marbury, a well-known literary agent, who came up with an idea: why not put on a series of musicals? "Everyone seems to be reforming the drama," she told him. "Various societies are doing their best to elevate it. It seems to me that now is the time for someone to do the same thing for musical comedy." Comstock agreed to give the plan a trial. He also made Bessie Marbury his co-producer and, at her suggestion, hired Guy Bolton and Jerome Kern to supply the librettos and the music.

The Princess Theatre musicals gave the thirty-year-old composer the chance he had been waiting for. The new shows would have modern stories dealing with people caught in comic but believable situations, uncluttered by massed choruses or spectacular scenery. The casts would be limited to about thirty, the orchestra would consist of eleven pieces, and there would be only two sets in each production. But most important to Kern was that he could at last create songs that would be introduced logically and meaningfully into the action of the play without the usual lengthy and obvious song cues.

The project was undeniably risky. Broadway audiences seemed to be satisfied with the elaborate costume musicals that were still the biggest drawing card in the musical theatre. Also, many theatre people doubted that such an adventurous scheme could attract customers to the tiny playhouse. Indeed, the first of the Princess Theatre series, *Nobody Home,* was a compromise between new and old. It was based on Paul Rubens' English musical, *Mr. Popple of Ippleton,* and even contained a few interpolated songs. However, Kern and Bolton (aided by at least three other lyricists) managed to turn it into what the ads called "a zippy, fox trotty musical treat," and its run of four months was decidedly encouraging. (It later toured with Fanny Brice succeeding Adele Rowland in the leading feminine role.)

By December, 1915, when they offered the second attraction, *Very Good Eddie,* Kern and his associates had perfected the new technique to such a degree that the show was an instant hit. The original libretto by Philip Bartholomae and Guy Bolton may not have been marked by any literary distinction, but it told a credible, human story about two average honeymooning couples and the comic situations that arise when they become separated on a Hudson River steamboat. As Bolton wrote in his book *Bring on the Girls!:* "It was the first of its kind to rely on situation and character laughs instead of using clowning and Weberfieldian cross-talk with which the large-scale musical filled in between the romantic scenes."*

---

* From *Bring on the Girls!* by P. G. Wodehouse and Guy Bolton. New York: Simon and Schuster, Inc.

VERY GOOD EDDIE (1915).
Eddie (Ernest Truex) finds
himself in the embarrassing
situation of going on a honeymoon with another man's
bride. The equally embar-
rassed lady is Alive Dovey.

In addition, *Very Good Eddie* had a particularly winning score which included "Some Sort of Somebody" (the lyric was by Elsie Janis, who had previously introduced it in *Miss Information*); Ernest Truex's "Thirteen Collar," and the plaintive "Babes in the Wood." The show played one year in New York (it moved to a larger theatre after five months at the Princess), and then toured for another year.

At the opening night of *Very Good Eddie*, Kern met an old friend, P. G. (Pelham Granville) Wodehouse, with whom he had once collaborated on some songs for a London musical, *The Beauty of Bath*. Kern introduced Bolton to Wodehouse, the three had supper together, and before the evening ended they had agreed to form a partnership with Bolton and Wodehouse collaborating on the librettos and Wodehouse writing the lyrics to Kern's compositions.

The new team lost little time. During 1917, Bolton, Wodehouse, and Kern collaborated on four musicals—*Have a Heart, Oh, Boy!, Leave It to Jane*, and *Miss 1917* (an unsuccessful revue with music also by Victor Herbert). *Have a Heart* was originally intended to follow *Very Good Eddie* at the Princess. Unknown to Kern and Bolton, however, Wodehouse had already promised the musical to Col. Henry W. Savage, the producer of

69

OH BOY! *(1917). Tom Powers and Marie Carroll are the ones in the center being joined in matrimony by a justice of the peace. To their left are Hal Forde and Anna Wheaton. Edna May Oliver is second from the right. Justine Johnstone (far left) and Marion Davies (third from left) were recent graduates of the* Ziegfeld Follies.

The Merry Widow. Billed as "An Up-to-Date Musical Comedy," *Have a Heart* had some attractive melodies ("And I Am All Alone," "The Road That Lies Before"), and an amusing title song which revealed the deep concern felt by a remarkably solicitous department-store owner for the welfare of his employees.

Kern and Bolton (plus Wodehouse) returned to the Princess Theatre shortly thereafter for their greatest triumph, *Oh, Boy!* According to Bolton's claim at the time, the musical was one in which "every song and lyric contributed to the action. The humor was based on situation, not interjected by the comedians." Recruited for its cast were Marion Davies and Justine Johnstone, two of Ziegfeld's most celebrated showgirls, who had small but decorative roles in support of the principals, Anna Wheaton, Tom Powers, Marie Carroll, Hal Forde, and Edna May Oliver. The sprightly "Till the Clouds Roll By" was the most popular song.

Although it was not presented at the Princess Theatre, *Leave It to Jane* was created for the Princess Theatre management, and everyone concerned made sure that it adhered to the prescribed rules of integration and intimacy. As one of the earliest musicals to use a college campus for a setting, it gave the composer and lyricist the opportunity to write songs dealing with such historical and literary subjects as "Sir Galahad," "Cleopatterer," and the legend of the Lorelei in the willowy "Siren's Song." More modern sentiments

70

were expressed in the go-getter's anthem, "Just You Watch My Step," while the entire company energetically joined in the advice to leave it to Jane, Jane, Jane. The show was so coherent and logical in its libretto, lyrics, and music that Alan Dale was moved to comment in the New York *American*: "No more are we asked to laugh at the bottle-nosed comedian as he falls down stairs; no longer is the heroine a lovely princess masquerading as the serving maid, and no more is the scene Ruritania or Monte Carlo. Today is rationally American, and the musical show has taken on a new lease of life."

The second and last musical by Bolton, Wodehouse, and Kern to play the Princess was the exclamatory successor to *Oh, Boy!*, called *Oh, Lady! Lady!!* The plot of the new work was concerned with pre- and post-marital complications on Long Island and in Greenwich Village, and its cohesion between song and story was equal to that achieved in its predecessor. Seldom before had Kern's music or Wodehouse's lyrics been more delectable. In "Before I Met You," both Vivienne Segal and Carl Randall, in the leading

LEAVE IT TO JANE (1917). *Posing on the campus of good old Atwater College are Arlene Chase, Oscar Shaw, Helen Rich, Olin Howland, Tess Mayer, and Ruloff Cuttin.*

71

OH, LADY! LADY!! *(1918). The happy newlyweds, Mollie (Vivienne Segal) and Willoughby French (Carl Randall). (Setting by Clifford Pember.)*

roles, admitted to previous loves—she had had a crush on John Drew when she was nine and he had been enamored of Lillian Russell when he was fourteen. "Not Yet" was an amusingly coquettish postponement of marriage, and in "Greenwich Village" Broadway had its first musical description of New York's Latin Quarter.

One song sung by Miss Segal during the tryout was dropped from the score before the New York première. It was a torch ballad in which the singer, after dreaming of her ideal man in the verse, then admitted:

> Along came Bill
> Who's quite the opposite
> Of all the men
> In story books.
> In grace and looks
> I know that Apollo
> Would beat him all hollow . . .*

This lyric, however, did not accurately describe the talented and handsome Carl Randall (who played the part of Willoughby French). Therefore, another song, "Do Look at Him," in which Bill did live up to the man of Miss

* Copyright © 1918 by T. B. Harms Company, New York. Copyright renewed.

72

Morris Gest (coproducer of Leave It to Jane), *P. G. Wodehouse, Guy Bolton, F. Ray Comstock, and Jerome Kern.*

Segal's dreams, had to be substituted. Three years later, attempts were made to fit "Bill" into *Sally,* but Marilyn Miller's voice was too small to make it effective. In fact, it was not until 1927, when a tearful lament was needed for Helen Morgan in a cabaret scene in *Show Boat,* that the song was revived (and revised) and at last heard on a New York stage.

The Princess Theatre shows of Guy Bolton, P. G. Wodehouse, and Jerome Kern were the first real advancements in the development of a truly native musical theatre—despite the fact that two of the members of the trio were born in England! Not only did their musicals point up the foolishness of many of the contemporary extravaganzas and operettas, but they also made the formulas of George M. Cohan seem crude and obvious. Today, this "integration" might appear somewhat awkward to modern audiences, but it is important to point out that all the Princess Theatre musicals were conscientious efforts to break away from the conventions of the theatre at that time and to establish a genuinely new form of musical comedy. Kern said, "It is my opinion that the musical numbers should carry the action of the play and should be representative of the personalities of the characters who sing them. Songs must be suited to the action and the mood of the play." That view was expressed in 1917.*

* Two more Princess Theatre shows followed *Oh, Lady! Lady!!,* though neither *Oh, My Dear* by Bolton, Wodehouse, and Louis Hirsch, nor *Toot-Sweet* by Richard A. Whiting and Leo Egan was successful. The theatre itself attracted little notice until twenty years later when the International Ladies Garment Workers Union bought it, renamed it the Labor Stage, and presented a modest revue of its own titled *Pins and Needles.*

73

Jerome Kern was undeniably sincere in his aims for the musical comedy theatre, but he had little opportunity to put them into practice when he again began to write for the regular Broadway stage. His successes at the Princess had given him prestige equal to any other theatre composer, yet when Henry Savage, or Charles Dillingham, or Florenz Ziegfeld wanted him for a lavish new production he found that they cared little for his theories of how musicals should be constructed. They wanted love songs, specialty songs, chorus songs, and, above all, hit songs, and whether a song fitted a situation in a story meant little to them. Kern had no other choice than to go along with what they wanted—if he wanted to stay active in the Broadway theatre. Therefore, it was not until he wrote *Show Boat* in 1927 that the composer again contributed anything notable to the form of musical comedy. His biggest hits of the first half of the Twenties were two conventionally ornate star vehicles with almost indistinguishable titles, *Sally* (1920) and *Sunny* (1925).

Ziegfeld planned *Sally* with meticulous care. It was to be the first starring appearance in a book musical of the delightful Marilyn (then spelled "Marilynn") Miller. To give her the strongest possible support, the producer

SALLY *(1920). Walter Catlett obviously feels he can make a glamorous star of Marilyn Miller, the poor dishwasher of the Alley Inn. Mary Hay, however, seems momentarily distracted. (Setting by Joseph Urban.)*

BROWN BROS.

signed two expert comedians, Leon Errol and Walter Catlett, for important roles. Originally, it was to have been another Bolton, Wodehouse, and Kern collaboration, but as Wodehouse was in England writing a novel, most of the lyrics were written by another English-born writer, Clifford Grey. The book, a durable Cinderella fable about a poor slavey who becomes a *Ziegfeld Follies* star, was patterned along lines similar to a recent hit called *Irene*. (Indeed, *Sally* was also related to two other shows that followed it: *Mary* and the all-inclusive *Sally, Irene and Mary.*)

Though the eminent Victor Herbert was called upon to provide a "Butterfly Ballet" for the finale, it was Jerome Kern whom Alexander Woollcott was now referring to as "that fount of melody." Three of Kern's songs for *Sally* were originally intended for two unproduced musicals—from *The Little Thing,* he took "The Church 'round the Corner" (lyric by Wodehouse), and from *Brewster's Millions,* he added the airy "Whip-poor-will" and the poignant "Look for the Silver Lining" (both lyrics by George Gard "Bud" DeSylva). The New York run of *Sally* was 570 performances, just two less than the initial run of *Show Boat.*

Sunny, which opened five years after *Sally,* made every effort to capitalize on the fame of its predecessor. Produced by Charles Dillingham, its "box-office" cast was headed by Marilyn Miller (again in the title role), Jack

SUNNY *(1925). The "particularly luminous beauty of Marilyn Miller" (to use the* Times's *phrase) is here displayed in a circus costume designed by James Reynolds.*

BROWN BROS.

75

Donahue, Clifton Webb, Mary Hay (who had also been in *Sally*), Joseph Cawthorn, Cliff "Ukulele Ike" Edwards (succeeded during most of the run by Borrah Minevitch), Pert Kelton, and George Olsen and his Orchestra. It also marked the first association between Jerome Kern and the team of Otto Harbach and Oscar Hammerstein II. As in *Sally*, there was little attempt to tell a coherent tale in dialogue and songs ("Our job was to tell a story with a cast that had been assembled as if for a revue," recalls Hammerstein). But the performances were excellent, the James Reynolds settings and costumes were sumptuous, and the songs, especially the still-popular "Who?," were whistled and hummed as soon as they were heard. Among them were the title number (with its nonconformist advice, "Never comb your hair, Suuuunny!"); the consoling duet, "Two Little Bluebirds"; "D'Ye Love Me?"; and the joyfully expectant "When We Get Our Divorce."

Secure in his fame and prestige, Kern was anxious to try something more daring than the frothy entertainments he was regularly called upon to turn

SHOW BOAT (1927). *The dramatic scene in which Julie, the mulatto entertainer of the "Cotton Blossom," faints after her white husband, Steve Baker, has sucked the blood from one of her fingers. Francis X. Mahoney as Rubber Face, Charles Ellis as Steve, Helen Morgan as Julie, Norma Terris as Magnolia, Eve Puck as Ellie, Charles Winninger as Cap'n Andy, and Edna May Oliver as Parthy. (Costumes by John Harkrider; setting by Joseph Urban.)*

BROWN BROS.

out. The breezy intimacy of the Princess shows had given way to opulent star-studded attractions, as inane in their way as the turgid operettas for which he had once supplied additional songs. Both Kern and Hammerstein discussed the matter often, and they finally agreed to undertake an adult musical together if either one ever found a good enough story.

Relaxing one evening, Kern began to read a new novel by Edna Ferber called *Show Boat*. Even before he had finished it, he knew that here, at last, was the perfect work to transform into a musical. Not only did it have a great title, but it also had a romantic yet credible story, colorful characters, and nostalgic locales. Hammerstein, also excited about its possibilities, promptly agreed to do the adaptation and the lyrics.

Many "old pros" in the theatre thought the scheme was impractical. *Show Boat* shattered too many musical comedy conventions and taboos. It dealt with two unhappy marriages. It showed the harsh life of southern Negroes. Part of its dramatic conflict resulted from the delicate subject of miscegenation. The biggest surprise of the year came when Florenz Ziegfeld agreed to produce it. Perhaps the Great Glorifier had some notion about glorifying the American Negro, but he soon realized that in this production the authors would need a free hand in most artistic matters.

Show Boat broke with tradition right from the start. In the first scene on the Natchez levee, there were no rows of leggy young ladies all chirping in unison about how it feels just dandy to be with Cap'n Andy. The writers took the bold step of opening the play with a group of colored dock workers lamenting the drudgery of lifting the back-breaking bales of cotton. When

SHOW BOAT *(1927). Cap'n Andy quiets the crowd during a performance of* The Parson's Bride, *after a backwoodsman, in the box directly above his head, has threatened to shoot the villain in the play. Charles Winninger as Cap'n Andy. (Costumes by John Harkrider; setting by Joseph Urban.)*

77

the ladies of the town arrived with their beaux to welcome the showboat troupe, both whites and Negroes sang about the "cotton blossom"—the townspeople referring to the name of the ship and the stevedores still concerned only with the weight of the cotton bales. Other numbers were equally valid with regard to character and to mood. "Make Believe"—which came right after the self-doubting "Where's the Mate for Me?", sung by the gambler, Gaylord Ravenal—was a sentiment both Ravenal and Magnolia Hawks could express naturally upon first meeting. Later, the expansive, "You Are Love" revealed their more mature emotions. To provide a unifying theme for the somewhat sprawling plot, "Ol' Man River" was sung by a Negro dock worker to convey the hopelessness he felt in contrast to the might and indifference of the Mississippi River.

For the tragic mulatto, Julie LaVerne, there were two songs to reveal her deep attachment to her worthless man—"Can't Help Lovin' Dat Man" and "Bill," the song that had been discarded from *Oh, Lady! Lady!!* Ravenal's "Till Good Luck Comes My Way" was a swaggering piece in which Kern skillfully repeated four bars from "Make Believe" in order to point up Magnolia's hold on the outwardly indifferent gambler. The comic dancers, Frank and Ellie, had an amusing duet in "I Might Fall Back on You," and Ellie, as a solo, did the mocking lament, "Life upon the Wicked Stage."

Ziegfeld wanted to make *Show Boat* the initial attraction at his newly constructed Ziegfeld Theatre, with Elizabeth Hines, Guy Robertson, and Paul Robeson signed for the leading parts. Production delays, however, forced him to substitute *Rio Rita* (score by Harry Tierney and Joseph McCarthy) as the Ziegfeld Theatre's first tenant in February, 1927.*

Heralded as "An All-American Musical Comedy," *Show Boat* began its tryout tour in Washington, D. C., with a cast headed by Charles Winninger (Cap'n Andy), Norma Terris (Magnolia), Howard Marsh (Ravenal), Jules Bledsoe (Joe), Helen Morgan (Julie), and the team of Sammy White and Eva Puck as Frank and Ellie. At its first public performance, the show ran an hour and a half overtime. This caused the deletion of seven songs, including "Mis'ry's Comin' 'Round," parts of which still remain in the score as background themes. "Why Do I Love You?," the third major love duet, was added in Philadelphia.

Show Boat arrived at the Ziegfeld Theatre on December 27, 1927, preceded by the largest advance ticket sale up to that time. It became such a substantial hit that, within a year after its opening, the producer made plans to assemble another company to run concurrently in New York, with Raymond Hitchcock as Cap'n Andy, Libby Holman as Julie, and Paul Robeson as Joe.

---

* The producer's cancellation of the *Show Boat* contracts provoked a $55,000 law suit by Miss Hines. She later settled for $12,000.

These plans, however, never materialized. At the completion of its run, *Show Boat* toured for seven months with its original cast, except that Miss Terris was succeeded by her understudy, Irene Dunne.

Ziegfeld revived the musical only three years after its first New York engagement. Apart from the replacements of Dennis King for Howard Marsh and Paul Robeson for Jules Bledsoe, the featured performers were the same as in the original company. A second major revival in 1946 ran for a year at the Ziegfeld Theatre. Its cast was headed by Ralph Dumke, Jan Clayton, Carol Bruce, Kenneth Spencer, and Buddy Ebsen.

Of all his musicals, *Show Boat* is undeniably Jerome Kern's most impressive work. It remains as warm and colorful to today's audiences as it was to those of thirty years ago. Its magnificent score is such an essential part of the story that even the time-worn sequences still have the power to move audiences. By at least attempting to deal with the serious aspects of society, Kern and Hammerstein broadened the scope of subject matter and treatment in the musical theatre and thus laid the foundation for *Porgy and Bess, South Pacific,* and other serious musical plays. In his review of *Show Boat* in *McCalls,* Stark Young accurately predicted: "Some of its best numbers are so successful in their combination of the theatrical elements, music, acting, scene, as to suggest openings for the development not of mere musical comedy, but of popular opera."

The great success scored by Helen Morgan in *Show Boat* prompted Kern and Hammerstein to write a musical specifically for her, *Sweet Adeline,* which was frankly designed to capitalize on the singer's great popularity. Nevertheless, with a score that included such pieces as "Why Was I Born?" and "Don't Ever Leave Me," the authors made effective use of music to enhance the sweet, delicate, turn-of-the-century atmosphere of the story.

During the early Thirties, the musical theatre offered many sophisticated and satirical works that reflected the mood of a country going through a depression. This was not the theatre of Jerome Kern. In his musicals he tried to capture a quality of timelessness that would have no relation either to the artificial operettas of the past or to the glossy smartness of most contemporary productions. Particularly with *The Cat and the Fiddle* (written with Otto Harbach) and *Music in the Air* (written with Oscar Hammerstein), Kern shut out the world around him and replaced it with a very personal theatrical world of his own. Both of these musicals were set in modern Europe (but contained no political implications), both were concerned with backstage romances, and both depended completely on music to tell their stories. Each work even avoided a conventional designation—*The Cat and the Fiddle* was billed as "A Musical Love Story," while *Music in the Air* was "A Musical Adventure."

THE CAT AND THE FIDDLE
(1931). *Georges Metaxa and
Bettina Hall are serenaded by
George Meader singing "The
Night Was Made for Love."
(Setting by Henry Dreyfuss.)*

MUSIC IN THE AIR *(1932) Oscar
Hammerstein II and Jerome
Kern photographed in the
orchestra pit of the Alvin
Theatre during a rehearsal.*

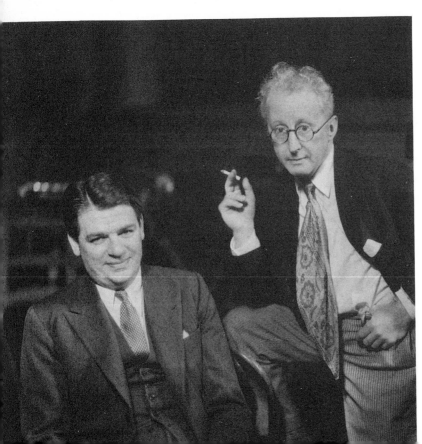

"Broadway has not heard lovelier music in all its life," was the glowing verdict of the *American's* critic, Gilbert Gabriel, in his review of *The Cat and the Fiddle*. As for the spell cast by *Music in the Air*, it was potent enough to have Alexander Woollcott hail it as "that endearing refuge, that gracious shelter from a troubled world . . . so drenched in melody that it is an unfailing delight." Both productions—particularly *The Cat and the Fiddle*—were burdened by a stodgy plot, but the songs and the adroit way in which they contributed to the action brought a quality of lyricism to the Broadway theatre that no other musical of the period could match. Among the melodies of *The Cat and the Fiddle* were "The Night Was Made for Love," "She Didn't Say, 'Yes,'" "Try to Forget," "One Moment Alone," and "I Watch the Love Parade." From *Music in the Air* have come "I've Told Every Little Star," "And Love Was Born," "The Song Is You," and "In Egern on the Tegern See."

Although Kern and Harbach's *Roberta* attempted to follow the pattern of *The Cat and the Fiddle* and *Music in the Air*, it was far too dependent on

PHOTO BY VANDAMM

MUSIC IN THE AIR (1932). *Following their adventures in the sophisticated theatrical world of Munich, Karl and Sieglinde return to their simple life in Edendorf, in the Bavarian mountains. Reinald Werrenrath as Cornelius, Al Shean as Dr. Lessing, Mary McQuade as Tila, Katherine Carrington as Sieglinde, and Walter Slezak as Karl. (Costumes by John Harkrider; setting by Joseph Urban.)*

ROBERTA (1933). *Bob Hope has difficulty tearing Ray Middleton away from Lyda Roberti and Sydney Greenstreet. (Costumes by Kiviette; setting by Clark Robinson.)*

the stock formulas of musical comedy. The show was a commercial success, however, partly due to its now famous cast (Tamara, Ray Middleton, Bob Hope, Sydney Greenstreet, Fay Templeton, and George Murphy, plus Fred MacMurray as a member of a vocal and instrumental group known as the California Collegians), and partly due to its many attractive Jerome Kern melodies. One of them, "Smoke Gets in Your Eyes," ranks among the composer's most inspired creations, but some found its beauties hard to detect upon first hearing. In his review in the *World-Telegram*, critic Robert Garland complained: "There's no tune you can whistle when you leave the theatre. I tried to pucker on the one about smoke getting in your eyes, but it turned out to be 'The Last Roundup' before I reached the sidewalk."

From 1934 on, Jerome Kern made his permanent home in California, where he composed many songs for the films. He returned to New York twice for theatre assignments. In 1939, he collaborated with Oscar Hammerstein

II on *Very Warm for May*, a commercial failure in spite of a frequently witty book and a score that contained the classic "All the Things You Are."

Six years later Kern returned to New York. He planned to produce a revival of *Show Boat* with Hammerstein, and he was also preparing a score for a musical sponsored by Rodgers and Hammerstein based on the life of Annie Oakley. A few days after his arrival in the city he suffered a fatal heart attack. He died on November 11, 1945, at the age of sixty.

Jerome Kern was the first real pioneer in the creation of a genuinely native musical theatre, the "daddy of modern musical comedy music," as Arthur Schwartz once called him. Apart from his unrivaled gifts as a melodist, he was a brilliant creator of purely functional theatrical music. It was in the application of this ability that he had such a profound influence on the structure of the American musical stage. Frequently dogmatic about the manner in which his songs were to be performed, he was nonetheless the first major composer to become actively interested in raising the level of musical comedy librettos and lyrics. From the Princess Theatre shows, through *Show Boat*, *The Cat and the Fiddle*, and *Music in the Air*, Kern was a leader in establishing the pattern for the modern musical theatre.

VERY WARM FOR MAY (*1939*). *Robert Shackleton, Richard Quine, Grace McDonald, and Eve Arden in an amorous predicament. (Setting by Vincente Minnelli.)*

Irving Berlin.

Irving Berlin

Both TIN PAN ALLEY and the Broadway musical theatre are ostensibly concerned with popular music, but the attitudes and approaches of song-writers in both localities are almost entirely different. Tin Pan Alley writers are only interested in creating hit songs with the widest possible appeal to the record and sheet-music buying public. Composers and lyricists for the theatre, however, are interested in the finer points; how songs fit characters and situations in a story, and how they are sung and performed. That many show tunes become individual hits is proof of their power to surmount the many theatrical elements—settings, costumes, dancing, singing, plot—that are also vying for the audience's attention.

Geographically, Tin Pan Alley is just around the corner from Shubert Alley, but only a surprisingly few writers have managed to turn that corner successfully. The prolific Walter Donaldson wrote two scores in the Twenties, the flop *Sweetheart Time* and the hit *Whoopee* (written with the equally prolific pop lyricist, Gus Kahn). More recently such Brill Building alumni as Bob Merrill ("Doggie in the Window"), Ervin Drake ("I Believe"), and John Kander and Fred Ebb ("My Coloring Book") have gone on to win new fame on the musical stage. Conversely, theatre writers occasionally take a stab at writing strictly commercial pieces. Such standards as the Gershwin brothers' "The Man I Love," Rodgers and Hart's "Blue Moon," and Kern and Hammerstein's "The Last Time I Saw Paris" achieved popularity unaided by their introduction in a play or a movie.

Irving Berlin is unique among his colleagues. He has lived and thrived in both worlds. Some of his most enduring songs were first heard across the footlights, but just as many were composed with no other purpose than to strike a responsive chord in as many people as possible. Not only has Berlin thrived, he has been a leader in both areas. A creator of music and lyrics for over half a century, he has written songs that have become so much a part of our lives that it is a bit difficult to think of him as once having been the most daring and influential innovator in the field of popular music.

Berlin popularized ragtime with "Alexander's Ragtime Band," thereby starting the dance craze and paving the way for the popular acceptance of jazz. He introduced ragtime into the theatre with *Watch Your Step*, and later wrote the music for four *Music Box Revues*, probably the most tasteful, melodious series ever offered. In the Thirties, he kept up with the times by contributing to the politically satirical musicals born of the depression years. Then, in 1946, after forty years as a song-writer, Berlin was able to achieve his greatest theatrical success, *Annie Get Your Gun*.

As a creator of popular songs, Irving Berlin has the wonderful ability to communicate his own emotions in words and music. Frequently working with a title idea or an accidental phrase, he has developed many of his most famous songs from everyday expressions that are instantly understood and appreciated. Four of his ballads, "All Alone," "What'll I Do," "Always," and "Remember," which were inspired by events in his own life, are considered today as the apotheosis of the romantic waltz. Yet each one begins with an almost conversational phrase ("All alone, I'm so all alone . . ."; "What'll I do . . ."; "I'll be loving you, always . . ."; "Remember the night . . .") and then goes on to unexpected musical and lyrical ideas. Berlin himself has said, "There's no such thing as a new melody. Our work is to connect the old phrases in a new way, so that they will sound like a new tune. Do you know that the public, when it hears a new song, anticipates the next line? Well, the writers who do *not* give them something they are expecting are those who are successful."

Famous for the apparent simplicity of many of his songs, Berlin has also created melodies and lyrics of remarkable ingenuity. Of these, "Lazy," composed in 1924, is a notable example. Its melodic line, which switches every four or eight bars without repeating a previous musical phrase, is so artfully constructed that the singer is made to sound as if he is actually getting lazier and lazier. Moreover, it mated to a lyric abounding in such intricate rhyming as:

> I wanna peep through the deep
> Tangled wildwood
> Counting sheep till I sleep
> Like a child would.

With a great big valise-full
Of books to read where it's peaceful,
While I'm killing time
Being lazy.*

Irving Berlin was born in the little Russian town of Temun (he himself is not sure of the exact spelling) on May 11, 1888, the youngest of eight children of Cantor Moses and Leah Baline. His real first name is Israel. At the age of two, he was taken by his family to the United States in their escape from the anti-Semitic raids of the Cossacks. Along with many other immigrant families, the Balines went to live on the lower East Side of New York. As Berlin recalls, "There were ten of us in four rooms, and in the summer some of us slept on the fire escape or on the roof. I was a boy with poor parents, but I didn't starve; I wasn't cold or hungry. There was always bread and butter and hot tea. I guess I never felt poverty because I'd never known anything else."

Irving was eight when his father died. Just six years later, to avoid being a burden to his mother, he ran away from home. To a runaway boy, the Bowery was the only place to go. There Berlin earned pennies by favoring saloon patrons with his vocal renditions of the tearful ballads of the day. One evening he discovered an abandoned upright piano in the back room of a saloon, and he would return there night after night to try to pick out tunes on the worn keyboard. This was as far as his musical education ever went; he still can play only in the key of F sharp.

In the early years of the century, it was not particularly difficult to get a part in the chorus of a touring musical show. Berlin was only fourteen when he was seen briefly in Edward E. Rice's production, *The Show Girl.* The show eventually reached Broadway, but Berlin was left stranded in Binghamton.

Despite reverses, Berlin became convinced that his future lay in the field of music. He next got a job as a song plugger for Harry Von Tilzer, a leading composer and publisher. One of Von Tilzer's songs was then being introduced by Buster Keaton and his family at Tony Pastor's Music Hall. Berlin's job was simple. After the song was sung, he would rise from his seat in the balcony—as if spontaneously inspired—to reprise the refrain of the song. For this he received five dollars a week.

Berlin soon acquired a steadier position as a singing waiter at the fashionably named Pelham Café in Chinatown. It was while working there that the young minstrel wrote his first lyric. The song was "Marie from Sunny Italy," and the music was created by "Nick" Nicholson, the pianist at the café. It came to be written because Nicholson and the proprietor, Mike Salter, became irritated when they discovered that two waiters at a rival tavern had already written a song and had had it published. As Berlin was already known for his parodies of popular songs, Nicholson asked him to write the words for the new piece. They even found a publisher, Joseph W. Stern and Company (which later published Romberg's first compositions), but all "Marie from Sunny Italy" ever netted the neophyte lyricist was thirty-seven cents. The song, however, started both a career and a new name: "I. Berlin" was the way he was credited on the sheet music.

Undaunted by the meager returns from his first effort, Berlin tried writing other songs, this time creating both the words and the music. His initial attempts resulted in "The Best of Friends Must Part," "Queenie, My Own," and "Dorando." The last song (an Italian dialect number about a famous marathon runner) was the one that really started Berlin's career as a full-time song-writer. It had been commissioned by a vaudeville performer who never returned to claim it and to pay the promised ten dollars. Unwilling to let his

Irving Berlin working for Ted Snyder as a $25 a week composer.

efforts go unrewarded, young Berlin bravely took the manuscript to Ted Snyder, a composer and publisher. To Berlin's surprise, Snyder liked the lyric so much that he offered twenty-five dollars for both the words and the music. There was just one difficulty—Berlin had written only the words. Putting on a bold front, he nervously improvised a hesitant melody while an arranger took down the notes. Fortunately, he got away with the ruse and the song was published. It did fairly well. Even more successful was "Sadie Salome, Go Home," an operatic parody, which prompted Snyder to hire Berlin as a staff lyricist at twenty-five dollars a week, plus royalties. As Alexander Woollcott, Berlin's biographer, wrote, "He had turned a corner and found himself in Tin Pan Alley."

Berlin worked hard, even painfully, on his songs. His ambition was to write the music as well as the words, and in order to show Snyder that he could do both, the young man would return to the office every morning at two and work until dawn. He turned out songs in such profusion—with an impressive amount of hits—that Snyder took him in as a partner. The two men also appeared together in a revue, *Up and Down Broadway*, in which they were attired as tennis playing men-about-town and sang a medley of their creations.

In 1911, Berlin, as a successful music publisher and writer of more than fifty songs, was elected to membership in the exclusive theatrical club, The Friars. The club was then preparing its first annual *Friars' Frolics* revue. Berlin was going to appear in it with his idol, George M. Cohan, and he was anxious to introduce a new song in honor of the occasion. He had already published a song called "Alexander and his Clarinet"; although it did not do very well, Berlin felt that the lyric could still be salvaged if combined with a stronger melody. He tried it out with an untitled instrumental piece he had composed, and found that with certain changes in the words it not only could be made to fit but that it also had a particularly infectious quality. He called it "Alexander's Ragtime Band." Encouraged by its reception in the *Friars' Frolics*, Berlin submitted it to the management of the *Folies Bergère*, a vaudeville show, who promptly rejected it. "Alexander" finally found a home on Broadway—if only temporarily—as part of the musical accompaniment at the Columbia Burlesque House.

The first real response to "Alexander's Ragtime Band" came when it was trumpeted out by the dynamic Emma Carus during a vaudeville engagement in Chicago. Audiences quickly responded to the compelling invitation to "Come on an' hear! Come on an' hear!" and before long the entire nation was singing it and dancing to it. Technically, except in a few places, the song is not authentic ragtime. But Berlin, who had tried to popularize the "ragged meter" before, felt that it would be uncommercial at the time and so used a melody that combined a march rhythm, simulated bugle calls, and a deliberately borrowed line from Stephen Foster's "Old Folks at Home." To the public, however, the song was different enough and exciting enough to be accepted as something brand new. Tin Pan Alley had safely broken with the past, ragtime ballroom dancing (with its menagerie of Turkey Trots, Bunny Hugs, and Grizzly Bears) became the latest dance craze, and at twenty-three, Irving Berlin was the most successful song-writer in the United States.

Just as Berlin was beginning to enjoy his sudden eminence, his young bride, the former Dorothy Goetz (sister of song-writer and producer E. Ray Goetz) died after contracting typhoid fever on their wedding trip to Cuba. This tragedy inspired his first real ballad, "When I Lost You," a marked departure from the earlier comic dialect numbers he had written to cover his lack of grammatical assurance.

Although many of Berlin's early creations had been added to musical comedies and revues, it was not until 1914 that he was given the opportunity to compose an entire score. At the urging of producer Charles Dillingham, Berlin wrote the songs for *Watch Your Step*, "A Syncopated Musical Show" designed specifically to show off the dancing skills of Vernon and Irene Castle. The program credited "plot, if any" to the ubiquitous Harry B. Smith, though the show was basically a revue. Smith, who had served as lyricist for many of the theatre's greatest composers, admired Berlin's facility with rhymes, particularly one in the song of the matinee idol, "They Always Follow Me Around":

> The matinee I play on Wednesday
> Is what I've nicknamed my old hen's day.°

The number that has remained the most popular is "Play a Simple Melody," in which a counter melody is ingeniously used to comment musically and verbally on the old-fashioned sentiments of the main theme. But there was such a native vitality and freshness about the entire score that the anonymous critic of *Theatre Magazine* summed up his appraisal of the music by stating unequivocally, if ungeographically, "Berlin is now a part of America."

Other musicals followed in rapid succession. Among them were *Stop! Look! Listen!*, *The Century Girl* (with songs also by Victor Herbert), and *Dance and Grow Thin*, one of the then-fashionable midnight revues that entertained theatregoing insomniacs.

During the First World War, Sgt. Irving Berlin received a special commission to write the songs for *Yip, Yip, Yaphank*, "A Musical 'Mess' Cooked Up by the Boys of Camp Upton." George M. Cohan may have conveyed the spirit of aggressive patriotism in his rousing "Over There," but it was Berlin who caught the more human emotions of the lowly soldier in such poignant pieces

---

° Copyright © 1914 Irving Berlin. Copyright renewed. Reprinted by permission of Irving Berlin Music Corporation.

WATCH YOUR STEP (1914).
*The Castle Walk as performed
by Vernon and Irene Castle.*

BROWN BROS.

as "Oh, How I Hate to Get Up In the Morning" and "Kitchen Police," the later with its mocking, mournful lines:

> Against my wishes
> I wash the dishes
> To make
>   this
>   wide
>   world
> Safe for democracy*

The highlight of the minstrel show that opened the first act of *Yip, Yip, Yaphank* was the joyous cakewalk, "Mandy." Berlin used the number in the *Ziegfeld Follies* the following year. In the new production, it became the first act finale, and it brought down the curtain on a strutting spectacle featuring Van and Schenck, Marilyn Miller as the famous minstrel, George Primrose, and Ray Dooley as Mandy.†

* Copyright 1918 Irving Berlin. Copyright renewed. Reprinted by permission of Irving Berlin Music Corporation.

† Another song first intended for *Yip, Yip, Yaphank* was never used because its author felt that it was too full of patriotic zeal to fit comfortably into the revue's lighthearted format. This was "God Bless America," which remained unpublished until twenty years later when it was introduced by Kate Smith at an Armistice Day celebration.

The *Follies of 1919* contained other delightful Irving Berlin songs—"A Pretty Girl Is like a Melody" (which became the unofficial theme song of *all* the *Follies*); "You'd Be Surprised" (a wide-eyed piece of suggestiveness sung by Eddie Cantor); and an anti-Prohibition Bert Williams specialty, "You Cannot Make Your Shimmy Shake on Tea," co-authored with Rennold Wolf.

When he was still in uniform, Berlin once made a casual suggestion to Sam Harris that led to one of his most ambitious and successful ventures. Meeting the Broadway producer at the Friars Club one day, he remarked, "Sam, if you ever build a theatre just for musicals, why not call it the Music Box?" Several weeks later, Harris telephoned Berlin. "Remember that Music Box idea of yours? Well, I've just bought a piece of land on the Astor property on West 45th Street. You can have your Music Box whenever you want it."

In association with film producer Joseph Schenck, Harris and Berlin built the intimate, elegantly appointed Music Box as the only theatre ever intended to display the musical creations of just one composer in a series of annual revues. The *Music Box Revues* were as lavish as anything Ziegfeld

COURTESY IRVING BERLIN

MUSIC BOX REVUE OF 1921. *Irving Berlin as he appeared in the next-to-closing spot with the young ladies known as the Eight Notes. The eighth note (extreme right) is Miriam Hopkins.*

put on, but they showed decidedly more imagination in stagecraft and in settings. Writing of the second edition, Alexander Woollcott once commented that for a while it looked as if none of the players "would be permitted to resort to any such routine and hackneyed entrance as merely walking on the stage. No, they emerge from tree trunks and bird cages, spring up out of trap doors and lightly swing down from high trapezes. When this is not possible they walk groggily down interminable staircases of black velvet, managing the perilous descent as nonchalantly as possible under the circumstances of having to carry with them gowns of silver sequins weighing about a ton each."

In addition to their technical innovations, the *Music Box Revues* were so distinguished by the quality of their humor and their music that people eagerly parted with the unusually high price of $5.50 per ticket in order to experience the myriad pleasures of sight and sound (and in two editions, even smell) that were assembled under the guidance of director Hassard Short.

At a cost of $947,000 for the theatre (including the land) and almost $188,000 for the first *Music Box Revue,* both were officially opened on September 22, 1921. Customers came to see the theatre and the revue in such numbers that construction and production expenses were paid back before a year had gone by. Among the musical attractions of this edition were the Brox Sisters tearing through the masterful rag, "Everybody Step"; Sam Bernard commenting wryly on dance-floor gyrations in "They Call It Dancing" ("A man can squeeze all the she's/With his arms and his knees"*); and Paul Frawley and Wilda Bennett singing the graceful theme song, "Say It with Music." Unlike "A Pretty Girl Is like a Melody," which developed into the anthem of the *Ziegfeld Follies* almost accidentally, "Say It with Music" was composed especially to be the official song of all the *Music Box Revues.* However, this "molten masterpiece" (in Percy Hammond's phrase) was completed long before the theatre itself was finished, and Berlin, still the irrepressible song-plugger, could not wait until the première to hear it played by an orchestra. One night he gave the manuscript to the band leader at the Sixty Club to play just once. But the customers kept demanding it again and again, and "Say It with Music" was whistled and sung by New Yorkers for months before its official introduction.

Other *Music Box Revues* were also filled with musical riches. The lilting jewel, "Lady of the Evening," was in the second edition, in which it was sung by John Steel who stood alone on the stage in front of a simple rooftop background. In the same show, Grace La Rue, wearing a dress with a hoop skirt that filled almost the entire stage, yearned tenderly for "those dear old Crinoline Days," while Charlotte Greenwood revealed the plight of a long-legged girl in "I'm Looking for a Daddy Long Legs." The first-act finale,

* Copyright © 1921 Irving Berlin. Copyright renewed. Reprinted by permission of Irving Berlin Music Corporation.

93

MUSIC BOX REVUE OF 1924. *Bobby Clark and Fanny Brice in the sketch, "Adam and Eve," by Bert Kalmar and Harry Ruby. Note Miss Brice's snake headdress. (Costumes by James Reynolds.)*

CULVER PICTURES, INC.

depicting Satan's Palace, had the McCarthy Sisters leading the cast through the fiery "Pack Up Your Sins and Go to the Devil."

The third *Music Box Revue* added Grace Moore to the·roster to sing "An Orange Grove in California" with John Steel, against a setting of orange trees which sprayed the audience with orange-scented perfume. "What'll I Do?," also sung by Miss Moore and Mr. Steel, was added during the run of the show. "Learn to Do the Strut," led by the Brox Sisters, had the full company dancing on a raised stage that was slanted down to the footlights. The 1923 *Music Box Revue* was also responsible for the professional acting debut of Robert Benchley, then the drama critic for the old *Life*. Benchley had appeared with a number of other literary celebrities in an amateur revue called *No, Sirree!* at the Hotel Algonquin. His routine was a parody of all the dull treasurers' reports he had ever heard, and it was so funny that Berlin and Harris, who were at the performance, asked him to do the act in their next revue. Because he did not feel that a drama critic should also be a professional entertainer, Benchley demanded what he considered the outlandish fee of $500 a week. When Harris agreed to the figure, the humorist reluctantly gave in. His bumbling "Treasurer's Report" has since become a classic.

"All Alone" was interpolated briefly in the fourth and final *Music Box Revue*. Grace Moore and Oscar Shaw sang it to each other via illuminated telephones as they stood on opposite sides of a bare, darkened stage. Others present were Fanny Brice to wail the song of the immigrant, "Don't Send Me Back to Petrograd," and to confess, with appropriate relish, "I Want to Be a

94

Ballet Dancer"; Clark and McCullough to tell the sibilant tale of "A Couple of Senseless Censors"; and Grace Moore to sing the romantic "Tell Her in the Springtime," accompanied by more perfume spraying.

Although they were still popular, four *Music Box Revues* were apparently the limit for the series. Ideas no longer seemed quite so fresh or daring, even with John Murray Anderson of the *Greenwich Village Follies* succeeding Hassard Short as director of the last edition. (It was an even exchange, as Short then replaced Anderson for the 1925 *Follies*.) Berlin, convinced that he needed a change, agreed to supply the songs for the Marx Brothers' *The Cocoanuts*, one of his lesser efforts.

Grace Moore once wrote that whenever she sang a romantic ballad in one of the *Music Box Revues* she always felt as if she were a singing telegram. For it was about that time that Irving Berlin had met and fallen in love with Ellin Mackay, daughter of the socially prominent president of Postal Tele-

ZIEGFELD FOLLIES OF 1927. *Backstage shot of Eddie Cantor, Florenz Ziegfeld, Irving Berlin, and dance director Sammy Lee surrounded by the ladies of the chorus.*

graph, Clarence Mackay. In spite of the opposition of Ellin's father, she and Berlin were married after one of the most widely reported courtships of the Twenties. Some of Berlin's most tender songs, notably "Remember" and "Always," were inspired by his personal emotions.

In the early Thirties, the elaborate revues and musical comedies were rapidly becoming out of date; the unhappy state of the United States had provoked a deeper social awareness in the theatre of Broadway, even in its most customarily frivolous branch. Not that musicals could not and should not be lighthearted and entertaining, but the song-and-dance entertainments, just as every other aspect of American life, reflected the times. The Gershwin brothers with Morrie Ryskind and George S. Kaufman had inaugurated the era of adult, satirical musicals when they wrote *Strike Up the Band* and *Of Thee I Sing*. Berlin, along with librettist Moss Hart, was quick to move along in the new direction with *Face the Music* in 1932 and *As Thousands Cheer* in 1933.

Both Berlin shows were daring. *Face the Music* dealt with the general theme of the depression and the specific theme of police and political corruption. It also managed to aim some of its darts at the more vulgar and elaborate forms of musical shows. Although Irving Berlin is not generally thought of as a lyricist in the socially conscious vein of E. Y. Harburg or Harold Rome, he easily adapted himself to the demands of the script. However, while his

FACE THE MUSIC (*1932*). *Mary Boland, as Mrs. Martin Van Buren Meshbesher, is perched atop the elephant for the grand finale. (Costumes by Kiviette; setting by Albert Johnson.)*

PHOTO BY VANDAMM

AS THOUSANDS CHEER *(1933).*
Marilyn Miller, Clifton Webb,
and Helen Broderick about to
stroll down Fifth Avenue in
the Easter Parade of 1883.
(Costumes by Irene Sharaff.)

PHOTO BY VANDAMM

lyrics contained topical references and comments, he never forgot that he was still writing songs for a gay musical comedy. Thus we find him either cheerfully optimistic about the economic situation in "Let's Have Another Cup o' Coffee," or bravely indifferent in "I Say It's Spinach" ("And the hell with it"), or completely in a melodious world of his own in "Soft Lights and Sweet Music."

As Thousands Cheer had a strikingly original format: the entire revue was created out of sections of a daily newspaper, with individual scenes depicting news events, the funnies, the lonelyhearts column, the society page, and other features. Real names of famous people were used, so that in one evening an audience might see Prince Mdivani (Clifton Webb) wooing Barbara Hutton (Marilyn Miller) with "How's chances, for one of those glances . . ."; or Aimee Semple MacPherson (Helen Broderick) trying to get Mahatma Gandhi (Mr. Webb) to end his hunger strike; or John D. Rockefeller (Mr. Webb) going after his children with a carving knife after they have made him a present of Rockefeller Center on his ninety-fourth birthday; or Josephine Baker (Ethel Waters) admitting that, in spite of her fancy French chateau, she still had "Harlem on My Mind."

97

Miss Waters made even more lasting impressions with her interpretations of two other headlines. "HEAT WAVE HITS NEW YORK" offered her as a highly animated weather report, relating the sizzling tale of the lady from Martinique who started the heat wave by making her seat wave; "UNKNOWN NEGRO LYNCHED BY FRENZIED MOB" showed her as the man's widow who wonders aloud as she sets the table how she will be able to tell her children that their father "ain't comin' home no more." Before the show opened in Philadelphia to begin its tryout tour, there were many who felt that such a threnody had no place in a lavish revue. Both Berlin and producer Sam Harris were adamant; the number stayed in and became one of the most moving pieces ever sung by Ethel Waters. "If one song can tell the whole tragic history of a race," she wrote in her autobiography, *His Eye Is on the Sparrow*, " 'Supper Time' was that song."*

* From *His Eye Is On the Sparrow* by Ethel Waters and Charles Samuels. Garden City, N.Y.: Doubleday & Company, 1951.

PHOTO BY VANDAMM

AS THOUSANDS CHEER *(1933* *Ethel Waters sings "Suppe* *Time."*

LOUISIANA PURCHASE (1940). *Victor Moore as the investigating Sen. Oliver P. Loganberry looks the other way as a disguised political boss (William Gaxton) sets the table for his rendezvous with Vera Zorina. Critic John Anderson uncompromisingly labeled Mr. Moore "the most endearing comedian of our stage." (Costumes and setting by Tom Lee.)*

PHOTO BY FRED FEHL

For the first-act finale, Berlin went back to a tune he had composed sixteen years before under the title, "Smile and Show Your Dimple." The scene in *As Thousands Cheer* was the rotogravure section showing an old-fashioned Easter Parade on Fifth Avenue. And leading the grand parade was the debonair Clifton Webb serenading the lovely Marilyn Miller with the old melody set to a new lyric, "In your Easter bonnet. . . ."

Eight years later (after writing three film scores for Fred Astaire and Ginger Rogers), Irving Berlin returned to Broadway—and another musical about politics. Unfortunately, the satire of *Louisiana Purchase* was not very barbed, even though the show dealt with such a likely subject as the attempts of a Huey Long-type boss (William Gaxton) to blackmail an investigating senator (Victor Moore) by getting him involved with three attractive ladies (Vera Zorina, Carol Bruce, and Irene Bordoni). Berlin's output was up to his best—two appealing ballads, "It's a Lovely Day Tomorrow" and "You're Lonely and I'm Lonely"; Moore's plaintive "What Chance Have I?"; the spiritual-derived "Lord Done Fixed Up My Soul"; and the amorously tenacious "You Can't Brush Me Off."

Except for the brilliant World War II all-soldier show, *This Is the Army* (with the composer back in uniform to bleat again, "Oh, How I Hate to Get Up in the Morning"), a number of years elapsed before Berlin wrote his next show. During that time, the musical theatre, like almost everything else in the world, was going through important changes. The emergence of Rodgers and Hammerstein had placed greater emphasis on the book value of musicals, and

99

THIS IS THE ARMY (1942). *Irving Berlin, once again in his World War I uniform is about to break out into "Oh, How I Hate to Get Up in the Morning."*

100

composers were forced to become more concerned with the way their songs were integrated with the librettos.

Annie Get Your Gun presented a challenge to Irving Berlin for two reasons: it was being produced by Rodgers and Hammerstein themselves, and he had been asked to take over the assignment only after the death of Jerome Kern, the original composer. When he was first approached in the fall of 1945, Berlin frankly admitted to Hammerstein that he just did not think he was capable of such a task. Hammerstein's insistence that he was the only one who could do the score made the composer reconsider, and he agreed to go away to Atlantic City for a week to think over the proposition. Not only did he think, he worked, composing songs such as "Doin' What Comes Natur'lly," "There's No Business like Show Business," and "They Say It's Wonderful."

PHOTO BY FRED FEHL

ANNIE GET YOUR GUN *(1946).* *Wrote Wolcott Gibbs: "Ethel Merman, whose voice might easily have tumbled the walls of Jericho, has some songs that will probably do the same thing for the Imperial Theatre." Here she is seen trumpeting "You Can't Get a Man with a Gun." (Costume by Lucinda Ballard.)*

Still uncertain, Berlin returned to New York. He told Rodgers and Hammerstein that he had written a few songs and wanted to audition for them. Once the songs were heard, of course, Berlin easily demonstrated to the producers' satisfaction—if not to his own—that he was still a master at writing musical comedy numbers. Moreover, these were songs that fitted logically into the story and perfectly suited the characters for whom they were intended. Berlin was also able to create something of a new stage personality for Ethel Merman, the star of the show. Before she played Annie, Miss Merman had always had to have some comic angle injected into her love songs, because composers and lyricists felt that the usual Merman characterization of a brassy but bighearted dame would not be believable in a sincere romantic expression. Berlin gave her such straight ballads as "They Say It's Wonderful" and "I Got Lost in His Arms" to help reveal the genuine warmth and femininity of the character. Even the exuberant pieces, "You Can't Get a Man with a Gun," "Doin' What Comes Natur'lly," and "I Got the Sun in the Morning," were still part of the personality of the determined but

COURTESY IRVING BERLIN

womanly sharpshooter. As Merman herself admits, "Irving Berlin made a lady out of me."

Although *Annie Get Your Gun* produced the unofficial anthem of the theatre, "There's No Business like Show Business," the song was almost thrown out of the score because Berlin mistakenly thought Rodgers did not like it. While he himself continually has such doubts about his work, Berlin is convinced that the opinion of the public is never wrong. As Howard Dietz has written, "He does not care to be considered witty or brilliant or artistic. He wants to be a hit." Surely, the musical's Broadway run of 1,147 performances gave Berlin exactly what he wanted, and was more responsible than anything else for wiping out the feeling of uncertainty that he felt when he first undertook the assignment. (Once, when a friend described *Annie Get Your Gun* as old-fashioned, Berlin replied, "Yes, a good old-fashioned smash!")

Three years after *Annie Get Your Gun*, Berlin had a fair success in *Miss Liberty*, on which he collaborated with Robert E. Sherwood (book) and Moss

ANNIE GET YOUR GUN *(1946). The final tableau. Ray Middleton as Frank Butler and Ethel Merman as Annie Oakley are in the center, flanked by William O'Neal as Buffalo Bill and George Lipton as Pawnee Bill. (Costumes by Lucinda Ballard; setting by Jo Mielziner)*

103

Hart (direction). The tale of the search for the model who posed for the Statue of Liberty is best remembered for the composer's moving musical setting to Emma Lazarus' poem, "Give Me Your Tired, Your Poor" (which is inscribed on the base of the statue), and the sight of the seventy-one-year-old Ethel Griffies kicking up her heels and croaking "Only for Americans."

CALL ME MADAM *(1950) Backstage shot of Raoul Pène DuBois (settings and costumes), Leland Hayward (producer), Jerome Robbins (choreographer), Howard Lindsay (co-librettist), Russel Crouse (colibrettist), Ethel Merman, Paul Lukas, Irving Berlin, and, kneeling, George Abbott (director).*

N.Y. PUBLIC LIBRARY

Call Me Madam, another vehicle for Ethel Merman, brought Irving Berlin back to Broadway in 1950. Inspired by the appointment of Washington party-giver Perle Mesta as President Truman's ambassador to Luxembourg, Howard Lindsay and Russel Crouse created a harmless spoof that offended no one. Even Harry Truman, in the person of former musical comedy juvenile Irving Fisher, nightly took a curtain call with Miss Merman. The song that has lingered the longest from the score is "You're Just in Love," with its down-to-earth counter melody commenting sympathetically on the starry-eyed emotions of the main theme. "They Like Ike," a relatively nonpartisan specialty number, soon became both a campaign song and a much-chanted slogan merely by changing the pronoun to the first person.

Twelve years later, Irving Berlin bounced back into the theatre—and back into politics. The vehicle, *Mr. President,* was again written with the usually dependable Lindsay and Crouse. This time, however, they failed to come up with much that was original or pointed about the political scene, and Berlin's generous score—19 numbers!—was still not enough to compensate. The best of them were Nanette Fabray's rousing affirmation, "They Love Me," and the pounding chorale, "Glad to Be Home Again." Despite a near-record advance ticket sale of more than $2,650,000, *Mr. President* remained in office a little over seven months and left with a deficit of $100,000.

Irving Berlin has been called the "Last of the Troubadours." It is an accurate title. The troubadours of the Middle Ages may not have been trained musicians, but they did have the rare faculty of being able to communicate their sentiments and their songs to vast numbers of people. Possibly no other song-writer in history has had this gift to such an extent as Irving Berlin. Whether he is writing about a soldier who hates to get up in the morning, a lonely lover who waits by the telephone, the thrills of taking a bow on the stage, the simple joys of getting out on a dance floor, or any of the hundreds of other human emotions, and thoughts, and experiences he has written about, Irving Berlin knows how to express feelings in such a way that they are universally shared.

Jerome Kern's succinct tribute to Berlin's ability to embody a nation's music is justly famous: "Irving Berlin has no *place* in American music. He *is* American music," was the way he once ended a letter to Alexander Woollcott, when Woollcott was preparing a biography of the composer. Preceeding this, Kern summed up beautifully the ways in which Berlin's music epitomized the average American: "Both the typical Yankee and the Berlin tune have humor, originality, pace, and popularity; both are wide-awake, and both are sometimes a little loud-but what might unsympathetically be mistaken for brass,

MR. PRESIDENT (1962). *President Robert Ryan and First Lady Nanette Fabray get away from the cares of the day "In Our Hideaway."*

PHOTO BY FRIEDMAN-ABELES

is really gold . . . He doesn't attempt to stuff the public's ears with pseudo-original, ultra modernism, but he honestly absorbs the vibrations emanating from the people, manners and life of his time, and in turn, gives these impressions back to the world—simplified—clarified—glorified."

Ira and George Gershwin.

108

George and Ira Gershwin

THE DEATH OF George Gershwin on July 11, 1937, was a stunning, almost unbelievable event. At the age of thirty-eight, at the height of his creative powers, he died in Hollywood of a brain tumor—a tragedy made all the sadder by the lingering doubts of many that if a certain brain specialist had been located in time, Gershwin's life might have been saved. The consolation that he is kept alive through the continuous performing of his music is always tempered by speculation as to what he might have gone on to achieve. Oscar Levant wrote in *A Smattering of Ignorance:* "No quantity of music could compensate for the loss of his corporeal presence, the cessation of his creative being—especially when we could have had both."[*] Vernon Duke, in his autobiography, *Passport to Paris,* echoed the sentiment: "Death can be kind and it can be just; but it had no business taking our George, who was in the full flower of his fine youth and who was unquestionably doing his best work."[†]

The frustration that many felt was understandable. For, in many ways, Gershwin represented the exciting, daring, adventuresome spirit of American

[*] From *A Smattering of Ignorance* by Oscar Levant. Garden City, N. Y.: Doubleday and Company.

[†] From *Passport to Paris* by Vernon Duke. Boston: Little, Brown and Company.

youth itself. Not only did he capture the pulse of the people, but, as Arthur Schwartz has commented, "he quickened it." To his friends and co-composers, he was an acknowledged leader—warm, understanding, and just as eager to praise someone else's music as he was to delight in his own. Indeed, this feeling about his own music, which led many to think of him as conceited, was nothing more than an almost detached and honest appreciation of his own worth, and he showed equal enthusiasm for the songs of Irving Berlin, Jerome Kern, and others. It was Gershwin who helped Vincent Youmans get his first assignment on Broadway, and composers such as Arthur Schwartz, Vernon Duke, and Harold Arlen have attested to Gershwin's encouragement and help. The people who knew George Gershwin only through his music felt his death almost as keenly as did his friends. Even though his audience may not have been fully conscious of it, the personality of Gershwin and of his music was the same. According to Arlen, "He bubbled just as much as his music does. That is why I believe that anyone who knows George's work, knows George. The humor, the satire, the playfulness of most of his melodic phrases were the natural expression of the man."

In a literal sense, Gershwin and his songs were seldom parted during the composer's life. He was an expert pianist with an almost-compulsive urge to play his own music. People gave parties for him because they knew he would be delighted to spend the entire evening entertaining them at the piano. Frequently, Gershwin became so excited about a new score that he would play the songs in public well in advance of the première of the show for which they were intended. "George's music gets around so much before an opening," George S. Kaufman once remarked dryly, "that the first night audience thinks it's at a revival."

Gershwin had the remarkable ability of projecting his own magnetism through the bright, athletic rhythms of his songs. He was also the first—and, at this writing, the only—song-writer who started out in Tin Pan Alley ever to be accepted with equal honors as a composer of concert and opera music. Herbert, Friml, Duke, Weill, and Bernstein all came to Broadway after years of training and experience as "classical" musicians and composers; Gershwin's apprenticeship as a "classical" musician and composer was spent as a song-plugger, vaudeville accompanist, rehearsal pianist, and the creator of the music for *George White's Scandals*. Today, his greatness rests not only on his succession of outstanding show tunes, but also on such works as the *Rhapsody in Blue*, the *Piano Concerto in F*, *An American in Paris*, and *Porgy and Bess*. None of the other composers discussed in this book—no matter what their backgrounds—ever mastered as many forms of musical expression as did George Gershwin. And he did it in less than twenty years.

Gershwin was born in Brooklyn, on September 26, 1898. His parents were Morris and Rose Gershvin, who later substituted the more Americanized *w* for the *v*. George was the second of four children; his older brother, Ira, was born on December 6, 1896. Their father was constantly becoming involved in a variety of business activities (turkish baths, bakeries, restaurants, etc.) that required the family to move from one neighborhood to another almost yearly. While they were living on the lower East Side of Manhattan, Mrs. Gershwin bought a piano. She wanted Ira to take lessons, but when George showed the greater musical aptitude, he was substituted for his reluctant brother. George's first important teacher was Charles Hambitzer, who later brought him to Edward Kilenyi for instructions in theory.

Music quickly became Gershwin's life. He left the High School of Commerce to take a job as a pianist for the Jerome H. Remick Music Publishing Company; at fifteen, he was the youngest pounder in Tin Pan Alley. His first attempts at composing, "Since I Found You," and "Ragging the Traumerei," went unpublished, although he did manage to sell his third effort to publisher Harry Von Tilzer for five dollars. Murray Roth's lyric was almost self-contained in the title—"When You Want 'Em, You Can't Have 'Em; When You Have 'Em, You Don't Want 'Em." It referred, of course, to the eternal problem of men—women.

At the beginning of Gershwin's career, his two idols were Irving Berlin and Jerome Kern. ("Many things I wrote at this period sounded as though Kern had written them himself," he later admitted.) He not only admired Kern's songs, he also admired Kern's success in getting his early works interpolated in musicals. Trying to emulate this success, Gershwin quit his job at Remick's to become a vaudeville accompanist. Then when he heard of an opening for a rehearsal pianist for a musical (with a score provided by both Jerome Kern and Victor Herbert), he applied for the job and was hired. Though the show itself, *Miss 1917*, lasted only forty-eight performances, the job proved to be an important step in the fledgling composer's career. The revue was housed at the Century Theatre, where, as a possible impetus to business, a series of Sunday evening variety "concerts" was presented. Gershwin, who had been hired to play at these performances, persuaded Vivienne Segal to introduce two of his songs, "You-oo Just You," a romantic ballad of Old Dixie, and "There's More to the Kiss Than the X-X-X," which made use of the simulated sounds of a kiss as part of the lyric. Someone brought the songs to the attention of publisher Max Dreyfus who thought so highly of them that he engaged Gershwin, not as a lowly song plugger or salesman, but as a regular staff composer.

In 1918, George and Ira wrote their first professional song together, "The Real American Folk Song" ("Is a rag—a mental jag"). Nora Bayes sang it in *Ladies First*. The same year, Dreyfus recommended George Gershwin to a

111

producer who was planning a revue starring Joe Cook. The show was called *Half-Past Eight,* with Gershwin contributing five songs. The attraction turned out to be so poor that it never got any closer to New York than Syracuse.

A more significant advancement occurred a few months later. Alex A. Aarons, a musician and incipient producer, had become fascinated by the many original touches Gershwin put into his music. Soon the two men began making plans for the show that was to mark their mutual debuts on Broadway, *La La Lucille* ("The New Up-to-the-Minute Musical Comedy of Class and Distinction"). Though it was initially presented by Alex's father, Alfred E. Aarons, within a few weeks the names of Alex A. Aarons and George B. Seitz appeared on the program as co-sponsors.

La La Lucille, a moderately amusing bedroom farce, served well enough as a showcase for the talents of the twenty-year-old composer, and it had a

LA LA LUCILLE *(1919). The first Broadway musical for which Gershwin wrote the entire score. The scene below shows Marjorie Bentley surrounded by four dapper gentlemen of the chorus.*

respectable run. Appraising its score, Heywood Broun wrote in the *Tribune:* "The music is spirited rather than melodious. 'Tee-Oodle-Um-Bum-Bo' was the song most appreciated by the first-night audience. This may furnish some clue to the nature of the lyrics." "Personally," countered Alan Dale of the *American,* "I prefer 'Tee-Oodle-Um-Bum-Bo' to bed, bath, or plot. In the favorite parlance of the theatre, it has 'ginger.' "

The "ginger" of "Tee-Oodle-Um-Bum-Bo" was rather bland compared to the ingredients found in "Swanee," Gershwin's first really big hit, which he wrote with Irving Caesar. "At that time," Caesar recalls, "there was a raging one-step sensation, 'Hindustan.' I said to George that we ought to write a one-step and give it an American flavor." The two men discussed the idea at dinner, took a bus ride up to Gershwin's home on Washington Heights, and completed the entire song in about fifteen minutes. "Swanee" attracted little notice when it was first introduced in 1919 in a revue at the newly constructed Capitol Theatre at Broadway and 50th Street. However, Al Jolson, who was then starring in *Sinbad* at the Winter Garden across the street, liked it so much that he reintroduced it in his own show. There was no doubt that Jolson's spirited delivery made the difference; before long, "Swanee" became the biggest hit in the country.

The composer's reputation as a result of "Swanee" made it easy for him to convince George White that he should be given the commission to supply songs for the next edition of the *George White's Scandals.* White had begun his series of annual revues the previous year; they were youthful, fast-moving affairs, and the driving excitement of Gershwin's songs made him well-suited to provide the proper kind of music. While his output covered five successive editions, from 1920 to 1924, few of these songs are known today. Only the gracefully flowing "Drifting Along with the Tide" and the pseudo-tropical "South Sea Isles" have survived the first two editions—and even they are rarely performed. However, the 1922 *Scandals* did have the remarkably constructed "Stairway to Paradise" (revised from an earlier song, "New Step Every Day") for an elaborate first-act finale in which the entire company joined in the ascent. Otherwise, there were such undistinguished items as "I Found a Four-Leaf Clover" ("And the next day I found you") and "Cinderelatives," a serenade to the rags-to-riches heroines of such recent Broadway musicals as *Irene, Sally, The Love Nest, The O'Brien Girl,* and *Good Morning Dearie.*

The most unusual item of the 1922 *Scandals* was a twenty-minute "jazz opera" by Gershwin and B. G. DeSylva called *Blue Monday.* While it was a tentative step in the direction that the composer was later to follow in *Porgy and Bess,* it proved so out of place in its Scandalous surroundings that it was cut from the show after the opening-night performance. As in Gershwin's later folk opera, the work dealt with the theme of infidelity among Negroes,

113

although in the custom of the day, white members of the cast appeared in blackface.

The critics were a little confused by *Blue Monday*. Kenneth Macgowan of the *Globe* called it "a very painful and long-drawn incident, a sort of rag-time opera, that drags the tedious 'Mammy' motif to unbearable lengths"; Charles Pike Sawyer of the *Post* was of the opinion that, "from an artistic point of view, it was the best number in the show"; the unspecified critic of the *Telegram* (who must have been at a different theatre) referred to it as "a delicious bit of musical fun"; Charles Darnton of the *Evening World* hit the hardest with "the most dismal, stupid, and incredible blackface sketch that has probably ever been perpetrated"; while the *Sun's* Stephen Rathbun summed up his verdict with "It's not successful from any angle—comedy, burlesque, opera or tragedy."

Admittedly, Gershwin had much to learn before he could master the operatic form. Yet, in spite of its apparent defects, *Blue Monday* (later re-titled *135th Street*) did have some moving themes. Of these, "Blue Monday Blues" still remains a haunting, expressive piece that conveys so well the feeling of frustration and hopelessness on a day when everything goes wrong.

The year 1924 was a memorable one for Gershwin; he began his career as a composer and performer of concert music, and he wrote his first Broadway musical comedy in collaboration with his brother, Ira. The first important event took place at Aeolian Hall in February. Paul Whiteman, who had been featured with his orchestra in the *Scandals of 1922*, was one of the few who had always had a fondness for *Blue Monday*. While working on the show, Whiteman told Gershwin about an idea he had for a concert devoted to American music. Would George be able to contribute a serious composition for the occasion? The result was the *Rhapsody in Blue*, which Gershwin himself performed with Whiteman's augmented "Palais Royal Orchestra." The enthusiastic reception to the *Rhapsody* (which had been given the choice "next-to-closing" spot on the program) presaged the eminence Gershwin would later attain as both a "serious" composer and performer.

Lady, Be Good!, which opened in December, was Gershwin's second major musical event of the year. Not only was it the first success on which he and Ira collaborated (*A Dangerous Maid* had failed on the road in 1921), but it also inaugurated a series of seven musicals they were to write for a producing firm Alex Aarons had recently organized with a former actor, Vinton Freedley. Excluding the unsuccessful *Tell Me More!* which was produced by Aarons alone, the seven productions were: *Lady, Be Good!* (Fred and Adele Astaire); *Tip-Toes* (Queenie Smith, Allen Kearns, Jeanette MacDonald); *Oh, Kay!* (Gertrude Lawrence, Oscar Shaw, Victor Moore); *Funny Face* (the Astaires, Victor Moore); *Treasure Girl* (Gertrude Lawrence, Clifton Webb); *Girl Crazy* (Willie Howard, Ginger Rogers, Ethel

114

LADY, BE GOOD! *(1924). Adele and Fred Astaire perform their famous run-around step to "Swiss Miss."*

Merman); and *Pardon My English* (Jack Pearl, Lyda Roberti). Of these, only *Treasure Girl* and *Pardon My English* were failures. Indeed, the last production was such a fiasco that it was one of the direct causes of the termination of the ten-year Aarons and Freedley partnership.

At first, it was the producers' intention to have these shows follow the bright, witty pattern of the old Princess Theatre attractions, only, according to Guy Bolton, on a larger scale. (Bolton was co-librettist on four of the musicals, and was joined on *Oh, Kay!* by his Princess Theatre collaborator, P. G. Wodehouse.) Despite these intentions, the shows soon became star vehicles rather than closely coordinated book-and-music shows. But in choosing a composer like Gershwin, Aarons and Freedley were motivated by the same considerations that had prompted F. Ray Comstock and Elisabeth Marbury to choose Jerome Kern—he was the freshest, most original composer of theatre music on Broadway. Though he was again following in the pat-

115

TIP-TOES (1925). *The distracted lady about to have her
pocket picked is Jeanette Mac-
Donald. The pranksters are
Allen Kearns and Robert Halliday.*

tern of his first idol, Kern, Gershwin could no longer be accused of imitating
him. His own sparkling music had already established its individuality; the
Aarons-Freedley succession of hits merely provided him with greater opportunities to develop his skills. For although these shows pioneered no new
theatrical ground, they did feature a number of outstanding performers who
inspired the composer to produce some of his most enduring music.

Lady, Be Good! gave Fred and Adele Astaire their second Broadway
triumph. They had just returned from England where they had captivated
audiences in Alex Aarons' production of *Stop Flirting* (called *For Goodness
Sake* in New York). With the Gershwins' help they scored an even greater
success in the new musical. *Lady, Be Good!* had a whole hopper of engaging
tunes—the wistful "So Am I"; "Fascinating Rhythm"; the lonely, lighthearted
plea, "Oh, Lady, Be Good!"; and the ragtime lament of the ardent suitor,
" 'The Half Of It, Dearie' Blues."

One of the scenes early in the first act of *Lady, Be Good!* has always been
considered as something of a classic in the field of pure mid-Twenties musical
comedy. As the curtain rises, Fred and Adele, as brother and sister, have

116

just been evicted from their apartment. Surrounded by their furniture, they try to cheer each other up by arranging the tables and chairs as if they were in their own home. Adele even hangs up a GOD BLESS OUR HOME sign on the nearest lamppost. When it begins to rain, Fred and Adele duck under a huge umbrella and break out into a consoling song-and-dance duet, "Hang On to Me."

"The Man I Love," one of the composer's most popular songs, had been intended for *Lady, Be Good!*, but it was dropped before the show reached New York. It fared no better three years later, when it was added to the first version of *Strike Up the Band*; then the musical itself closed on the road. The following year, after an attempt to fit "The Man I Love" into *Rosalie*, the song was dropped again. That it was never sung on Broadway did not disturb Gershwin. "The song is not a production number," he once explained. "It allows little or no action while it is being sung. It lacks a soothing, seducing rhythm; instead, it has a certain slow lilt that disturbs the audience instead of lulling it into acceptance. Then, too, there is the melody, which is not easy to catch; it presents too many chromatic pitfalls." Pitfalls or not, "The Man I Love" did manage to succeed on its own, unaided by a theatrical presentation.

Tell Me More!, which opened in April, 1925, was unsuccessful. But it did have one distinction: during its tryout tour it was known as *My Fair Lady*. This was also the name of one of the songs, with the musical derivation of its title line stemming from "London Bridge Is Falling Down."

The same year, Aarons and Freedley offered a more profitable Gershwin attraction called *Tip-Toes*. "Looking For a Boy," "Sweet and Low-Down" (sung to the accompaniment of a group of kazoo trumpets), and "That Certain Feeling" were some of its musical pleasures. In his book *Lyrics on Several Occasions*, Ira Gershwin claims that *Tip-Toes* had the first score in which he noticed any development in his skills as a lyricist. He was particularly pleased with "These Charming People," which he felt was at last equal to the kind of witty lyrics that P. G. Wodehouse had created for the Princess Theatre shows.

The gay, modern pattern of musical comedy was scrupulously adhered to in a tale of rum-running and Long Island society called *Oh, Kay!* For their star, Aarons and Freedley were able to secure Gertrude Lawrence, then very much in demand as a result of her success in the imported *Charlot's Revues*. Her reason for choosing *Oh, Kay!* as her first American musical was simple: "George Gershwin was writing the music especially for me."

After its première on November 8, 1926, the score of the Gershwin-Gershwin-Bolton-Wodehouse musical prompted critic Percy Hammond to dub the composer as the "premier music-master," and to reveal how "all of us simply floated away on the canoodling notes of 'Maybe,' and were brought

117

OH, KAY! *(1926). Gertrude Lawrence, of whom Bide Dudley wrote: "Here is an artiste from bob to toe."*

PHOTO BY VANDAMM

back to Broadway by such flesh and bony anthems as 'Fidgety Feet' and 'Clap Yo' Hands.' " As for "Someone to Watch Over Me," Hammond testified that Gershwin had "wrung the withers of even the most hard-hearted of those present."

After creating another sensation in England in *Lady, Be Good!*, the Astaires returned to Broadway in *Funny Face*. Although its book was initially to have been the product of Fred Thompson and Robert Benchley, the humorist withdrew during its hectic out-of-town tryout and was succeeded by Paul Gerard Smith. Almost to everyone's surprise, when the show opened in November, 1927, at the newly built Alvin Theatre ("Al" for Alex Aarons, "vin" for Vinton Freedley), it turned out to be an unqualified smash. The combination of the singing and the dancing of Fred and Adele and the songs of George and Ira again proved irresistible, particularly in such numbers as "He Loves and She Loves," "High Hat," "My One and Only," "Funny Face" (a forerunner of Rodgers and Hart's "My Funny Valentine" as a paean to physical plainness), and the brilliant compilation of conversational cliches, "The Babbitt and the Bromide," during which the Astaires performed their celebrated "run-around" dance.

Apparently, neither the presence of Gertrude Lawrence nor the Gershwin songs could help *Treasure Girl*. It lasted only two months, in spite of a score that included "I've Got a Crush on You," "Where's the Boy?," "Oh, So Nice," "Feeling I'm Falling," and "I Don't Think I'll Fall in Love Today"

118

(which dared to rhyme the seven syllable word "incompatibility" with "A B C").

Aarons and Freedley and the Gershwin brothers came back successfully in 1930 with *Girl Crazy*. Perhaps its simple-minded story was already old-fashioned (the Gershwins' *Strike Up the Band* had opened earlier that year), but there were enough other attractions to compensate for the book. In a part originally intended for Bert Lahr, Willie Howard gave an immensely comic performance as a New York taxi driver who takes a fare to Custerville, Arizona, and ends up as the sheriff. The leading female character was played by a nineteen-year-old dancer named Ginger Rogers, who had already attracted notice in *Top Speed* and in the film *Young Man of Manhattan*. She was given the romantic songs ("But Not for Me" and "Embraceable You") which were suitable for her small but attractive voice. The more raucous, direct numbers, however, needed someone who could really belt them out. Freedley found the girl he wanted at the Brooklyn Paramount where, for the first time, Ethel Zimmerman from Astoria, Long Island, was singing professionally as Ethel Merman. At the opening night of *Girl Crazy* it was she who scored the greatest personal triumph with her delivery of "Sam and Delilah," Boy! What Love Has Done to Me!", and "I Got Rhythm." During the last number, as *Newsweek* magazine once noted, Miss Merman made history by holding one note for the full second chorus in defiance of the second law of thermodynamics, i.e., all forces must eventually come to rest.

But for a world going through the Depression, the completely meaningless, anything-for-a-laugh musical was rapidly losing its flavor and, beginning with *Strike Up the Band*, the Gershwin brothers and their collaborators were

CULVER PICTURES, INC.

FUNNY FACE *(1927). The ladies Fred Astaire is pointing to are Betty Compton, Adele Astaire, and Gertrude McDonald.*

119

STRIKE UP THE BAND *(1930).*
Paul McCullough and Bobby
Clark.

GIRL CRAZY *(1930). Ethel Mer-*
man as Kate Fothergill. Miss
Merman, according to Time
Magazine, "approaches sex in
song with the cold fury of a
philosopher. She aims at a
point slightly above the en-
trails, but she knocks you out
just the same."

OF THEE I SING (*1931*). *Lyricist Ira Gershwin, composer George Gershwin, colibrettists George S. Kaufman and Morrie Ryskind.*

in the forefront of the change. *Strike Up the Band* was originally to have been presented in 1927, but the anti-war sentiments of the George S. Kaufman book were so uncompromising—even to the ending in which the United States is seen preparing for war with the Soviet Union—that it folded on the road. Morrie Ryskind's revised script three years later blunted the edge somewhat by having the action take place in a dream, changing the enemy to Switzerland, and giving the leads to two zany comics, Bobby Clark and Paul McCullough. Nevertheless, *Strike Up the Band* was a bold innovation in the musical theatre, capable of inspiring William Bolitho to comment in the *World:* "I don't remember ever before in a musical comedy having noticed or understood what it was all about. Here all is not only clear but really startling. Of all things in the world, here is a bitter, rather good satirical attack on war, genuine propaganda at times, sung and danced on Broadway to standing room only."

"I've Got a Crush on You" was salvaged from the unsuccessful *Treasure Girl,* while others in the amorous spirit were the mellifluous "Soon" and the bashful lover's stammering proposal, "I Mean to Say." Most of the numbers, however, were used to fill a more important need—commenting satirically upon developments in the plot and upon the characters. "The Unofficial Spokesman," inspired by the career of President Wilson's adviser, Colonel House, gave advice on how to reach the top in politics (keep your mouth shut), and "A Typical Self-Made Man" detailed the steps that must be taken

121

for the go-getter in business. The mocking title song (which, ironically, has since become accepted as a sincerely patriotic march) set the tone of the entire show both in words and music.

Strike Up the Band was a satirical musical comedy. *Of Thee I Sing* was more in the style of a Gilbert and Sullivan satirical comic opera. Produced by Sam H. Harris, it united for the first time the comedy team of William Gaxton and Victor Moore as the immortal John P. Wintergreen and Alexander Throttlebottom, candidates, respectively, for President and Vice President of the United States. The script by Kaufman (he also directed) and Ryskind was careful to aim its darts not at individuals but at various aspects of society— political conventions, the Congress, the Supreme Court, bathing beauty contests, even motherhood. Yet, it was all done so artfully and entertainingly that there was never a hint of viciousness or of preaching.

In 1931, *Of Thee I Sing* received the Pulitzer Prize for drama. Although this was the first time that the writers of a musical comedy were so honored, the judges refused to include the name of George Gershwin in its citation on the strict technicality that he had not contributed to the actual story. The

OF THEE I SING (1931). *The final scene in the musical. The proud parents of twins are President John P. Wintergreen (William Gaxton) and Mary Turner Wintergreen (Lois Moran). Vice President Alexander Throttlebottom (Victor Moore) beams approvingly at the far left. (Setting by Jo Mielziner.)*

N.Y. PUBLIC LIBRARY

fact was, of course, that the entire production was built on the music, either in its satirical commentary or in its dramatic use to propel and develop the action of the play.

The proper mood is set immediately. When the curtain rises the stage is full of a group of noisy campaigners and voters marching up and down and singing the stirring "Wintergreen for President" while waving banners with such slogans as "TURN THE REFORMERS OUT," "VOTE FOR PROSPERITY AND SEE WHAT YOU GET,' and "WINTERGREEN—THE FLAVOR LASTS." The music itself, Oscar Levant once observed, contains "an actual feeling of social comment," particularly with the intermingling of various airs including "Tammany," "The Sidewalks of New York," and "Hail, Hail, the Gang's All Here."

The song, "Of Thee I Sing," in which the word "baby" is irreverently added to the familiar line from "America," is another example of the deftness of the Gershwin brothers' touch. But, more than consisting of mere touches, the music for *Of Thee I Sing* was employed throughout in what was unquestionably the most closely integrated manner of any Broadway show to that time. Almost all of the Atlantic City bathing-beauty pageant episode was set to music, carrying the action from the selection of Diana Devereaux as queen to the conclusion, in which Wintergreen refuses to marry her because she cannot bake corn muffins. The last scenes of the play, with their profusion of political, judicial, diplomatic, amorous, and natal complications, were sung in a series of arias, choruses, and recitatives. Indeed, almost everything about *Of Thee I Sing* was created with a skill that has rarely been equaled in the musical comedy theatre.

Sequels seldom succeed. In 1933, *Let 'Em Eat Cake*, the successor to *Of Thee I Sing*, adhered faithfully to the rule. With the same producer, librettists, director, and stars, the new work was more astringent, more cutting than the first. An almost grim mood penetrated its discordant, contrapuntal score. Indeed, even the single love song "Mine" used a chorus to interject a sarcastic commentary during Wintergreen's serenading of Mary Turner. In spite of its failure at the box office, however, Gershwin still felt that *Let 'Em Eat Cake* was his best work to that date, calling it "the composer's claim to legitimacy."

LET 'EM EAT CAKE *(1933). John P. Wintergreen (William Gaxton) establishes a dictatorship of the proletariat and sings "Let 'Em Eat Cake" as the first act finale. Joining him on the White House portico are the faithful Mary (Lois Moran) and Alexander Throttlebottom (Victor Moore). (Setting by Albert Johnson.)*

Ever since a particularly trying day in 1926 when nothing seemed to go right at a rehearsal of *Oh, Kay!*, George Gershwin's ambition had been to compose an opera based on DuBose Heyward's short novel, *Porgy*. After returning home that day, he picked up the book hoping that it would lull him to sleep. He read it straight through, however, and became so excited about its possibilities for the theatre that, at four in the morning, he scribbled a letter to Heyward expressing his interest in transforming the novel into an opera. To his surprise, Gershwin soon learned that Dorothy Heyward, the author's wife, had already begun to dramatize his story of the lame beggar of Catfish Row. But this did not really matter; Gershwin, with a remarkable cool personal insight, knew that it would take him years of study before he would have sufficient command of his medium to undertake such an ambitious project. DuBose Heyward collaborated with his wife on the play, the Theatre Guild produced it in 1927, and *Porgy* became one of the dramatic hits of the Broadway season.

Its success only fortified Gershwin's conviction that he must, someday, create an opera out of *Porgy*. In fact, the composer made no secret of this conviction even when the play opened. Critic Gilbert Gabriel of the *Sun*, who was one of the few who did not like the play, prophetically summed up his observations with: "It seems all bits, and nothing but. Or else nothing but the beginnings of the opera George Gershwin hopes to make of it."

In 1932, the Gershwin-Heyward correspondence began again. Although the composer was still interested in *Porgy*, he advised Heyward that there would have to be further delays because of his commitments to write the music for *Pardon My English* and *Let 'Em Eat Cake*. Heyward was particularly disappointed by this news; he had hoped that Gershwin's proposed operatic version of *Porgy* would bring a reverse in the financial difficulties he was having at the time. The Theatre Guild had already approached him with the tempting idea of letting Jerome Kern and Oscar Hammerstein II make a musical of the story with Al Jolson in the title role. Heyward, however, agreed to wait for Gershwin when the composer gave his assurance that he would definitely begin the opera once *Let 'Em Eat Cake* had opened on Broadway. Five days after the première, contracts were signed with the Theatre Guild; shortly thereafter, the actual writing of *Porgy and Bess* was begun.

Most of the collaboration between November, 1933, and July of the following year was done by mail, as Heyward preferred writing in the South and Gershwin was kept in New York by a radio contract. Their postal teamwork was arranged so that scenes and lyrics would be written first, and then mailed north to Gershwin to supply the appropriate music. A few months after the project had started, Ira Gershwin joined the collaboration as co-lyricist and general liaison man. (Heyward once wrote how, upon receiving

PORGY AND BESS *(1935). The citizens of Catfish Row are about to go off on a picnic on Kittiwah Island. Sportin' Life (John W. Bubbles) stands on a table at the left; Porgy (Todd Duncan) and Bess (Anne Brown) are seated on the steps at the right. (Setting by Sergei Soudekine.)*

the scenes, "the brothers Gershwin, after their extraordinary fashion, would get at the piano, pound, wrangle, swear, burst into weird snatches of song, and eventually emerge with a polished lyric.")

Including visits to Charleston, South Carolina, where the Heywards lived, Gershwin worked on the score for eleven months. Nine more were devoted to orchestrations. During its creation, the opera was called *Porgy,* but to avoid confusion with the original play—and to give it a more "operatic" flavor—the name was changed to *Porgy and Bess.* Rouben Mamoulian (who had also directed the nonoperatic *Porgy*) staged the new work, and the cast, consisting mostly of unknown singers and actors, was headed by Todd Duncan (Porgy), Anne Brown (Bess), and John W. Bubbles (Sportin' Life). Alexander Smallens conducted the forty-two-piece orchestra. Billed as "An American Folk-Opera," *Porgy and Bess* opened at the Alvin Theatre on October 10, 1935.

Convinced that *Porgy and Bess* was worthy of both dramatic and musical appraisal, the larger daily newspapers sent both drama and music critics to the première, and then ran their reviews in adjoining columns. There were wide differences of opinion within both groups, although, in general, the drama reviewers liked it better than the music critics. Burns Mantle (*News*) gave it his highest rating of four stars; Brooks Atkinson (*Times*) wrote: "The story gained by its musical investiture"; John Mason Brown (*Post*): "A memorable production"; Robert Garland (*World-Telegram*): "A modern masterpiece." There were also varying degrees of approval from Richard Watts, Jr., (*Herald Tribune*), Gilbert Gabriel (*American*), and Walter Winchell (*Mirror*). Among those who disapproved were John Anderson of the *Journal*, who felt that it was too long; George Jean Nathan of *Life* ("indeterminate, wobbly, and frequently dull"); Stark Young of the *New Republic* ("curiously monotonous"), and Joseph Wood Krutch of *The Nation* ("I never felt myself profoundly interested or deeply moved").

The music critics seemed to have had some difficulty in trying to determine what *Porgy and Bess* really was. Samuel Chotzinoff (*Post*) called it a "hybrid"; Robert A. Simon (*The New Yorker*): "forceful and often brilliant"; Leonard Liebling (*American*): "the first authentic American opera"; Winthrop Sargeant: "no advance in American operatic composition"; Pitts San-

PORGY AND BESS (1935). *The picnic at Kittiwah Island. John W. Bubbles, as Sportin' Life, sings "It Ain't Necessarily So." (Setting by Sergei Soudekine.)*

born (*World-Telegram*): "an unquestionable advance in Gershwin's art"; Paul Rosenfeld: "the score sustains no mood"; Marcia Davenport (*Stage*): "qualities of conviction and genuineness and importance"; Virgil Thomson (*Modern Music*): "falsely conceived and rather clumsily executed, but it is an important work"; Olin Downes (*Times*): "much to recommend it even though it does not utilize all the resources of the operatic composer."

Whether *Porgy and Bess* is really an opera is still being debated; that it is surely one of the most fully realized musical plays of the American theatre there is no doubt. By combining elements of the Broadway stage that he knew so well with the more challenging features of opera with which he was less familiar, Gershwin created a theatrical and musical entity that, more than twenty-five years later, still stands as a drama of towering emotional power and vitality. More than any other work, it is the one that is most universally accepted as a truly American form of opera.

Although its initial production lasted a bare 124 performances in New York (remarkable for a new opera, but a flop according to Broadway standards), the subsequent major revivals of *Porgy and Bess* in 1942 (Cheryl Crawford production) and in 1953 (as part of the Blevins Davis–Robert Breen international tour) have now raised the total number of its Broadway performances to 715.

What would George Gershwin have accomplished had he not died in 1937? His entire career had been the most steady, step-by-step advance of any theatre composer. There was some overlapping, but it is remarkable that his rise was so chronologically systematic—from revues (1920–1924), to musical comedies (1924–1930), to satirical comic operas (1931–1933), to an American folk-opera (1935). This continual striving after new means of expression certainly would have continued. In their book *The Gershwin Years*, Edward Jablonski and Lawrence D. Stewart reveal that before he died, the composer was planning a film ballet for George Balanchine, a symphony, and a concert tour of Europe. For the theatre he was considering three proposals: a musical cavalcade of American history for the Theatre Guild; a musical about the writing of a musical, with a book by George S. Kaufman and Moss Hart; and an opera with a libretto by Lynn Riggs. Nor had he forgotten DuBose Heyward. According to Frank Durham, the novelist's biographer, Gershwin wrote to his *Porgy and Bess* collaborator just six months before his death to discuss the possibilities of adapting Heyward's book *Star-Spangled Virgin* for the musical stage.

No matter what Gershwin would have chosen to do, however, this much is certain: it would have revealed yet another facet of the endlessly searching and inquisitive nature that distinguished both the man and the musician.

Vincent Youmans.

128

Vincent Youmans

IF EVER A PERIOD of musical comedy belonged to its composers and lyricists it was the decade between 1920 and 1930. The war had succeeded in doing what Cohan, and later Kern and Berlin, had been trying to do since the turn of the century—it cut to a minimum the influx of European operettas, thus enabling the works of a rising generation of American writers to be heard. "Back in those days," Douglas Watt once wrote in *The New Yorker*, "a sense of gaiety predominated among songwriters, but there was also a sense of pride—pride in the stimulating little island called Manhattan, pride in breaking away from European-influenced operettas, and, most of all, pride in their own audacity, for almost all of them were young men."

The twenty-year-old George Gershwin had led the way in 1919 with *La La Lucille*. Oscar Hammerstein II was twenty-four when he wrote the book and lyrics for his first musical, *Always You,* the following year. A few months later, Richard Rodgers, then all of eighteen, and Lorenz Hart, then twenty-five, were represented by their first show, *Poor Little Ritz Girl*. When he was twenty-one, Vincent Youmans composed the music for his initial entry, *Two Little Girls in Blue,* with lyrics by the twenty-four-year-old Ira Gershwin. Cole Porter, though he had written two scores before the Twenties, came back from Europe at the age of thirty-one to do *The Greenwich Village Follies of 1924*. The same year, Howard Dietz was twenty-eight when he wrote the words to Jerome Kern's music for *Dear Sir*; two years later, his future partner, Arthur Schwartz, contributed his first numbers to *The Grand Street Follies* when he was twenty-five.

Of all the young composers, however, none was more the product of, or is more directly associated with, the Broadway musical theatre of the 1920's than Vincent Youmans. All his successful stage productions were presented during that period, including three, *Wildflower, No, No, Nanette,* and *Hit the Deck*, that were among the biggest hits of the decade.

Youmans' career has always been somewhat overshadowed by that of the more prolific George Gershwin. Indeed, there are several striking, if superficial, parallels in their lives and works. Youmans was born on September 27, 1898, just one day after Gershwin. Both worked for Max Dreyfus when they were young, and both were given their first Broadway assignments by Alex Aarons. The Youmans show, *Two Little Girls in Blue*, even had a book written by Fred Jackson, the author of Gershwin's *La La Lucille*, and the lyricist was George's brother, Ira. Toward the end of the 1920's, Gershwin and Youmans attempted to broaden the scope of the musical theatre, though only Gershwin was able to succeed in his more adventuresome undertakings. And, of course, the tragedy of the two composers is that their careers came to an end when they were both young—Gershwin died at thirty-eight and Youmans was forced into retirement because of tuberculosis when he was thirty-five.

The personalities of the men, however, were entirely different. Gershwin was gregarious, warmhearted, pulsating with his own vibrant excitement with life; Youmans was a genuinely shy person whose constant illnesses were partly responsible for making him seem cold and aloof. In their careers, Gershwin was surely the more fortunate of the two in having such a close working arrangement with his brother; Youmans seldom was able to find a lyricist worthy of his music, and, in fact, seldom worked with the same one twice. But perhaps the most unfortunate aspect of Youmans' life was that he had to stop working when he was so young; Gershwin, at least, was spared the mental and physical strain of a prolonged invalidism.

Vincent Millie Youmans (he was the third in his family with that name) was born in New York. His father was a prosperous maker of men's hats, and his mother, Lucy (Gibson) Youmans, came from a socially prominent family. At the age of four, young Vincent could play chords on the piano; soon afterward, encouraged by his mother, he began to take lessons. Although he first wanted to become an engineer, he took his father's advice and got a job with a Wall Street brokerage firm. After enlisting in the Navy at the outbreak of the war, Youmans was assigned to the Great Lakes Naval Training Station, where he began to compose songs and produce shows for his fellow servicemen.

This experience changed his mind about his future career; upon his return to civilian life, he was determined to become a song-writer. To achieve this aim, he followed the familiar path of song-plugger (for Max Dreyfus) and rehearsal pianist (mostly for Victor Herbert operettas). In 1920, inspired by the motion picture *The Country Cousin*, Youmans wrote his first published song and gave it the same title. Alfred Bryan, the veteran lyricist, wrote the words.

Youmans and Gershwin first met and became good friends when they were both working for Harms. Gershwin, highly appreciative of Youmans' talent, played a number of his friend's songs to convince producer Alex Aarons that he should hire Youmans for his next musical, *Two Little Girls in Blue*. Aarons was impressed, and Youmans got the job as co-composer with Paul Lannin, with lyrics supplied by Ira Gershwin (then modestly known by the pseudonym Arthur Francis).

CULVER PICTURES, INC.

TWO LITTLE GIRLS IN BLUE *(1921). Madeline and Marion Fairbanks (as Dolly and Polly Sartoris) have many shipboard adventures on their way to India to claim an inheritance. It was the first Broadway musical for both Vincent Youmans and Ira Gershwin.*

Just before rehearsals began, Aarons sold the musical to A. L. Erlanger for $100,000. The composer and lyricist were retained but Ned Wayburn, Erlanger's director, warned Youmans and Ira Gershwin to stay away from rehearsals lest the producer become panicky over their youthful appearances. Erlanger really had no cause to worry. *Two Little Girls in Blue*, which opened in May, 1921, had a respectable run of 135 performances and produced three songs ("Who's Who with You," "Dolly," and "Oh, Me! Oh, My!") that sold a good many reams of sheet music.

Youmans' second musical, *Wildflower*, was one of the biggest successes of the Twenties. Responsible for its plot and lyrics were Otto Harbach and Oscar Hammerstein II, who had been brought together in 1920 by producer Arthur Hammerstein. Harbach, the older of the two, had already written such hits as *The Three Twins*, *Madame Sherry*, and *The Firefly*, and the producer felt that he would be of great help to his young nephew, then beginning to write for the theatre. The year that they met, Harbach and Hammerstein

WILDFLOWER (1923). *Edith Day as the strong-willed Nina Benedetto, who can inherit her grandfather's millions only by keeping her temper under control for six months. (Costume by Charles LeMaire; setting by Frank E. Gates and E. A. Morange.)*

CULVER PICTURES, INC.

NO, NO, NANETTE (1925). Louise Groody & Charles Winninger sing "I Want to Be Happy."

collaborated on the successful *Tickle Me* (for Frank Tinney) and the unsuccessful *Jimmie*, both with music by Herbert Stothart. In 1923, the trio of Harbach, Hammerstein, and Stothart—augmented by Vincent Youmans—was reunited by Arthur Hammerstein for *Wildflower*.

Wildflower gave Edith Day her biggest success since Harry Tierney's and Joseph McCarthy's *Irene*. The score contained many delightful numbers, among them the ever-recurrent "Bambalina," which told of an eccentric old fiddler at a country fair who liked to stop playing in the middle of a number just to embarrass the dancers. The critics were far from happy about the story. The *News's* Burns Mantle dismissed it as "one of those 'here come the girls and boys now' operettas," though Robert Benchley of *Life*, while conceding that the book was weak, concluded his review on a philosophical note: "If you're going in for books, you might as well stay home and tell stories every evening."

In spite of its shorter Broadway run, *No, No, Nanette* had a far more impressive history than *Wildflower*. Indeed, if we consider its worldwide reception and its numerous touring companies, *No, No, Nanette* was probably the biggest international hit of any of the conventional musical comedies of the decade. Without being pioneering or even particularly original, it was nonetheless a skillful combination of many of the stock farce elements then so common in musical comedy—the philandering husband, the domineering wife, the innocent ingenue, and the amorous complications resulting from mistaken identity.

133

At first, *No, No, Nanette* showed all the symptoms of pre-Broadway egg-laying. Immediately following the coolly received opening performance in Detroit, in April, 1924, producer H. H. Frazee made some drastic changes: he took over as director, made librettists Frank Mandel and Otto Harbach rewrite the script, and threw out five songs. After frantic effort, Youmans and lyricist Irving Caesar produced four new numbers, including two, "I Want to Be Happy" and "Tea for Two," that became the most durable songs in the score.

Frazee continued making changes even after the show opened in Chicago. In June, he replaced almost all of the original leads, with the two most important roles, the negatively admonished heroine and the playboy husband, taken over by Louise Groody and Charles Winninger. The musical quickly became such a hit that the producer kept it in Chicago for almost a year. Even before this company was to arrive in New York, Frazee took the unprecedented step of sending out three other companies to tour the United States, and of allowing the musical to be presented in London and other foreign localities. When, on September 16, 1925, *No, No, Nanette* at last opened in New York at the Globe Theatre (now the Lunt-Fontanne), it settled down to a respectable run of 321 performances. (Youmans always maintained that it could have run much longer if it had not toured so extensively both before and during the Broadway engagement.)

The music and lyrics of *No, No, Nanette* are full of the irresistibly buoyant spirit of the Twenties. Indeed, the words occasionally seem to be unconsciously parodying the entire era. When the curtain rises on the first scene (the reception room in the home of wealthy Jimmy Smith), a covey of boys and girls are seen as they arrive to call on Nanette, Jimmy's ward. While waiting for her, they prance merrily down to the footlights to reveal gleefully in song that they are all "flippant and fly and free," and that they only have time for "petting parties with the smarties." Much of the period flavor is also captured in "You Can Dance with Any Girl at All," "Too Many Rings around Rosie" ("Will never get Rosie a ring!"), and the sparkling title song (whose melody Youmans appropriated from his own "My Boy and I," heard briefly in *Mary Jane McKane*).*

By 1927, although his output was limited by ill health, Youmans had become recognized as one of the leading composers of the theatre. Yet he was seldom satisfied with the way his songs were sung or performed. His first seven scores had been created with at least nine lyricists for six different producers, and his relationship was not close with any of them. He knew that he would always have to depend on others for lyrics, but there was nothing to

* Two years after *No, No, Nanette* opened in New York, producer Frazee presented an alliterative sequel, *Yes, Yes, Yvette*, with lyrics by Caesar and music by Phil Charig and Ben Jerome. Despite its affirmative title, however, the show was a quick failure.

HIT THE DECK *(1927). "Bilge" Smith (Charles King) surrounded by the admiring ladies of the ensemble. (Costumes by Mark Mooring; setting by Ward and Harvey.)*

prevent him from becoming his own producer. Therefore, at twenty-eight, Youmans formed a partnership with Lew Fields (who withdrew shortly after the opening) to present *Hit the Deck,* "A Nautical Musical Comedy" written by Fields's son, Herbert. "For the first time in my life," Youmans said at that time, "I am able to select my own singers and my own cast to interpret my music and to play the parts as I would like to have them played. For the past six or seven years, I have been completely at the mercy of the managers and of the actors."

Hit the Deck, with a cast headed by Louise Groody, Charles King, and Stella Mayhew, became Youmans' third big hit of the Twenties. To critic Percy Hammond, though he allowed that it did contain a "few fleshly jots and tittles,"the show was "clean, pretty, bright, and happy," with quantities of jolly dancing, three good songs, and romance teeming with badinage and bon mots." Its story was also considered stronger than most musical comedies

135

RAINBOW (1928). *Libby Holman, as Lotta, about to sing the torch song, "I Want a Man." (Costume by Charles LeMaire.)*

of the day as it was based on a popular play, *Shore Leave*, which had been shown on Broadway five years before.

Two of the "three good songs" mentioned by Hammond were undoubtably "Sometimes I'm Happy" and "Hallelujah!" Coincidentally, both had melodies that were not specifically created for *Hit the Deck*. "Hallelujah!", the first song Youmans had ever written, was composed during the First World War at Great Lakes. Somewhat timidly, he showed the manuscript to "Red" Carney, the bandmaster of his group, who liked the piece very much. According to Youmans, Carney was the first man ever to encourage him to become a composer, though, paradoxically, he never played the number.

"Sometimes I'm Happy" had been known as "Come on and Pet Me" when Oscar Hammerstein II and William Cary Duncan first put words to it for the 1923 musical *Mary Jane McKane*. However, it was cut before the show reached New York. In 1925, with a new lyric by Irving Caesar and Clifford Grey, "Sometimes I'm Happy" was added to the score of *A Night Out*. This time it was the show itself that did not reach New York. Youmans had faith that the song would eventually become a hit, and he made sure that a suitable place was found for it in *Hit the Deck*.

Vincent Youmans never again had a theatrical hit for which he composed the entire score. Because of failing health, he agreed to relinquish his producing activities temporarily to write the songs for Philip Goodman's production of *Rainbow*. The prospects of the show were decidedly favorable: the libretto, by Laurence Stallings and Oscar Hammerstein II, was an especially strong one, and Hammerstein's lyrics and Youmans' music were combined into a surging, dramatic score. Set in 1849 during the California gold rush, the story told of a young scout at Fort Independence, Missouri, who kills an officer in self-defense, joins a wagon train heading West, and eventually wins both a pardon and the colonel's daughter. With its realistic situations, lusty dialogue, three-dimensional characters, and intelligent use of music, *Rainbow* was in the grand tradition of *Show Boat*, with which it was favorably compared.

Unfortunately, when presented on the stage, the production lacked pace, and almost everything went wrong with it during its première on November 21, 1928. The first-act curtain didn't fall until ten minutes to eleven, a mule misbehaved on stage, the backdrops twitched and shook throughout the entire evening, and, as Gilbert Gabriel wrote, "One intermission was so long and lapsy that the orchestra played everything but 'Dixie' to fill it up." Moreover, as a result of a disagreement between Youmans and the producer, the single love duet, "Who Am I That You Should Care for Me?" (lyric by Gus Kahn), had been removed during the tryout, leaving the score with stirring marches, torch songs, comic numbers, but not one real ballad. Most of the critics, fortunately, overlooked its faults to comment

137

enthusiastically about the daring and originality of the work. The cast included Allan Prior, Charles Ruggles, Louise Brown, Mae Barnes, and the torrid Libby Holman, who achieved her first notice on Broadway by intoning the languorous "I Want A Man." The show never recovered from its opening-night problems, and lasted only thirty performances.

After his disappointment with *Rainbow*, Youmans again tried to be his own producer. He bought the Cosmopolitan Theatre at Columbus Circle, renamed it the "Youmans Cosmopolitan," and set about preparing *Great Day!*, with "Characters and locale of the story conceived by Vincent Youmans." But nothing went the way he wanted it. During the four months of tryouts before its October, 1929, opening in New York, writers, directors, actors, and even the costume designer quit or were fired. Moreover, of its ten original songs, only "Happy Because I'm in Love," "More Than You Know," "Without a Song," and "Great Day" were in the show by the time it had its Broadway première. (Among the casualties was Harold Arlen, who played the part of the piano player in the scene in the Hot Ace Dance Hall, and sang a song called "Doo-Dah-Dey.") *Great Day!* lasted six performances longer than *Rainbow*.

Youmans' misfortunes continued. In 1930, Ziegfeld wanted him for a production that appeared to be a certain hit: the combined talents of Marilyn Miller and Fred and Adele Astaire in a story based on an idea by Noël Coward. The show was called *Smiles*, though few were seen during either its preparation or its presentation. From the start, Youmans had difficulties with both Ziegfeld (who added Walter Donaldson's "You're Driving Me Crazy" and "Keep Smiling and Carry On" to the score during its brief New York run), and Marilyn Miller (who, for some inexplicable reason, refused to sing "Time on My Hands," the hit song of the show). On the bright side there was a dance routine to "Say, Young Man of Manhattan," in which Fred Astaire, in top hat and tails, danced around chorus boys in similar costume and shot them down with his cane. The idea was later used in the film *Top Hat*, with which it has since become identified.

Through the Years, based on *Smilin' Through*, was another ambitious musical and another flop. Youmans produced it himself, gave it a painstaking production (including a forty-five piece orchestra), but the story was heavy and old-fashioned. The title song was always the composer's favorite.

In 1932, Youmans was called in to bolster the score of a musical called *Humpty Dumpty*, then floundering in its pre-Broadway tryout. Renamed *Take a Chance*, its original score by Richard A. Whiting, Herb Brown Nacio (better known as Nacio Herb Brown), and B. G. DeSylva was then augmented by seven songs by Youmans, two of which were dropped before New York. The show was one of Ethel Merman's early triumphs. The final curtain was delayed almost every night by Merman's exciting delivery of

TAKE A CHANCE (1932). *One of the musical numbers in a Broadway-bound revue called* Humpty Dumpty *was "Eadie Was a Lady," sung by Ethel Merman. "She sings it," wrote Percy Hammond, "in an anteprohibition New Orleans supper club, where, surrounded by chorus girls disguised as amorous sailors from the U.S. battleship* Tampico, *she mourns the death of Eadie, a sister in sin. Ere she is through with the jocular threnody her audience is clapping its hands and waving its handkerchiefs in deserved approval." (Costumes by Kiviette and Charles LeMaire; setting by Cleon Throckmorton.)*

such show-stopping numbers as the Whiting-DeSylvia-Nacio "Eadie Was a Lady" (with additional lyrics by Roger Edens), and the Youmans-DeSylva optimistic, revivalistic "Rise 'n Shine." Other Youmans efforts included the schizophrenic dilemma of "pop" singers, "Should I Be Sweet?" (". . . or hot? It's up to yooooou!"), and two attractive duets, "So Do I" and "Oh, How I Long to Belong to You," both sung by June Knight and Jack Whiting.

In all, the Vincent Youmans catalogue consists of less than one hundred songs, published within a thirteen-year period. But in this group are some of the most continually performed "standards" of popular music. Because his more ambitious works such as *Rainbow, Great Day!,* and *Through the Years* failed to win popular support, Youmans has become far better remembered for the quality of his music than for his innovations in the musical theatre. His intriguing harmonies and syncopations combined with a disarming economy of notes have become something of a trademark, as have such spiritual-inspired, emotionally compelling pieces as "Hallelujah!," "Great Day," and "Rise 'n Shine." But Youmans could also create songs that overflowed with rich melody and sentiment, distinguished by warmth and genuine musicianship.

Although he died on April 5, 1946, at the age of forty-seven, "new" songs by Vincent Youmans may yet be heard. During his years as an invalid, he spent almost all of his time studying and writing. There are approximately 175 manuscripts of music in his "trunk," most of which were composed after his retirement. If suitable musical comedy librettos can be found, these songs, outfitted with new lyrics, will then be used. The years ahead will surely be musically enriched if once again the credit line, "Music by Vincent Youmans," is associated with a Broadway musical.

Lorenz Hart and Richard Rodgers.

CHAPTER TEN

Richard Rodgers
and Lorenz Hart

APART FROM THOSE men who not only create music but also write their own lyrics, the theatre composer, as a rule, has outshone the lyricist. In the early days of the twentieth century, words of popular songs were usually so uninspired that the reputations of Victor Herbert, Sigmund Romberg, and others were far greater than those of their lesser endowed collaborators. Even more modern song-writers, such as Kern or Youmans, were better known than most of the writers who joined words to their melodies. Although the Gershwin brothers were a closely welded team, the billings usually listed "Music by George Gershwin" ahead of all other credits, and, in some cases, in larger letters than those allotted to Ira. The first composer-lyricist team that made a change in this trend and created musicals for which both men were given equal recognition was that of Rodgers and Hart.

In his entire career, Richard Rodgers has had only two partners, Lorenz Hart and Oscar Hammerstein II. In each case, the partnership has been entirely equal. No one has ever referred to a "Richard Rodgers musical"; it has always been "Rodgers and Hart" or "Rodgers and Hammerstein." This "collaborative fidelity of Rodgers," Hammerstein has written, "is significant, I think, because it illustrates a sense of pattern and constructive purpose which never leaves him. This is not just professional habit, but a view of life."*

It also illustrates why a song by Rodgers, whether its lyric was written by Hart or Hammerstein, seems to have been the product of just one man. There is always the effect of not only a singleness of expression but of a single-mindedness as well. For to fuse lyrics with music so that each seems to belong totally and indivisibly with the other, both composer and lyricist must yield a little so that neither element in the song is given sustained prominence. It is this ability to compromise that has marked the most successful song-writing teams. That Rodgers has been able to achieve a close unity with two such disparate lyricists as Hart and Hammerstein, and to produce brilliant music with both, is a mark of his dedication and his uniqueness.

Richard Charles Rodgers was born on June 28, 1902, near Arverne, Long Island, where his parents, William and Mamie Rodgers, were spending the summer. His mother was a fine pianist and his father, a doctor, was a good baritone. They frequently held family concerts in their New York apartment of all the latest musical comedy and operetta successes. By the time Dick was four, he could pick out melodies on the piano; at six, he was able to play with both hands. From an early age he was enchanted by the theatre, particularly the musical theatre. When he was in his teens, Saturday afternoon would find him at the matinée of a musical; if it were by Jerome Kern, he would see it over and over again. As he recently told Arnold Michaelis in a recorded interview, "If you were at all sensitive to music, Kern had to be your idol. You had to worship Kern."

It was at a summer camp in Maine, Camp Wigwam (later to be attended by Frank Loesser), that the fourteen-year-old Richard Rodgers wrote his first song, the words and music to "Campfire Days." The same year he multigraphed and distributed his first copyrighted song, "Auto Show Girl," with a lyric by David Dyrenforth.

Unlike most song-writers, Rodgers was fortunate in having a father who encouraged and helped him in his musical interests. Dick's older brother, Mortimer, however, was responsible for giving him his first chance to write for the theatre. Mortimer belonged to a social group known as the Akron Club. In 1917, when the club decided to put on an original musical comedy for the benefit of the New York *Sun* Tobacco Fund for servicemen, he managed to convince his fellow members that his fifteen-year-old brother should be allowed to write the songs. Called *One Minute Please*, the show was presented at the Grand Ballroom of the Plaza Hotel. Among the numbers were such intriguingly titled compositions as "When They Rub Noses in Alaska," "I'm a Vampire," and "At the Movies" ("If your sweetie should prove fickle, You can love her for a nickel").

* From *The Rodgers and Hart Song Book*, with Foreword by Oscar Hammerstein II. New York: Simon and Schuster, Inc., 1951.

142

Rodgers' score was so well received that the following year he was asked to contribute the music and lyrics for the second Akron show, *Up Stage and Down*. With his father assisting him on some of the melodies, and his brother helping out with the lyrics, Rodgers contributed sixteen numbers to the show. Five of them were considered good enough to be published, but the young composer did not have to find a receptive music company. His father gave him the money and he published the songs himself.

When Rodgers was only seventeen, the first Rodgers and Hart song was sung in a Broadway musical. The two young men had been brought together the previous year by a mutual friend, Philip Leavitt, who felt that they would make a good song-writing team.

Lorenz Milton Hart was born May 2, 1895, in New York City. His parents were Max and Frieda Hart, and, on his father's side, Larry descended from Heinrich Heine, the German poet. He was an inveterate reader with a great interest in both classical literature and the classical theatre. Hart was only seven when he saw his first play; from then on, he attended the theatre as regularly as he could. At Columbia University, he was active in the Varsity Shows, but he left Morningside Heights after three years to work for the Shubert brothers as a play translator. In recalling his first meeting with Hart, Rodgers once wrote in *Theatre Arts Monthly:* "He was violent on the subject of rhyming in songs, feeling that the public was capable of understanding better things than the current monosyllabic juxtaposition of 'slush' and 'mush.' It made great good sense, and I was enchanted by this little man and his ideas. Neither of us mentioned it, but we evidently knew we'd work together, and I left Hart's house having acquired in one afternoon a career, a partner, a best friend and a source of permanent irritation."

The new partners began to work together almost immediately. Leavitt, the man who had introduced them, was a neighbor and a good friend of Lew Fields, the famous comedian and producer. In the summer of 1919, he arranged an audition for the new team to be held at Fields's Far Rockaway home. "In those days," Rodgers recalls, "all a show tune needed to be acceptable was attractiveness and a potential hit quality." Thus, after listening to all the material, Fields promptly decided to add one song, "Any Old Place with You," to the score of *A Lonely Romeo*, a musical in which he was then appearing on Broadway. The number was fitted into the show rather handily, and it became the first published song by Rodgers and Hart. "Any Old Place with You" remains an enjoyable, bouncy piece with a clever lyric that makes use of the names of geographic locations ("I'll go to hell for ya—or Philadelphia!") to create a series of original and unexpected rhymes.

Rodgers entered Columbia University in the fall of 1919. When Deems Taylor once asked him why he chose Columbia, his answer was simple: the Varsity Show. He was there only a few months when he and Hart wrote the score for a musical, *Fly with Me*, which was accepted by the Varsity Show

POOR LITTLE RITZ GIRL (1920). *Lulu McConnell, of the* Poor Little Ritz Girl *company, does some heavy emoting for the benefit of stage manager Grant Simpson. Aileen Poe, another member of the cast, looks rather disdainfully at the performance.*

committee. Oscar Hammerstein II, a member of the committee, even collaborated with Rodgers on one song for the show, "Room for One More." *Fly with Me* was a satire on undergraduate life on an island ruled by the Soviets. It was greeted so enthusiastically that S. Jay Kaufman of the *Globe* wrote of the young composer: "Several of his tunes were capital. We have not heard of Mr. Rodgers before. We have a suspicion we will hear of him again."

Another member of the audience who was impressed was Lew Fields. Once again he made a quick decision: he would use some of the songs in his next musical comedy, *Poor Little Ritz Girl.* This, of course, was exciting news to Rodgers and Hart. In addition to three songs from *Fly with Me* ("Don't Love Me Like Othello," "Peek in Pekin," and "Dreaming True," which became, respectively, "You Can't Fool Your Dreams," "Love's Intense in Tents," and "Love Will Call"), the team turned out twelve new songs for the production. That was as far as their association with *Poor Little Ritz Girl* went. Fields bought the songs outright, and never felt it necessary to consult such inexperienced talent during the show's preparation. Consequently, Rodgers and Hart were not advised of the producer's decision to cut eight of their numbers right after the Boston tryout, replacing them with eight by the more experienced Sigmund Romberg and Alex Gerber. Perhaps Fields had become nervous about entrusting an entire score to an eighteen-year-old college freshman and his twenty-five-year-old partner. Whatever the reason, the first the partners knew about the change was when they arrived at the Central Theatre for the première on July 27, 1920.

Poor Little Ritz Girl was a lightweight comedy of mistaken identity, using the musical-show-within-a-musical-show technique to present many of

144

the songs. In spite of their decimated contribution, Rodgers and Hart did succeed in gaining some recognition. Kenneth Macgowan and the *Globe* liked Rodgers' "hard, brisk tunes," and Heywood Broun of the *Tribune* commented that "the neglected lyric also gets more of its due than usual, for 'Mary, Queen of Scots' seems to us the most rollicking ballad we have heard in a twelvemonth. It is perhaps fitting to mention that Richard C. Rodgers composed the music for this ditty as well as that for another excellent song, 'What Happened Nobody Knows.' The more serious songs are from Sigmund Romberg, and they are pleasing, but hardly as striking as the lighter numbers."

Such favorable comments, however, made little impression on Broadway producers who were reluctant to take a chance on two brash young men and their unorthodox approach to songs. Rodgers reluctantly returned to Columbia and, with Hart, wrote the next Varsity Show, *You'll Never Know* (which included two songs, "Will You Forgive Me?" and "Let Me Drink in Your Eyes," that had been written for *Poor Little Ritz Girl* but were never used). Oscar Hammerstein II directed the show. After his second year at Columbia, Rodgers left to enroll in the nearby Institute of Musical Art (now the Juilliard School of Music). During his two years there, he found time to continue writing musicals with Hart for the Akron Club and almost any other social group that asked him. In many of these undertakings, the partners were joined by Lew Fields's son, Herbert, as either book director or dance director.

In 1924, under the perhaps protective *nom de drame* of "Herbert Richard Lorenz," Fields, Rodgers, and Hart collaborated on a comedy for Lew Fields called *The Melody Man*. Though it was about the music-publishing business and included two songs ("I'd Like to Poison Ivy" and "Moonlight Mama"), the play was not really a musical. Nor was it a hit. But it did accomplish two things: it helped to launch the career of a young actor named Fredric March, and it inaugurated the most successful musical comedy-writing trio since Bolton, Wodehouse, and Kern.

Just before the beginning of the long string of Fields, Rodgers, and Hart book musicals, the trio was associated in the production of a now-legendary revue of the mid-Twenties, *The Garrick Gaieties*. Fields's position as dance director, however, made the show a far less important assignment for him than it was for Rodgers and Hart.

The Garrick Gaieties provided the song-writers with the opportunity they badly needed. Rodgers and Hart had started auspiciously enough with *Poor Little Ritz Girl* in 1920. Yet for five years they had been unable to interest producers or music publishers; except for *The Melody Man*, they had had to devote their energies exclusively to creating amateur shows. Benjamin Kaye, a lawyer and close friend of the Rodgers family, was anxious to do what he could to help the young composer. A sometimes writer himself (he had once written the words to a Rodgers song, "Prisms, Plums and Prunes," which was in the Akron Club show *Up Stage and Down*), Kaye was helping to organize an intimate revue with a group of young actors who had appeared in the Theatre Guild plays. It was their hope that the Theatre Guild itself might sponsor the entertainment; the Guild had just built the Guild Theatre (now the ANTA), but had run short of money and could not buy new tapestries. The revue would serve a double purpose: it would give young talent a chance to be seen, and it would raise the necessary amount for the tapestries.

At Kaye's suggestion, Rodgers was chosen as composer; at Rodgers' insistence, Hart was chosen as lyricist. Lawrence Langner and Theresa Helburn, the managers of the Guild, agreed to sponsor the show and to allow it to be shown for two Sunday performances at the Garrick Theatre. With a top price of $2.20 a ticket, *The Garrick Gaieties* featured a cast of unknown performers including Sterling Holloway, Elisabeth (Libby) Holman (in her first Broadway appearance), Edith Meiser, Romney Brent, Philip Loeb (who also directed), Lee Strasberg, and Sanford Meisner. Harold Clurman was the stage manager, and Rodgers himself conducted the tiny pit orchestra. Although it had been planned to show *The Garrick Gaieties* only on Sunday, May 17, 1925, the demand for tickets was so great that six extra performances were given. When the demand continued unabated, the show settled down for a six-month run.

The Garrick Gaieties followed the pattern set by the *Greenwich Village Follies* and *The Grand Street Follies*. It was a fresh, youthful, impudent, seemingly spontaneous revue with some of its satirical barbs aimed at the Theatre Guild itself and its fondness for heavy dramatic productions. There was in both the first and the second *Gaieties* (the second was given in 1926) such a high level of wit and melody that they have since become landmarks in the history of the revue. (Wells Root of the *World*, who attended that first Sunday performance, predicted with some accuracy that its program "will be dug up from nowhere in ten years and conned with reminiscent chuckles.")

"Manhattan," an almost wistfully bucolic tune combined with a bright, intricately rhymed lyric, was the hit of the 1925 edition, though "Sentimental Me," in which the excessively ardent emotions of popular love ballads were parodied, was also outstanding. In the 1926 *Gaieties*, the most popular item was "Mountain Greenery," a brisk number that was something of a companion piece to "Manhattan" as it sang the praises of vacations in the country. Each edition also contained a lengthy musical production as the first-act finale. In the first *Gaieties, The Joy Spreader* was an attempt at a jazz opera, with the inspiration for its book credited to Gilbert Seldes, "who is therefore primarily responsible for this outrage." The second *Gaieties* included a devastating lampoon of operettas called *Rose of Arizona*. As the title indicates, one of

THE GARRICK GAIETIES *(1925)*
Philip Loeb, Sterling Hollo-
way, and Romney Brent as
"The Three Musketeers."
(Costumes by Carolyn Han-
cock.)

PHOTO BY VANDAMM

the main targets was *Rose-Marie*. with the setting changed from the Canadian Rockies to the Mexico–Arizona border. The Rodgers and Hart work had a chorus line of muscular soldiers, eight chorus girls depicting different flowers, and a group of songs all obviously plagiarized from well-known tunes ("It May Rain When the Sun Stops Shining" was an especially wicked takeoff on "Till the Clouds Roll By.")*

Although most of the critics hailed the two revues, there seems to have been a slight preference for the first one. Robert Benchley felt that "Rodgers and Hart's music and lyrics, together with the burlesque sketches and the playing of half-a-dozen hitherto unknown youngsters, should be a standing taunt and source of chagrin to those uptown revue managers who keep putting on the same old thing each year." On viewing the second *Gaieties,* Percy Hammond commented, "Last year it seemed to be saying 'Ain't I Cute, I'm only six'; which it was. But this time it is a wise and flippant ingenue, well versed in the ways of the world, though a bit awkward in pursuing them."†

Between the 1925 and 1926 *Garrick Gaieties,* two Fields, Rodgers, and Hart book musicals, *Dearest Enemy* and *The Girl Friend,* were shown in New York. *Dearest Enemy,* which was written even before the first *Gaieties,*

* *Rose of Arizona,* apparently, was the grandmother of *Little Mary Sunshine,* Rick Besoyan's clever spoof of the same type of musical theatre, produced over thirty years later.

† In 1930, a third *Garrick Gaieties,* with songs by many different writers, was presented by the Theatre Guild. Although some of the members of the original company were present, and many of the original Rodgers and Hart songs were used, it was far less successful than its predecessors. The cast included Albert Carroll, Edith Meiser, Philip Loeb, Sterling Holloway, Imogene Coca, and, making her musical comedy debut, Rosalind Russell.

147

DEAREST ENEMY (1925)
Charles Purcell, as Capt. Sir
John Copeland, is temporarily
at the mercy of Helen Ford, as
patriotic Betsy Burke, in this
tale of the American Revolution. (Costumes by James
Reynolds; setting by Clark
Robinson.)

was variously described as an "operetta with more than a chance flavor of
Gilbert and Sullivan" (Times); "something very akin to a genuine comic
opera" (Arthur Hornblow, Theatre magazine), and "a baby grand opera"
(Percy Hammond, Herald Tribune). The trio had originally taken the manu-
script to Lew Fields, but he had feared that its story of how Mrs. Robert
Murray (of Manhattan's Murray Hill) detained General Howe during the
American Revolution would not be commercial. The musical was eventually
sponsored by the husband of Helen Ford, the star of the show.

There was a well-sustained attempt to fit the music into both the story
and the period. The ballads, "Here in My Arms," "Bye and Bye," and "Here's
a Kiss," were dainty, charming pieces, while the comic numbers, among them
"Old Enough to Love" (a gayer approach to mature love than Kurt Weill's
"September Song") and "War Is War," were both funny and appropriate.
"Sweet Peter" went back to an even earlier New York as it told how the
boom-boom-boom of Peter Stuyvesant's wooden leg always alerted his wife
when he came home drunk. In summing up his opinion of Dearest Enemy,
Frank Vreeland of the Telegram wrote: "We have a glimmering notion that
someday they [Fields, Rodgers, and Hart] will form the American counter-
part of the once great triumvirate of Bolton, Wodehouse, and Kern."

The new triumvirate's next show, The Girl Friend, was indeed in the
spirit of the bright, up-to-date productions once offered at the Princess
Theatre. Presented by Lew Fields, with Sammy White and Eva Puck in the
leads, the musical won critical and popular favor. Its book, according to Abel

Green of *Variety*, "is the best libretto Fields has contributed so far and is only parred by the songs with ultra-smart lyrics and oddly rhythmed and fetching tunes." Among them were the classic of city-life contentment, "The Blue Room," and the jagged ode to "The Girl Friend."

"From the beginning," wrote an unspecified *Times* critic in his review of *Peggy-Ann*, "Fields, Rodgers, and Hart have brought freshness and ideas to the musical comedy field, and in their new piece they travel a little further along their road." The show, which opened in December, 1926, was daring in almost every respect but its title. Roughly based on a 1910 Marie Dressler musical called *Tillie's Nightmare*, the entire story was a dream, with the exception of a prologue and an epilogue. Many of the conventions of musical comedy were both shattered and satirized as the slightly Freudian saga took the heroine (Helen Ford) from her home in Glens Falls, New York, to New York City's Fifth Avenue, out to sea in a yacht and then a raft, and finally to a Havana race track. There was no opening chorus, nor were there any songs at all for the first fifteen minutes. When the dancing girls did arrive, they were used functionally within the plot rather than as unrelated ornaments. The ending, when Peggy-Ann finally awoke from her three-hour dream, was actually performed in semidarkness.

That such an adult and original work could succeed commercially in the mid-Twenties so encouraged its trio of writers that they followed it with another dream fantasy. Early in 1921, Fields, Rodgers, and Hart had taken a six-month option on Mark Twain's *A Connecticut Yankee in King Arthur's Court*, but they were unable to interest a producer. Six years later, they had little difficulty in getting Lew Fields and Lyle D. Andrews, the co-producers of *Peggy-Ann*, to sponsor it as the next attraction at the Vanderbilt Theatre. In inventiveness and wit it may have been a less-inspired offering than its predecessor, but *A Connecticut Yankee* nevertheless attracted audiences in such throngs that it became the first Rodgers and Hart musical to run over

PHOTO BY VANDAMM

A CONNECTICUT YANKEE *(1927). "That irrepressible young trinity" (as Gilbert Gabriel called them), Herbert Fields, Richard Rodgers, and Lorenz Hart, photographed backstage at the Vanderbilt Theatre.*

149

400 performances. The music and lyrics were an important factor in its popularity. "My Heart Stood Still" (originally sung earlier in the year by Jessie Matthews and Richard Dolman in a London revue, *One Dam Thing After Another*) was a warm, rich melody wedded to an uncommonly expressive lyric, made all the more effective by Hart's use of simple monosyllabic words. Another hit of the score, "Thou Swell," revealed the lyricist in a more characteristic vein as he mixed old English and new American.

In 1943, after Rodgers and Hammerstein had begun their collaboration with *Oklahoma!*, Rodgers himself produced an up-dated version of *A Connecticut Yankee*. This time, the Yankee was a lieutenant in the Navy and the girl a corporal in the W.A.C. Another change enlarged the relatively minor character of Queen Morgan Le Fay to fit the major talents of Vivienne Segal. It was in this production that she introduced the hilariously macabre inventory, "To Keep My Love Alive," which, in Rodgers's words, showed "the inability on Larry's part to succumb to a cliché or to rhyme any way but brilliantly."

Rodgers and Hart had three shows on Broadway in 1928, *She's My Baby*, *Present Arms*, and *Chee-Chee*. Following the quick failure of *She's My Baby* (in spite of the efforts of Beatrice Lillie, Clifton Webb, and Irene Dunne), the composer and lyricist went back to the Fields family for their next musical. Herbert Fields, having recently written a libretto about the Navy in *Hit the*

PHOTO BY VANDAMM

A CONNECTICUT YANKEE (1927). Queen Morgan Le Fay (Nana Bryant) seems to have hypnotized the Yankee (William Gaxton). (Costumes by John Hawkins, Jr.)

Deck, now turned his attention to the Marines in *Present Arms.* This, too, became a well-attended attraction, with critics comparing it to both *Hit the Deck* and the DeSylva-Brown-Henderson musical *Good News.* The songs, happily, were pure Rodgers and Hart—among them the unregretful "You Took Advantage of Me."

Chee-Chee, also with a book by Herbert Fields, was an ambitious work that tried to make all the songs adhere firmly to the story line. Rodgers and Hart had been anxious to write this kind of show for a long time. As Hart described it before the opening, it would be "a new form of musical show," in which "the songs are going to be a definite part of the progress of the piece, not extraneous interludes without rhyme or reason." Even its program note—similar to that of *Rose-Marie*—contained the following information: "The musical numbers, some of them very short, are so interwoven with the story that it would be confusing for audiences to peruse a complete list." Only six, including "Moon of My Delight" and "I Must Love You," were then specified by title. Everything, in fact, seemed promising about *Chee-Chee* except a plot that related the fairly indelicate account of how the son of the Grand Eunuch of old China avoided inheriting his father's exalted position. The show lasted thirty-one performances.

The quick failure of *Chee-Chee* ended Rodgers and Hart's association with Lew Fields and temporarily halted their collaboration with Herbert Fields. It also made them a little cautious. *Spring Is Here* and *Heads Up!,* their next two shows, were formula entertainments, both produced by Alex A. Aarons and Vinton Freedley. *Spring Is Here* did have "With a Song in My Heart" (though it had to be sung by the "other man," John Hundley, because the star, Glenn Hunter, could not sing); *Heads Up!* offered the gently lapping "Ship without a Sail." This was also the first Broadway musical to provide a young dancer named Ray Bolger with sufficient opportunity to demonstrate his remarkable talent.

Nor was there anything outstanding about *Simple Simon,* a lavish Ziegfeld production of 1930 in which Ed Wynn starred. Of the Rodgers and Hart songs, the maudlin "Ten Cents a Dance" has become the most popular. It was introduced by Ruth Etting, who had succeeded Lee Morse only twenty-four hours before the New York opening. During the tryout, Ziegfeld insisted that one song, "Dancing on the Ceiling," would have to be cut. Luckily, Rodgers and Hart were able to salvage it for Jessie Matthews to sing in a London musical, *Ever Green.*

America's Sweetheart, in 1931, was the last original musical comedy written by Fields, Rodgers, and Hart. As the Mary Pickford allusion in the title suggests, it was a satire on Hollywood, where the trio had just spent some time working on a film called *The Hot Heiress.* For the leading female role of an aspiring movie actress, the authors chose an unknown singer, Harriette

151

SIMPLE SIMON (1930). *Ed Wynn comes to the rescue of Cinderella in this musical Mother Goose fantasy. "Wynn has never seemed so indisputably great," wrote Brooks Atkinson.*

AMERICA'S SWEETHEART *(1931). Rodgers and Hart's musical about the movies had Jack Whiting and Harriette Lake (better known as Ann Sothern) as two ambitious young actors. In this scene, Miss Lake is obviously not amused at Mr. Whiting's gift of a success horseshoe consisting of fruits and vegetables. (Costumes by Charles Le-Maire; setting by Donald Oenslager.)*

Lake, whom they had seen in a brief part in *Smiles* during its Boston tryout. Described by *Time* as "a lovely synthesis, one part Ginger Rogers, one part Ethel Merman," Miss Lake soon emerged with a definite personality of her own under the name of Ann Sothern.

In general, although Dorothy Parker commented in *The New Yorker* that Hart's rhymes were "less internal than colonic," greater praise was bestowed on the score than on the script. According to Brooks Atkinson, there was "a rush about the music and a mocking touch in the lyrics that make the score more deftly satirical than the production."

Despite the attitude they had shown toward the movie industry in *America's Sweetheart,* Rodgers and Hart spent the next three and one-half years in Hollywood. Upon their return to New York in 1935, their first assignment was to create the songs for Billy Rose's mammoth *Jumbo*, the final production to play at the Hippodrome Theatre. With John Murray Anderson as over-all director and George Abbott staging the book (his first musical), *Jumbo* was, according to Percy Hammond, "a sane and exciting compound of opera, animal show, folk drama, harlequinade, carnival, circus, extravaganza, and spectacle." Jimmy Durante headed the cast of ninety humans and almost as many animals.

The myriad problems of such a huge undertaking—financial as well as creative—compelled Billy Rose to delay the première for almost three months beyond its scheduled date. Surprisingly, after it did open, Broadway customers kept it running for only five months. After closing in New York, it

JUMBO (1935). The "Circus Wedding" finale with Donald Novis and Gloria Grafton as the groom and bride. (Costumes by Raoul Pène du Bois; production designed by Albert Johnson.)

PHOTO BY VANDAMM

reopened at the Dallas Exposition with Eddie Foy, Jr., in the Durante part. But eventually, as a headline in *Variety* sadly revealed:" 'JUMBO' DISINTEGRATES INTO 50-CENT CIRCUS; TEXAS DATE ANOTHER FLOP, RAN SHOW $30,000 FURTHER INTO RED."

Although they were always anxious to explore novel ideas for the musical stage, Rodgers and Hart were never completely successful in contributing to the structure of the musical theatre until *On Your Toes* in 1936. This time the partners decided to write the book themselves, which they did in collaboration with George Abbott. Thus, they were able to create a strikingly unified production that not only offered a coherent story but also utilized dancing as an integral part of the action. For the important post of dance director, they secured George Balanchine, the ballet choreographer, whose only previous Broadway experience had been in staging some of the dances for the *Ziegfeld Follies of 1936*. The most memorable sequence in *On Your Toes* was the *Slaughter on Tenth Avenue* ballet, in which Balanchine's choreography, the dancing of Ray Bolger and Tamara Geva, the sleazy excitement of Rodgers' music, and the ballet's dramatic importance all combined to lift *On Your Toes* to a position as one of the supreme theatrical achievements of the mid-Thirties.

The producer of *On Your Toes* was Dwight Deere Wiman. For the next two years he followed it with annual spring musicals bearing the credits,

ON YOUR TOES (1936). *George Balanchine's* Slaughter on Tenth Avenue *ballet. Tamara Geva as the Strip Tease Girl, George Church the Big Boss, and Ray Bolger the Hoofer. (Costumes by Irene Sharaff; setting by Joe Mielziner.)*

BABES IN ARMS (1937). Aljan de Loville, as a French pilot, makes a forced landing in the midst of Mitzi Green, Rolly Pickert, Alfred Drake, Duke McHale, and Wynn Murray. (Costumes by Helene Pons; setting by Raymond Sovey.)

PHOTO BY LUCAS-PRITCHARD

"Book, music, and lyrics by Rodgers and Hart," and "Choreography by George Balanchine." In 1937, their combined efforts created *Babes in Arms;* in 1938, it was *I Married an Angel.*

Babes in Arms was full of *Garrick Gaieties* youthfulness, with a cast headed by such youngsters as Mitzi Green, Ray Heatherton, the Nicholas Brothers, Wynn Murray, and, in minor roles, Alfred Drake and Dan Dailey. More important, it was another serious attempt to make each song serve a purpose in the story, which, conveniently, was concerned with young people putting on an amateur musical. Seldom has one show produced so many enduring hits—the saga of the vocal phenomenon known as "Johnny One Note"; the almost psychological "Where or When"; "My Funny Valentine," in which the warmth of the music conveys so perfectly the true intent of the slightly exaggerated lyric; the duet, "I Wish I Were in Love Again," with its unusual combination of disillusionment and ebullience; and the brazen confession of the nonconformist, "The Lady Is a Tramp."

John Anderson in the *Journal-American* hailed *I Married an Angel* as "a winged wonderwork from the musical heavens of Rodgers and Hart," an appraisal that may have been only slightly excessive. The story, which Rodgers and Hart had originally adapted for the movies in collaboration with Moss Hart, was an imaginative tale of a Budapest banker (Dennis King) who vows that he will marry only an angel, and the awkward situations that arise when a real angel (Vera Zorina) actually becomes his bride. The cast was particularly notable. Both King and Walter Slezak had recently distinguished themselves in straight dramas. After an eight-year self-imposed exile from the musical stage, Vivienne Segal returned to Broadway in the kind of light comedy part she had been trying to get ever since *The Three Musketeers,* her last musical, in which she had also appeared opposite Dennis King. Vera

I MARRIED AN ANGEL (1938). *Audrey Christie, Walter Slezak, and Dennis King. (Costumes by John Hambleton; setting by Jo Mielziner.)*

"Beauty is truth, truth beauty / Gabriel blow your root-toot-tooty," sing Vera Zorina and fellow angels in "Angel without Wings."

Zorina, who had scored a hit in the Tamara Geva role in the London production of *On Your Toes,* gave her most fondly remembered performance as the lovely angel-bride.

I Married an Angel was the first musical to be directed by Joshua Logan. Jo Mielziner's decor, which incorporated treadmills and a curtain that functioned like a huge Venetian blind, was an especially important contribution to the effectiveness of the play.

The score offered such glittering Rodgers and Hart gems as "Did You Ever Get Stung?" ("Where the doctor can't help you"), "I Married an Angel," "I'll Tell the Man in the Street," "A Twinkle in Your Eye," and the poignant "Spring Is Here," in which the beauties of spring are found to have little appeal when one is unloved. Of all, perhaps, the real show-stopper was the audacious travesty of every Roxy and Radio City Music Hall stage spectacle, "The Roxy Music Hall" ("It's a Wonderland where everyone is Alice/Where the ladies room is bigger than a palace".*)

Between *Babes in Arms* and *I Married an Angel,* Rodgers and Hart and librettists George S. Kaufman and Moss Hart collaborated on a musical social satire, *I'd Rather Be Right.* Following the precedent set by Moss Hart's and Irving Berlin's *As Thousands Cheer,* actual living people were portrayed. Instead of offering impersonations in a number of blackout sketches, however, *I'd Rather Be Right* was a regular book musical with President Franklin D. Roosevelt as the leading character. Portraying the role was the semiretired, but still agile, George M. Cohan.

Because of the news value of such a production, newspapers and news magazines treated the preparation of *I'd Rather Be Right* as a major event. There were headlines when, during the Boston tryout, Cohan refused to sing an uncomplimentary line about his friend, Al Smith, in the song, "Off the Record." There were more headlines when Noël Coward was called in to help rewrite and restage some of the material. There were still more headlines concerning the friction between Cohan and Rodgers and Hart, whom the star disparagingly referred to as "Gilbert and Sullivan." Even the New York *Times* devoted an editorial to "Spoofing the Great" (they were for it). All these helped give the show a record advance sale of $300,000. ("Why the idea of calling George M. Cohan Franklin D. Roosevelt should have engendered so intense an interest I cannot figure out," wrote George Jean Nathan in *Newsweek,* "unless it was because Franklin D. Roosevelt, on the other hand, has been called everything under the sun but George M. Cohan.")

Almost inevitably, when *I'd Rather Be Right* at last arrived at the Alvin Theatre in New York on November 2, 1937, there were some who felt disappointed. Richard Lockridge, whose review was carried on page 1 of the *Sun* and contained almost every punch line in the show, commented that it was

* Copyright © 1938 Robbins Music Corporation. Used by special permission.

157

I'D RATHER BE RIGHT (1937). *Gathered around the piano in Sam Harris' office are producer Harris, lyricist Lorenz Hart, composer Richard Rodgers, colibrettists Moss Hart and George S. Kaufman, and star George M. Cohan.*

not always brilliant satire. In comparing it with *Of Thee I Sing*, which almost everyone did, the general feeling was that Gershwin, Gershwin, Kaufman, and Ryskind were more skillful than Rodgers, Kaufman, and the *Zwei Herzen* (as John Mason Brown referred to the unrelated Moss and Lorenz). George M. Cohan, however, scored a great personal triumph that might well have elected *him* President, and audiences were made acutely aware that nowhere else in the world could so outspoken a production be shown.

The score for *I'd Rather Be Right* was written in just three weeks. It contained only one moderately popular song, "Have You Met Miss Jones?"; the rest of the numbers being too satirical and too close to the theme for any of them to catch on.

After their three-in-a-row springtime musicals for Dwight Deere Wiman, Rodgers and Hart evened their seasonal average by writing three successive fall shows for producer-director George Abbott—*The Boys from Syracuse* (libretto by Abbott) in 1938, *Too Many Girls* in 1939, and *Pal Joey* in 1940. The first of these, an uninhibited but skillful adaption of Shakespeare's *The Comedy of Errors,* so impressed Richard Watts, Jr., of the *Herald Tribune,* that he wrote: "If you have been wondering all these years just what was wrong with *The Comedy of Errors,* it is now possible to tell you. It has been waiting for a score by Rodgers and Hart and direction by George Abbott."

158

The long-awaited score still remains one of the team's finest, high-lighted by "This Can't Be Love," "You Have Cast Your Shadow on the Sea," "Falling in Love with Love" (one of Rodgers and Hart's best waltzes), and the romantic tribute to the winter solstice, "The Shortest Day of the Year." The two Dromios were played by Jimmy Savo and Teddy Hart (Larry's brother), and their masters were Eddie Albert and Ronald Graham.

Too Many Girls had a collegiate setting (Pottawatomie College, Stop Gap, New Mexico) which gave it a football backfield of Hal LeRoy, Eddie Bracken, Desi Arnaz, and Richard Kollmar, cheered on by coeds Marcy West-cott, Mary Jane Walsh, and Diosa Costello. One of the energetic undergradu-ates was Van Johnson, who later succeeded Kollmar for the tour. The pro-duction had so much vitality and so many fine Rodgers and Hart songs that few were troubled by its old-fashioned book or the awkward way some of the numbers were incorporated into it.

The idea of fashioning a musical out of a series of short stories about a conniving hoofer named Joey Evans was first suggested by the author himself, John O'Hara, in a letter to Rodgers. It took Rodgers and Hart only five minutes to decide to do it, and they promptly notified O'Hara that they would be glad to write the songs if he supplied the book. For the leading part, Rodgers chose a young actor named Gene Kelly, whom he had seen in a dancing role in William Saroyan's *The Time of Your Life*. As his middle-aged, worldly patroness there could be no other actress than Vivienne Segal, who had recently demonstrated her gifts as a brittle comedienne in *I Married an Angel*.

In many ways, *Pal Joey* was the pinnacle of the Rodgers and Hart col-laboration. The score was purposely unsentimental and sardonic, allowing only one love song, "I Could Write a Book," and even that was an insincere

PHOTO BY VANDAMM

THE BOYS FROM SYRACUSE *(1938). Marcy Westcott, Wynn Murray and Muriel Angelus stopping the show with "Sing for Your Supper." (Costumes by Irene Sharaff.)*

TOO MANY GIRLS (1939). Desi Arnaz, as the football hero of Pottawatomie College, leads the students in the torrid "Spic and Spanish" number. On the right is an equally animated Diosa Costello, and behind them is Van Johnson. (Costumes by Raoul Pène du Bois.)

PAL JOEY (1940). Joey's dream of the Chez Joey night club at the end of the first act. Gene Kelly and Vivienne Segal are in the center. Van Johnson is at the extreme right. (Costumes by John Koenig; setting by Jo Mielziner.)

expression. Throughout, there was a cohesion of mood between music and plot that was remarkable, though not all the songs were used to advance the action. Some of the best ("Happy Hunting Horn," "The Flower Garden Of My Heart," "That Terrific Rainbow") were part of a nightclub floor show; "Zip" was an out-of-nowhere, in-front-of-the-curtain routine; "Do It the Hard Way" was a specialty number for tumbler Jack Durant. Others, however, such as "In Our Little Den of Iniquity," "Bewitched, Bothered, and Bewildered," and "Take Him," were all intelligently introduced as part of the story. In whatever manner they were introduced, however, all the songs shed light on the smoky characters who sang them and about whom they were sung.

Peopled by characters who were either unattractive or just stupid, *Pal Joey* was too far from musical comedy orthodoxy for many of the patrons and some of the critics. "Although it is expertly done, can you draw sweet water from a foul well?" asked Brooks Atkinson. To Wolcott Gibbs, however, it was that rarity, "A song-and-dance production with living, three-dimensional figures, talking and behaving like human beings."

Pal Joey may well have been ahead of its time. When it was revived in 1952 by Jule Styne and Leonard Key, it met with much greater success. "While Joey himself may have been fairly adolescent in his thinking and his morality," Rodgers observed shortly before the second opening, "the show bearing his name certainly wore long pants, and in many respects forced the entire musical comedy theatre to wear long pants for the first time." With Vivienne Segal in her original role, with Joey played by Harold Lang (understudied by Bob Fosse), and with hardly a line changed, the musical had the longest run (542 performances) of any Rodgers and Hart production. The once divided critics were now almost unanimous in their praise. Words like "masterpiece" and "classic" were in their reviews, and some compared it to the Kurt Weill–Bert Brecht *Die Dreigroschenoper*. Even Brooks Atkinson could now feel that "it renews confidence in the professionalism of the theatre," while a slightly gloating Wolcott Gibbs noticed that "standards

PHOTO BY EILEEN DARBY—GRAPHIC HOUSE

PAL JOEY *(1952). Vivienne Segal recreates her original role of Vera Simpson, and Harold Lang is the new Joey Evans. Here they sing "In Our Little Den of Iniquity." (Costumes by Miles White; setting by Oliver Smith.)*

BY JUPITER *(1942). Ray Bolger as Sapiens and Benay Venuta as Hippolyta in a musical remake of Julian Thompson's* The Warrior's Husband. *(Costumes by Irene Sharaff.)*

apparently have changed, because up to now I have met nobody who found anything embarrassing in the goings on."

The April before the first *Pal Joey* opened, Dwight Deere Wiman tried to revive his streak of spring musical successes with Rodgers and Hart's *Higher and Higher,* but it was a failure. The producer was more fortunate in the summer of 1942 when he joined Rodgers (in association with Richard Kollmar) to present *By Jupiter.* Starring the nimble Ray Bolger, it was a formula Rodgers and Hart show full of what the customers could easily appreciate as pre-World War II glamour, and it became one of the team's most profitable undertakings.

The partnership of Rodgers and Hart, however, was all but finished. Hart, a brilliant, unstable man given to mysterious disappearances for weeks at a time, was becoming extremely difficult for Rodgers to work with. In 1941, the composer had secretly aligned himself with George Abbott as co-producer of *Best Foot Forward* (score by Hugh Martin and Ralph Blane), and early in September of that year had discussed with his old friend, Oscar Hammerstein II, the possibility of a partnership if the time ever came when Hart could no longer continue. When Theresa Helburn of the Theatre Guild approached Rodgers with the idea of adapting Lynn Riggs's play, *Green Grow the Lilacs,* into a musical, he immediately became enthusiastic about the project. Hart demurred. He didn't feel well, it wasn't their kind of show, and if Rodgers really wanted to do the show, why didn't he choose another lyricist. It was then that Rodgers and Hammerstein agreed to work together on the play that eventually became *Oklahoma!* Hammerstein, in fact, had long wanted to make a musical out of *Green Grows the Lilacs,* and had even tried unsuccessfully to interest Jerome Kern in collaborating on it.

The last show Lorenz Hart worked on was the 1943 production of *A Connecticut Yankee.* Throughout the opening-night performance, Hart remained in the rear of the theatre, walking back and forth and muttering to himself. When Rodgers looked for him after the final curtain, he was nowhere to be found. Two days were spent in frantic efforts to locate him. When he was finally found unconscious in a hotel room, Hart was immediately rushed to Doctors Hospital, suffering from acute pneumonia. Rodgers and his wife were with him almost constantly for three days, but he never regained consciousness. On November 22nd, in the midst of an air-raid-drill blackout, Lorenz Hart died. He was forty-eight years old.

The collaboration between Rodgers and Hart was a unique one in many ways. Aside from its productivity and longevity, it was a near-perfect combination of frequently sharp, sophisticated lyrics set to music that was just as frequently warm and lyrical. The remarkable thing, of course, is how well each man complemented the other's style, adding something both inseparable from, and indispensable to, the total effect. (The Rodgers and Hart technique, incidentally, was somewhat opposite from that of the Gershwin brothers. George's hard-driving, jagged rhythms were often smoothed down by what Vernon Duke has called the "lazy, good-natured, placidly *gemutlich* fun with words that was Ira's characteristic.")

Freshness, charm, and daring, coupled with an unquenchable spirit of youthfulness, were present in almost everything that Rodgers and Hart wrote. The methodical, outwardly calm composer and his excitable, cigar-chewing partner were continually seeking new ideas in songs and in stories, and the range of subject matter in their musicals attests to their inquisitive, experimental nature. *Time* magazine wrote, in 1938: "As Rodgers and Hart see it, what was killing musicomedy was its sameness, its tameness, its eternal rhyming of June with moon. They decided it was not enough to be just good at the job; they had to be constantly different also. The one possible formula was: *Don't have a formula;* the one rule for success: *Don't follow it up.*"

B. G. DeSylva, Lew Brown and Ray Henderson.

B.G. DeSylva
Lew Brown and
Ray Henderson

FROM THE STANDPOINT OF PRODUCTIVITY—at least—there has never been, nor will there ever be again, a period like the Twenties. At no time during the decade did the number of new Broadway musicals, both book shows and revues, drop below thirty-seven per season. During two seasons, 1920-21 and 1927-28, the figure reached the staggering total of forty-eight! Reasons for this musical plethora along Broadway are easy to find: costs were relatively low and, except for night clubs and vaudeville, there just was no competition from any other media offering light theatrical entertainment embellished by songs.

Such multiplicity of attractions naturally required a corresponding multiplicity of composers and lyricists. Operetta was special. That was still primarily for the European-trained, classically oriented. But musical comedy and revue required writers who were not only versatile but adept at creating self-sustaining songs, songs that could tell their stories and express their emotions succinctly and completely, with only a nodding relationship to the stories to which they were affixed. Apart from their quality, musical numbers stood out because they literally stood out; they were spotlighted and illuminated as soon as the boy tossed a line at the girl that set up the song cue.

In musical construction and in lyrical expression many of the songs for the average musical of the Twenties were undeniably period pieces. They sighed and they bubbled with the innocence of the decade. They were created solely for the entertainments of their time and they reflected it. Yet while that time has long since faded, the songs of the decade continue to exert an emotional hold on the listener. They transport us, as no play or costumed operetta could, into a more naive but unquestionably happier period of our national life.

There were hundreds of writers then, pouring out song after song, and meeting almost any requirement of the usually patchquilt productions then being offered. Harry Tierney and Joe McCarthy emphasized sweet romance in *Irene*, knockabout comedy in the Eddie Cantor vehicle, *Kid Boots*, and south-of-the-border spectacle in *Rio Rita*. Harry Ruby and Bert Kalmar kept things light and lively in such farcical diversions as *The Ramblers* (for Clark and McCullough), *The Five O'Clock Girl*, *Good Boy*, and the Marx Brothers' *Animal Crackers*.

But among the creators of hummable, durable "period" songs, no team ever enjoyed the success of B. G. ("Buddy") DeSylva, Lew Brown and Ray Henderson. It was their special knack to take an up-to-date topic— be it college life or country club life or aviation or whatever—and deck it out with a serviceable book, some bright numbers for raucously funny clowns like Bert Lahr or personality boys like Harry Richman, and then tie the whole bundle together into an uptempoed, youthful, gag-filled package. The songs could be whistled by anyone and their lyrics—beginning with a catch phrase like "You're the cream in my coffee" or "Button up your overcoat"—were hard to forget. The credit line, "Songs by DeSylva, Brown and Henderson," was enough to stamp the entertainment with the writers' own particularly well-meshed personalities; to this day, it still symbolizes a body of works that was especially endemic both to period and locale.

Although their creativity frequently overlapped and specific credits for lyrics or music were seldom listed, in general DeSylva and Brown worked on the words and Henderson on the music. Taking them in the order of their billing, B. G. DeSylva—known as "Bud" or "Buddy" but christened "George Gard"—was born in New York on January 27, 1895. His father, an actor-turned-lawyer, moved the family to Los Angeles when young Buddy was two. At four the precocious youngster appeared in a

SINBAD *(1918). Sinbad (Forrest Huff) discovers Inbad (Al Jolson) prowling about the harem. Jolson sang DeSylva's first hit, " 'N Everything," in this show.*

local benefit show billed as "Baby Gard," and was even offered a contract to tour the B. F. Keith vaudeville circuit. Mother wouldn't hear of it, however, and Buddy remained home to attend the local high school and, briefly, the University of Southern California. The summer following his sophomore year, he joined three classmates as singing and ukulele-strumming "Hawaiians" at a nearby country club. He had also begun making up songs which he sang for the club's members and their guests including, one night, Al Jolson. Ever on the lookout for new material, Jolson particularly liked one DeSylva song, " 'N Everything," bought a half interest in it, and sang it in *Sinbad* later that year. That was all the impetus DeSylva needed; he promptly came east to see if he could make a fulltime career of song writing. Six months later he received his first royalty check— $16,000.

DeSylva needed no further convincing. He signed with the Remick Publishing Company, and began turning out even bigger hits for Jolson —"Avalon" written with Vincent Rose, "April Showers" with Louis Silvers,

167

"California, Here I Come" with Joe Meyer. In 1919, when he was twenty-four, DeSylva joined with a twenty-year-old piano-pounder named George Gershwin to write his—and Gershwin's—first Broadway score, *La La Lucille*. Other distinguished collaborations soon followed. With Jerome Kern, De-Sylva wrote "Look for the Silver Lining," the song hit from *Sally*, and, with Victor Herbert, the score for *Orange Blossoms* (including "A Kiss in the Dark"). The team of DeSylva and Gershwin was reunited for the *George White's Scandals* of 1922, which they followed with two other annual editions (among their songs: "I'll Build a Stairway to Paradise" and "Somebody Loves Me"). When Gershwin gave up composing music for the George White extravaganzas to concentrate on writing for book shows, the producer decided to replace him with a promising young Tin Pan Alley composer named Ray Henderson. But Henderson, who had been writing on and off with lyricist Lew Brown, was anxious to establish a steady partnership with Brown. This put White in an awkward position since he had already signed DeSylva for the next edition of his *Scandals*. His solution: why don't the three try to work together? They did, found that their talents meshed, and thus began a song-writing triumvirate that was to last until 1931.

Lew Brown had been the first of the trio to meet with success. Born in Odessa, Russia, on December 10, 1893, he was brought to the United States by his immigrant parents when he was five. At sixteen, while serving as a lifeguard at a Rockaway beach, he began jotting down parodies of popular songs of the day. Then he tried a few original lyrics and, at the urging of friends, showed them to veteran composer Albert Von Tilzer. Von Tilzer liked Brown's lyrics, and the two began a fruitful collaboration. At nineteen, Lew Brown had had his first success with Von Tilzer, "I'm the Lonesomest Gal in Town," which the team soon followed up with "Give Me the Moonlight, Give Me the Girl," "I May Be Gone for a Long, Long Time" (Grace LaRue introduced it in *Hitchy-Koo, 1917*), and "I Used to Love You but It's All Over Now."

In 1922, publisher Louis Bernstein, of Shapiro-Bernstein, spotted Brown as the perfect partner for a young composer he had under contract named Ray Henderson. The first Brown and Henderson song, "Georgette," did pretty well and was interpolated in the *Greenwich Village Follies*. Henderson, who was born in Buffalo, N.Y., on December 1, 1896, was taught piano by his mother even before he went to grammar school. After studying at the Chicago Conservatory, he joined local dance bands as a pianist. From Chicago, he went to New York where he climbed the musical ladder from song-plugger, to arranger-pianist, to composer. During the early Twenties, Henderson's gifts became recognized with such efforts as "That Old Gang of Mine" (lyric by Billy Rose and Mort Dixon), "Bye Bye Blackbird" (lyric by Dixon alone), "Five Foot Two, Eyes of Blue" and "I'm Sitting on Top of the World" (the last two with Sam Lewis and Joe Young). The first Henderson melody mated to words by Buddy De-Sylva (in collaboration with Bud Green) was "Alabamy Bound," identified with both Al Jolson and Eddie Cantor. The song was introduced early in 1925, the same year DeSylva, Brown and Henderson were united for their first *George White's Scandals*.

Surprisingly, the special DeSylva-Brown-Henderson chemistry took a little while to become apparent. The maiden effort for the *Scandals* produced nothing memorable at all—not even with the inspiration of Helen Morgan in her Broadway debut. But the trio's second score the following year turned out to be one of the glories of the mid-Twenties revues, contributing much to achieving what Wells Root dubbed in the *World*, "the master *Scandals* of the series."

George White was determined, right from the outset, to make it exactly that. He was so confident that he would have the triumph of his career that he charged $55.00 per ticket for the first nine rows on opening night (thereafter it dropped to the still steep price of $5.50). No one was heard demanding his money back. The show had, for its day, everything. There was Harry Richman, in straw hat and cane, strutting through "Lucky Day" (in which "horseshoe" rhymed with "of course you"), rimmed by lovelies apparelled as a Wishbone, a Horseshoe, a Four-Leaf Clover, a Star, a New Moon, and a Haystack. There were the Howard brothers, Willie and Eugene, cavorting through a wild sketch about a woman barber (Frances Williams), and another one about their dear old days at the Winter Garden. There was the eye-boggling "Triumph of Women" montage, with the likes of Mme. Sans-Gene, Salome, Mme. DuBarry, Lucretia Borgia, Cleopatra, and Eve serenaded to the tune of "Lady Fair." There were Richman and Miss Williams mutually cooing "The Girl Is You and the Boy Is Me." There was dimple-kneed Ann Pennington, the *Scandals'* celebrated dancing doll. There was the new dance craze (Mr. White had to have one every year), "The Black Bottom," "a slap-foot, drag-foot, oozy sort of dance (to quote John Anderson in the *Post*) from the mud flats of the Suwanee River, moaning a little swampily as it lags through its sinuous gyrations."

And there was, most certainly, "The Birth of the Blues." In the first act finale, a jazz-versus-classics duel, Willie Howard played Beethoven, brother Eugene was Liszt, and Harry Richman was the champion of that native musical form, the blues, assisted by the McCarthy sisters personifying the "St. Louis Blues" and the "Memphis Blues." To prove to the obdur-

GEORGE WHITE'S SCANDALS
(1926).   Producer - director
George White teaching the
intricacies of "The Black Bottom" to Tom Patricola and
Ann Pennington.

ate longhairs that this was indeed music worthy of their admiration, Richman offered in evidence, "The Birth of the Blues," tracing its genesis to the breeze in the trees singing weird melodies, the wail of a down-hearted incarcerated frail, and a note from a whippoorwill high on a hill. In addition to these disparate pregenital origins, there was a further evidential piece, Gershwin's "Rhapsody in Blue" (with lyrics!). That did it. The immortals of music grandly let open the heavenly gates, and the curtain fell on a glimpse of Paradise with indigo-spotlighted angels perched on a flight of steps trilling the final notes.

There was no official *George White's Scandals* in 1927. However, to many, the DeSylva-Brown-Henderson almost bookless book show, *Manhattan Mary*, produced by George White, was an acceptable substitute. It had a great clown (Ed Wynn), a new dance step ("The Five Step"), and, as part of its slender story, the heroine (Ona Munson) actually ended up as the queen of the *Scandals.*

All the principal performers of the 1926 *George White's Scandals*—plus the song-writing trio—were reunited for the ninth edition of the revue in 1928. Again in full-throated command of most of the songs was the ebullient Harry Richman, sailing into "Crest of a Wave" ("Do I theem to efferveth!"), and, in "What D'Ya Say?," crooning into Frances Williams' ear, "You're so very cute you're/Bound to have a future." According to Richman's autobiography, *A Hell of a Life*, "It seems hard to realize that song writers could have written material so perfectly styled to an entertainer. It was as though they somehow had got inside my skin and joined forces with my brains and lungs."

CULVER PICTURES, INC.

GOOD NEWS (1927). *College roommates Gus Shy and John Price Jones sing the praises of Jones' latest flame. (Costumes by Kiviette; setting by Donald Oenslager.)*

171

HOLD EVERYTHING (1928). *Cook Victor Moore, trainer Harry T. Shannon and prize-fighter Bert Lahr have their problems at the training camp. (Setting by Henry Dreyfuss.)*

FOLLOW THRU (1929). *The antics of Jack Haley attract the attention of Constance Lane, Dorothy Christy and Yvonne Grey. (Costumes by Kiviette; setting by Donald Oenslager.)*

172

Sandwiched in between the last two editions of the *Scandals* that all three writers did together was their first major book musical, *Good News!* The show was unquestionably the quintessence of the DeSylva-Brown-Henderson musical comedy genre, and set the stage for no less than three successes in the general mold—*Hold Everything, Follow Thru* and *Flying High. Good News!* did it simply by taking a lively modern subject—collegiate life—as a peg to hang any number of situations and songs that reflected the naively hedonistic attitude of the period. It was all speed and youth and fun, and those concerned made sure the audience got into the proper spirit right from the start: before the show began, George Olsen's band filed down the aisles in college sweaters, and gave out with a rah-rah cheer before settling down to playing the overture. The story line concerned one Tom Marlowe (played by John Price Jones), dear old Tait's football star and ladies' man (he had a song called "He's a Ladies' Man"), his romantic entanglements, scholastic hurdles, and eventual gridiron victory. (Tom was allowed to play in the big game, despite a failing grade in astronomy, simply because the professor liked him.)

The presentation of the show, somewhat akin to a series of highly animated John Held cartoons, was perfectly complemented by the musical episodes. The opening number lost no time, lest there be any lingering

FLYING HIGH *(1930). Wrote Gilbert Gabriel in the "American": "By the sweat of his crazily corrugated brows and all the Indian contortions of his comical mug and his grotesquely quaky shoulder blades, Bert Lahr wrung such laughter out of the audience as no clown of this season's lot could." Here is Bert, surrounded by Grace Brinkley, Henry Whittemore and Kate Smith, broadcasting the story of his record-breaking flight. (Costumes by Charles Le-Maire.)*

CULVER PICTURES, INC.

doubt, in establishing the prevailing point of view: "Learning to sin—not how to think. How to mix our gin right in the sink." Other pieces were equally sturdy examples of musical comedy requirements of the period. 1) A number about flaming youth (titled "Flaming Youth"). 2) A new dance routine, the combustible down-on-the-heels-up-on-the-toes "Varsity Drag." 3) A revivalistic chorale, the pie-in-the-sky harbinger, "Good News." 4) A philosophical interlude, "The Best Things in Life Are Free," which they managed to shoehorn into a scene by having the poor heroine (played by Mary Lawlor) admit her lower social station in order that our hero might advise her, in song, that a lot of things make up for a shortage of money. The show received honor grades from the critics, with most of them getting into the proper descriptive spirit. "They sway from the hips," described Burns Mantle in the *News*. "They wear their trousers baggy and their panties short. They sing with raucous abandon and dance like all get out. They rah-rah with gusto. They are very collegiate. Oh, very!" Mantle went on to admire the musical's "flaming, flaring, infectious youth," an alliterative bent that also overtook Walter Winchell who proclaimed the evening "flip, fast, furious, free and flaming festive."

With a good thing going for them, DeSylva, Brown and Henderson next found inspiration in another youthfully energetic subject, prize fighting. *Hold Everything* (the title makes one wonder if the original idea might not have dealt with wrestling) was held together by the slender thread of a plot involving a handsome boxer (Jack Whiting), whose knockout victory resulted from a mistaken notion that his adversary had insulted his beloved. But the story counted for little. For the show had in its corner the new clown prince of Broadway, Bert Lahr, to gnong-gnong his way through a maze of hilarious boxing routines and one-line gags (when asked in the locker room what book he is reading, Lahr blinked his beady eyes and answered haughtily, "Da Woiks, by William Shakespeare"). The notices weren't quite as enthusiastic as they had been for *Good News!*, but there was enough journalistic approval to help keep audiences in attendance for over 400 performances. To wit, Percy Hammond in the *Herald Tribune*: "...a likeable jamboree, boisterous, light on its feet, and with a flair for minor melody and romance. Its grim story of the wars in Madison Square Garden is mitigated by pretty girls in leggy maneuvers, nonsense both quiet and loud, and a velvet love affair involving a tony pugilist and a soubrette of the better type."

The songs continued to be lively, contagious variations on themes expressing emotions ranging from the universal to the up-to-the-minute. The reverse title song, "Don't Hold Everything" ("Just let everything go") was a peppy panegyric to unrestricted behavior based, according to the verse,

174

on the teachings of Sigmund Freud. There were love songs, both simpering ("To Know You Is to Love You") and exuberant ("Too Good to Be True"). But nothing quite caught the public fancy as did "You're the Cream in My Coffee," that engaging, pre-Cole Porter compilation in which the individual serenaded is likened to those everyday adjuncts designed to add taste and convenience to the necessities of life.

College football, then boxing, then . . . golf. *Follow Thru* was the name of the new game, billed as "A Musical Slice of Country Club Life," and guaranteed to be a fitting successor to its athletic precursors. The score, apart from the musical banality of "My Lucky Star" and the lyrical banality of "You Wouldn't Fool Me, Would You?," contained such bright new pieces as the latest flapper confession, "I Want to Be Bad" ("What can you do when you're loaded with hell-th and vigor?") and the adroitly worded hymn to postponed romance, "Then I'll Have Time for You." Again it was a novelty love song, "Button Up Your Overcoat," that became the most reprised number, with audiences responding readily to its healthful pre-scriptions to eat proper food, be careful crossing streets ("oo-oo"), get to bed by three (!), and keep away from bootleg hootch. Gilbert Gabriel echoed the critical consensus in the *American*: "They seem dedicated to the task of making youth flame and love shout out, with crisp, crazy, lusty, ankle-loosing, hip-seizing songs, and lyrics that give this whole razzing, jazzing society circus its cue to get gay. Wild-faced, free-legged kids shouted catch lines across the footlights that fairly roped and yanked the audience onto the stage."

Flying High, presented in 1930, turned the boys away from the sporting page to an equally topical tale about aviation. Luckily, Bert Lahr was on hand again to play the role of an aviator who sets a world record for time in the air simply because he doesn't know how to get his plane to land. In spite of the generally conventional story, the musical did break with tradition by not having the chorus appear until the third scene. The show opened on the roof of an apartment house in Manhattan, with wide-eyed Grace Brinkley pining away for an unknown love in the song "I'll Know Him." Then, on cue, there is an explosion above her head, she looks up in fear and amazement, and a handsome pilot (Oscar Shaw) parachutes to her feet.

The song writers contributed a moody, insistently throbbing tune in "Without Love"; a tasteless teasing number in "Good for You—Bad for Me" (containing, as an inside joke, the line, "But some things in life are not free"); a rhythmic ode, "Red Hot Chicago," in which that metropolis is celebrated as the origin of jazz ("If you think I'm wrong then you're a nincompoop! Poop-poop-a-doop!"); and another one of their justly popu-

GEORGE WHITE'S SCANDALS *(1931). Rudy Vallee, surrounded by bridesmaids, about to croon "This Is the Missus." Note bridesmaid Alice Faye on the extreme right. (Costumes by Charles LeMaire; setting Joseph Urban.)*

lar roundabout love songs, "Thank Your Father." In this one, the boy's love is conveyed through his gratitude for the girl's conception which, if the lyric is to be taken literally, was apparently illegitimate.

After writing songs for three early "talkies" (Al Jolson's *The Singing Fool* and *Say It with Songs,* and also *Sunny Side Up*), DeSylva, Brown and Henderson decided to make a permanent move to the West Coast in 1930. But within a year irreconcilable differences forced the trio to break up. De-Sylva remained in Hollywood (except for a temporary interruption to co-produce *Take a Chance* in New York and to write its lyrics), and rose rapidly in his new career as a film producer. Brown and Henderson, how-ever, stuck together as song writers; their first DeSylva-less assignment brought them back to Broadway for the 1931 *George White's Scandals*. Confounding the Sardi set, they did initially well as a duo, turning out such fondly remembered pieces as "This Is the Missus" for Rudy Vallee, "The Thrill Is Gone" and "That's Why Darkies Were Born," both for Everett Marshall, as well as that stirring antidote to the Depression, "Life Is Just a Bowl of Cherries," trumpeted by Ethel Merman, who had been rushed into the show just before its Broadway première. Other pleasures: Ray Bolger as a fleetfooted Al Smith, Willie and Eugene Howard in their classic "Pay the Two Dollars" sketch, and the musical stage debut of Ethel Barrymore Colt, whose one duet with Vallee, "My Song," turned out to be Merman's song by the time the revue officially opened.

A second Brown-Henderson offering, *Hot-Cha!*, incredibly subtitled "Laid in Mexico," opened the same season as the *Scandals*. With Bert Lahr and Lupe Velez in the cast, and a fast-moving story about bullfighting, the show was an obvious attempt to revive the same sort of book musical that had established the team's reputation during their heyday with De-Sylva. But times had changed. In a season that had produced *The Cat and the Fiddle, Of Thee I Sing* and *Face the Music*, the anything-for-a-laugh *Hot-Cha!* was an anachronism*. The following year, Brown and Henderson were back with a revue, *Strike Me Pink*. It had Jimmy Durante, Hope Williams, Lupe Velez, and mobster Waxey Gordon's $150,000, but it didn't last more than three months. The show also marked the termination of the partnership of Lew Brown and Ray Henderson.

In 1934, Henderson joined lyricist Ted Koehler in writing the score for a short-lived Harry Richman opus, *Say When*, and Brown teamed with composer Harry Akst for a revue, *Calling All Stars*, which turned out to be more of a cry for help than a prideful announcement. That same year, Brown went to Hollywood and, like DeSylva, became a film producer.

After an absence of over four years, George White brought back his *Scandals*—the twelfth in line—in 1935. Rudy Vallee was in it, along with the Howard brothers and Bert Lahr, and the occasion also introduced the new song writing team of Ray Henderson and Jack Yellen. But the revue was dismissed as being too much of an echo of the past and it had a run of only 110 performances. Henderson's whilom partner, Lew Brown, returned to Broadway in 1939. He teamed with co-lyricist Charles Tobias and composer Sam Stept to produce a cornball musical yclept *Yokel Boy*, best recalled for Phil Silvers' musical comedy debut and a still popular song, "Comes Love."

---

* Brown and Henderson were not particularly happy about the new trend toward politically slanted musicals. In one of their *Hot-Cha!* songs, they derided "Park Avenue librettos by children of the ghettos," an obvious swipe at the creators of *Of Thee I Sing* and *Face the Music*.

177

1939, however, was a particularly important year in the career of the Hollywood-based Buddy DeSylva. Brooding over his lack of public acclaim as a film executive, DeSylva was anxious to see his name back in lights on Broadway. His friend librettist Herbert Fields outlined a rough story idea, suitable for someone like Mae West, about an up-to-date Mme. DuBarry. At the same time DeSylva was dreaming about a tale of a washroom attendant in a swank night club smitten with the likes of Brenda Frazier. Together the two men pooled and altered their respective outlines; within two weeks they were ready to sign Bert Lahr to play the part of a washroom attendant who dreams about being Louis XV to Ethel Merman's DuBarry. All that was needed was Cole Porter to supply words and music and voilà—DuBarry Was a Lady. In December, 1939, the name "B. G. DESYLVA" was blinking above the marquee at the 46th Street Theatre as both producer and co-librettist of the season's biggest smash.

The biggest smash, that is, until DeSylva's next musical, Louisiana Purchase, came along the following May. For this one he hired the services of librettist Morrie Ryskind (adapting his story from an original DeSylva concept), composer-lyricist Irving Berlin, and performers William Gaxton, Vera Zorina and Victor Moore. Then, in October, 1940, DeSylva made it three hits in a row. Intrigued by the song, "Katie Went to Haiti," in DuBarry, Herbert Fields and Buddy DeSylva decided to expand its basic idea into an entire Merman musical. The Haitian locale, however, was switched to Panama, which conveniently lent itself to a ready-made show title, Panama Hattie. Again they finished the book within two weeks, and again they had Cole Porter to join them in another DeSylva-Fields-Merman festival. For about a month and a half after the show's opening, DeSylva became the first producer since Ziegfeld* to have three musical successes running simultaneously in New York.

Once satisfied that his personal prestige had been fully restored, DeSylva was content to quit while he was ahead. There also may have been a more practical reason. Within a month after the opening of Panama Hattie, he was California-bound to succeed William LeBaron, another ex-lyricist-librettist, as head of Paramount Studios. DeSylva held the post for about four years, then turned to independent film production, and finally retired because of ill health. On July 11, 1950, at the age of 55, he died of a heart attack in Los Angeles. Lew Brown, whose last Broadway assignment had been as director-writer of a revised 1941 revue, Crazy with the Heat, also succumbed to a heart attack. That was on February 5, 1958, when he was 64.

* From March 13 through April 7, 1928, Ziegfeld's three concurrently running musicals were Rio Rita, Show Boat and The Three Musketeers.

ZIEGFELD FOLLIES *(1943). In-*
spired by Carmen Jones, *the*
first act finale, Carmen in
Zoot, *had Milton Berle as a*
peg-trousered Escamillio (sic).
(Costumes by Miles White).

PHOTO BY GRAPHIC HOUSE, INC.

Ray Henderson, who has survived both his former partners, returned to Broadway in 1943 as composer—with Jack Yellen as lyricist—of one of the last successful large-scale revues, the *Ziegfeld Follies.* Starring the unlikely trio of Milton Berle, Ilona Massey and Arthur Treacher, it turned out to be a particularly gala wartime treat, possibly made all the more so by stirring memories of a bygone era when shows such as this were the rule rather than the exception.

Although the team of DeSylva, Brown and Henderson flourished for not quite five years, the unique personality of the theatre they represented is still savored today. They personified a form of musical comedy that was bound to disappear in a rapidly changing and brutal world. Only during the Twenties was there time for just fun and games along Broadway. And when it came to fun-and-games musicals, no writers were more adept at calling the tune than DeSylva, Brown and Henderson.

179

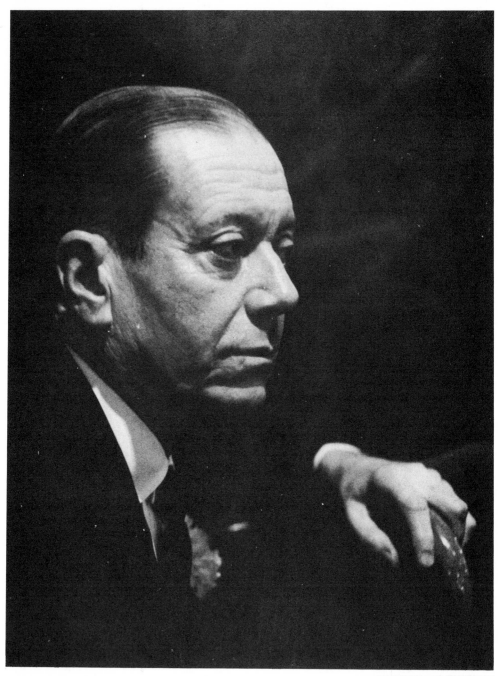

Cole Porter.

Cole Porter

THE LIVES OF the most prominent theatre composers have been distinguished by extreme dedication to their occupations. Apart from Rodgers, who got his apprenticeship writing amateur shows, the leading figures during the Twenties usually followed a set routine as they went from song plugger (usually for Max Dreyfus), to vaudeville accompanist, to rehearsal pianist. Then, if they were lucky, they would have a song interpolated in a show, or, if they were even luckier, they would be asked to compose an entire score. But no matter what the exact path may have been, all the major talents first decided on their goal when they were in their early or middle teens, and then went after it with diligence and determination.

Cole Porter was the notable exception. He never had to struggle or to perform lowly tasks either in Tin Pan Alley or in Shubert Alley. He never had to bother with amateur shows to attract attention. He never had to make the rounds of producers and publishers. Competition never disturbed him, nor was he particularly concerned about money. He was twenty-three when his first Broadway show, *See America First,* opened in 1916, but for the next twelve years he spent most of his time living in Europe, traveling around the world, and, in general, making sure that there was not one pleasurable place anywhere that he had not visited. Chronologically, his initial offering places

Porter after Romberg, Friml, and Berlin, and before Gershwin, Youmans, and Rodgers, but his theatrical career only began in earnest at the very end of the 1920's. From then on, however, Porter's rise was rapid. He turned out a series of scores—both words and music—for musical comedies celebrated for their glossy opulence, outstanding performances, melodic inventiveness, and sophisticated wit.

During the Thirties, when other composers were writing social satires and experimenting with new and different theatrical forms, Porter was creating songs that did what they could do to perpetuate all that was glamorous in the Twenties. For Porter, that was the decade of luxurious apartments in Paris, special trains to the Lido, ballets staged by Diaghilev for his own private parties, years spent at the Palazzo Rezzonico in Venice (at a rental of $4,000 a month), cruises down the Rhine, and incessant traveling to distant, exotic places. During this period, whenever a friend would suggest that he try Broadway again, Porter's answer was that he much preferred writing his songs for the amusement of his friends. His attitude was summed up once when, to an entreaty that he turn professional song-writer, he answered simply, "Suppose I had to settle down on Broadway for three months just when I was planning to go to the Antibes."

Nonetheless, wherever Porter was, or whatever he was supposed to be doing, he was always busily composing songs. These songs, among them "Two Little Babes in the Wood," "Let's Do It," and "What Is This Thing Called Love?," were certainly not the product of an amateur or a dabbler. In melody and in lyrics, his work at the time showed a professionalism made all the more impressive by his absence from Broadway. For though he was aware of what the Gershwin brothers and Rodgers and Hart were accomplishing, he was not directly under the influence of the rising young generation of song-writers of the Twenties. Completely independently and far from the Broadway scene, Cole Porter was creating his own distinctive style, one that would later characterize all his contributions to the musical theatre.

Cole Albert Porter was born on a 750-acre farm in Peru, Indiana, on June 9, 1891. His parents were Samuel Fenwick and Kate (Cole) Porter. By the time he was ten, young Cole had already composed two songs, a feat that so delighted his proud mother that she had one of them, "The Bobolink Waltz," published in Chicago. This musical interest, however, did not please Porter's wealthy grandfather, J. O. Cole. Cole, who had made a fortune in the lumber business in West Virginia, was anxious to leave his grandson a large inheritance, but only on the condition that the boy become a lawyer.

Porter's grandfather sent him to Worcester Academy in Massachusetts, and to Yale, with the hope that he would become interested in his studies and get his mind off music. Porter still found time to write. When he was seventeen, Remick published an early effort called "Bridget", and within the next two years he created those immortal college tunes, "Bingo Eli Yale" and "Yale Bulldog Song." Although music interested him far more than his regular studies, Porter dutifully entered Harvard Law School. His obvious lack of interest in the law soon became apparent to the dean, who suggested that he might make a more impressive scholastic record at the Harvard School of Music. Once grandfather Cole finally gave his grudging consent, Porter enthusiastically began his study of music.

While still at Harvard, Porter and a fellow student, T. Lawrason Riggs, collaborated on a professional Broadway show, *See America First*. On one of his frequent trips to visit friends in East Hampton, Porter had met Elisabeth Marbury, the socially prominent literary agent who had recently co-sponsored the immensely successful *Very Good Eddie*. Hoping to do as much for Porter's career as she had for Kern's, Miss Marbury agreed to produce the show that Porter and Riggs had recently written. *See America First* ("A Patriotic Comic Opera") may have seemed like a clever idea on paper, but when it was performed on the stage it was a complete failure. The story dealt with the efforts of an anti-British U. S. senator to keep his daughter from meeting anyone from across the Atlantic. Of course, inevitably, after being taken out West, the girl does meet a titled Englishman (Clifton Webb), they fall in love, and, eventually, the senator loses his prejudices. Apparently, the fact that this was a spoof of the George M. Cohan flag-wavers—particularly *George Washington, Jr.*—was lost on the unnamed critic of the *New York Dramatic Mirror*, who wrote: "The lyrics are studiously copied after the Gilbertian pattern in the long and complicated rhyme effects achieved. The music, however, gives the impression that its composer, after the first hour, gave up the task of recreating a Sullivan atmosphere, preferring to seek his inspiration in our own George M. Cohan."

Following the brief run of *See America First*, Porter, partly out of disappointment and partly out of a desire for adventure, joined the French Foreign Legion.* While in service in North Africa, he entertained the troops by playing his songs on a specially constructed portable piano which could be carried on his back with the rest of his equipment. When the United States entered the First World War, Porter was transferred to the French Artillery School at Fontainebleau. The charms of Paris soon proved irresistible to him; after the war, he rented a large apartment and decided to remain there.

Although he was rather well provided for, Porter felt that he needed a still larger allowance from his grandfather, especially since he wanted to marry the wealthy Linda Lee Thomas. Such an important request required a personal confrontation, and Porter sailed back to the United States in 1919.

---

* T. Lawrason Riggs also gave up thoughts of a musical career after *See America First*. He soon entered the priesthood, and later became Roman Catholic chaplain at Yale.

Also on board ship was Raymond Hitchcock, the popular comedian and producer. After hearing Porter play some of his songs (and possibly not unmindful of the young man's financial status), Hitchcock commissioned the young composer to write the music and lyrics for the third edition of his *Hitchy-Koo* revues. Joe Cook made his New York debut in the show singing "When I Had a Uniform On," but it was the uncharacteristically sentimental "An Old-Fashioned Garden" that gave Cole Porter his first song hit.

Grandfather Cole's refusal to allow him more money was of little concern to Porter now. With his royalty checks from "An Old-Fashioned Garden" giving his bank account a much-needed boost, he returned to Paris, married Linda Lee, and began his life of party-giver and pleasure-seeker. He did not abandon music, however, devoting much time to the study of harmony and counterpoint under Vincent d'Indy at the Schola Cantorum in Paris. In 1923, Porter's affluence was enhanced even more when J. O. Cole died and left his grandson over $1 million. Then, as Porter once put it, "I could go to Venice."

During the early Twenties, Porter interrupted his life of ease only twice: to write songs for another *Hitchy-Koo* revue that never came to New York, and to contribute the score for John Murray Anderson's *Greenwich Village Follies of 1924*. Of the numbers in the *Follies*, "I'm in Love Again," sung by the Dolly Sisters and danced by future Broadway choreographer Robert Alton, was the only one to win popularity.

Among the many people who never gave up their efforts to induce Porter to return to the Broadway theatre, the only one to succeed was E. Ray Goetz. Goetz, an enterprising producer and occasional song-writer himself, journeyed to the Lido in the summer of 1928 with the express purpose of talking the reluctant composer into creating another score. Finding Porter sunning himself on the Lido beach, Goetz introduced himself and immediately offered what he was sure would be an attractive proposal. The score would be for a musical that was so Parisian it was actually called *Paris*, the star of the show would be Goetz's vivacious wife, Irene Bordoni, and Porter would only have to compose eight songs. Somewhat to his own surprise, Porter found himself agreeing to take the assignment.

Paris, though it was billed, *Time*-fashion, as "A Musicomedy," and though it did well at the box office, was little more than an incidental comedy with incidental music. In fact, of the eight Cole Porter songs, only five were used, with two others supplied by the producer. All the numbers were sung by Miss Bordoni accompanied by Irving Aaronson's Commanders, an eleven-piece orchestra seated on stage in what was supposed to be a hotel suite.

In the song, "Let's Misbehave" (cut from *Paris* before it reached New York), Porter's lyric mentioned briefly the love life of lovebirds, bears, and camels. This interest in the animal kingdom was slight compared to the zoölogical survey in "Let's Do It," the number that replaced "Let's Misbe-

PARIS *(1928). Irene Bordoni surrounded by Irving Aaronson's Commanders. (Setting by William Castle.)*

have." Bluebirds, bluebells, sponges, oysters, clams, jellyfish, electric eels, shad, sole, goldfish, dragonflies, centipedes, mosquitoes, katydids, lady bugs, moths, locusts, bees, fleas, chimpanzees, kangaroos, giraffes, hippopotamuses, sloths, guinea pigs, bears, and Pekinese dogs—in addition to various types of humans—all had their amatory habits covered in a manner that immediately established Cole Porter as one of the most ingenious creators of sly and imaginative lyrics.

The reception to his songs for *Paris* convinced Porter that there were pleasures to be had in the world of musical comedy as well as in the world of international society. The next year, he and Goetz again worked together on another musical with a Parisian locale, *Fifty Million Frenchmen*. Featuring William Gaxton, Genevieve Tobin, and Helen Broderick, it was the first of seven Cole Porter musicals to have librettos written or co-written by Herbert Fields. It was also the first musical directed by Edgar Montillion "Monty" Woolley, who had been an instructor at Yale while Porter was an undergraduate.

Fifty Million Frenchmen, which became a bigger box office success than *Paris*, had a score that abounded in unhackneyed sentiments. "I Worship You" revealed Porter's interest in the mythology of the Greeks, Phoenicians, and Egyptians, while "Find Me a Primitive Man" went back to an earlier age for inspiration. There was even a jaunty, insouciant air about the more traditional love duets, "You Do Something to Me" and "You've Got That Thing."

185

"When it comes to lyrics," wrote George Jean Nathan in *Judge*, "this Cole Porter is so far ahead of the other boys in New York that there just is no race at all."

Just one month after the première of *Fifty Million Frenchmen*, an English show, *Wake Up and Dream!*, opened with Jack Buchanan, Jessie Matthews, and Tilly Losch. Porter did not contribute all the songs to it, but he was responsible for the dark, brooding "What Is This Thing Called Love?," which was based on a native chant he had first heard in Marrakech, Morocco, and the somewhat more emotionally fulfilling "Looking at You." Although the eternal dilemma of the modern maiden called "Which?" had been intended originally for *Paris*, it was first sung on Broadway by Miss Matthews in *Wake Up and Dream!*

The New Yorkers, in 1930, was another Porter musical written by Herbert Fields for E. Ray Goetz. Monty Woolley again directed. There were some interpolations in it from the repertory of Clayton, Jackson, and Durante, and also that of Fred Waring's Pennsylvanians, but the score was chiefly Porter's. Hope Williams and Charles King sang "Where Have You Been?," a rather heavy ballad, and Kathryn Crawford intoned the dolorous saga of a street walker in "Love for Sale." The composer also described the rival pleasures of staying at home ("The Great Indoors") and of taking off for a tropical island ("Let's Fly Away").

Porter's skill at combining opposites within a single song was strikingly demonstrated in "Night and Day," which was first sung by Fred Astaire in the 1932 success, *Gay Divorce*. The song, a somewhat extended piece, was another example of a less ethereal, more carnal approach to love, with its verse suggesting a heartbeat and its release a tegumentary revelation of the yearning burning under one's hide. Luella Gear and Eric Blore contributed most of the comedy, with Miss Gear making something both funny and touching of the mad life of the social-climbing "Mister and Missus Fitch."

After the debacle of the Gershwin brothers' *Pardon My English* ended the Alex A. Aarons–Vinton Freedley partnership in 1934, Freedley and his

FIFTY MILLION FRENCHMEN (1929). *William Gaxton and a bevy of beauties. (Costumes by James Reynolds.)*

GAY DIVORCE (1932). There were many complications in this tale of an unhappy wife who hires a professional corespondent to help her secure a divorce. In this scene, Luella Gear discovers the wife (Claire Luce) with both the presumed corespondent (Fred Astaire) and the real one (Erik Rhodes). (Setting by Jo Mielziner.)

wife took a lengthy ocean voyage to enable him to reflect on the possibility of a career as a solo producer. As Freedley recalls: "The idea came to me when I was fishing peacefully in the Pacific Ocean near the Pearl Islands. While waiting for a bite, I began, with no special purpose, to consider the ideal people for a musical show." William Gaxton and Victor Moore were obvious choices, particularly as a result of their Wintergreen and Throttle-bottom characterizations in *Of Thee I Sing* and *Let 'Em Eat Cake*. So was Ethel Merman, whom Freedley had discovered for *Girl Crazy*. George and Ira Gershwin would have been the logical song-writers, but it was apparent from their toiling over *Porgy and Bess* that they would have little interest in doing another musical comedy. The bright and brittle rhythms of Cole Porter suggested themselves immediately; so did the idea of having a book created by the Princess Theatre masters, P. G. Wodehouse and Guy Bolton.

The more he thought of the idea, the more plausible it became. When he arrived back in New York, Freedley immediately signed the stars, the composer, and, finally, the librettists. In those days, as Ethel Merman wrote in her autobiography, *Who Could Ask for Anything More*, "the writers who used to think up the books that were wrapped around Gershwin or Cole Porter scores, started from scratch, with only their bare cupboards and an unmanageable sense of humor to guide them. First a producer signed a cast; then he hired writers to rustle up some material for that cast to use. 'I've got Bert Lahr,' he'd say; 'write me a part for Bert Lahr.' Or 'I've signed Victor Moore. Get goin' buddy. Make with the Moore-type yoks.' "[*]

[*] From *Who Could Ask for Anything More* by Ethel Merman. Garden City, N. Y.: Doubleday & Company.

ANYTHING GOES *(1934). Ethel Merman sings "Anything Goes" accompanied by Marshall Smith, Ray Johnson, Dwight Snyder, and Del Porter. (Costume by Jenkins.)*

The story Wodehouse and Bolton concocted for the new show was based on some general ideas Freedley had given them. The producer wanted it to take place on board a ship, but when the script arrived he found that the authors had written a libretto about a shipwreck. Such a theme would not have been disastrous in itself, but just two months before the scheduled opening of the musical, the S.S. *Morro Castle* went down in flames off Asbury Park, New Jersey, with a loss of 125 lives. With Wodehouse in London and Bolton in Paris, the harried producer had to find someone quickly to rewrite the book. His director, Howard Lindsay, had had some experience as a playwright, but with so little time Lindsay insisted on having a collaborator. Through a mutual friend he was introduced to Russel Crouse, a Theatre Guild press agent and occasional librettist. The two agreed to be partners. "We went into rehearsal with only two-thirds of a first act and there was no second act at all," Lindsay later admitted. Somehow, everything was miraculously pulled into shape before the opening night; once the curtain went up on November 21, 1934, there was little doubt that *Anything Goes* would become one of the decade's superior achievements in musical comedy.

"A thundering good song-and-dance show," thundered Brooks Atkinson; and so it was. With Moore in the incongruous role of Public Enemy Number 13 (a superstitious man, he was anxious to bump off Number 12 so that he might rise in the hierarchy), with Gaxton bursting with kinetic energy, and with Ethel Merman trumpeting her way through some of Cole Porter's most inspired numbers, *Anything Goes* was the quintessence of the lavish, bawdy, swift-paced, uninhibited Music Comedy of the mid-Thirties. Almost every musical number was a highly polished gem, including "All through the Night," with its throbbing description of an imaginary nocturnal romance; the propulsive "Blow, Gabriel, Blow"; the blasé, but sincere "I Get a Kick out of You"; and "You're the Top," the classic of catalogued superlatives set to music.

Most of the songs for *Anything Goes* were written while Porter was cruising down the Rhine. For *Jubilee,* the following year, he extended his

188

quest for geographical inspiration by composing the score during a world-wide tour with librettist Moss Hart. Wherever he went, Porter was able to find ideas for his songs. The melody for "Begin the Beguine" came to him as he was listening to native music on the island of Kalabahi, in the Dutch East Indies; "The Kling-Kling Bird on the Top of the Divi-Divi Tree" was actually seen and heard in Jamaica, British West Indies; the music for the "Judgment of Paris" ballet emanated from ethnic themes heard on the island of Bali. Among the less exotic rhythms, "A Picture of Me without You" strung out a varied list of improbable separations to affirm love's constancy (Fritzi Kreisler without his fiddle, Philadelphia without a Biddle); "Why Shouldn't I?" expressed the youthful desire for even a temporary romance; and "Just One of Those Things" conveyed a disillusioned, though realistic, acceptance of a passing affair.

Mary Boland and Melville Cooper were the queen and king of an Anglified (though unspecified) country in *Jubilee*. Members of the royal family included Charles Walters, Margaret Adams, and fifteen-year-old Montgomery Clift. Unfortunately, when a film contract forced Miss Boland to return to Hollywood, a satisfactory replacement could not be found, and the musical was forced to close after only 169 performances.

In 1936, hoping to repeat the success of *Anything Goes*, Vinton Freed-

JUBILEE *(1935). The collaborators: Cole Porter (music and lyrics) and Moss Hart (libretto).*

JUBILEE (1935). *King Melville Cooper is momentarily distracted from his rope trick to glance at a picture of Queen Mary Boland's favorite Hollywood star. (Costumes by Irene Sharaff and Connie De Pinna; setting by Jo Mielziner.)*

RED, HOT AND BLUE! *(1936). Vivian Vance, Jimmy Durante, Ethel Merman, Bob Hope, and Grace Hartman have a large audience for their conversation. (Costumes by Constance Ripley; setting by Donald Oenslager.)*

ley signed Cole Porter, Howard Lindsay, and Russel Crouse to create *Red, Hot and Blue!* It was originally intended as a vehicle for Ethel Merman, Jimmy Durante, and William Gaxton, but, according to Miss Merman, Gaxton refused to appear in it after overhearing Lindsay and Crouse telling her what a big part she would have. To replace Gaxton, Freedley hired Bob Hope, who had previously revealed his comic talent in *Roberta* and the *Ziegfeld Follies of 1936*.

In spite of its authors and performers, *Red, Hot and Blue!* was not a success. The chief fault was the book, a fairly elementary piece concerned with the search for a missing heiress whose identity could only be determined by a waffle-iron mark on her behind. Porter's contributions were more inspired. "Down in the Depths (on the 90th Floor)," sung by Miss Merman in a gold lamé gown illuminated by a single gold spotlight, brilliantly heightened the heroine's loneliness by contrasting it with her surrounding luxury. The exultant "Ridin' High," however, brought Miss Merman back to her more accustomed sanguine emotions. There was also the cleverly intricate "It's De-Lovely," which told, via a self-kidding verse and four choruses, the blissful saga of a boy and girl from the night they fell in love, through their marriage and wedding trip, and right up to the arrival of their first born.

Apart from its songs, *Red, Hot and Blue!* is remembered today chiefly because of the ridiculous battle of the billing. Both Miss Merman's and Durante's agents wanted their clients to have top billing, i.e., the name on the left-hand side above the title of the show. Although it still seemed to give the preferential billing to Durante, the following compromise was finally worked out:

In the summer of 1937, while Porter was horseback riding on a friend's estate on Long Island, his horse suddenly slipped, threw him, and then fell on top of him. Both of his legs were broken, and extreme damage was done to his nervous system. After submitting to thirty-one operations over a period of about twenty years in order to save his legs, Porter eventually had to have his right leg amputated in 1958.

191

Shortly after the accident, the Shubert brothers tried to take Porter's mind off his misfortune by commissioning him to supply the score for *You Never Know*. It was not, however, one of his—or their—major efforts. The next year, the composer had far better luck with *Leave It to Me!*, which was also written while he was bed-ridden. Adapted by Sam and Bella Spewack from their play *Clear All Wires*, the musical had a stellar cast including William Gaxton, Victor Moore, Sophie Tucker, and Tamara. While Moore, as usual, was singled out for his hilarious performance as Alonzo P. Goodhue, the American ambassador to the Soviet Union, a twenty-four-year-old singer named Mary Martin made an auspicious Broadway debut as she sang, and coyly stripped to, "My Heart Belongs to Daddy," while waiting at a freezing Siberian railway station. (Some people even noticed a dancer in that scene named Gene Kelly, who was also appearing on the New York stage for the first time.)

Leave It to Me! was a generally funny spoof of communism and American diplomacy, with such irreverences as "The Internationale" performed as the first-act finale and Stalin dancing around in true musical comedy fashion. The sight of the timid Mr. Moore kicking the Nazi ambassador in the stomach was treasured by audiences as both a wish-fulfillment and a reminder of the unique freedom that the Broadway theatre has always enjoyed.

LEAVE IT TO ME! *(1938). "A new girl named Mary Martin is gay, fresh, and attractive,"* wrote Richard Watts, Jr., in the Herald Tribune. *Here at a freezing Siberian railroad station she sings "My Heart Belongs to Daddy," accompanied by a quintet including (to her immediate right) Gene Kelly. (Costumes by Raoul Pène du Bois; setting by Albert Johnson.)*

PHOTO BY VANDAMM

DUBARRY WAS A LADY (1939). Bert Lahr, as the washroom attendant at the Club Petite, dreams that he is King Louis XV and that Ethel Merman is DuBarry. (Costumes by Raoul Pène du Bois.)

From December, 1939, to January, 1944, Cole Porter created the songs for five box-office smashes in a row—*DuBarry Was a Lady, Panama Hattie, Let's Face It!, Something for the Boys,* and *Mexican Hayride.* Each one of these shows ran over 400 performances, and all were co-authored by Herbert Fields (he wrote the first two with B. G. DeSylva, the other three with his sister, Dorothy Fields). Although only *Let's Face It!* was produced by Vinton Freedley, all five musicals seemed to capture the bright, star-studded, flavor of the Gershwin shows that Aarons and Freedley had offered in the Twenties. Like Gershwin at that time, Porter was particularly adept at writing for star personalities (Ethel Merman, Bert Lahr, Danny Kaye, Bobby Clark), without too much concern for the logic of plot development or the manner in which the songs were suited to the story. But just as the early Gershwin entertainments were attuned to the period in which they were presented, so the five Porter musicals of the early Forties could offer the amusement-seeking audiences of the Second World War a much-needed escape into a spangled, melodic, and glamorous world.

DuBarry Was a Lady was described by John Mason Brown as "a rowdy, boisterous, high-spirited extravaganza which stops at just this side of nothing and makes much of little." Ethel Merman played May Daley, a nightclub

DUBARRY WAS A LADY *(1939). Charles Walters and Betty Grable in a burlesque routine at the Club Petite. (Costumes by Raoul Pène du Bois.)*

PANAMA HATTIE *(1940). Rags Ragland registers complete approval of Ethel Merman's rather garish outfit. (Costumes and setting by Raoul Pène du Bois.)*

singer, and Bert Lahr was the washroom attendant at the Club Petite who dreams that he is Louis XV and Ethel is DuBarry. Among the songs, "Do I Love You?" was another beguine-tempoed ballad; "Katie Went to Haiti" related the rhythmic saga of a girl who was, according to critic John Anderson, "obviously a business and musical relation of the immortal Eadie"; and "Well, Did You Evah?" was made up of a series of gossipy social notes, delivered by Betty Grable (in her first stage role) and Charles Walters. Surprisingly, the song with the greatest popular appeal was the mocking hillbilly duet in which Miss Merman and Mr. Lahr vowed their eternal "Friendship."

Ethel Merman received solo star billing for the first time in *Panama Hattie*. Again she played the part of a nightclub singer (this time called Hattie Maloney) whose heart of gold could only be revealed through a voice of brass. In "I've Still Got My Health," she gaily proclaimed that her physical soundness was ample compensation for her lack of social graces, but in "Make It Another Old Fashioned, Please," she sadly concluded that the only thing to do with her sorrow was to drown it. The most fondly remembered sequence in the show involved Miss Merman and eight-year-old Joan Carroll, an occasion so touching that Brooks Atkinson predicted: "Gruff old codgers are going to choke a little this winter when tot and temptress sing 'Let's Be Buddies' and bring down the house."

The performance that Danny Kaye had given in *Lady In the Dark* fully merited the stardom he won in *Let's Face It!* Its tale of three middle-aged married ladies who go on a spree with three young servicemen was found to be, in the words of John Mason Brown, "an exuberant and irresistible show which does not hesitate to call a shovel a spade." In addition to Kaye, the cast was comprised of a superior roster of musical comedy talent, including Mary Jane Walsh, Eve Arden (with Carol Channing as understudy), Edith

PHOTO BY VANDAMM

LET'S FACE IT! *(1941). Extra marital entanglements among three discontented wives and three eager servicemen. Eve Arden, Danny Kaye, Edith Meiser, Benny Baker, Jack Williams, and Vivian Vance. (Costumes by John Harkrider; setting by Harry Horner.)*

MEXICAN HAYRIDE (1944). *Bobby Clark (alias Joe Bascom, alias Humphrey Fish) and June Havoc as the bullfighter known as Montana. (Costumes by Mary Grant.)*

Meiser, Vivian Vance, Nanette Fabray, and Benny Baker. Among the outstanding Porter songs were "Farming," which ridiculed celebrities who had just discovered the soil; "Ev'rything I Love," a straight love duet for Kaye and Miss Walsh, and "You Irritate Me So," a comic love duet sung by Miss Fabray and Jack Williams.

Cole Porter's two musicals for Michael Todd, *Something for the Boys* and *Mexican Hayride* were successful as moneymakers, though neither one represented the composer's best work. Originally known as *Jenny Get Your Gun, Something for the Boys* doubtlessly benefited from the presence of Ethel Merman who was cast as a defense worker who could receive wartime radio messages through the fillings in her teeth. The show-stopping routine was one in which Miss Merman and Paula Laurence, decked out as squaws for no apparent reason, romped through a number about their husbands who wait for them "By the Mis-sis-sis-sis-sis-sis-sis-sis-sin-e-wah."

Just as *Something for the Boys* was indebted to Ethel Merman for its success, so *Mexican Hayride* was equally indebted to Bobby Clark. As Joe Bascom (alias Humphrey Fish), Clark was cast as a numbers racketeer who flees to Mexico, assumes various disguises, and becomes involved with a female bullfighter (played by June Havoc). "I Love You," which followed the pattern of "Do I Love You?" has been the most durable song from the score, but two others, "Sing to Me, Guitar" and "Carlotta," were especially successful in capturing the atmosphere of a languid and romantic Mexico.

By the mid-Forties, the belief was that Cole Porter was no longer capable of creating the outstanding scores that had distinguished most of his early

196

musicals. Neither *Something for the Boys* nor *Mexican Hayride* was a major effort, and there was little of merit in Porter's music and lyrics for Billy Rose's revue, *Seven Lively Arts*, or Orson Welles's adaptation of Jules Verne's *Around the World in Eighty Days*. Few, therefore, had high expectations when it was announced in 1948 that librettists Sam and Bella Spewack were collaborating with Porter on *Kiss Me, Kate*, a musical based on Shakespeare's *The Taming of the Shrew*. Nor did the stars indicate success. Since his first important role in *Oklahoma!*, Alfred Drake had appeared in four failures in a row, and Patricia Morison, who was to play opposite him, had not been in a Broadway musical in over ten years. (Her last appearance had been in *The Two Bouquets*, in which Drake also had had a part.)

Like Irving Berlin with regard to *Annie Get Your Gun*, Porter was apprehensive about the new project, which was completely unlike the usual gossamer star vehicles with which he was customarily associated. Moreover, in common with everyone else in the musical theatre, he was well aware of the strides taken since the formation of the Rodgers and Hammerstein partnership. "The librettos are much better," he once told reporter Gilbert Millstein, "and the scores are much closer to the librettos than they used to be. Those two made it much harder for everybody else." Nevertheless, partially spurred on by Berlin's example ("His having so much music in *Annie Get Your Gun* made me feel like trying a similar thing"), Porter created a score for *Kiss Me, Kate* that is universally conceded to be his masterpiece. Although, as was his customary professional habit, he still remained somewhat aloof from the actual production, he was extremely concerned with the way his music and lyrics fit the characters and the situations, and frequently called upon the Spewacks for opinions and suggestions.

Porter's unique accomplishment in *Kiss Me, Kate* lay in his facility for creating melodies and lyrics of uncommonly high standards while, at the same time, successfully bridging the completely different worlds of Broadway and the Bard. From the general area of Times Square, he produced "Another Op'nin', Another Show," a rousing show business anthem to rival Berlin's "There's No Business like Show Business"; the plaintive torch ballad, "Why Can't You Behave?"; "Too Darn Hot," with its galvanic melody in direct contrast to the inaction proposed in the lyric; and the tender confession, "So in Love," another melody in Porter's soft beguine tempo. "Always True to You in My Fashion" was pure Broadway also, even though its title stemmed from a line in a poem by Ernest Dowson. In its avowel of fidelity to one true love, the song expressed a reverse sentiment to the composer's previous "My Heart Belongs to Daddy," in which fidelity was pledged to the wealthy "daddy."

The Taming of the Shrew itself provided the direct inspiration for four of the songs. "I've Come to Wive It Wealthily in Padua" was based on

197

KISS ME KATE (1948). "We open in Venice," sing Patricia Morison, Alfred Drake, Lisa Kirk, and Harold Lang as a group of strolling players about to appear in Shakespeare's The Taming of the Shrew. (Costumes and setting by Lemuel Ayers.)

Petruchio's first revelation of his quest for a rich wife, in which the concluding lines were:

> . . . were she as rough
> As are the swelling Adriatic seas:
> I come to wive it wealthily in Padua;
> If wealthily then happily in Padua.

"Where Is the Life That Late I Led?" was a line in a song actually sung by Shakespeare's hero, while the rather mystical "Were Thine That Special Face" was prompted by Bianca's admission:

> Believe me, sister, of all the men alive,
> I never yet beheld that special face
> Which I could fancy more than any other.

For the last number in the show, "I Am Ashamed That Women Are So Simple," Porter set almost all of Shakespeare's original words to music for the reformed Kate to explain how women should behave toward their husbands.

Such numbers as "Tom, Dick or Harry," "We Open in Venice," and "I Hate Men," while they are all completely Porter, fit perfectly into the story and spirit of the ancient tale. Indeed, Brooks Atkinson has termed "I Hate Men" "the perfect musical sublimation of Shakespeare's evil-tempered Kate."

"Wunderbar" is, of course, far from either Shubert Alley or Shakespeare. Though Porter wrote the melody in strict three-quarter time, the song is actually a satire on all the sentimental waltzes ever performed in a Viennese operetta. This is immediately revealed in the first line of the verse, "Gazing down on the Jungfrau," a rather difficult feat since the Jungfrau is one of the highest peaks in the Alps.

Arnold Saint Subber and Lemuel Ayers, the producers of *Kiss Me, Kate*, also produced Cole Porter's next musical, *Out of This World*. As *Kiss Me, Kate* had contrasted show business with Shakespeare, so *Out of This World* combined the Amphitryon legend with the adventures of a modern American couple visiting Greece on their wedding trip. In the role of Juno, Charlotte Greenwood made a gangling, triumphal return to the musical stage after an absence of almost twenty-four years.

The now-standard "From This Moment On" was dropped from the score before the musical opened in New York, but there were still many superb songs among those left—"Where, Oh Where?," with its sweet, lilting melody mated to a coldly calculating lyric; the ever-present beguine, "I Am Loved" (with a release almost identical to that of the earlier "I Love You"); the forthright stand of the contented wife called "No Lover"; and the paean to the satisfactions of old age, "I Sleep Easier Now," which Miss Greenwood sang with particular relish. There were also some delightful Cole Porter incongruities: "I Jupiter, I Rex" ("Reck-eck-o-weck-o-wex!") brought the spirit of the Yale cheering section to Mount Olympus, while "Climb Up the Mountain" turned a quasi-Negro spiritual into the perfect musical expression for gods and goddesses. Two bright sagas of itemization were "Cherry Pies Ought to Be You" (in the "You're the Top" vein), and the Rabelaisian, rapid-fire account of Mercury's romantic conquests, "They Couldn't Compare to You."

Can-Can (1953) and *Silk Stockings* (1955) were presented by Cy Feuer and Ernest Martin, the team that had previously produced *Where's Charley?*

KISS ME, KATE *(1948). Fred Graham (Alfred Drake) gives vent to his feelings toward his leading lady, Lilli Vanessi (Patricia Morison), by administering a sound spanking during a performance of* The Taming of the Shrew. *Lisa Kirk is beneath the balcony at the right. (Costumes and setting by Lemuel Ayers.)*

CAN-CAN (1953). Gwen Verdon, Hans Conried, and Lilo. (Costumes by Motley.)

and *Guys and Dolls*. Both shows were written and directed by Abe Burrows, although in the case of *Silk Stockings* he revised a script already completed by George S. Kaufman and Leueen McGrath. *Can-Can* dealt with Parisian life in the days of Toulouse-Lautrec. Its story may have been inconsequential, but the dances created by Michael Kidd and the show's breezy pace helped make it a huge financial success. The songs, if not among Porter's best work, nonetheless enabled him to recapture the Parisian flavor of some of his earliest scores with such pieces as "Allez-Vous-En," "I Love Paris" (written, according to Porter, because Jo Mielziner had designed such a beautiful scenic sky line of the city), "Montmart'," and "C'est Magnifique." Of the rest, "I Am in Love" was constructed from the "Do I Love You?–I Love You–So in Love–I Am Loved" matrix, and "It's All Right with Me" was a wry serenade sung by a disillusioned young man whose heart still longs for another.

Lilo, the French star, was imported especially to play La Mome Pistache, which she did in a strikingly ebullient manner. However, a greater success was scored by a twenty-eight-year-old dancer named Gwen Verdon, despite the fact that her part had been cut drastically to please the star. Miss Verdon's two previous Broadway appearances had been as a dancer in *Alive and Kicking*, a revue, and in the Villa-Lobos operetta, *Magdalena*.

Silk Stockings, an adaptation of the movie, *Ninotchka*, was set in modern Paris, with the leading roles played by Hildegarde Neff, Don Ameche, and Gretchen Wyler. Porter's lyrics had fun at the expense of the movies ("Josephine," "Stereophonic Sound") and the Russians ("Too Bad," "Siberia," and the exercise in verbal frugality, "The Red Blues"). Amatory emotions were expressed cartographically in "All of You," selflessly in "Without Love," and dispassionately in "It's a Chemical Reaction."

After almost thirty years of physical suffering, Cole Porter died on October 16, 1964, in Santa Monica, California. He succumbed at the age of 73 following surgery for a kidney stone. Of all the major musical comedy composers and lyricists, Porter possessed a style that was least affected by the passage of time. If we listen to his earliest efforts and compare them

SILK STOCKINGS (1955). *Don Ameche as Steve Canfield and Hildegarde Neff as Ninotchka, in the musical version of one of Garbo's most popular films. (Costumes by Lucinda Ballard.)*

with the songs he wrote toward the end of his career, we can find little change in their basic attitudes or musical construction. There was an undeniable aura of the glittering Twenties about almost everything he ever wrote. For in spite of developments within the theatre, in spite of changes in world conditions, Cole Porter's art remained completely personal, completely inpervious to outside influence.

In his so very civilized outlook revealed through his urbane verses and his compelling music, Cole Porter never stopped writing the kind of songs he once did merely to amuse his friends. In fact he never ceased writing to amuse his friends. This did not mean he was a dilettante; on the contrary, he was always a meticulous, painstaking craftsman. Yet his detached manner toward the theatre (which kept him far from the day-to-day problems of actual production) did allow him to take pleasure in his own works in much the same ingenuous manner of George Gershwin. The premières of Cole Porter musicals invariably found the composer, surrounded by the smartest of the smart set, enjoying himself thoroughly from an orchestra seat as if he were listening to his own creations for the very first time. Nor was he above leaning over to one of his guests after a particular number and whispering, with guileless relish, "Good, isn't it?"

As Jule Styne once said, "Cole Porter has a brand of sophistication that is commercial, the type that makes a shopgirl know 21 or El Morocco without ever having been there." This communication was possible because there was nothing ever spurious or derivative about his style. It was simply the genuine expression of what always was, to Cole Porter, the only way of life.

Arthur Schwartz and Howard Dietz.

Howard Dietz
and Arthur Schwartz
Dorothy Fields

THE OPPORTUNITIES AVAILABLE to aspiring young writers of the musical theatre have always been limited. By the mid-Twenties, they could no longer depend on the heavy European operettas of the kind that had served Jerome Kern so propitiously in the early decades of the century. However, there were still the revues. Whether extravagant or intimate, on-Broadway or off-Broadway, hackneyed or imaginative, these shows were the chief outlets for the budding talents of young composers and lyricists, their first chance to get their work on the professional stage.

The composer and lyricist who have been most closely identified with this form of musical theatre are Howard Dietz and Arthur Schwartz. Moreover, from their very first collaboration, *The Little Show*, they were among the leaders in creating a new form of revue. Eschewing the opulence of Ziegfeld or the make-shift modesty of the off-Broadway attractions, the new shows were closer to the spirit of the impeccably produced *Charlot's Revues*, which had introduced Beatrice Lillie, Gertrude Lawrence, and Jack Buchanan to American audiences in the mid-Twenties. Intimate, sophisticated, and callid, these revues were marked by the brilliant performances of their stars, some revolutionary innovations in stagecraft, and a general air of sleek but exuberant professionalism.

In addition to *The Little Show*, Dietz and Schwartz were associated with other memorable revues—*Three's a Crowd, The Band Wagon, Flying Colors, At Home Abroad,* and *Inside U.S.A.* All of these attractions were well suited to the skillful cohesion of words and music created by the team. For both men were of similar background and outlook, and their urbane, literate songs caught perfectly the flavor of the shows for which they were created. Though his music has always shown great variety, Schwartz's most distinguished ballads are frequently marked by a brooding soulfulness that is perhaps matched only by some of Cole Porter's work. Dietz's lyrics are characterized by their brittle wit and subtle poetic imagery; while they may lack a certain warmth, they nevertheless contain a keenness and originality that make them ideally suited to Schwartz's music.

Arthur Schwartz was born in Brooklyn, on November 25, 1900. His father, a lawyer, was so strongly opposed to his son's early interest in music that he punished the youth whenever he found him trying to play the family piano. Secretly encouraged by his mother, young Arthur learned to play well enough to make his professional debut at the age of fourteen when he was hired to furnish musical accompaniment to silent films at the Cortelyou Movie Emporium in Flatbush.

After graduating from New York University, Schwartz continued his studies at Columbia University. Although he briefly considered a writing career, he acceded to his father's wishes and entered Columbia Law School. During his four years there, he helped support himself by teaching English at various high schools in New York. He also began to devote whatever free time he had to composing popular songs. At twenty-three, he wrote his first published song, "Baltimore, Md., You're the Only Doctor for Me." It netted him about eight dollars, but the urge to write melodies continued to be strong. One thing was obvious even from the title: he needed a good lyricist.

At first, Schwartz hoped to form a partnership with Lorenz Hart. The summer after graduating from Columbia Law School, he took a job as a counselor at a summer camp for the sole reason that Hart was also a counselor there. They wrote several songs together for camp shows, plus one, "I Know My Girl by Her Perfume," that was later used in a vaudeville act.

The success Hart achieved with Rodgers when they wrote the songs for *The Garrick Gaieties* ended the possibility of a permanent Schwartz-Hart collaboration. In 1926, Schwartz had some songs in *The Grand Street Follies* and the following year he was one of three composers responsible for another off-Broadway revue, *The New Yorkers* (not to be confused with the Cole Porter musical of three years later). Finding himself being drawn more to music than to law, Schwartz felt that he had to make a definite choice between the two. Encouraged by Larry Hart, he quit his law practice in 1928 to devote himself exclusively to music and the theatre.

Although some of his earliest assignments—for vaudeville acts and "tab" shows (tabloid versions of Broadway plays that played the vaudeville circuits)—were not profitable, he continued to feel that things would change once he found the right lyricist. The man he eventually decided on was a part-time writer for the theatre and a full-time publicist for M-G-M named Howard Dietz.

Dietz was born in New York City, on September 8, 1896. He attended Columbia University at the same time as Oscar Hammerstein II and Lorenz Hart. While still an undergraduate, he had his first light verse published in Franklin P. Adams' *Conning Tower* and Don Marquis' *Sun Dial* newspaper columns. He also won a $500 prize for submitting the winning advertising copy in a contest sponsored by Fatima cigarettes. This led to his getting a job as copywriter for an advertising agency. One of the agency's accounts was the Goldwyn Pictures Corporation, and one of Dietz's first assignments was to give the new company a trademark (Leo the Lion, inspired by the mascot of Columbia University) and a slogan (*Ars Gratia Artis*). After serving in the Navy during World War I, Dietz did free-lance publicity for various film companies until Samuel Goldwyn appointed him director of advertising and publicity. When, in 1924, the Goldwyn company merged with Metro and Mayer, Dietz continued with the new company in a similar capacity. (Goldwyn, however, sold his interest soon after the merger to continue as an independent producer.) Dietz remained an executive at M-G-M for over thirty years; during that period he also wrote sketches, librettos, and lyrics for twelve Broadway musicals, plus English versions of *La Bohème* and *Fledermaus* for the Metropolitan Opera.

Dietz first began to write for the theatre in 1923, when he fashioned a lyric to Arthur Samuel's music for the song "Alibi Baby." It was sung by Luella Gear in *Poppy*, one of W. C. Fields's greatest stage successes. (Fame was not Dietz's, however, because Dorothy Donnelly, the librettist-lyricist of the show, would not allow his name on either the program or the sheet music.)

The following year, Jerome Kern agreed to collaborate with the young lyricist on the score for *Dear Sir*. One evening when Dietz reported to the composer at his home in Bronxville, Kern played twelve numbers of the score on the piano, and asked him to get to work and return in a few days. Somewhat overawed by writing his first complete score with such an illustrious composer, Dietz thought he was expected to have all twelve sets of lyrics completed by that time. He then worked for fifty hours straight to finish the assignment, only to discover upon his return to Kern's home that the composer had expected him to have just one lyric ready.

Dear Sir was a quick failure, but *Merry-Go-Round*, a revue which Dietz wrote with Jay Gorney and Morrie Ryskind in 1927, did have a long enough

205

run to make many people recognize his talent. One of those most impressed was Arthur Schwartz.

Schwartz became convinced that in Dietz he would have a partner equally as inventive and as bright as Larry Hart. So determined was he to form a collaboration that he barraged the lyricist with telegrams and telephone calls. Dietz, however, was not receptive to the entreaties; he felt that since both men were relatively new to the theatre they would benefit more from associating with writers of greater experience.

The matter was allowed to rest until 1929 when Tom Weatherly joined with William A. Brady, Jr., and Dwight Deere Wiman to produce a revue called *The Little Show*. This was the outgrowth of a series of Sunday evening *Divertissements* that Weatherly and James Pond had presented at the Selwyn Theatre. "They were really nothing more than high-class vaudeville shows," recalls Weatherly, "but they were far more artistic than the Sunday night variety programs then being offered at the Winter Garden. They became so successful that I was convinced there would be an audience for a really smart and sophisticated revue." Upon reading the first newspaper announcement of the plans for *The Little Show*, Schwartz immediately went to see Weatherly. After some further persuasion on Schwartz's part, Dietz finally yielded and agreed to become associated with the project.

The Little Show, which played at the Music Box, was an elegantly intimate affair featuring Clifton Webb, Libby Holman, and Fred Allen. Most of the songs were composed by Schwartz and Dietz, but, as in most revues, there were many interpolated numbers. In fact, Schwartz had nothing to do with two of Miss Holman's biggest hits, "Can't We Be Friends?" and "Moanin' Low." "Can't We Be Friends?" was written by Kay Swift and her husband, James Warburg, a banker and occasional lyricist who wrote under the name of Paul James; "Moanin' Low" was the work of Howard Dietz and Ralph Rainger, one of the two featured pianists in the pit orchestra. During the out-of-town tryout of the revue, prospects did not seem very promising until Dietz suggested that "Moanin' Low" be given the next-to-closing spot on the program; somehow this strengthened the entire entertainment and helped assure its success. The scene in which Libby Holman expressed this excruciating sentiment was a squalid Harlem tenement flat. After rousing her lover (Clifton Webb) from a drunken stupor, she brings him to his feet and they perform a particularly torrid dance. As a climax to the scene, and to prove the line in the song about being mean as can be, Webb strangles his devoted paramour.

The Dietz-Schwartz creations, however, were not completely overlooked. Among them was the open-hearted tribute to New York's celebrated nuts-and-bolts emporium, "Hammacher Schlemmer, I Love You," and the

THE LITTLE SHOW *(1929)"One of the most striking things in the revue,"* wrote critic Richard Lockridge, *"is a song that is neither amusing nor forgettable. It is 'Moanin' Low,' which Libby Holman sings in that powerfully throbbing voice of hers while Clifton Webb dances with her in mad grotesque."* The climax of that dance is shown here. *(Costumes by Ruth Brenner.)*

CULVER PICTURES, INC.

debonair admission of the spurned lover, "I Guess I'll Have to Change My Plan."*

With *The Little Show* such an impressive hit, Messrs. Brady, Wiman, and Weatherly soon made plans for a sequel to be produced in the fall of 1930. At first they considered starring Webb, Holman, and Allen again. Then, remembering that even with Lillie, Lawrence, and Buchanan, the second *Charlot's Revue* had run less than half the number of performances of the first, the producers decided upon an entirely new cast for *The Second Little Show*. The show lasted just two months.

Once it became known that Webb, Holman, and Allen would not be in the new production, Max Gordon, a former agent and associate of Sam Harris, promptly signed the three for his own production, *Three's a Crowd*. He also hired Dietz and Schwartz to supply most of the songs, and gave Dietz the additional task of selecting all the material and the other performers to be in the show.

Again, although Dietz and Schwartz wrote most of the songs together, Dietz also collaborated on numbers with Phil Charig, Burton Lane, and Vernon Duke. The piece that made the biggest hit, however, was the only one that Dietz was not associated with—"Body and Soul," by Johnny Green,

* "I Guess I'll Have to Change My Plan" was based on a melody Schwartz had written the summer he spent at the camp with Lorenz Hart. Hart's original lyric went, in part:

> I love to lie awake in bed.
> Right after taps
> I pull the flaps
> Above my head . . .

THREE'S A CROWD *(1930). Clifton Webb, Libby Holman, and Fred Allen.*

PHOTO BY VANDAMM

Robert Sour, and Edward Heyman. As intoned by Libby Holman, this masochistic lament became the "Moanin' Low" of the new revue. The best of the Dietz and Schwartz inspirations was "Something to Remember You By,[*] a ballad of unhappy leave-taking sung by Miss Holman to a sailor who stood with his back to the audience. He was played by Fred MacMurray. Fred Allen achieved new stature as a comedian with his uproarious sketch about Admiral Byrd at the South Pole.

By the time they signed with Max Gordon to supply the songs for *The Band Wagon,* Dietz and Schwartz were the acknowledged masters of the revue form. Dietz again agreed to supervise the production but only on two conditions: George S. Kaufman would have to write most of the sketches, and Fred and Adele Astaire would have to be signed for the leads. "In many ways, it was an experimental production," Dietz has observed, "combining as it did the best features of the so-called intimate type of revue that had come into vogue with *The Garrick Gaieties* and *The Little Show,* with the more spectacular backgrounds associated with the productions of Ziegfeld."

One of its most unusual innovations was the use of the revolving stage, which before that had been used mainly to change scenery. Now, as created by Albert Johnson, it was employed to enhance the musical and dramatic effectiveness of a scene. The sketches by Kaufman and Dietz were well above the average in wit and substance, particularly the satire on the Old South called "The Pride of the Claghornes."

Shortly after the June 3, 1931, opening of *The Band Wagon,* Olin Downes, the music critic of the New York *Times,* handed down the following verdict: "Each scene or episode serves to display a new angle of approach and craftsmanship. And—mirabile dictu—we have a composer whose melodic

[*] "Something to Remember You By," with a much faster tempo, was called "I Have No Words" when it was first sung in an English musical, *Little Tommy Tucker,* the previous year.

vein is not only graceful but characterized at its best by refinement and artistic quality. . . . He is able in many places to deliver a quality of musical workmanship which would command the respect of the most serious composer, and perhaps also the envy."

The still-enviable score—possibly the finest ever written for a revue—included the gaily optimistic "New Sun in the Sky" for Astaire to sing as he preened before a mirror; the saucy "Hoops" for Fred and Adele as two frolicking Parisian *enfants;* the almost ethereal "High and Low"; and the contagious oom-pah rhythm of "I Love Louisa" which ended the first act on a roistering Bavarian scene with the cast astride a swirling, festively decorated merry-go-round.

During rehearsals one day, it was discovered that there was need for what Schwartz describes as a "dark song, somewhat mystical, yet in slow, even rhythm." The following morning, he awoke with the entire melody so fixed in his mind that he was able to go immediately to the piano and play it through without faltering. The song, "Dancing in the Dark," was sung by John Barker, and danced by Tilly Losch on a slanted, mirrored floor illuminated by continually changing colored lights.

The third and final Max Gordon revue was *Flying Colors.* Judging by its cast (Clifton Webb, Tamara Geva, Patsy Kelly, Charles Butterworth, Larry Adler), it was the equal of *Three's a Crowd* and *The Band Wagon.* Yet,

THE BAND WAGON *(1931). "I Love Louisa," sung by the cast on a merry-go-round at a Bavarian amusement park, was the first act finale. Adele and Fred Astaire are seated on the tortoise, Frank Morgan wears the lederhosen, and Helen Broderick is on the lamb. (Costumes by Kiviette; setting by Albert Johnson.)*

PHOTO BY VANDAMM

though Dietz (chief sketch writer, director, and lyricist) and Schwartz made notable contributions, there were many who felt that the show was merely repeating same of the proven formulas of their previous offerings. "Meine Kleine Akrobat," for example, sought to recapture the flavor of "I Love Louisa," while the sultry "Alone Together" was performed in a manner so similar to "Dancing in the Dark" that John Mason Brown referred to it as "Dancing in the Schwartz." "A Shine On Your Shoes," a piece of didactic exuberance tapped out by Monette Moore and Vilma and Buddy Ebsen around a shoe-shine stand, and the joyous chorale, "Louisiana Hayride," were also originally heard in this revue. *

The sameness that was creeping into their revues and their natural desire to try something fresh prompted Dietz and Schwartz to write their first book musical, *Revenge with Music*, in 1934. Inspired by a trip to Spain, Dietz adapted his libretto from the same Spanish novel, *El Sombrero de Tres Picos* by Pedro de Alarcón, that had previously served as the basis for Manuel de Falla's ballet of the same name and Hugo Wolf's comic opera, *Der Corregidor*. The story, a fairly elementary tale, concerned the attempt of a governor of a Spanish province to make love to the wife of a poor miller, and the miller's counter (and more successful) attempt to make love to the governor's wife.

Schwartz's score was distinguished by its melodic richness and its faculty for capturing all the fire and romance of Spain. Because Libby Holman, as the miller's wife, was given the fervent "You and the Night and the Music," it was necessary to have an equally strong solo for Georges Metaxa, as her husband. Among the many songs Dietz and Schwartz had written the previous year for a radio serial, *The Gibson Family,* was one called "If There Is Someone Lovelier Than You," which they felt would be perfectly suited to the requirements of *Revenge with Music*. Although melodically it may have lacked the proper Spanish coloration, Mr. Metaxa's European accent and the orchestral arrangement combined to give it just the right atmosphere for the locale.

There were two other collaborations by the team in the Thirties. *At Home Abroad* (1935) used one of the oldest frameworks for a revue, the around-the-world tour. Thus, Beatrice Lillie was given the opportunity to extoll the charms of "Paree," become hopelessly confused in London while ordering "two double-damask dinner napkins," and, in "Get Yourself a Geisha," slyly reveal some of the quaint customs of Japan, the land where "it's better with your shoes off." Ethel Waters, Eleanor Powell, Herb Williams, and Reginald Gardiner (he mimicked trains and gave an impersonation of wallpaper) were also members of the tour.

---

* Agnes de Mille was to have done the choreography—her first for a Broadway musical—for *Flying Colors,* but because of differences with almost everyone but Howard Dietz, she quit during the tryout and was succeeded by Albertina Rasch.

REVENGE WITH MUSIC *(1934)*. *Libby Holman and Georges Metaxa as the young Spanish couple in a musical based on an old Spanish tale of cuckolds and cuckolders. (Costumes by Constance Ripley.)*

Between the Devil (1937), the last Dietz-Schwartz musical for eleven years, was their second book show. Its tale of an English bigamist whose life was complicated by an English wife (Evelyn Laye) and a French wife (Adèle Dixon) was a time-worn farce situation (it turned up again twenty-one years later in *Oh Captain!*), and neither the authors nor the players could extract much life from it. As the bigamist, Jack Buchanan sang the jauntily self-pitying "By Myself" while being pursued by bobbies through London's foggy streets. The show ran three months.

Because of increased pressure on Dietz to concentrate on his salaried chores at M-G-M, Schwartz was compelled to seek other collaborators during the latter part of the Thirties. Shortly before *Between the Devil*, he became associated with an elaborate production called *Virginia* which the Rockefeller family produced at the Center Theatre in Radio City. As the Rockefellers had already invested a considerable sum toward the restoration of the Colonial village of Williamsburg, Virginia, they thought it would be a fine idea to offer a musical set in that locale during the American Revolution. To write the book they chose Laurence Stallings (later succeeded by Owen Davis), and as Schwartz's partner they assigned Albert Stillman, the Radio City's staff lyricist.

The musical, which turned out to be a costly but dull extravaganza, was the last stage musical shown at the theatre. After becoming a showplace for Sonja Henie's ice revue and a television studio, the Center Theatre was torn out in 1954 to be converted into office space.

Stars In Your Eyes, in 1939, was Schwartz's first score with Dorothy Fields. Miss Fields, the daughter of producer-comedian Lew Fields and the sister of librettist Herbert and librettist-playwright Joseph, was born in

211

Herbert and Dorothy Fields.

Allenhurst, New Jersey, where her parents had rented a summer home, on July 15, 1905. Determined that none of his children would suffer the inherent agonies of a theatrical career, Papa Fields at first vainly tried to steer them into other pursuits. Dorothy attended the Benjamin School for Girls and, following graduation, became the school's drama instructor. Her first literary efforts were light verses she submitted to magazines, and her first lyrics were improvisations she made up to fit the classical piano pieces she was studying. When she was twenty-two, Dorothy met composer Jimmy McHugh, who had already written a number of hits, including "When My Sugar Walks Down the Street" and "I Can't Believe that You're in Love with Me," both for Harlem's famed Cotton Club. Impressed by Dorothy's poems and lyrics, McHugh took her on as a collaborator for the next Cotton Club revue, featuring Duke Ellington and his Orchestra. Their work attracted the attention of producer Lew Leslie who was convinced they would be the perfect combination to write the score for his all-Negro Broadway revue, *Blackbirds of 1928*, starring Adelaide Hall and Bill Robinson. The show contained a remarkable string of song hits—"I Can't Give you Anything but Love, Baby" (inspired by an overheard remark made by an indigent swain while peering into Tiffany's window), "Diga Diga Doo," "I Must Have that Man," and "Porgy" (a pre-Gershwin plaint prompted by the Dorothy and DuBose Heyward play).

The great success of *Blackbirds* (the longest-running Negro show ever presented on Broadway*) assured the new song-writing team of steady employment in a variety of locales and media. Ziegfeld hired them to write songs for his final *Midnight Frolic* (1928), headlining Eddie Cantor and

Helen Morgan. Lew Fields put them to work on *Hello, Daddy*, which he kept pretty much of a family affair by starring in it himself and assigning son Herbert to do the book. Leslie next signed McHugh and Fields for his *International Revue*, a Broadway flop despite the stellar presence of Gertrude Lawrence, Harry Richman and Jack Pearl, plus songs such as "Exactly Like You" and "On the Sunny Side of the Street." The team also did the songs for Leslie's Chicago revue, *Clowns in Clover* (including "Don't Blame Me"), for New York's Palais Royale night club floorshow, and for the opening bill at the Radio City Music Hall.

During most of the period between 1930 and 1939, Dorothy Fields worked in Hollywood, writing film songs primarily with McHugh ("I'm

STARS IN YOUR EYES *(1939). Every night, in the midst of the song called "It's All Yours," Ethel Merman and Jimmy Durante would break each other up with supposedly spontaneous wisecracks and stories. (Costumes by John Hambleton.)*

PHOTO BY JEROME ROBINSON

in the Mood for Love," "Dinner at Eight") and Jerome Kern (scores for *I Dream Too Much* and *Swing Time*). This movie background made her particularly well equipped to collaborate on Arthur Schwartz's new musical comedy project, *Stars in Your Eyes*. For this was to be a movie satire with a particularly novel idea. It was Schwartz's notion that a very funny show could be built around the making of a Hollywood musical by leaders of New York's left-wing theatre, with the humor derived from superimposing social significance on a glamorous Hollywood production. After J. P. McEvoy completed the script—then called *Swing to the Left*—Dwight Deere Wiman agreed to produce it with Ethel Merman as a movie queen and Jimmy Durante as a labor-union organizer. Upon reading the book and listening to the songs, however, director Joshua Logan objected to the social commentary. Liberal themes were fine for revues, he told the authors, but why clutter up a gay story with anything so weighty? Eventually, Schwartz, Fields and McEvoy capitulated. The labor leader became a studio idea man, a song about the South's economy was thrown out, and, in general, what might have been a sharp, unconventional spoof of the movies became a standard product by the time *Swing to the Left* was transformed into *Stars in Your Eyes*. Nevertheless, with all the concessions to what the public was supposed to want, the show lasted only 127 performances.

Soon after *Stars in Your Eyes* opened, Schwartz accepted an offer to work in Hollywood. He remained there until 1946. Among the films for which he wrote complete scores were *Thank Your Lucky Stars* (lyrics by Frank Loesser) and *The Time, the Place and the Girl* (lyrics by Leo Robin). For Columbia, he produced the Gene Kelly–Rita Hayworth *Cover Girl* (score by Jerome Kern and Ira Gershwin), and for Warners, the romanticized biography of Cole Porter, *Night and Day*.

By the mid-Forties, the Broadway musical theatre had become saturated with serious costume musical plays. As something of an antidote to *Bloomer Girl, The Song of Norway, Up in Central Park, Carousel,* and the like, George S. Kaufman and Nunnally Johnson decided to collaborate on a sophisticated modern musical comedy. *Park Avenue,* the show they wrote, was concerned with nothing more serious than the compulsion of socialites to shed their mates with as much frequency as possible. As the production was also to mark the return to Broadway of both Arthur Schwartz and Ira Gershwin in their first assignment as a team, there was, understandably, great expectation for the enterprise. Unfortunately, although the songs were attractive, the book

* Leslie had first presented a *Blackbirds* revue in London in 1926, with Florence Mills starred. His attempts to mount subsequent *Blackbirds* editions on Broadway in 1933 and in 1939—even with Lena Horne in the latter—were dismal failures. West End audiences, however, continued to prove receptive in 1934, 1935, and 1936.

was too much of a one-joke affair, and the show had a very brief run.

Schwartz's duties in both New York and in Hollywood have compelled him to cross the country many times. Yet it was not until the summer of 1947, when he drove from the East Coast to the West Coast, that he actually saw something of the country and the people. This gave him an idea: a musical revue that, instead of using the format of an around-the-world tour as in *At Home Abroad*, would be restricted to topics and locales indigenous to the United States. John Gunther presented him with a perfect title for it—*Inside U. S. A.*

Inside U. S. A., which co-starred Beatrice Lillie and Jack Haley, was the only musical Schwartz ever produced himself. It also reunited him with Howard Dietz, and their score gave undeniable proof that in the wit and originality of their songs the collaborators had lost none of the skill that had marked their earlier efforts. In "Haunted Heart," they returned to the kind of throbbing torch ballad to which they have always given a certain distinction; in "Rhode Island Is Famous for You," they created a punning inventory of the most famous products of almost every state in the Union; in "Come, O Come to Pittsburgh," they supplied Beatrice Lillie with a mocking madrigal celebrating the industrial wonders of that city. Two particularly original musical notions were "Blue Grass," the lament of a girl who has lost her boy friend to the horses at Churchill Downs, and "My Gal Is Mine Once More," a loping Western number sung by a cowboy celebrating his remarriage to his first wife.

For his next two undertakings, *A Tree Grows in Brooklyn* in 1951, and *By the Beautiful Sea* in 1954, Schwartz again became affiliated with lyricist Dorothy Fields. Both shows starred Shirley Booth (whose previous musical comedy experience had been as Louhedda Hopsons in *Hollywood Pinafore* five years earlier), both were set in Brooklyn just after the turn of the century, and both lasted exactly 270 performances.

Judged on musical merits, *A Tree Grows in Brooklyn* was the more impressive work. The famous Betty Smith novel provided both Schwartz and Miss Fields with the opportunity to create songs of far greater depth and meaning than they had previously done. In place of sophisticated patter and soulful ballads of the type they had provided for *Stars in Your Eyes*, the writers produced a score overflowing with nostalgia and sentiment, one that caught all the poignance and emotion of the gallant Nolan family. For Schwartz, it was an opportunity to return to the people and the places he had once known during his boyhood in Brooklyn, and he took long walks through the tenement areas of the city in order to steep himself in the proper atmosphere. Miss Fields also strove for authenticity. "The lyrics reflect the simplicity of these people," she once said. "There are no high-flown poetic sentiments." Yet, though there may not be any deliberate attempts at poetry, there is a rich vein of the poetry of everyday speech in the lyrics, just as there is a feeling of genuine eloquence in the music. Indeed, the characters and locale came more vividly to life in the songs than in the somewhat awkward libretto devised by George Abbott and Betty Smith.

Because it had an even weaker book and score, *By the Beautiful Sea* was more dependent on the charm and personality of Shirley Booth. As Lottie Gibson, a vaudeville performer who owned a theatrical boarding house in Coney Island, her performance was so disarming that Brooks Atkinson had to confess, "Everyone has long since lost his heart to Miss Booth." It is interesting to note that while both *A Tree Grows in Brooklyn* and *By the Beautiful Sea* were financial failures, they ran ten performances longer than had the hugely successful *Band Wagon* in 1931.

In 1960, Howard Dietz retired from his duties at Metro-Goldwyn-Mayer to devote himself full time to writing with Arthur Schwartz. The first product of their resumed partnership, *The Gay Life*, adapted from Schnitzler's *Affairs of Anatol*, was a slightly frayed bedroom farce redeemed by a score of unfailing melodic richness and lyrical grace. The Italian comic Walter Chiari was miscast as the roving Anatol, but the lovely Barbara Cook made the most of such musical delights as "Magic Moment" and

INSIDE U.S.A. *(1948). The gay opening number of the second act with Beatrice Lillie as the queen of the Mardi Gras. The kneeling swain at the right is Jack Cassidy. (Costumes by Eleanor Goldsmith and Castillo; setting by Lemuel Ayers.)*

PHOTO BY EILEEN DARBY—GRAPHIC HOUSE

A TREE GROWS IN BROOKLYN (1951). *Aunt Cissy breaks out into a spirited rendition of "Look Who's Dancing." The scene is a furniture store where she and newlyweds Kate and Johnny Nolan have gone to purchase a bed. Shirley Booth, Marcia VanDyke, and Johnny Johnston. (Costumes by Irene Sharaff.)*

PHOTO BY EILEEN DARBY—GRAPHIC HOUSE

"Who Can? You Can!" Another Dietz-Schwartz collaboration, *Jennie*, starting Mary Martin as a fictitious Laurette Taylor, suffered through a brief life in 1963.

The striking irony in the career of Arthur Schwartz is that in spite of the high quality of his melodic creations for such book musicals as *Revenge with Music, Virginia, Between the Devil, Stars in Your Eyes, Park Avenue, The Gay Life*, and especially *A Tree Grows in Brooklyn*, the composer's only commercial successes have been the revues he wrote in partnership with Howard Dietz. The fault has seldom been his or his lyricist's; in almost every case it has been the librettist who has somehow failed to supply a script worthy of its score. Thus, at this writing, Schwartz remains a composer looking for a good librettist—just as in the mid-Twenties he was a composer looking for a good lyricist.

To date, the contributions of Dietz and Schwartz to the revue form are still their most significant collaborative achievement in the development of the musical theatre. Chiefly due to their efforts, the revue reached a peak of perfection that has never been surpassed. Indeed, in the event that this form of entertainment ever does return to its former eminence, it will need the very qualities of smartness, originality, wit and melody that have so distinguished the works of Howard Dietz and Arthur Schwartz.

E. Y. Harburg.

CHAPTER FOURTEEN

E. Y. Harburg,
Vernon Duke, Harold Arlen,
Burton Lane

IN ADDITION TO Arthur Schwartz, there were many other composers who first won recognition for their work in the Broadway revues of the late Twenties and early Thirties. Chief among them were Vernon Duke, Harold Arlen, and Burton Lane, though none of these men was as closely identified with this form of entertainment as Schwartz.

In fact, each one of these composers won far more lasting fame with serious musical plays during the Forties—Duke with *Cabin in the Sky*, Arlen with *Bloomer Girl*, and Lane with *Finian's Rainbow*. Apart from the similarity of their progress in the theatre, what is interesting about these men is that they were part of the rising group of writers—which included Schwartz—who were inspired by George Gershwin. Just as Jerome Kern had been the idol of Rodgers, Gershwin, and other composers of the Twenties, so it was now Gershwin himself who was the inspiration for the new generation. The relationship of these men to the Gershwin family has even been professional, as all have collaborated with George's brother, Ira. The lyricist, however, who has been most closely associated with the careers of Duke, Arlen, and Lane—and who has also been a close friend of the Gershwins—is the prodigious E. Y. Harburg.

219

E. Y. Harburg

E. Y. (Edgar "Yip") Harburg was born on April 8, 1898, in New York City. His parents were poor, and as a boy he sold newspapers, lighted street lamps, and did other odd jobs to help pay for his education. At Townsend Harris High School, he was co-editor with Ira Gershwin of the literary column in the school newspaper. The friendship of the two men continued when they both attended the City College of New York. While at college, Harburg, like Ira Gershwin and Howard Dietz, began to contribute light verse to Franklin P. Adams' *Conning Tower* column. After graduation, he traveled through South America for about three years, spending a year writing for a newspaper in Montevideo, Uruguay.

While in South America, he made up his mind to become a lyricist. On his return to New York in the early Twenties, he was advised by Ira Gershwin that he would do well to find a more remunerative way of earning a living. Harburg then started an electrical appliance business and did well until the 1929 stock market crash wiped him out. "I had my fill of this dreamy abstract thing called business," he once said," and I decided to face reality by writing lyrics."

Fortunately, at that time, composer Jay Gorney was looking for a lyricist. A few years before, having read some poems in F.P.A.'s column signed "Freckles," Gorney had discovered the man behind the nickname to be Howard Dietz, and an informal partnership had developed. But because Gorney had recently been appointed head of the music department of Paramount Picture's Astoria Studio and Dietz was the chief publicist for M-G-M, the composer had to find another lyricist. Again he scanned F.P.A.'s column, where some verses signed "Yip" attracted his attention. Abetted by a high recommendation from Ira Gershwin, Harburg soon had both a partner and a contract with a motion picture company. About the same time, five songs by Gorney and Harburg were accepted for *Earl Carroll's Sketchbook*, an extremely successful revue which ran for a year and one-half. So outstanding were Harburg's initial efforts that he was given assignments to contribute the major share of lyrics to *The Garrick Gaieties, Earl Carroll Vanities of 1930, Shoot the Works, Ballyhoo,* and *Americana.* In *Americana,* produced in 1932, Harburg was represented by contributions written with Vernon Duke ("Let Me Match My Private Life with Yours"), Harold Arlen and Johnny Mercer ("Satan's Li'l Lamb"), and Burton Lane ("You're Not Pretty but You're Mine"). The biggest hit of the show was the memorable Depression anthem, "Brother, Can You Spare a Dime?," which Harburg wrote with Jay Gorney. The song was one of the first examples of the kind of socially conscious viewpoint that would mark many of Harburg's later lyrics.

220

Vernon Duke.

Vernon Duke

Along with Kurt Weill, Vernon Duke had the most thorough musical education of any of the leading theatre composers who won recognition during the Thirties. Yet, unlike most well-trained composers, Duke has led a somewhat schizophrenic musical life, writing symphonies, ballets, and concertos in a style completely unlike that employed in his musical comedies and revues. Indeed, for many years, he even used two different names: his real name, Vladimir Dukelsky, for the concert hall, and Vernon Duke, a pseudonym suggested by George Gershwin, for Broadway.

Duke was born in Parafianovo, Russia, on October 10, 1903. His early studies were under Reinhold Glière and Marian Dombrovsky, and at the age of thirteen was admitted to the Kiev Conservatory of Music. After the Russian Revolution, his family fled the country. For a time, Duke tried to pursue his musical career in the United States, but found few opportunities. He returned to Europe, where he soon became acquainted with Sergei Diaghilev, the director of the Ballet Russe. Diaghilev was so impressed with

221

WALK A LITTLE FASTER *(1932).*
Bobby Clark, Beatrice Lillie,
and Paul McCullough.

the twenty-year-old composer that he commissioned him to write the music for the ballet, *Zéphyr et Flore,* which was subsequently performed throughout Europe. In the mid-Twenties, Duke moved to London. There his first assignment for the musical theatre was to supply additional music for *Katja, the Dancer.* The following year he performed a similar task for *Yvonne,* which won immortality when Noël Coward dubbed it "*Yvonne* the Terrible." Duke's first complete score was written in 1928 for *The Yellow Mask,* an English musical with a book by Edgar Wallace.

Soon after settling permanently in the United States in 1929, Duke wrote his first "American" song, "I Am Only Human after All," with a lyric by Ira Gershwin and E. Y. Harburg. Although the song was accepted for Ruth Selwyn's *9:15 Revue,* it was dropped from the score even before rehearsals began. Later, it was introduced in the 1930 edition of *The Garrick Gaieties* and became Duke's first commercial success.

Duke's romantic background as a Russian emigré soon made him a popular figure in the social life of New York. Courtney Burr, a wealthy young man with a great interest in the theatre, was anxious to produce a revue in the sophisticated style inaugurated by *The Little Show.* Burr was impressed by Duke's musical talent and hoped to induce Dorothy Parker to contribute the lyrics. On Duke's insistence, however, the assignment went to Harburg. The revue, *Walk a Little Faster,* opened in December, 1932, with the leading parts played by Beatrice Lillie and Clark and McCullough. The show may have been hindered by its continual striving for unusual artistic effects, but there was no sign of strain in the smoothly constructed melodies or in their deft lyrics.

"April in Paris," which quickly established the reputation of Duke and Harburg (even though Evelyn Hoey, who introduced it, had laryngitis on

222

opening night), was written one April afternoon while Duke and some friends were reminiscing about Paris in a small restaurant in New York. Suddenly, someone paraphrased Browning by crying out "Oh, to be in Paris now that April's here." "April in Paris" struck the composer as a perfect title for a song; he dashed over to an upright piano and, within a relatively short time, created the refrain that still remains the most popular melody he has ever composed.

In the mid-Thirties, the Shuberts were the successors to Ziegfeld in the creation of elaborate revues. In fact, after Ziegfeld's death in 1932, his former rivals secured the rights to produce the *Ziegfeld Follies*. The first Shubert-sponsored *Follies* was presented in 1934, with Mrs. Billie Burke Ziegfeld as titular producer. Duke and Harburg created most of the score for this revue. Two years later, an equally resplendent edition reunited Duke with Ira Gershwin. Fanny Brice was the stellar attraction in both productions, though the second served to introduce American audiences to the charms of the St. Louis-born and Paris-acclaimed Josephine Baker. The 1936 *Follies* was also the first Broadway attraction to have choreography by George Balanchine.

On Christmas night, 1936, the Shuberts offered another opulent revue, *The Show Is On,* which was designed and directed by Vincente Minnelli. The bulk of the score was the product of Vernon Duke and Ted Fetter (Cole Porter's cousin). By the time the show reached New York, however, many of their numbers had been cut and replaced by contributions by some of the most illustrious song-writers of the theatre: George and Ira Gershwin, "By Strauss"; Rodgers and Hart, "Rhythm" (for an aggressively rhythmic Beatrice Lillie); Hoagy Carmichael and Stanley Adams, "Little Old Lady"; and Harold Arlen and E. Y. Harburg, "Song of the Woodman" (bellowed out by Bert Lahr). Among the remaining Duke-Fetter songs was one of their loveliest inspirations, the graceful, economically titled "Now."

PHOTO BY MURRAY KORMAN

ZIEGFELD FOLLIES OF 1936. *The irrepressible Baby Snooks (Fanny Brice) is beginning to get on the nerves of a Hollywood director (Bob Hope) in one of the sketches from the revue. This was Miss Brice's last appearance on the Broadway stage.*

THE SHOW IS ON (1936). *Beatrice Lillie invites the audience to "Buy yourself a balloon, fly up to the moon," as she is swung way out over the orchestra. As a climax to the number, Miss Lillie unfastened a garter and flung it to a favored gentleman. (Costume by Vincente Minnelli.)*

Although his previous works would not have indicated his suitability for the task, Vernon Duke became associated in 1940 with a musical fantasy of Negro life called *Cabin in the Sky*. The Lynn Root libretto was initially brought to George Balanchine, who was anxious to do it as his first assignment as director of an entire Broadway production. Balanchine took the script to Duke, who became fascinated by the story. Nevertheless, he hesitated to write the music as he feared that his lack of familiarity with the Negro people would be too much of a handicap. (The word around Broadway at the time was that the wrong Duke had been chosen.)

The more he thought about it, however, the more Duke became intrigued by the challenge. Because both he and Balanchine were Russian and Root was a Hollywood script-writer, the composer wanted a lyricist with some direct contact with Southern Negroes. Duke first thought of Ira Gershwin because of *Porgy and Bess,* but Gershwin was already committed to *Lady in*

CABIN IN THE SKY *(1940).*
Dooley Wilson listens as Ethel
Waters sings "Cabin In the
Sky." "Without once stepping
out of character or assuming
the airs of a star performer,"
wrote Brooks Atkinson, "Miss
Waters captures all the inno-
cence and humor of a story-
book character, investing it
also with that rangy warmth
of spirit that distinguishes her
acting."

the Dark. E. Y. Harburg, Duke's second choice, diplomatically told the composer that he thought the story lacked significance, though his true feeling
was that the composer was incapable of writing the kind of score the play
required. (Later, Harburg readily admitted he was wrong.) Finally, Duke
turned to the willing John Treville Latouche, a twenty-three-year-old poet
from Richmond, Virginia, whose lyric to *Ballad for Americans* (music by Earl
Robinson) had recently won wide acclaim.

When it was finally presented in October, 1940, *Cabin in the Sky* offered
audiences an imaginative tale that combined elements of both *The Green
Pastures* and *Liliom.* As a parable of the struggle between good and evil, the
play may have been, as Richard Watts, Jr., wrote, "merely a white man's self-
conscious attempt to write a pseudo-folk fable of another race." Yet in its
pioneering effort to create something bold and unconventional, it did provide
Ethel Waters with her only dramatic role in the musical theatre, while also
demonstrating the remarkable versatility of the composer. Despite the fact
there were no blues or rhythm songs to convey the authentic emotions of
American Negroes, the score was still authentic enough as purely theatre
music to delineate characters skillfully and to set the proper mood. Such
varied, yet appropriate creations as the deeply felt "Cabin in the Sky," or the

225

slinky "Honey in the Honeycomb" (for temptress Katherine Dunham), or the hedonistic "Do What You Wanna Do," all demonstrated their creators' talents for using music and lyrics to achieve maximum dramatic effectiveness.

Shortly before the New York opening, the authors felt that a comic number was badly needed for Miss Waters to offset some of her more impassioned solos. With the New York première only three days off, Duke came up with a song called "Foolin' around with Love," which he had once written with Ted Fetter. Latouche rewrote the lyric and retitled it "Takin' a Chance on Love." With Miss Waters delivering it through chorus after chorus, it became one of the most memorable show-stoppers in the history of Broadway musicals.

One of the great enigmas of the American musical theatre is that, to this writing, Vernon Duke has been unable to follow up his work for *Cabin in the Sky* with anything else that has revealed so much creative talent for the stage. As in the case of Arthur Schwartz, Harold Arlen, and other gifted composers, the fault has not been in the quality of Duke's contributions but rather in the quality of the productions for which they were written. Just one year after *Cabin in the Sky*, Duke became involved in a minor vehicle for Eddie Cantor called *Banjo Eyes*, which was also Cantor's final Broadway appearance. In 1944, great expectations were held for *Sadie Thompson*, a musical version of Somerset Maugham's *Rain* that had a libretto by Howard Dietz (he also did the lyrics) and Rouben Mamoulian. However, the production was foredoomed when Ethel Merman, the intended star, refused to appear in it because she objected to Dietz's lyrics. June Havoc was an excellent replacement, but the damage had been done: *Sadie Thompson* lasted only two months on Broadway.

In the Fifties, Duke became involved in the ill-advised Bette Davis revue, *Two's Company*, which also included an abbreviated musical treatment of *Rain* as the first-act finale. Two of the composer's most exquisite numbers, "Roundabout" and "Out of the Clear Blue Sky" (both with lyrics by Ogden Nash), were also sung in this revue. Ben Bagley's off-Broadway *Littlest Revue* in 1956 was a modest effort with an equally modest run.

Probably no other composer, with the possible exception of Arthur Schwartz, contributed so many good songs to the revues of the Thirties than Vernon Duke. With *Cabin in the Sky*, however, he showed definite indications of the broadening of his scope as a creator of well-integrated scores for adult, meaningful book musicals. The bad luck that has since plagued him in the commercial theatre cannot obliterate the sound musicianship and superior quality that have distinguished his work for the musical stage. Graceful, elegant, imaginatively constructed, the songs of Vernon Duke have a durability and individuality that has made them part of the permanent literature of American popular songs.

Harold Arlen.

Harold Arlen

Harold Arlen became a composer almost by accident. He was born in Buffalo, New York, on February 15, 1905. At seven, he sang in the choir of the synagogue where his father was a cantor. Because his parents wanted him to become a music teacher, they encouraged young Harold's interest in music. In his early teens, Arlen began to play piano at local clubs and on lake steamers. When he was fifteen, he helped organize an instrumental group known as The Snappy Trio. He later joined another group, The Yankee Six, which eventually expanded into a full-sized dance orchestra known as the Buffalodians. While performing as a pianist, vocalist, and arranger for the group during an engagement at a New York nightclub, Arlen attracted the attention of Arnold Johnson, a well-known orchestra leader. Johnson liked Arlen's singing and playing so much that he hired him for his own orchestra, which was then about to appear in *George White's Scandals of 1928*.

Because Arlen's chief ambition at the time was to become a singer, Johnson allowed him to sing one of the songs from the DeSylva-Brown-Henderson score during the intermission. Thus for the six-and-one-half-month run of the *Scandals*, Arlen serenaded nonsmoking spectators with his crooning of Harry

227

Richman's hit song, "On the Crest of a Wave." One of those who were impressed with the twenty-three-year-old between-the-acts entertainer was Vincent Youmans, who was just beginning to organize the cast for his forthcoming production, *Great Day!* Youmans promptly hired Arlen to play the role of Cokey Joe, the piano player, in the musical. Arlen never quite made it on the Broadway stage, however; after the first tryout performance on Long Island, both the character and the song he sang, "Doo-Dah-Dey," were eliminated.

Great Day! may have ended Arlen's career as a performer, but it was responsible for beginning his career as a full-time composer. One day at rehearsal, the regular pianist had become ill. As Arlen recalls: "I was asked to sit at the piano and play ta-tum, ta-tum-tum, TUM—the phrase that's always used to start a dance chorus off at rehearsals. I gave them the standard pick-up the first day, but the next day I played it a little differently. On the third day, I worked it around a bit more, and suddenly the whole company was asking, 'Say, what *is* that you're playing?' "

Urged to turn his variation into a commercial song, the neophyte composer took the piece to his friend, Harry Warren, then on the staff at Remick's. Warren introduced Arlen to Ted Koehler, who gave the melody a lyric and the title, "Get Happy." When they learned of Ruth Selwyn's plans for the *9:15 Revue*, the two men auditioned the song. Unlike the less-fortunate team of Duke, Harburg, and Gershwin, whose "I Am Only Human after All" had not been used, Arlen and Koehler had their new song accepted and given to Ruth Etting to sing in the first-act finale. George Gershwin, who saw the show during its tryout, was so impressed with "Get Happy" that he told the composer it was the most exciting finale he had ever heard. After receiving such encouragement—especially since the *9:15 Revue* was a dismal failure—Arlen promptly decided to end his career as a singer and pianist to devote all his time to composing.

Though he contributed songs to a few minor Broadway attractions in the early 1930's, Harold Arlen first won fame for the songs he and Koehler wrote for a series of Cotton Club revues. These were probably the only night-club floor shows ever to produce so many numbers of enduring appeal, among them "Between the Devil and the Deep Blue Sea," "Kickin' the Gong Around," "I Love a Parade," "I've Got the World on a String," "Stormy Weather," and "Ill Wind."

In 1938, "Yip" Harburg had an idea for a musical that was eventually turned into a successful vehicle for Ed Wynn and called *Hooray for What!* Concerned with the chaotic world situation at that time, the lyricist was anxious to become associated with a musical comedy that would not only be entertaining but would also have something to say about the need for preserving peace and the dangers of the armament race. Unsure of his own ability

228

as a librettist, he took the idea to Howard Lindsay and Russel Crouse, who agreed to write the book. Arlen then joined Harburg to write the score. In spite of its overtones of a message (it even made reference to the atom bomb), *Hooray for What!* was still very much within the framework of conventional musical comedy. Ed Wynn again played his customary zany clown, although this time the character was called upon to save the world from destruction by using laughing gas. In the score were many superior numbers, including "God's Country," a merry flag-waver in which Popeye and Gypsy Rose Lee were extolled as ample compensation for being deprived of Mussolini and Oswald Mosley.*

From the Thirties to the mid-Forties, the uncertain condition of the Broadway theatre forced most of the creative musical talent, including Arlen and Harburg, to accept Hollywood contracts. By the early Forties, however, writers on the West Coast were becoming eager to return to a Broadway that was being transformed as a result of the impact of *Cabin in the Sky, Pal Joey, Lady in the Dark,* and, most significantly, *Oklahoma!* A book show now had to have a really sturdy libretto, with songs and dances an inseparable part of the entire production. During World War II, there was also a greater emphasis on American themes from which audiences might derive some measure of hope for the future.

While still in California, "Yip" Harburg became intrigued with the idea of doing a musical with a Civil War setting. Lilith and Dan James had written a play about the introduction of bloomers during that period. Harburg liked the story, but he felt the theme needed further development and suggested to writers Sig Herzig and Fred Saidy that they strengthen it by putting greater emphasis on the issues of women's rights and Negro rights. In that way, he felt, audiences of 1944 could accept the theme as pertaining to the struggle for freedom everywhere. To provide the score, Harburg was joined by Arlen, with whom he had last collaborated on the film *The Wizard of Oz.*

Bloomer Girl emerged as a charming and colorful musical play with an almost inescapable kinship to *Oklahoma!* This, however, was due more to its cast and production staff than to its subject matter or music. Both Celeste Holm (in her first starring role) and Joan McCracken had previously been in the Rodgers and Hammerstein musical and both plays shared the same set designer (Lemuel Ayers), costume designer (Miles White), choreographer (Agnes de Mille), and orchestral arranger (Robert Russell Bennett). Miss de Mille's chief contribution, a Civil War Ballet, was particularly impressive in its moving depiction of the longing of women who must wait at home while their men are at war.

* *Hooray for What!* was the second musical intended to begin the Broadway career of choreographer Agnes de Mille. As in *Flying Colors,* however, she withdrew prior to the show's New York opening.

BLOOMER GIRL (1944). Agnes de Mille's eloquent Civil War Ballet. Joan McCracken is the girl with her arms upraised, third from the left. (Costumes by Miles White; setting by Lemuel Ayers.)

The songs by Arlen and Harburg caught the mood and the spirit of the story. "The Eagle and Me" and "I Got a Song" sang eloquently of the Negro's yearning for freedom, while "It Was Good Enough for Grandma" burst out in animated defiance of old-fashioned convention. The eternal subject of love was melodiously treated in "Evelina," with its quasi-folk flavor, and in the more conventional "Right as the Rain." "Sunday in Cicero Falls" was a mocking, stately march that conveyed so perfectly the starched atmosphere of the Sabbath in a small, mid-nineteenth-century American town.

After *Bloomer Girl*, Harold Arlen continued to divide his time between film assignments and Broadway. In 1946, he joined Johnny Mercer in creating the songs for *St. Louis Woman*,* an all-Negro musical in which Pearl Bailey made an auspicious Broadway debut singing "Legalize My Name" and "A Woman's Prerogative." In spite of a superior score, however, the show was not a success. Neither was Arlen's next musical, *House of Flowers*, produced almost nine years later. Truman Capote made the adaptation from his own short story, and collaborated with Arlen on the lyrics. Although the idea was

* *St. Louis Woman* was subsequently expanded into a "blues opera," *Free and Easy*, which incorporated some early songs by the composer. After opening in Amsterdam, Holland, in the fall of 1959, it was forced to close soon afterward in Paris.

promising, the story of an innocent girl living in a brothel on a Caribbean island proved to be too weak and undramatic to be successful as a musical comedy libretto. This was particularly unfortunate; Arlen's score was one of his most distinguished, the Oliver Messel décor was stunning, and the cast, headed by Pearl Bailey and Diahann Carroll, was widely acclaimed.

When Harburg first approached Arlen to write the music for *Jamaica*, the composer was reluctant. The Caribbean locale of the story was almost identical with that of *House of Flowers*, and, though his music has always shown a certain Negroid influence, he was understandably anxious to try something different. But the prospect of again working with Harburg was hard to resist, and he was intrigued by the simple charm of the story. Originally, Harburg's script was about a poor fisherman on a tropical island (to be played by Harry Belafonte) who was unique among his fellow islanders in that he had no desire to live in the United States. Why, he reasoned, should he trade his values for those of the people on the mainland when tourists obviously like his way of life so much that they continuously visit his island?

Because the producer, David Merrick, had different ideas about the show, this theme was completely lost by the time *Jamaica* opened on Broadway in the fall of 1957. The character of the fisherman (now played by Ricardo Montalban) was made subordinate to that of the leading female character (Lena Horne), and the plot was almost nonexistent. Although the

ST. LOUIS WOMAN *(1946). Pearl Bailey made her first appearance on Broadway in this musical. Here she is seen urging Fayard Nicholas to "Legalize My Name." (Costumes by Lemuel Ayers.)*

231

HOUSE OF FLOWERS (1954). Ottilie (Diahann Carroll) and the townspeople of a Caribbean island give a joyous welcome to Royal (Rawn Spearman), who has just barely escaped being drowned at sea. (Costumes and setting by Oliver Messel.)

show was a financial success because of the lure of Miss Horne in her first starring role, in almost every department it was a curiously heavy-handed production.

Faults of production were also apparent in *Saratoga*, for which Arlen was joined by his *St. Louis Woman* lyricist, Johnny Mercer. In his first attempt as librettist, director Morton Da Costa evolved a rather plodding book out of Edna Ferber's novel, *Saratoga Trunk*, which left Cecil Beaton's almost overpoweringly elegant settings as the chief feature of the attraction.

In Harold Arlen, the musical theatre has, quite possibly, the most distinguished native composer to emerge since the Twenties. George Gershwin called him "the most original of us all." Irving Berlin, with typical succinctness, has said, "Harold's best *is* the best." To E. Y. Harburg, Harold Arlen is

JAMAICA (1957). Ricardo Montalban and Lena Horne. Of Miss Horne, Life Magazine wrote, "She shines like a tigress in the night, purring and preening and pouncing into the spotlight." (Costumes by Miles White.)

SARATOGA (1959). "Cecil Beaton's sets and costumes depicting New Orleans and the title resort in the lavish glories of the '80s provide a really breathtaking pictorial loveliness," was the opinion of Richard Watts, Jr. The above scene shows Howard Keel, Carol Lawrence, Odette Myrtil, Tun Tun, and Carol Brice at the Waterfront Market in New Orleans.

a genius. "He writes with his own genes. An Arlen song is completely individual, completely uninfluenced by anyone else. His songs are the kind that last. His contributions are colorfast."

Though he can write in a variety of moods, Arlen is best known for his blues and rhythm songs that have a strong affinity with the emotions of Negroes. Many of his numbers have been written specifically for shows with all-Negro or predominantly Negro casts—the Cotton Club revues, *St. Louis Woman* (and *Free and Easy*), *House of Flowers,* and *Jamaica.* Other musicals, such as *Bloomer Girl* and *Saratoga,* were concerned with Negro themes. Yet Arlen's ability to invest his songs with so much inventiveness and musicianship has kept them from seeming repetitive, and his great theatrical sense has endowed them with an indisputable fitness for the stage.

"Does it work theatrically?" is the question he continually asks himself about his songs. "Does it motivate the action? Is the song, in a sense, a part of the dialogue? Does the music capture character without getting out of the framework of the show?" The hard, relentless questioning of the requirements of his music has, happily, resulted in songs that can be appreciated even apart from the circumstances for which they were written. For though he understands fully the theatrical requirements of music, Arlen has frequently been associated with enterprises that have not always utilized his gifts to their fullest. A dedicated, sensitive artist, he has put the stamp of his own creativity far more on the songs he has written than on the productions for which they were created. The obstacles of a weak libretto cannot be surmounted even by a composer such as Harold Arlen. That so many of his songs have outlasted their original surroundings is a testament to the inherent quality with which they have been endowed.

233

Burton Lane.

Burton Lane

Although *Bloomer Girl* was a success, commitments in Hollywood forced Harburg to remain on the West Coast for the next few years. While there, he continued to think of ideas for the stage. He had tentative ideas for two nonmusical plays, but neither one seemed to work out. One was about a bigoted Southern senator who miraculously turns black and thus becomes a victim of his own discriminatory laws. The other was a fantasy about a leprechaun with three wishes. "Then it occured to me," Harburg recalls, "Why not combine the two stories by having one of the leprechaun's wishes be to turn the senator black? Then I knew I had something!"

Harburg decided to write the story himself in collaboration with Fred Saidy. After finishing the libretto, he approached composer Burton Lane to supply the music. "All it needs is something like *Porgy and Bess*," Harburg told him. Lane, a highly regarded song-writer, but one who had never before attempted anything of this scope, at first felt that Harburg had gone to the wrong man. But Harburg was so positive that Lane eventually joined the project that resulted in *Finian's Rainbow.*

Burton Lane was another composer who had begun his career in the early Thirties by having songs interpolated in revues. He was born in New York City, on February 2, 1912, of well-to-do parents. While still in high school, he showed so much musical talent that J. J. Shubert hired him to compose the score for a proposed edition of the *Greenwich Village Follies.* The sixteen-year-old composer had more than twenty songs ready for the show, but when the intended star, James Barton, fell ill, Shubert abruptly cancelled the production. After getting a job as a pianist at Remick's, Lane became acquainted with many rising young song-writers. One of them, Howard Dietz, liked two of his melodies so much that he put words to them and added the songs to *Three's a Crowd.* The composer was still in his teens when "Forget All Your Books" and "Out in the Open Air" were sung in the revue.

Many of the numbers for the 1931 edition of the *Earl Carroll Vanities* were written by Lane in collaboration with lyricist Harold Adamson. Two years later, Lane went to Hollywood. He remained there until 1954, creating many film songs with such lyricists as Adamson, Harburg, Ted Koehler, Frank Loesser, Alan Jay Lerner, and Ira Gershwin.

During the twenty-one years he lived in California, Lane returned to New York for three Broadway assignments. In 1940, he and Harburg wrote a bright score for *Hold On to Your Hats,* a satire on radio Westerns, in which Al Jolson made a highly acclaimed return to the stage after an absence of almost ten years. Jolson scored a personal hit, but the show lasted only about four months because of the star's ill health at the time. It was his last appearance in a musical comedy. Lane returned to Broadway again in 1944 when he contributed both words and music to Olsen and Johnson's madhouse variety show, *Laffing Room Only.* Created from the same mold as the immensely successful *Hellzapoppin* and *Sons o' Fun,* the attraction is probably best remembered for the song "Feudin' and Fightin'," later made famous by Dorothy Shay.

In 1947, *Finian's Rainbow* brought Lane back to New York for the third time. That its intermingling of fantasy and social comment could cohere so smoothly into a unified musical attests to the uncommon skill brought to it by all those responsible for its creation. The feeling of a message may have been apparent throughout, but *Finian's Rainbow* was never allowed to become a sermon. It was light, it was imaginative, and it had its own brand of simpleminded logic. For example, Finian, an Irishman newly arrived in the state of Missitucky, is anxious to bury a crock of gold at Fort Knox. His

235

reason is that if gold is buried there it will have to grow, for what other purpose would the United States government have to put all of its gold in the ground? Harburg was anxious to make two important points in the story: one was that people would find riches not in burying gold but in trusting one another more, and the other, as exemplified by the situation of the senator, was the inanity of racial intolerance.

The score aided immeasurably in keeping the various elements complementing rather than competing with each other. The Irish motif was found in the wistful "How Are Things in Glocca Morra?" and "Look to the Rainbow," both sung by Ella Logan in her customary Scottish burr. The whimsical spirit of the leprechaun, played by David Wayne, came through in "Something Sort of Grandish" and "When I'm Not Near the Girl I Love." Two rousingly optimistic numbers describing the vision of a bright future were the satirical "When the Idle Poor Become the Idle Rich," and the more impassioned "That Great Come-and-Get-It-Day."

Almost eighteen years elapsed before Burton Lane was once again represented on Broadway. This time it was as collaborator with Alan Jay Lerner on the score for Lerner's production of *On a Clear Day You Can See Forever*. Although faults were found in the book, Lane's contributions

FINIAN'S RAINBOW *(1947). Og, a leprechaun (played by David Wayne), sings a reprise of* "Something Sort of Grandish" *to the children of Rainbow Valley, Missitucky. (Costumes by Eleanor Goldsmith.)*

236

were among the most noteworthy of the season. According to Howard Taubman's verdict in the *Times,* his tunes have "more melodic grace and inventive distinction than has been heard in some years."

Lane has been active in the musical theatre far less frequently than any other major composer who first won recognition in the Thirties. Nevertheless, his scores for *Finian's Rainbow* and *On a Clear Day* unquestionably place him among the most gifted and original of the post-Twenties com-

PHOTO BY BERT ANDREWS

ON A CLEAR DAY YOU CAN SEE FOREVER *(1965). Dr. Mark Bruckner (John Cullum) trying to cure Daisy Gamble (Barbara Harris) of the smoking habit. Wrote Ted Kalem in Time: "Barbara Harris can fumble a cigarette between her teeth like a crazed nicotine addict and fire off machine gun bursts of smoke . . . She can chew grammer like bubble gum, or make English ring with the elegance of George III's crystal."*

posers. It was Yip Harburg who gave him the ultimate accolade. Of all the modern composers, Harburg once said, Burton Lane comes closest to capturing that special effervescence so characteristic in the songs of George Gershwin.

Of the composers discussed in this chapter, Arlen has been the most prolific, though the contributions of Duke and Lane, particularly with respect to their work for *Cabin in the Sky* and *Finian's Rainbow,* have ensured their lasting fame. Yet the inability of these men to continue the pursuit of their careers in the theatre with the constancy of the composers of the first three decades of the century is unfortunate. The drastic reduction in the number of musicals being produced, the length of time that it takes to prepare a musical, and the almost prohibitive cost of such a venture have all been factors resulting in the relative infrequency of their efforts on Broadway.

Another important change has been the growing importance of the librettist. No other writer has appreciated this more than E. Y. Harburg. His entire career has reflected the transformations through which the musical theatre has gone. Starting as a writer of sophisticated lyrics for revues in the early Thirties, he soon moved away from revues to concentrate his attention on book musicals. In the Forties, he originated the plot of *Bloomer Girl* and also directed it. With *Finian's Rainbow,* he became his own librettist, in collaboration with Fred Saidy. The Harburg-Saidy team was also responsible for the books of *Flahooley* (music by Sammy Fain) and *Jamaica* (music by Arlen). In 1961, Harburg supplied both inspiration and outline for *The Happiest Girl in the World,* a short-lived musical satire for which he mated his lyrics to melodies by Jacques Offenbach.

By his growing concern with every phase of a production, Harburg has been able to make his musicals more totally a part of himself than have the composers with whom he has worked. Rather than merely setting words to another man's melody or blocking out the rudiments of a story to hold the songs together, he has become the motivating force behind each production of which he is a part. Usually it is Harburg who first gets the idea and then finds collaborators he believes will be best suited to a particular project. Moreover, particularly in the cases of Harold Arlen and Burton Lane, he has been able to inspire composers to turn out their most successful efforts.

Though he is occasionally accused of injecting too much social consciousness in his plays, "Yip" Harburg is one of the most consistently adventurous men of the theatre today, both in his lyrics and in his librettos. To him, his purpose in writing for the musical stage is neither to provide escapist entertainment nor to depict life realistically. "I don't believe the theatre is a place for photographic reproduction," he says. "That's why I'm attracted to fantasy, to things with a poetic quality. Through fantasy, I feel that a musical can say things with greater effectiveness about life. It's great for pricking balloons, for exploding shibboleths. Of course, I want to send people out of the theatre with the glow of having had a good time, but I also believe the purpose of a musical is to make people think."

Harold Rome.

Harold Rome

THE ECONOMIC CLIMATE of the early Thirties inevitably nurtured the socially conscious revues and musical comedies that came along during the second half of the decade. Of course, there had been such pioneering work as *Strike Up the Band, Of Thee I Sing,* and *Face the Music,* but these did not hit specific individuals or situations; the country had to wait until after the worst years of the Depression for serious topics to again be treated with a certain amount of detachment and humor.

Parade, in 1935, was intended as the first revue of social significance, though its edge was considerably blunted by its sponsor, the Theatre Guild. The season of 1937–1938 provided theatregoers with four political musicals containing viewpoints ranging from mildly liberal to radical: *I'd Rather Be Right* (President Roosevelt and his administration); Marc Blitzstein's *The Cradle Will Rock* (the evils of capitalism and the virtues of the working class); *Hooray for What!* (the need for international disarmament); and *Pins and Needles.*

Of them all, it was *Pins and Needles* that won the largest following. Produced by the International Ladies Garment Workers Union and with a cast composed entirely of union members, the revue ran for more than three years, went through at least three editions, toured the major cities of the

241

United States, and was responsible for giving composer-lyricist Harold Jacob Rome the most auspicious debut of any song-writer of the decade.

Rome was born in Hartford, Connecticut, on May 27, 1908. He began to play the piano at an early age and, in his teens, joined many local dance bands. At Yale, he was a member of the University Orchestra, with which he made four trips to Europe. After graduation, he spent a year at the Yale Law School. Like Cole Porter, he had little interest in poring over law books, and soon switched to the School of Architecture. In 1934, he became a draftsman with an architectural firm in New York. As the Depression was then at its most severe, he augmented his small salary by playing the piano at social functions.

After quitting his job as a draftsman, Rome joined the entertainment staff at Green Mansions, an adult summer camp in upstate New York. There he wrote many topical songs for camp revues. Encouraged by the reception the guests gave his efforts, he returned to New York determined to succeed as a song-writer. Producers and publishers, however, were almost unanimous in their reactions: Nobody, they chorused, wanted to hear songs about the nation's current problems while the economic situation was still so serious. Though he did manage to get a few numbers published—one was sold to Gypsy Rose Lee—it was not until Louis Schaffer, the head of the I.L.G.W.U. drama activities, heard his songs that Rome at last was given his opportunity.

Schaffer was then preparing a revue to be shown at the Labor Stage (the new name of the Princess Theatre), with the cast recruited entirely from the ranks of the union. After assembling all the sketches and songs necessary for the show, Schaffer discovered that his union actors were against doing anything so frivolous as a musical revue. They wanted a grim drama depicting the hardships of the economically exploited masses. In order to convince them that a song-and-dance show would be even more effective in presenting the union's point of view, Schaffer hired a group of W.P.A. actors to perform the show exclusively for the benefit of the cast. With Harold Rome and Earl Robinson providing two-piano accompaniment, the first showing of *Pins and Needles* took place on June 14, 1936, in a small studio above the regular Labor Stage auditorium.

As soon as they saw the sketches and heard Rome's bright, pungent music and lyrics, those who had objected to the entertainment were won over. For a year and a half, the I.L.G.W.U. Players rehearsed almost every night after they had finished their day's work in New York's garment center. They were eager to learn, but their lack of experience and the brevity of rehearsal periods were responsible for many delays. When the show finally had its pre-mière, neither critics nor a large audience turned out to greet it. Within weeks, however, word-of-mouth reports turned *Pins and Needles* into such a popular attraction that the small playhouse soon had a hit equal to those it had once enjoyed during the days of Bolton, Wodehouse, and Kern.

The revue was intelligent and funny, with the enthusiasm of the cast making up for what it may have lacked in professional skill. Perhaps the show's most winning trait was the ability to laugh at the labor movement itself while also, of course, taking jabs at the foibles of those on the other side of the bargaining table. After running about a year and one-half, a somewhat altered version, *Pins and Needles 1939*, was introduced. Later that year, it moved uptown to the larger, on-Broadway Windsor Theatre ($1.65 top) where a third edition, *New Pins and Needles*, was presently displayed. Including all its versions, the show had a run of 1,108 performances, though this impressive record must be "weighted" as the Labor Stage seated only about 300.

"Sing me a song with social significance" demanded the opening chorus in feigned earnestness. Rome obliged with a group of songs that were remarkable in their ability to express a fresh, original viewpoint within a colloquial speech pattern that was completely natural for the untrained performers. "It's Better with a Union Man" was a turn-of-the-century tearjerker given a sly, up-to-date twist; "Nobody Makes a Pass at Me" revealed the plight of the girl whose love life is completely unaided by any of the advertised products she tries; "Sunday in the Park" (as if in answer to Irving Berlin's elegant "Easter Parade") proclaimed the verdant pleasures of Central Park as a haven for the working man; and "One Big Union for Two" expressed eternal love through the language of collective bargaining.

The sketches and songs tried to keep up with the daily headlines as much as possible. "Four Little Angels of Peace" were Hitler, Mussolini, Eden, and an unnamed Japanese. After Munich, the composer substituted Chamberlain

PINS AND NEEDLES (1937). *Two of the "Four Little Angels of Peace": Berni Gould as Hitler and Harry Clark as Stalin. (Setting by S. Syrjala.)*

for Eden. With the signing of the Hitler–Stalin nonaggression pact, another angel was added. "Britannia Waives the Rules" had to be cut when World War II started. In "The Red Mikado," Rome and sketch-writer Joseph Schrank had fun at the expense of both communism and the two jazz versions of the same Gilbert and Sullivan operetta, *The Hot Mikado* and *The Swing Mikado*, then running concurrently in New York.

Even before *Pins and Needles* ended its run, *Sing Out the News,* another topical revue with words and music by Harold Rome, was offered on Broadway. This time, although the view was still from the left of the political stage, the show was a completely professional affair produced by Max Gordon in association with George S. Kaufman and Moss Hart. Rome's observations continued to be remarkably trenchant, but the novelty of his kind of revue had apparently already worn off. Although *Sing Out the News* lasted only three months, it did contain one truly electric number—the exultant "F.D.R. Jones," sung by Rex Ingram and chorus at a joyous Harlem christening.

Rome was inducted into the Army in 1943. During most of his time in the service, he wrote and organized soldier shows. While still in uniform, Rome and Arnold Auerbach, a former radio script-writer, began planning a Broadway revue. The show's theme would be soldiers returning to civilian life, with songs and sketches depicting in a generally lighthearted manner various aspects of life in and out of the Army. Only ex-servicemen, ex-WACs, and ex-USO entertainers would be in the cast, which was headed by Betty Garrett. (Her credentials were numerous appearances in the *G.I. Jane* shows that toured Army bases and hospitals.)

Titled *Call Me Mister,* the revue was presented in the spring of 1946 under the combined sponsorship of Herman Levin (who was to produce *My Fair Lady* ten years later) and Melvyn Douglas. The mood of the show was almost completely optimistic. Although Rome's songs were less concerned with the class struggle, they were equally as original as those of his previous revues. "The important element of a song is neither the words nor the tune, but the basic idea," Rome explained at the time *Call Me Mister* opened. "Take 'Little Surplus Me.' Once I had the picture of the girl pleading with the President to bring back her uniformed boy friends, the rest was merely a matter of variations on the original thesis. Similarly with 'Military Life.' Having conceived the notion that the soldier who went away a jerk might return still a jerk, all that remained was improvisations on the established theme."

The two serious numbers (both sung by Lawrence Winters) in *Call Me Mister* illustrated the composer's sociopolitical outlook. Contrasted with the jubilation of "F.D.R. Jones" in *Sing Out the News,* was the quietly touching tribute to Roosevelt called "The Face on the Dime." There was also a bitter sequence in which Winters, a Negro, after singing of the wartime exploits

244

CALL ME MISTER (1946). Betty Garrett, as a U.S.O. hostess, expresses her opinion of Latin American music in "South America, Take It Away." The attentive soldiers are Alan Manson, Chandler Cowles, George Hall, and Harry Clark.

PHOTO BY EILEEN DARBY—GRAPHIC HOUSE

of the Transportaton Corps in the stirring "Red Ball Express," was the only one of a group of applicants to be refused a job.

Harold Rome was the last of the major revue writers of the Thirties to compose a score for a book musical. In 1950, he and Arthur Kober decided to adapt Kober's play *Having Wonderful Time* into a musical appropriately called *Wish You Were Here*. The story dealt with middle-class New Yorkers on a two-week vacation at a summer camp in the mountains, and it gave Rome the chance to draw from his youthful experiences at Green Mansions.

Wish You Were Here was also an early example of the importance that directors were to assume in the musical theatre during the Fifties. When Joshua Logan agreed to produce the show, he also became its director, co-librettist, and choreographer. His insistence on putting in a $15,000 swimming pool made it impossible to take the musical on the customary tryout tour. Consequently, without the necessary "break-in" period, the play was greeted with generally unfavorable reviews following its June 25, 1952, première.

Logan still thought he had a potential hit. With the cooperation of Kober and Rome, he completely rewrote the script, changed many songs, and had the dances restaged by Jerome Robbins. *Wish You Were Here* became a sell-out within three weeks, and ran for two years. (So many alterations had taken place after its faltering start that Harold Clurman once called it the only experimental theatre left in New York.)

Logan was also associated with Rome on his next musical, *Fanny*. In 1951, Producer David Merrick had brought the property, which was based on Marcel Pagnol's trilogy *Marius, César,* and *Fanny*. The musical took three

245

PHOTO BY SLIM AARONS

WISH YOU WERE HERE (1952). *Joshua Logan directing. So many changes were continually being made even after the show opened that Harold Clurman once called it "the only truly experimental theatre in New York."*

Happy vacationers at Camp Karefree, a summer camp for adults, "where friendships are formed to last a whole lifetime through." In the center are Jack Cassidy, Patricia Marand, and Sheila Bond. (Costumes by Robert Mackintosh; setting by Jo Mielziner.)

PHOTO BY SLIM AARONS

years of preparation before it reached Broadway, with Ezio Pinza and Walter Slezak in the leads. After working more than a year with other writers and composers, Merrick called in Logan, who promptly became co-producer, co-author (with S. N. Behrman), and director. Because of their association on *Wish You Were Here,* Logan brought in Rome.

The score of *Fanny* presented the composer with a greater challenge than any other work for which he had written. Previously, he had been more celebrated for the ingenuity and wit of his lyrics than for his gifts as a composer. For *Fanny* he was called upon to create an expansive, melodious score, matched by lyrics that expressed deep emotions. As Marseilles was the locale and the people were uneducated waterfront characters, it was necessary to give the music a certain French feeling, while keeping the lyrics both simple and direct. Another major problem, according to Logan, was "... how to get jubilation into an essentially tragic story. Here was the tale of two lovers who are so completely separated that it is difficult to dream of them ever getting together. The songs in *Fanny* did not solve the problem completely, but Harold Rome's resourceful score was able to satisfy the audience's need for happy music without sacrificing the integrity of the story."

PHOTO BY ZINN ARTHUR

FANNY *(1954). Ezio Pinza as César and Walter Slezak as Panisse. This was Pinza's last role in the theatre.*

During the run of *Fanny*, it occurred to David Merrick that there had never been a real western musical comedy in the classic good-guys-versus-bad-guys movie tradition. He immediately decided that the time had come to musicalize that durable sagebrush saga, *Destry Rides Again*, and secured both the rights to the story from Universal Pictures and the services of Harold Rome for the score. The musical opened in the spring of 1959 with Andy Griffith as the violence-hating deputy sheriff, and Dolores Gray as the frontier saloon singer. While the show added neither satire nor a new dimension to the familiar tale, it was skillfully staged by Michael Kidd, whose crackling dance routines were among the most exciting of the season. Rome's songs ably captured the spirit of the terrain but, unfortunately, the

DESTRY RIDES AGAIN (1959). *Tom Destry (Andy Griffith) causes Frenchy (Dolores Gray) some momentary embarrassment by accidentally tearing off part of her skirt. The villainous Kent (Scott Brady) thinks it's all rather amusing. (Costumes by Alvin Colt.)*

PHOTO BY FRIEDMAN-ABELES

book offered him little inspiration for a distinguished score.

For *I Can Get It for You Wholesale*, produced by Merrick three years later, Rome returned to the more familiar *Pins and Needles* milieu of New York's Garment District. This time, however, he and librettist Jerome Weidman (who had adapted his own novel) were more concerned with skullduggery among employers than with the social slant of the workers. Seldom has a composer been more perfectly in tune with his subject, with both music and lyrics beautifully conveying the pains and pleasures of toiling along Manhattan's Seventh Avenue. But little could be done to atone for the lack of appeal of the central characters. Wrote John Chapman in the *News*: "I couldn't find one to whom I could give either affection or admiration. Well, I guess there was one—but she is just a minor mouse in the story. She is a harried, frantic, put-upon, homely frump of a secretary, and she is hilariously played by a nineteen-year-old newcomer, Barbra Streisand. Her song, 'Miss Marmelstein,' is the happiest number in Rome's copious score."

The revues that Harold Rome was identified with during the Thirties and Forties were reactions to current events. *Pins and Needles* and *Sing Out the News* were outgrowths of the Depression. *Call Me Mister* reflected the spirit of the country immediately after the war. When timely revues were no longer in style, and Rome at last began to write scores for book shows, he was able to bring to them the same understanding and natural warmth that had shown through in his earlier works. Moreover, to his already well established skill with words, Rome soon added a greater richness of musical style, one that served him with equally winning effect in his scores for *Wish You Were Here, Fanny* and *I Can Get It for You Wholesale*. The ability to express in songs the honest emotions of those who are least articulate has been one of his most distinguishing characteristics. For Rome is, essentially, a people's composer and lyricist, one who, without being sentimental or patronizing, provides the common man with uncommon musical expressions.

Kurt Weill

PHOTO BY HOYNINGEN-HUENE. COURTESY NEW YORK CITY OPERA

250

Kurt Weill

UNLIKE OTHER EUROPEAN-BORN composers who have settled in the United States, Kurt Weill had achieved a worldwide reputation even before he began to write for the American musical theatre. His *Die Dreigro-schenoper* (*The Threepenny Opera*), written in 1928, was performed over 10,000 times throughout Central Europe within a period of five years. It was translated into eighteen languages and, in 1933, even had a brief run on Broadway. The musical was universally accepted as the most revealing depiction of the moral decadence that was then eating away the fabric of society at almost every level all over Europe. Bertolt Brecht's libretto may have been a social preachment but, particularly when combined with Weill's jingly, beer-hall tunes, it emerged as popular entertainment that reflected the cynicism and desperate gaiety of the times.

To the Nazis, however, the work was that of a *Kultur-Bolshevist*, and one of the first things the new regime did when it came to power in Germany in 1933 was to ban the production. Weill and his wife, Lotte Lenya, were soon forced to flee the country. For a time they settled in Paris where the composer quickly learned the techniques of the French theatre. Within two years, he had collaborated with French playwright Jacques Deval on *Marie Galante* and, with fellow-refugee Bertolt Brecht, he composed the ballet *The Seven Deadly Sins*.

Though his career in France seemed assured, Weill was anxious to leave Europe as quickly as possible. He had little confidence that France or England could stand up to Hitler; only in the United States, he felt, was there hope for the future. His opportunity to leave the Continent came in 1935. Max Reinhardt, the Viennese director and producer, was then preparing a Biblical pageant, *The Eternal Road,* for a Broadway production. Knowing of Weill's urgent desire to go to America, he offered the composer the commission of creating the background music.

Almost as soon as he arrived in New York, Weill became so much a part of his adopted country that he made up his mind never to return to Europe. Indeed, it was characteristic of the man, in both his work and in his personal life, that he never looked backward. The challenge of the present was what concerned him, whether it was a new country or a new musical project. His impatience with self-pity, combined with his complete disinterest in anything that was not of immediate concern, enabled him to adjust to every new situation within the shortest possible time and with the most efficient results.

Kurt Weill was born in Dessau, Germany, on March 2, 1900. Like Irving Berlin and Harold Arlen, he was the son of a cantor. As a youth, he showed such musical aptitude that at sixteen he was sent to Berlin to study under Engelbert Humperdinck. When Humperdinck retired from teaching, Weill accepted the post of director of a small opera company at Ludenscheid. During his one year there, he gained valuable experience in every phase of theatrical production.

Weill returned to Berlin in the early Twenties to continue his studies under Ferruccio Busoni. His first important attempts at composition resulted in many concert pieces greatly influenced by the modern atonal technique. At the time, Weill cared little for audience acclaim. His ideas began to change, however, when he was commissioned to compose a children's ballet, *Die Zaubernacht.* Upon seeing the reactions of the children to the work, Weill, with characteristic decisiveness, made up his mind to devote his career to creating music that would make a direct appeal to the largest number of people. "I am not struggling for new forms or new theories," he said in the mid-Twenties. "I am struggling for a new public."

Three years later, Weill's first opera, *Die Protagonist,* with a libretto by playwright Georg Kaiser, won such favorable notice that he received a commission from the Berlin State Opera. This resulted in *Royal Palace,* in which may be detected some of the earliest influences of jazz in an opera.

With *Die Dreigroschenoper* and the even more sardonic *Aufsteig und Fall der Stadt Mahagonny (Rise and Fall of the City of Mahagonny),* the composer broke completely with the classical past. Even the opera house had become too confining for these examples of *Zeitoper,* a form of popular opera created to reflect the spirit of the times in which it was written.

KURT WEILL

After he had come to America in 1935, Weill found that the Broadway theatre offered him a greater latitude than he had ever had before. There was no censorship, no storm troopers, nothing to stand in his way of reaching the wide public he so fervently desired. He reacted to this freedom by shedding some of the astringent pessimism inherent in his German works and by revealing a far greater lyricism than had previously been apparent.

One of the exciting developments of the Broadway theatre during the mid-Thirties was the formation of the Group Theatre, a repertory company dedicated to introducing new works by promising playwrights. Because he admired the aims of the organization, Weill confided in Lee Strasberg, one of the Group's directors, that he would like to work on an original musical play with a dramatist Strasberg would recommend. Strasberg suggested Paul Green. The result of the Weill-Green collaboration was *Johnny Johnson*, a bitter yet funny anti-war "folk legend," with a cast including many who later won fame as both actors and directors: Russell Collins (in the title role), Lee J. Cobb, John (then Jules) Garfield, Robert Lewis, Elia Kazan, Luther Adler, and Morris Carnovsky. The production also marked the first Broadway assignment of musical director Lehman Engel.

JOHNNY JOHNSON (1936). The scene in the French churchyard in which Johnny Johnson, an American soldier, captures a German sniper who has been hiding behind a statue of Christ. When Johnny learns that the German (whose name is also Johnny) longs for peace, he releases him. John Garfield played the German and Russell Collins had the title role. (Setting by Donald Oenslager.)

KNICKERBOCKER HOLIDAY *(1938). Led by Councilman Roosevelt (George Watts), the City Council of New Amsterdam turns against Governor Pieter Stuyvesant (Walter Huston) and refuses to pull the rope that would hang the outspoken Brom Broeck (Richard Kollmar). (Costumes by Frank Bevan; setting by Jo Mielziner.)*

Although *Johnny Johnson* was not a commercial success, its daring fusion of music and satiric fantasy won many champions. At the opening-night performance, Lorenz Hart, who was seated behind Weill, tapped the composer on the shoulder and inquired in mock rage: "What are you trying to do, put people like me out of business?" And Robert Benchley, indignant at the indifference of both critics and the public, particularly in a mediocre theatrical season, exclaimed: "My God, if we don't grab onto something really big when it comes along, even if it does have flaws, the theatre may go right on as it started this year. This is the first anti-war play to use laughing gas in its attack on the stupidity of mankind, and to my mind it is the most effective of all satires in its class."

Knickerbocker Holiday, in 1938, united Kurt Weill with playwright Maxwell Anderson. As both men were deeply concerned with the world situation, they longed to say something pertinent, yet entertaining, about the evils of dictatorship and the value of freedom. To express their convictions they drew modern parallels with the attempts of the tyrannical Pieter Stuyvesant to suppress the liberties of the people of New Amsterdam. The theme of the play was posed in the song, "How Can You Tell an American?" To Anderson and Weill, the answer was simple: an American is someone who loves freedom and hates any restrictions on his thoughts or on his actions.

At the suggestion of director Joshua Logan, the role of Stuyvesant was given to the fifty-four-year-old Walter Huston, a former vaudeville song-and-dance man who had never before appeared in a Broadway musical. Because Huston was living in California when he signed the contract, Weill sent him the following telegram: "WHAT IS RANGE OF YOUR VOICE." The actor's reply came promptly: "I HAVE NO RANGE STOP APPEARING TONIGHT ON BING CROSBY PROGRAM WILL SING SONG FOR YOU." Upon hearing Huston's transcontinental radio audition that night, Weill turned to Anderson and said, "Let's write a sentimental, romantic song for him." Both men went to work at once and within a few hours produced the most enduring number of the show, "September Song."

In spite of its brief run of about four months, *Knickerbocker Holiday* is generally accepted as a significant milestone in the development of the American musical theatre. Apart from its close integration of music and story, it was one of the first musicals to use a historical subject as a means through which pertinent observations could be made about contemporary political problems.

Moss Hart was the one who first thought of the idea of *Lady in the Dark*. Having recently undergone psychoanalysis, he was anxious to write a serious play about the subject and to cast Katharine Cornell in the central role of an emotionally disturbed fashion-magazine editor. As the work progressed, however, he found it taking shape more as a musical. With Miss Cornell eliminated by the play's metamorphosis, the author could think of no other actress for the part than Gertrude Lawrence. Kurt Weill, who was to have written some incidental music for the original concept, readily agreed to supply the entire score, and Ira Gershwin was signed as lyricist for his first Broadway musical since the death of his brother.

Lady in the Dark was an advanced work in both theme and music. Even allowing for the convenient device of keeping the musical portions within the dream sequences until the final scene, the music and lyrics, as Moss Hart has written, were "part and parcel of the basic structure of the play. One cannot separate the play from the music, and vice versa. More than that, the music and lyrics carry the story forward dramatically and psychologically."

The most memorable scene of *Lady in the Dark* takes place in the Circus Dream during the second act. Here the inability of the magazine editor, Liza Elliott, to make up her mind becomes the motivation for a trial presided over by the Ringmaster (Danny Kaye), with the handsome movie star (Victor Mature) as Liza's lawyer. For no apparent reason (except that tongue-

LADY IN THE DARK (1941). *Musical director Maurice Abravanel, composer Kurt Weill, and lyricist Ira Gershwin.*

"As for Gertrude Lawrence," wrote Brooks Atkinson in his review, "she is a goddess, that's all." Miss Lawrence is shown here in the Circus Dream sequence as she related all the misadventures of the unfortunate lady known as Jenny. (Costumes by Irene Sharaff.)

twisting numbers were a Danny Kaye specialty), the Ringmaster rattles off the names of forty-nine Russian composers in thirty-nine seconds in a piece called "Tschaikowsky."* Soon after this feat of vocal dexterity, Liza follows it with her own lubriciously uninhibited "Saga of Jenny," in which she relates all the misfortunes that once befell a lady because she "would make up her mind." Doing "Jenny" so soon after Kaye's ovation-winning rendition was a challenge to Miss Lawrence; she met it by giving an interpretation of such unbounded magnetism that audiences were once again brought to their feet.

Lady in the Dark, which opened January 23, 1941, was the third major musical to move onto Broadway within a period of three months. Following so soon after *Cabin in the Sky* and *Pal Joey*, it inspired Brooks Atkinson to predict: "The American musical stage is a sound basis for a new centrifugal dramatic form, and *Lady in the Dark* takes a long step forward in that direction."

If *One Touch of Venus* was not the daring work usually associated with Kurt Weill, the musical nevertheless provided many unusual touches on the familiar Pygmalion-Galatea theme. The S. J. Perelman libretto may have floundered occasionally between low comedy and highly polished wit, but the songs by Weill and poet-turned-lyricist Ogden Nash maintained a high level of musicianship and verbal ingenuity. Although *One Touch of Venus* was originally written with Marlene Dietrich in mind, the part was eventually given to Mary Martin as her first starring role on Broadway. Apart from the brooding, haunting "Speak Low," the most impressive musical interlude came when Miss Martin, in elegant simplicity, leaned over the back of an ordinary straight chair to describe her ideal man in the tender, amusing (and intentionally ungrammatical) "That's Him."

From the very beginning of his theatrical career, Kurt Weill zealously recruited outstanding writers from other fields to become active in the musical theatre. By the time he began work on the musical version of *Street Scene*, some of his American collaborators had been playwrights Paul Green, Maxwell Anderson, and Edwin Justus Mayer (with whom Weill had adapted the short-lived *Firebrand of Florence* from Mayer's own play, *The Firebrand*), humorist S. J. Perelman, and poet Ogden Nash. For *Street Scene*, produced in 1947, the composer persuaded Elmer Rice to supply the libretto based on his own Pulitzer Prize-winning play, and secured Langston Hughes to write the lyrics. "Not until *Street Scene*," Weill once wrote, "did I achieve a real blending of drama and music in which the singing continues naturally

---

* "Tschaikowsky" was based on a humorous poem called "The Music Hour," which Ira Gershwin had written under the pen name of Arthur Francis. It was published in the June 12, 1924, issue of the old *Life* magazine. Before listing the Russian composer's names, Gershwin introduced them with the following couplet:

> I'll mention some composers who are known to us as Russian.
> Please note them down. Tomorrow we shall have them for discussion.

ONE TOUCH OF VENUS (1943). *Mary Martin singing "That's Him." (Costume by Mainbocher; setting by Howard Bay.)*

STREET SCENE (1947). *Norman Cordon, as the suspicious husband, threatens his wife, Polyna Stoska, as Anne Jeffreys, their daughter, tries to intervene. (Costumes by Lucinda Ballard; setting by Jo Mielziner.)*

where the speaking stops, and the spoken word, as well as the dramatic action, is embedded in the over-all musical structure."

Even though it was billed as "A Dramatic Musical," *Street Scene* was very close to genuine opera. Taking a compassionate look at the varied inhabitants of a single New York tenement (much as DuBose Heyward and George and Ira Gershwin had done with the citizens of Catfish Row in *Porgy and Bess*), the authors created a work that was, in the opinion of critic Olin Downes, "the most important step toward significant American opera yet encountered in the musical theatre." Of its arias, "Somehow I Never Could Believe" (sung by Polyna Stoska) was an overpowering exposition of the causes of a woman's bitterness and frustration, and there were deeply affecting passages in Anne Jeffreys' and Brian Sullivan's duets, "Remember That I Care" and "We'll Go Away Together." The musical even had a "pop" hit, "Moon-faced, Starry-Eyed," energetically danced by Sheila Bond and Danny Daniels over fire hydrants, garbage pails, and a front stoop.

A temporary cessation in the partnership of Alan Jay Lerner and Frederick Loewe enabled Lerner to become associated with Weill for an imaginative musical called *Love Life*. Designated simply as "A Vaudeville," it depicted the disintegration of marriage in the United States—from the colonial era up to that time (1948)—in a series of sketches and vaudeville acts. The couple through whom the story was told never grew any older during the entertainment; they were still the same age in the last scene, when the tensions of modern life had made it increasingly difficult for them to remain in the same blissful matrimonial state as they had been at the play's beginning. If its stagecraft technique occasionally seemed like too much of a theatrical device, *Love Life* was nevertheless a welcome departure from conventional musical fare, containing many sharp observations on marital mores in America.

Weill was reunited with Maxwell Anderson for his last work, *Lost in the Stars*, produced in 1949. For years, Weill and Anderson had been looking for the right story on which to base a musical dealing with racial problems. At the recommendation of Mrs. Oscar Hammerstein II, they read Alan Paton's novel, *Cry, the Beloved Country*, and immediately felt that it was the story they needed. Through this drama of negro-white relations in South Africa, Weill sought to convey a "message of hope that people, through a personal approach, will solve whatever racial problems exist." Avoiding obvious "native" devices in his score, the composer made effective use of music to set the proper emotional atmosphere, though the integration of music as part of the action of the story was never completely realized.

Kurt Weill was only fifty years old when he died of a heart attack on April 3, 1950. During the fifteen years that he devoted himself to the American musical theatre, he brought to it an affection and pride that was, perhaps,

PHOTO BY KARGER-PIX

LOST IN THE STARS (1949). *Rev. Stephen Kumalo (Todd Duncan) visits his brother (Warren Coleman) in Shantytown, outside of Johannesburg, in a vain attempt to enlist his help in finding his missing son. (Setting by George Jenkins.)*

partly motivated by the circumstances responsible for his becoming part of it. His undeviating faith in the commercial theatre was effectively summed up when, in an interview, he said, "You hear a lot of talk about the 'American opera' that's going to come along some day. It's my opinion that we can and will develop a musical-dramatic form in this country, but I don't think it will be called 'opera,' or that it will grow out of the opera which has become a thing separate from the commercial theatre. It will develop from, and remain a part of, the American theatre—'Broadway' theatre, if you like. I'm convinced that many modern composers have a feeling of superiority toward their audiences. But the great 'classic' composers wrote for their contemporary audiences. As for myself, I write for today. I don't give a damn about writing for posterity."

Posterity, however, does give a damn about the writing of Kurt Weill. *Street Scene* and *Lost in the Stars* have become part of the repertory of the New York City Opera Company, and *The Seven Deadly Sins* is one of the most popular attractions of the New York City Ballet Company. *Down in the Valley,* a half-hour opera based on American themes that Weill wrote with Arnold Sundgaard, is continually being performed in schools throughout the country. Kurt Weill concerts are sell-out programs in New York, both at Lewisohn Stadium and at Carnegie Hall.

Just four years after the composer's death, Stanley Chase and Carmen Capalbo raised $10,000 to present an off-Broadway production of Marc Blitzstein's English adaptation of *The Threepenny Opera*. With Lotte Lenya appearing in the same role she had created in Berlin in 1928, the show ran for twelve weeks before it was forced to vacate the theatre due to a prior booking of another play. But interest in *The Threepenny Opera* would not die. In response to genuine public demand, it reopened, a year and a half later, on September 20, 1955. At this writing, it is still being performed at the 299-seat Theatre de Lys.

What is the reason for its continued durability? In the twilight years of the Weimar Republic in Germany, audiences could see in its raffish, sardonic story all the venality and bitterness then so much a part of daily life in Central Europe. An empathy was created between the play and audience that no other work of that period could approach. The social illnesses within the United States thirty years later may not be so pronounced, but they have caused many sociologists to express concern at the decline of moral values within an apparently healthy society. Thus, *The Threepenny Opera* still has something pertinent to say, while, at the same time, delivering its message with broad humor, a certain romantic charm, and an unflagging musical appeal.

Kurt Weill was a complete man of the theatre. The only major composer since Victor Herbert to do his own orchestrations, he was also vitally interested in every phase of theatre production. Moreover, from his very first American score, he was a motivating force in organizing and giving direction to every musical with which he was associated. Never lured to Hollywood for a lengthy stay, this soft-spoken, timid-looking man was able to devote all his considerable energies to the creation of a popular musical theatre that, he felt, had as its essence "a simple, strong story told in musical terms, inter-

THE THREEPENNY OPERA (1954). *Lotte Lenya, Kurt Weill's widow, as Jenny. As Jay Harrison wrote: "During the second act, Lotte Lenya stepped to the front of the stage to sing her air about Pirate Jenny. At that moment the miniature confines of the theatre stretched and were replaced by a broad and sweeping arena of genuine sentiment. For that's what art can do, and that's what an artist does."*

weaving the spoken word and the sung word so that the singing takes over naturally whenever the emotion of the spoken word reaches a point where the music can 'speak' with greater effectiveness."

Weill's devotion to the commercial theatre never made him deaf to uncommercial ideas. In fact, the theory of the *Zeitoper* theatre that he had brought to such acceptance in Germany continued to dominate his thinking in his American works. Though he believed in the mass appeal of music, he would never condescend to his audiences. Nothing was too daring for him. He built his musicals around such "unpopular" subjects as war, dictatorship, psychoanalysis, tenement living, race relations, and political and moral decay. That so many of his works are still performed today attests not only to the durability of the popular theatre in which Weill had so much faith, but also to his own indestructible place in it.

Richard Rodgers and Oscar Hammerstein II.

CHAPTER SEVENTEEN

Richard Rodgers
and Oscar Hammerstein II

A̲T A FEW SECONDS past eight-thirty on the evening of March 31, 1943, the house lights at the St. James theatre dimmed, the excited chatter of the audience died down, musical director Jacob Schwartzdorf* raised his baton, and the orchestra struck up the overture to the first New York performance of *Oklahoma!*

Everyone connected with the production had reason to feel especially apprehensive at that moment. To Theresa Helburn and Lawrence Langner, the co-directors of the Theatre Guild which produced it, the new work represented their last hope. The once affluent Guild had only $30,000 in the bank when it occurred to Miss Helburn that a twelve-year-old play by Lynn Riggs, *Green Grow the Lilacs*, might make a good musical. A series of theatrical failures had depleted the number of financial backers who would even consider investing in a Guild project; countless time-consuming auditions had to be given before, little by little, the required amount was raised.

To actors Alfred Drake, Joan Roberts, and Celeste Holm, *Oklahoma!* was their first opportunity to be seen in major roles in a Broadway musical. To director Rouben Mamoulian, it was a challenge to repeat the great success he had achieved with *Porgy and Bess*, his last Broadway assignment more

* During the run of *Oklahoma!*, Mr. Schwartzdorf anglicized his name to Jay S. Blackton.

than seven years before. To choreographer Agnes de Mille, it was the first real chance to create something meaningful in the musical theatre.

To composer Richard Rodgers and librettist-lyricist Oscar Hammerstein II, *Oklahoma!* had probably the greatest significance of all. For twenty-five years, Rodgers had never written a note with any lyricist other than Lorenz Hart. They had been an inseparable team that had created some of the greatest musical comedy scores ever heard on Broadway. It was almost impossible to think of one without the other. As for Hammerstein, though he had had many successes in the Twenties, his record since *Music In the Air*, in 1932, had consisted of an almost unbroken chain of failures.

The new partners also knew they were giving the public a work that broke with conventional musical comedy on many levels. While it was no longer an innovation to begin a show without a high-kicking chorus line, it was unusual for the curtain to rise on a simple farm scene of a woman sitting alone on the stage churning butter, with the opening song, "Oh, What a Beautiful Mornin'," begun offstage by the leading baritone. About forty minutes later, when the dancing girls finally did arrive, they were all garbed in correct, though less-than-appealing, period costumes. No great conflicts were posed in Act I; the action was concerned primarily with finding out which man, Curly McLain or Jud Fry, would take Laurey Williams to a

OKLAHOMA! *(1943). The Post Cards in Agnes de Mille's dream ballet, "Laurey Makes Up Her Mind": Joan McCracken, Kate Friedlich, Margit DeKova, Bobby Barrentine, and Vivian Smith. (Costumes by Miles White; setting by Lemuel Ayers.)*

PHOTO BY VANDAMM

PHOTO BY VANDAMM

OKLAHOMA! (1943). *The final scene just before Curly and Laurey (Alfred Drake and Joan Roberts) drive off in the surrey with the fringe on top. Kneeling in front of the happy couple is Joseph Buloff as Ali Hakim, the peddler. Other well-wishers are Marc Platt (Chalmers), George Church (Jess), Katharine Sergava (Ellen), Lee Dixon (Will Parker), Celeste Holm (Ado Annie), Betty Garde (Aunt Eller), Owen Martin (Cord Elam), and four of the bridesmaids. (Costumes by Miles White; setting by Lemuel Ayers.)*

The lively "Farmer and the Cowman" dance at the party at the Skidmore ranch. Photo below is of the National Company which toured for ten and a half years, beginning in New Haven, October 15, 1943, and ending in Philadelphia, May 1, 1954. It was seen in 153 cities in the United States and 10 in Canada, with frequent return performances in most of the larger cities. In 1951, it was presented in Berlin, Germany, as part of the International Theatre Festival. The longest run of the National Company was 60 weeks in Chicago.

PHOTO BY VANDAMM

dance. The second act introduced only three new songs, all the others being reprised from the first.

Many of the facts concerning the production were known to the audience at the first-night performance. Indeed, as the reports from Boston—where the show had opened under the title of *Away We Go!*—were not overwhelmingly enthusiastic, there were empty seats at the première. But almost as soon as they heard the rich, true baritone of Alfred Drake singing "Oh, What a Beautiful Mornin'," the audience succumbed to the open-air charm of the production. After the intermission, as the people were returning to their seats for the second act, Hammerstein recalls that "the glow was like the light from a thousand lanterns. You could *feel* the glow, it was that bright."

The critical reception the next morning was equally incandescent. "Wonderful," exclaimed Lewis Nichols of the *Times*. "Jubilant and enchanting," cheered Howard Barnes of the *Herald Tribune*. "The most thoroughly and attractive American musical comedy since *Show Boat*," was the verdict of the *News's* Burns Mantle. To Burton Rascoe of the *World-Telegram*, it was "fresh, lively, colorful and enormously pleasing." Wolcott Gibbs of *The New Yorker* happily admitted, "I feel nothing but the greatest affection for everybody in it. To the Theatre Guild my gratitude is practically boundless."

Oklahoma! ran for five years and nine weeks, to achieve a total run of 2,212 performances. Until it was surpassed by *My Fair Lady*, this held the record as the greatest number of continuous performances ever achieved by a musical on Broadway.

The first lyric Hammerstein wrote for *Oklahoma!* was for "Oh, What a Beautiful Mornin'." "When Oscar handed it to me," Rodgers recalls, "and I read it for the first time, I was a little sick with joy because it was so lovely and so right. When you're given words like 'the corn is as high as a elephant's eye,' you've got something to say musically." In its happy description of a sun-drenched morning on a farm in the American Southwest, the song set the proper mood for both play and audience.

The mood continued throughout. Early in the first act there was need for a love duet between the hero and the heroine. As they had just had a quarrel, however, it was necessary for them to express their emotions in an indirect way. Rodgers and Hammerstein adroitly solved the problem in "People Will Say We're in Love" by having the boy and girl warn each other against appearing too friendly lest they give people the impression that they are really in love. "The Surrey with the Fringe on Top" was a brilliant piece of scene painting in the way it fused music and lyric to convey the simple pleasures of a young couple riding in a horse and buggy. In "Pore Jud," the authors succeeded in creating something both ludicrous and touching in the imagined death of the story's villain. As a finale, they produced a roaring title song that was so charged the audience could almost feel the wind come sweeping down the plain.

Apart from the charm and inventiveness of the individual songs, what was unique about *Oklahoma!* was the synthesis of its component parts into a complete theatrical entity of great beauty and imagination. Everything fit into place. For the first time, not only were songs and story inseparable, but the dances devised by Agnes de Mille heightened the drama by revealing the subconscious fears and desires of the leading characters.

One factor in the success of *Oklahoma!* that cannot be overlooked was the attitude of the American people at the time it was presented. World War II was more than a year old when the musical opened, and those who remained at home were becoming increasingly aware of the heritage they enjoyed as a free people. Seeing the happier, sunnier days that were so much a part of this heritage gave spectators both an escape from daily headlines and a feeling of optimism for the future.

Rodgers was forty years old and Hammerstein forty-seven when *Oklahoma!* began its historic run on Broadway. Though they had never written together professionally before, they had known each other almost all of their lives. In fact, Rodgers had met Hammerstein about a year before he met Larry Hart. Mortimer Rodgers, Dick's older brother and Oscar's fraternity brother, had taken Dick to see a Columbia Varsity Show in which Hammerstein was appearing. Later, backstage, the awestruck twelve-year-old Rodgers was introduced to his future partner, then a worldly nineteen-year-old Junior.

Oscar Greeley Clendenning Hammerstein was born July 12, 1895, in New York City. Named for his paternal grandfather, the opera impressario and producer of *Naughty Marietta*, young Oscar soon adopted the "II" in order to rid himself of the cumbersome middle names. His father, William Hammerstein, was the manager of the Victoria Theatre, a vaudeville house owned by Oscar I. It was there that the youth first experienced the fascination of the theatre. But his parents were well aware of the hazards of show business and thought that their son might be happier if he became a lawyer. At Columbia, Oscar's first writing for the stage was an additional scene in the Varsity Show of 1916, *The Peace Pirates*, in which both he and Lorenz Hart appeared.

Even though the theatre was becoming increasingly important to him, Hammerstein acceded to his parents wishes and entered Columbia Law School. After a few months, however, he left to enter the professional theatre. His uncle, producer Arthur Hammerstein, gave him his first job as stage manager for three Rudolf Friml musicals—*You're in Love*, *Sometime*, and *Tumble In*.

Hammerstein also continued to be active in Columbia Varsity Shows.

He shared credit for writing the book and lyrics of the 1917 edition, *Home, James,* and the following year assumed full responsibility for the book, lyrics, and direction of the "War Show," *Ten for Five.* He was also on the committee that-chose Rodgers and Hart's *Fly with Me* as the Varsity Show of 1920. In addition to having the first complete Rodgers and Hart score, the musical also had the first song by Rodgers and Hammerstein, "Room for One More," a rather debonair piece with just a touch of John Donne in the lyric:

> My heart is an airy castle
>   Filled with girls I adore.
> My brain is a cloud of memories
>   of peaches galore.
> There were Jane and Molly,
>   And Ruth and Sue;
> Camilla, Kit,
>   and Patricia, too.
> My heart is filled to the brim with you—
> But there's always room for one more!

In 1919, Hammerstein created his first professional work for the theatre, a nonmusical play called *The Light.* It lasted four performances in New Haven, where it was described by one critic as *"The Light* that failed." The following year, Hammerstein wrote the book and lyrics for his first musical, *Always You,* with music by Herbert Stothart. The show had a very brief Broadway run. Because Hammerstein exhibited far greater talent as a lyricist than as a librettist, Arthur Hammerstein, who had produced both of his nephew's plays, suggested that he collaborate with the more experienced Otto Harbach, who had written both book and lyrics for most of the early Friml operettas. Their maiden effort, *Tickle Me,* had a good run due chiefly to its star, Frank Tinney. Later they worked on four of the leading musicals of the Twenties—*Wildflower, Rose-Marie, Sunny,* and *The Desert Song.* Still later, as the sole author of both libretto and lyrics, Hammerstein joined Jerome Kern in creating *Show Boat, Sweet Adeline, Music In the Air,* and *Very Warm for May.*

When Rodgers first proposed to Hammerstein that they collaborate on the musical version of *Green Grow the Lilacs,* the librettist was immediately enthusiastic—he had already tried in vain to interest Jerome Kern in the same project. Rodgers believed that their basically similar outlook on the theatre and on life itself would help to make theirs a harmonious partnership. With Larry Hart, it had been a matter of combining warm, tender melodies with frequently biting lyrics. With Hammerstein, it would now be a matter of combining these same musical qualities with lyrics that also possessed great warmth and tenderness. This fact, coupled with Rodgers' sound musician-ship, his explorative nature, and his maturity as a composer, indicated how well he would be able to suit his style to that of his new collaborator. To a writer of such innate gifts, turning from the sardonic quality of a *Pal Joey*, or the slickness of a *By Jupiter*, to the rustic pleasures of an *Oklahoma!* was both natural and, perhaps, even inevitable.

The lyrics of Oscar Hammerstein II differ from those of Lorenz Hart in many ways, just as in appearance, working habits, and temperament, the men themselves were entirely different. For example, unless it is something like "Thou Swell," it is hard to recall a dialect lyric by Hart. Hammerstein, however, has always made use of dialects and idioms; his rare gift for en-hancing the varied, colloquial speech patterns of an Oklahoma cowboy or a Siamese monarch is equally as brilliant as Hart's more facile ability with polysyllabic and internal rhymes. A Hammerstein lyric seldom calls attention to itself; at its best it seems to be the spontaneous and honest expression of the character who sings it. Yet there is always an inherent quality that once prompted Irving Berlin to remark, "The difference between Oscar and the rest of us lyric writers is that he is a poet." Moreover, Hammerstein has been able to convey his basic philosophy more firmly in his work than did Hart. "I believe not that the whole world and all of life is good," he has said, "but I do believe that so much of it is good, and my inclination is to emphasize that side of life. It's a natural inclination, not one that I've developed."

Shortly after *Oklahoma!* opened, the team split up temporarily— Rodgers to produce the new version of *A Connecticut Yankee* and Hammer-stein to complete work on *Carmen Jones*, adapted from Georges Bizet's opera *Carmen*. While adhering faithfully to the original tempos (except in the wildly exciting "Beat out Dat Rhythm on a Drum"), Hammerstein updated the story more than one hundred years and changed the characters and locale from Basques in southern Spain to Negroes in the southern United States. What resulted was a vividly idiomatic theatrical piece, beautifully sung and acted, and stunningly produced.

Rodgers and Hammerstein resumed their partnership to create *Carousel*, a musical version of Ferenc Molnar's play, *Liliom*. As in *Oklahoma!*, it was Theresa Helburn of the Theatre Guild who first suggested the idea. At first, the partners thought it was too tragic for the musical stage, but they finally decided that the story could be made acceptable by adding a strong note of hopefulness at the end. They also felt that the play's locale of Budapest should be changed to somewhere in the United States; Rodgers' suggestion of the New England coast met with a favorable response because they could then have choruses of mill workers, sailors, and fishermen. Another task was in keeping the leading character, a carnival barker, basically sympathetic even though he is shiftless and frequently unattractive. But the authors were able

CAROUSEL (1945). Mrs. Mullin, the owner of the carousel, warns Julie Jordan and Carrie Pipperidge to stay away from her barker, Billy Bigelow. John Raitt, Jean Casto, Jan Clayton, and Jean Darling. (Costumes by Miles White; setting by Jo Mielziner.)

to treat the theme with so much insight and compassion that the work emerged as a remarkably affecting musical drama, one that could be accepted on its individual merits without comparison to the play from which it had been adapted.

The use of music as in integral part of the story was maintained to an even greater degree than in the authors' first collaboration. Early in the play, when two young girls, Julie Jordan and Carrie Pipperidge, are seated on a park bench, their dialogue is first synchronized over the music. As their conversation continues, it develops naturally into song: first the duet, "You're a Queer One, Julie Jordan," and then Carrie's starry-eyed revelation that she is in love with Mr. Snow. Shortly thereafter, Julie meets Billy Bigelow, the barker. Because it is too soon for them to admit their love, Rodgers and Hammerstein created "If I Loved You," a song in which the characters imagined how they would act if they really were in love.

As with "Oh, What a Beautiful Mornin'," "June Is Bustin' Out All Over" was inspired by the effect of weather. However, while the song in *Oklahoma!* was a lazy, arm-stretching ode to the beauties of a farm in summertime, the song in *Carousel* is a sprightly account of the odd effects summer has on the behavior of normally well-adjusted individuals. The final feeling of hope, so essential to the story, is conveyed through the simple, moving hymn, "You'll Never Walk Alone."

The most ambitious musical undertaking of the score was Billy Bigelow's "Soliloquy," which had taken Hammerstein several weeks to write and Rodgers just two hours to compose. The song contains many contrasting melodic and emotional themes as the barker imagines what it would be like to be the father of a boy and what it would be like to be the father of a girl. Expressing the frequently conflicting feelings of the joys and fears of fatherhood, the authors created one of the most probing expositions of a man's inner thoughts ever written for the Broadway stage.

In addition to its Theatre Guild sponsorship, *Carousel* kept intact most of the production staff that had worked on *Oklahoma!* Rouben Mamoulian directed, Agnes de Mille did the choreography, and Miles White designed the costumes. Again the cast consisted of comparatively unknown performers, among them John Raitt, Jan Clayton, Murvyn Vye, Jean Darling, and, from *Oklahoma!*, Bambi Linn. The new musical opened on April 19, 1945, at the Majestic Theatre, directly across the street from the St. James where *Oklahoma!* was playing. Thus, for about two years, Rodgers and Hammerstein had two musicals facing each other on West 44th Street.

CAROUSEL *(1945). The final scene of the musical in which the graduating class of a local school sings "You'll Never Walk Alone." Bambi Linn, as Louise, is seated at the far right of the front row. At the far right of the stage are Jan Clayton, John Raitt, and Jay Velie. (Costumes by Miles White; setting by Jo Mielziner.)*

PHOTO BY VANDAMM

Allegro, produced by the Theatre Guild in 1947, was Rodgers and Hammerstein's first original musical play. Directed entirely by Agnes de Mille, it was a boldly experimental work detailing the life of a young doctor from his birth to his thirty-fifth year. The authors used the story to probe the reasons why dedicated men sometimes begin to lose their integrity after they have won success. "I wanted to write a large, universal story, and I think I overestimated the physchological ability of the audience to identify itself with the leading character," Hammerstein admits.

The story was told with many original theatrical effects, particularly in the elimination of formal sets and in the use of a modern Greek chorus to comment on the happenings in the play. The authors also made a deliberate attempt to make the score serve the function of the plot, although some pieces, "A Fellow Needs a Girl," "So Far" (the only number that was not germane to the story), and "The Gentleman Is a Dope," have won favor as individual popular songs.

Allegro had the critics divided. Brooks Atkinson thought it "just missed the final splendor of a perfect work of art," while Howard Barnes felt it was a "show to be remembered with *Show Boat* and *Oklahoma!*" However, Wolcott Gibbs referred to it as "spectacular banality," and George Jean Nathan called it "as pretentious as artificial jewelry, and just as valuable."

ALLEGRO *(1947). "Yatata, yatata, yatata, yatata" sing the guests at a party at the home of Dr. and Mrs. Joseph Taylor. John Battles and Roberta Jonay, as the host and hostess, are in the center foreground. John Conte, as Joe's best friend, is third from the left holding the brandy snifter. (Costumes by Lucinda Ballard.)*

PHOTO BY VANDAMM

SOUTH PACIFIC *(1949). Mary Martin, Ezio Pinza, and "Some Enchanted Evening."*

South Pacific, which opened in 1949, is probably the most universally admired achievement of Rodgers and Hammerstein. In a realistic wartime setting, they created a warm, credible romance between a worldly French planter and a naïve Army nurse from Little Rock, while managing to keep this somewhat idyllic relationship in perfect balance with the far-from-idyllic circumstances that brought them together.

The idea of turning James A. Michener's collection of stories, *Tales of the South Pacific,* into a dramatic work first occurred to Kenneth MacKenna, then the head of M-G-M's story department. When the studio decided against filming it, MacKenna suggested to his friend, Joshua Logan, that it would make an excellent property for the stage. Logan read the book and took the idea to producer Leland Hayward; when it seemed to be developing into a musical, they approached Rodgers and Hammerstein. All four men agreed to become associated as co-producers, with Logan also serving as director. Originally, the libretto was to have been written entirely by Hammerstein, but because of Logan's experience in the Navy, he joined Hammerstein as co-author. One thing everyone was agreed on from the start: there would be no formal choreography to jar the mood.

Almost four months were devoted to conferences before a word or a note was put on paper. The tale they decided to use for the story was the one called "Fo' Dollah," which related the unhappy love affair between Lieutenant Joe Cable and a Tonganese girl, Liat. The writers soon felt, however, that there was too much *Madama Butterfly* in the romance to make it acceptable as the main plot. Another tale, "Our Heroine," about the planter Emile DeBecque and the nurse Nellie Forbush, seemed to work out better. The story of Cable and Liat was retained as a secondary theme and the two stories were fused by adding the dramatic situation of Cable and DeBecque going off together on a secret mission behind enemy lines.

For the part of DeBecque, Rodgers and Hammerstein needed a mature man with an excellent singing voice. When they heard that Metropolitan Opera basso Ezio Pinza was anxious to appear in a Broadway musical, they promptly signed him to a contract. For Nellie, they chose Mary Martin, who had just finished touring in the National Company of *Annie Get Your Gun*, another Rodgers and Hammerstein production.

The skill with which the action flowed from the music just as smoothly as the music flowed from the action prompted some music critics to liken Rodgers' technique to that of an operatic composer. Moreover, the authors created each song to fit perfectly with the occasion and the character singing it. Nellie's straightforward, buoyant, warmhearted quality is expressed through "A Cockeyed Optimist," "I'm Gonna Wash That Man Right outa My Hair," and "I'm in Love with a Wonderful Guy." In fact, this last song

SOUTH PACIFIC *(1949). Myron McCormick leads the Seabees in singing "There Is Nothing like a Dame." (Setting by Jo Mielziner.)*

276

had such a contagious effect on audiences that Harold Clurman once wrote: "When Mary Martin tells us, with radiant good nature, 'I'm in love, I'm in love, I'm in love with a wonderful guy,' one doesn't murmur 'Who cares?' but 'Congratulations, congratulations, congratulations to you both!' '"

DeBecque's impulsive, romantic emotions come through in his ardent affirmation of love at first sight, "Some Enchanted Evening," and in the touching song of a fleeting romance, "This Nearly Was Mine." The raucous, restless Seabees beautifully contrast this idealized attitude with their single-minded desires in the rollicking "There Is Nothing like a Dame." The haunting dissonance of "Bali Ha'i" (which the composer wrote in less than ten minutes during lunch one day) captures the flavor of the entire South Pacific, while "Younger Than Springtime" and the plea for understanding, "Carefully Taught," give meaning to the character of the earnest young Joe Cable.

South Pacific had a New York run of 1,925 performances and, until *My Fair Lady*, held the record for the highest gross receipts ($9,000,000) of any Broadway musical. In 1950, it became the second musical ever to win the Pulitzer Prize for drama. As the *Herald Tribune* editorialized, it was one award that "will receive confirming cheers from coast to coast."

After traveling to Oklahoma, New England, the Middle West, and the South Pacific, Rodgers and Hammerstein journeyed to the Far East in 1951 for *The King and I*. The play was adapted from the book, *Anna and the King of Siam* by Margaret Landon, which had been based on the real adventures of a Victorian Englishwoman who went to Siam to become tutor and governess to the royal children. The novel made such an impression on Gertrude Lawrence that she approached Rodgers and Hammerstein about adapting it as a musical for her. Miss Lawrence was persuasive, and the partners were especially intrigued by the prospect of doing a play with an Oriental locale.* Finding an actor to play the part of the king proved to be more difficult. They finally decided on a little-known, bald-headed actor named Yul Brynner who, for his audition, sat cross-legged on the stage, played a guitar, and sang gypsy songs.

The possibility of creating a story around the characters of the straight-laced Anna Leonowens and the semibarbaric monarch fascinated Rodgers and Hammerstein. "The intangibility of their strange union," they once wrote, "was a challenge to us as librettist and composer. In dealing with them musically, we could not write songs which said 'I love you' or even 'I love him' or 'I love her.' We were dealing with two characters who could indulge themselves only in oblique expressions of their feeling for each other, since they themselves do not realize exactly what these feelings mean."

---

* Gertrude Lawrence died on September 6, 1952, during the run of *The King and I*. She was succeeded by Constance Carpenter.

PHOTO BY VANDAMM

PHOTO BY VANDAMM

THE KING AND I *(1951). The royal Siamese children bow down as the king enters their classroom. Standing are Gertrude Lawrence, Yul Brynner, and Dorothy Sarnoff. (Costumes by Irene Sharaff; setting by Jo Mielziner.)*

To the music of "Shall We Dance?," Gertrude Lawrence teaches Yul Brynner how couples dance in Western countries. Wrote John Mason Brown: "Her incredible grace remains with her as she moves about in her great hoopskirts. So do her glamour, her beauty, and her charm."

Again Rodgers and Hammerstein created a score to implement the action and to reveal characters and motivations, but at times with even greater effectiveness than in previous works. The king's soliloquy, "A Puzzlement," so different from the emotional outpouring of Billy Bigelow in *Carousel*, illuminates much of the personality of the untutored yet crafty ruler; "My Lord and Master" is a moving expression of pent-up secret defiance; the light, dainty "Getting to Know You" is an affirmative answer to Cable's troubled "Carefully Taught" in *South Pacific*; Anna's "Hello, Young Lovers" is a gentle, eloquent song of consolation and encouragement.

No better example of the way Rodgers and Hammerstein use a song to illuminate a dramatic situation can be found than the scene from *The King and I* in which Lady Thiang, the king's number-one wife, pleads with Anna to remain at court after she has decided to leave. Nothing can sway the determined governess. Then, as a final effort, Lady Thiang sings "Something Wonderful." In the song, while admitting all the ruler's faults, she emphasizes his hopes and aspirations and expresses her own belief that with Anna's help he could accomplish "something wonderful." This alone changes Anna's mind, and she agrees to remain at court.

The exotic locales of *South Pacific* and *The King and I* made Rodgers and Hammerstein anxious to try something completely different. As both men had been stagestruck from early youth, they decided to express their feelings about the theatre in a modern musical comedy. *Me and Juliet*, produced in 1953, was their valentine to show business. For their cast, they chose such bright young performers as Isabel Bigley, Bill Hayes, and Joan McCracken, and for their director, George Abbott.

PHOTO BY EILEEN DARBY—GRAPHIC HOUSE

ME AND JULIET *(1953). A tense moment backstage, as Bob, the electrician (Mark Dawson), warns Larry, the assistant stage manager (Bill Hayes), to keep away from his girl. In the center of the group of onlookers are Joan Mc-Cracken and Arthur Maxwell. (Costumes by Irene Sharaff.)*

Hammerstein's libretto was his first original script since *Allegro*. Unfortunately, it was an occasionally awkward combination of backstage story and onstage story that never quite succeeded in fitting together as a completely realized plot. The real distinction of the production was the spectacular scenic effects devised by Jo Mielziner, which enabled audiences to see both backstage and onstage simultaneously. "No Other Love," originally written as a theme for Rodgers' thirteen-hour television score for *Victory at Sea,* was the song with the greatest popularity.

Pipe Dream, in 1955, had the shortest run of any Rodgers and Hammerstein musical—246 performances. Originally, the rights to do a musical version of John Steinbeck's *Sweet Thursday* were held by producers Cy Feuer and Ernest Martin; when they were unable to secure Frank Loesser to write the score, they suggested to Rodgers and Hammerstein that it might be suitable for them. R & H agreed, but the public did not. A leisurely story with little conflict, *Pipe Dream* took such a warmhearted look at the denizens of a West Coast skid row that there was little opportunity for theatrical excitement or genuine gaiety. In the leading female role of the owner of a brothel, the Metropolitan's Helen Traubel found herself in rather strange surroundings.

In 1957, playwright Joseph Fields read the novel, *The Flower Drum Song*, by Chin Y. Lee, and felt that it was an almost-perfect property for the stage. After securing the rights, he and his friend Oscar Hammerstein discussed the possibility of turning it into a musical. Hammerstein believed that while it did not have a strong plot, it was "strong on character and background, like a Chinese *Life with Father*. I just fell in love with it." With Rodgers in agreement, Hammerstein and Fields then became collaborators on the libretto.

PIPE DREAM *(1955). Helen Traubel leads the group in "The Bums' Opera." Seated at the left are Mike Kellin and George Wallace. (Costumes by Alvin Colt; setting by Jo Mielziner.)*

PHOTO BY KARGER—PIX

FLOWER DRUM SONG *(1958). Oscar Hammerstein II leans across the footlights to polish a lyric.*

Flower Drum Song opened on December 1, 1958. It told a placid, somewhat predictable tale of the conflicts between Old World and New World Chinese living in San Francisco's Chinatown. Miyoshi Umeki, who was born in Japan, played the part of a tradition-bound Chinese girl, while Pat Suzuki, an American of Japanese descent, played a Chinese-American strip-tease dancer. Of the songs, the masterfully constructed "I Enjoy Being a Girl" has probably become the most popular, but the gliding, pseudo-Oriental "You Are Beautiful" and the searching lament, "Love, Look Away," are equally fine examples of the art of Rodgers and Hammerstein. *Flower Drum Song* was a box-office success in spite of wide differences among the critics— from Robert Coleman's "everything about it is just right," to Brooks Atkinson's "a pleasant interlude," to Kenneth Tynan's "a world of woozy song."

Even before the opening of *Flower Drum Song*, Rodgers and Hammerstein had become associated with one of those rare productions that seems, from the outset, to be incapable of failure. Theatre director Vincent J. Donehue, after being approached by Paramount Pictures to direct a movie based on a German film, *The Trapp Family Singers*, became convinced that the story should be done only as a Broadway musical. Once the film company allowed

FLOWER DRUM SONG (1958). *Pat Suzuki and the chorus of the Celestial Bar singing of the wonders of Grant Avenue, the main street of San Francisco's Chinatown. (Costumes by Irene Sharaff; setting by Oliver Smith.)*

its option to lapse, Donehue contacted Mary Martin; as soon as she saw the German film, she too became excited about the project.

Securing the rights, however, turned out to be rather difficult. Miss Martin's husband, Richard Halliday, spent eight fruitless months trying to locate Baroness Von Trapp, who was somewhere in the South Pacific doing missionary work. Eventually, he found her in an Austrian hospital, where she was being treated for malaria. Co-producer Leland Hayward made six trips to Munich before he came to terms with the German film company that had made the original movie. Then the producer had to search for the widely scattered Trapp children to secure their permission to be portrayed on the stage.

After all of this preliminary work was over, there was still the important task of finding the writers best suited to tell the story of the courageous Trapp family. The first to be signed were librettists Howard Lindsay and Russel Crouse. For the score, the producers wanted to use the authentic folk and religious songs that the family actually sang in its concerts, plus some additional songs. When Hayward suggested to Rodgers and Hammerstein that they supply the new material, the partners were against the idea. If you are going to use authentic Trapp family music, that's fine, Rodgers told the producer; the important thing is that old songs should never be mixed with new. It did not take Hayward long to come to a decision: if Rodgers and Hammerstein would supply an entirely new score, he would be glad to postpone production until they had completed *Flower Drum Song*.

The effect of the new alliance was not hard to foresee. The combination of Mary Martin and Rodgers and Hammerstein (who also became co-producers) was enough to guarantee an advance ticket sale for *The Sound of Music* of $3,325,000, the highest ever achieved for a Broadway production.

Opening on November 16, 1959, the play that audiences waited for so eagerly was cheerful, wholesome entertainment, possibly more in the style of a Sigmund Romberg operetta than in the integrated style that Rodgers and Hammerstein themselves had done so much to develop. Wisely, the team decided against a formal overture. Instead, nuns at an abbey sang a moving *a capella* "Preludium," which helped set the tone and spirit of the play. The title song told appealingly of the beauties of music and nature, while a bubbly quartet, "Maria," was described by Walter Kerr as having "the lilt and sprightliness proper to lucky princesses living in an enchanted castle." Of the

THE SOUND OF MUSIC *(1959). To allay the Van Trapp children's fears during a storm. Maria (Mary Martin) teaches them a song about "The Lonely Goatherd." (Costumes by Lucinda Ballard; setting by Oliver Smith.)*

PHOTO BY FRIEDMAN-ABELES

numbers Miss Martin sang with the seven Trapp children, the most popular has become "Do-Re-Mi," a brisk march which served to teach the children the rudiments of music by having the lyric develop from the notes on the scale. "My Favorite Things," possibly the loveliest song in the play, deftly employed an abruptly contrasting release to emphasize the wistfulness of the chief melodic line. The moving theme of the story, "Climb Ev'ry Mountain," had something of the simple faith expressed in "You'll Never Walk Alone" from *Carousel*.

Again, as in most recent Rodgers and Hammerstein works, the critics were divided. Although he lamented the book, Brooks Atkinson found that "the sound of music is always moving. Occasionally, it is also glorious." Richard Watts, Jr., thought the entire production "wonderfully endearing," and John McClain of the *Journal-American* called it "the most mature product of the Rodgers-Hammerstein team." However, Walter Kerr felt that it "will be most admired by people who have always found Sir James M. Barrie pretty rough stuff," and Henry Hewes of the *Saturday Review* questioned whether everything about the play "was decided by a committee of craftsmen all too willing to please each other and to avoid risk." Nevertheless, audiences were far less divided, and *The Sound of Music* became one of the longest-running musicals in Broadway history.

THE SOUND OF MUSIC (1959). *Maria (Mary Martin) and Capt. Von Trapp (Theodore Bikel) first begin to realize that they are in love as they dance to the "Laendler" during a party at the captain's home. (Costumes by Lucinda Ballard.)*

Oscar Hammerstein's death, as a result of cancer, on August 23, 1960, terminated the most successful partnership in theatre history. From the beginning of their association, Rodgers and Hammerstein made their influence felt both in the audience and behind the footlights. Once, when Cole Porter was asked to name the most profound changes in musical comedy in forty years, he replied simply, "Rodgers and Hammerstein." Chiefly because of them, writers for the musical stage who might have spent the rest of their lives in Hollywood suddenly began to think again of the challenge and the opportunities inherent in the Broadway musical theatre. By their pioneering, Rodgers and Hammerstein conditioned the public to accept the kind of adventurous musicals that have been presented since *Oklahoma!* For in spite of the gradual changes that were taking place before that memorable production, it was *Oklahoma!* that demonstrated to composers, lyricists and librettists the indisputable truth that if they do create a work of merit, no matter how unconventional, there will be a large and responsive audience waiting for it.

As did the team of Rodgers and Hart, the team of Rodgers and Hammerstein always avoided formula musicals. "We believe that writers who repeat themselves will eventually bore themselves," they once wrote. "And this condition is a short and automatic step toward boring the public." In spite of the variety of their plays, however, there was always something of the basic philosophy of the two men present in their works. Ironically, although they helped bring about a more mature musical theatre through their contributions both before and after their partnership, Rodgers and Hammerstein were frequently accused of radiating too much of an unreal aura of sweetness and light. Rodgers was always quick to answer. "What's wrong with sweetness and light? It's been around quite a while. Even a cliché has a right to be true. I'm not interested in cracking out at anything, and I'm certainly not interested in kicking sentiment around. I love satire but I just couldn't write it." For his part, Hammerstein readily admitted he was a sentimentalist. "There's nothing wrong with sentiment because the things we're sentimental about are the fundamental things in life— the birth of a child, the death of a child, or anybody falling in love. I couldn't be anything but sentimental about these basic things. To be anything else is being a poseur."

Apart from their influence and philosophy, Rodgers and Hammerstein were particularly concerned about creative integrity. Once they decided upon their subject and the manner in which it would be developed, they proceeded in a direction that conformed solely to their own convictions. "I think it is disaster to try to do what the public wants if you don't feel that way yourself," Rodgers once said. "It's only when you and the public have the same mind that you are successful." To which Hammerstein

285

added, "You can't deliberately say, 'I will please the public although I don't like what I'm doing.' There must be a faith behind every work to make it succeed."

Following Hammerstein's death, Rodgers waited over a year before announcing his future plans—a collaboration with Alan Jay Lerner (which never materialized) and an original musical, *No Strings*, which, for the first time, would have lyrics as well as music by Richard Rodgers. *No Strings* proved to be an especially daring undertaking in many ways. Impressed with the talents of singer Diahann Carroll, the composer joined with playwright Samuel Taylor to fashion a vehicle expressly for her. Their conception took the form of an interracial love affair, set amid the elegant world of modern Paris and St. Tropez, but with the racial angle deliberately de-emphasized. Then with relative newcomers Joe Layton as director, Peter Matz as music director, and Ralph Burns as arranger, Rodgers worked out a scheme for taking the orchestra out of the pit, placing it backstage, and utilizing the services of specific instrumental soloists on stage both as part of the action and to lend appropriate atmosphere. He further did away with conventional scene changes by having the ladies of the chorus serve as decorative stage hands shifting sets and properties

NO STRINGS *(1962). Diahann Carroll and Richard Kiley strolling down a stylized Parisian boulevard. (Costumes by Fred Voelpel and Donald Brooks; setting by David Hays.)*

within full view of the audience. Then, as a touch of whimsy, he even had the instrumentation—save for a harp and bass violin—live up to the play's title by consisting of nothing that could be bowed or plucked. But there was more than mere whimsy in the over-all concept of *No Strings*. "I wanted the orchestra on stage," Rodgers explained, "in order to blend the orchestral sounds with the other elements so completely that they would seem to be an integral part of the proceedings, just as much as the dialogue, the lyrics or the action. I also wanted to eliminate the chasm between the audience and the stage that has always existed because of the orchestra pit."

There was general rejoicing at the boldness of the presentation, though some critical reservations were expressed with regard to the book itself. As for the music, Howard Taubman happily announced in the *Times* that the composer was "still a magician of the musical theatre," who had "written a score full of romance and vivacity" with lyrics that "have a touch of the wholesome ease of Hammerstein and a soupçon of the peppery impertinence of Lorenz Hart. If Mr. Rodgers is not yet as polished as either of his unforgettable colleagues, he is good enough to walk—and sing— alone." As for Miss Carroll, she was unquestionably the most electric personality appearing on Broadway that season—though, unfortunately, she hasn't been back since.

A far less friendly reception greeted Rodgers' second post-Hammerstein musical, *Do I Hear a Waltz?*, written in concert with lyricist Stephen Sondheim, a protege of Hammerstein, and librettist Arthur Laurents, who adapted the work from his own play, *The Time of the Cuckoo*. Here the main problem was possibly insurmountable—how to musicalize a rueful tale about a middle-aged American secretary's desperate romantic fling with a middle-aged married Venetian shopkeeper. By making them both somewhat younger and prettier, the writers did much to destroy the believability of the situation, despite the obvious integrity and taste that went into the adaptation.

In the history of the American musical theatre, there has, quite simply, never been another figure to match Richard Rodgers, both in his influence in shaping the course of this form of theatrical entertainment and in the longevity of his creative powers. It is, in fact, a bit staggering to realize that if all his Broadway musicals could be presented consecutively in their original number of performances, they would run for a total of almost thirty-seven and a half years. But Rodgers, with a lifetime of unparalleled accomplishment behind him, still looks to the future with the same unblinking gaze that he had when he first began writing for the musical stage. The sweetest sounds he'll ever hear, to paraphrase his own Keatsian lyric, may still be inside him.

Leonard Bernstein.

Leonard Bernstein

WITH THE GROWING emphasis on well-constructed librettos, young writers of the Forties and Fifties could no longer rely on the gradually disappearing revue as a means of getting their first songs on Broadway. Diverse media of entertainment, however, were still available to provide training for many aspiring composers and lyricists. The profusion of movie musicals in the Thirties and Forties gave Jule Styne and Frank Loesser the opportunity to write their first hits. Betty Comden and Adolph Green began their careers performing their own material in night clubs. Radio script-writing was Alan Jay Lerner's first professional job. For many years, Meredith Willson was known coast to coast as a radio conductor and composer. The most ancient training locale of all, Tin Pan Alley, was responsible for the emergence of Richard Adler and Jerry Ross, and Bob Merrill.

Although it is no longer a rarity for the concert hall to produce composers for the musical stage, not since Victor Herbert has there been anyone quite as successful in both areas as Leonard Bernstein. As a conductor, pianist, lecturer, and composer for the concert hall, he is an acknowledged leader in the world of classical music; as the composer of *On The Town, Wonderful Town, Candide,* and *West Side Story,* he is also an acknowledged leader in the world of musical comedy.

Born in Lawrence, Massachusetts, on August 25, 1918, Leonard Bernstein first became interested in music at a relatively advanced age. He was ten when an aunt presented his parents with a discarded upright piano; the gift so fascinated the youth that his father eventually yielded to his entreaties and permitted him to take lessons. At Harvard, where he majored in music, Bernstein became acquainted with Dimitri Mitropoulos, who was so impressed by the young man's talents that he urged him to become a conductor. After graduating from Harvard, Bernstein studied under Fritz Reiner at the Curtis Institute of Music in Philadelphia. In the summer of 1940, Serge Koussevitzky hired him as an assistant at the Tanglewood Summer Music Festival. The famed conductor soon developed a fatherly affection for Bernstein, who returned to Tanglewood for the next two summers.

Artur Rodzinski, then the musical director of the New York Philharmonic, thought the twenty-five-year-old conductor showed so much promise that he made him his assistant. One evening in the fall of 1943, Bruno Walter, the scheduled guest conductor of the Philharmonic, was suddenly taken ill. With Rodzinski out of town, and with no time for a rehearsal, Bernstein was suddenly called on to take over as conductor of the concert. His success prompted a front page story in the New York *Times* and an editorial in the *Daily News*. Hailed as a *Wunderkind*, Bernstein quickly found himself sought after for a wide variety of musical commissions.

The first one he accepted was to compose the music for a ballet, *Fancy Free*, choreographed by a young man named Jerome Robbins. The work, which depicted the escapades of three brash sailors on a twenty-four-hour spree in New York, became such a popular attraction of the Ballet Theatre that its creators decided to enlarge it into a Broadway musical. At Bernstein's suggestion, producers Oliver Smith and Paul Feigay signed Betty Comden and Adolph Green to write the libretto and lyrics.

Bernstein and Green had known each other since 1937 when Bernstein had been the music counsellor at a summer camp where Green had been hired to play the pirate king in a production of *The Pirates of Penzance*. Two years later, they shared an apartment in Greenwich Village. At the time, Green wrote for a nightclub act, The Revuers, which consisted of himself, Betty Comden, and Judy Holliday. Bernstein spent almost every evening with the group, which was then performing at the Village Vanguard.

Because of the inexperience of all those connected with *On the Town*, they chose as over-all director one of the most experienced men in the theatre, George Abbott. The show, which opened in December, 1944, was bright, swift-paced, and engagingly youthful. Its skillful blending of music, lyrics, book, and dances was the result of the unusually close rapport among the creators. The score was not only melodically and rhythmically appealing, but it had a technical mastery and unity of design that was uncommon. For

ON THE TOWN (1944). *The collaborators at work. Leonard Bernstein (composer), Jerome Robbins (choreographer), Betty Comden, and Adolph Green (co-librettists and co-lyricists).*

Three sailors enjoying the night life of New York. Adolph Green, Cris Alexander, and John Battles are the sailors; Allyn Ann McLerie, Betty Comden, and Nancy Walker are the girls. (Costumes by Alvin Colt; setting by Oliver Smith.)

example, the melody of "New York, New York," which opens the show and sets its invigorating pace, was later used by Bernstein in a much slower tempo to establish the proper mood for the contrasting expression, "Lonely Town." Comden and Green also had parts in the show (to bellow out their song of suppressed desires, "I Get Carried Away"), and Nancy Walker, as a female taxi driver, was especially funny as she boasted of her culinary and amatory prowess in "I Can Cook, Too."

Bernstein's major occupation as a symphony conductor (with the short-lived New York City Symphony and, since 1956, with the New York Philharmonic) has severely limited his theatrical output since *On the Town*. His second musical, *Wonderful Town,* was written eight years later and came about when he was called in to replace another composer. Because of differences with Joseph Fields and Jerome Chodorov (who had adapted the story from their own play, *My Sister Eileen*), the original lyricist and composer had quit five weeks before rehearsals were to start. This posed a problem; if rehearsals did not begin by December 15, 1953, producer Robert Fryer would lose his star, Rosalind Russell. In desperation, director George Abbott called in Betty Comden and Adolph Green. They agreed to undertake the assignment on the condition that Leonard Bernstein would compose the music.

According to Green, neither he nor Miss Comden was optimistic about the show. *My Sister Eileen* had seemed to him "so awfully Thirties-bound, sort of a post-Depression play, full of overexploited plot lines and passé references." Bernstein, however, was bursting with enthusiasm. "The Thirties! My God, those were the years! The excitement that was around! The political awareness! F.D.R.! Fiorello! Real personalities! And the wonderful fashions! Glorious! And the songs! What beat!" The composer's attitude proved so contagious that the trio seldom left his studio during the five weeks it took to finish the score.

All the numbers in *Wonderful Town* caught the pace and spirit of New York of the mid-Thirties, with such tunes as "Swing!" and "Conga!" written in the specific style of the then-current rhythmic phenomena. "Conversation Piece," in which five people at a party make self-conscious, embarrassed attempts at conversation, has always been one of the composer's favorites. "That's the kind of thing I like to do in the theatre. The background is pure theatre music, operating exclusively in theatre terms, not with an eye on Tin Pan Alley, and not to create a memorable tune, but something which is an integral part of the story."

As in *On the Town*, Bernstein used many devices to give the score unity. For example, themes from "What a Waste" were adroitly repeated at the beginning of "Pass that Football" and "A Quiet Girl," while the melody of "A Little Bit in Love" was used in the introductions to "Conversation Piece" and "It's Love."

WONDERFUL TOWN (1953).
*Rosalind Russell, in the arms
of a Brazilian naval officer,
gives some pointers on the
American dance called the
conga. Wrote Walter Kerr:
"Instead of attacking a song,
she inhabits it, moving around
in it with such confidence,
grace, and honest exuberance
as to make it entirely her
own."*

PHOTO BY BOB GOLBY

The most important single element that assured the box-office success of *Wonderful Town* was the performance of Rosalind Russell. After eighteen years in Hollywood, the forty-five-year-old actress romped through her part with such magnetic verve that audiences happily overlooked her limitations as a singer and dancer.

Being a thorough musician, Bernstein has not been limited by either subject matter or locale. For the unsuccessful *Candide* in 1956 he was able to capture the flavor of the Voltaire classic in a score that abounded in melodic grace and satiric invention. Such rhythms as the tango, mazurka, waltz, gavotte, and schottische were employed with striking effect, as were parodies of the styles of various classical composers. In particular, "Glitter and Be Gay" provided a delightful operatic coloratura aria in which the heroine, who has temporarily become a *demimondaine,* trills gaily of the materialistic compensations of her sad life.

For many years, Bernstein and Jerome Robbins had discussed the idea of doing a special kind of musical. Was it possible, they wondered, to tell a tragic story with a theme of some depth in terms of musical comedy without becoming operatic? A specific idea occurred to Robbins early in 1949: an up-to-date version of *Romeo and Juliet*, with the lovers played by a Jewish girl and an Italian Catholic boy living on the lower East Side of Manhattan. Playwright Arthur Laurents, a friend of Robbins, was called in to write the libretto of *East Side Story*, as it was then called, but the project soon had to be abandoned because of conflicting schedules.

About six years later, the writers decided to try again. By this time, it was apparent that the original concept was dated; the clashes between native-born teenagers and newly arrived Puerto Ricans offered them a far more timely and dramatic conflict. Now, in partnership with a young television writer named Stephen Sondheim as lyricist, they moved the play's locale across town and retitled it *West Side Story*. Although the work had to be interrupted because of Bernstein's commitment to compose the score for *Candide*, the four men were reunited early in 1957.

To Bernstein, creating *West Side Story* was like walking on a tightrope. The important thing was to keep it from ever getting too poetic or too realistic. In the "Rumble," for instance, the composer felt that if it "had been too balletic, we would have fallen off on one side—all you'd have is just another ballet. And if it had been too realistic, we would have fallen off on the other side— there would have been no poetry to it, no art."

The great triumph of *West Side Story*, which eventually was presented on Broadway in September, 1957, is that it is impressionistic but at the same time it gives the illusion of reality. The costumes, the settings, the dialogue, the music, and the dances were all combined with a theatrical expressiveness that transcended mere naturalism to establish a truly lyrical mood. Here were young city toughs moving with agility through the dance patterns, spewing out their pent-up hatreds and revealing secret longings through music that could be, by turns, both nervously agitated and almost ethereal. Moreover, the story was told without resorting to wisecracks or a happy ending. It made few compromises, yet *West Side Story* contained sufficient entertainment value to last more than two years on Broadway, and to return in 1960 after a successful cross-country tour.

PHOTO BY FRED FEHL

WEST SIDE STORY *(1957). Larry Kert and Carol Lawrence, as the Romeo and Juliet lovers, use a fire escape as a balcony. (Costumes by Irene Sharaff; setting by Oliver Smith.)*

WEST SIDE STORY *(1957). The Jets and their girls dance in the local drugstore just before their rumble with the rival gang known as the Sharks. Larry Kert, seated alone at a table, is worried about the outcome. (Costumes by Irene Sharaff; setting by Oliver Smith.)*

With time for only four musicals within thirteen years, Bernstein has nevertheless left a strong mark on the theatrical scene, particularly as something of a *minnesinger* of Manhattan. The brash spirit of *On the Town*, the nostalgia of *Wonderful Town*, and the jagged impact of *West Side Story* reveal a city of many faces and a composer of many facets. Perhaps only one not native to the city could capture it so well in music. "This town still gets me," Bernstein exclaims. "No wonder I keep composing about it. It's so dramatic and alive. New York! The amazing, confusing beauty of the place!"

Paradoxically, this concern with one geographical locale has not endowed Bernstein's creations with any discernible personal style. Partly due to his knowledge of, and his involvement in, all kinds of music, Bernstein has shown a certain eclecticism in his work for the theatre that has made it less of an individual expression than highly technical, remarkably effective music with each score sounding almost as if it were the work of different men.

Leonard Bernstein has become the most public personality of today's composers. On television, his witty, incisive commentaries have shown him to be a zealous crusader for a wider appreciation of almost every type of music, including the music of the theatre. "Out of our natural musical theatre," he once said, "which is wholly an outgrowth of our culture, is emerging our opera, intelligible to all." The firmness of this belief would suggest that Bernstein is the successor to Kurt Weill, and, indeed, *West Side Story* is a direct extension of the *Zeitoper* that Weill had been instrumental in creating in Germany. Unfortunately, Bernstein has been unable to devote all his prodigious energies to the musical theatre. In spite of his multiple activities, however, he has always brought to his work for the Broadway stage the same kind of affection, originality, and painstaking care that has distinguished his career in every one of the numerous musical pursuits to which he is devoted.

Frederick Loewe and Alan Jay Lerner.

Alan Jay Lerner
and Frederick Loewe

THE SPECIAL CHEMISTRY that takes place between two individuals to enable them to produce a successful blending of words and music has never been distilled in any laboratory's test tube. Some famous song-writing teams— Rodgers and Hammerstein, for example, or Schwartz and Dietz—have had markedly similar backgrounds and outlook; others—Rodgers and Hart, the Gershwin brothers—may have had similar, and even identical, backgrounds, but they have been made up of men with almost completely different personalities and tastes.

In background, in personality, and in temperament, Alan Jay Lerner and Frederick Loewe would seem to be two of the most dissimilar men in the theatre. Loewe, Lerner's senior by fourteen years, was born in Berlin, on June 10, 1904. He was the son of Edmund Loewe, a well-known Viennese tenor who sang in the popular operettas of the day. By the time he was seven, young Fritz could pick out tunes on the piano. He studied in Berlin under Ferruccio Busoni (Kurt Weill's teacher), Eugène d'Albert, and Emil Nikolaus von Reznicek. At thirteen, he was the youngest piano soloist ever to appear with the Berlin Symphony. Two years later, he wrote a popular song, "Katrina," which became one of the biggest song hits throughout Europe.

In 1924, Frederick Loewe confidently journeyed to New York to continue his career. His difficulties with the English language and his seeming inability to write in an "American" style made it extremely hard for him to adjust to the new country. Instead of continuing his career as a composer, he was soon forced to take a job as a pianist at a Greenwich Village nightclub, and, for a time, he was even a bus boy in a cafeteria.

With his career in music apparently over, Loewe, a solidly built, athletic man, next became a riding instructor at a New Hampshire resort and, later, a prize fighter at a Brooklyn athletic club. His pugilistic career, however, was painfully terminated when his teeth were knocked out in his ninth bout. After a few years in the West (where he was a cow puncher, gold prospector, and horseback mail deliverer), Loewe took a job as a pianist on board ships transporting thirsty citizens from Miami to Havana during Prohibition. When repeal ended this ferrying service in the early Thirties, he became a pianist at a *Brauhaus* in Yorkville, New York City's German section.

During this period, he again began to compose. As one acquaintance remembers, "Even though Fritz wasn't doing well in those days, I knew he had a tremendous inner fire just burning to create great songs." To help his career, Loewe joined the Lambs, the famous theatrical club. There he became friendly with Dennis King, who was so fond of one of Loewe's songs, "Love Tiptoed through My Heart," that he sang it in the play *Petticoat Fever*.

The following year, 1935, Loewe formed a partnership with Earle Crooker, a radio and Hollywood script-writer, who had contributed lyrics to *The Little Show*. Their first song, "A Waltz Was Born in Vienna," was danced by Gomez and Winona in the unsuccessful *Illustrators' Show*. It was subsequently added to the score for *Salute to Spring*, an original musical Loewe and Crooker wrote for the St. Louis Opera Association.

Salute to Spring was one of the most popular attractions offered in St. Louis in the summer of 1937. Producer Dwight Deere Wiman was so delighted with their work that he signed Loewe and Crooker to create the songs for *Great Lady*, a costly operetta which he produced on Broadway the following year. Neither music nor lyrics was distinguished, nor was there much merit in the story of how Eliza Bowan, a notorious adventuress of the early nineteenth century, broke into New York society by marrying the wealthy Stephen Jumel. Musical comedy sentimentalists may have been delighted to see Norma Terris, Irene Bordoni, and Helen Ford in the same play, but the future stars of the ballet, opera, and musical theatre were in the singing and dancing groups. The dancers, led by André Eglevsky, included Alicia Alonso, Nora Kaye, Paul Godkin, and Jerome Robbins; Dorothy Kirsten and Walter Cassel were among the singers.

It had taken Loewe almost fourteen years to get the opportunity to compose his first Broadway score. Unfortunately, *Great Lady* closed after twenty performances, and he was once again forced to return to his job as a piano player in a restaurant. Then, one day in 1942, he introduced himself to a young writer named Alan Jay Lerner.

Unlike Loewe, Lerner had never had to spend years toiling at strange occupations in an alien country. He was born in New York City, on August 31, 1918, the son of the founder of a chain of women's specialty shops, the Lerner Shops. Instead of smothering his ability, the advantages of wealth and education only instilled in him a strong determination to succeed unaided by any parental assistance. Lerner was only eight when he first made up his mind to become a writer for the theatre. His father neither opposed nor encouraged this ambition; his only advice to his son was that he would have to work hard at his profession if he really wanted to succeed. Young Lerner learned to play the piano at an early age, and later took courses at the Juilliard School of Music. At Harvard, he wrote music and lyrics for two Hasty Pudding shows. Two songs were even considered worthy enough to be commercially published: "Chance to Dream" from the 1938 production, *So Proudly We Hail*, and "From Me to You" from the 1939 show, *Fair Enough*. After graduating Lerner became a radio script-writer, turning out about five hundred scripts in two years.

Desperation brought Loewe to Lerner in 1942. Henry Duffy, a producer, wanted to present a series of original musical comedies at a theatre he owned in Detroit. The previous year he had offered a musical adaptation of Barry Connors' play, *The Patsy*, in San Francisco, but he wanted an entirely different treatment of the same story for the Detroit production. Two weeks before rehearsals were to begin, Duffy met with Loewe at the Lambs Club to discuss the possibility of using the bulk of the Loewe-Crooker score for *Salute to Spring*. What Loewe needed to ensure the commission, however, was a librettist who could also update some of the earlier lyrics. Because he admired the sketches and lyrics Lerner had contributed to *The Lambs Gambol*, a revue put on by Lambs Club members, Loewe immediately thought of him for the new project. Seeing Lerner at the club that day playing cards, the composer introduced himself with the businesslike: "You are Alan Jay Lerner? You write good lyrics. I am Frederick Loewe. I have something to say to you."

Two days later, they were on a train bound for Detroit, the show was written within the prescribed two weeks, and in October, 1942, Detroit audiences saw the initial collaboration of Alan Jay Lerner and Frederick Loewe—*Life of the Party*, starring Dorothy Stone and Charles Collins. There was nothing memorable about the musical, but Lerner's work convinced Loewe that they might succeed as a team. For their next musical, *What's Up*—and for every one of their collaborations since then—Alan Jay Lerner has written the book and lyrics and Frederick Loewe has composed the music.

What's Up opened in November, 1943. Even with Jimmy Savo in the cast and George Balanchine as director, it was not an auspicious debut. Their next work, however, *The Day before Spring*, turned out to be a highly literate and imaginative fantasy which just missed being a hit. Wolcott Gibbs called it "my kind of show," adding that "the songs that go with it are fresh and bright and seem to spring spontaneously from the action rather than from spasmodic impulses on the part of the singers."

The Day before Spring was more of an artistic than a commercial success. *Brigadoon* was both. Lerner, long fond of the works of Sir James M. Barrie, had been eager to write a musical with a Scottish setting. "One day, while working on *The Day before Spring*, Fritz mentioned something about faith moving mountains. This started me thinking. For a while, I had a play about faith moving a mountain. From there we went to all sorts of miracles occurring through faith, and, eventually, faith moved a town."

In less skilled hands, the legend of the sleeping Scottish town that awakens once in every one hundred years could easily have been too precious or maudlin, but so ably were the theatrical ingredients blended—story, music, lyrics, dancing, settings, costumes—that the result became what Brooks Atkinson unequivocably labeled a "vibrant work of art." Never before had Agnes de Mille's talents been better realized than in the way she made each dance sequence an integral part of the story, most notably in the Sword Dance, the Chase, and the Funeral Dance. Robert Lewis directed *Brigadoon* with rare sensitivity, and Oliver Smith's evocative settings enhanced the total effect.

The score that Frederick Loewe and Alan Jay Lerner created was especially distinguished for its appropriateness to locale, story, and characters. Lerner's lyrics captured much of the highland flavor, and his ability to use simple, genuine imagery was marked in the songs "Brigadoon," "Come to Me,

PHOTO BY EILEEN DARBY—GRAPHIC HOUSE

WHAT'S UP *(1943). Johnny Morgan as an American sergeant and Jimmy Savo as an East Indian potentate.*

BRIGADOON *(1947). James Mitchell about to begin the Sword Dance. (Costumes by David Ffolkes; setting by Oliver Smith.)*

Bend to Me," and "The Heather on the Hill." Loewe's music was equally suffused with the atmosphere of the play, and, when required, attained a certain eloquence. The wisdom of the authors' approach was notably demonstrated in the way the one sophisticated song, "Almost Like Being in Love," was first introduced by the rich American tourist (played by David Brooks) before being reprised by the simple highland maid (Marion Bell).

Soon after writing *Love Life* with Kurt Weill in 1948,. Lerner began thinking of an idea for a musical he could write with Loewe. He was determined that it would have a story with a positive point of view, "a musical that would embrace all the robustness and vitality and cockeyed courage that is so much a part of our American heritage." To both Lerner and Loewe, the saga of the California gold rush filled that specification.

Paint Your Wagon opened in New York in November, 1951. With the exception of director Daniel Mann, almost all of the principal members of the production staff had been associated with *Brigadoon*—producer Cheryl Crawford, choreographer Agnes de Mille, designer Oliver Smith, musical director Franz Allers, and musical arranger Ted Royal. James Barton, who had not appeared in a Broadway musical in over twenty years, played the part of a grizzled old prospector, and Olga San Juan appeared as his daughter. Throughout the score, the songs projected a genuine flavor of Americana; many of them, in fact, seemed to be not Broadway show tunes but authentic folk ballads handed down from the miners themselves. The booming theme song, "Wand'rin' Star," sung at the beginning and end of the play, served as an appropriate frame for such numbers as the stirring "I'm on My Way"; the rushing legend "They Call the Wind Maria"; the misty-eyed "I Still See

PAINT YOUR WAGON *(1951). Agnes de Mille's lively dance to "Hand Me Down That Can o' Beans." (Costumes by Motley; setting by Oliver Smith.)*

Elisa," touchingly sung by Barton; the rousing dances "Whoop-Ti-Ay" and "Hand Me Down That Can o' Beans"; and the almost chilling expression of loneliness, "Another Autumn."

In their research for *Paint Your Wagon,* Lerner and Loewe became so steeped in the subject that they incorporated actual incidents and miners' dialogue as part of the play. Possibly, as Lerner later admitted, they may have done too much research. According to Walter Kerr, "Writing an *integrated* musical comedy—where people are believable and the songs are logically introduced—is no excuse for not being funny from time to time. But the librettist of *Paint Your Wagon* seems to be more interested in the authenticity of his background than in the joy of his audience."

Including *Paint Your Wagon,* Lerner's books for his first five musicals had all been based on original stories. He became convinced that the main reason why some of his musicals were not more successful was that they had faulty librettos. Quite logically, he decided that henceforth he would adapt his stories from plays or novels that had already won favor with both critics and the public. His opportunity came in 1952, when Gabriel Pascal, the celebrated Hungarian movie producer, suggested to him that he transform Bernard Shaw's *Pygmalion* into a musical play.

Pascal, the only man ever to win Shaw's permission to film his plays, had made a motion picture of *Pygmalion* in the mid-Thirties. Sometime after that he became interested in producing a musical version of the work. Shaw, who had voiced public indignation over Oscar Straus's *The Chocolate Soldier* (based on his *Arms and the Man*), had always been unalterably opposed to the idea of a musical *Pygmalion*. In 1948, when a friend once interceded in behalf of two other writers, the playwright shot back a typically Shavian response: "I absolutely forbid such outrage. If *Pygmalion* is not good enough for your friends with its own verbal music, their talent must be altogether extraordinary. Let them try Mozart's *Cosi fan tutti*, or at least Offenbach's *Grand Duchess*."

After Shaw's death in 1950, Pascal felt free to proceed with his plan. In rapid succession, he importuned such distinguished writers of the musical stage as Noël Coward, Cole Porter, E. Y. Harburg and Fred Saidy, Schwartz and Dietz, and Rodgers and Hammerstein. Each one, however, turned him down.* When Lerner and Loewe finally agreed to undertake the project, the producer did not even have the rights to present the play as a musical. So persuasive were his arguments, however, that the Shaw estate granted him a two-year option.

Lerner and Loewe at first could not agree on the proper approach to the Shaw work. After struggling with it for about three months, they had to admit to Pascal that they saw no way in which the adaption could be accomplished. For the next two years, Lerner and Loewe went their separate ways, each becoming involved in projects that were never realized. Lerner tried to transform *Li'l Abner*† into a musical, first with Burton Lane and later with Arthur Schwartz. Loewe joined with Joseph Fields, Jerome Chodorov, and Leo Robin in attempting a musical version of Paul Vincent Carroll's *Saints and Sinners*.

While Lerner and Loewe were occupied with other pursuits, Pascal continued his vain hunt for other writers who might be induced to make a musical of *Pygmalion*. It had become such an obsession with him that he obtained a two-year extension after his option had expired. The tenacious producer, however, never lived to see his dream fulfilled. He died in New York in the summer of 1954, soon after beginning another search.

Ironically, it was about the time of Pascal's death that Lerner and Loewe resumed their partnership to make one last attempt at setting *Pygmalion* to music. The problem, according to Lerner, "was how to enlarge it into a big musical without hurting its content. It was a big surprise—we hardly had to enlarge the plot at all. We just added what Shaw had happening offstage." Once they found the way to do it, the authors went ahead with their adapta-

* Harburg refused to do the adaptation because he felt *Pygmalion* was a perfect work of art and should not be touched. Hammerstein's reason was based on Shaw's insistence that it was not a love story, and he did not want to oppose the author's wishes.

† The rights to *Li'l Abner* were presently acquired by Norman Panama, Melvin Frank, and Michael Kidd. With a score by Johnny Mercer and Gene de Paul, the musical opened in New York in the fall of 1956. It had a run of almost 700 performances.

PHOTO BY FRIEDMAN-ABELES

MY FAIR LADY (1956). *The first day of rehearsals on the roof of the New Amsterdam Theatre. Julie Andrews, Rex Harrison, Alan Jay Lerner, and Frederick Loewe. Moss Hart can be seen just behind Lerner and Loewe.*

tion, even though they no longer had Pascal or the rights. They took the finished script to producer Herman Levin. After some delays, he was able to secure the rights from the Pascal estate.

From the very beginning, Rex Harrison was the choice of Lerner and Loewe to play Professor Higgins. Following Shaw's specifications that Eliza Doolittle should be played by an actress between eighteen and twenty, the authors diligently auditioned every girl in her late teens they could find. While so occupied, they received word that Mary Martin was interested in the part. "Forgetting Shaw's directions," Levin recalls, "we paged Mary. She wasn't twenty, but she was box-office dynamite. Mary quickly dissipated any qualms we may have had about flouting Shaw's blueprint. Lerner and Loewe played five songs for her and she didn't like any of them." They next tested a young English actress, Julie Andrews, then making an impressive Broadway debut in Sandy Wilson's *The Boy Friend*. Although she fitted Shaw's concept perfectly, they still were not completely sure that she was right for the part. After auditioning about fifty English girls in London, however, the producer and the writers returned to New York and signed Miss Andrews to a two-year contract.

In October, 1955, a press release announced the forthcoming adaptation, then known as *My Lady Liza*. Rehearsals began early the following January. Moss Hart was the director, Hanya Holm the choreographer, Oliver Smith the set designer, Cecil Beaton the costume designer, and Franz Allers the musical director. The supporting cast was headed by Stanley Holloway

MY FAIR LADY (1956). *The first scene between Eliza Doolittle (Julie Andrews) and Professor Higgins (Rex Harrison), as they meet outside Covent Garden. (Costumes by Cecil Beaton.)*

Stanley Holloway (as Alfred P. Doolittle) explains his philosophy in "With a Little Bit of Luck" to cronies Gordon Dilworth and Rod McLennan.

Eliza (Julie Andrews) Professor Higgins (Rex Harrison), and Col. Pickering (Robert Coote) join in a spontaneous dance to the tune of "The Rain in Spain." This was, in Wolcott Gibbs's opinion, "just about the most brilliantly successful scene I remember seeing in a musical comedy."

MY FAIR LADY (1956). *The scene at the Ascot Races. Freddy Eynsford-Hill and Henry Higgins's mother are amused at Liza's difficulties with the English language. John Michael King, Julie Andrews, and Cathleen Nesbitt. (Costumes by Cecil Beaton.)*

PHOTO BY FRIEDMAN-ABELES

(Alfred P. Doolittle), Cathleen Nesbitt (Professor Higgins' mother), and Robert Coote (Col. Pickering). After opening in New Haven, two songs, "Say a Prayer" (later used in the film *Gigi*) and "Come to the Ball," and a ballet, "Decorating Eliza," were cut from the score.

Since its première on March 15, 1956, the legends about the difficulties of getting tickets to *My Fair Lady* and the reports of weekly box-office grosses have become part of the folklore of the theatre. In December, 1958, the show established the all-time record for gross receipts with $10 million, thus exceeding the record of $9 million established by *South Pacific* at a lower price scale.

"For years, Fritz and I floundered around, trying to find our natural way of writing," Lerner once confessed in an interview in the New York *Times*. "*My Fair Lady* revealed it to us. The property dictates it. The characters in the story. We are the means by which they express themselves, not vice versa. When we felt we really knew them, then we began to work on the score. We try to find some thought of a character that motivates him and, in turn, the story."

This approach is evident throughout. In the songs for Professor Higgins, there is the biting disdain for his inferiors in "Why Can't the English?"; his witty defense of his own way life in "I'm an Ordinary Man"; his petulent admiration for masculine traits in "A Hymn to Him"; and, in the simply stated "I've Grown Accustomed to Her Face," his admission that he has finally fallen in love with Eliza. Eliza's character is also revealed through song. First, as a poor flower-seller, she dreams only of a life of physical comforts in "Wouldn't It Be Lovely?" Later, after having gone through the rigors of the professor's speech classes, she expresses her secret defiance in "Just You Wait," and her thrill at having succeeding in speaking correctly in "I Could Have Danced All Night." The girl's impatience with all men bursts through in "Show Me," and, at the end, in a bolt of sarcastic fury, she tells Higgins her real opinion of him in "Without You."

The secondary characters are equally well served by the songs. For Alfred Doolittle, Eliza's philosophical, high-spirited father, Lerner and Loewe created two appropriate music-hall turns, "With a Little Bit of Luck" and "Get Me to the Church on Time." For the faithful Freddy Eynsford-Hill (played by Dennis King's son, John Michael King) they wrote the worshipful ballad "On the Street Where You Live."

The most musically and dramatically effective episode comes midway through the first act when Eliza is at last able to say "The rain in Spain stays mainly in the plain" without a Cockney accent. As Walter Kerr described the scene, "You listen astonished—because you believe in her so completely that you didn't really suppose she could make it. Suddenly, her delight becomes yours. And when Mr. Harrison, together with an equally astonished Robert Coote, bounces irresistibly to the center of the stage and begins to kick out a tango rhythm to the sound she has just made, there is no controlling the joy in the theatre."

The unprecedented success of *My Fair Lady,* which has given Lerner and Loewe a stature almost equal to that of Rodgers and Hammerstein, has produced a rather philosophical attitude in both men. "Neither Fritz nor I believe we're *that* good," says Lerner. "It's just that the time was ripe for something gay and theatrical, something that was not two lonely people finding each other in a dark alley. *My Fair Lady* filled the bill."

They had, in fact, purposely set out to make their musical as glamorous, as stylish, as visually stunning as they possibly could, something that would be in the grand manner of the romantic musicals of the past. (Even their story was a variation on the oldest plot of all, the Cinderella legend, including the ball.)

How does one follow *My Fair Lady?* If a tale originally inspired by the legendary Pygmalion, King of Cyprus, could succeed so spectacularly, why not a musical based on another legendary king, Arthur of Britain? Lerner's specific source was T. H. White's *The Once and Future King,* though he was indebted to it more for approach and style than for plot. In partnership with director Moss Hart, Lerner and Loewe produced the musical themselves, and gave it the name of Arthur's court and castle, Camelot.

Trouble plagued the enterprise from the start. During the out-of-town tryout Lerner was hospitalized with bleeding ulcers and Hart was felled by a heart attack. Once Lerner was well enough to be discharged, he assumed responsibility for the direction which, among other things, included slicing off more than an hour from the show's original four hour running time. After two months on the road, the cost of the production had soared to a record $635,000. But these *were* the people who had created *My Fair Lady,* and there *was* Fair Lady Julie Andrews, *plus* Richard Burton. Little wonder that expectations ran so high that the pre-opening ticket sale was well over $3 million.

CAMELOT (1960). As the queen, Julie Andrews listens while King Arthur (Richard Burton) sings "What Do the Simple Folk Do?" (Costumes by Adrian and Tony Duquette.)

PHOTO BY FRIEDMAN-ABELES

A distinct let-down was felt following the December, 1960, première at the Majestic Theatre. The reviews ran the gamut, with the majority praising the richness of the decor but decrying the poverty of the plot. Obviously the play wasn't ready for the opening and obviously something had to be done—fast. Within a month a partially recovered Moss Hart began the major task of overhauling. Lerner wrote and rewrote, shaved another twelve minutes from the script, and, at the suggestion of critic John Chapman, substituted a more upbeat but still consistent ending. The result was that—aided by the huge advance ticket sale—Camelot soon found its audience, and ended its Broadway run nearly 900 performances later.

Few of the songs seemed to be fully appreciated when the musical was first unveiled. The stirring saga of "Camelot" and the jaunty "What Do the Simple Folk Do?" caused a slight stir and, thanks to a pop record-ing, "If Ever I Would Leave You," that throbbing declaration of multi-seasonal devotion, managed to catch on. After a while, "How to Handle a Woman," "The Lusty Month of May," "Follow Me," and "I Wonder What the King Is Doing Tonight" became better known and won deserved favor. After the play had been running a year, author Lerner summed up the expectations and realities inherent in being responsible for a musical work unlucky enough to follow My Fair Lady: "In the jargon of Times

308

Square, a play that comes unheralded to Broadway and becomes a success is known as a 'sleeper.' *Camelot* was a 'waker': exhausting, infuriating, unraveling at times; but now, twelve months later, gratifying indeed."

Camelot turned out to be the sixth and final Lerner and Loewe collaboration. In looking back upon the contributions of the two men, we find their musicals were, to a great extent, the successors to the Viennese school of Lehár and Strauss and Herbert—only welded more firmly together with all the theatrical arts developed through the years. Instead of pasteboard characters theirs had depth and believability. Instead of illogical, frequently infantile stories, theirs dealt coherently with a wide variety of adult themes. Instead of bland, artificial lyrics mated to usually unmotivated melodies, their songs were created to serve a purpose in the stories and to spring naturally from the characters who sang them.

Modern though their plays were in inspiration and execution, the distinguishing trait of Lerner and Loewe was in their preservation of the values and traditions of the past—a 200-year-old Scottish village that has vanished in the highland mist . . . the adventurous life of gold prospectors in mid-19th century California . . . London's social standards immediately preceding World War I . . . the idealistic court of King Arthur's round table. Such works have endowed bygone places and people not only with authenticity but with illumination and warmth. The musical world of Alan Jay Lerner and Frederick Loewe may not have been concerned with the problems of today, but it surely was created for today's audiences. It remains a world in which the past comes excitingly alive, while still being romantic, and gay, and eternally appealing.

In 1962, differences in temperament compelled the team of Lerner and Loewe to dissolve. Loewe vowed he would retire and never write another note. So far he has kept his word. Lerner's plans included a partnership with Richard Rodgers to create a musical about extrasensory perception tentatively known as *I Picked a Daisy*. With the cast and production crew practically set, the new team broke off and Lerner went in search of a new composer. He found him in Burton Lane, whose last efforts for the stage had been *Finian's Rainbow* in 1947. The musical, now called *On a Clear Day You Can See Forever*, turned out to be a somewhat uneasy amalgam of *Bridey Murphy* and *Berkeley Square*. But the songs were radiantly tuneful and the enterprise had a special plus factor in co-star Barbara Harris, a moon-faced hoyden who had first attracted notice in *The Second City* revues. Along with the theme of extrasensory perception, a subject dear to Lerner, the librettist also dealt with an equally favorite theme, contrasting ancient with modern living. Even without Frederick Loewe, the past continues to furnish inspiration for one of our most forward-looking of contemporary theatre craftsmen.

Jule Styne, Betty Comden and Adolph Green.

310

Jule Styne
Betty Comden and Adolph Green

THERE ARE MANY REASONS for the reduction in the number of Broadway musicals since the 1920's and the corollary lessening in the output of major theatrical composers. Among the most apparent have been the increasingly longer runs of hit shows, the greater time spent on all the component parts of a production, the competition from other entertainment media, and, possibly the strongest deterrent of all, the mounting production costs.

As a consequence, some striking paradoxes emerge regarding the musical theatre of the Twenties and the Fifties, particularly as reflected in the career of composer Jule Styne. By working on twelve Broadway musicals over a period of about eleven and a half years, Vincent Youmans was the least prolific among the leading composers of his day; by working on eight Broadway musicals over a similar period of time, Styne established himself as the most prolific composer currently writing for the theatre. In fact, judging by the popularity of his shows, he is undoubtably one of the most successful musical comedy composers of all time. The total number of original Broadway performances of Styne's first thirteen musicals easily exceeds that of the entire seventeen musicals with complete scores by

Irving Berlin, or the twenty-three with scores by George Gershwin, or the twenty-five with scores by Rodgers and Hart.

No yardstick is intended here other than to point out the changing face of Broadway both in the productivity of its writers and the longevity of their creations. Yet it is strange that with a record of accomplishment such as this that the name Jule Styne is still less familiar to the average person than the aforementioned Messrs. Youmans, Berlin, Gershwin or Rodgers. Here too the reason is tied in with the theatrical changes that have developed through the years. Today it isn't just enough to create a varied and tuneful collection of songs to keep a show running. The composer and lyricist contribute only one part—an indispensable one to be sure, but still only a part—of the total creation. A musical succeeds because of its over-all style and the way all the components have been pulled into shape, not, generally speaking, because of the predominance of any single factor.

Except possibly the star. And that's another reason for Styne's lack of due recognition. Almost every one of his hits has been dominated by the personality of an authentic star—or two authentic stars. *High Button Shoes* had the swaggering clowning of Phil Silvers and the vivacity of Nanette Fabray. *Gentlemen Prefer Blondes* became a vehicle for a saucer-eyed comedienne named Carol Channing. *Two on the Aisle* gave us both Bert Lahr and Dolores Gray. *Peter Pan* relied for much of its appeal on the charms of Mary Martin. *Bells Are Ringing* owed its marathon run primarily to the incandescent Judy Holliday. *Gypsy* offered Ethel Merman at the height of her powers. *Funny Girl* revealed the magnetism of Barbra Streisand. *Fade Out—Fade In* was known as "the Carol Burnett Show." And *Hallelujah, Baby!*, though it aimed at significance, owed its limited success to the sparkling performance of Leslie Uggams.

There is, of course, ample evidence that the stature of Jule Styne is being more and more recognized despite the enumerated roadblocks. Surely his work for *Gypsy* and *Funny Girl* has clearly demonstrated that musical scores such as these are equally as important to the artistic merits of their respective productions as the stars. In these two musicals especially it is evident that in quality as well as in proficiency and popularity, Jule Styne is in the front ranks of composers for the modern musical theatre.

Styne was born Jules Stein in London, England, on December 31, 1905. He had his first taste of the theatre at the age of three when he bounded up on the stage to sing a duet with Sir Harry Lauder, the legendary Scottish entertainer. When he was eight, young Jule and his parents moved to Chicago. There the youth quickly showed such musical talent that within a year he was guest piano soloist with the Chicago and Detroit Symphonies. At thirteen, he won a scholarship to the Chicago College of Music where he studied piano, harmony, composition and theory.

In the Twenties, Styne became fascinated by the songs being written by the rising young composers of Tin Pan Alley and Broadway. Responding to this kind of music to a far greater extent than he did to the works of classical composers, he abandoned his concert career to become a pianist in a dance band. In 1931, he organized his own orchestra, for which he served not only as leader but also as arranger and occasional song writer (his first song and his first hit, "Sunday," had been composed in 1926). Writing eventually became more important to Styne than fronting an orchestra; in the mid-Thirties he disbanded his group to sign a contract with Twentieth Century-Fox as both composer and vocal coach.

During the Thirties and Forties, Styne turned out many hits for the movies. With lyricist Frank Loesser, he wrote "I Don't Want to Walk without You, Baby"; later, with Sammy Cahn, he created a string of Hit Parade occupants including "I've Heard That Song Before," "I'll Walk Alone," "It's Been a Long Long Time," "Time After Time," and "It's Magic." Living in California was pleasant and profitable, but Styne deeply felt the lack of recognition or of any artistic fulfillment. He had only one ambition: he wanted to write a Broadway score. (As Styne once said, "In Hollywood you're a song writer, in New York you're a composer.") Styne and Cahn received their first opportunity in 1944, when they supplied the songs for the Broadway-bound *Glad to See You*, but the show never made it any closer to New York than Boston.

High Button Shoes, three years later, not only opened on Broadway

HIGH BUTTON SHOES *(1947). Phil Silvers, as Harrison Floy, and Nanette Fabray, as Sara Longstreet. Of Mr. Silvers, Brooks Atkinson wrote: "He is an uproarious comic. He has the speed, the drollery, and the shell-game style of a honky tonk buffoon." (Costumes by Miles White.)*

GENTLEMEN PREFER BLONDES
(1949). Lorelei Lee (Carol
Channing) demonstrates her
prowess on a diminutive
Frenchman (Mort Marshall).
Looking on is another Frenchman (Howard Morris). Ac-
cording to John Chapman,
Miss Channing "got the most
enthusiastic notices of any
musicomedienne of this generation."

but remained there for about two and one-half years. With a book by
Stephen Longstreet, it was a bright, funny, though formula musical heavy
with nostalgic charm. Its main appeal was the brash performance of Phil
Silvers as con man Harrison Floy and the hilarious Keystone Kops ballet
devised by Jerome Robbins. Of the songs, "Papa, Won't You Dance with
Me?" and "I Still Get Jealous," both engagingly performed by Nanette
Fabray and Jack McCauley, are still recalled for their infectious period
flavor.

Despite the success of *High Button Shoes*, Cahn preferred to return
to the sunkissed hills of Hollywood, and Styne formed a winning but brief
partnership with lyricist Leo Robin. For *Gentlemen Prefer Blondes*,
produced in 1949, they contributed a lively, atmospheric score perfectly
suited to Anita Loos's hedonistic tale of the torrid Twenties. Yet it was
Carol Channing, as gold-digging Lorelei Lee, who captivated both critics
and public, particularly with her renditions of "Diamonds Are a Girl's Best
Friend" and "A Little Girl from Little Rock." Miss Channing,
whose only previous experience on Broadway had been as Eve Arden's
understudy in *Let's Face It!* and in the Charles Gaynor revue, *Lend an
Ear*, was elevated to stardom during the run. The producers could hardly
have avoided twinkling her name above the theatre marquee since it was
her strangely grotesque yet winningly feminine portrayal that won the
season's loudest hurrahs.

In 1951, Jule Styne began his association with his most frequent collaborators, Betty Comden and Adolph Green. The inseparable lyricists had
met thirteen years before while Miss Comden was a drama major at New
York University and Green was a self-styled bum. From then on, neither

one has ever written a lyric or a libretto or a screenplay without the other. Their—to date—nearly thirty-year partnership is surely the most remarkable example of tenacious teamwork in the annals of the musical stage.

Betty Comden was born in Brooklyn on May 3, 1915; Adolph Green first saw daylight in the Bronx on December 2, 1915. Originally their mutual ambition was to scale the heights of thespian stardom and, to that end, they formed a quintet of acting and singing comedians known as The Revuers. Another member of the troupe, Judy Tuvim, a bright-eyed, baby-voiced blonde, later changed her last name to Holliday. Because they couldn't afford writers, Comden and Green found themselves dreaming up most of the scripts and the lyrics. The act was a hit at the Village Vanguard, flopped at the Rainbow Room, and disbanded after a disastrous fling at the movies.

Comden and Green, however, stuck together. It was while appearing at the Blue Angel, a New York supperclub, that they were approached by a young composer named Leonard Bernstein to collaborate on the score for a musical that would become known as *On the Town*. Bernstein, a former roommate of Green's, had been asked to expand his ballet, *Fancy Free*, into a musical comedy, and he was firm in his conviction that none but Comden and Green would do for the story and lyrics. The team promptly gave up their night club performing career in favor of writing —but they also made sure that two fat parts in the show would be played by Betty Comden and Adolph Green.

On the Town was a resounding smash, and Comden and Green were immediately hailed as the freshest, brightest lyric writers of the year. But the cheers quickly died. In December 1945, almost exactly one year after *On the Town*, the team had a less-than-brilliant entry in *Billion Dollar Baby*, a spoof of the Twenties with a score by Morton Gould. Even more disastrous was *Bonanza Bound*, which they wrote two years later with composer (now movie producer) Saul Chaplin. It folded in Philadelphia. Hollywood—finally—beckoned, and for about two years Comden and Green were gainfully employed as scenarists and/or lyricists for such M-G-M musicals as *Good News*, *On the Town*, and *The Barkleys of Broadway*.

The team returned to New York in 1951. That year saw the first Broadway score with lyrics by Comden and Green, music by Jule Styne. The musical, *Two on the Aisle*, was a revue with a show biz slant for which the lyricists also contributed most of the sketches. The entertainment's main attraction was Bert Lahr hilariously ranging from impersonating Queen Victoria to playing a member of New York's Sanitation Department who lives in constant dread of being demoted to the dump. Among the songs blasted out by Dolores Gray was an inspired creation, "If You Hadn't but You Did," a rapid-fire apologia detailing the reasons why a distraught woman has just bumped off her husband.

Styne was both producer and composer of *Hazel Flagg*, a disappointing musical version of the celebrated movie, *Nothing Sacred*. Ben Hecht adapted the story from his own screenplay, and Bob Hilliard supplied the lyrics. The score was not on a level with most of Styne's work, but it did contain an especially affectionate tribute to New York City, "Every Street's a Boulevard in Old New York," sung and soft-shoed by Jack Whiting as a dapper Jimmy Walker-type mayor. Just fourteen days after the opening of *Hazel Flagg*—on February 25, 1953, to be exact—Comden and Green plus Leonard Bernstein had their second smash in a row, *Wonderful Town*.

The following year, when Jerome Robbins decided to stage a new production of Sir James M. Barrie's *Peter Pan* with Mary Martin as Peter and Cyril Ritchard as Captain Hook, he initially planned to use only a few incidental songs by composer Mark ("Moose") Charlap and lyricist Carolyn Leigh. When the production began to evolve into a full-scale musical, he went to Styne, Comden and Green to supply the additional songs. Following its world première in San Francisco, *Peter Pan* opened in New York in October. The reviews were generally favorable and Miss Martin won special acclaim for her ability to sing and fly through the air at the

BELLS ARE RINGING (1956). *Sydney Chaplin and Judy Holliday perform an impromptu entertainment for passersby in New York's Central Park.*

PHOTO BY FRIEDMAN-ABELES

same time. The play's disappointing run (152 performances) was due primarily to the fact that it had opened only about four and one-half years after the highly successful Jean Arthur-Boris Karloff version. That one, incidentally, had five songs written by Leonard Bernstein.

Styne, Comden, Green and Robbins were reunited in 1956 for *Bells Are Ringing*. Ever since Betty Comden and Adolph Green first worked with Judy Holliday in their night club act, they had hoped someday to write a musical especially for her. Their inspiration came when they thought of casting Judy as a meddlesome switchboard operator at a telephone answering service. The resultant libretto owed much to the already proven *Wonderful Town* formula of depicting New York as just a gay, warmhearted small town, where people dance and sing in subways, and where a mousey telephone operator can find both adventure and the man of her dreams.* Miss Holliday, in her first musical, had an irresistible winsomeness that helped audiences overlook many of the sophomoric twists of the plot. Even her untrained singing voice proved remarkably suitable at interpreting the sentiments of such diverse musical contributions as "Is It a Crime?" which satirizes bathetic pleas for happiness, the poignant "The Party's Over," and the rousing "Mammy"-styled "I'm Going Back" ("To the Bonjour Tristesse Brassière Company").

Say, Darling, the fourth Jule Styne-Betty Comden-Adolph Green collaboration, was something of a theatrical oddity. After having co-authored *The Pajama Game*, a musical version of his novel, *7½ Cents*, Richard Bissell wrote another novel based on his adventures in the world of musical comedy. Called *Say, Darling*, it too was converted into a musical, or to be precise, "A Comedy About a Musical." Nine songs were in it, none really distinguished.

Once *Say, Darling* was unveiled on Broadway in the spring of 1958, audiences took special pleasure in trying to identify some of the individuals who had been connected with *The Pajama Game*. David Wayne, as the smalltown author, was obviously Bissell himself. Robert Morse, as a young producer, was doubtlessly Harold Prince, and Jerome Cowan, as an experienced musical comedy director, could be none other than George Abbott. Whether the egotistical song writer (played by Johnny Desmond) was a composite of Richard Adler and Jerry Ross was never made clear, nor was the true identity of the glamorous star of the show (played by Vivian Blaine).

---

* The leading character in *Bells Are Ringing* was not too dissimilar from the one in *The Five O'Clock Girl*, a Bert Kalmer-Harry Ruby musical comedy hit of 1927. In that show, the heroine worked in a cleaner's shop and carried on a telephone flirtation with an unknown man every day at five.

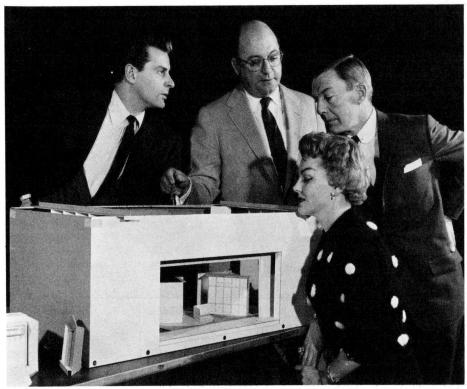

SAY, DARLING *(1958). Director Abe Burrows explaining a scene to Johnny Desmond, Vivian Blaine and David Wayne. (Setting by Oliver Smith.)*

Producer David Merrick first saw the musical possibilities in *Gypsy*, the autobiography of Gypsy Ross Lee, when he read only a chapter from it in *Harper's Magazine*. Without even bothering to read the entire book, he went ahead and secured the theatrical rights. Ethel Merman, who did read the complete biography, was so determined to play the part of Gypsy's ambitious mother that she threatened to shoot anyone else who got the part. She got it without firing a shot. At first *Gypsy* was supposed to have been another Styne, Comden and Green enterprise, but after working on it for some time, all three came to the conclusion that it could not be adapted. Director Jerome Robbins, however, was sure it could—if librettist Arthur Laurents, with whom he had worked on *West Side Story*, were given a crack at it. Then, according to Stephen Sondheim, the eventual lyricist, "they auditioned a number of song writers, including Cy Coleman and Carolyn Leigh, Marshall Barer and Dean Fuller, and myself. I was

318

chosen to do both music and lyrics. That was in April of 1958; Arthur and I began preliminary discussions on the play, awaiting Ethel Merman's approval. She came to New York in August and announced that since she had just been burned by two young writers in *Happy Hunting*, she didn't want to take a chance on an unknown again. Her agent suggested Jule. Arthur and Jerry said they'd accept him if I would. I said no, since I didn't want to be pigeonholed as a lyricist forever. But Oscar Hammerstein, who brought me up, and Arthur, who said that he wouldn't do the show with any other lyricist, persuaded me to stop licking my wounds. And I *did* like the project."

The book of *Gypsy* may have been another variation on the familiar rags-to-riches Cinderella tale, but all those responsible resisted the temptation to make it just another backstage saga about a domineering mother. "This woman is a classic," says Laurents. "What we've got here is a mother

GYPSY *(1959). Rose, the ambitious stage mother, coaches her children, Louise and June, in the first scene of the play. Karen Moore, Ethel Merman, and Jacqueline Mayro. (Costumes by Raoul Pène du Bois.)*

PHOTO BY FRIEDMAN-ABELES

GYPSY (1959). "Salute to Christmas" à la Minsky.

who has to learn that if you try to live your children's lives, you'll end up by destroying yourself." Creating music to match the uncompromising libretto was the most severe challenge Styne ever faced as a composer. To achieve the proper musical setting, Styne and Sondheim evolved a superbly congruous score that illuminated all the courage, misplaced ambition, and singleness of purpose of the central character. They achieved this principally through three numbers—"Some People," "Ev'rything's Coming Up Roses," and "Rose's Turn"—each individually compelling, yet each firmly linked to the other, with the haunting "I had a dream" passage effectively used as a leitmotif.

On a lighter though equally meaningful level, the composer and lyricist were able to capture all the tinselled gaudiness of small-time vaudeville and big-time burlesque. One particularly original and striking touch was their variations on a single melody, "May We Entertain You?" (later called "Let Me Entertain You"), which was the "onstage" music for all scenes involving Gypsy Rose Lee and her sister, June Havoc. First, it was sung by two frightened kids as they auditioned for a seedy vaudeville show; later it became a more aggressive invitation as the girls acquired greater experience; finally, it turned into the slinky, blaring accompaniment to

320

Gypsy's first strip tease. Other remarkably effective pieces dealing with varied aspects of show business were "All I Need Is the Girl," the slightly pathetic attempt of a young hoofer to do the suave Fred Astaire bit, and the vulgar, riotous show-stopper, "You Gotta Have a Gimmick," in which three strippers offered highly animated expatiations on their art.

Gypsy did win Jule Styne a measure of long-delayed recognition. It may have had Ethel Merman to attract the customers, but the show could not be called a Merman vehicle. For just as the musical required more of Styne, it also required more of Merman; both met the challenges of the story with gifts never before revealed because they had never before been tested.

For his next two musicals, *Do Re Mi* and *Subways Are for Sleeping*,

DO RE MI *(1960). "Watch Nancy Walker," advised critic Walter Kerr, "as she larrups into a honey of a lyric called 'Adventure,' whipping husband Phil Silvers' wardrobe like a lariat beneath her feet while she sends forth the mating call of a triumphant coyote." (Costumes by Irene Sharaff; setting by Boris Aronson.)*

Styne was rejoined by Comden and Green. Both shows dealt with aspects of modern-day big city life. The former, with a book by Garson Kanin based on his own novel, was a wild satire on the music business with special emphasis on the jukebox industry. The latter, a Comden and Green adaptation of Edmund Love's novel, was a wacky look at the city's disaffected and indigent. Both productions, though cut pretty much to formula, did have rewarding features. *Do Re Mi*, which was reminiscent of *Guys and Dolls* and a few other recent musicals (the solo breast-beating ending was right out of *Gypsy*), gave us two brilliant clowns in Phil Silvers, as Hubie Cram, the pushiest of patsies, and Nancy Walker, as his long-suffering spouse. At a recording session, Phil knowledgeably instructed a group of musicians how and what to play ("You hang around, you learn," was his bland explanation for such expertise), and, at a flashy night club, went into hilariously full details of gangland behavior gleaned from watching old movies on television's Late Late Show. Miss Walker was at her slack-jawed best in the rampageous musical account, "Adventure," in which she contrasted her abandoned middle class security with her frenetic, unpredictable life with Phil. Apart from such specialties, the score contained two standout pieces, the folkish "Cry Like the Wind," sung by Nancy Dussault, and that bit of homey philosophy, "Make Someone Happy," sung by John Reardon.

While *Subways Are for Sleeping* was a far less skillful piece of stagecraft ("woebegone," "painful" and "vapid" were among the critical adjectives used in the press), it did give audiences the opportunity—as did *On the Town, Wonderful Town* and *Bells Are Ringing* —of going along on another of Comden and Green's wide-eyed, affectionate guided tours through the brick and concrete playground called Manhattan. With composer Styne, they revealed the lonely heart of a big city office worker ("Girls Like Me"), showed how astonishingly agile are the city's George Price-ish street corner Santas ("Be a Santa"), and, in a truly inspired creation, "Ride Through the Night," cut through the babble of subway riders' voices to reveal the magic carpet wonders of a twisting, turning express ride underground. Two other appealing items, "Taking My Time" and "Comes Once in a Lifetime," prescribed proper attitudes for achieving happiness in the tough but of course basically friendly city.

At various times before its opening, Jule Styne's next musical was called *A Very Special Person, My Man* and *The Luckiest People*. At various times, the leading role was announced—or rumored—for Mary Martin, Anne Bancroft and Carol Burnett. But when *Funny Girl* did, after much pre-Broadway travail, arrive at the Winter Garden late in March, 1964, there was no doubt that the musical and its star, Barbra Streisand, would

FUNNY GIRL (1964). *Composer Jule Styne and lyricist Bob Merrill go over the score with Sydney Chaplin and Barbra Streisand.*

be as inextricably linked as if the one had been created specifically for the other.

Mounting a dramatic work based on the life of comedienne Fanny Brice had long been the dream of producer Ray Stark, an understandable ambition since he also happens to be the husband of Fanny's daughter, Frances. But since Stark was—and still is—primarily a Hollywood executive, he first visualized it as a screen adaptation. It was only after reading scenarist Isobel Lennart's first draft that he saw it emerging as a musical for the stage. Styne and lyricist Bob Merrill, who heretofore had written music as well as words for the theatre, were then signed to supply the songs. By the time rehearsals began in November, 1963, a year and a half had already been spent in writing. By the time the show opened on Broadway four months later, there had been four changes of directors (Jerome Robbins, Bob Fosse, Garson Kanin, and back to Robbins), innumerable script alterations including forty rewrites of the final scene alone (main problem: should Fanny leave husband Nicky Arnstein after he gets out of prison or should he leave her?), and five postponements of the première. But once the show opened, nothing that had gone on before really mattered. For *Funny Girl*, thanks mainly to its dynamic star and its superior score, was a boxoffice smash that continued to attract customers for almost 1,400 performances.

Most of the attention was focused, quite logically, on the twenty-one-year-old Barbra Streisand, whose only previous theatrical experience had been in a short-lived off-Broadway revue, *Another Evening with Harry Stoones* (whence also came Diana Sands and Dom DeLuise), and in her brief but memorable role in *I Can Get It for You Wholesale*. Melvin Gussow in *Newsweek* commented that the actress was given "plenty of

FUNNY GIRL *(1964). Barbra Streisand, as Fanny Brice, is hoisted by her friends and neighbors following her rendition of the song of the happy newlywed, "Sadie, Sadie." (Costumes by Irene Sharaff; setting by Robert Randolph.)*

elbow room to prove she's a star—and she seems to have a dozen elbows," and described her movements as "more gnu than gazelle." A similarly physical appraisal of Miss Streisand's performance was voiced by *Time* critic Ted Kalem, who both heralded the actress as "the theatre's new girl for all seasons," and called her "an anthology of the awkward graces, all knees and elbows, or else a boneless wonder, a seal doing an unbalancing act." But it was Walter Kerr of the *Herald Tribune* who outdid everyone by likening the lady to a grasshopper, an oak with the spine of a willow inside, an eel, and a second cousin to an octopus. Oh, yes, he also proclaimed her a star.

Musically and lyrically, Styne and Merrill had to balance their score between personal expressions and songs that were supposedly part of theatrical productions—just as Styne and Sondheim had done in *Gypsy*. Indeed, there were a few parallels between the two scores that were perhaps impossible to avoid. In *Gypsy*, the spirit of out-of-my-way determination was revealed early in the show through "Some People"; in *Funny Girl*, "I'm the Greatest Star" carried a similar message as, after a tentative start, it builds to a blaring declaration of self-confidence. Both musicals brought down their first act curtains on their respective stars, all alone at deserted railway terminals, in self-deluding affirmations of their single-minded goals. Just as "I had a dream" became part of "Ev'rything's Coming Up Roses," so an interpolation from "I'm the Greatest Star"—the staccato buildup beginning, somewhat anachronistically, "Who is the pip with piz-azz?"—was added, with a different lyric, to the curtain dropper, "Don't Rain on My Parade." As for the endings of both shows, each contained throat-catching bits in which the star appeared solo on stage to strip herself emotionally bare. Merman in *Gypsy* had the explosive "Rose's Turn"; Streisand in *Funny Girl* the equally affecting, though more conventional, "The Only Music that Makes Me Dance" (also serving as substitute for the real Fanny Brice's tearstained theme, "My Man"). But the song from *Funny Girl* that became most closely identified with the "new" Fanny was unquestionably "People," a soaring, wide-ranged testament to the brotherhood of man that was that theatrical rarity, a show-stopping ballad.

Just two months after the opening of *Funny Girl*, Jule Styne had another show on the boards, *Fade Out—Fade In*, an original Comden and Green concept spoofing Hollywood in the Thirties. The musical, both tailor-made and jerry-built, spotlighted the gawky gamboling of Carol Burnett, and received a generally favorable press. Though slated for a good run, the show was forced to close after only a few months because of Miss Burnett's back injuries. It faded in again the following February, but faded out permanently after two months—this time because of Miss Burnett's pregnancy.

FADE OUT - FADE IN (1964). Tiger Haynes and Carol Burnett do the Bill Robinson and Shirley Temple bit as they strut through the number, "You Mustn't Be Discouraged." (Costumes by Donald Brooks.)

The score tried hard for nostalgia and satire, and succeeded most impressively in a starry-eyed clarion, "The Usher from the Mezzanine."

Hallelujah, Baby!, at this writing the most recent Styne-Comden-Green musical, had a bright, imaginative idea behind it—a lighthearted look at the Negro's struggle for equality since the turn of the century, but with none of the characters aging a day.* What looked particularly promising was that the trio was being joined in the venture by *West Side Story* and *Gypsy* librettist, Arthur Laurents. But regrettably the musical turned out to be rather patronizing, with ill-defined characters, a fuzzy point of view, and a story that simply gave up midway in the second act. The show, however, did have one important thing in its favor. Leslie Uggams, in her Broadway debut, was, in the words of Walter Kerr, "One of the most complete personalities to have descended upon us in many a mournful moon, ready-

---

* A similar technique had been used by Alan Jay Lerner and Kurt Weill in their 1948 collaboration, *Love Life*. In that musical, the principle characters remained the same age from 1791 to the then present.

326

made, able for anything, proud as silk, intimate as velvet, cheery as ging-ham." Apart from one hand-me-down item ("Witches Brew," with a differ-ent lyric, had been "Call Me Savage" in *Fade Out—Fade In*), the song writ-ers matched her personality with appropriately fresh material. Such as: "My Own Morning," a suitably lofty air for the show's hope-for-the-future theme; "Being Good Isn't Good Enough," an almost excruciatingly intense personal credo; and the foot-stomping, hand-clapping, tambourine-jangling title song.

"Without the rendition there is no song," maintains Jule Styne em-phatically, and his career proves it. With Nanette Fabray, Charol Chan-ning, Dolores Grey, Mary Martin, Judy Holliday, Ethel Merman, Barbra Streisand, Carol Burnett, and Leslie Uggams to sing them, his songs have benefited from some of the most individualistic and compelling renditions ever heard in the theatre. But obviously they needed something to render. To compose songs to fit particular talents—especially when they are as out-standing as the ones for whom Styne has written—requires a creativity no less demanding than composing songs to fit particular characters or situa-tions. When a composer can create a melody that fits all three—the per-former. the character and the dramatic situation—he demonstrates the rarest kind of theatrical skill. The measure of Jule Styne's contributions to the world of musical comedy may best be appreciated not alone by what per-formers have done for his songs, but also by what his songs have meant to the careers of the performers who have sung them.

Frank Loesser.

CHAPTER TWENTY-ONE

Frank Loesser
Richard Adler and Jerry Ross
Meredith Willson

THE FREQUENTLY BACK-BITING rivalry usually associated with the theater is, of course, very real, and there is no point in denying that it exists. Yet with regard to composers, the rule seems to be more one of mutual admiration, even mutual assistance. Victor Herbert took a keen interest in the career of Jerome Kern, and, for a while, Kern had an almost paternal feeling toward George Gershwin. Gershwin himself did what he could to help many budding talents; in the early Thirties, he even introduced new works by various young composers on his radio program. More recently, Rodgers and Hammerstein offered *Annie Get Your Gun* with a score by Irving Berlin, and Jule Styne was responsible for reviving Rodgers and Hart's *Pal Joey*. He also presented *Mr. Wonderful* and *First Impressions,* both with scores by other song-writers. Of all the composers discussed in this book, however, it is Frank Loesser who has probably been in the most advantageous position of being of help to others, a fact that is strikingly revealed in the careers of Richard Adler, Jerry Ross, and Meredith Willson.

Frank Loesser

The multiple activities of Frank Loesser in the musical theatre—composer, lyricist, librettist, producer — have given him a special distinction among his colleagues. Of equal importance to his own accomplishments, however, has been his unflagging interest in, and assistance to, new writers for the stage. Loesser is, in fact, able to offer very tangible aid. As president of the Frank Music Company, one of the leading music-publishing companies in the country, he has published the works of many promising composers and lyricists—in addition, of course, to his own songs.

It has been a particular mark of his foresight that Frank Loesser has been instrumental in furthering the careers of the three most successful songwriters of the theatre to emerge during the Fifties—Richard Adler, Jerry Ross, and Meredith Willson. In 1951, anxious to find the most promising talent among the young writers of Tin Pan Alley, he signed the team of Richard Adler and Jerry Ross to a contract. A few years later, after Loesser was approached to write the score for *The Pajama Game*, he suggested to George Abbott that Adler and Ross would make excellent replacements. In the case of Meredith Willson, it was Loesser who first urged him to turn the story of his Iowa boyhood into a musical. Loesser even introduced Willson to Cy Feuer and Ernest Martin, who were originally to have been the producers of *The Music Man*. Eventually, when it opened in New York in 1957, Frank Productions was the associate producer with Kermit Bloomgarden and Frank Music was the music publisher.

Such a variety of activities is completely natural to the restless, energetic Loesser. A hard-working, hard-driving man, he gets no more than four hours sleep a night and is usually awake by six-thirty in the morning. "I get bored otherwise," he says. "I like to have a song, a list of figures, and a business problem all around me."

Frank Henry Loesser was born in New York City, on June 29, 1910. His father was a piano teacher whose only interest was in the classics. His older brother, Arthur, has been a concert pianist, critic, and music teacher. In this environment, Loesser became interested in music at an early age. At six, he wrote a song called "The May Party" in celebration of the children's processions he saw in Central Park. A year later, he amused himself by fitting words to the clicking of the elevated railroad as it roared through his neighborhood.

Because his father disapproved of popular music, Loesser had to teach himself how to play the piano when he was in his early teens. After failing in his studies at the City College of New York, he took a variety of jobs. One that he particularly liked was as a reporter for a short-lived New Rochelle newspaper. When he was assigned to cover a local dinner of the

Lions Club, he obliged one of the officers by supplying rhymed couplets celebrating the exploits of all the members at the dinner. According to his brother Arthur, the local fame he achieved as the author of such lines as "Secretary Albert Vincent, Read these minutes right this instant," gave him his first inspiration to become a lyricist.

Soon Loesser began to write sketches and lyrics for vaudeville acts. During the Depression, he wrote occasional material for radio. In those days, Loesser recalls, "Somehow you had to find a way of getting a job. You had to keep alert all of the time. I suppose that's where this tremendous energy of mine originated."

In 1931, Loesser wrote his first published song, "In Love with a Memory Of You." It had a melody by William Schuman, who was to become a celebrated composer of concert music. A few years later, Loesser got a job singing and playing at the Back Drop, a 52nd Street nightclub. Many of the songs he sang where original numbers with music by Irving Actman. Five of these were used in *The Illustrators' Show*, the same revue in which Frederick Loewe's "A Waltz Was Born in Vienna' was first heard.

As a result of their work for *The Illustrators' Show*, Loesser and Actman were signed to a contract by Universal Pictures. Soon afterward, Loesser joined Paramount. His first song hit, "The Moon of Manakoora," (music by Alfred Newman) was written for *The Hurricane* in 1937. Among his most frequent collaborators during his eleven years in Hollywood were Burton Lane, Hoagy Carmichael, Frederick Hollander, Jimmy McHugh, Victor Schertzinger, Jule Styne, and Arthur Schwartz.

Loesser often wrote the words to songs before composers had written the music. Because the very construction of his lyrics almost dictated the melodies that would carry them, many of his collaborators urged him to write music as well as words. The first song with music and lyrics created exclusively by Frank Loesser was "Praise the Lord and Pass the Ammunition," written while he was in the Army during World War II. Its success gave Loesser the confidence to compose all of his own melodies from then on.

After his army stint was over, Loesser returned to Hollywood in 1946. His friends, Cy Feuer, the former head of the music department at Republic Pictures, and Ernest Martin, a former television executive, had formed a partnership to produce musical plays. Through attorney Howard Reinheimer (who was also Rodgers and Hammerstein's lawyer), they had secured the rights to Brandon Thomas' ancient farce, *Charley's Aunt*, as a vehicle for Ray Bolger, and they wanted Loesser to contribute the music and lyrics. In common with many other theatrical beginners, the producers then called upon the experienced George Abbott to serve as both director and librettist.

Where's Charley?, as the play was retitled, opened on October 11, 1948, and became an unqualified hit. It was the first of Feuer and Martin's five

331

WHERE'S CHARLEY? (1948). George Abbott directing Ray Bolger.

successful musicals in a row (the other four were *Guys and Dolls, The Boy Friend, Can-Can,* and *Silk Stockings*), and it also established Loesser as a Broadway composer and lyricist of great promise. His ballads ("My Darling, My Darling" and "Once in Love with Amy") had a simple, direct appeal, though even more impressive musical gifts were revealed in "The Red Rose Cotillion" and "The New Ashmoleon Marching Society and Student Conservatory Band." Moreover, in "Make a Miracle," he created a number in which words and music were brilliantly combined to produce a complete musical vignette as the ardent suitor tries vainly to gain the attention of his daydreaming sweetheart.

For their next musical, Feuer and Martin decided on a more ambitious work. Long fond of Damon Runyon stories and characters, they decided to do a Runyon fable based on a short story, *The Idyll of Miss Sarah Brown.* They also had a good title for it: *Guys and Dolls.* Their first choice for librettist was a Hollywood scenarist named Jo Swerling, but the producers were dissatisfied with the result. By the time they approached Abe Burrows, then a radio script-writer, they had already read librettos by eleven different authors. Although the Burrows script at last provided them with the right approach, contractural arrangements compelled them to retain Swerling's name on the program as co-author.

Feuer and Martin had signed Loesser even before they hired Burrows. Later, they secured George S. Kaufman as director and Michael Kidd to stage the dances. What emerged, when the show opened in 1950, was one of the most tightly coordinated musicals ever created. As Howard Barnes of the *Herald Tribune* wrote: "The work uses music and dancing as embellishments to the libretto, rather than making the latter a loose clothesline for assorted capers and vocal numbers."

GUYS AND DOLLS (1950). *The oldest established permanent floating crap game in New York takes up temporary residence in a sewer. Throwing the dice is Sky Masterson (Robert Alda), and standing behind him is Big Julie (B. S. Pully). Nicely Nicely Johnson (Stubby Kaye) and Nathan Detroit (Sam Levene) are kneeling on either side of them. (Costumes by Alvin Colt; setting by Jo Mielziner.)*

PHOTO BY EILEEN DARBY—GRAPHIC HOUSE

In writing the score, Loesser found inspiration in many of the actual guys and dolls he had known when he was a pianist at the Back Drop. It was his ability to capture the racy, hard-shelled, but basically soft-hearted characters of the gamblers and racketeers of the Runyon fable that gave his songs their special distinction. These people speak in awkwardly cultivated tones, their emotions are explosive but unassailably pure, and when Sister Sarah Brown of the Save a Soul Mission comes along to urge them into living more respectable lives, there is never any doubt that she will eventually succeed.

Loesser's score had great variety, yet it also had a singleness of design and purpose that caught the appealing ambivalence of the highminded low-lifes. Dignified and classical forms, such as a college alma mater for "The Oldest Established," or the Bachlike fugue for a description of a horse race, were completely right because, in spite of the incongruity, the characters themselves were essentially dignified and classical. So too, a grandly operatic duet, "Sue Me," was used with unerring effect as Adelaide, a nightclub singer, (played by Vivian Blaine) flails away at Nathan Detroit, her fiancé of fourteen years (played by Sam Levene), only to be met by his unnerving acquiescence. For the two sequences at the Hot Box nightclub, Loesser had his fun on two levels. "A Bushel and a Peck" is a purposely inane number which becomes all the more ridiculous as it is squealed by the chorus girls, while "Take Back Your Mink" achieves its humor from the shocked attitude of the girls whose virtues are about to be imperiled.

One song, "Adelaide's Lament," was written well before the final libretto was completed. Originally, Adelaide was to have been a stripper who catches cold from overexposure; later, when it was decided that she would be more sympathetic as a singer, Loesser changed the lyric to make her suffer from psychosomatic ailments because her marriage to Nathan has been postponed so often. "Adelaide's Lament," one of the most brilliant of all comic love songs, is a perfect example of Loesser's dictum: "I try to examine characters, not events."

THE MOST HAPPY FELLA (1956). Robert Weede as Tony, the aging winegrower of Napa Valley, California, and Jo Sullivan as Rosabella, his mail-order bride.

PHOTO BY ARTHUR CANTOR

In 1952, a friend suggested to Loesser that he create a musical out of Sidney Howard's *They Knew What They Wanted*. Loesser read it and was immediately intrigued with the idea. "I figured take out all this political talk, the labor talk, and the religious talk. Get rid of all that stuff and you have a good love story." The tender tale of the elderly Italian winegrower in California who falls in love at first sight with a waitress seemed to Loesser to have an emotional intensity especially well suited to a musical adaptation. "Go spell what you sound like when you're laughing or crying. You have to say it in music."

Writing *The Most Happy Fella*—music, lyrics, libretto—took Loesser more than four years. He felt like giving it up many times, but inevitably a period of depression would be followed by one of extreme enthusiasm, and he would again plod forward. Once the work was finished, there still remained the problem of finding a suitable actor for the leading role of the winegrower. Loesser even made a trip to Italy in a vain search for someone with the right quality of voice and acting ability. Eventually, he engaged Robert Weede, formerly of the Metropolitan Opera, who made his Broadway debut in the musical.

The Most Happy Fella, which opened in New York on May 5, 1956, was probably the most ambitiously operatic work ever created for the Broadway musical theatre. Included among its more than thirty separate musical numbers were recitatives, arias, duets, trios, quartets, and choral passages, yet all of them were created to fit within the framework of the commercial musical theatre. Big, booming arias, such as "Rosabella" and "My Heart Is So Full of You," are interspersed with such traditional Broadway specialty numbers as "Big 'D'" and "Standing on the Corner." Other selections, particularly "Abbondanza" and "Benvenuta," reveal their composer's knack of parodying the effulgences of Neapolitan singers. Perhaps most charming of all are the duet between Weede and Jo Sullivan (as his mail-order bride), "Happy to Make Your Acquaintance," and the evocative quartet, "How Beautiful the Days."

334

Although in the manner of an opera, the program for *The Most Happy Fella* did not list the individual songs, the work was designated simply as "A Musical." To those who prod him on the matter, Loesser says, "I may give the impression this show has operatic tendencies. If people feel that way—fine. Actually all it has is a great frequency of songs. It's a musical with music." Or, as arranger Don Walker has put it, "This is a musical comedy expanded. Not an opera cut down."

Apparently, once Frank Loesser becomes identified with a particular type of music or musical, he feels he must move on to something more challenging. In his next production, *Greenwillow*, starring Anthony Perkins in his first appearance in a musical, Loesser abruptly abandoned the colorful big-city world of Damon Runyon and the melodramatic world of Sidney Howard in favor of the pastoral world of novelist B. J. Chute. This time, Loesser (and co-librettist Lesser Samuels) sought to capture the elusive flavor of an imaginary community located somewhere along the banks of the Meander River. With little plot, the musical relied on a certain synthetic charm derived from imaginary quaint rural customs (the baptism of a cow, for example), that were perhaps somewhat difficult to accept on the musical stage. "Folklore," wrote Walter Kerr following its March 8, 1960, première, "may just be one dish that can't be cooked to order."

Loesser's score provided a rich variety of bucolic themes, demonstrating again that the composer is a master at recreating familiar musical styles, while still endowing his songs with his own individual style. Included are wistful old English ballads ("Walking Away Whistling," "Faraway Boy"), a religious hymn (an amusing bit in which two ministers offer contrasting sermons

THE MOST HAPPY FELLA *(1956). The "Big D" number led by Texans Susan Johnson and, at the far right, Shorty Long. (Costumes by Motley.)*

PHOTO BY FRIEDMAN-ABELES

on the same theme), and a Christmas carol ("Greenwillow Christmas"). Loesser also created two moving songs for Mr. Perkins, "Summertime Love," which fairly bursts out its message of love's constancy, and the touching renunciation, "Never Will I Marry." All these numbers have an authenticity and feeling for mood that somehow escaped the production as a whole.

For his next musical, Loesser had no such problem. *How to Succeed in Business Without Really Trying* offered a perfect theme for his special musical gifts. Certainly the challenge was still great: to write a score that would hew so closely to this satire on big business shenanigans that it would permit no compromise in the form of dragged-in, commercially-motivated songs. Every number was made to fit. Every number was part of the overall design. "The Company Way" was the organization man's ode to the organization. "I Believe in You" was a narcissistic serenade our hero —to the accompanying buzz of an electric razor—sang to himself while shaving. "Grand Old Ivy" turned out to be every old grad's tribute to every Alma Mater. "A Secretary Is Not a Toy" was a perkey compendium of office etiquette ("Her pad is to write in/Not spend the night in"), punctuated by the clatter of typewriters.

Loesser's fidelity to form and content was typical of the integrity of the entire show. The work had originated as a comedy without music by Willie Gilbert and Jack Weinstock, adapted from Shepherd Mead's humorous non-fictional guidebook on how to get ahead in business. But pro-

GREENWILLOW *(1960). Anthony Perkins vows his devotion to his "Summertime Love." (Costumes by Alvin Colt.)*

PHOTO BY FRED FEHL

HOW TO SUCCEED IN BUSI-
NESS WITHOUT REALLY TRYING
*(1961). Alma Mater "Grand
Old Ivy" is ardently sung by
old-grad J. B. Biggley (Rudy
Vallee) and would-be young-
grad J. Pierpont Finch (Robert Morse).*

ducers Cy Feuer and Ernest Martin had other ideas; they saw it as a musical
comedy that was perfect for their *Guys and Dolls* cohorts, composer Frank
Loesser and librettist Abe Burrows. Long before they had put a word on
paper, Loesser and Burrows held endless sessions thrashing out the vital
questions posed by the specific nature of the project. How do you sing a
show about big business? What kind of songs would business people sing?
When and why would they sing them? Bob Fosse, who had been hired
to do the musical staging, ventured the idea that a soft-shoe number would
have the right sound for a business office. That became "A Secretary Is
Not a Toy." Burrows came up with the notion of having the musical's big
love song sung by the leading man to himself. That became "I Believe in
You." Only after working out about nine or ten musical ideas—not even
knowing exactly where they would go—did Loesser and Burrows then sit
down to write the songs and the libretto. "We declared," declared Burrows,
"that our show would be as impudent as we could make it. We wanted it
to be funny and sharp. Our people were going to be interesting and exciting,
not just wilted violets drooping away with fraudulent broken hearts and
stems. We promised ourselves that every song would make a point and
that no one would stop dead, center stage, in order to sing a song that had
no purpose in the story."

After a full year of self-imposed discipline, the men eventually came up with a working script. Everything connected with the mores and morals of corporation life—from the mailroom to the board room—became frequently devastated targets, with shots aimed as such institutions and fixtures as the coffee break, the office party (in which all the girls show up in the identical "Paris Original"), the fawning yes men, and even the prestigious confines of the executive washroom.

From the very beginning of the project, there was agreement that the role of the baby-faced, two-timing "hero," J. Pierpont Finch, would go to Robert Morse, who had been in only two previous musicals. Despite a tendency toward mugging, Morse was unquestionably the season's musical comedy find. The part of the stuffy tycoon, J. B. Biggley, president of World Wide Wicket Co., Inc., was played by Rudy Vallee in his first Broadway appearance since the *George White's Scandals of 1936*. The general hat-tossing reception the musical received following its October, 1961, opening, fully justified the determination of the authors to keep their work free from moralizing or sentimentality. Howard Taubman of the *Times* ranked it among "the blue chips of modern musicals," and Walter Kerr in the *Herald Tribune* found it "crafty, conniving, sneaky, cynical, irreverent, impertinent, sly, malicious, and lovely, just lovely." So did the Pulitzer Committee, which handed the show its prize as the best play of the year—the fourth musical so honored.

Frank Loesser's multiple activities have limited him to only six musicals (one, *Pleasures and Palaces* in 1965, didn't make it to New York) since he first began his theatre career in 1948. Yet he is universally acknowledged to be among the most creative practitioners in the field. Moreover, his work has been marked by the most steady advance of any composer since George Gershwin. From formula musical comedy (*Where's Charley?*), he plunged right into a modern comic opera (*Guys and Dolls*). Then, in *The Most Happy Fella,* he proceeded to write the first successful Broadway opera since Gershwin's *Porgy and Bess. Greenwillow,* despite its faults, was still commendably daring in subject and treatment, and *How to Succeed in Business Without Really Trying* capped Loesser's career to date with a second modern comic opera even more unconventional than the first. Also noteworthy is that, just as he has extended himself in themes, Loesser has also expanded his creative activities—from lyricist to composer-lyricist to composer-lyricist-librettist-producer.

Frank Loesser is an original who has established his own high standards in the Broadway theatre. Combining the sensitivity of the artist with the acumen of the businessman, he has labored to preserve these standards not alone through his own works but through the works of others whom he has encouraged and sponsored.

Richard Adler and Jerry Ross.

Richard Adler and Jerry Ross

When, in 1951, Frank Loesser asked another music publisher to send him the most promising young song-writers he knew, the publisher immediately thought of Richard Adler and Jerry Ross. Loesser was so impressed with their songs that he promptly signed the two young composers to an exclusive contract with his publishing company. Many things about the versatile team—each man could write both music and lyrics—made Loesser confident that they would eventually fulfill his expectations. Their music showed both originality and a rhythmic accessibility that indicated commercial appeal. Their lyrics were full of the argot of modern, idiomatic speech that Loesser himself has captured so well. Above all, both men, like Loesser, were anxious to break down the walls that had, for so many years, created barriers between Tin Pan Alley and the Broadway theatre.

During their relatively brief partnership (Ross died of a lung ailment in 1955), these "two young Loessers," as Leonard Bernstein has called them, showed a special aptitude for communicating with contemporary audiences. "Subconsciously, and from our training, we're writing for the man in the street," Ross once remarked. To which Adler added: "We try to write universal truths in colloquial terms. We're just trying to bring out the expression of the times in which we live in terms of the people with whom we're dealing. We're writing the way our generation demands we write."

Both men were born in New York—Adler on August 23, 1923, and Ross on March 9, 1926. Adler's family life was quite similar to Frank Loesser's, as his father, Clarence Adler, was a concert pianist and music teacher. Classical music, however, never interested the young Adler; in fact, his original ambition was to become a writer. After graduating from the University of North Carolina (where he studied playwrighting under Paul Green), he spent three years in the Navy. Upon his discharge, he got a job writing advertising copy for a large corporation. About this time he began to compose songs; at first, during his spare time and later even during office hours. Inevitably, this resulted in his dismissal, but, as Adler had already decided to become a song-writer, he welcomed the opportunity to devote all of his time to music. He met with little success, however, until he met Jerry Ross in 1950.

Ross was born in the East Bronx of poor parents. At ten, while singing in a synagogue choir, he was approached to join the Bronx Art Theatre, a Yiddish acting company. After acting in one of its productions, he joined other companies then presenting plays on the Jewish stage. Because Ross attended high school in the Bronx and most of these groups were on the lower East Side of Manhattan, he was forced to stay up until all hours commuting. As a result, during this period he developed chronic bronchietasis, which was eventually responsible for his death. Ross was still in his teens when he wrote his first song. He continued composing at New York University, where he took courses in music, and at summer resorts in the Catskills. Like Adler, Ross had little luck as a song-writer until he met his partner.

Adler and Ross's first success for Frank Loesser was "Rags to Riches," which they wrote in 1953. The same year they were signed to write most of the songs for *John Murray Anderson's Almanac*, a revue starring Hermione Gingold, Billy DeWolfe, and Harry Belafonte. Even before this show opened, the team was hired by George Abbott to create the entire score for *The Pajama Game*. Adler and Ross had previously auditioned for Abbott on two occasions; each time, though he was encouraging, the old master told them that they were not yet ready. When Loesser recommended them for *The Pajama Game*, the partners again auditioned. This time, the director was

THE PAJAMA GAME (1954). *Eddie Foy, Jr., Janis Paige, and John Raitt.*

DAMN YANKEES (1955). Choreographer Bob Fosse rehearsing the chorus.

so excited about their work that he rushed over to Frederick Brisson, Robert Griffith, and Harold Prince, the show's producers, and insisted that the team be hired.

The Pajama Game opened in May, 1954. Following the frequent pattern of George Abbott musicals, most of the people responsible for the production were newcomers to the theatre—including the producers (Griffith and Prince had been stage managers for many of Abbott's productions) and choreographer Bob Fosse. Apart from Abbott, the only other experienced member of the staff was Jerome Robbins, the co-director, though this marked his first assignment directing an entire show. By thus dividing the directing chores, Abbott was given more time to work on the libretto with Richard Bissell, the author of *7½ Cents*, the novel from which the book was adapted.*

The Pajama Game was a fast-paced, human story based on the unlikely subject of a threatened strike in a pajama factory. There was, however, nothing socially conscious about it in the manner of *Pins and Needles;* the rights of the workers were not nearly as important as their fun and romantic complications. Although the unmistakable George Abbott touch was evident throughout, the contributions of Adler and Ross were of sufficient merit to establish them as the brightest new song-writing team to emerge during the decade. *The Pajama Game* also provided new opportunities for its stars, John Raitt, Janis Paige, and Eddie Foy, Jr., as well as for Carol Haney, a young dancer making her Broadway debut. (For a few performances soon after the opening, Miss Haney was replaced by her understudy, Shirley MacLaine.)

The flavor—if not the ingredients—of *Damn Yankees,* produced exactly one year later, was similar to *The Pajama Game.* It had the same production

---

* Bissell subsequently based his novel, *Say, Darling,* on his experiences working on *The Pajama Game.* This, in turn, became "A Comedy about a Musical," with songs by Jule Styne, Betty Comden, and Adolph Green.

341

staff—producers, choreographer, musical director (Hal Hastings), arranger (Don Walker)—plus director George Abbott and Adler and Ross. Abbott also collaborated on the libretto with Douglass Wallop, whose novel, *The Year the Yankees Lost the Pennant,* furnished the basis for the musical. Again, the swift-moving show had the style and the spirit that has long distinguished its director's work; even the Faustian overtones of the story were treated in a breezy manner, particularly with Ray Walston playing the devil and Gwen Verdon (in her first starring role) as his most efficient temptress. The Adler and Ross contributions, while not as striking as those in their first score, nevertheless provided such commercially successful pieces as "Whatever Lola Wants" and "Heart."

There is little doubt that the firm hand of director and co-librettist George Abbott was chiefly responsible for the lengthy runs of both *The Pajama Game* and *Damn Yankees.* Yet the work of Adler and Ross cannot be overlooked in appraising their success. Just as Frank Loesser had before them, they brought a new commercial flair to the Broadway theatre; they were remarkably adept at combining a wide range of catchy, familiar rhythms —plus original sound effects—within the framework of a single score. Thus, in *The Pajama Game* there was a lively march ("7½ Cents"), a roaring Western ballad ("There Once Was a Man"), a novelty item with a hissing noise as part of its lyric ("Steam Heat"), a lilting waltz ("I'm Not at All in Love"), a solo love song that became a duet when played back over a dictaphone ("Hey, There"), and a spooky tango ("Hernando's Hideaway"). For *Damn Yankees,* the team created a satirical barbershop quartet ("Heart"), a spirited hoedown ("Shoeless Joe from Hannibal, Mo."), a sultry tango ("Whatever Lola Wants"), a soft-shoe vaudeville number ("Those Were the Good Old Days"), and a comic mambo ("Who's Got the Pain?").

The Adler-Ross partnership, so full of promise, was terminated on November 11, 1955, when Ross died of a lung ailment at the age of 29. Since then, except for the ambitious but short-lived *Kwamina* in 1961, Adler has devoted most of his energies to writing television commercials. But in the team's two whopping, durable hits, *The Pajama Game* and *Damn Yankees,* Adler and Ross made a major—if brief—breakthrough. By proving conclusively that good theatre music could become good commercial music, they succeeded in closing the ever-widening gulf existing between the world of Broadway and the world of pop.

Meredith Willson

One day in 1949, Meredith Willson was indulging in one of his favorite indoor pastimes: reminiscing to a group of friends about his boyhood in

Rini and Meredith Willson.

Mason City, Iowa. Among his listeners was Frank Loesser. Suddenly, Loesser jumped to his feet. "What an idea!" he shouted, "Why don't you write a musical about it?" Then he started to pace up and down. "Maybe you can start with the fire chief. Let's make him the leader of the town band. Maybe *you* can play the fire chief. And maybe instead of a pit orchestra, you can have a real brass band in the pit. And you're the leader of the band. You could also be sort of a narrator and talk directly to the people in the audience. That way you could tell everybody about your town. It would be real Americana!"

When *The Music Man* finally opened on Broadway eight years later, it bore little resemblance to Loesser's original concept. But Loesser had planted an idea in Willson's mind about doing a musical with an Iowa background, something that would capture all the nostalgia and warmth inherent in a story of a small Midwestern town in the early days of the century. "Innocent, that was the adjective for Iowa," Willson has said. "I didn't have to make anything up for *The Music Man*. All I had to do was remember."

Meredith Willson was born in Mason City, on May 18, 1902. His mother gave piano lessons, and young Meredith dutifully studied that instrument as well as the piccolo and the flute. In his youth, he played piccolo in the high-school band, enjoyed the county fairs, had a job pumping water for Saturday night baths, and, in general, absorbed everything he could of the folk-lore of his small Iowa community. After high school, he went to New York to pursue a career in music. There he studied at the Institute of Musical Art (later Juilliard School of Music), and, at the age of nineteen, was hired by

343

John Philip Sousa as first flutist in his band. Three years later, he joined the New York Philharmonic, where he played under Toscanini. In 1929, Willson became musical director of the Northwest Territory for the American Broadcasting Company; soon afterward, he joined the staff of the National Broadcasting Company.

Willson's first symphony ("San Francisco") was written when he was thirty-three. From 1937 on, with the exception of the years spent in the Army during World War II, he was associated with many radio programs as both conductor and performer. His first song hit, "You and I," was written in 1941; nine years later, he wrote the popular "May the Good Lord Bless and Keep You" as the theme song for Tallulah Bankhead's radio program, *The Big Show*.

Because of his other work, Willson did not begin to write the musical about Iowa until nearly three years after Loesser had first suggested it. After abandoning the idea of the fire chief and also of appearing in the show himself, Willson then thought of telling a story about a kindly music teacher. Later, the main character was changed to a traveling salesman of non-existent musical instruments. The leading female part, a librarian who also gives piano lessons, was modeled after Willson's mother.

Through Loesser, Willson met producers Cy Feuer and Ernest Martin. They became so enthusiastic about the script that they promised to put it into production immediately after the opening of *Silk Stockings* in February, 1955. They even suggested *The Music Man* as the title. Soon, however, the producers lost interest because of what they felt were basic weaknesses in the story. This was a serious blow to Willson, but he had already put so much effort and time on the musical by then that he was determined to continue to work on it and try to interest other producers. In the summer of 1956, he re-wrote much of the libretto with playwright Franklin Lacey. By the following November, Willson had already gone through thirty-two drafts of *The Music Man* and he was still unable to find a producer. Then, remembering that Kermit Bloomgarden had co-sponsored Frank Loesser's *The Most Happy Fella*, he telephoned the producer from California. When Bloomgarden agreed to let him audition, Willson and his wife, Rini, flew to New York, and played and sang the entire production the following evening. The next morning, Bloomgarden called Willson to his office. "Meredith," he asked, "may I have the privilege of producing your beautiful play?"

Many actors were considered for the leading role of Professor Harold Hill, the persuasive but unscrupulous music man. According to Willson's book, *But He Doesn't Know the Territory*, Danny Kaye was the original choice, but Kaye did not feel he was right for the part. Dan Dailey never kept his appointment to discuss the matter with Willson. Phil Harris did not even return his telephone call. Gene Kelly just was not interested. Finally, at the insistence of director Morton DaCosta and musical director Herbert Greene, Robert Preston, best known for his performances in movie Westerns, was signed for the part.

In his score for *The Music Man,* Willson made great use of the technique of rhythmic, but not rhyming, lyrics. This is apparent in the very first number of the show, "Rock Island," in which the rhythm of a moving train is simulated in dialogue as a group of traveling salesmen discuss the problems of their trade. The same device later occurs in both "Piano Lesson," which uses the musical scale as accompaniment to a conversation between Barbara Cook, as the librarian–music teacher, and Pert Kelton, as her mother, and in "Trouble," a rousing sermon exploded into the midst of the townspeople by the fast-talking Professor Hill. Willson also adds a dramatic touch by employing the same melody for both Miss Cook's wistful "Goodnight, My Someone" and Preston's spirited "Seventy-Six Trombones," in order, as he has explained, "to suggest that these two people have something more in common than meets the eye."

Despite the fears of those who felt that *The Music Man* would be too old-fashioned for Broadway, it received unanimously favorable reviews following its December 19, 1957, opening. It then settled down for the first marathon run since *My Fair Lady.* What distinguished the show were the

THE MUSIC MAN (1957). In "Seventy Six Trombones," Robert Preston, as a bogus instrument salesman, wins over the children of River City, Iowa, with his description of the most mammoth parade of all times. "Though he never danced or sang before on stage," wrote Life Magazine, "he displays both zing and polish and follows triumphantly in the tradition of George M. Cohan." (Costumes by Raoul Pène du Bois.)

qualities of conviction and affection that so obviously went into its creation. Every type of musical expression used—soft-shoe, ragtime, barbershop quartet, march—had a feeling of genuineness that helped to bring alive the flavor of a naïve American town circa 1912. In his capacity as composer, lyricist, and librettist, Willson brought to his work a musical proficiency and a unity of purpose that made *The Music Man* a completely irresistible show.

The play's successful combination of breeziness and sentimentality were reminiscent of the works of another man of the theatre who also wrote books, music and lyrics—George M. Cohan. There was the same fondness for typically American characters and locales, the same electric excitement in the swiftly paced production, the same theatrical contrast between the city slicker and various rural types. *The Music Man* even took place on Cohan's favorite holiday, the Fourth of July. Thus, in spite of the skills of production and the advances in theatrical techniques, the musical theatre could still find welcome room for a production with the same basic appeal of the earliest examples of strictly American musicals based on strictly American themes.

Willson's two subsequent musicals, *The Unsinkable Molly Brown* (book by Richard Morris) and *Here's Love* (book by Willson), were equally representative—though not equally felicitous—examples of the composer's general style and outlook. *Molly Brown,* which provided Tammy Grimes with her most rewarding role to date, retold the saga of a near-legendary figure of the Colorado silver mines, who pulled herself up from

PHOTO BY FRIEDMAN-ABELES

THE UNSINKABLE MOLLY BROWN *(1960). Harve Presnell and Tammy Grimes cavorting to "I Ain't Down Yet." (Costumes by Miles White; setting by Oliver Smith.)*

poverty by marrying a lucky prospector named Leadville Johnny Brown. Here the situation was something of a reversal of *The Music Man.* Harold Hill had been a big city con man who made a living bilking rubes; Molly Brown was a rustic who triumphed over the big city swells. Also, perhaps coincidentally, Molly's saga took her from the turn of the century to late April, 1912—just two months short of the period in which the story of *The Music Man* was set. Musically, the new work had the by-now familiar Willson trademarks—an optimistically breezy march ("I Ain't Down Yet"), a boisterous male chorale ("Belly Up to the Bar, Boys"), a back country dance number ("Keep a-Hoppin'"), and a revivalistic exhortation ("Are You Sure?") that almost matched the feverous pitch of "Trouble."

In *Here's Love,* which arrived in the fall of 1963, Willson jumped from the rural past to the urban present. Just as he had found inspiration in the Fourth of July celebration in *The Music Man,* he now made full and colorful use of another indigenously American holiday, Thanksgiving. Shunning an overture, the show simply took off by presenting, to the tune of a lighter-than-air march, "The Big Calown Balloons," the Macy's Parade in New York. The festive opening, of course, was almost inevitable since Willson had adapted his story from that happy cinema fantasy, *The Miracle on 34th Street,* which was all about a real Santa Claus who gets a job in a department store. Again the composer had provided parents with a suitable-for-the-kiddies show, possibly less congenial to his muse than his previous works, but still retaining much of the innocent charm and freshness of the original.

All three Meredith Willson musicals have revealed his world to be a thoroughly affirmative one, full of simple faith that is easily reinforced by a miracle or two. Although his roots may be in the rich soil of the heartlands of America, Willson has proved that, with conviction and talent, they can be transplanted with ease to the steel and concrete of Broadway.

Bob Merrill.

Bob Merrill
Stephen Sondheim
Jerry Bock and Sheldon Harnick
Charles Strouse and Lee Adams
Tom Jones and Harvey Schmidt

BECAUSE OF THE RELATIVELY few musicals being produced today, writers for the theatre must wait longer than ever before they develop a sizeable catalogue, much less a specific niche in the evolution of the musical stage. For that reason, this chapter and the one following are devoted to a number of composers and/or lyricists in more or less chronological order, without regard to their relationships to other writers discussed in the same chapter. Chapter Twenty-Two traces the work of the most prolific and accomplished creators of music and lyrics who first attracted notice during the period 1957 through 1960; Chapter Twenty-Three covers those who first emerged within the period 1961 through 1966.

Bob Merrill

There are few practitioners in the musical theatre today with as widely varied a theatrical background as Bob Merrill. Before settling down in 1957 to concentrate on being a composer-lyricist for the stage, Merrill had been an actor, radio writer and producer, film director, television casting director and industrial consultant, and Tin Pan Alley song writer. It is that last calling that, to many, still makes him suspect as a serious craftsman for the theatre.

For the songs with which Merrill first became identified were juvenile novelty items, and the biggest cross that he has had to bear is not that they were flops but that they were all runaway hits. Following his first brain child, "If I Knew You Were Comin' I'd've Baked a Cake" (written with Al Hoffman and Clem Watts), Merrill produced another gastronomical absurdity, "Candy and Cake." From then on there were "Sparrow in the Treetop," "My Truly, Truly Fair," "Belle, Belle, My Liberty Belle," "Mambo Italiano," "Honeycomb," and his most notorious, "How Much Is That Doggie in the Window?" ("Yip! Yip!"). Surely not one harbinger among them of a talent that would be responsible for musicalizing two plays by Eugene O'Neill, or of furnishing Barbra Streisand with the lyrics of some of the best songs in her repertory.

Bob Merrill was born in Atlantic City, New Jersey, on May 17, 1921. Raised in Philadelphia, he first set his sights on becoming an actor and, while in his teens, became something of a protege of Richard Bennett. During World War II, he wrote and produced army radio shows, an experience that spurred him, once the war was over, to try his luck in Hollywood. With no opportunities open and little cash on hand, Merrill took a job as a porter at C.B.S. In true *How to Succeed in Business* fashion, one day during his lunch hour he put on his best suit and walked boldly into the writers' department at N.B.C. He merely told them that he was at C.B.S., wanted to switch, and they hired him as a writer. No one thought to ask him what he had written. Within three weeks he became supervisor of the entire department. In the mid-Forties, Columbia Pictures hired Merrill as a dialogue director (mostly for westerns), a post that allowed him enough free time to try his hand at a new hobby—song writing (he still creates his melodies by beating them out on a toy xylophone). Merrill returned to C.B.S. in 1948, spent a year as television casting director, and then became production consultant to the Liggett & Myers Tobacco Company.

It was about this time that Merrill started thinking of song writing as more than a hobby, and he began making the rounds of music publishers. Nothing doing, he was told. His stuff was too sophisticated for the commercial market. What people wanted were novelty numbers with simple, catchy tunes. Bob Merrill obliged—so well, in fact, that he soon became the most prolific and proficient song writer in the field. But now he had a new ambition; he wanted to write a score for a Broadway musical. However, as the master of "Doggie in the Window," he found the situation reversed. Producers refused to believe he was capable of writing a sophisticated number and wouldn't even give him a hearing.

Undaunted, Merrill tried Hollywood again in 1956, only this time he went to the film studios. Johnny Green, then head of M-G-M's music department, was so impressed with Merrill's work that he helped him secure a contract with the studio to write, compose and produce between five to ten musicals over a seven-year period. The first one planned was to be based on Eugene O'Neill's drama, *Anna Christie*, retitled *A Saint She Ain't*. Merrill had already completed sixteen songs when the movie company abruptly scrapped the entire project. Maybe it was that title.

Director George Abbott, then in Hollywood filming the screen version of *The Pajama Game*, heard about the songs, listened to them, liked them, and got Broadway producers Robert Griffith and Harold Prince to secure the rights to *Anna Christie* from M-G-M. Somehow, none of the sixteen songs that had won over George Abbott (except for "It's Good to Be Alive") was suitable for the stage adaption, *New Girl in Town*, and Merrill had to start from scratch to supply a brand new score.

NEW GIRL IN TOWN *(1957). Gwen Verdon and companions Harvey Hohnecker and Harvey Jung have a high kicking time at the Check Apron Ball. (Costumes by Rouben Ter-Arutunian.)*

PHOTO BY FRIEDMAN-ABELES

351

TAKE ME ALONG (1959). "There are many quite wonderful moments in Take Me Along," Richard Watts, Jr., wrote in his review, "but the one I think I treasure most is that in which the Messrs. Gleason and Pidgeon go into a soft shoe dance to the accompaniment of the title song."

Transforming the dour saga of the woebegone Anna into a high-kicking musical presented too many problems to be solved to everyone's satisfaction. As Wolcott Gibbs wrote in The New Yorker, "Abbott and Merrill have done their best to say that incest, prostitution, and terrible despair are simultaneously the stuff of high tragedy and also somehow of low comedy, but it is uphill work." Still, the musical did have the stellar presence of Gwen Verdon and the appealingly abrasive Thelma Ritter. And, while the romantic expressions never really added very much to the story or the characters, there were a number of atmospheric pieces—"Roll Yer Socks Up," "At the Check Apron Ball," and, most assuredly, "The Sunshine Girl" ("has raindrops in her eyes")—that were skillful examples of period-flavored pastiche. One well-remembered touch: the first act curtain fell as Miss Verdon was leading the dancers in the middle of "There Ain't No Flies on Me"; the second act began by picking up the dancers exactly where they had left off.

Eugene O'Neill again furnished the basis for Merrill's second musical, Take Me Along, which came along in September, 1959. Since the original, Ah, Wilderness!, was just about the sunniest play the gloom-obsessed play-

352

wright ever wrote, the theme was far more congenial to a musical treatment than had been *Anna Christie*. This one, however, suffered from casting problems. Although Eileen Herlie as Aunt Lily and Robert Morse as teenager Richard Miller were ideally cast, neither Jackie Gleason as Uncle Sid nor Walter Pidgeon as Nat Miller was especially comfortable in his role.

Merrill's score represented the peak of his accomplishments as a composer-lyricist. Again he showed his flair at creating a turn-of-the-century mood, particularly in the soft shoe title song performed by Gleason and Pidgeon. But the character songs were even more felicitous. Pidgeon's "Staying Young" said almost as much about the feeling of growing old as did the classic in the field, "September Song." Gleason's "Sid Ol' Kid" and "Little Green Snakes" were splendidly realized comic pieces. Miss Herlie sang the quietly affecting "We're Home" and "Promise Me a Rose." Morse had two appropriate adolescent expressions, "I Would Die" and "Nine O'Clock." All fine, fresh musical ideas without a false note. The musical-dramatic highpoint, however, occurred when Gleason, in a more-or-less serious moment, dropped to one knee to propose to the fluttery Miss Herlie. In their duet, "I Get Embarrassed," he delivered a fairly ribald proposal to which the lady responded in hysterical spasms, alternating genuine embarrassment with ill-concealed delight at the matrimonial prospects.

Carnival, which opened in the spring of 1961, offered a special kind of challenge to composer-lyricist Merrill. Since the work was based on that cinematic charmer, *Lili,* there was the problem of what to do about a theme song since the film's theme, "Hi-Lili, Hi-Lo," had become almost inextricably linked with the story. Merrill simply met the problem head-on by coming up with a similarly wistful variation on the model, known alternately as "Theme from *Carnival*" and "Love Makes the World Go Round." Also, for the first time, Merrill was called upon to create songs with a fairly wide range to suit the vocal prowess of the stage Lili, Anna Maria Alberghetti. The results—including "Mira," "Yes, My Heart"—were particularly attractive, though the score, as a whole, lacked the special distinction of *Take Me Along*.

Carnival was the second musical staged by Gower Champion and written by librettist Michael Stewart, both of whom had started their Broadway careers with *Bye Bye Birdie* the previous year. The new musical left no doubt that Champion had easily jumped to the forefront among directors for the musical theatre. For an opener, he did away with the overture: *Carnival* begins on a bare, pre-dawn stage with the theme music first heard from a wheezing concertina as, one by one, the members of a down-at-the-heels French carnival troupe straggle on to arrange the lights, hang the bunting, and set up the tents for their performance. Later, Champion had the disillusioned, somnolent performers snap wide awake with bright-eyed, high-kicking anticipation as Pierre Olaf describes the fame that will be theirs once they are again hailed as the Grand Imperial Cirque de Paris. *Carnival's* 719-performance-run was a highly deserved success for a work that, as Howard Taubman wrote in the *Times*, turned "sentiment and show business razzle-dazzle into a flashy, eye-filling and occasionally touching entertainment."

Prior to *Funny Girl*, Bob Merrill's record as a composer-lyricist was respectable enough. But the new project gave him two firsts: it was the first time he had set his lyrics to another composer's melodies, in this case Jule Styne's, and it was the first time—with "People" and "Don't Rain on My Parade"—that he had any song successes comparable to those he had written during his Tin Pan Alley days.

Since that memorable production, however, Bob Merrill's career has been less than notable. One score had the misfortune to have been written for the most publicized flop of all time, David Merrick's *Breakfast at Tiffany's*. Amid fanfare comparable to that heralding a hit, the show packed up its diamond-studded cornflakes before risking a New York opening. Dazed but unfazed, Merrill then wrote the score for *Henry, Sweet Henry*, which opened in the fall of 1967. Based on the film, *The World of Henry Orient* (which had been based on Nora Johnson's novel based on her own schoolgirl infatuation with pianist Oscar Levant), the show was well-paced, had a hilarious first act finale, and even contained a few genuinely touching moments. But the score was surprisingly deficient in its suitability for the characters and the period.

As of this writing, Bob Merrill has been represented on Broadway by five musicals in ten and one-half years, four of them as composer-lyricist and one as lyricist. At his best Merrill has made substantial contributions and his potential is still unquestionably high. It surely cannot be ignored that his greatest commercial success, *Funny Girl*, was achieved when he abandoned dual creativity in favor of concentrating on one area of writing.

Stephen Sondheim

Like Bob Merrill, Stephen Sondheim is also both a composer and a lyricist. Also like Bob Merrill, his greatest commercial successes have been scored as a lyricist. But comparisons end right there. For Sondheim, though three of his five Broadway musicals to date contained music created by others, is a thoroughly trained composer who far prefers writing melodies

Stephen Sondheim.

PHOTO BY FRIEDMAN-ABELES

to writing the words that go with them. "Lyric writing," he has said, "is, at best, a very limited art—if it is an art at all. It's largely a matter of sweat and time consumption. Once a basic idea for a lyric has been set, it's like working out a crossword puzzle. But composing music is genuinely creative. And it's much more fun."

Sondheim, whose father Herbert Sondheim, was a leading New York dress manufacturer, was born in the city on March 22, 1930. He attended the George School in Newtown, Pa., where he struck up a friendship with a fellow student, James Hammerstein, son of Oscar II. It was through Jimmy that, at fifteen, young Sondheim met the elder Hammerstein, who

355

promptly took a paternal interest in his work and served for many years as both critic and mentor. At Williams College, where he majored in music, Sondheim wrote the book, lyrics and music for two musicals, one an adaptation of the George S. Kaufman-Marc Connelly play, *Beggar on Horseback*.

Following graduation, Sondheim was awarded the Hutchinson Prize to study composition under Milton Babbitt for two years. During that period he won his bread by turning out scripts for the *Topper* series on television. His first musical theatre break-through occurred in 1954 when his original musical, *Saturday Night* (script by Julius Epstein), was scheduled for production by Lemuel Ayers. Although Ayers died before the production was able to be mounted, the numerous backers' auditions had given Sondheim the opportunity to make his work familiar to many people in the theatre. One of the most impressed was Arthur Laurents, who was then working on the musical that was to become *West Side Story*. Leonard Bernstein, the composer of the new musical, was desperately looking for a lyricist. Once Bernstein heard Sondheim's songs, he enthusiastically welcomed the twenty-seven-year-old theatrical neophyte as his collaborator. Sondheim more than held his own. When *West Side Story* was followed by *Gypsy* (music by Jule Styne), there was no doubt that he had become a major creative force in the Broadway musical stage.

But he still felt unfulfilled. He was, after all, primarily a composer and he did not want to spend the rest of his career writing words to someone else's music. In 1961, writer Bert Shevelove came to Sondheim with an idea—turning some of the characters and stories by the Roman playwright Plautus into a wild, far-out musical farce to be called *A Funny Thing Happened On the Way to the Forum*. Best of all, Shevelove wanted Sondheim to create both music and lyrics. As the work developed, it was decided that the songs would be employed in a somewhat different manner than in most musicals. "The intent of each song," Sondheim once pointed out, "was to provide periods of respite from the relentlessness of the farce as one farcial situation piles upon another. They pinpoint moments of joy or delight or desire and they give the performers a chance to perform. Though they're not used to develop character, they still had to be written with a specific personality since the characters are all prototypes."

To get the show off the ground, Sondheim wrote an opening number —between the Washington tryout and the New York première—in which the entire cast explains that the entertainment to follow will be a "Comedy Tonight" ("No royal curse, no Trojan Horse/And a happy ending, of course!") The proper mood thus established, the composer went on to deal in a lighthearted fashion with man's ambivalent desire for freedom ("Free"), to give detailed plans ("Pretty Little Picture") for two lovers to

356

A FUNNY THING HAPPENED ON THE WAY TO THE FORUM *(1962). Four gentlemen of ancient Rome—Lycus (John Carradine), Hysterium (Jack Gilford), Senex (David Burns) and Pseudolus (Zero Mostel) —lustily agree "Everybody Ought to Have a Maid." (Costumes and setting by Tony Walton.)*

PHOTO BY VAN WILLIAMS

make their getaway, to sing the praises of domestic service ("Everybody Ought to Have a Maid"), and to provide a trumpeting command ("Bring Me My Bride") for the impatient warrior hero, Miles Gloriosus. For the two dimwitted lovers, there were equally appropriate sentiments—her ingenuously self-praising "Lovely," and his love-starved "Love, I Hear" ("I pine, I blush, I squeak, I squawk/Today I woke too weak to walk").

With a cast headed by such seasoned buffoons as Zero Mostel (in a role originally intended for Milton Berle), Jack Gilford and David Burns, the frenetically complicated story was whipped through its pellmell paces by the knowledgeable hand of director George Abbott, with an uncredited assist from Jerome Robbins (he was the one who worked out the highly inventive opening number). After carefully researching all twenty-one surviving comedies by Plautus, co-authors Shevelove and Larry Gelbart ended up by writing an original script, though incorporating characters and situations found in the original plays. One of them concerned a doddering old man who is kept from entering his house because he is made to believe it is haunted. Incredibly enough, the scene had been found in a play with the strangely prophetic title, *Mostellaria.*

357

A FUNNY THING HAPPENED ON THE WAY TO THE FORUM (1962). *A riotous complication in the plot finds Jack Gilford mistaken for a honey-haired virgin. Here Miles Gloriosus (Ronald Holgate), Senex (David Burns) and Erronius (Raymond Walburn) attempt to prevent the beauty from fleeing.*

"I wouldn't mind putting my name to a flop if it has done something that hadn't been tried before," Stephen Sondheim said in an interview in 1961. Three years later he had his chance. The show was *Anyone Can Whistle*, with a book by Arthur Laurents, and with both words and music by Sondheim. Though it had what critics have long been pining for, an original satirical libretto that tried to deal with contemporary problems, the musical was greeted by unmerciful clobbering by most of the reviewers: "Exasperating"—Kerr, *Herald Tribune* . . . "Acute pretentiousness"—Thompson, *Life* . . . "Sick"—Taubman, *Times* . . . "Ponderously heavy-handed"—Watts, *Post* . . . "Boxoffice dodo"—Morrison, *Variety.*

Perhaps it was ahead of its time, but there was little question that *Anyone Can Whistle,* concerned as it was with the bizarre theme that madness was the only hope for world sanity, had an impossible task in overcoming the critical reception. It lasted only nine performances. Sondheim's score was a perfectly congruous complement to the theme, emerging from the situations and dialogue with consummate skill. And there have surely been few songs of recent date—both in musical and lyrical content—to surpass his title song or "A Parade in Town."

Sondheim limited himself to writing lyrics for *Do I Hear a Waltz?*, his first collaboration with composer Richard Rodgers and his fourth with librettist Arthur Laurents. Though battered by the press, the show was, in many ways, a work of considerable style and integrity.

To date, the Sondheim record on Broadway is about par for current productivity. But his accomplishments and influence, particularly among young writers, have far transcended quantity of output or even public acceptance. To contemporaries he occupies a singular position. Fellow lyricist Sheldon Harnick has written: "If I have one favorite lyricist it is Stephen Sondheim. I invariably look forward to a new Sondheim score with a special excitement, because I know it will have a particularly high level of invention, wit, meticulous craftsmanship, taste and content." According to frequent collaborator Laurents, "without question the best Broadway lyricist past or present is Stephen Sondheim. I think Sondheim is the only lyricist who writes a lyric which could *only* be sung by the character for which is was designed, who never pads with unnecessary fillers, who never sacrifices meaning or intention for a clever rhyme and who knows that a lyric is the shortest of one-act plays, with a beginning, a middle and an end."

Sondheim's self-appraisal is, understandably, more critical. "I don't really have a philosophy of life," he insists. "That's why my work doesn't show it. I have nothing large to say, just a lot of small things. I think I have a style but I don't think I have a tone. The tone varies from piece to piece."

Jerry Bock and Sheldon Harnick

So far, only four musicals have won the Pulitzer Prize in drama. When *Of Thee I Sing* became the first in 1931, the show was the Gershwin brothers' eleventh musical collaboration over a period of seven years. When Rodgers and Hammerstein's fourth production, *South Pacific,* was similarly honored, the prize came at a time when both men could look back on

Jerry Bock and Sheldon Harnick.

theatrical activity that had spanned almost thirty years. When, in 1961, Frank Loesser took home a Pulitzer for his musical contributions to *How to Succeed in Business Without Really Trying*, his fifth score in thirteen years, he had spent a life in music also totalling about thirty years. For all these men the recognition came after years of musical and theatrical experience, at the apex of their careers. But when composer Jerry Bock and lyricist Sheldon Harnick were presented with the most prestigious accolade in American letters, their prize-winner, *Fiorello!*, was only their second collaboration in a partnership that had been in existence less than two years. Bock, before Harnick, had begun his theatrical writing career in 1955 with three numbers in a short-lived revue and had followed it up with one musical comedy score; Harnick, before Bock, had first attracted notice in 1952 with one song, "The Boston Beguine," had written some revue pieces, but had never done a complete score. Little wonder that winning a Pulitzer at such an early stage in their careers made both men apprehensively philosophical. "I think I'll quit

360

when I'm ahead," Harnick said at the time. "What else is left for me—the Nobel Peace Prize?"

Harnick, the older of the two, was born in Chicago, on December 27, 1924. As a child he showed his musical talent by learning to play the violin and his lyric-writing talent by making up verses honoring family celebrations. After a hitch in the army during World War II, he attended Northwestern University where he contributed songs—both words and music—to the undergraduate Waa-Mu shows. After college, Harnick became a professional violinist in dance orchestras in the Chicago area; he abruptly abandoned this calling, however, when he was fired by Xavier Cugat after working for the band leader only one night. By this time he had a new ambition—he wanted to write songs for the theatre. He came to New York in 1950, getting most of his theatrical experience initially at Green Man-

FIORELLO! *(1959). A young New York lawyer named Fiorello LaGuardia shows picketing workers how to put some spirit in what they are doing. In the opinion of critic Henry Hewes, "Actor Tom Bosley, as a fine artist should, captures more of LaGuardia's essence than the man did himself when he was alive." (Costumes by William and Jean Eckart.)*

COURTESY CAPITOL RECORDS

sions, the same summer resort where Harold Rome had first tried out *his* earliest efforts. The reception accorded "The Boston Beguine," sung by Alice Ghostley in *New Faces of 1952*, led to opportunities to contribute to other revues. Most notably: "The Merry Minuet" ("They're rioting in Africa..."), which Orson Bean introduced in *John Murray Anderson's Almanac*.

Harnick was building a reputation if not a bank account. It was "Yip" Harburg who convinced him that while his lyrics were good, he'd better start looking around for a composer to work with. Harnick found him at a bar the night of June 13, 1956. The lyricist had gone there following the opening of *Shangri-La*, a short-lived musical for which he had made some last-minute, uncredited interpolations. Also at that particular bar was Jack Cassidy, a member of the cast, who introduced Harnick to his future partner, Jerry Bock.

Bock was born in New Haven, on November 23, 1928. His father, a machine salesman, moved the family to Flushing, New York, when Jerry was a tot. He studied piano with local teachers, and soon discovered that he could play songs by ear—even venturing variations on their themes. At high school, he won limited fame by writing the words and music for a war bond show, *My Dream*. When Bock enrolled at the University of Wisconsin, he was fully prepared to pursue a career in journalism; on impulse, however, he auditioned for and was accepted by the university's music school. At college he wrote another original musical, *Big as Life*, which toured the surrounding cities, including a one-night stand in Chicago. After that he had no doubts about his future career; there could be no other life for him than composing songs for the theatre. Following graduation, Bock returned to New York when he got a job writing for Max Liebman's television revues starring Sid Caesar and Imogene Coca. Summers were spent mastering his craft at Tamiment, an adult summer camp in the Pennsylvania Poconos. There he turned out ten revue scores each season for three years.

Bock's first lyric-writing collaborator was Larry Holofcener, with whom he contributed three songs to the Broadway revue, *Catch a Star*. The team of Bock and Holofcener—augmented by George Weiss—did well enough with their first book musical, *Mr. Wonderful*, a Sammy Davis vehicle co-produced by Jule Styne. The show even spawned two durable hits—the title song and "Too Close for Comfort." *Mr. Wonderful* opened just three months before Bock and Harnick met for the first time.

Tommy Valando, who published the *Mr. Wonderful* score, sent the newly allied team to Richard Kollmar, then preparing a musical about prize fighters called *The Body Beautiful*. Bock and Harnick were hired but their partnership debut was less than auspicious. The show was panned and so were the songs, though at least two, "Summer Is" and "All of These and

362

More," are still part of the audition repertory of aspiring young singers.

One of the few who was impressed with the songs for *The Body Beautiful* was George Abbott, then about to go into production on a musical based on the life of New York's peppery Mayor, Fiorello H. LaGuardia. Producers Robert Griffith and Harold Prince had secured the rights to a musical dramatization of LaGuardia's life, and Griffith had persuaded his Connecticut neighbor, novelist Jerome Weidman, to write the adaptation with Abbott. But no one was signed for the songs. What Abbott wanted was a new team who could write with a satirical slant but who could also give the score the period flavor it required. As an audition Bock and Harnick wrote a nostalgic waltz suggestive of the World War I period of La-Guardia's younger days. Abbott hired them on the basis of that number, "Till Tomorrow," one of the memorable moments in the score.

Casting an actor who could sing and dance and look and act like New York's "Little Flower" was an even bigger problem. About two hundred—ranging from Mickey Rooney to Eli Wallach—were tested before the producers settled on 32-year-old Tom Bosley who had never appeared in a Broadway play before. In voice, stance and general magnetism he caught the spirit of LaGuardia to an uncanny degree, and scored a resounding success. As for Bock and Harnick, there was no questions that they too had arrived. Apart from the romantic contributions, their score admirably captured all the ward-heeling double-dealing of New York politics, particularly with "Politics and Poker," a waltzing tribute to the interrelationship of the two games, and "Little Tin Box" (written two weeks before the Broadway opening). In the latter, various politicos, found with their hands in the till, explain their wealth in shocked innocence by detailing how they saved their pennies by giving up smoking, returning empty bottles to the grocer, and going without lunches for a week. There was also wonderful contrast in the campaign songs—a thumpingly idealistic march, "The Name's LaGuardia" for the pugnacious reformer and a razzmatazz Charleston, "Gentleman Jimmy" to describe the incumbent mayor, Jimmy Walker.

Everyone connected with the creation of *Fiorello!*—Griffith, Prince, Abbott, Weidman, Bock and Harnick—got along so well that they decided to stick together for their next musical, *Tenderloin*. The show, which gave Maurice Evans his first singing role since *Ball at the Savoy* in London, 1933, again dealt with a stubbornly crusading white knight battling corruption in a bygone, wicked New York. But Dr. Parkhurst's fight against the red light section known as the Tenderloin suffered from a stuffy leading character and a wavering point of view—and from the inevitable comparison with *Fiorello!* The Bock-Harnick contributions, however, were delectable recreations of a bawdy and sentimental era, particularly in the tear-stained "Artificial Flowers," the jolly tale of the virtues of vice known as "The Picture of

PHOTO BY GRAPHIC HOUSE, INC.

TENDERLOIN *(1960). Maurice Evans, as a crusading minister, puts on a disguise to learn from first hand experience all about New York's most sinful section, the Tenderloin. (Costumes and setting by Cecil Beaton.)*

Happiness," and the innocent compilation of childhood games, "Good Clean Fun."

On April 23, 1963, producer Harold Prince became producer-director Harold Prince with the opening of *She Loves Me.** It also reunited him with Jerry Bock and Sheldon Harnick. Initially, however, the producers were to have been Lawrence Kasha and Philip McKenna who had wanted to put

---

* Prince's first Broadway directorial assignment had been A *Family Affair,* presented by Andrew Siff early in 1962.

on a musical version of Ernst Lubitsch's film, *The Shop Around the Corner*, ever since they had seen a revival of it. The musical version of the film (which in turn had been based on a play called *Parfumerie* by Miklos Laszlo) deserved a far better fate than its relatively meager three hundred or so performances. Perhaps in the waning theatrical season the play was just too gentle, too intimate, and too free from Broadway razzle-dazzle to attract the customers. Critics could find no adjectives more helpful to the show's press agents than "charming," "delightful," "enjoyable," and "darling." And surely the lone nay-sayer, Walter Kerr, in the *Herald Tribune*, didn't help with his crack, "things seem a little shopworn around the corner."

But for eyes that could see and ears that could hear, *She Loves Me* will

SHE LOVES ME *(1963). After much misunderstanding, boy (Daniel Massey) finally gets girl (Barbara Cook) on Christmas day in front of Maraczek's Parfumerie.*

365

stand as a model in its use of songs as an indispensable adjunct to the plot. It was, in fact, a musical told *through* music and lyrics, with no less than twenty-three set musical pieces. This in no way diminishes the worthy contribution of librettist Joe Masteroff, in his first assignment in the musical theatre. It was agreed from the start that he would write a complete play —not a libretto—in order that Bock and Harnick could best find areas in which to substitute songs for dialogue, as well as utilizing the dialogue itself as a springboard for the musical expressions. In keeping with the proper spirit, most of the songs were done as solos and duets, only occasionally by the rather limited chorus. Everything jelled, nothing stood out in applause-milking desperation. Little wonder that Jerry Bock could later recall, "It was a show that we dearly loved doing. There was a feeling of give and take throughout. There was a feeling of inspiration throughout. A feeling of group chemistry."

Even before starting work on *She Loves Me,* Bock and Harnick had begun laying the groundwork for the musical that was to become *Fiddler on the Roof.* They had read a novel by Sholom Aleichem, thought it had theatrical possibilities, and had turned it over to librettist Joseph Stein, with whom they had worked on *The Body Beautiful.* Though Stein did not think that this particular story could be converted into a musical, Bock and Harnick had become completely hooked on doing something by Sholom Aleichem. At a friend's suggestion, they read another one of his books, *Tevya's Daughters.* There was no question about it. This was it. For the first time in their careers, both composer and lyricist had the satisfaction of initiating a project rather than having a producer call them in to work on an already-scheduled show.

Fiddler on the Roof became the fourth Bock and Harnick musical to be produced by Harold Prince. In many ways it was a far from commercial undertaking. Recalling the famous telegram that Mike Todd sent after seeing *Oklahoma!* during its tryout ("NO GAGS NO GALS NO CHANCE"), here was a musical that had no pretty scenery, no pretty costumes, no pretty girls, and no pretty story. Its plot dealt with a people vainly trying to keep alive traditions in an alien, hostile world, and of their hopeless attempts to establish roots in a place where they had none and from which they are eventually forced to flee. But though the libretto was concerned specifically with impoverished Jews in Czarist Russia, its theme is so universal that audiences of all backgrounds have responded to it. Notwithstanding its special ethnic quality, *Fiddler on the Roof* has managed to create an empathetic bond with everyone who has ever had to deal with mindless cruelty, or has ever been compelled to leave a home or a family.

The guiding hand of director Jerome Robbins was in evidence throughout in soaking the production in authentic atmosphere—despite an occasional intrusion of a line or piece of business that seemed like unnecessary concessions to musical comedy taste. In the central role of Tevya, the dairy-man, Zero Mostel scored the unquestioned theatrical triumph of the year, with many critics, incorrectly as it turned out, crediting him for the production's success. Bock and Harnick, who initially conceived of Tevya as a thin, wasted little man, not only had to rethink the role along physical lines but also were inspired to create songs with Mostel specifically in mind. Of one of them, "If I Were a Rich Man," and the way it was performed, the *Herald Tribune's* Walter Kerr wrote, "Mr. Mostel dreams his dreams in vocalized snuggles, not in words. For every other line of the lyric he simply substitutes gratifying gargles and cascading coos until he has arrived, mystically, at a kind of cabalistic coloratura. The effect is what we all had in mind when we last thought of satisfaction in depth." There is much color and emotion too in the foot-stomping opening number, "Tra-

FIDDLER ON THE ROOF (1964). *Zero Mostel leads his fellow villagers in the joyful toast, "to life, to life, l'chaim."*

PHOTO BY FRIEDMAN-ABELES

PHOTO BY EILEEN DARBY-GRAPHIC HOUSE

FIDDLER ON THE ROOF *(1964). The men of Anatevka do a traditional bottle dance at the wedding of Tevya's daughter, Tzeitel. (Costumes by Patricia Zipprodt.)*

dition," in the wistful "Matchmaker, Matchmaker," in the robust "To Life" ("L'Chaym"), and, in the excruciatingly poignant, "Sunrise, Sunset," the gentlest of all commentaries on the unbelievability of passing years.

At this writing, the fiddler is still perched precariously on the roof of Boris Aronson's version of Tevya's house, more than three years after the musical's New York première. The belief held by many that it was a Mostel showcase has not been borne out. Mostel played the role a little under a year, was followed by Luther Adler (his first musical) for three months, by Herschel Bernardi for two years, and then—to no sudden drop in attendance—by the virtually unknown Harry Goz.

As two of the most adventurous writers of musicals today, Bock and

368

Harnick are both believers in and practitioners of daring previously untrodden paths. Thus, in mid-1965, they went in a new direction, a musical that would contain three separate short stories connected by the unifying theme of man, woman and the devil. After trying out stories by de Maupassant, Bernard Malamud and Marcel Aymé, they settled on Bruce Jay Friedman's *Show Biz Connections* (illustrating modern-day permissiveness), Nathaniel Hawthorne's *Young Goodman Brown* (early American Puritanism), and Mark Twain's *The Diary of Adam and Eve* (dawn of humanity innocence). The original title was *Come Back! Go Away! I Love You!*, the original director was Jerome Robbins, and the original librettist was Jerome Coopersmith. But things didn't work out as planned. Robbins was replaced by Mike Nichols (his first Broadway musical), who drastically altered both concept and contents. Frank Stockton's *The Lady or the Tiger* was substituted for the Hawthorne, Jules Feiffer's *Passionella* for the Friedman, the order of the stories was reversed, and Coopersmith's work was taken over by Bock and Harnick themselves. Under the new title of *The Apple Tree*, the finished product, when it was premièred in the autumn of 1966, turned out to be three musical vignettes with hardly a discernable thread. Sharp ears, though, could spot certain interrelating musical themes—the melody of the lullaby, "Go to Sleep Whatever You Are," in *Adam and Eve*, showed up as the final song in *Passionella*, and the music for the snake's "Forbidden Fruit," was likewise repeated for the Balladeer's song in *The Lady or the Tiger*.

What is noteworthy about the career of Jerry Bock and Sheldon Harnick is that they are always willing to take chances on new forms and new means of expression. What is fortunate for all of us is that they have, most often, succeeded so brilliantly.

THE APPLE TREE *(1966). In* The Lady or the Tiger, *the second of three one-act musicals offered on the same program, Larry Blyden played the Balladeer, Alan Alda Captain Sanjar, and Barbara Harris the seductive Princess Barbára. (Costumes by Tony Walton.)*

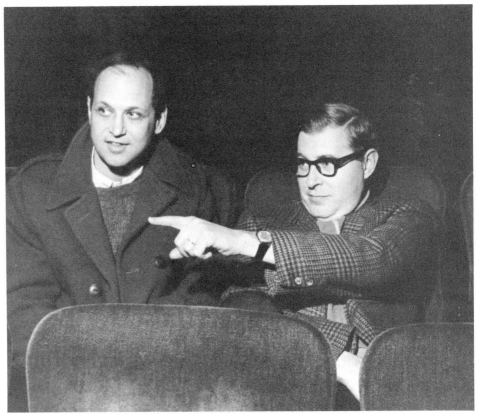

Charles Strouse and Lee Adams.

Charles Strouse and Lee Adams

Among our current creators of musical theatre songs, no team has been as successful in cornering the contemporary youth market as composer Charles Strouse and lyricist Lee Adams. Look at their first four shows. In *Bye Bye Birdie*, it was the influence of a rock-and-roll singer on the acne and apple cheeks generation. In *All American*, it was college life and football. In *Golden Boy*, alienated Negro youth battling to win recognition in the fight ring. In *It's a Bird It's a Plane It's Superman*, the literature of youth as exemplified by the comic strip. Obviously, Strouse and Adams are not limited to subject matter or to age group; in fact, they have since gone on to themes involving more mature characters. Yet since our musical stage combines so many of the attributes and characteristics of young people, it is only natural that their crushes, crises and cartoons should provide particularly suitable inspirations. And surely through the consid-

370

erable talents of Strouse and Adams, the youth of our land have been given uncommonly winning and perceptive musical expressions.

Charles Strouse, who was born in New York, June 7, 1928, began his composing career at the age of twelve. Music was his life from then on, though initially his goal was in the area of the concert hall. He attended the Eastman School of Music at Rochester, received a scholarship to study with Aaron Copland at Tanglewood, and later studied in Paris with Nadia Boulanger. Once his student days were over, however, Strouse discovered, without too much surprise, that popular music offered more gainful employment, both as performer and as composer. At first he played piano in dance bands; soon he gravitated toward the theatre—in the Jerome Kern-George Gershwin tradition—via the rehearsal pianist route.

Lee Adams, a native of Mansfield, Ohio, was born on August 14, 1924. At Ohio State University, where he was a journalism major, he wrote occasional lyrics for the varsity shows though with nary a thought about song writing as anything else but a hobby. Upon graduation, Adams came to New York where he did graduate work at Columbia University's Pulitzer School of Journalism. For almost four years he served on the staff of *Pageant* magazine, which he followed with a stint as an articles editor of *This Week.*

Strouse and Adams met through a mutual friend in 1949. Their first collaborative efforts for the theatre were heard at the Green Mansions summer resort, where they followed the customary training route of preparing a new revue score every week for ten weeks. In all, they wrote songs for some ten revues both off-Broadway and in London, including three for Ben Bagley—*Shoestring Revue* in 1955 (for which Strouse doubled as music director), *The Littlest Revue,* and *Shoestring '57.*

It was Edward Padula who ended Strouse's career as a rehearsal pianist and Adams' career as a magazine editor. He wanted the team to collaborate on the songs for *Bye Bye Birdie,* his first venture as a Broadway producer. Padula's aim was to do an original story about modern teenagers, but one that would show their healthier, sunnier, far from the *West Side Story* side. And he wanted the songwriting team to come up with a fresh, youthful score to match the fresh, youthful script being devised by Michael Stewart, another Green Mansions alumnus. In all, over two and a half years were devoted to creating some fifty-five songs for three separate versions of the story—as well as holding over eighty-five backers' auditions. "Our problem," Strouse has said, "was to satirize a kind of music—rock-and-roll —that was so new it was hard to maintain a perspective about it as we could, say, the Charleston or swing. And not only did we have to satirize it, we also had to use the form for real musical value. In 'The Telephone Hour,' we did a kind of fugal development, with real rock-and-roll har-

371

BYE BYE BIRDIE *(1960). His teenage fans swoon whenever they hear rock and roll idol, Conrad Birdie (Dick Gautier), sing "Honestly Sincere." Michael J. Pollard and Susan Watson are at the left. (Costumes by Miles White.)*

monies and rhythm. In 'One Last Kiss' we satirized it by going overboard, the way we imagined our singing idol, Conrad Birdie, would do it." Other songs also captured the spirit of a restless but not alienated youth. In "One Boy" ("One boy to laugh with, to joke with, have Coke with"), an adolescent girl dreams of the pleasures of going steady. The rhythmic "A Lot of Livin' to Do" was a beltable ode to a future life of uninhibited pleasure. And "Kids" gave the adult point of view as the elders bewailed, "Why can't they be like we were, perfect in every way?"

What added greatly to the show's style were the contributions of director Gower Champion. For "The Telephone Hour," for example, he had his teenagers wriggling and writhing through telephone conversations staged in a huge honeycomb set representing their rooms. Memorable too was the madcap disruption of a Shriners convention in which Chita Rivera enticed all of the befezzed celebrants under the table. "Everything about the musical," gushed Kenneth Tynan in *The New Yorker*, "was filled with a kind of affectionate freshness that we have seldom encountered since Mr. Rodgers collaborated with Mr. Hart on *Babes in Arms*." (Mr. Tynan, bless his faultless memory, was all of eleven at the time.)

The high school kids of *Bye Bye Birdie* gave way to the college kids of *All American*, Strouse and Adams' second musical, which came along two years later. Ray Bolger, absent from Broadway musicals since *Where's Charley?*, made a none too auspicious return in the role of an immigrant engineering professor who comes to this country to teach at Southern Baptist Institute of Technology and ends up as the football coach. Many opportunities for spoofing American education and huckstering were somehow lost in the Mel Brooks libretto, which simply deteriorated into an old-fashioned star vehicle. The score, surprisingly, was strongest in the sentimental pieces—including "Once Upon a Time" sung by Bolger and Eileen Herlie as the dean of women.

The inspiration for transforming Clifford Odets' drama, *Golden Boy*, into a musical drama originated with Hillard Elkins, a personal manager, who was anxious to break into the ranks of producers. It occurred to him that switching the central part of an Italian-American boxer named Joe Bonaparte into a Negro American boxer named Joe Wellington would give the story the same significance for modern audiences as had the earlier concept for the audiences of the Thirties. Once Sammy Davis had become enthusiastic about doing the part, Elkins signed Strouse and Adams (two

GOLDEN BOY *(1964). "Don't forget 127th Street," harmonize Joe Wellington (Sammy Davis) and his brother-in-law, Ronnie (Johnny Brown). (Costumes by Tony Walton.)*

PHOTO BY FRIEDMAN-ABELES

373

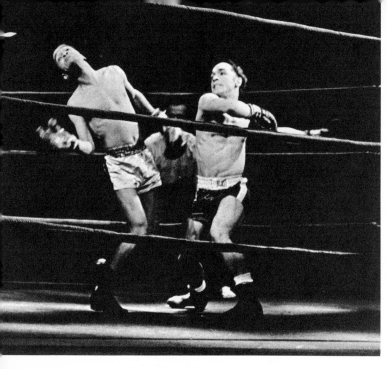

GOLDEN BOY (1964). *"Into the ring," wrote Walter Kerr in the* Herald Tribune, *"choreographer Donald McKayle throws Sammy Davis and dancer Jaime Rogers with nothing but drums to guide them. There are instant haymakers but on metronome beat ... The view from the ringside is breath-taking as Mr. Rogers spins his last spin and drops; it is as though rhythm had died while you were looking."*

of his former clients) for the songs, and then managed to talk a slightly startled Clifford Odets into writing the adaptation.

The work did not proceed smoothly or quickly. Then, with the second revision almost completed, Odets died of cancer in August, 1963. At first Adams, who had worked closely with the playwright, tried taking over the book-writing assignment, but in August, 1964, with only two months to go before the Broadway opening, playwright William Gibson, a close friend of Odets, was persuaded to do a complete rewrite. Disagreements forced the replacement of director Peter Coe by Arthur Penn, and there were some major cast changes. Nerves were frayed and no one seemed to have a clear idea of exactly what was going on from one day to the next. But the miracle happened: the show opened on schedule, got respectable notices, and, thanks largely to the appeal of Sammy Davis, had a run of over 500 performances.

There was no question that the production suffered from its too numerous changes, and that the seams showed quite obviously. Yet the show captured its audience through the dynamic performance of its star and its inherent theatricality (highlighted by a musicalized gym workout as an opener, and a stunner of a choreographed fight sequence). The Strouse-Adams score caught just the right qualities of pathos and impending doom in the love songs, particularly in "I Want to Be with You" and "Lorna's Here." But larger issues were not overlooked. In "Night Song," the writers gave musical dimension to the feelings of frustration and tension of Negro youth; in "127th Street," they turned out a lively, nosethumbing salute to Harlem, made all the more telling through its parodying of sentimental home-and-hearth ballads.

374

In *It's a Bird It's a Plane It's Superman*, produced and directed by Harold Prince in 1966, Strouse and Adams ventured into the camp camp via a takeoff on the well-known comic strip. Everyone connected with the show —including librettists Robert Benton and David Newman—was scrupulous in avoiding the above-it-all, exaggerated approach; everything was done to make the ridiculous appear natural and matter-of-fact. The musical contributions worked well within the show's framework, allowing for some wonderfully foursquare statements for the hero ("Everyman has a job to do, and my job is doing good") that beautifully contrasted with the generally breezy pieces Strouse and Adams gave to almost everyone else.

Verve, vitality, and a thorough comprehension of the function of songs in the modern musical have been among the major contributions of Charles Strouse and Lee Adams. In addition, they are deeply committed to their belief in the song as an entity, as an inextricable union of music and lyrics. "What we are aiming for," Strouse says, "is to make the lyric almost indistinguishable from the music. Not merely a wedding of words and music; but the words and music as a total concept, a complete and inevitable part of the character's expression of the moment. As we see it, neither the melody nor the lyrics should be able to exist without the other."

Tom Jones and Harvey Schmidt

As the first two sons of Texas to achieve renown in the musical theatre, lyricist Tom Jones and composer Harvey Schmidt might have been expected to reflect the generous air of excess and elaboration for which the state's citizens have long been famous. Yet Jones (born in Littlefield in February 17, 1928) and Schmidt (born in Dallas on September 12, 1929) have run completely contrary to expected form. So far at least, they have made it big by doing things small. Theirs has been the theatre of the intimate and the compressed, be it in subject matter, time span or casting.

To date, Jones and Schmidt have written the scores for three book musicals. Their first, *The Fantasticks*, still playing at the 150-seat Sullivan Street Playhouse, has a cast of eight (shaved down from the original nine). Their second, *110 in the Shade*, a more conventional enterprise and their first on Broadway, managed to compress the entire action within one day, from dawn to midnight. Their third, *I Do! I Do!*, became the first musical in history to have a cast consisting entirely of two actors. Equally characteristic has been the subject matter of their musicals. Tom and Harvey are genuine romantics. They believe firmly in the miracle of love, and are unabashed at expressing its various manifestations. They sang of innocent young love in *The Fantasticks*, probed the yearnings of the unloved in *110*

375

in the Shade, and rejoiced at fifty years of connubial love in *I Do! I Do!.*

Tom Jones and Harvey Schmidt met when they were both students at the University of Texas. Tom, who was studying to be a stage director, was anxious to become part of the world of music; Harvey, an art major, was able to play piano by ear and was anxious to become part of the world of the theatre. They were brought together by their activities in a campus theatrical group, the Curtain Club, and their first collaborative effort was something called *Hippsy-Boo.* Harvey wrote the title song and Tom the sketches. A second collegiate effort, *Time Staggers On* (an inherited title) was their maiden attempt at writing songs together.

Following graduation, both men served time in the army—at different camps—and continued to collaborate via mail. Jones reached New York first. He began his professional career writing and directing a night club

Harvey Schmidt and Tom Jones.

THE FANTASTICKS *(1960). Jerry Orbach, as El Gallo, crosses swords with hero Kenneth Nelson, as heroine Rita Gardner watches with apprehension.*

act featuring Tom Posten and Gerry Matthews. The act was booked into the Reuben Bleu, a since deceased bistro, whose revelries were presided over by Julius Monk. By the time Schmidt had arrived to join his partner, Monk had moved to the Upstairs at the Downstairs, where he offered his series of numerically progressive revues (*Four Below, Demi-Dozen, Pieces of Eight, etc.*). These were frequently studded with the efforts of Jones and Schmidt. (At the time, Schmidt, who had become a much sought-after commercial artist, also co-authored, with Robert Benton, the bible of the trivia set known as *The In and Out Book.*)

Early in June, 1959, Word Baker, a fellow Texas U. graduate, telephoned Tom and Harvey. He knew that they had been struggling for years over a musical adaptation of Edmond Rostand's first play, *Les Romanesques*, and he was wondering if they could possibly whip it into shape in about two months. He thought it might do nicely at a summer theatre then being run at Barnard College. But Baker, who was to direct the show, insisted that the play be cut down to a one-act musical. This presented a real problem. Originally, true to their Lone Star heritage, Jones and Schmidt had conceived of the work as an elaborate spectacle, called *Joy*

377

Comes to Dead Horse. They had reset the story in the American southwest, and had concerned it with the rivalry between a Mexican family and an Anglo family living on adjoining ranches. The Mexican girl was named Maria, and there was even a song about her with that title. What they had, of course, was a Texas version of *West Side Story*—only theirs had come first.

It wasn't until Jones and Schmidt got together with Baker in New York that the musical finally crystallized. It was all too easy. They just decided to do an uncluttered version of the Rostand play, without elaborate staging or nationalistic overtones. The rewriting took three weeks, and, as a one-act musical, *The Fantasticks* (the title of an earlier translation of the play) had a week-long run at Barnard. Among the most enthusiastic members of the first night audience was a young producer, Lorenzo "Lore" Noto, who offered the boys a proposition: expand the show into a full evening entertainment and he'd produce it off Broadway. They did and he did—nine months later.

The Fantasticks cost a mere $12,000 to open. After steadily declining business for the first nine weeks, the producer was ready to put up the closing notice. But business began picking up and by Christmas it had repaid the entire original investment. By Christmas, 1961, it had earned a 100 per cent profit; at the present writing it's well over 2,000 per cent.

Those who look upon theatre critics as omnipotent arbiters would do well to take a look at the opening-night reviews. Walter Kerr, in the *Herald Tribune*, figured that it "averages out a little less than satisfactory." Richard Watts, Jr., was of a somewhat divided mind in the *Post*: "While the virtues it possesses are modest and less than exhilarating, it has freshness, youthful charm and a touch of imagination." The *News* gave it a brief but glowing notice, but the *Times* was as reserved as Kerr. The *Saturday Review's* Henry Hewes, however, went all out, calling it "one of the happiest off-Broadway events in a season that has been happier off Broadway than on . . . Jones and Schmidt have worked with a professional expertness equalling the best Broadway has to offer and with a degree of artistic taste that Broadway seldom attains anymore."

Broadway, in the person of David Merrick, apparently thought it could use a little of that artistic taste itself. Merrick signed the team for a musical version of N. Richard Nash's play, *The Rainmaker*, first renamed *Rainbow*, then finally *110 in the Shade*. The theme of an unattractive girl whose brief fling with a fast-talking rainmaker helps rid her of her insecurity was, in fact, even more congenial to the song writers than to the not too successful adaptation Nash made of his own play. The private longings of the touching ballad, "Love Don't Turn Away," and the controlled exultation of "Is It Really Me?" reached the height of American art songs. So

PHOTO BY FRIEDMAN-ABELES

I DO! I DO! *(1966). Gathered around the piano on the first day of rehearsal: Jean Rosenthal (lighting), Oliver Smith (scenery), David Merrick (producer), Robert Preston and Mary Martin (cast), Gower Champion (director), Freddy Wittop (costumes), Tom Jones (lyrics), and Harvey Schmidt (music).*

too the vivid contrast of the rainmaker's fantastic saga of "Melisande" and the girl's explanation of her desire for "Simple Little Things" were almost spine-tinglingly effective. As the awkward Lizzie, Inga Swenson gave a shiningly memorable performance, though Robert Horton's rainmaker failed to make the character thoroughly convincing.

I Do! I Do!, also produced by Mr. Merrick, came along in December, 1966. At first the prospect of turning Jan de Hartog's two-character play, *The Fourposter*, into a two-character musical did not light any sparks. But director Gower Champion was persistent, and soon Jones and Schmidt began seeing the possibilities in the concept. Mary Martin had agreed to play the role of Agnes almost from the very start; in June, 1966, Robert Preston agreed to play Michael. Thus the musical took shape with the most important advantage a two-character musical could possibly have—two authentic superstars.

379

I DO! I DO! *(1966). Mary Martin and Robert Preston doing their shoeless old soft shoe to the tune of "I Love My Wife."*

Keeping things hopping for a meandering, crisis-free saga of a half century of wedded bliss was a severe test for Jones, Schmidt and Champion. They dreamed up a soft shoe routine without shoes. They devised a top hat and cane strutaway for Preston, and an uninhibited whatever-it-was in a big hat for Miss Martin. They created a lark happy duet for both of them called "When the Kids Get Married," and topped it off with Preston playing a saxophone and Miss Martin doing her stuff on a violin. To show the aging of the two stars, Champion simply had them come down to the footlights and apply wrinkle lines and grey wigs out of their makeup kits. *I Do! I Do!*, despite its theatrical ingenuity, received a mixed press; critics,

380

for the most part, appreciated the high points but questioned the play's basic sentimentality.

The remarkable thing about Tom Jones and Harvey Schmidt is that, so far, they have been able to stick to their firm belief in the virtues of simplicity in the musical theatre. "I'm convinced," Jones says, "that the simpler you do a thing the better off its going to be. All too often in the musical theatre a great deal of effort is expended on things that have only a momentary effect without producing a genuine emotional response. The proper words and music can evoke a spectacle in the mind that's so much more satisfying than anything the most skillful scenic designer could possibly devise."

Cy Coleman.

CHAPTER TWENTY-THREE

Cy Coleman
Carolyn Leigh
Jerry Herman
Mitch Leigh and Joe Darion
John Kander and Fred Ebb

Cy Coleman
Carolyn Leigh

The musical theatre composer who also doubles as a professional performer is surely nothing new. But from Victor Herbert, through George Gershwin, and on up to Leonard Bernstein, he has usually been someone whose interpretive skills have largely been confined to the concert hall. Composer Cy Coleman has broken with this tradition; not only has he written three Broadway scores, he is also in demand as a pianist and singer in the flossier supper clubs. Unquestionably, this is a great advantage to a composer; he can break in new songs before living, breathing audiences, and he can help keep alive the old ones. Besides, performing is the area of music that Coleman really loves. "When you sit down and write," he once explained, "it's in a lonely room and you spend a great deal of time just staring at your collaborator. That's why it's so great to get out and perform in clubs. Your social life is taken care of, and, best of all, you're able to get instant reaction to what you're doing."

Carolyn Leigh.   PHOTO BY FRIEDMAN-ABELES

Despite his subsequent career, Coleman initially started out—and at a remarkably tender age—to become a concert pianist. Born in the Bronx, New York, on June 14, 1929, he began playing when he was four, picking out tunes he heard on the radio. This feat so impressed his family that they arranged to get him a piano scholarship. By the time he was six, he had already given recitals at both Steinway Hall and Town Hall. He continued his piano studies under Rudolph Gruen, attending the New York College of Music at the same time he was going to classes at the High School of Music and Art. In his mid-teens, Coleman played in servicemen's canteens where he found himself becoming increasingly involved in jazz. After graduating from high school, he formed a trio and promptly got a booking at the Little Club. The success of this engagement insured steady work and gave him a name even before his composing skills were recognized.

Cy Coleman's first lyric writing partner was Joe McCarthy (his father, also named Joe McCarthy, had been the lyricist of *Irene*, *Kid Boots* and *Rio Rita*). Their biggest hits were "I'm Gonna Laugh You Right Out of My Life" and "Why Try to Change Me Now?" In 1953, the Coleman-McCarthy song, "Tin Pan Alley" ("Just think of a catchy tune/ Come up with a rhyme for June") served as the first act finale of *John Murray Anderson's Almanac*.

About four years later, Coleman accidentally met lyricist Carolyn Leigh on the street. They had known each other slightly before and, partly to make conversation, Cy asked Carolyn if she'd like to write a song with him sometime. "How about right now?" she suggested, and off they went. "A Moment of Madness," the tune that resulted, was written in two days, was published almost immediately, and was quickly recorded by Sammy Davis, Jr. Convinced that they had a good thing going, Coleman and Leigh soon began turning out songs on a regular basis. Among their pre-Broadway hits: "Witchcraft," "Firefly" (written as a Twenties-type production number for *Gypsy*, for which they auditioned but lost out to Styne and Sondheim), "I Walk a Little Faster," "You Fascinate Me So" (sung in the Julius Monk supper club revue, *Demi-Dozen*), "The Best Is Yet to Come," and "It Amazes Me."

Carolyn Leigh's debut as a writer for the theatre occurred some six years before her first score with Coleman. Born on August 21, 1926, also in the Bronx, she started writing poems and doggerel when she was nine. After attending Queens College and New York University, she entered the literary world by writing continuity for WQXR and serving as chief—because she was the only—copywriter at an advertising agency. In 1951, a music publisher, impressed with some verse she had written, offered her a year's contract to write song lyrics. Her first big success, "Young at Heart" (music by Johnny Richards), came along two years later.

While driving home one night following a theatre performance, Mary Martin heard the song on her automobile radio. Struck with the quality of the words, she felt that the person who had written them would be ideal to write the lyrics for her next musical, *Peter Pan*. The following day, Miss Martin's husband, producer Richard Halliday, telephoned Miss Leigh and simply asked her if she'd be interested in the assignment. With a new partner, composer Mark ("Moose") Charlap, she wrote about ten pieces for what was then a "play with music"; when, during the production's West Coast break-in, director Jerome Robbins decided to increase the musical content, he turned to the more seasoned team of Jule Styne, Betty

WILDCAT *(1960). Flanked by Swen Swenson and Al Lanti, Lucille Ball does her own version of the Mexican Hat Dance in "El Sombrero." (Costumes by Alvin Colt.)*

Comden and Adolph Green for the additional songs. Still, the best-remembered songs from *Peter Pan*, "I've Gotta Crow" and "I'm Flying," were the work of Leigh and Charlap.

Despite her skill with words dealing with the emotions of the young, Carolyn Leigh, once she had begun writing with Cy Coleman, showed she could match the rhythmically sophisticated music of her partner with suitably adult, worldly lyrics. Their Broadway debut as a team was prompted by a long distance telephone call from director Michael Kidd. Kidd, then in Hollywood, was about to co-produce a musical in partnership with librettist N. Richard Nash, that would star the reigning queen of video, Lucille Ball. Coleman and Leigh eagerly snapped at the chance. Unfortunately, *Wildcat,* when it was unveiled on Broadway in December, 1960, was met by a generally lukewarm press. Due to the boxoffice appeal of the star, however, the show did well enough financially, but then had to shut down in June because of Miss Ball's illness.

The Coleman-Leigh score had several attractive pieces and one smash

386

hit—"Hey, Look Me Over." This was the first song in the show sung by Lucille Ball, and the writing of it posed many serious problems. Originally, the team was thinking of something very sophisticated, very Broadway, but whatever they tried always came out sounding like an Ethel Merman opener. Finally, after two weeks, Carolyn said, "Cy, if you didn't care at all, if it wasn't the opening number and it wasn't for Lucille Ball making her stage debut, and it was just a simple number for the scene and the character, what would you write?" And Cy replied, "If this number weren't so important, I'd just write something as corny and as simple as this . . ." And he played the opening measures of "Hey, Look Me Over." They laughed and quickly vetoed the idea, but Carolyn couldn't get the melody out of her head. Two days later, she called her partner, "Remember that tune you played for Lucy's opening number? As long as we're making jokes, how's this for a lyric, 'Hey, look me over, lend me an ear/ Fresh out of clover, mortgaged up to here . . .' Isn't that funny, Cy?"

There were fewer uncertainties about the next Coleman-Leigh venture, *Little Me*, which opened two years later. The hilarious saga of the rise of Belle Poitrine, née Schlumpfert, had been a successful novel by

LITTLE ME (1962). Sid Caesar as Mr. Pinchley, the richest man in the world, takes a shine to our little Belle (Virginia Martin.)

Patrick Dennis, the libretto was the work of Neil Simon, and the star was Sid Caesar playing no less than seven roles. The reviews ranged from mild to wild approval, but somehow the customers didn't come in the expected drove-like packs. The musical contributions were certainly superior to the work Coleman and Leigh had done for *Wildcat*. The ethereal "Real Live Girl," a striking contrast to the generally brash, spoofing nature of the rest of the score, provided a memorable ballet for soldiers in a World War I dugout. "The Other Side of the Tracks" emerged from a sentimental day-dream into a clarion battle cry. The slinky "I've Got Your Number" was a show-stopping, tantalizing mating call for the gracefully agile Swen Swenson. Mr. Caesar had five comic turns, most notably "I Love You," in which a snobbish young man ardently professes his love for the heroine, "Considering you're riffraff and I am well-to-do."

Two Broadway scores and over twenty published songs—and the team of Cy Coleman and Carolyn Leigh decided to call it quits. Of the two, Coleman has fared better on Broadway since the breakup. One day he called veteran lyricist Dorothy Fields and asked her—in much the same way as he had first asked Carolyn Leigh—if she'd like to write a song with him. Miss Fields said why not, and not long afterward they became involved in writing the score for *Sweet Charity*, starring Gwen Verdon.

Coleman was working on two film scores at the time he agreed to supply the music for the new musical, and, in setting about the new task, he injected some of the techniques he had picked up in Hollywood. In

SWEET CHARITY *(1966). Composer Cy Coleman and lyricist Dorothy Fields talk over a problem backstage with director-choreographer Bob Fosse.*

SWEET CHARITY *(1966). Gwen Verdon, Helen Gallagher and Thelma Oliver belting out "There's Gotta Be Something Better than This." (Costumes by Irene Sharaff.)*

true cinematic fashion, he deliberately composed a perky, chipper instrumental piece as an identifying theme everytime Miss Verdon, as Charity, appeared on the stage. He also made great use of underscoring to heighten the dramatic situations of the story. As for the set pieces, Coleman and Fields constructed a musically unified score that dramatically exposed the heroine's variety of moods and emotions—"Where Am I Going" to point up her frustration, "There's Gotta Be Something Better than This" her determination to seek a better life, "If My Friends Could See Me Now" her amazement at fleeting good fortune. In one memorably atmospheric number, "Big Spender," the dance hall hostesses at the Fan-Dango Ballroom draped themselves around a railing in awkwardly seductive poses to coax the audience, as lethargically as possible, to "spend a little time with me."

The origin of the musical had been Federico Fellini's *Nights of Cabiria,* but on Broadway in the newly refurbished Palace Theatre the prostitute of the film had become a presumably more sympathetic dime-a-dance girl. Initially conceived to be presented with another one-act musical writ-

389

ten by Elaine May, *Sweet Charity* was subsequently fleshed out to two acts by Neil Simon when the other work was abandoned. The padding, however, was all too apparent, with many scenes extended beyond their proper length and with seemingly endless, though imaginatively staged, dance routines devised by Bob Fosse.

Both Cy Coleman and Carolyn Leigh are writers of the current scene. Both have a way of creating for and communicating beyond the theatre. Coleman's most apparent traits are his musical sophistication and structural experimentation, generally revealed through hard-driving, brisk melodies; in partnership with the supremely gifted and adaptable Dorothy Fields, his *Sweet Charity* score stands as a model for our vibrant, restless age. Though Carolyn Leigh's first post-Coleman musical, *How Now, Dow Jones* (written with Hollywood's Elmer Bernstein), received a more bearish than bullish reception, the lyricist remains unquestionably one of the musical theatre's most polished and meaningful writers, with a complete understanding of her craft. "I'm experienced enough," she has said, "to know that what you may think is the most monumental work can be less than monumental when it's translated to the stage, surrounded by the story, the costumes, the mood, the lights, performed by the performers. I'm only concerned with success in terms of the audience understanding what's been done, enjoying it, feeling it. The theatre is no place for an individual to try to make a particular production his or her vehicle."

Jerry Herman

If Charles Strouse and Lee Adams have—so far—been our musical youth leaders among modern writers, composer-lyricist Jerry Herman has —so far—been our musical champion of the middle and post-middle aged. The fact that Herman is also the youngest writer represented in this book (born July 10, 1932) makes it doubly distinctive that his book shows to date have been concerned with two mature romances in *Milk and Honey,* the machinations of an ancient fraud in *Madame Aphrodite,* and the madcap careers of those two antic post-debs, Dolly Gallagher Levi and Mame Dennis Burnside.

Jerry, né Gerald, Herman was born in New York (as were about half of the heroes of this book), but moved with his family to Jersey City, New Jersey, at an early age. Though Herman's mother was a piano and voice teacher, she never forced him to take lessons; he picked up his musical knowledge by playing piano by ear and never did have a formal musical education (a condition he shares with, among other composers, Irving Berlin, Frank Loesser, Richard Adler, Bob Merrill and Harvey Schmidt). At Miami University, which he attended primarily because of their experi-

Jerry Herman.   PHOTO BY FRIEDMAN-ABELES

mental drama department, Herman was active as a composer, lyricist,
author, director and designer.

One of Jerry Herman's college revues was called *I Feel Wonderful.*
Apparently, it gave enough patrons a similarly affirmative attitude; in 1954,
after Herman had graduated from Miami, the show was bankrolled by
local enthusiasts and presented at an off-Broadway theatre. Not too many
customers came, but the reviews were favorable ("Fresh and entertaining
without a tedious number in it," opined Louis Kronenberger). *Nightcap,*
a night club revue, was offered at the showplace, where Herman was
earning steady money as a pianist. Its 400-performance run spurred producer Lawrence Kasha to commission Herman to whip up another off-

Broadway revue, *Parade*, though its success was only moderate.

That was early in 1960. Herman, with three revues—plus assorted television and nightclub assignments—now felt himself ready for Broadway. His agent introduced him to another client, playwright Don Appell, and the two began tossing ideas around. Suddenly, Appell blurted out, "How about a musical set in Israel?" With no idea of what they would put into a musical set in Israel, the two men agreed to collaborate. Aided by a financial assist from realtor-turned-producer Gerard Oestreicher, they took off for Israel where they spent five weeks soaking up atmosphere and dreaming up a story and the songs to go with it. Because Herman didn't want to confine himself to writing an entire score in a minor key, the writers decided to make their principal characters Americans rather than Israelis, with appropriately indigenous music added for local color.

When it opened in October, 1961, *Milk and Honey* won respectable notices, with generous praise for the performances of Robert Weede, Mimi Benzell and Molly Picon, and the bright, travel poster way the Israeli spirit was captured. As for Jerry Herman, Howard Taubman wrote in the *Times*, "He has provided songs that range from functional to exultant. His hora has the necessary rhythmic fervor; his 'Shalom' and 'Milk and Honey' pay genial respects to Israel, and in 'That Was Yesterday' and 'I Will Follow You,' he conveys the conviction of personal emotion."

Notwithstanding the gay, satirical pieces Jerry Herman had written for revues, he now found, as a result of *Milk and Honey*, that his creative image had become so altered that he was besieged with scripts dealing with somber romances between men and women of the post-forties generation. What he needed was a quick change of pace. Hearing that David Merrick was about to produce a musical version of Thornton Wilder's slam-bang farce, *The Matchmaker*, Herman went about getting the song writing assignment in the most direct manner possible. He simply auditioned. After listening to four songs, Merrick, in fabled Hollywood style, turned to Herman and said, "Kid, the show is yours."

Because he had also sponsored *The Matchmaker*, Merrick had an especially proprietary attitude about the musical adaptation, and he was determined to do everything he could to insure that it would be the biggest success of his career. For librettist, he hired Michael Stewart, and for director, Gower Champion, both of whom had worked on two previous winners, *Bye Bye Birdie* and *Carnival*. His star was the superpowered, larger-than-life Carol Channing. Couldn't miss? Well, it almost did. The prospects looked so bleak, in fact, during the Detroit tryout that Merrick almost shut down the production.

But major alterations were quickly and skillfully made. Three songs were dropped, three were added (including the Act I finale). Possibly the

HELLO, DOLLY! *(1964). Carol Channing and her welcoming committee at the Harmonia Gardens. (Costumes by Freddy Wittop; setting by Oliver Smith.)*

most significant change was in holding up Miss Channing's second act entrance until the second—or "Hello, Dolly!"—scene. Following the January 16, 1964, New York première at the St. James Theatre, *Hello, Dolly!* was joyously welcomed by hat-tossing but not completely uncritical critic. While proclaiming it "a musical shot through with enchantment," Howard Taubman in the *Times* nevertheless objected to its "unnecessarily vulgar and frenzied touches." The *Post's* Richard Watts, Jr., although hailing it as "big, bouncing, handsome, rapid-paced and filled with the shrewdest ingredients of successful showmanship," still lamented the lack of "whimsically playful humor and charm it had originally." Ted Kalem of *Time*, however, disagreed. He found it "has eye appeal, ear appeal, love appeal, and laugh appeal, but its most insinuating charm is its nostalgic appeal," but he did admit it "occasionally gets bogged down in a plot hole." As for Henry Hewes, the *Saturday Review* reviewer called it "a triumph of staging over a book, lyrics and music that are not in themselves extraordinary."

Among other touches that helped him score his triumph, director Champion made use of a circular runway around the rim of the orchestra pit which was particularly effective in the show's biggest applause-catcher,

HELLO, DOLLY! *(1964). Horace Vandergelder (David Burns) is rather distracted by the ability of Dolly Levi (Carol Channing) to consume endless quantities of dumplings.*

the "Hello, Dolly" number. It is useless to cavil, of course, that the scene advances the story not a whit, or that Dolly Levi's return to a once-favored haunt is hardly a significant enough event to warrant such riotous celebrating. What counts, obviously, is the exciting theatricality of the number—the waiters strutting and racing through a split-second whirlwind galop, manipulating trays, food and shish-kebab skewers . . . the descent down the center staircase of the scarlet-gowned, plume-topped mistress of the revels . . . the opening up of the scene practically in the audience's lap as Dolly leads her fleet-footed admirers across the runway. It was an electric occasion, one that Walter Kerr summed up as "the best single piece of sheer musical comedy staging I have ever seen since I went to my first minstrel show."

After Miss Channing had relinquished her role on Broadway to tour in the musical for over a year, the part was taken over by a succession of ex-movie queens—Ginger Rogers (year and a half), Martha Raye (four months), Betty Grable (five months), and in a touring edition, Dorothy Lamour. At this writing, thanks to an effusive all-Negro cast headed by Pearl Bailey and Cab Calloway, *Hello, Dolly!* is almost as much of a Broadway boxoffice attraction as it ever was.

Following the success of *Hello, Dolly!*, Jerry Herman had no further image problem. Obviously no longer in need of proving his versatility, he next became involved with the saga of another zany, flamboyant female, Auntie Mame. Jerome Lawrence and Robert E. Lee had already turned Patrick Dennis' novel into a play that had somehow given the impression of being a musical comedy without music; now Lawrence and Lee were taking the inevitable step of converting it into a musical comedy *with* music. After flirting with the title *My Best Girl*, they eventually settled for the simplest appellation possible, *Mame*.

Herman worked closely with the librettists at all times, almost as a third book collaborator. What the authors were determined to do was to try to forget everything that they had done in fashioning *Auntie Mame* as a play. They wanted *Mame* to have a life of her own, not merely be a

MAME *(1966). "It's Today!," sings Angela Lansbury, and all the invited guests at her party are in exuberant agreement. (Costumes by Robert Mackintosh; settings by William and Jean Eckart.)*

PHOTO BY FRIEDMAN-ABELES

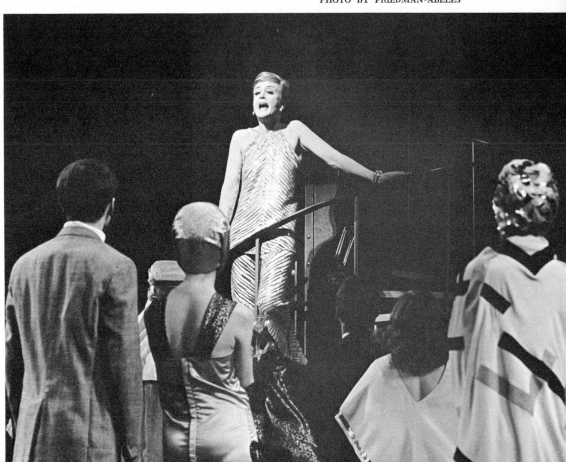

blaring, overblown cartoon of the previous incarnation. With Angela Lansbury as the redoubtable, zestful Mame (after almost forty ladies of the theatre had been considered or tested), they achieved a laudable blending of music, lyrics and story that, if anything, made the leading character and her picaresque story more human and fully developed than it had been before.

Mame offered Jerry Herman an inescapable challenge—to write another "Hello, Dolly!" song. For the title number of the new work (slotted as the first act finale), he came up with a prancing, cake-walking dear-old-Southland tribute to the heroine, containing such imaginative encomia as "You make our black-eyed peas and our grits, Mame/Seem like the bill of fare at the Ritz, Mame." But the composer's own favorite, and justifiably so, was Mame's tender "If He Walked into My Life," in which the hedonistic heroine muses about the things she may have done wrong ("Did he need a stronger hand? Did he need a lighter touch?") in bringing up her charge, young Patrick Dennis. "It's Today," reworked from Herman's earlier, "No Tune Like a Show Tune" in *Parade*, was an effulgent credo to living life to the fullest, while "Open a New Window" sounded a challenging call to risk the unknown.

"I don't want to be a song writer," Jerry Herman once wrote. "I want to be a composer-lyricist for the American musical theatre. There's a great difference. The composer-lyricist is no longer a song writer, he's a musical playwright. He can heighten an emotion with the addition of music because he is appealing to another sense in the audience; when that fiddle begins to play it can transport us to an emotion that might not be reached by the spoken word. It's this roller coaster between the two, this homogenizing of the spoken word and the sung word, that makes a career in the present American musical theatre so fascinating."

Mitch Leigh and Joe Darion

It is symptomatic of the times that, in addition to the popular music field, summer resorts, off-Broadway, night clubs, films, and the concert hall, there has emerged a new training ground for musical theatre composers—radio and television commercials. To date, Mitch Leigh, the composer of the score for *Man of La Mancha*, is the most celebrated practitioner but undoubtably others will be following. "Writing a jingle or a pop song or a symphony or a Broadway score," he insists, "involves a profound training in the craft and that's exactly what Madison Avenue gives a writer."

Leigh, however, has not been artistically limited to Madison Avenue. Born in Brooklyn, New York, on January 31, 1928, he studied music at Yale University under Paul Hindemith and earned his master's degree. In

Mitch Leigh.

1954, in collaboration with another writer, he sold his first television commercial to Revlon. After completing their assignment, the two men asked the advertising agency how much they could expect for their labors. When they were told "seven-fifty," Leigh was shocked. He had figured at least ten dollars, with five apiece. How could they split $7.50? When it was explained that the fee would be seven hundred and fifty, Leigh was no longer concerned about simple division. He also quickly realized that writing jingles is an extremely lucrative business. Three years later, he founded Music Makers, Inc., which has become the largest company in the country specializing in television and radio musical commercials.

Leigh first ventured into the theatre in 1963 when he composed the background music for an all-star cast revival of Bernard Shaw's *Too True*

397

Joe Darion.

to Be Good. Albert Marre was the director. In August of the same year, *The New York Times* announced that Music Makers was about to enter the Broadway production ranks by sponsoring a musical treatment of Dale Wasserman's television play, *I, Don Quixote,* to be called *Man of La Mancha.* Albert Marre would do the staging, and the score would be written by Mitch Leigh and, as co-lyricists, W. H. Auden and Chester Kallman. Michael Redgrave was then the likeliest prospect for the title role. By the time the production was unveiled two years later, the production had been turned over to Albert W. Selden and Hal James, Richard Kiley was the Don, and the lyrics had become the work of Joe Darion.

Like Mitch Leigh, Joe Darion has felt at home in all areas of writing. A native New Yorker, born January 30, 1917, he attended the City College of Journalism, and has written for radio, television, films, and the concert hall. He is responsible for "The Ho-Ho Song" (music by Jack Wolf) for

Red Buttons, and "The Growing Up Tree" (music by George Kleinsinger) for the Camp Fire Girls, plus assorted pop hits. He has written words to song cycles and cantatas, and his oratorio, *Galileo*, with music by Ezra Laderman, was commissioned by CBS-TV. For the theatre, he was responsible for the lyrics—to George Kleinsinger's music—of *Shinbone Alley*, a musical version of Don Marquis' *archie and mehitabel*, which was seen briefly in 1957. Darion was also the lyricist of the 1967 musical, *Illya Darling*, starring the explosive Melina Mercouri. Manos Hadjidakis, who had created the background score for the film *Never on Sunday*, the basis of the musical, was the composer.

Playwright Wasserman first thought of writing a play about Cervantes' *Don Quixote* when, in Madrid, he read a totally erroneous newspaper account that that was his purpose for being in Spain. This spurred him to read the book, which convinced him to attempt, not a dramatization, but a play that would be "a tribute to the spirit of Don Quixote's creator. The motif of the attempt I found in a quotation by another brilliant writer, Miguel Unamuno, who said: 'Only he who attempts the ridiculous may

PHOTO BY ARTHUR CANTOR.

MAN OF LA MANCHA *(1965).* *"I am I, Don Quixote," booms the Don (Richard Kiley), as he and his servant, Sancho Panza (Irving Jacobson), set off on their adventure astride two remarkable steeds. (Costumes by Howard Bay and Patton Campbell.)*

MAN OF LA MANCHA *(1965).*
The deathbed scene - Sancho
(Irving Jacobson), the Don
(Richard Kiley), and Aldonza
(Joan Diener).

achieve the impossible.' In that quixotic spirit the play was written, a
deliberate denial of the prevailing spirit of our time which finds its
theatrical mood in black comedy and the deification of despair."

Once his television play had been presented, Wasserman rewrote it as
a play for Broadway. But director Albert Marre, to whom he showed it,
persuaded him to rewrite it again as a musical. This opened up many new
problems in construction, staging and style. For composer Leigh and lyricist Darion, the challenge was primarily to write songs that *sounded* authentic, without necessarily being authentic in music or lyrics. Leigh spent hours
researching the music of the early seventeenth century, the period of the
story, but found it totally uninteresting. Then he turned to Flamenco,
which, though only about one hundred and fifty years old, seemed to have
the proper period flavor and theatrical effectiveness. "It became evident,"
the composer has explained, "that a single continuing sound was required,
on which variations would have to be 'leaned.' The humorous songs and
the wilder numbers could not stray too far from the emotional content of
the piece."

Apart from these considerations, the music and lyrics had a rightness
about them in content as well as in form. Don Quixote's innocent faith was
never permitted to become farcical, whether in his declaration of his mission ("I am I, Don Quixote, the Lord of La Mancha/My destiny calls and
I go"), or in extolling the whore Aldonza as his spotless Dulcinea, or in

400

dreaming his impossible dream. Aldonza actually did come to believe herself to be Dulcinea, a transformation calling for musical emotions ranging from bitter resignation in "It's All the Same" to her final, anguished plea, as the knight lay dying, to "bring me back the bright and shining glory of Dulcinea."

Man of La Mancha was tried out at the Goodspeed Opera House, in East Haddam, Connecticut, in the summer of 1965. After much alteration, it opened five months later far from the theatre district at the ANTA Washington Square Theatre, on east 4th Street. At this writing, the musical is still a near sell-out. (It was however, forced to move to a more central location because of the impending demolition of the theatre.)

Surely, few musicals have ever matched *Man of La Mancha* for the sheer theatricality of its physical production—at least in its original home. The suspended stage platform, jutting out into the banked, semi-circular auditorium, was tilted toward the audience. Behind it towered a huge staircase suspended whenever necessary to provide a link between the outer world and the dungeon into which Cervantes and his servant have been thrown. The orchestra was split in two and placed on both sides of the arena stage. The transformation of Cervantes into Don Quixote and his servant into Sancho Panza was done simply with makeup kits in full view of the audience, and their subsequent horseback ride was accomplished on two wooden frames attached to two dancers wearing horse head masks.

Despite the geographical inconvenience of the play's location and the physical inconvenience to theatregoers of running without an intermission, the play soon found its audience. This is, perhaps, even more surprising when we reread some of the reviews that greeted it. Though Richard Watts and John Chapman were unstinting in their praise, Howard Taubman of the *Times* and Walter Kerr of the *Herald Tribune* took strong exception to what both called its vulgarities. However, former *Times* appraiser Brooks Atkinson came out of retirement to dub it "one of the most imaginative theatre events of the decade." Others were quick to fault the production for distorting Cervantes; instead of making the work a satire on the foolishness of the dying age of knight errantry, it now became a pathetic tale of vision and faith in a cynical world. Certainly the Wasserman-Leigh-Darion approach is more applicable today, and one which can strike the far more responsive chord. Where is self-deluding chivalry now? Idealism and morality are among the very qualities our age is most in need of. The huge success of *Man of La Mancha* would make it appear that audiences are well aware of the need, and can wishfully empathize with a dreamer who dared to see the world as a better place than it is.

CABARET (1966). *Composer John Kander, lyricist Fred Ebb, actress Jill Haworth, producer Harold Prince, and librettist Joe Masteroff on the first day of rehearsal.*

John Kander and Fred Ebb

The curtain is already up as the audience enters the theatre—and sees itself. Suspended from the flies is a huge, slanted, distorted mirror, the only prop on the darkened stage. To the left of the proscenium arch is a spiral staircase. Dimly seen receding street lamps are on both sides of the stage. Suddenly, an illuminated sign blinks on, letter by letter—C A B A R E T. As it is hoisted away, there is a low, ominous roll on the drums, the cymbals clash, and the Master of Ceremonies enters. His patent leather hair is parted in the middle, his face is clown white, his cheeks rouged, his lips scarlet, his eyes mascaraed, his smile leering. To an oompah, beerhall beat, he bids us in a steely, German-accented voice, "Willkommen, bienvenue, welcome im Cabaret, au Cabaret, to Cabaret!" Here in the Kit Kat Klub, he tells us, "life is beautiful . . . even the orchestra is beautiful"—and a platform containing a quartet of musical harpies, pounding and blasting away at their instruments, is rolled onstage. With another effusive introduction ("each

402

and every one a virgin"), the bra-less, bare-thighed, black-stockinged, frozen-faced doxies of the chorus appear to join in the song of welcome, as the slanted mirror tilts upward now reflecting the performers. Then, to the wail of the tenor saxes, the tables—complete with telephones—roll on stage, as does the bar, and out come the waiters, busboys, bartenders, entertainers, customers. Willkommen, bienvenue, welcome, they all sing, high-kicking their way down to the footlights—and we are right there in the frenzied midst of a garish Berlin night club of the late Twenties.

Thus *Cabaret* begins, making it perfectly clear that, despite the desperate gaiety of the opening number, there will be nothing truly gay or escapist about the musical. From then on, it proceeds to an ending of complete despair as our cabaret master of ceremonies, his enthusiasm drained, his voice husky and his face now a death mask, welcomes us for the last time. Hitler has now come to power, the dancers goosestep wearing swastika armbands, and the music is nightmarish and discordant. At the end of *Man of La Mancha*, Don Quixote may still dream his impossible dream.

CABARET (1966). *The Master of Ceremonies (Joel Grey) bidding one and all "Willkommen, bienvenue, welcome." (Costumes by Patricia Zipprodt; setting by Boris Aronson.)*
PHOTO BY FRIEDMAN-ABELES

CABARET *(1966). Overcome by the gift of a pineapple, Lotte Lenya conveys her thanks to Jack Gilford in "It Couldn't Please Me More."*

PHOTO BY FRIEDMAN-ABELES

At the end of *Fiddler on the Roof,* Tevya may still have his faith. But when the curtain falls on *Cabaret,* no one is left with anything. Hero has left heroine to her doomed life and the world is about to plunge into its most devastating war. The fact that *Cabaret* has succeeded so well on a commercial level indicates that audiences accept it as reflecting more than a decadent period of the past. Despotism and discord will not disappear, it seems to say, if we close our eyes and heed only the beckoning call to come to the cabaret old chum, come to the cabaret . . .

The musical was adapted by Joe Masteroff from both the play, *I Am a Camera* by John van Druten, and the play's source, Christopher Isherwood's *Berlin Stories.* Masteroff and producer-director Harold Prince began working on a treatment even before they approached composer John Kander and lyricist Fred Ebb to write the score. As the musical began to take shape, little of *I Am a Camera,* except for the character of Sally Bowles, was retained; increasingly, the collaborators found themselves going back to the flavor and situations of the Isherwood stories. But the form of the musical

404

began to jell only when they hit upon the idea of the Master of Ceremonies, an entirely original character, who provided the thematic thread woven through a series of vulgar night club specialties.

Cabaret was the second Broadway musical on which John Kander and Fred Ebb worked as a team. Kander, born in Kansas City, Missouri, on March 18, 1927, studied music at both Oberlin College and Columbia University. He received his master's degree in 1953. During the next nine years his theatrical training included conducting at summer theatres, serving as rehearsal pianist and, eventually, creating the dance arrangements for *Gypsy* and *Irma la Douce*. In 1962, Kander joined with James and William Goldman to fashion both songs and story for *A Family Affair*, Harold Prince's first directorial assignment. Though the presentation was short-lived, Kander's score won the "sleeper of the year" prize from fellow composer Vernon Duke, who wrote in his book, *Listen Here!*: "The music bristles with delightful surprises, new departures in song construction, and a sort of unrestrained lust for tonal adventure exceedingly rare to come by these days."

The same year, Kander collaborated with Fred Ebb on their first song, "My Coloring Book," which, though created for Kaye Ballard, went on to long-playing fame via a recording by Sandy Stewart. The second Kander-Ebb song, "I Don't Care Much," became a Barbra Streisand specialty. It also helped put the partnership on a permanent basis.

A native New Yorker, Fred Ebb was born on April 8, 1932. He attended both New York University and Columbia. With his first collaborator, Paul Klein, he turned out some strikingly fresh night club pieces, among them "The Insecure Tango" (a girl's confession that she's not even sure she's insecure), and a hilarious bit dealing with communal psychiatry called "Group Therapy." In 1960, in partnerships with both Paul Klein and Norman Martin, Ebb contributed material to the revue, *From A to Z*, starring Hermione Gingold.

The first Kander and Ebb musical comedy score was written for *Flora, the Red Menace* which, under the sponsorship of Harold Prince, endured a brief existence in 1965. This didn't dampen Prince's admiration for the team a bit; convinced that they were the right ones to do the songs for *Cabaret*, the producer simply went after them and talked them into doing it.

Following the opening of *Cabaret* in November, 1966, it was obvious that Kander and Ebb had finally made it. Indeed it was their atmospheric score, the George Grosz influence of the decor, and some first-rate performances by Joel Grey (the epicene Master of Ceremonies), Lotte Lenya (a pragmatic landlady), and Jack Gilford (a mushy Jewish fruit dealer) that made the most lasting impact. Tying the disparate elements together into a unified entertainment was the accomplishment of Harold Prince, whose direction was never surer or more effective as he recreated the clownish tragedy of a world in decay.

Walter Kerr, writing in the *N. Y. Times,* found something even more noteworthy in the production—a breakthrough in musical theatre form. Here, he wrote, was a rarity, a musical that did not really concern itself with the integration of song into the story; the musical numbers for the most part were done within the framework of set pieces in the night club—which itself provided the framework for the entire production. "Instead of putting the narrative first," wrote Kerr, "and the singers and dancers wherever a small corner can be found for them, it pops the painted clown and gartered girls directly into our faces, making them, in effect, a brightly glazed window—with a musical staff scrawled all over it—*through* which we can perceive the people and the emotional pattern of the plot."

Will *Cabaret* herald a breakthrough in form? At this writing the signs are hard to find. (None surely in Kander and Ebb's subsequent entry, *The Happy Time,* a far more conventional bit of sentimental fluff.) But, most certainly, *Cabaret* does represent yet another breakthrough in the never-ending attempt at utilizing the form of the musical theatre in the service of more meaningful expression. Wrote Fred Ebb: "A few short years ago it would have been impossible for a musical with this kind of subject to succeed. I think the same is true of *West Side Story* and *Fiddler on the Roof.* All of these musicals have been supported by the public. Maybe there are fewer 'verboten' topics now. Maybe the musical theatre can experiment on a large scale for the first time. And still be 'commercial.'" Maybe.

CHAPTER TWENTY-FOUR

Epilogue

In so viable an art form as the musical theatre, no one knows which writers will be responsible for the next major innovation in content or in form. Or even the next hit. Thus in addition to those writers discussed in previous chapters, there are many other talented composers and lyricists whose works have already been applauded and whose development bears watching. This brief Epilogue is devoted to sketching the highlights of some of the more promising talents who have emerged since 1959.

Composer MARY RODGERS (daughter of Richard) and lyricist MARSHALL BARER got off to an auspicious start in 1959 with their off-Broadway success, *Once Upon a Mattress*. Seven years later, still off-Broadway, they came back with another popular attraction, *The Mad Show*. Another meritorious debut of 1959 was scored by composer-lyricist-librettist RICK BESOYAN with his spoof of the world of Friml and Romberg called *Little Mary Sunshine*. Its run of 1,143 performances made it the fourth longest-running off-Broadway musical to date.

Also offered far from the Main Stem was the well-received *Ernest in Love*, which librettist-lyricist ANNE CROSWELL and composer LEE POCKRISS adapted from Oscar Wilde's *The Importance of Being Ernest*. Three years later, the team made it on Broadway with *Tovarich*, co-starring Vivien Leigh (in her only musical) and Jean Pierre Aumont. *Riverwind*, for which JOHN JENNINGS supplied music, lyrics and libretto, was the off-Broadway success story of 1962. The following year, that distinction

ONCE UPON A MATTRESS (1959). *Carol Burnett as Princess Winifred ("Fred" to her friends) bellows to the assembled courtiers that she's "Shy." (Costumes by William and Jean Eckart.)*

LITTLE MARY SUNSHINE (1959). *Little Mary Sunshine (Eileen Brennan) demurely turns her head as the brave Capt. Big Jim Warington (William Graham) serenades her with "You're the Fairest Flower." (Costumes by Howard Barker.)*

HIGH SPIRITS *(1964). Beatrice Lillie, as Mme. Arcati, kicks up her heels as she puts over the number, "Talking to You."*

easily went to *The Streets of New York*, written by BARRY ALAN GRAEL and RICHARD CHODOSH.

ERVIN DRAKE, who had had a succession of pop hits to his credit ("I Believe," "Tico-Tico," "It Was a Very Good Year"), first embarked on a Broadway career in 1964. His musical, *What Makes Sammy Run?*, for which he supplied words and music, starred Steve Lawrence and ran over 500 performances. Later the same season newcomer TIMOTHY GRAY joined veteran HUGH MARTIN to write *High Spirits*. This was a musical version of Noel Coward's *Blithe Spirit*, which boasted the stellar trio of Beatrice Lillie, Tammy Grimes and Edward Woodward.

The 1964-65 Broadway season introduced the talents of five writers who somehow managed to circumvent the customary off-Broadway apprenticeship route: librettist-lyricist SIDNEY MICHAELS and composer MARK SANDRICH, Jr., who wrote *Ben Franklin in Paris*, starring Robert Preston; composer-lyricist WALTER MARKS, who created the score for *Bajour* (and, in 1968, *Golden Rainbow*); and co-composers-lyricists MARION GRUDEFF and RAYMOND JESSEL, responsible for the songs in the Sherlock Holmes saga, *Baker Street*.

YOU'RE A GOOD MAN, CHARLIE BROWN (1967). *The baseball game, as played by Karen John-son (Patty), Reva Rose (Lucy), Bill Hinnant (Snoopy), Bob Balaban (Linus), Skip Hinnant (Schroeder,) and Gary Burghoff (Charlie Brown).*

Off-Broadway, however, still manages to provide the greatest opportunities for musical comedy debuts. Four successful productions on view within recent years revealed creative talents in widely varied areas. Librettist-lyricist BEN TARVER and composer JOHN CLIFTON recreated the charms of eighteenth-century England in *Man with a Load of Mischief* (1966). Librettist-lyricist-composer CLARK GESNER humanized and musicalized Charles Schulz's cartoon characters in *You're a Good Man, Charlie Brown* (1967), which is well on its way to becoming a long-run phenomenon. Lyricists GEROME RAGNI and JAMES RADO along with composer GALT MacDERMOT broke new ground with their first "American Tribal Love-Rock Musical," yclept *Hair* (1967), subsequently transferred to Broadway in a somewhat altered version. Still another rock musical, *Your Own Thing* (1968) switched the Illyria of Shakespeare's *Twelfth Night* to mod Manhattan, and won the New York Drama Critics Circle

410

palm for the best musical of the season. HAL HESTER and DANNY APOLINAR were credited with the songs.

Thus we can see healthy stirrings in diverse directions. Ultimate changes in the paths of the musical stage may come through the efforts of writers mentioned in this Epilogue or discussed more fully in previous chapters—or from voices yet to be heard. We live in hope and we watch and we listen.

YOUR OWN THING *(1968). A rock group known as The Apocalypse (co-author Danny Apolinar, Michael Valenti and John Kuhner) are joined by masquerading pop singer Viola (Leland Palmer) to blast out their affirmation to "The Now Generation." (Costumes by Albert Wolsky; setting by Robert Guerra.)*

411

Musical Productions & Discography

The following lists include opening dates, theatres, number of performances, collaborators, producers, directors, choreographers, leading cast members, and principal songs of every Broadway (and off-Broadway) musical with scores written by the composers and lyricists discussed in this book. Modern director-choreographers are credited only as directors. In addition to productions with complete scores by these writers, others with four or more interpolated songs have been included.

All original cast (O.C.), film version cast (F.V.), television cast (TV), and studio cast (S.C.) 12-inch long playing records are noted and discussed briefly. When two record numbers are used, the second one represents the stereo release. An "X" indicates that the record has been cut from the catalogue.

The exact number of performances, especially, of some of the earlier musicals, is difficult to determine. In general, references have been *The Best Plays* series, *The Billboard, Variety*, and Daniel Blum's *Theater World* series. Wherever a noticeable discrepancy exists in these sources, the number has been used that most closely corresponds to the total months a show has played on Broadway.

Names of cast members have been listed according to the spelling found in programs of each musical. In cases where actors or writers have since changed their names so that they are no longer identifiable by this listing, the more familiar names appear in parentheses.

412

CHAPTER TWO
VICTOR HERBERT
composer

PRINCE ANANIAS
Opened: Nov. 20, 1894, Broadway Th.
(No record of performances)
Book & lyrics by Francis Neilson.
Produced by The Bostonians.
Cast included: Mena Cleary, W. H. Mac-Donald, Eugene Cowles, Henry Clay Barnabee, George Frothingham, Jessie Bartlett Davis, Josephine Bartlett.
Principal songs: Ah! Cupid, Meddlesome Boy!; Ah! List to Me; It Needs No Poet; I Am No Queen; Amaryllis.

THE WIZARD OF THE NILE
Opened: Nov. 4, 1895, Casino Th.
105 *performances.*
Book & lyrics by Harry B. Smith.
Produced by Kirke LaShelle & Arthur F. Clark; directed by Napier Lothian, Jr.
Cast included: Frank Daniels, Walter Allen, Edwin Isham, Dorothy Morton, Helen Redmond.
Principal songs: Pure and White Is the Lotus; Star Light, Star Bright; My Angeline; Stonecutters' Song.

THE GOLD BUG
Opened: Sept. 21, 1896, Casino Th.
1 *week.*
Book & lyrics by Glen MacDonough.
Produced by Thomas Canary & George W. Lederer; directed by Max Freeman.
Cast included: Marie Cahill, Max Figman, Molly Fuller, Bert Williams & George Walker.
Principal songs: One for Another; The Owl and the Thrush; Gold Bug March.

THE SERENADE
Opened: Mar. 16, 1897, Knickerbocker Th.
79 *performances.*
Book & lyrics by Harry B. Smith.
Produced by The Bostonians; directed by W. H. Fitzgerald.
Cast included: Alice Nielsen, Eugene Cowles, Henry Clay Barnabee, Josephine Bartlett, W. H. MacDonald, George Frothingham, Jessie Bartlett Davis.
Principal songs: With Cracking of Whip and Rattle of Spur; I Love Thee, I Adore Thee; The Monk and the Maid; Cupid and I.

THE IDOL'S EYE
Opened: Oct. 25, 1897, Broadway Th.
7 *weeks.*
Book & lyrics by Harry B. Smith.
Produced by Frank Daniels; directed by Julian Mitchell.
Cast included: Frank Daniels, Helen Redmond, Maurice Darcy, Alf. C. Whelan, Will Danforth.
Principal songs: I'm Captain Cholly Chumley of the Guards; The Lady and the Kick; Song of the Priestess; Cuban Song.

THE FORTUNE TELLER
Opened: Sept. 26, 1898, Wallack's Th.
40 *performances.*
Book & lyrics by Harry B. Smith.
Produced by Fred J. Perley; directed by Julian Mitchell.
Cast included: Alice Nielsen, Eugene Cowles, Joseph Herbert, Joseph Cawthorn, Frank Rushworth, May Boley.
Principal songs: Always Do as People Say You Should; Romany Life; Gypsy Love Song; Czardas.

CYRANO DE BERGERAC
Opened: Sept. 18, 1899, Knickerbocker Th.
28 *performances.*
Book by Stuart Reed; lyrics by Harry B. Smith.
Produced by Francis Wilson; directed by A. M. Holbrook.
Cast included: Francis Wilson, Lulu Glaser, Josephine Intropidi, Charles H. Bowers.
Principal songs: Since I Am Not for Thee; Cadets of Gascony; I Wonder; Let the Sun of My Eyes.

THE SINGING GIRL
Opened: Oct. 23, 1899, Casino Th.

80 *performances.*
Book by Stanislaus Stange; lyrics by
Harry B. Smith.
Produced by Fred J. Perley; directed by
Julian Mitchell.
Cast included: Alice Nielsen, Eugene
Cowles, Joseph Herbert, Joseph Caw-
thorn, Richie Ling.
Principal songs: If Only You Were Mine;
Love Is Tyrant; Well Beloved; The Song
of the Danube.

THE AMEER

Opened: Dec. 4, 1899, Wallack's Th.
51 *performances.*
Book & lyrics by Frederic Ranken &
Kirke LaShelle.
Produced by Frank Daniels; directed by
John Stapleton.
Cast included: Frank Daniels, Helen
Redmond, George Devoll, Will Dan-
forth, Josephine Bartlett.
Principal songs: Sweet Clarissa; Fond
Love, True Love.

THE VICEROY

Opened: Apr. 9, 1900, Knickerbocker Th.
28 *performances.*
Book & lyrics by Harry B. Smith.
Produced by The Bostonians; directed
by William H. Fitzgerald.
Cast included: Henry Clay Barnabee,
Helen Bertram, Grace Cameron, Wil-
liam H. MacDonald, Frank Rushworth,
George B. Frothingham, William H.
Fitzgerald.
Principal songs: The Robin and the
Rose; Tell Me; 'Neath the Blue Neapoli-
tan Skies; Just for Today.

BABES IN TOYLAND

Opened: Oct. 13, 1903, Majestic Th.
192 *performances.*
Book & lyrics by Glen MacDonough.
Produced by Fred R. Hamlin & Julian
Mitchell; directed by Mitchell.
Cast included: George W. Denham, Ma-
bel Barrison, William Norris, Bessie
Wynn, Amy Ricard, Nella Webb.
Principal songs: Never Mind, Bo Peep;

I Can't Do the Sum; Go to Sleep, Slum-
ber Deep; March of the Toys; Toyland.
Recorded Versions
Decca DL 8458 (S.C.).
Buena Vista (S) 4022 (F.V.) (1962).
Six numbers from the charming score
are well sung by Kenny Baker and Karen
Kemple on one side of the Decca (Her-
bert's *Red Mill* is on the reverse). The
soundtrack version, with Tommy Sands,
Annette, Ray Bolger & Ed Wynn, is a
pretty bowdlerized affair.

BABETTE

Opened: Nov. 16, 1903, Broadway Th.
59 *performances.*
Book & lyrics by Harry B. Smith.
Produced by Charles Dillingham; di-
rected by Fred G. Latham & A. M. Hol-
brook.
Cast included: Fritzi Scheff, Eugene
Cowles, Richie Ling, Louis Harrison, Er-
roll Dunbar, Josephine Bartlett.
Principal songs: Letters I Write All the
Day; I'll Bribe the Stars; There Once
Was an Owl.

IT HAPPENED IN NORDLAND

Opened: Dec. 5, 1904, Lew Fields Th.
154 *performances.*
Book & lyrics by Glen MacDonough.
Produced by Fred R. Hamlin, Julian
Mitchell, Lew Fields; directed by
Mitchell.
Cast included: Marie Cahill, Lew Fields,
Joseph Herbert, Harry Davenport, May
Robson, Bessie Clayton, Pauline Fred-
erick.
Principal songs: Absinthe Frappé; Com-
manderess-in-Chief; Al Fresco; The Knot
of Blue; Bandanna Land.

MISS DOLLY DOLLARS

Opened: Sept. 4, 1905, Knickerbocker
Th.
56 *performances.*
Book & lyrics by Harry B. Smith.
Produced by Charles Dillingham; di-
rected by A. M. Holbrook.
Cast included: Lulu Glaser, Melville

Stewart, Carter DeHaven, Elsie Ferguson, Ralph Herz.
Principal songs: A Woman Is Only a Woman but a Good Cigar Is a Smoke; An American Heiress; Ollendorff Duet.

WONDERLAND
Opened: Oct. 24, 1905, Majestic Th.
73 performances.
Book & lyrics by Glen MacDonough.
Produced & directed by Julian Mitchell.
Cast included: Sam Chip, Lotta Faust, Eva Davenport, Bessie Wynn.
Principal songs: The Nature Class; Love's Golden Day; The Only One.

MLLE. MODISTE
Opened: Dec. 25, 1905, Knickerbocker Th.
202 performances.
Book & lyrics by Henry Blossom.
Produced by Charles Dillingham; directed by Fred G. Latham.
Cast included: Fritzi Scheff, William Pruette, Walter Percival, Claude Gillingwater, Josephine Bartlett.
Principal songs: Kiss Me Again; The Time, the Place and the Girl; When the Cat's Away; I Want What I Want when I Want It; The Mascot of the Troop.

THE RED MILL
Opened: Sept. 24, 1906, Knickerbocker Th.
274 performances.
Book & lyrics by Henry Blossom.
Produced by Charles Dillingham; directed by Fred G. Latham.
Cast included: Fred Stone, David Montgomery, Augusta Greenleaf, Joseph Ratliff, Allene Crater.
Principal songs: The Isle of Our Dreams; When You're Pretty and the World Is Fair; Everyday Is Ladies' Day With Me; The Streets of New York; Because You're You; Moonbeams.
Recorded Versions
Decca DL 8458 (S.C.).
Capitol T 551 (S.C.).
Eileen Farrell, Wilbur Evans & Felix

Knight are heard in six selections on one half of the Decca LP (*Babes in Toyland* is on the reverse). This version is also paired with *Up in Central Park* on Decca DL 8016. Capitol's release, with Gordon MacRae, offers more of the music but still manages to share the disc comfortably with *Naughty Marietta*.

DREAM CITY AND THE MAGIC KNIGHT
Opened: Dec. 25, 1906, Weber's Th.
102 performances.
Book & lyrics by Edgar Smith.
Produced by Joe Weber; directed by Al. Holbrook.
Cast included: Joe Weber, Otis Harlan, Cecilia Loftus, Maurice Farkoa, Lillian Blauvelt.
Principal songs: I Don't Believe I'll Ever Be a Lady; In Vaudeville; Nancy, I Fancy You.

THE TATTOOED MAN
Opened: Feb. 18, 1907, Criterion Th.
59 performances.
Book by Harry B. Smith & A. N. C. Fowler; lyrics by Smith.
Produced by Charles Dillingham; directed by Julian Mitchell.
Cast included: Frank Daniels, Sallie Fisher, Herbert Waterous, Harry Clarke, May Vokes.
Principal songs: Boys Will Be Boys and Girls Will Be Girls; The Land of Dreams; Nobody Loves Me.

ALGERIA
Opened: Aug. 31, 1908, Broadway Th.
48 performances.
Book & lyrics by Glen MacDonough.
Produced by Frank McKee; directed by George Marion.
Cast included: Ida Brooks Hunt, William Pruette, George Marion, George Leon Moore, Harriet Burt.
Principal songs: Rose of the World; Twilight in Barakeesh; Love Is Like a Cigarette; Ask Her While the Band Is Playing.

LITTLE NEMO

Opened: Oct. 20, 1908, New Amsterdam Th.

111 *performances.*

Book & lyrics by Harry B. Smith.

Produced by Klaw & Erlanger; directed by Herbert Gresham.

Cast included: Joseph Cawthorn, Billy B. Van, Harry Kelly, Master Gabriel, Florence Tempest, Sunshine Ijames (Marion Sunshine), Rose Beaumont.

Principal songs: Won't You Be My Valentine?; The Happy Land of Once-Upon-a-Time; In Happy Slumberland.

THE PRIMA DONNA

Opened: Nov. 30, 1908, Knickerbocker Th.

72 *performances.*

Book & lyrics by Henry Blossom.

Produced by Charles Dillingham; directed by Fred G. Latham.

Cast included: Fritzi Scheff, William Raymond, William K. Harcourt, St. Clair Bayfield, Josephine Bartlett.

Principal songs: I'll Be Married to the Music of a Military Band; A Soldier's Love; Espagnola; If You Were I and I Were You.

THE ROSE OF ALGERIA

(revised version of *Algeria*)

Opened: Sept. 20, 1909, Herald Square Th.

40 *performances.*

Book & lyrics by Glen MacDonough.

Produced by Lew Fields; directed by Ned Wayburn.

Cast included: Lillian Herlein, Eugene Cowles, Anna Wheaton, Frank Pollock.

Principal songs: Same as *Algeria*.

OLD DUTCH

Opened: Nov. 22, 1909, Herald Square Th.

88 *performances.*

Book by Edgar Smith; lyrics by George V. Hobart.

Produced by Messrs. Shubert & Lew Fields; directed by Ned Wayburn.

Cast included: Lew Fields, Alice Dovey, Ada Lewis, Charles Judels, John Bunny, Eva Davenport, Vernon Castle, John E. Henshaw, William Raymond, Helen Hayes.

Principal songs: I Want a Man to Love Me; Climb, Climb; U, Dearie.

NAUGHTY MARIETTA

Opened: Nov. 7, 1910, New York Th.

136 *performances.*

Book & lyrics by Rida Johnson Young.

Produced by Oscar Hammerstein; directed by Jacques Coini.

Cast included: Emma Trentini, Orville Harrold, Edward Martindel, Marie Duchene, Peggy Wood.

Principal songs: Tramp! Tramp! Tramp!; Naughty Marietta; 'Neath the Southern Moon; Italian Street Song; I'm Falling in Love with Someone; Ah! Sweet Mystery of Life.

Recorded Version

Capitol T 551 (S.C.).

Gordon MacRae & Marguerite Piazza star in arias from Herbert's most celebrated score. *The Red Mill* selections are on the reverse.

WHEN SWEET SIXTEEN

Opened: Sept. 14, 1911, Daly's Th.

12 *performances.*

Book & lyrics by George V. Hobart.

Produced by Harry J. Everall & Samuel A. Wallach; directed by R. H. Burnside & Hobart.

Cast included: Harriet Standon, Josie Intropidi, Roy Purviance, Frank Belcher, William Morris.

Principal songs: The Wild Rose; In the Golden Long Ago; Laughs.

THE DUCHESS

Opened: Oct. 16, 1911, Lyric Th.

24 *performances.*

Book by Joseph Herbert; lyrics by Joseph Herbert & Harry B. Smith.

Produced by Messrs. Shubert; directed by J. C. Huffman.

Cast included: Fritzi Scheff, George

Anderson, John E. Hazzard, May Boley.
Principal songs: Cupid, Tell Me Why;
The Land of Sultans' Dreams; It's the
Bump.

THE ENCHANTRESS

Opened: Oct. 19, 1911, New York Th.
72 *performances.*
Book by Fred DeGresac; lyrics by Harry
B. Smith.
Produced by Joseph M. Gaites; directed
by Fred G. Latham.
Cast included: Kitty Gordon, Harold
(Hal) Forde, Ralph Riggs, Hattie Ar-
nold.
Principal songs: To the Land of My Own
Romance; Rose, Lucky Rose; All Your
Own Am I; They All Look Good when
They're Far Away.

THE LADY OF THE SLIPPER

Opened: Oct. 28, 1912, Globe Th.
232 *performances.*
Book by Anne Caldwell & Lawrence
McCarty; lyrics by James O'Dea.
Produced by Charles Dillingham; di-
rected by R. H. Burnside.
Cast included: Fred Stone, David Mont-
gomery, Elsie Janis, Vernon Castle,
Queenie Vassar, Peggy Wood, Allene
Crater, Douglas Stevenson, Vivian Rush-
more, Lydia Lopokova.
Principal songs: Bagdad; Meow! Meow!
Meow!; Punch Bowl Glide; Drums of
All Nations.

SWEETHEARTS

Opened: Sept. 8, 1913, New Amsterdam
Th.
136 *performances.*
Book by Harry B. Smith & Fred De-
Gresac; lyrics by Robert B. Smith.
Produced by Werba & Luescher; di-
rected by Fred G. Latham; dances by
Charles S. Morgan, Jr.
Cast included: Christie MacDonald,
Thomas Conkey, Tom McNaughton,
Edwin Wilson.
Principal songs: Sweethearts; Angelus;
Every Lover Must Meet His Fate; Jean-
nette and Her Little Wooden Shoes;
Pretty as a Picture; The Cricket on the
Hearth.
Recorded Version
RCA Camden CAL 369 (S.C.) X.
With Al Goodman conducting, soloists
sing six numbers from the operetta, plus
"To the Land of My Own Romance" &
"I Might Be Your Once-in-a-While."

THE MADCAP DUCHESS

Opened: Nov. 11, 1913, Globe Th.
71 *performances.*
Book & lyrics by David Stevens & Justin
Huntly McCarthy.
Produced by H. H. Frazee; directed by
Fred G. Latham.
Cast included: Ann Swinburne, Glenn
Hall, Josephine Whittell, Peggy Wood,
Harry Macdonough.
Principal songs: Aurora Blushing Rosily;
Love and I Are Playing; The Deuce,
Young Man; Goddess of Mine.

THE ONLY GIRL

Opened: Nov. 2, 1914, 39th St. Th.
240 *performances.*
Book & lyrics by Henry Blossom.
Produced by Joe Weber; directed by
Fred G. Latham.
Cast included: Thurston Hall, Wilda
Bennett, Jed Prouty, Ernest Torrence,
Adele Rowland, Josephine Whittell,
Richard Bartlett.
Principal songs: When You're Away; Tell
It All Over Again; You're the Only Girl
for Me; Personality; When You're Wear-
ing the Ball and Chain.

THE DÉBUTANTE

Opened: Dec. 7, 1914, Knickerbocker Th.
48 *performances.*
Book by Harry B. Smith; lyrics by Rob-
ert B. Smith.
Produced by John C. Fisher; directed
by George Marion; dances by Allan K.
Foster.
Cast included: Hazel Dawn, Wilmuth
Merkyl, Zoe Barnett, Robert G. Pitkin,
William Danforth.

Principal songs: All for the Sake of a Girl; The Golden Age; The Love of the Lorelei; The Springtime of Life.

THE PRINCESS PAT

Opened: Sept. 29, 1915, Cort Th.
158 performances.
Book & lyrics by Henry Blossom.
Produced by John Cort; directed by Fred G. Latham.
Cast included: Eleanor Painter, Joseph R. Lertora, Al Shean, Eva Fallon, Robert Ober, Doris Kenyon, Ralph Riggs.
Principal songs: Love Is the Best of All; Neapolitan Love Song; All for You; Two Laughing Irish Eyes.

THE CENTURY GIRL

Opened: Nov. 6, 1916, Century Th.
200 performances.
Sketches uncredited; Herbert lyrics by Henry Blossom; music & lyrics also by Irving Berlin.
Produced by Charles Dillingham & Florenz Ziegfeld, Jr.; directed by Fred G. Latham, Leon Errol, Edward Royce, Ned Wayburn.
Cast included: Hazel Dawn, Sam Bernard, Marie Dressler, Leon Errol, Elsie Janis, Harry Kelly, Gus Van & Joe Schenck, Frank Tinney, John Slavin, Lillian Tashman, Irving Fisher, James Doyle & Harland Dixon, Maurice & Florence Walton.
Principal Herbert-Blossom songs: The Century Girl; When Uncle Sam Is Ruler of the Sea; You Belong to Me (lyric by Harry B. Smith).

EILEEN

Opened: Mar. 19, 1917, Shubert Th.
64 performances.
Book & lyrics by Henry Blossom.
Produced by Joe Weber; directed by Fred G. Latham.
Cast included: Walter Scanlan, Greek Evans, Edward Martindel, Olga Roller, Grace Breen.
Principal songs: Free Trade and a Misty Moon; When Shall I Again See Ireland?;

When Love Awakes; Thine Alone; The Irish Have a Great Day Tonight; Eileen Alanna Asthore.
Recorded Version
RCA Camden CAL 210 (S.C.) X.
  Six pieces from Herbert's own favorite score are heard on one side of the LP; music from *Polonaise* is on the other.

MISS 1917

Opened: Nov. 5, 1917, Century Th.
48 performances.
Sketches by Guy Bolton & P. G. Wodehouse; lyrics by Wodehouse; music also by Jerome Kern.
Produced by Charles Dillingham & Florenz Ziegfeld, Jr.; directed by Ned Wayburn.
Cast included: Lew Fields, Cecil Lean, Cleo Mayfield, Vivienne Segal, Andrew Tombes, Harry Kelly, Elizabeth Brice, Marion Davies, Charles King, Peggy Hopkins, Bessie McCoy Davis, Gus Van & Joe Schenck, Irene Castle, Lilyan Tashman, George White, Ann Pennington, Bert Savoy, Emma Haig, Herbert Fields.
Principal Herbert songs: The Society Farmerettes; The Singing Blacksmith of Curriclough (based on songs by Samuel Lover).

HER REGIMENT

Opened: Nov. 12, 1917, Broadhurst Th.
40 performances.
Book & lyrics by William LeBaron.
Produced by Joe Weber; directed by Fred G. Latham.
Cast included: Donald Brian, Audrey Maple, Hugh Chilvers, Frank Moulan, Josie Intropidi.
Principal songs: Soldier Men; 'Twixt Love and Duty; Art Song.

THE VELVET LADY

Opened: Feb. 3, 1919, New Amsterdam Th.
136 performances.
Book & lyrics by Henry Blossom.
Produced by Klaw & Erlanger; directed

by Edgar MacGregor & Julian Mitchell. *Cast included:* Fay Marbe, Alfred Gerrard, Ray Redmond, Ernest Torrence, Georgia O'Ramey, Jed Prouty, Eddie Dowling, Minerva Coverdale, Marie Flynn.
Principal songs: Life and Love; Fair Honeymoon; Spooky Ookum.

ANGEL FACE

Opened: Dec. 29, 1919, Knickerbocker Th.
57 *performances.*
Book by Harry B. Smith; lyrics by Robert B. Smith.
Produced & directed by George W. Lederer; dances by Julian Alfred.
Cast included: Marguerite Zender, John E. Young, Tyler Brooks, Emilie Lea, George Schiller, Jack Donahue, Mary Milburn.
Principal songs: I Might Be Your Once-in-a-While; Someone Like You; Angel Face.

MY GOLDEN GIRL

Opened: Feb. 2, 1920, Nora Bayes Th.
105 *performances.*
Book & lyrics by Frederic Arnold Kummer.
Produced by Harry Wardell; directed by J. Clifford Brooke.
Cast included: Victor Morley, Marie Carroll, Helen Bolton, George Trabert, Ned A. Sparks, Edna May Oliver.
Principal songs: Darby and Joan; I Want You; A Song Without (Many) Words; Ragtime Terpsichore.

THE GIRL IN THE SPOTLIGHT

Opened: July 12, 1920, Knickerbocker Th.
56 *performances.*
Book & lyrics by Richard Bruce (Robert B. Smith).
Produced & directed by George W. Lederer; dances by Julian Alfred.
Cast included: Mary Milburn, Ben Forbes (Bechtel Alcock), Johnny Dooley, Hal Skelly, John Reinhard.

Principal songs: I Cannot Sleep Without Dreaming of You; I Love the Ground You Walk On; Catch 'Em Young, Treat 'Em Rough, Tell 'Em Nothing.

ZIEGFELD FOLLIES
(15th Edition)

Opened: June 21, 1921, Globe Th.
119 *performances.*
Sketches by Willard Mack, Raymond Hitchcock, James Reynolds; Herbert lyrics by Gene Buck; music & lyrics also by Henry Creamer & Turner Layton, James Hanley & Grant Clarke, David Stamper, Rudolf Friml & B. G. DeSylva, Maurice Yvain & Channing Pollock, Harry Carroll & Ballard Macdonald.
Produced by Florenz Ziegfeld, Jr.; directed by Edward Royce & George Marion.
Cast included: Gus Van & Joe Schenck, Fannie Brice, Raymond Hitchcock, Mary Milburn, W. C. Fields, Mary Eaton, Vera Michelena, Ray Dooley, Florence O'Denishawn, Channing Pollock, Consuelo Flowerton.
Principal Herbert-Buck songs: Princess of My Dreams; The Legend of the Golden Tree.

ORANGE BLOSSOMS

Opened: Sept. 19, 1922, Fulton Th.
95 *performances.*
Book by Fred DeGresac; lyrics by B. G. DeSylva.
Produced & directed by Edward Royce.
Cast included: Edith Day, Queenie Smith, Hal Skelly, Robert Michaelis, Pat Somerset, Jack Whiting, Robert Fischer.
Principal songs: A Kiss in the Dark; This Time It's Love; The Lonely Nest; A Dream of Orange Blossoms.

ZIEGFELD FOLLIES
(18th Edition)

Opened: Oct. 20, 1923, New Amsterdam Th.
233 *performances.*
Sketches by Eddie Cantor & Gene Buck;

Herbert lyrics by Buck; music & lyrics also by David Stamper, Harry Tierney & Joe McCarthy, Rudolf Friml, Bert Kalmar & Harry Ruby, Leo Edwards & Blanche Merrill.
Produced by Florenz Ziegfeld; directed by Ned Wayburn.
Cast included: Bert & Betty Wheeler, Fannie Brice, Brooke Johns, Harland Dixon, Lew Hearn, Olga Steck, Edna Leedom, David Stamper, Roy Cropper, Robert Quinault, Paul Whiteman Orchestra.
Principal Herbert-Buck songs: That Old-Fashioned Garden of Mine; I'd Love to Waltz Through Life with You; Legend of the Drums.

THE DREAM GIRL
Opened: Aug. 20, 1924, Ambassador Th.
117 *performances.*
Book by Rida Johnson Young & Harold Atteridge; lyrics by Mrs. Young.
Produced by Messrs. Shubert; directed by J. C. Huffman; dances by David Bennett.
Cast included: Fay Bainter, Walter Woolf, George Lemaire, Billy B. Van, Maude Odell, William O'Neal, John Clarke.
Principal songs: My Dream Girl; If Somebody Only Would Find Me; Bubble Song.

CHAPTER THREE
GEORGE M. COHAN
composer-lyricist

All books, music & lyrics by Mr. Cohan unless otherwise noted.

THE GOVERNOR'S SON
Opened: Feb. 25, 1901, Savoy Th.
32 *performances.*
Produced by L. C. Behman & Cohan; directed by R. A. Roberts.
Cast included: The Four Cohans, Ethel Levey, Will Sloan, Josephine Kirkwood.
Principal songs: Too Many Miles from Broadway; The Story of the Wedding

March; A Regular William Gillette.

RUNNING FOR OFFICE
Opened: Apr. 27, 1903, 14th St. Th.
48 *performances.*
Produced by Fred Niblo; directed by C. W. Valentine.
Cast included: The Four Cohans, Ethel Levey.
Principal songs: If I Were Only Mr. Morgan; I Want to Go to Paree, Papa; I'll Be There in the Public Square.

LITTLE JOHNNY JONES
Opened: Nov. 7, 1904, Liberty Th.
52 *performances.*
Produced by Sam H. Harris; directed by Cohan.
Cast included: George M. Cohan, Jerry Cohan, Helen Cohan Ethel Levey, Donald Brian, Tom Lewis, Truly Shattuck, Sam J. Ryan.
Principal songs: The Yankee Doodle Boy; Good-Bye Flo; Give My Regards to Broadway; Life's a Funny Proposition After All; If Mr. Boston Lawson Had His Way; I'm Mighty Glad I'm Living and That's All.

FORTY-FIVE MINUTES FROM BROADWAY
Opened: Jan. 1, 1906, New Amsterdam Th.
90 *performances.*
Produced by Klaw & Erlanger; directed by Cohan.
Cast included: Fay Templeton, Victor Moore, Donald Brian, Julia Ralph, Lois Ewell, Marion Singer.
Principal songs: I Want to Be a Popular Millionaire; Mary's a Grand Old Name; So Long, Mary; Forty-Five Minutes from Broadway; Stand Up and Fight Like H---.

GEORGE WASHINGTON, JR.
Opened: Feb. 12, 1906, Herald Square Th.
81 *performances.*
Produced by Sam H. Harris; directed

by Cohan.
Cast included: George M. Cohan, Jerry Cohan, Helen Cohan, Ethel Levey, Truly Shattuck, Eugene O'Rourke, Willis Sweatman.
Principal songs: You're a Grand Old Flag; I Was Born in Virginia; All Aboard for Broadway; If Washington Should Come to Life; Washington, He Was a Wonderful Man.

THE HONEYMOONERS
(revised version of *Running for Office*)
Opened: June 3, 1907, Aerial Gardens.
167 *performances.*
Produced by Sam H. Harris; directed by Cohan.
Cast included: George M. Cohan, Jerry Cohan, Helen Cohan, Gertrude Hoffman.
Principal songs: I'm a Popular Man; If I'm Going to Die I'm Going to Have Some Fun; I'll Be There in the Public Square.

THE TALK OF NEW YORK
Opened: Dec. 3, 1907, Knickerbocker Th.
157 *performances.*
Produced by Cohan & Harris; directed by Cohan.
Cast included: Victor Moore, Emma Littlefield, Gertrude Vanderbilt, Jack Gardner, Rosie Green, Stanley Forde.
Principal songs: When We Are M-A-Double R-I-E-D; When a Fellow's on the Level with a Girl that's on the Square; I Want the World to Know I Love You; Under Any Old Flag at All.

FIFTY MILES FROM BOSTON
Opened: Feb. 3, 1908, Garrick Th.
32 *performances.*
Produced by Cohan & Harris; directed by Cohan.
Cast included: Edna Wallace Hopper; Lawrence Wheat, Emma Janvier, George Parsons, James C. Marlowe.
Principal songs: Harrigan; A Small Town Girl; Ain't It Awful.

THE YANKEE PRINCE
Opened: Apr. 20, 1908, Knickerbocker Th.
28 *performances.*
Produced by Cohan & Harris; directed by Cohan.
Cast included: The Four Cohans, Tom Lewis, Stella Hammerstein, Jack Gardner, Donald Crisp.
Principal songs: Come On Down Town; I'm Awfully Strong for You; I'm to Marry a Nobleman; The ABC's of the U.S.A.; Cohan's Rag Babe.

THE AMERICAN IDEA
Opened: Oct. 5, 1908, New York Th.
64 *performances.*
Produced by Cohan & Harris; directed by Cohan.
Cast included: George Beban, Gertrude Vanderbilt, Stella Hammerstein, Trixie Friganza, Rosie Green, Robert Daly.
Principal songs: Too Long from Longacre Square; That's Some Love; F-A-M-E; Cohan's Pet Names.

THE MAN WHO OWNS BROADWAY
Opened: Oct. 11, 1909, New York Th.
128 *performances.*
Produced by Cohan & Harris; directed by Cohan.
Cast included: Raymond Hitchcock, Flora Zabelle, Stanley Forde.
Principal songs: There's Something About a Uniform; The Man who Owns Broadway; I've Always Been a Good Old Sport.

THE LITTLE MILLIONAIRE
Opened: Sept. 25, 1911, George M. Cohan Th.
192 *performances.*
Produced by Cohan & Harris; directed by Cohan.
Cast included: George M. Cohan, Jerry Cohan, Helen Cohan, Tom Lewis, George Parsons, Donald Crisp.
Principal songs: Barnum Had the Right Idea; Any Place the Old Flag Flies; Oh, You Wonderful Girl.

HELLO, BROADWAY!

Opened: Dec. 25, 1914, Astor Th.
123 performances.
Produced by Cohan & Harris; directed by Cohan; dances by Ned Wayburn & James Gorman.
Cast included: George M. Cohan, William Collier, Louise Dresser, Peggy Wood, Lawrence Wheat, Rozsika Dolly, Florence Moore, Tom Dingle.
Principal songs: Hello, Broadway; My Flag; Pygmalion Rose.

THE COHAN REVUE 1916

Opened: Feb. 9, 1916, Astor Th.
165 performances.
Produced by Cohan & Harris; directed by Cohan; dances by James Gorman.
Cast included: Elizabeth Murray, Fred Santley, Charles Winninger, Valli Valli, Richard Carle, Harry Bulger, Harry Delf, Miss Juliet.
Principal songs: It's a Long Way from Broadway to Edinboro Town; You Can Tell that I'm Irish; Julia, Donald and Joe; Won't You Let Me Be Your Little Edna May?

THE COHAN REVUE 1918

Opened: Dec. 31, 1917, New Amsterdam Th.
96 performances.
Music & lyrics also by Irving Berlin.
Produced by Cohan & Harris; directed by Cohan; dances also by Jack Mason & James Gorman.
Cast included: Nora Bayes, Charles Winninger, Irving Fisher, Fred Santley, Sydney Jarvis.
Principal Cohan songs: The Eyes of Youth See the Truth; Their Hearts Are Over Here; Our Acrobatic Melodramatic Home.

THE VOICE OF McCONNELL

Opened: Dec. 25, 1918, Manhattan Opera House.
30 performances.
Produced by Cohan & Harris; directed by Cohan & Sam Forrest.

Cast included: Chauncey Olcott, Arthur Shields, Roy Cochrane.
Principal songs: Ireland, the Land of My Dreams; You Can't Deny You're Irish; When I Look in Your Eyes, Mavourneen.

THE ROYAL VAGABOND

Opened: Feb. 17, 1919, Cohan & Harris Th.
208 performances.
Book by Stephen Ivor Szinnyey; music & lyrics also by Anselm Goetzl & William Cary Duncan.
Produced by Cohan & Harris; directed by Cohan, Julian Mitchell & Sam Forrest.
Cast included: Tessa Kosta, Fred Santley, Mary Eaton, Dorothy Dickson, Carl Hyson.
Principal Cohan songs: Opera, Comic Opera; In a Kingdom of Our Own; Goodbye, Bargravia.

LITTLE NELLIE KELLY

Opened: Nov. 13, 1922, Liberty Th.
276 performances.
Produced & directed by Cohan; dances by Julian Mitchell.
Cast included: Elizabeth Hines, Robert Pitkin, Georgia Caine, Charles King, Arthur Deagon, Frank Parker, Barrett Greenwood.
Principal songs: You Remind Me of My Mother; Till Good Luck Comes Rolling Along; Nellie Kelly, I Love You; The Voice in My Heart.

THE RISE OF ROSIE O'REILLY

Opened: Dec. 25, 1923, Liberty Th.
87 performances.
Produced by Cohan; directed by Cohan & John Meehan; dances by Julian Mitchell.
Cast included: Virginia O'Brien, Jack McGowan, George Bancroft, Mary Lawlor, Emma Haig, Georgie Hale, Margaret Dumont, Bobby Watson, Ruby Keeler.
Principal songs: Born and Bred in Brook-

lyn; When June Comes Along with a Song; Let's You and I Say Goodbye; The Ring to the Name of Rosie.

THE MERRY MALONES

Opened: Sept. 26, 1927, Erlanger's Th. 208 *performances.*
Produced by Cohan; directed by Edward Royce & Sam Forrest; dances by Jack Mason.
Cast included: George M. Cohan, Polly Walker, Alan Edwards, Robinson Newbold.
Principal songs: Molly Malone; God's Good to the Irish; Like a Wandering Minstrel; Like a Little Ladylike Lady Like You; The Bronx Express.

BILLIE

Opened: Oct. 1, 1928, Erlanger's Th. 112 *performances.*
Produced by Cohan, directed by Edward Royce & Sam Forrest.
Cast included: Polly Walker, Robinson Newbold, John Wagstaff, June O'Dea, Charles Sabin, Al Stanton, Ernie Stanton, Chantall Sisters (duo-pianists).
Principal songs: Every Boy in Town's My Sweetheart; Where Were You, Where Was I?; Billie; Go Home Ev'ry Once in a While.

GEORGE M!

Opened: Apr. 10, 1968, Palace Th.
(Still running as of Sept. 1, 1968)
Book by Michael Stewart, John & Fran Pascal.
Produced by David Black, Konrad Matthaei, Lorin E. Price; directed by Joe Layton.
Cast included: Joel Grey, Betty Ann Grove, Jerry Dodge, Jill O'Hara, Bernadette Peters, Jamie Donnelly, Jacqueline Alloway, Danny Carroll.
Principal songs: Ring to the Name of Rose; Give My Regards to Broadway; Forty-Five Minutes from Broadway; So Long, Mary; Mary; Yankee Doodle Dandy; Over There; You're a Grand Old Flag.

Recorded Version
Columbia KOS 3200 (O.C.).
Almost all the Cohan favorites given the proper razzle-dazzle treatment.

CHAPTER FOUR
RUDOLF FRIML
composer
THE FIREFLY

Opened: Dec. 2, 1912, Lyric Th. 120 *performances.*
Book & lyrics by Otto Hauerbach.
Produced by Arthur Hammerstein; directed by Fred G. Latham.
Cast included: Emma Trentini, Roy Atwell, Melville Stewart, Sammy Lee, Audrey Maple, Craig Campbell.
Principal songs: Giannina Mia; When a Maid Comes Knocking at Your Door; Love Is Like a Firefly; Sympathy.

HIGH JINKS

Opened: Dec. 10, 1913, Lyric Th. 213 *performances.*
Book & lyrics by Otto Hauerbach.
Produced by Arthur Hammerstein; directed by Frank Smithson.
Cast included: Elaine Hammerstein, Robert Pitkin, Mana Zucca, Tom Lewis, Elizabeth Murray, Gladys Feldman, Ignacio Martinetti.
Principal songs: Love's Own Kiss; Not Now but Later; The Bubble; Something Seems Tingle-ingleing.

THE PEASANT GIRL

Opened: Mar. 2, 1915, 44th St. Th. 111 *performances.*
Book by Edgar Smith; lyrics by Herbert Reynolds (M. E. Rourke) & Harold Atteridge; music also by Oskar Nedbal.
Produced by Messrs. Shubert; directed by J. H. Benrimo; dances by Jack Mason.
Cast included: Emma Trentini, Clifton Crawford, Ernest Hare, John Charles Thomas.
Principal Friml songs: Listen, Dear (Reynolds); Love Is Like a Butterfly

(Reynolds); The Flame of Love (Atteridge); And the Dream Came True (Atteridge).

KATINKA

Opened: Dec. 23, 1915, 44th St. Th.
220 *performances.*
Book & lyrics by Otto Hauerbach.
Produced by Arthur Hammerstein; directed by Frank Smithson.
Cast included: Adele Rowland, Franklyn Ardell, May Naudain, Samuel Ash, A. Robbins, Count Lorrie Grimaldi.
Principal songs: 'Tis the End So Farewell; Allah's Holiday; Rackety Coo; My Paradise.

YOU'RE IN LOVE

Opened: Feb. 6, 1917, Casino Th.
167 *performances.*
Book & lyrics by Otto Hauerbach & Edward Clark.
Produced by Arthur Hammerstein; directed by Clark.
Cast included: Lawrence Wheat, Clarence Nordstrom, May Thompson, Harry Clarke.
Principal songs: I'm Only Dreaming; You're in Love; That's the Only Place Where Our Flag Shall Fly.

KITTY DARLIN'

Opened: Nov. 7, 1917, Casino Th.
14 *performances.*
Book by Otto Hauerbach; lyrics by Hauerbach & P. G. Wodehouse.
Produced by William Elliott, F. Ray Comstock, Morris Gest; directed by Edward Royce.
Cast included: Alice Nielsen, Glen Hall, Jackson Hines, Edwin Stevens, Frank Westerton.
Principal songs: When She Gives Him a Shamrock Bloom (Hauerbach); The Land Where Dreams Come True (Wodehouse); Dear Old Dublin (Wodehouse); Kitty Darlin' (Hauerbach).

SOMETIME

Opened: Oct. 4, 1918, Shubert Th.
283 *performances.*
Book & lyrics by Rida Johnson Young.
Produced by Arthur Hammerstein; directed by Oscar Eagle; dances by Allan K. Foster.
Cast included: Ed Wynn, Mae West, Francine Larrimore, Beatrice Summers, Betty Stivers.
Principal songs: Sometime; Spanish Maid; The Tune You Can't Forget; Keep on Smiling.

GLORIANNA

Opened: Oct. 28, 1918, Liberty Th.
96 *performances.*
Book & lyrics by Catherine Chisholm Cushing.
Produced by John Cort; directed by Clifford Brooke.
Cast included: Eleanor Painter, Alexander Clark, Ralph Whitehead, Dorothy South.
Principal songs: When a Girl; Toodle-oo; My Climbing Rose.

TUMBLE IN

Opened: Mar. 24, 1919, Selwyn Th.
128 *performances.*
Book & lyrics by Otto Hauerbach.
Produced by Arthur Hammerstein; directed by Bertram Harrison; dances by Bert French.
Cast included: Peggy O'Neil, Charles Ruggles, Zelda Sears, Edna Hibbard, Johnny Ford.
Principal songs: The Thoughts I Wrote on the Leaves of My Heart; I've Told My Love; Snuggle and Dream.

THE LITTLE WHOPPER

Opened: Oct. 13, 1919, Casino Th.
224 *performances.*
Book by Otto Harbach; lyrics by Bide Dudley & Harbach.
Produced by Abraham Levy; directed by Oscar Eagle; dances by Bert French.
Cast included: Vivienne Segal, David Torrence, Harry C. Browne, Sydney

Grant, Rose & May Wilton, Inez Courtney.

Principal songs: You'll Dream and I'll Dream; 'Round the Corner; Oh! What a Little Whopper.

JUNE LOVE

Opened: Apr. 25, 1921, Knickerbocker Th.

50 *performances.*

Book by Otto Harbach & W. H. Post; lyrics by Brian Hooker.

Produced by Sherman Brown; directed by George Vivian.

Cast included: Else Alder, Clarence Nordstrom, Johnny Dooley, W. B. Davidson.

Principal songs: Dear Love, My Love; June Love; The Flapper and the Vamp; Don't Keep Calling Me Dearie.

ZIEGFELD FOLLIES
(15th Edition)

Opened: June 21, 1921, Globe Th.

119 *performances.*

Sketches by Willard Mack, Raymond Hitchcock, James Reynolds; Friml lyrics by Gene Buck, Brian Hooker, B. G. DeSylva; music & lyrics also by Henry Creamer & Turner Layton, James Hanley & Grant Clarke, David Stamper, Victor Herbert, Maurice Yvain & Channing Pollock, Harry Carroll & Ballard Macdonald.

Produced by Florenz Ziegfeld, Jr.; directed by Edward Royce & George Marion.

Cast included: Gus Van & Joe Schenck, Fannie Brice, Raymond Hitchcock, Mary Milburn, W. C. Fields, Mary Eaton, Vera Michelena, Ray Dooley, Florence O'Denishawn, Channing Pollock, Consuelo Flowerton.

Principal Friml songs: Bring Back My Blushing Rose (Buck-Hooker); Four Little Girls with a Future and Four Little Girls with a Past (DeSylva).

THE BLUE KITTEN

Opened: Jan. 13, 1922, Selwyn Th.

140 *performances.*

Book & lyrics by Otto Harbach & William Cary Duncan.

Produced by Arthur Hammerstein; directed by Edgar Selwyn, Leon Errol, Julian Mitchell.

Cast included: Joseph Cawthorn, Lillian Lorraine, Lorraine Manville, Victor Morley, Robert Woolsey, Marion Sunshine, Douglas Stevenson, Frances Grant & Ted Wing, Dallas Welford.

Principal songs: Cutie; I Found a Bud Among the Roses; Blue Kitten Blues; When I Waltz with You.

CINDERS

Opened: Apr. 3, 1923, Dresden Th.

31 *performances.*

Book & lyrics by Edward Clark.

Produced & directed by Edward Royce.

Cast included: Queenie Smith, Nancy Welford, Jack Whiting, Douglas Stevenson, George Bancroft, Margaret Dale, Roberta Beatty, Kitty Kelly, Ralph Riggs.

Principal songs: Cinders; One Good Time; I'm Simply Mad About the Boys; Belles of the Bronx.

ROSE-MARIE

Opened: Sept. 2, 1924, Imperial Th.

557 *performances.*

Book & lyrics by Otto Harbach & Oscar Hammerstein II; music also by Herbert Stothart.

Produced by Arthur Hammerstein; directed by Paul Dickey; dances by David Bennett.

Cast included: Mary Ellis, Dennis King, William Kent, Edward Ciannelli, Dorothy Mackaye, Pearl Regay, Arthur Deagon.

Principal Friml songs: Rose-Marie; The Mounties (with Stothart); Indian Love Call; Totem Tom-Tom (with Stothart); The Door of My Dreams; Pretty Things.

Recorded Versions

RCA Victor LOP/ LSO 1001 (S.C.) X.

MGM E 3769 (F.V.) (1954).

Pathé 30146 (French S.C.) X.

On the RCA release, Julie Andrews & Giorgio Tozzi star in the only complete version of the enduring score. The soundtrack MGM LP, with Howard Keel, Ann Blyth & Fernando Lamas, has only three songs from the original production. It occupies one side of the record, as does the well sung French version.

THE VAGABOND KING
Opened: Sept. 21, 1925, Casino Th.
511 *performances.*
Book & lyrics by Brian Hooker & W. H. Post.
Produced by Russell Janney; directed by Max Figman; dances by Julian Alfred.
Cast included: Dennis King, Carolyn Thomson, Max Figman, Herbert Corthell, Herbert Delmore, Jane Carroll.
Principal songs: Song of the Vagabonds; Some Day; Only a Rose; Huguette Waltz; Love Me Tonight; Nocturne; Love for Sale.
Recorded Versions
RCA Victor LM/ 2004 (F.V.) (1956) X.
Capitol T 219 (S.C.).
Decca DL 8362 (S.C.).
RCA Victor LM/ LSC 2509 (S.C.).
Oreste & Jean Fenn (who was not in the film) cover most of the songs on the first RCA release, while Mario Lanza & Judith Raskin are heard on the second. Capitol's, featuring Gordon MacRae, is backed by Romberg's *New Moon;* Decca's, with Alfred Drake & Mimi Benzell, shares the record with Romberg's *Student Prince.*

NO FOOLIN'
(Title changed during run to *Ziegfeld's American Revue of 1926*).
Opened: June 24, 1926, Globe Th.
108 *performances.*
Sketches by J. P. McEvoy & James Barton; lyrics by Gene Buck & Irving Caesar; music also by James Hanley.
Produced by Florenz Ziegfeld; directed by John Boyle & Walter Wilson.
Cast included: James Barton, Charles King, Andrew Tombes, Ray Dooley, Irving Fisher, Arthur "Bugs" Baer, Moran & Mack, Barbara Newberry, Louise Brown, Edna Leedom, Polly Walker, Peggy Fears, Claire Luce, Paulette Goddard.
Principal Friml songs: Florida, the Moon and You (Buck); Wasn't It Nice? (Caesar); Gentlemen Prefer Blondes (Caesar).

THE WILD ROSE
Opened: Oct. 20, 1926, Martin Beck Th.
61 *performances.*
Book & lyrics by Otto Harbach & Oscar Hammerstein II.
Produced by Arthur Hammerstein; directed by William J. Wilson; dances by Busby Berkeley.
Cast included: William Collier, Desirée Ellinger, Joseph Santley, Joseph Macaulay, Gus Shy, Inez Courtney, Nana Bryant, Fuller Mellish.
Principal songs: Brown Eyes; Wild Rose; One Golden Hour; We'll Have a Kingdom.

THE WHITE EAGLE
Opened: Dec. 26, 1927, Casino Th.
48 *performances.*
Book & lyrics by Brian Hooker & W. H. Post.
Produced by Russell Janney; directed by Richard Boleslavsky; dances by Busby Berkeley.
Cast included: Allan Prior, Marion Keeler, Jay Fassett, Blanche Fleming.
Principal songs: Give Me One Hour; Gather the Rose; Regimental Song; Silver Wing.

THE THREE MUSKETEERS
Opened: Mar. 13, 1928, Lyric Th.
319 *performances.*
Book by William Anthony McGuire; lyrics by P. G. Wodehouse & Clifford Grey.
Produced by Florenz Ziegfeld; directed by McGuire & Richard Boleslavsky; dances by Albertina Rasch.

Cast included: Dennis King, Vivienne Segal, Lester Allen, Yvonne D'Arle, Douglass Dumbrille, Detmar Poppen, Louis Hector, Reginald Owen, Clarence Derwent, Harriet Hoctor.
Principal songs: March of the Musketeers; Ma Belle; Your Eyes; My Sword and I; Queen of My Heart.

LUANA
Opened: Sept. 17, 1930, Hammerstein Th.
21 *performances.*
Book by Howard Emmett Rogers; lyrics by J. Keirn Brennan.
Produced by Arthur Hammerstein; directed by Hammerstein & Rogers; dances by Earl Lindsey.
Cast included: Ruth Altman, Joseph Macaulay, Donald Novis, Lillian Bond, Robert Chisholm, Doris Carson, Sally Rand.
Principal songs: Luana; My Bird of Paradise; Son of the Sun; Aloha.

MUSIC HATH CHARMS
Opened: Dec. 29, 1934, Majestic Th.
29 *performances.*
Book by Rowland Leigh & George Rosener; lyrics by Leigh & John Shubert.
Produced by Messrs. Shubert; directed by Rosener; dances by Alex Yakovleff.
Cast included: Natalie Hall, Robert Halliday, Andrew Tombes, Paul Haakon, Constance Carpenter, William Kent.
Principal songs: My Palace of Dreams; My Heart Is Yours; It's You I Want to Love Tonight; Annina; Sweet Fool.

OTTO HARBACH
lyricist

All books & lyrics by Mr. Harbach unless otherwise noted.

THREE TWINS
Opened: June 15, 1908, Herald Square Th.
288 *performances.*
Book by Charles Dickson; music by Karl Hoschna.

Produced by Joseph M. Gaites; directed by Gus Sohlke.
Cast included: Bessie McCoy, Clifton Crawford, Joseph Allen, Stella Tracy, Joseph Kaufman.
Principal songs: Cuddle Up a Little Closer, Lovey Mine; Hypnotic Kiss; Boo-Hoo, Tee-Hee; Little Miss Up-to-Date.

BRIGHT EYES
Opened: Feb. 28, 1910, New York Th.
40 *performances.*
Book by Charles Dickson; music by Karl Hoschna.
Produced by Joseph M. Gaites; directed by Frederick A. Bishop.
Cast included: Florence Holbrook, Cecil Lean, Adelaide Sharp, Arthur Conrad.
Principal songs: Good Old Days of Yore; For You Bright Eyes; Cheer Up My Honey.

MADAME SHERRY
Opened: Aug. 30, 1910, New Amsterdam Th.
231 *performances.*
Music by Karl Hoschna.
Produced by A. H. Woods, H. H. Frazee & George Lederer; directed by Lederer.
Cast included: Lina Abarbanell, Ralph Herz, Elizabeth Murray, Frances Demarest, Ignacio Martinetti, Dorothy Jardon, Jack Gardner.
Principal songs: Every Little Movement; The Smile She Means for Me; The Birth of Passion; We Are Only Poor Weak Mortals.

DR. DELUXE
Opened: Apr. 17, 1911, Knickerbocker Th.
32 *performances.*
Music by Karl Hoschna.
Produced by Joseph M. Gaites; directed by Frank Smithson.
Cast included: Ernest Truex, Ralph Herz, William Pruette, Lillian Berry.
Principal songs: The Accent Makes No Difference in the Language of Love;

War Is Hell, but Oh You Jealousy; For Every Boy that's Lonely There's a Girl that's Lonely Too.

THE GIRL OF MY DREAMS

Opened: Aug. 7, 1911, Criterion Th.
40 *performances.*
Book with Wilbur Nesbit; music by Karl Hoschna.
Produced by Joseph M. Gaites; directed by Frank Smithson.
Cast included: Leila McIntyre, John Hyams, Harry Humphreys, Harry Clark, Ethel Marston.
Principal songs: The Girl who Wouldn't Spoon; Girl of My Dreams; Every Girlie Loves Me but the Girlie I Love.

THE CRINOLINE GIRL

Opened: Mar. 16, 1914, Knickerbocker Th.
88 *performances.*
Lyrics by Julian Eltinge; music by Percy Wenrich.
Produced by A. H. Woods; directed by John Emerson.
Cast included: Julian Eltinge, Maidel Turner, Herbert McKenzie.

THE FASCINATING WIDOW

Opened: Sept. 11, 1911, Liberty Th.
56 *performances.*
Music by Karl Hoschna.
Produced by A. H. Woods; directed by George Marion.
Cast included: Julian Eltinge, June Mathis, Winona Winter, Ed Garvie.
Principal songs: Don't Take Your Beau to the Seashore; You Built a Fire Down in My Heart; The Ragtime College Girl.

THE FIREFLY

(*See* Rudolf Friml).

HIGH JINKS

(*See* Rudolf Friml).

SUZI

Opened: Nov. 3, 1914, Casino Th.
55 *performances.*
Music by Aladar Renyi.

Produced by Lew Fields; directed by George Marion.
Cast included: Jose Collins, Melville Stewart, Lew Hearn, Tom MacNaughton.
Principal songs: I'll Not Let Love Disparage Marriage; Life Is a Garden.

KATINKA

(*See* Rudolf Friml).

YOU'RE IN LOVE

(*See* Rudolf Friml).

KITTY DARLIN'

(*See* Rudolf Friml).

GOING UP

Opened: Dec. 25, 1917, Liberty Th.
351 *performances.*
Music by Louis A. Hirsch.
Produced by George M. Cohan & Sam H. Harris; directed by Edward Royce & James Montgomery.
Cast included: Edith Day, Frank Craven, Ruth Donnelly, Donald Meek, Marion Sunshine.
Principal songs: The Tickle Toe; Kiss Me; Going Up; If You Look in Her Eyes.

TUMBLE IN

(*See* Rudolf Friml).

THE LITTLE WHOPPER

(*See* Rudolf Friml).

TICKLE ME

(*See* Oscar Hammerstein II).

MARY

Opened: Oct. 18, 1920, Knickerbocker Th.
219 *performances.*
Book with Frank Mandel; music by Louis A. Hirsch.
Produced by George M. Cohan; directed by Cohan, Julian Mitchell & Sam Forrest.
Cast included: Jack McGowan, Janet Velie, Charles Judels, Georgia Caine.
Principal songs: The Love Nest; Mary; Anything You Want to Do, Dear; That Might Have Satisfied Grandma.

JIMMIE
(*See* Oscar Hammerstein II).

JUNE LOVE
(*See* Rudolf Friml).

THE O'BRIEN GIRL
Opened: Oct. 3, 1921, Liberty Th.
164 *performances.*
Book with Frank Mandel; music by
Louis A. Hirsch.
Produced by George M. Cohan; directed
by Julian Mitchell.
Cast included: Elizabeth Hines, Robin-
son Newbold, Edwin Forsberg, Geor-
gia Caine, Ada Mae Weeks, Andrew
Tombes, Carl Hemmer.
Principal songs: I Wonder How I Ever
Passed You By; The Conversation Step;
That O'Brien Girl.

THE BLUE KITTEN
(*See* Rudolf Friml).

MOLLY DARLING
Opened: Sept. 1, 1922, Liberty Th.
99 *performances.*
Book with William Cary Duncan; lyrics
by Phil Cook; music by Tom Johnstone.
Produced by Moore & Mesley; directed
by Julian Mitchell & Walter Wilson.
Cast included: Mary Milburn, Jack Don-
ahue, Clarence Nordstrom, Hal Forde,
Albert Roccardi.

WILDFLOWER
(*See* Vincent Youmans).

JACK AND JILL
Opened: Mar. 22, 1923, Globe Th.
92 *performances.*
Book with Frederic Isham; lyrics also
by John Murray Anderson, Augustus
Barratt, Robert A. Simon, Irving Caesar;
music by Alfred Newman, William Daly,
Muriel Pollock, Augustus Barratt.
Produced by Chelsea Productions; di-
rected by John Murray Anderson;
dances by Larry Ceballos & Leon Barté.
Cast included: Ann Pennington, Clifton
Webb, Brooke Johns, Georgia O'Ramey,
Lennox Pawle, Roger Imhof, Leon Barté.

Principal Harbach songs: Voodoo Man
(Newman); I Want a Pretty Girl (Daly).

KID BOOTS
Opened: Dec. 31, 1923, Earl Carroll Th.
479 *performances.*
Book with William Anthony McGuire;
lyrics by Joseph McCarthy; music by
Harry Tierney.
Produced by Florenz Ziegfeld; directed
by Edward Royce.
Cast included: Eddie Cantor, Mary
Eaton, Jobyna Howland, Robert Barrat,
Paul Everton, Harry Fender, Ethelind
Terry, Harland Dixon, George Olsen
Orch.

ROSE-MARIE
(*See* Rudolf Friml).

BETTY LEE
Opened: Dec. 25, 1924, 44th St. Th.
111 *performances.*
Lyrics also by Irving Caesar; music by
Louis A. Hirsch, Con Conrad.
Produced by Rufus LeMaire; directed
by Bertram Harrison; dances by David
Bennett.
Cast included: Joe E. Brown, Hal Skelly,
Gloria Foy, Jack Kearns.
Principal Harbach songs: Arabian
Dreams (Caesar-Hirsch); Betty Lee
(Caesar-Conrad); Let's Kiss Goodbye
(Caesar-Hirsch-Conrad).

NO, NO, NANETTE
(*See* Vincent Youmans).

SUNNY
(*See* Jerome Kern).

SONG OF THE FLAME
(*See* George Gershwin).

KITTY'S KISSES
Opened: May 6, 1926, Playhouse Th.
170 *performances.*
Book with Philip Bartholomae; lyrics by
Gus Kahn; music by Con Conrad.
Produced by William A. Brady; directed

by John Cromwell; dances by Bobby Connolly.
Cast included: John Boles, Dorothy Dilley, Nick Long, Jr., William Wayne.

CRISS-CROSS
(*See* Jerome Kern).

THE WILD ROSE
(*See* Rudolf Friml).

THE DESERT SONG
(*See* Sigmund Romberg).

OH, PLEASE!
(*See* Vincent Youmans).

LUCKY
Opened: Mar. 22, 1927, New Amsterdam Th.
71 *performances.*
Book with Bert Kalmar & Harry Ruby; Kalmar & Harbach music by Ruby; Kalmar & Ruby music by Jerome Kern.
Produced by Charles Dillingham; directed by Hassard Short; dances by David Bennett & Albertina Rasch.
Cast included: Mary Eaton, "Skeet" Gallagher, Walter Catlett, Ruby Keeler, Ivy Sawyer, Joseph Santley, Paul Everton, Paul Whiteman Orchestra.
Principal Harbach-Kalmar-Ruby songs: Cingalese Girls; Dancing the Devil Away; The Same Old Moon.

GOLDEN DAWN
(*See* Oscar Hammerstein II).

GOOD BOY
(*See* Oscar Hammerstein II).

NINA ROSA
(*See* Sigmund Romberg).

THE CAT AND THE FIDDLE
(*See* Jerome Kern).

ROBERTA
(*See* Jerome Kern).

FORBIDDEN MELODY
(*See* Sigmund Romberg).

CHAPTER FIVE
SIGMUND ROMBERG
composer

THE WHIRL OF THE WORLD
Opened: Jan. 10, 1914, Winter Garden
161 *performances.*
Sketches & lyrics by Harold Atteridge.
Produced by Messrs. Shubert; directed by William J. Wilson; dances by Jack Mason.
Cast included: Lillian Lorraine, Bernard Granville, Ralph Herz, Eugene & Willie Howard, Walter C. Kelly, Rozsika Dolly, May Boley.
Principal songs: Ragtime Arabian Nights; My Cleopatra Girl; Life Is Just a Dress Parade.

THE PASSING SHOW OF 1914
Opened: June 10, 1914, Winter Garden
133 *performances.*
Sketches & lyrics by Harold Atteridge; music also by Harry Carroll.
Produced by Messrs. Shubert; directed by J. C. Huffman; dances by Jack Mason.
Cast included: Bernard Granville, Jose Collins, Marilynn Miller, Bessie Crawford, Robert Emmett Keane, Lew Brice, Frances Demarest, T. Roy Barnes.
Principal Romberg songs: Omar Khayyam (no lyric); Dreams of the Past; Bohemian Rag; California.

DANCING AROUND
Opened: Oct. 10, 1914, Winter Garden
145 *performances.*
Sketches & lyrics by Harold Atteridge; music also by Harry Carroll.
Produced by Messrs. Shubert; directed by J. C. Huffman; dances by Jack Mason.
Cast included: Bernard Granville, James Doyle & Harland Dixon, Al Jolson, Clifton Webb, Cecil Cunningham, Melville Ellis.
Principal Romberg songs: My Lady of the Telephone; He Is Sweet, He Is Good; My Rainbow Beau.

MAID IN AMERICA

Opened: Feb. 18, 1915, Winter Garden
108 *performances.*
Sketches & lyrics by Harold Atteridge;
music also by Harry Carroll.
Produced by Messrs. Shubert; directed
by J. C. Huffman; dances by Jack Mason.
Cast included: Mlle. Dazie, Blossom
Seeley, Harry Carroll, Harry Fox, Hal
Forde, Lew Brice, Nora Bayes, Joe Jackson, Yansci Dolly, Yvette.
Principal Romberg songs: Sister Susie
Started Syncopation; Only for You; Oh,
Those Days; The Girlie of the Cabaret.

HANDS UP

Opened: July 22, 1915, 44th St. Th.
52 *performances.*
Book by Edgar Smith; lyrics by E. Ray
Goetz.
Produced by Messrs. Shubert; directed
by J. H. Benrimo; dances by Jack Mason.
Cast included: George Hassell, Alice
Dovey, Irene Franklin, Ralph Herz, Will
Rogers, A. Robbins, Maurice & Florence
Walton.
Principal songs: Orange Blossom Time in
San José; The Levee Along Broadway;
Sing Sing Tango Tea (lyric by Harold
Atteridge).

THE BLUE PARADISE

Opened: Aug. 5, 1915, Casino Th.
356 *performances.*
Book by Edgar Smith; lyrics by Herbert
Reynolds (M. E. Rourke); music also
by Edmund Eysler.
Produced by Messrs. Shubert; directed
by J. H. Benrimo; dances by Ed Hutchinson.
Cast included: Cecil Lean, Cleo Mayfield, Vivienne Segal, Robert Pitkin, Ted
Lorraine, Frances Demarest.
Principal Romberg songs: Auf Wiedersehn; One Step into Love; My Model
Girl (lyric by Harold Atteridge); A
Toast to a Woman's Eyes.

A WORLD OF PLEASURE

Opened: Oct. 14, 1915, Winter Garden
116 *performances.*
Sketches & lyrics by Harold Atteridge.
Produced by Messrs. Shubert; directed
by J. C. Huffman; dances by Jack Mason.
Cast included: Kitty Gordon, Stella Mayhew, Clifton Crawford, Lew Holtz, Dan
Healy, Sydney Greenstreet, Venita Fitzhugh, Sahari Djeli.
Principal songs: I Could Go Home to a
Girlie Like You; The Ragtime Pipe of
Pan; Fascination; Girlies Are Out of My
Life.

ROBINSON CRUSOE, JR.

Opened: Feb. 17, 1916, Winter Garden
130 *performances.*
Book & lyrics by Harold Atteridge; music also by James Hanley.
Produced by Messrs. Shubert; directed
by J. C. Huffman; dances by Allan K.
Foster.
Cast included: Al Jolson, Barry Lupino,
Kitty Doner, Lawrence D'Orsay, Claude
Flemming.
Principal Romberg songs: When You're
Starring in the Movies; Minstrel Days;
Happy Hottentot; My Pirate Lady.

THE PASSING SHOW OF 1916

Opened: June 22, 1916, Winter Garden
140 *performances.*
Sketches & lyrics by Harold Atteridge;
music also by Otto Motzan.
Produced by Messrs. Shubert; directed
by J. C. Huffman; dances by Allan K.
Foster.
Cast included: Ed Wynn, Herman Timberg, James Hussey, Frances Demarest,
Florence Moore, Fred Walton, Stella
Hoban.
Principal Romberg songs: Ragging the
Apache; Sweet and Pretty; Ragtime Calisthenics.

THE GIRL FROM BRAZIL

Opened: Aug. 30, 1916, 44th St. Th.
61 *performances.*
Book by Edgar Smith; lyrics by Matthew
Woodward; music also by Robert Winterberg.

Produced by Messrs. Shubert; directed by J. H. Benrimo; dances by Allan K. Foster.
Cast included: Maude Odell, George Hassell, Hal Forde, Frances Demarest, Anita Baldwin.
Principal Romberg songs: Stolen Kisses; Come Back Sweet Dream; My Senorita.

THE SHOW OF WONDERS
Opened: Oct. 26, 1916, Winter Garden 209 *performances.*
Sketches & lyrics by Harold Atteridge; music also by Otto Motzan & Herman Timberg.
Produced by Messrs. Shubert; directed by J. C. Huffman; dances by Allan K. Foster.
Cast included: Willie & Eugene Howard, Ernest Hare, Marilynn Miller, McIntyre & Heath, Lew Clayton, Walter C. Kelly, Sam White, John T. Murray, Tom Lewis.
Principal Romberg songs: When Pavlova Starts Buck and Winging; Bring Your Kisses to Me; Love Is Like a Bubble.

FOLLOW ME
Opened: Nov. 29, 1916, Casino Th. 78 *performances.*
Book uncredited; lyrics by Robert B. Smith.
Produced by Messrs. Shubert; directed by J. H. Benrimo; dances by Jack Mason & Allan K. Foster.
Cast Included: Anna Held, Edith Day, Paul Porcasi, Harry Tighe, Wilmer Bentley.
Principal songs: Follow Me; I Am True to Them All; I Want to Be Good but My Eyes Won't Let Me; A Tete-à-Tete with You.

HER SOLDIER BOY
Opened: Dec. 6, 1916, Astor Th. 198 *performances.*
Book & lyrics by Rida Johnson Young; music also by Emmerich Kalman.
Produced by Messrs. Shubert; directed by J. J. Shubert; dances by Jack Mason.
Cast included: Clifton Crawford, John

Charles Thomas, Adele Rowland, Ralph J. Herbert.
Principal Romberg songs: Mother; All Alone in a City Full of Girls; Kiss Waltz; I'd Be Happy Anywhere with You; A Married Man Makes the Best Soldier.

THE PASSING SHOW OF 1917
Opened: Apr. 26, 1917, Winter Garden 196 *performances.*
Sketches & lyrics by Harold Atteridge; music also by Otto Motzan.
Produced by Messrs. Shubert; directed by J. C. Huffman; dances by Allan K. Foster.
Cast included: DeWolf Hopper, Jefferson De Angelis, Irene Franklin, Zeke Colvan, Yvette Rugel, Johnny Dooley, Tom Lewis.
Principal Romberg songs: Won't You Send a Letter to Me?; The Willow Tree; My Bedouin Girl.

MY LADY'S GLOVE
Opened: June 18, 1917, Lyric Th. 16 *performances.*
Book by Edgar Smith; lyrics by Edward A. Paulton; music also by Oscar Straus.
Produced by Messrs. Shubert; directed by J. C. Huffman; dances by Allan K. Foster.
Cast included: Charles Purcell, Vivienne Segal, Charles Judels, Maude Odell, Horace Sinclair, Arthur Geary, Charles McNaughton, Frances Demarest, Ned Monroe.
Principal Romberg songs: Foolish Little Maiden, I; No More Girls for Me; Do Buy Some Candy, Sir.

MAYTIME
Opened: Aug. 16, 1917, Shubert Th. 492 *performances.*
Book & lyrics by Rida Johnson Young.
Produced by Messrs. Shubert; directed by Edward Temple; dances by Allan K. Foster.
Cast included: Peggy Wood, Charles Purcell, Ralph J. Herbert, William Norris, Richard Morgan, Laura Arnold.

Principal songs: The Road to Paradise; Jump Jim Crow; Will You Remember?; In Our Little Home Sweet Home.

DOING OUR BIT

Opened: Oct. 18, 1917, Winter Garden
130 *performances.*
Sketches & lyrics by Harold Atteridge; music also by Herman Timberg.
Produced by Messrs. Shubert; directed by J. C. Huffman; dances by Allan K. Foster.
Cast included: Ed Wynn, Frank Tinney, Duncan Sisters, James J. Corbett, Charles Judels, Ada Lewis, Herman Timberg, Sam Ash.
Principal Romberg songs: Doing My Bit; Hello, Miss Tango; For the Sake of Humanity.

OVER THE TOP

Opened: Nov. 28, 1917, 44th St. Th.
78 *performances.*
Book by Philip Bartholomae & Harold Atteridge; lyrics by Charles Manning & Matthew Woodward; music also by Herman Timberg.
Produced by Messrs. Shubert; directed by Joseph Herbert; dances by Allan K. Foster.
Cast included: Justine Johnstone, Mary Eaton, Ted Lorraine, Fred & Adele Astaire, Joe Laurie, T. Roy Barnes, Craig Campbell, Oakland Sisters.
Principal Romberg songs: The Justine Johnstone Rag (music with Frank Carter, lyric by Manning); Oh, Galatea (lyric by Bartholomae); Golden Pheasant (lyric by Woodward).

SINBAD

Opened: Feb. 14, 1918, Winter Garden
164 *performances.*
Book & Romberg lyrics by Harold Atteridge; music & lyrics also by B. G. De-Sylva, George Gershwin & Irving Caesar, Jean Schwartz, Joe Young & Sam Lewis.
Produced by Messrs. Shubert; directed by J. C. Huffman; dances by Jack Mason & Alexis Kosloff.

Cast included: Al Jolson, Kitty Doner, Forrest Huff, Mabel Withee, Hazell Cox, Grace Washburn, Edgar Atchinson-Ely.
Principal Romberg-Atteridge songs: A Thousand and One Arabian Nights; The Rag Lad of Bagdad; Beauty and Beast; I Hail from Cairo.

THE PASSING SHOW OF 1918

Opened: July 25, 1918, Winter Garden
124 *performances.*
Sketches & lyrics by Harold Atteridge; music also by Jean Schwartz.
Produced by Messrs. Shubert; directed by J. C. Huffman; dances by Jack Mason.
Cast included: Willie & Eugene Howard, George Hassell, Fred & Adele Astaire, Charles Ruggles, Frank Fay, Lou Clayton, Sam White, Nita Naldi, Dave Dreyer.
Principal Romberg songs: My Baby-Talk Lady; Galli-Curci Rag; The Duchess of Devonshire; My Vampire Girl; I Can't Make My Feet Behave.

THE MELTING OF MOLLY

Opened: Dec. 30, 1918, Broadhurst Th.
88 *performances.*
Book by Maria Thompson Davies & Edgar Smith; lyrics by Cyrus Wood.
Produced by Messrs. Shubert; directed by Oscar Eagle; dances by Allan K. Foster.
Cast included: Charles Purcell, Gladys Walton, Ted Lorraine, Isabelle Lowe, Gloria Goodwin.
Principal songs: Jazz All Your Troubles Away (lyric by Augustus Barrett); Floating Down a Moonlight Stream; You Remember Me.

MONTE CRISTO, JR.

Opened: Feb. 12, 1919, Winter Garden
254 *performances.*
Book & lyrics by Harold Atteridge; music also by Jean Schwartz.
Produced by Messrs. Shubert; directed by J. C. Huffman.
Cast included: Charles Purcell, Ralph Herz, Chic Sale, Sam Ash, Rose Rolando,

Clem Bevins, Tom Lewis, William & Gordon Dooley.
Principal songs: Are You Stepping Out Tonight?; Broadway Butterfly; Jazzamarimba; There's a World of Beauty in You.

THE PASSING SHOW OF 1919
Opened: Oct. 23, 1919, Winter Garden 144 *performances.*
Sketches & lyrics by Harold Atteridge; music also by Jean Schwartz.
Produced by Messrs. Shubert; directed by J. C. Huffman; dances by Allan K. Foster.
Cast included: James Barton, Charles Winninger, Blanche Ring, Reginald Denny, Avon Comedy 4, Walter Woolf, George & Dick Rath, Harry Turpin, Ralph Riggs, Hazel Cox, Olga Cook, Haley Sisters.
Principal songs: So Long, Sing Song; Dreamy Florence; The Kiss Burglar.

THE MAGIC MELODY
Opened: Nov. 11, 1919, Shubert Th. 143 *performances.*
Book & lyrics by Frederic Arnold Kummer.
Produced by Max R. Wilner & Romberg; directed by J. C. Huffman; dances by Allan K. Foster.
Cast included: Charles Purcell, Fay Marbe, Julia Deane, Carmel Myers, Flavia Arcaro, Tom McNaughton.
Principal songs: The Little Church 'Round the Corner (lyric by Alex Gerber); Down by the Nile; Once Upon a Time; Dream Girl, Give Back My Dreams.

POOR LITTLE RITZ GIRL
Opened: July 28, 1920, Central Th. 119 *performances.*
Book by George Campbell & Lew Fields; Romberg lyrics by Alex Gerber; music & lyrics also by Richard Rodgers & Lorenz Hart.
Produced by Lew Fields; directed by Ned Wayburn.

Cast included: Charles Purcell, Eleanor Griffith, Lulu McConnell, Andrew Tombes, Aileen Poe, Grant Simpson.
Principal Romberg-Gerber songs: I Love to Say Hello to the Girls; When I Found You; In the Land of Yesterday.

LOVE BIRDS
Opened: Mar. 15, 1921, Apollo Th. 105 *performances.*
Book by Edgar Allan Woolf; lyrics by Ballard Macdonald. Produced by Max R. Wilner & Romberg; directed by Edgar MacGregor; dances by Julian Alfred.
Cast included: Pat Rooney, Marion Bent, Elizabeth Hines, Elizabeth Murray, Vincent Lopez.
Principal songs: I Love to Go Swimmin' with Wimmen; Is It Hard to Guess?; Trousseau Incomplete; Two Little Love Birds.

BLOSSOM TIME
Opened: Sept. 29, 1921, Ambassador Th. 516 *performances.*
Book & lyrics by Dorothy Donnelly; music based on Franz Schubert themes. Produced by Messrs. Shubert; directed by J. C. Huffman.
Cast included: Bertram Peacock, Olga Cook, Howard Marsh, William Danforth, Roy Cropper.
Principal songs: Song of Love; Tell Me Daisy; Only One Love Ever Fills the Heart; My Springtime Thou Art; Three Little Maids.

BOMBO
Opened: Oct. 6, 1921, Al Jolson Th. 219 *performances.*
Book & Romberg lyrics by Harold Atteridge; music & lyrics also by B. G. DeSylva, Con Conrad, Cliff Friend, Walter Donaldson, Sam Lewis & Joe Young.
Produced by Messrs. Shubert; directed by J. C. Huffman; dances by Allan K. Foster.
Cast included: Al Jolson, Janet Adair, Forrest Huff, Vivian Oakland, Russell Mack, Portland Hoffa.

Principal Romberg-Atteridge songs: Oh, Oh, Columbus; In Old Granada; Jazza-Da-Dadoo; The Very Next Girl I See.

THE BLUSHING BRIDE
Opened: Feb. 6, 1922, Astor Th.
144 *performances.*
Book & lyrics by Cyrus Wood.
Produced by Messrs. Shubert; directed by Frank Smithson.
Cast included: Cecil Lean, Cleo Mayfield, Tom Lewis, Clarence Nordstrom, Edythe Baker, Robert O'Connor, William Holbrook.
Principal songs: Mister and Missus; Rosy Posy; I'll Bet on Anything but Girls.

THE ROSE OF STAMBOUL
Opened: Mar. 7, 1922, Century Th.
111 *performances.*
Book & lyrics by Harold Atteridge; music also by Leo Fall.
Produced by Messrs. Shubert; directed by J. C. Huffman.
Cast included: Tessa Kosta, Marion Green, James Barton, Felicia Sorel.
Principal Romberg songs: My Heart Is Calling; Lovey Dove; Mazuma.

SPRINGTIME OF YOUTH
Opened: Oct. 26, 1922, Broadhurst Th.
68 *performances.*
Book uncredited; lyrics by Cyrus Wood.
Produced by Messrs. Shubert; directed by John Harwood; dances by Allan K. Foster.
Cast included: Olga Steck, J. Harold Murray, Harry K. Morton, George MacFarlane, Eleanor Griffith, Harry Kelly.
Principal songs: Starlight of Hope; Just Like a Doll; Pretty Polly.

THE DANCING GIRL
Opened: Jan. 24, 1923, Winter Garden
126 *performances.*
Book & lyrics by Harold Atteridge; music also by Alfred Goodman.
Produced by Messrs. Shubert; directed by J. C. Huffman.
Cast included: Trini, Marie Dressler,

Jack Pearl, Arthur Margetson, Edythe Baker, Lou Holtz, Ted & Kitty Doner, Benny Leonard, Nat Nazzaro, Jr.
Principal Romberg songs: Cuddle Me as We Dance; That Romance of Mine; Why Am I Sad?

THE PASSING SHOW OF 1923
Opened: June 14, 1923, Winter Garden
118 *performances.*
Sketches & lyrics by Harold Atteridge; music also by Jean Schwartz.
Produced by Messrs. Shubert; directed by J. C. Huffman; dances by Allan K. Foster.
Cast included: George Hassell, Walter Woolf, George Jessel, Barnett Parker, Helen Shipman, Alex Morrison, Nancy Carroll.
Principal Romberg songs: Lotus Flower (lyric by Cyrus Wood); Lovelit Eyes; The Ball Begins.

INNOCENT EYES
Opened: May 20, 1924, Winter Garden
126 *performances.*
Book by Harold Atteridge; lyrics by Atteridge & Tot Seymour; music also by Jean Schwartz.
Produced by Messrs. Shubert; directed by Frank Smithson; dances by Jack Mason & Seymour Felix.
Cast included: Mistinguett, Cecil Lean, Cleo Mayfield, Frances Williams, Lew Hearn, Edythe Baker, Ted Doner, Vera Lavrova (Baroness Michael Royce Garrett), Vanessi, Jack Oakie, Lucille Le Sueur (Joan Crawford).
Principal Romberg songs: Love Is Like a Pinwheel; Day Dreams.

THE PASSING SHOW OF 1924
Opened: Sept. 3, 1924, Winter Garden
106 *performances.*
Sketches by Harold Atteridge; lyrics by Atteridge & Alex Gerber; music also by Jean Schwartz.
Produced by Messrs. Shubert; directed by J. C. Huffman; dances by Max Scheck & Seymour Felix.

Cast included: James Barton, George Hassell, Allan Prior, Lulu McConnell, Olga Cook, Harry McNaughton, Lucille Le Sueur (Joan Crawford).

Principal songs: When Knighthood Was in Flower (Atteridge); Dublinola (Atteridge); Mooching Along (Gerber).

ARTISTS AND MODELS OF 1924

Opened: Oct. 15, 1924, Astor Th.
261 performances.

Sketches mostly by Harry Wagstaff Gribble; lyrics by Sam Coslow & Clifford Grey; music also by J. Fred Coots.
Produced by Messrs. Shubert; directed by J. J. Shubert; dances by Seymour Felix.
Cast included: Trini, Frank Gaby, Barnett Parker, Mabel Withee.
Principal songs: Tomorrow's Another Day; Take Me Back to Samoa Some More.

ANNIE DEAR

Opened: Nov. 4, 1924, Times Square Th.
103 performances.

Book by Clare Kummer; lyrics by Clifford Grey; music & lyrics also by Mrs. Kummer.
Produced by Florenz Ziegfeld; directed by Edward Royce.
Cast included: Billie Burke, Ernest Truex, Jack Whiting, Alexander Gray, Marion Green, Spencer Charters, Bobby Watson, May Vokes, Gavin Gordon, Catherine Littlefield.
Principal Romberg-Grey songs: Whisper to Me; One Man Is Like Another; Bertie.

THE STUDENT PRINCE IN HEIDELBERG

Opened: Dec. 2, 1924, Al Jolson Th.
608 performances.

Book & lyrics by Dorothy Donnelly.
Produced by Messrs. Shubert; directed by J. C. Huffman; dances by Max Scheck.
Cast included: Howard Marsh, Ilse Marvenga, Greek Evans, George Hassell, Fuller Mellish, Violet Carlson, Roberta Beatty.

Principal songs: Golden Days; To the Inn We're Marching; Drinking Song; Deep in My Heart, Dear; Serenade; Just We Two.

Recorded Versions
Columbia CL 826 (S.C.) X.
RCA Victor LM/LSC 2339 (F.V.) (1954).
Capitol (S)W 1841 (S.C.).
Decca DL 8362 (S.C.).
Columbia ML 4060 (S.C.) X.
Columbia OL 5980/OS 2380 (S.C.).

Romberg's melodic score is given its best all-around aural production on the last Columbia release listed above. Jan Peerce, Roberta Peters & Giorgio Tozzi are the stars. The two deleted Columbias feature Dorothy Kirsten & Robert Rounseville on the first, and Risë Stevens & Nelson Eddy on the second. RCA's soundtrack has Mario Lanza and additional songs from the film. The Capitol issue, with Miss Kirsten & Gordon MacRae is acceptable, but Decca's, with Lauritz Melchior, is outdated.

LOUIE THE 14TH

Opened: Mar. 3, 1925, Cosmopolitan Th.
319 performances.

Book & lyrics by Arthur Wimperis.
Produced by Florenz Ziegfeld; directed by Edward Royce.
Cast included: Leon Errol, Doris Patston, Ethel Shutta, Catherine Calhoun Doucet, Harry Fender, Evelyn Law, Catherine Littlefield, Lucy Monroe, Peggy Fears.
Principal songs: Little Peach; Homeland; Edelweiss (lyric by Clifford Grey).

PRINCESS FLAVIA

Opened: Nov. 2, 1925, Century Th.
152 performances.

Book & lyrics by Harry B. Smith.
Produced by Messrs. Shubert; directed by J. C. Huffman; dances by Max Scheck.
Cast included: Harry Welchman, Evelyn Herbert, John Clarke, Joseph C. Spurin (Joseph Calleia), William Danforth, Alois Havrilla, Douglass Dumbrille, Margaret Breen, Maude Odell.

Principal songs: What Do I Care?; Only One; I Dare Not Love You; Twilight Voices.

THE DESERT SONG
Opened: Nov. 30, 1926, Casino Th.
465 *performances.*
Book by Otto Harbach, Oscar Hammerstein II, Frank Mandel; lyrics by Harbach & Hammerstein.
Produced by Laurence Schwab & Mandel; directed by Arthur Hurley; dances by Bobby Connolly.
Cast included: Robert Halliday, Vivienne Segal, Eddie Buzzell, William O'Neal, Pearl Regay, Nellie Breen, Margaret Irving, Glen Dale.
Principal songs: The Riff Song; Margot; French Military Marching Song; Romance; Then You Will Know; It; The Desert Song; Let Love Go; One Flower Grows Alone in Your Garden; One Alone; Let's Have a Love Affair.
Recorded Versions
Columbia CL 831 (S.C.) X.
RCA Victor LOP/LSO 1000 (S.C.) X.
RCA Victor LM/LSC 2440 (S.C.).
Capitol (S)W 1842 (S.C.).
Angel (S) 35905 (S.C.).
The Angel release, with Edmund Hockridge & June Bronhill, gets the nod, followed by the Columbia, featuring Nelson Eddy & Doretta Morrow. The first RCA (Kathy Barr, Giorgio Tozzi) is an embarrassment, the second (Mario Lanza) not bad, and the lone Capitol entry (Gordon MacRae - Dorothy Kirsten) ok but unexciting.

CHERRY BLOSSOMS
Opened: Mar. 28, 1927, 44th St. Th.
56 *performances.*
Book & lyrics by Harry B. Smith.
Produced by Messrs. Shubert; directed by Lew Morton; dances by Ralph Reader & Michio Ito.
Cast included: Desiree Ellinger, Howard Marsh, Bernard Gorcey, Gladys Baxter.
Principal songs: 'Neath the Cherry Blossom Moon; Tell Me Cigarette; Wait and See.

MY MARYLAND
Opened: Sept. 12, 1927, Al Jolson Th.
312 *performances.*
Book & lyrics by Dorothy Donnelly.
Produced by Messrs Shubert; directed by J. C. Huffman; dances by Jack Mason.
Cast included: Evelyn Herbert, George Rosener, Nathaniel Wagner, Fuller Mellish, Warren Hull.
Principal songs: Boys in Gray; Won't You Marry Me?; Silver Moon; Mother; Your Land and My Land.

MY PRINCESS
Opened: Oct. 6, 1927, Shubert Th.
20 *performances.*
Book & lyrics by Dorothy Donnelly.
Produced by Alfred E. Aarons; directed by Sam Forrest; dances by David Bennett.
Cast included: Hope Hampton, Leonard Ceeley, Donald Meek, Robert Woolsey, Luis Alberni, Granville Bates.
Principal songs: I Wonder Why; My Mimosa; Follow the Sun to the South.

THE LOVE CALL
Opened: Oct. 24, 1927, Majestic Th.
88 *performances.*
Book by Harry B. Smith & Edward Locke; lyrics by Smith.
Produced by Messrs Shubert & L. Lawrence Weber; directed by J. C. Huffman & Lew Morton; dances by Earl Lindsay.
Cast included: Berna Dean, John Barker, W. L. Thorne, Barry Lupino, Joseph Macaulay, Veloz & Yolanda.
Principal songs: Eyes that Love; The Ranger's Song; 'Tis Love; I Live, I Die for You.

ROSALIE
Opened: Jan. 10, 1928, New Amsterdam Th.
327 *performances.*
Book by William Anthony McGuire & Guy Bolton; Romberg lyrics by P. G. Wodehouse; music & lyrics also by

437

George & Ira Gershwin.
Produced by Florenz Ziegfeld; directed by McGuire; dances by Seymour Felix.
Cast included: Marilyn Miller, Jack Donahue, Frank Morgan, Bobbe Arnst, Margaret Dale, Oliver McLennan, Clay Clement, Gladys Glad, Hazel Forbes.
Principal Romberg - Wodehouse songs: West Point March; Kingdom of Dreams; The King Can Do No Wrong; Why Must We Always Be Dreaming?

THE NEW MOON

Opened: Sept. 19, 1928, Imperial Th.
518 performances.
Book by Oscar Hammerstein II, Frank Mandel, Laurence Schwab; lyrics by Hammerstein.
Produced by Schwab & Mandel; director uncredited; dances by Bobby Connolly.
Cast included: Robert Halliday, Evelyn Herbert, Gus Shy, William O'Neal, Max Figman, Esther Howard, Olga Albani.
Principal songs: Marianne; Softly, as in a Morning Sunrise; Stouthearted Men; One Kiss; Wanting You; Lover, Come Back to Me; Try Her Out at Dances.
Recorded Versions
Capitol T 219 (S.C.).
Capitol (S)W 1966 (S.C.).

Coupled with Friml's *Vagabond King*, the first recording is a well sung collection featuring Gordon MacRae. The second, more complete version, also stars MacRae.

NINA ROSA

Opened: Sept. 20, 1930, Majestic Th.
137 performances.
Book by Otto Harbach; lyrics by Irving Caesar.
Produced by Messrs. Shubert; directed by J. C. Huffman.
Cast included: Ethelind Terry, Guy Robertson, Leonard Ceeley, Clay Clement, Armida, Cortez & Peggy.
Principal songs: My First Love, My Last Love (lyric with Harbach); Nina Rosa; Serenade of Love; Your Smiles, Your Tears.

EAST WIND

Opened: Oct. 27, 1931, Manhattan Th.
23 performances.
Book by Oscar Hammerstein II & Frank Mandel; lyrics by Hammerstein.
Produced by Lawrence Schwab & Mandel; directed by Hammerstein; dances by Bobby Connolly.
Cast included: Charlotte Lansing, J. Harold Murray, Joe Penner, William Williams, Greek Evans, Dennie Moore, Vera Marsh.
Principal songs: Are You Love; East Wind; I'd Be a Fool; You Are My Woman.

MELODY

Opened: Feb. 14, 1933, Casino Th.
79 performances.
Book by Edward Childs Carpenter; lyrics by Irving Caesar.
Produced & directed by George White; dances by Bobby Connolly.
Cast included: Evelyn Herbert, Walter Woolf, Everett Marshall, George Houston, Hal Skelly, Victor Morley, Jeanne Aubert, Mildred Parisette, Ina Ray (Hutton), Vivian Fay, Louise Kirtland, Milton Douglas, Rose Louise (Gypsy Rose Lee), Consuelo Flowerton, Barry Hyams.
Principal songs: Give Me a Roll on the Drum; I'd Write a Song; You Are the Song; Tonight May Never Come Again; Melody.

MAY WINE

Opened: Dec. 5, 1935, St. James Th.
213 performances.
Book by Frank Mandel; lyrics by Oscar Hammerstein II.
Produced by Laurence Schwab; directed by José Ruben.
Cast included: Walter Slezak, Nancy McCord, Walter Woolf King, Leo G. Carroll, Robert Fischer, Jack Cole, Alice Dudley, Vera Van, Earle MacVeigh.
Principal songs: I Built a Dream; Somebody Ought to Be Told; Something New Is in My Heart; Dance, My Darlings; Just Once Around the Clock.

FORBIDDEN MELODY

Opened: Nov. 2, 1936, New Amsterdam Th.

32 *performances.*

Book & lyrics by Otto Harbach.

Produced by Jack Kirkland & Sam H. Grisman; directed by Macklin Megley & José Ruben.

Cast included: Carl Brisson, Ruby Mercer, Jack Sheehan, Leo Chalzel, June Havoc, Ruth Weston, Joseph Greenwald.

Principal songs: Lady in the Window; You Are All I've Wanted; No Use Pretending; Moonlight and Violins.

SUNNY RIVER

Opened: Dec. 4, 1941, St. James Th.

36 *performances.*

Book & lyrics by Oscar Hammerstein II.

Produced by Max Gordon; directed by John Murray Anderson & Hammerstein; dances by Carl Randall.

Cast included: Muriel Angelus, Bob Lawrence, Helen Claire, Ethel Levey, Tom Ewell, Ivy Scott, Vicki Charles (Vicki Cummings), Richard Huey, Oscar Polk, Dudley Clements, Joan Roberts, William O'Neal, Howard Freeman, Gordon Dilworth.

Principal songs: My Girl and I; Call It a Dream; Along the Winding Road; Let Me Live Today; Sunny River.

UP IN CENTRAL PARK

Opened: Jan. 27, 1945, Century Th.

504 *performances.*

Book by Herbert & Dorothy Fields; lyrics by Miss Fields.

Produced by Michael Todd; directed by John Kennedy; dances by Helen Tamiris.

Cast included: Wilbur Evans, Maureen Cannon, Noah Beery, Betty Bruce, Daniel Nagrin.

Principal songs: The Big Back Yard; When You Walk in the Room; April Snow; Close as Pages in a Book; It Doesn't Cost You Anything to Dream; The Fireman's Bride.

Recorded Version

Decca DL 8016 (S.C.).

Seven songs from the score are well sung by Wilbur Evans, Celeste Holm & Eileen Farrell. Excerpts from Herbert's *The Red Mill* are on reverse.

MY ROMANCE

Opened: Oct. 19, 1948, Shubert Th.

95 *performances.*

Book & lyrics by Rowland Leigh.

Produced by Messrs Shubert; directed by Leigh; dances by Fred Kelly.

Cast included: Anne Jeffreys, Lawrence Brooks, Luella Gear, Rex Evans, Melville Ruick, Hazel Dawn, Jr., Doris Patston, Hildegarde Halliday, Melton Moore.

Principal songs: From Now Onward; If Only; Desire; In Love with Romance.

THE GIRL IN PINK TIGHTS

Opened: Mar. 5, 1954, Mark Hellinger Th.

115 *performances.*

Book by Jerome Chodorov & Joseph Fields; lyrics by Leo Robin.

Produced by Shepard Traube & Anthony Brady Farrell; directed by Traube; dances by Agnes de Mille.

Cast included: Jeanmaire, Charles Goldner, Brenda Lewis, David Atkinson, Alexander Kalioujny, Joshua Shelley, Dania Krupska, Marni Nixon, Herbert Banke.

Principal songs: Lost in Loveliness; Up in the Elevated Railway; In Paris and in Love; My Heart Won't Say Goodbye; Free to Love.

Recorded Version

Columbia OL 4890 (O.C.).

The only original cast recording of a complete Romberg score, this has some attractive pieces and the dynamic Jeanmaire.

CHAPTER SIX
JEROME KERN
composer

MR. WIX OF WICKHAM

Opened: Sept. 19, 1904, Bijou Th.

41 *performances.*
Book & lyrics by John Wagner; music also by Herbert Darnley & George Everard.
Produced & directed by Edward E. Rice.
Cast included: Julian Dalton Eltinge, David Lythgow, Harry C. Clarke, Frank Lalor, Thelma Fair.
Principal Kern songs: From Saturday til Monday; Waiting for You; Angling by the Babbling Brook.

FASCINATING FLORA

Opened: May 20, 1907, Casino Th.
113 *performances.*
Book by R. H. Burnside & Joseph Herbert; Kern lyrics by Paul West, James O'Dea, M. E. Rourke; music & lyrics mostly by Gustave Kerker & Burnside.
Produced by Burnside & F. Ray Comstock; directed by Burnside; dances by Jack Mason.
Cast included: Adele Ritchie, Ada Lewis, Louis Harrison, Fred Bond.
Principal Kern songs: Ballooning (West); The Subway Express (O'Dea); Little Church Around the Corner (Rourke).

THE DAIRYMAIDS

Opened: Aug. 26, 1907, Criterion Th.
86 *performances.*
Book by A. M. Thompson & Robert Courtneidge; Kern lyrics by M. E. Rourke; music & lyrics mostly by Paul A. Rubens, Frank A. Tours & Arthur Wimperis.
Produced by Charles Frohman; directed by A. E. Dodson; dances by Ad. Newberger.
Cast included: Julia Sanderson, George Gregory, Donald Hall, Eugene O'Rourke Arthur Conrad, Stella Thomas.
Principal Kern-Rourke songs: The Hay Ride; I've a Million Reasons Why I Love You; I'd Like to Meet Your Father.

FLUFFY RUFFLES

Opened: Sept. 7, 1908, Criterion Th.
48 *performances.*
Book by John J. McNally; Kern lyrics

by C. H. Bovill; music & lyrics mostly by William T. Francis & Wallace Irwin.
Produced by Charles Frohman; directed by Ben Teal.
Cast included: Hattie Williams, Violet Heming, John Bunny, Adele Rowland, Jack Gardner, George Grossmith, Jr.
Principal Kern-Bovill songs: Meet Her with a Taximeter; Won't You Let Me Carry Your Parcel?; There's Something Rather Odd About Augustus.

THE KING OF CADONIA

Opened: Jan. 10, 1910, Daly's Th.
16 *performances.*
Book by Frederick Lonsdale; Kern lyrics mostly by M. E. Rourke; music & lyrics also by Sidney Jones & Adrian Ross.
Produced by Messrs. Shubert; directed by Joseph Herbert.
Cast included: Marguerite Clark, William Norris, Melville Stewart, William Danforth, Robert Dempster, Clara Palmer.
Principal Kern-Rourke songs: Come Along, Pretty Girl; Coo-oo Coo-oo; Catamarang (lyric by Percival Knight).

LA BELLE PAREE

Opened: Mar. 20, 1911, Winter Garden
104 *performances.*
Sketches by Edgar Smith; lyrics by Edward Madden; music also by Frank Tours.
Produced by Messrs. Shubert; directed by J. C. Huffman; dances by William J. Wilson.
Cast included: Mitzi Hajos, Mlle. Dazie, Kitty Gordon, Stella Mayhew, Al Jolson, Barney Bernard, Dorothy Jardon, Cliff Gordon, Edgar Atchison-Ely, Tempest & Sunshine, Harry Fisher.
Principal Kern-Madden songs: I'm the Human Brush; Look Me Over, Dearie; Sing Trovatore.

THE KISS WALTZ

Opened: Sept. 18, 1911, Casino Th.
88 *performances.*
Book by Edgar Smith; lyrics by Matthew

Woodward; music mostly by Carl M. Ziehrer.
Produced by Messrs. Shubert; directed by J. C. Huffman; dances by Gus Sohlke.
Cast included: Adele Rowland, William Pruette, Eva Davenport, Charles Bigelow.
Principal Kern songs: Fan Me with a Movement Slow; Love Is Like a Little Rubber Band; Ta Ta, Little Girl.

THE GIRL FROM MONTMARTRE
Opened: Aug. 5, 1912, Criterion Th.
64 *performances.*
Book & most lyrics by Harry B. Smith & Robert B. Smith; music also by Henri Bereny.
Produced by Charles Frohman; directed by Thomas J. Reynolds.
Cast included: Hattie Williams, Richard Carle, William Danforth, Lennox Pawle.
Principal Kern songs: Don't Turn My Picture to the Wall (R. B. Smith); Bohemia (H. B. Smith); Ooo, Ooo, Lena! (lyric by John Golden); Hoop-La-La Papa (lyric by M. E. Rourke).

THE RED PETTICOAT
Opened: Nov. 13, 1912, Daly's Th.
61 *performances.*
Book by Rida Johnson Young; lyrics by Paul West.
Produced by Messrs. Shubert; directed by Joseph Herbert.
Cast included: Helen Lowell, William Pruette, Louise Mink, Frances Kennedy, Allen Kearns.
Principal songs: Little Golden Maid; Since the Days of Grandmama; The Ragtime Restaurant.

THE DOLL GIRL
Opened: Aug. 25, 1913, Globe Th.
88 *performances.*
Book & lyrics by Harry B. Smith; music mostly by Leo Fall.
Produced by Charles Frohman; directed by Thomas J. Reynolds; dances by Edward Royce.
Cast included: Hattie Williams, Richard Carle, Charles McNaughton.
Principal Kern songs: If We Were on Our Honeymoon; A Little Thing Like a Kiss; Will It All End in Smoke?

OH, I SAY!
Opened: Oct. 30, 1913, Casino Th.
68 *performances.*
Book by Sydney Blow & Douglas Hoare; lyrics by Harry B. Smith.
Produced by Messrs. Shubert; directed by J. C. Huffman; dances by Julian Alfred.
Cast included: Joseph Herbert, Cecil Cunningham, Nellie King, Walter Jones, Wellington Cross, Clara Palmer, Alice Yorke.
Principal songs: Each Pearl a Thought; Alone at Last; I Can't Forget Your Eyes; Katy-Did.

THE LAUGHING HUSBAND
Opened: Feb. 2, 1914, Knickerbocker Th.
48 *performances.*
Book by Arthur Wimperis; Kern lyrics by Harry B. Smith; music & lyrics mostly by Edmund Eysler & Wimperis.
Produced by Charles Frohman; directed by Edward Royce.
Cast included: Fred Walton, William Norris, Roy Atwell, Josie Intropidi, Venita Fitzhugh, Frances Demarest.
Principal Kern-Smith songs: Take a Step with Me; You're Here and I'm Here; Love Is Like a Violin.

THE GIRL FROM UTAH
Opened: Aug. 24, 1914, Knickerbocker
120 *performances.*
Book by James Tanner; Kern lyrics by Harry B. Smith; music & lyrics also by Paul Rubens, Sidney Jones, Adrian Ross & Percy Greenbank.
Produced by Charles Frohman; directed by J. A. E. Malone.
Cast included: Julia Sanderson, Donald Brian, Joseph Cawthorn, Queenie Vassar, Venita Fitzhugh, George Bishop.
Principal Kern-Smith songs: Same Sort of Girl; Why Don't They Dance the

Polka Anymore?; They Didn't Believe Me (lyric by Herbert Reynolds (M. E. Rourke)).

90 IN THE SHADE
Opened: Jan. 25, 1915, Knickerbocker Th.
40 *performances.*
Book & lyrics by Guy Bolton & Clare Kummer.
Produced by Daniel V. Arthur; directed by Robert Milton; dances by Julian Alfred.
Cast included: Richard Carle, Marie Cahill, Edward Martindel, Victor Morley, Otis Harlan, Pedro de Cordoba.
Principal songs: Where's the Girl for Me? A Package of Seeds; My Mindanao Chocolate Soldier.

NOBODY HOME
Opened: Apr. 20, 1915, Princess Th.
135 *performances.*
Book by Guy Bolton; lyrics by Schuyler Greene.
Produced by Elisabeth Marbury & F. Ray Comstock; directed by J. H. Benrimo; dances by David Bennett.
Cast included: Adele Rowland, Lawrence Grossmith, Alice Dovey, Charles Judels, Maude Odell, Helen Clarke, George Lydecker, George Anderson.
Principal songs: Any Old Night (music with Otto Motzan, lyric by Greene & Harry B. Smith); In Arcady (lyric by Herbert Reynolds (M. E. Rourke); The Magic Melody; You Know and I Know; The Chaplin Walk.

MISS INFORMATION
Opened: Oct. 5, 1915, George M. Cohan Th.
47 *performances.*
Book by Paul Dickey & Charles Goddard; lyrics by Elsie Janis.
Produced by Charles Dillingham; directed by Robert Milton.
Cast included: Elsie Janis, Irene Bordoni, Melville Ellis, Maurice Farkoa.
Principal songs: Some Sort of Somebody; A Little Love; On the Sands of Wah-Ki-Ki (music with Henry Kailimai).

VERY GOOD EDDIE
Opened: Dec. 23, 1915, Princess Th.
341 *performances.*
Book by Philip Bartholomae & Guy Bolton, lyrics by Schuyler Greene.
Produced by Elisabeth Marbury & F. Ray Comstock; directed by Frank McCormack; dances by David Bennett.
Cast included: Alice Dovey, John E. Hazzard, Oscar Shaw, Ernest Truex, Ada Lewis, Helen Raymond.
Principal songs: Babes in the Wood; Some Sort of Somebody (lyric by Elsie Janis); On the Shore at Le Lei Wi (music with Henry Kailimai, lyric by Herbert Reynolds (M. E. Rourke)); Thirteen Collar; Nodding Roses (lyric by Greene & Reynolds); Isn't It Great to Be Married?

ZIEGFELD FOLLIES
(10th Edition)
Opened: June 12, 1916, New Amsterdam Th.
112 *performances.*
Sketches by George V. Hobart & Gene Buck; Kern lyrics by Buck; music & lyrics also by Dave Stamper, Louis Hirsch.
Produced by Florenz Ziegfeld, Jr.; directed by Ned Wayburn.
Cast included: Frances White, Sam Hardy, Ina Claire, Carl Randall, Bernard Granville, Fanny Brice, W. C. Fields, Emma Haig, Bert Williams, Ann Pennington, Marion Davies, Lillian Tashman, Justine Johnstone.
Principal Kern - Buck songs: Have a Heart; Ain't It Funny What a Difference Just a Few Drinks Make?; My Lady of the Nile.

HAVE A HEART
Opened: Jan. 11, 1917, Liberty Th.
76 *performances.*
Book by Guy Bolton & P. G. Wodehouse; lyrics by Wodehouse.
Produced by Henry W. Savage; directed by Edward Royce & George Marion.

Cast included: Louise Dresser, Margaret Romaine, Thurston Hall, Billy B. Van, Flavia Arcaro.

Principal songs: Honeymoon Inn; And I Am All Alone; The Road that Lies Before; You Said Something.

LOVE O' MIKE

Opened: Jan. 15, 1917, Shubert Th.
192 *performances.*
Book by Thomas Sydney; lyrics by Harry B. Smith.
Produced by Elisabeth Marbury & Lee Shubert; directed by J. H. Benrimo.
Cast included: Peggy Wood, Clifton Webb, Luella Gear, Alan Edwards, George Hassell, Lawrence Grossmith, Helen Clarke.
Principal songs: Drift with Me; Don't Tempt Me; Baby Vampire; Simple Little Tune; It Wasn't My Fault (lyric by Herbert Reynolds (M. E. Rourke)).

OH, BOY!

Opened: Feb. 20, 1917, Princess Th.
463 *performances.*
Book by Guy Bolton & P. G. Wodehouse; lyrics by Wodehouse.
Produced by William Elliott & F. Ray Comstock; directed by Edward Royce & Robert Milton.
Cast included: Hal Forde, Marie Carroll, Tom Powers, Anna Wheaton, Edna May Oliver, Marion Davies, Justine Johnstone, Dorothy Dickson, Carl Hyson.
Principal songs: Till the Clouds Roll By; An Old-Fashioned Wife; You Never Knew About Me; Nesting Time in Flatbush; A Pal Like You.

LEAVE IT TO JANE

Opened: Aug. 28, 1917, Longacre Th.
167 *performances.*
Book by Guy Bolton & P. G. Wodehouse; lyrics by Wodehouse.
Produced by William Elliott, F. Ray Comstock & Morris Gest; directed by Edward Royce.
Cast included: Edith Hallor, Robert Pitkin, Oscar Shaw, Georgia O'Ramey, Olin Howland, Ann Orr.
Principal songs: Just You Watch My Step; Leave It to Jane; The Siren's Song; Cleopatterer; The Crickets Are Calling; The Sun Shines Brighter; Sir Galahad; Wait Till Tomorrow.
Recorded Version
Strand SL(S) 1002 (O.C.) (1959) X.
Members of the off-Broadway revival give a scintillating performance of the score. Kathleen Murray, Angelo Mango, Jeanne Allen, Dorothy Greener & George Segal head the cast.

MISS 1917

Opened: Nov. 5, 1917, Century Th.
48 *performances.*
Sketches by Guy Bolton & P. G. Wodehouse; lyrics by Wodehouse; music also by Victor Herbert.
Produced by Charles Dillingham & Florenz Ziegfeld, Jr.; directed by Ned Wayburn.
Cast included: Lew Fields, Cecil Lean, Cleo Mayfield, Vivienne Segal, Andrew Tombes, Harry Kelly, Elizabeth Brice, Marion Davies, Charles King, Peggy Hopkins, Bessie McCoy Davis, Gus Van & Joe Schenck, Irene Castle, Lilyan Tashman, George White, Ann Pennington, Bert Savoy, Emma Haig.
Principal Kern songs: Go Little Boat; The Land Where the Good Songs Go; Tell Me All Your Troubles, Cutie.

OH, LADY! LADY!!

Opened: Feb. 1, 1918, Princess Th.
219 *performances.*
Book by Guy Bolton & P. G. Wodehouse; lyrics by Wodehouse.
Produced by F. Ray Comstock & William Elliott; directed by Edward Royce & Robert Milton.
Cast included: Vivienne Segal, Carl Randall, Margaret Dale, Harry C. Browne, Carroll McComas, Janet Velie, Constance Binney.
Principal songs: Before I Met You; Not Yet; When the Ships Come Home; Greenwich Village; You Found Me and

I Found You.

TOOT-TOOT!

Opened: Mar. 11, 1918, George M. Cohan Th.

40 performances.

Book by Edgar Allan Woolf; lyrics by Berton Braley.

Produced by Henry W. Savage; directed by Woolf & Edward Rose; dances by Robert Marks.

Cast included: William Kent, Flora Zabelle, Louise Groody, Greek Evans, Alonzo Price.

Principal songs: If You Only Care Enough; Honeymoon Land; When You Wake Up Dancing; Every Girl in All America.

ROCK-A-BYE BABY

Opened: May 22, 1918, Astor Th.

85 performances.

Book by Edgar Allan Woolf & Margaret Mayo; lyrics by Herbert Reynolds (M. E. Rourke).

Produced by Selwyn & Co.; directed by Edward Royce.

Cast included: Louise Dresser, Frank Morgan, Carl Hyson, Dorothy Dickson, Alan Hale, Edna Hibbard, Florence Eldridge.

Principal songs: Little Tune Go Away; No Better Use for Time than Kissing; The Kettle Song.

HEAD OVER HEELS

Opened: Sept. 29, 1918, George M. Cohan Th.

100 performances.

Book & lyrics by Edgar Allan Woolf.

Produced by Henry W. Savage; directed by George Marion.

Cast included: Mitzi, Charles Judels, Dorothy Mackaye, Joe Keno, Robert Emmett Keane, Boyd Marshall.

Principal songs: The Big Show; Head Over Heels; Let's Build a Little Nest; Funny Little Something.

SHE'S A GOOD FELLOW

Opened: May 5, 1919, Globe Th.

120 performances.

Book & lyrics by Anne Caldwell.

Produced by Charles Dillingham; directed by Fred G. Latham & Edward Royce.

Cast included: Ivy Sawyer, Joseph Santley, Olin Howland, Rosetta & Vivian Duncan, James C. Marlowe, Ann Orr.

Principal songs: First Rose of Summer; I've Been Waiting for You All the Time; The Bullfrog Patrol; Teacher, Teacher.

THE NIGHT BOAT

Opened: Feb. 2, 1920, Liberty Th.

313 performances.

Book & lyrics by Anne Caldwell.

Produced by Charles Dillingham; directed by Fred G. Latham; dances by Ned Wayburn.

Cast included: Louise Groody, John E. Hazzard, Hal Skelly, Ernest Torrence, Wellington Cross, Ada Lewis, Lillian Kemble Cooper, Jeanette MacDonald.

Principal songs: Left All Alone Again Blues; Whose Baby Are You?; I Love the Lassies; A Heart for Sale.

HITCHY-KOO 1920

Opened: Oct. 19, 1920, New Amsterdam Th.

71 performances.

Sketches by Glen MacDonough; lyrics by Anne Caldwell.

Produced by Raymond Hitchcock; directed by Ned Wayburn.

Cast included: Raymond Hitchcock, Julia Sanderson, Grace Moore, G. P. Huntley, Charles Withers, Florence O'Denishawn, Bobby Connolly, Billy Holbrook.

Principal songs: Buggy Riding; Ding-Dong, It's Kissing Time; Moon of Love.

SALLY

Opened: Dec. 21, 1920, New Amsterdam Th.

570 performances.

Book by Guy Bolton; lyrics mostly by Clifford Grey.

Produced by Florenz Ziegfeld, Jr.; directed by Edward Royce.

Cast included: Marilynn Miller, Leon Errol, Walter Catlett, Irving Fisher, Mary Hay, Stanley Ridges, Dolores, Barbara Dean, Catherine Littlefield.

Principal songs: Wild Rose; Sally; The Church 'Round the Corner (lyric by Grey & P. G. Wodehouse); Look for the Silver Lining (lyric by B. G. DeSylva); Whip-Poor-Will (DeSylva); The Lorelei (lyric by Anne Caldwell).

GOOD MORNING DEARIE

Opened: Nov. 1, 1921, Globe Th.
347 *performances.*
Book & lyrics by Anne Caldwell.
Produced by Charles Dillingham; directed by Edward Royce.
Cast included: Louise Groody, Oscar Shaw, John Price Jones, Ada Lewis, William Kent, Marie Callahan, Harland Dixon, Mary Read, Consuelo Flowerton, Leo Reisman Quartet.
Principal songs: Ka-lu-a; Blue Danube Blues; Easy Pickin's; Rose-Marie; Good Morning Dearie.

THE BUNCH AND JUDY

Opened: Nov. 28, 1922, Globe Th.
63 *performances.*
Book by Anne Caldwell & Hugh Ford; lyrics by Miss Caldwell.
Produced by Charles Dillingham; directed by Fred G. Latham.
Cast included: Fred & Adele Astaire, Ray Dooley, Johnny Dooley, Grace Hayes, Philip Tonge, Six Brown Brothers, Roberta Beatty.
Principal songs: Pale Venetian Moon; Every Day in Every Way; Morning Glory; How Do You Do, Katinka.

STEPPING STONES

Opened: Nov. 6, 1923, Globe Th.
241 *performances.*
Book by R. H. Burnside & Anne Caldwell; lyrics by Miss Caldwell.
Produced by Charles Dillingham; directed by Burnside; dances by Mary Read & John Tiller.
Cast included: Fred Stone, Dorothy Stone, Allene Stone, Jack Whiting, Evelyn Herbert, Oscar ("Rags") Ragland, Roy Hoyer.
Principal songs: In Love with Love; Once in a Blue Moon; Raggedy Ann; Everybody Calls Me Little Red Riding Hood.

SITTING PRETTY

Opened: Apr. 8, 1924, Fulton Th.
95 *performances.*
Book by Guy Bolton & P. G. Wodehouse; lyrics by Wodehouse.
Produced by F. Ray Comstock & Morris Gest; directed by Fred G. Latham; dances by Julian Alfred.
Cast included: Queenie Smith, Frank McIntyre, Dwight Frye, Gertrude Bryan, Rudolph Cameron.
Principal songs: The Enchanted Train; A Year from Today; On a Desert Island with You.

DEAR SIR

Opened: Sept. 23, 1924, Times Square
15 *performances.*
Book by Edgar Selwyn; lyrics by Howard Dietz.
Produced by Philip Goodman; directed by David Burton; dances by David Bennett.
Cast included: Genevieve Tobin, Oscar Shaw, Walter Catlett, Claire Luce, George Sweet.
Principal songs: All Lanes Must Reach a Turning; If You Think It's Love You're Right; A Mormon Life.

SUNNY

Opened: Sept. 22, 1925, New Amsterdam Th.
517 *performances.*
Book & lyrics by Otto Harbach & Oscar Hammerstein II.
Produced by Charles Dillingham; directed by Hassard Short; dances by Julian Mitchell, David Bennett, Alexis Kosloff, John Tiller, Fred Astaire.
Cast included: Marilyn Miller, Jack Donahue, Clifton Webb, Mary Hay, Joseph Cawthorn, Paul Frawley, Cliff Edwards,

Esther Howard, Pert Kelton, Marjorie Moss & Georges Fontana, George Olsen Orchestra.
Principal songs: Sunny; Who?; D'Ya Love Me?; Two Little Bluebirds; When We Get Our Divorce; Let's Say Good-night Till It's Morning.

THE CITY CHAP
Opened: Oct. 26, 1925, Liberty Th.
72 performances.
Book by James Montgomery; lyrics by Anne Caldwell.
Produced by Charles Dillingham; directed by R. H. Burnside; dances by David Bennett.
Cast included: Richard "Skeet" Gallagher, Betty Compton, Irene Dunne, George Raft, Frank Doane, Phyllis Cleveland, George Olsen Orchestra.
Principal songs: Sympathetic Someone; Walking Home with Josie; Journey's End (lyric by P. G. Wodehouse).

CRISS-CROSS
Opened: Oct. 12, 1926, Globe Th.
206 performances.
Book & lyrics by Anne Caldwell & Otto Harbach.
Produced by Charles Dillingham; directed by R. H. Burnside; dances by David Bennett & Mary Read.
Cast included: Fred Stone, Dorothy Stone, Oscar ("Rags") Ragland, Roy Hoyer, Dorothy Francis, Lucy Monroe.
Principal songs: You Will, Won't You?; Cinderella Girl; In Araby With You (lyric by Otto Harbach & Oscar Hammerstein II).

LUCKY
Opened: Mar. 22, 1927, New Amsterdam Th.
71 performances.
Book by Otto Harbach, Bert Kalmar & Harry Ruby; Kern lyrics by Kalmar & Ruby; lyrics & music mostly by Harbach, Kalmar & Ruby.
Produced by Charles Dillingham; directed by Hassard Short; dances by David Bennett & Albertina Rasch.
Cast included: Mary Eaton, Richard "Skeet" Gallagher, Walter Catlett, Ruby Keeler, Ivy Sawyer, Joseph Santley, Paul Everton, Paul Whiteman Orchestra.
Principal Kern-Kalmar-Ruby songs: When the Bo-Tree Blossoms Again; That Little Something; Lucky.

SHOW BOAT
Opened: Dec. 27, 1927, Ziegfeld Th.
575 performances.
Book & lyrics by Oscar Hammerstein II.
Produced by Florenz Ziegfeld; directed by Hammerstein (uncredited) & Zeke Colvan; dances by Sammy Lee.
Cast included: Charles Winninger, Norma Terris, Howard Marsh, Helen Morgan, Edna May Oliver, Jules Bledsoe, Eva Puck, Sammy White, Aunt Jemima (Tess Gardella), Charles Ellis.
Principal songs: Make Believe; Ol' Man River; Can't Help Lovin' dat Man; Till Good Luck Comes My Way; I Might Fall Back on You; Life Upon the Wicked Stage; You Are Love; Why Do I Love You?; Bill (lyric with P. G. Wodehouse).
Recorded Versions
Columbia OL 4058 (O.C.) (1946).
RCA Victor LM 2008 (S.C.).
RCA Victor LOP/LSO 1505 (S.C.).
MGM E 3767 (F.V.) (1951).
Epic LN 3512 (S.C.) X.
RCA Victor LOC/LSO 1126 (O.C.) (1966).
Columbia OL 5820/OS 2200 (S.C.).
The 1946 revival on Columbia is the most theatrical. The first RCA, with Patrice Munsel, Robert Merrill & Risë Stevens, uses the London score. The second RCA, with Anne Jeffreys, Howard Keel & Gogi Grant, has especially good aural presence. Keel is also on the MGM soundtrack, along with Kathryn Grayson & Ava Gardner. The Doreen Hume-Bruce Trent on Epic can be ignored. The third RCA, with the Lincoln Center revival cast (Barbara Cook, Stephen Douglass, William Warfield),

is notable for Constance Towers as Julie. Cook, Warfield & John Raitt are on the admirable second Columbia set.

SWEET ADELINE
Opened: Sept. 3, 1929, Hammerstein Th.
234 performances.
Book & lyrics by Oscar Hammerstein II. Produced by Arthur Hammerstein; directed by Reginald Hammerstein; dances by Danny Dare.
Cast included: Helen Morgan, Charles Butterworth, Robert Fischer, Irene Franklin, Robert Emmett Keane, Robert Chisholm, John D. Seymour, Violet Carson, Max Hoffman, Jr.
Principal songs: Here Am I; 'Twas Not So Long Ago; Molly O'Donahue; Why Was I Born?; Don't Ever Leave Me; The Sun About to Rise.

THE CAT AND THE FIDDLE
Opened: Oct. 15, 1931, Globe Th.
395 performances.
Book & lyrics by Otto Harbach. Produced by Max Gordon; directed by José Ruben; dances by Albertina Rasch.
Cast included: Bettina Hall, Georges Metaxa, George Meader, Odette Myrtil, Eddie Foy, Jr., José Ruben, Doris Carson, Flora LeBreton, Lawrence Grossmith.
Principal songs: The Night Was Made for Love; She Didn't Say "Yes"; One Moment Alone; Poor Pierrot; Try to Forget; A New Love Is Old; I Watch the Love Parade.
Recorded Version
Epic LN 3569 (S.C.) X.
Six selections, all well sung by Doreen Hume & Denis Quilley.

MUSIC IN THE AIR
Opened: Nov. 8, 1932, Alvin Th.
342 performances.
Book & lyrics by Oscar Hammerstein II. Produced by Peggy Fears; directed by Kern & Hammerstein.
Cast included: Walter Slezak, Natalie Hall, Al Shean, Katherine Carrington, Reinald Werrenrath, Nicholas Joy, Tullio Carminati, Ivy Scott, Marjorie Main, Vivian Vance.
Principal songs: There's a Hill Beyond a Hill; I've Told Ev'ry Little Star; And Love Was Born; One More Dance; In Egern on the Tegern See; I'm Alone; The Song Is You; We Belong Together.
Recorded Version
RCA Victor LK 1025 X.
This was to have been the original cast recording of the 1951 revival. However, because the production was not successful, RCA signed only Jane Pickens of the cast to record the songs.

ROBERTA
Opened: Nov 18, 1933, New Amsterdam Th.
295 performances.
Book & lyrics by Otto Harbach. Produced by Max Gordon; directed by Hassard Short (uncredited); dances by José Limon & John Lonergan (uncredited).
Cast included: Lyda Roberti, Bob Hope, Fay Templeton, Tamara, George Murphy, Sydney Greenstreet, Raymond Middleton, Helen Gray, William Hain, Roberta Beatty, California Collegians (incl. Fred MacMurray).
Principal songs: You're Devastating; Yesterdays; The Touch of Your Hand; Smoke Gets in Your Eyes; Let's Begin; I'll Be Hard to Handle (lyric by Bernard Dougall).
Recorded Versions
Columbia OL 7030/OS 2530 (S.C.).
Decca DL 8007 (S.C.).
Capitol T 384 (S.C.).
MGM E 3230 (F.V.) (1952) X.
The best all-around version is on Columbia, featuring Jack Cassidy, Joan Roberts & Kaye Ballard. The Decca release stars Kitty Carlisle & Alfred Drake. Both the Capitol & the MGM feature selections on just one side. Gordon MacRae & Lucille Norman are on the former; Howard Keel, Kathryn Gray-

son, Red Skelton & the Champions are on the latter, known as *Lovely to Look At.*

VERY WARM FOR MAY
Opened: Nov. 17, 1939, Alvin Th.
59 *performances.*
Book & lyrics by Oscar Hammerstein II.
Produced by Max Gordon; directed by Vincente Minnelli & Hammerstein; dances by Albertina Rasch & Harry Losee.
Cast included: Jack Whiting, Eve Arden, Hiram Sherman, Grace McDonald, Frances Mercer, Donald Brian, Richard Quine, Don Loper & Maxine Barrat, Hollace Shaw, Ray Mayer, Robert Shackleton, Evelyn Thawl, Avon Long, Max Showalter, Helena Bliss, June Allyson, Billie Worth, André Charise, Webb Tilton, Matty Malneck Orchestra (incl. Milton DeLugg).
Principal songs: In Other Words; Seventeen; All The Things You Are; Heaven in My Arms; That Lucky Fellow; In the Heart of the Dark; All in Fun.

CHAPTER SEVEN
IRVING BERLIN
composer-lyricist

ZIEGFELD FOLLIES
(5th Edition)
Opened: June 26, 1911, Jardin de Paris.
80 *performances.*
Sketches by George V. Hobart; music & lyric also by Maurice Levi, Raymond Hubbell & Hobart, Jerome Kern & Bessie McCoy.
Produced by Florenz Ziegfeld, Jr.; directed by Julian Mitchell; dances by Gus Sohlke & Jack Mason.
Cast included: Leon Errol, Walter Percival, Fanny Brice, Bessie McCoy, Dolly Sisters, Bert Williams, Lillian Lorraine, George White, Harry Watson, Jr., Vera Maxwell, Clara Palmer.
Principal Berlin songs: Ephraham Played

Upon the Piano (with Vincent Bryan); Woodman, Woodman, Spare that Tree (with Bryan); Doggone that Chilly Man; You've Built a Fire Down in My Heart.

WATCH YOUR STEP
Opened: Dec. 8, 1914, New Amsterdam Th.
175 *performances.*
Book by Harry B. Smith.
Produced by Charles Dillingham; directed by R. H. Burnside.
Cast included: Vernon & Irene Castle, Frank Tinney, Harry Kelly, Justine Johnstone, Charles King, Elizabeth Brice, Sallie Fisher, Elizabeth Murray.
Principal songs: Play a Simple Melody; Settle Down in a One Horse Town; The Syncopated Walk; When I Discovered You; They Always Follow Me Around; Lock Me in Your Harem and Throw Away the Key.

STOP! LOOK! LISTEN!
Opened: Dec. 25, 1915, Globe Th.
105 *performances.*
Sketches by Harry B. Smith.
Produced by Charles Dillingham; directed by R. H. Burnside.
Cast included: Gaby Deslys, Justine Johnstone, Harry Fox, Florence Tempest & Marion Sunshine, Joseph Santley, Frank Lalor, Marion Davies, Marion Harris, Tot Qualters, James Doyle & Harland Dixon, Harry Pilcer, Maurice & Florence Walton.
Principal songs: The Girl on the Magazine Cover; I Love a Piano; When I Get Back to the U.S.A.

THE CENTURY GIRL
Opened: Nov. 6, 1916, Century Th.
200 *performances.*
Sketches uncredited; music & lyrics also by Victor Herbert & Henry Blossom.
Produced by Charles Dillingham & Florenz Ziegfeld, Jr.; directed by Fred G. Latham, Leon Errol, Edward Royce, Ned Wayburn.
Cast included: Hazel Dawn, Sam Ber-

nard, Marie Dressler, Leon Errol, Elsie Janis, Harry Kelly, Gus Van & Joe Schenck, Frank Tinney, John Slavin, Lillian Tashman, Irving Fisher, James Doyle & Harland Dixon, Maurice & Florence Walton.
Principal Berlin songs: The Chicken Walk; Alice in Wonderland; It Takes an Irishman to Make Love.

THE COHAN REVUE 1918
Opened: Dec. 31, 1917, New Amsterdam Th.
96 *performances.*
Sketches by George M. Cohan; music & lyrics also by Cohan.
Produced by Cohan & Harris; directed by Cohan; dances also by Jack Mason & James Gorman.
Cast included: Nora Bayes, Charles Winninger, Irving Fisher, Fred Santley, Sydney Jarvis.
Principal Berlin songs: Down Where the Jack O'Lanterns Grow; King of Broadway; Polly, Pretty Polly.

YIP, YIP, YAPHANK
Opened: Sept. 2, 1918, Century Th.
32 *performances.*
Sketches by the Boys of Camp Upton.
Produced by Uncle Sam; directed by William Smith.
Cast included: Danny Healy, Harry Green, Bob Higgins, Sammy Lee, Benny Leonard, Irving Berlin.
Principal songs: Bevo; What a Difference a Uniform Will Make; Kitchen Police; Mandy; Oh, How I Hate to Get Up in the Morning; I Can Always Find a Little Sunshine in the Y.M.C.A.

THE CANARY
Opened: Nov. 4, 1918, Globe Th.
152 *performances.*
Book uncredited; music & lyrics also by Ivan Caryll, Anne Caldwell & P. G. Wodehouse.
Produced by Charles Dillingham; directed by Fred G. Latham & Edward Royce.

Cast included: Julia Sanderson, Joseph Cawthorn, Sam Hardy, James Doyle & Harland Dixon, Maude Eburne, Edna Bates, Wilmer Bentley, Marie Callahan.
Principal Berlin songs: You're So Beautiful; Julia and Her Johnnies; I Wouldn't Give That for the Man who Couldn't Dance.

ZIEGFELD FOLLIES
(13th Edition)
Opened: June 23, 1919, New Amsterdam Th.
171 *peformances.*
Sketches by Rennold Wolf, George Lemaire, Eddie Cantor, Gene Buck & David Stamper; music & lyrics also by Stamper & Buck, Harry Tierney & Joe McCarthy, Victor Herbert, Albert Von Tilzer, Lew Brown & Eddie Buzzell, Robert Hood Bowers & Francis DeWitt.
Produced by Florenz Ziegfeld, Jr.; directed by Ned Wayburn.
Cast included: Eddie Dowling, Mary Hay, Ray Dooley, Johnny Dooley, Fairbanks Twins, Delyle Alda, Marilynn Miller, Bert Williams, Gus Van & Joe Schenck, Eddie Cantor, John Steel, George Lemaire, Hazel Washburn, Billie Dove.
Principal Berlin songs: Bevo; Mandy; A Pretty Girl Is Like a Melody; You Cannot Make Your Shimmy Shake on Tea (lyric with Rennold Wolf); I'm the Guy who Guards the Harem.

ZIEGFELD FOLLIES
(14th Edition)
Opened: June 22, 1920, New Amsterdam Th.
123 *performances.*
Sketches by W. C. Fields, George V. Hobart, James Montgomery; music & lyrics also by Victor Herbert, Harry Tierney & Joe McCarthy, David Stamper & Gene Buck, Abner Silver & Alex Gerber, George Fairman & Sidney Mitchell, Harry Carroll & Ballard Macdonald.
Produced by Florenz Ziegfeld, Jr.; directed by Edward Royce; dances by

Ray Dooley & Jack Donahue.
Cast included: Charles Winninger, Fannie Brice, W. C. Fields, Moran & Mack, Delyle Alda, Ray Dooley, Carl Randall, Bernard Granville, Gus Van & Joe Schenck, Mary Eaton, John Steel, Art Hickman Orchestra.
Principal Berlin songs: Bells; The Girls of My Dreams; Tell Me, Little Gypsy; The Syncopated Vamp.

MUSIC BOX REVUE

Opened: Sept. 22, 1921, Music Box Th. 440 *performances.*
Sketches by Frances Nordstrom, William Collier, Thomas Gray, George V. Hobart.
Produced by Sam H. Harris; directed by Hassard Short & William Collier; dances by Bert French.
Cast included: William Collier, Wilda Bennett, Paul Frawley, Sam Bernard, Ivy Sawyer, Joseph Santley, Rose Rolando, Emma Haig, Florence Moore, Brox Sisters, Margaret Irving, Chester Hale, Hugh Cameron, Ethelind Terry, Miriam Hopkins, Irving Berlin.
Principal songs: Everybody Step; Say It With Music; They Call It Dancing; The Legend of the Pearls.

MUSIC BOX REVUE

Opened: Oct. 23, 1922, Music Box Th. 330 *performances.*
Sketches by Frances Nordstrom, George V. Hobart, Walter Catlett, Paul Gerard Smith.
Produced by Sam H. Harris; directed by Hassard Short & Sam Forrest; dances by William Seabury & Stowitts.
Cast included: Charlotte Greenwood, Grace LaRue, William Gaxton, Margaret & Dorothy McCarthy, Fairbanks Twins, John Steel, Bobby Clark & Paul McCullough, Margaret Irving, Robinson Newbold, Hal Sherman, Ruth Page, Stowitts, Olivette, William Seabury.
Principal songs: Crinoline Days; Pack Up Your Sins and Go to the Devil; Lady of the Evening; Will She Come from

the East?; I'm Looking for a Daddy Long Legs.

MUSIC BOX REVUE

Opened: Sept. 22, 1923, Music Box Th. 273 *performances.*
Sketches by Edwin Burke, Stanley Rauh, Irving Strouse, George S. Kaufman, Bertram Block, Robert Benchley.
Produced by Sam H. Harris; directed by Hassard Short & Sam Forrest; dances by Sammy Lee & Alex Oumansky.
Cast included: Frank Tinney, Joseph Santley, Ivy Sawyer, John Steel, Robert Benchley, Phil Baker, Columbus & Snow, Grace Moore, Florence O'Denishawn, Brox Sisters, Florence Moore, Solly Ward, Mme. Dora Stroeva, Hugh Cameron, Dorothy Dilley.
Principal songs: Learn to Do the Strut; An Orange Grows in California; Tell Me a Bedtime Story; The Waltz of Long Ago; Little, Butterfly.

MUSIC BOX REVUE

Opened: Dec. 1, 1924, Music Box Th. 184 *performances.*
Sketches by Bert Kalmar & Harry Ruby, Bobby Clark & Paul McCullough, Ralph Bunker, Ned Joyce Heaney, Gilbert Clark.
Produced by Sam H. Harris; directed by John Murray Anderson & Harris; dances by Carl Randall & Mme. Serova.
Cast included: Fannie Brice, Bobby Clark & Paul McCullough, Oscar Shaw, Grace Moore, Carl Randall, Ula Sharon, Brox Sisters, Hal Sherman, Claire Luce, Joseph Macaulay.
Principal songs: Don't Send Me Back to Petrograd; Tell Her in the Springtime; Unlucky in Love; Listening; Rock-a-bye Baby.

THE COCOANUTS

Opened: Dec. 8, 1925, Lyric Th. 276 *performances.*
Book by George S. Kaufman.
Produced by Sam H. Harris; directed by Oscar Eagle; dances by Sammy Lee.

Cast included: The Marx Brothers, Janet Velie, Georgie Hale, Margaret Dumont, Mabel Withee, Basil Ruysdael, Frances Williams, Brox Sisters.
Principal songs: Florida by the Sea; A Little Bungalow; Lucky Boy; Monkey Doodle-Doo.

ZIEGFELD FOLLIES
(21st Edition)

Opened: Aug. 16, 1927, New Amsterdam Th.
167 *performances.*
Sketches by Harold Atteridge & Eddie Cantor.
Produced by A. L. Erlanger & Florenz Ziegfeld; directed by Zeke Colvan; dances by Sammy Lee & Albertina Rasch.
Cast included: Eddie Cantor, Ruth Etting, Andrew Tombes, Harry McNaughton, Dan Healy, Franklyn Baur, Claire Luce, Irene Delroy, Cliff Edwards, Brox Sisters, Paulette Goddard, Edgar Fairchild & Ralph Rainger (duo-pianists).
Principal songs: It All Belongs to Me; It's Up to the Band; Oooh, Maybe It's You; Shaking the Blues Away; Rainbow of Girls.

FACE THE MUSIC

Opened: Feb. 17, 1932, New Amsterdam Th.
165 *performances.*
Book by Moss Hart.
Produced by Sam H. Harris; directed by Hassard Short & George S. Kaufman; dances by Albertina Rasch.
Cast included: Mary Boland, Hugh O'Connell, J. Harold Murray, Katherine Carrington, Andrew Tombes, Edward Gargan, David Burns, Jack Good.
Principal songs: I Say It's Spinach; Let's Have Another Cup o' Coffee; On a Roof in Manhattan; Soft Lights and Sweet Music.

AS THOUSANDS CHEER

Opened: Sept. 30, 1933, Music Box Th.
400 *performances.*
Sketches by Moss Hart.
Produced by Sam H. Harris; directed by Hassard Short; dances by Charles Weidman.
Cast included: Marilyn Miller, Clifton Webb, Helen Broderick, Ethel Waters, Leslie Adams, Jerome Cowan, Hal Forde, Harry Stockwell, José Limon, Letitia Ide, Hamtree Harrington, Katherine Litz.
Principal songs: Harlem on My Mind; Easter Parade; How's Chances?; Heat Wave; Not for All the Rice in China; Supper Time; Lonely Heart.

LOUISIANA PURCHASE

Opened: May 28, 1940, Imperial Th.
444 *performances.*
Book by Morrie Ryskind.
Produced by B. G. DeSylva; directed by Edgar MacGregor; dances by George Balanchine & Carl Randall.
Cast included: William Gaxton, Vera Zorina, Victor Moore, Irene Bordoni, Carol Bruce, Nick Long, Jr., April Ames, Robert Pitkin, Ralph Riggs, Edward H. Robins, Ray Mayer, Hugh Martin, Ralph Blane, Georgia Carroll.
Principal songs: Fools Fall in Love; It's a Lovely Day Tomorrow; Latins Know How; Louisiana Purchase; You Can't Brush Me Off; You're Lonely and I'm Lonely.

THIS IS THE ARMY

Opened: July 4, 1942, Broadway Th.
113 *performances.*
Produced by Uncle Sam; directed by Ezra Stone; dances by Robert Sidney & Nelson Barclift.
Cast included: Ezra Stone, Fred Kelly, Gary Merrill, Burl Ives, Philip Truex, Julie Oshins, Anthony Ross, Earl Oxford, James MacColl, Robert Sidney, Ross Elliot, Hank Henry, Nelson Barclift, Stuart Churchill, Robert Shanley, Alan Manson, Irving Berlin.
Principal songs: This Is the Army, Mr. Jones; I Left My Heart at the Stage Door Canteen; I'm Getting Tired So I

Can Sleep; Mandy; American Eagles; With My Head in the Clouds; The Army's Made a Man out of Me; Oh, How I Hate to Get Up in the Morning.

ANNIE GET YOUR GUN
Opened: May 16, 1946, Imperial Th. 1,147 *performances.*
Book by Herbert & Dorothy Fields.
Produced by Rodgers & Hammerstein; directed by Joshua Logan; dances by Helen Tamiris.
Cast included: Ethel Merman, Ray Middleton, Marty May, Kenny Bowers, Betty Anne Nyman, William O'Neal, Lea Penman, Ellen Hanley, George Lipton, Milton Watson, Warren Berlinger, Daniel Nagrin, Lubov Roudenko, Harry Bellaver, Christina Lind, Leon Bibb, Franca Baldwin.
Principal songs: Doin' What Comes Natur'lly; The Girl that I Marry; You Can't Get a Man With a Gun; There's No Business Like Show Business; They Say It's Wonderful; My Defenses Are Down; I'm an Indian, Too; I Got Lost in His Arms; I Got the Sun in the Morning; Anything You Can Do.
Recorded Versions
Decca DL (7)9018 (O.C.).
MGM E 3768 (F.V.) (1950).
Capitol W 913(TV) (1958).
RCA Victor LOC/LSO 1124 (O.C.) (1966).
Columbia OL 5960/OS 2360 (S.C.).

Merman in the same role 20 years apart may be compared on the Decca & the RCA releases. The ebulient Betty Hutton almost makes the part her own on the MGM soundtrack with Howard Keel, and the more sedate Mary Martin is heard with John Raitt on the Capitol. The Columbia is recommended only to the most devoted fans of Doris Day & Robert Goulet.

MISS LIBERTY
Opened: July 15, 1949, Imperial Th. 308 *performances*

Book by Robert E. Sherwood.
Produced by Berlin, Sherwood & Hart; directed by Moss Hart; dances by Jerome Robbins.
Cast included: Eddie Albert, Allyn McLerie, Mary McCarty, Charles Dingle, Philip Bourneuf, Ethel Griffies, Herbert Berghof, Tommy Rall, Dolores (Dody) Goodman, Janice Rule, Maria Karnilova, Eddie Phillips, Erik Kristen.
Principal songs: A Little Fish in a Big Pond; Let's Take an Old-Fashioned Walk; Homework; Paris Wakes Up and Smiles; Only for Americans; Just One Way to Say I Love You; Give Me Your Tired, Your Poor (poem by Emma Lazarus).
Recorded Version
Columbia OL 4220 (O.C.).

Many attractive pieces in this rather unappreciated score.

CALL ME MADAM
Opened: Oct. 12, 1950, Imperial Th. 644 *performances.*
Book by Howard Lindsay & Russel Crouse.
Produced by Leland Hayward; directed by George Abbott; dances by Jerome Robbins.
Cast included: Ethel Merman, Paul Lukas, Russell Nype, Pat Harrington, Alan Hewitt, Henry Lascoe, Galina Talva, Muriel Bentley, Geoffrey Lumb, Jay Velie, E. A. Krumschmidt, Tommy Rall, Nathaniel Frey.
Principal songs: The Hostess with the Mostes' on the Ball; Marrying for Love; It's a Lovely Day Today; Something to Dance About; They Like Ike; You're Just in Love; The Best Thing for You.
Recorded Versions
RCA Victor LOC 1000 (O.C.) X.
Decca DL (7)9022.

Miss Merman's Decca contract prevented her from making the original cast disk for RCA, and she was replaced by Dinah Shore. On the Decca LP she is supported by Dick Haymes.

MR. PRESIDENT

Opened: Oct. 20, 1962, St. James Th.
265 *performances.*
Book by Howard Lindsay & Russel Crouse.
Produced by Leland Hayward; directed by Joshua Logan; dances by Peter Gennaro.
Cast included: Robert Ryan, Nanette Fabray, Anita Gillette, Jack Haskell, Jack Washburn, Stanley Grover, Jerry Strickler, David Brooks, Charlotte Fairchild, Wisa D'Orso, John Cecil Holm.
Principal songs: Let's Go Back to the Waltz; Meat and Potatoes; Is He the Only Man in the World?; They Love Me; Pigtails and Freckles; Don't Be Afraid of Romance; Empty Pockets Full of Love; This Is a Great Country.
Recorded Version
Columbia KOL 5870/KOS 2270 (O. C.).

Not exactly a landslide, but there are still plenty of winners here.

CHAPTER EIGHT
GEORGE GERSHWIN
composer

IRA GERSHWIN
lyricist

All music by George Gershwin & lyrics by Ira Gershwin unless otherwise noted. For other musicals with Ira Gershwin lyrics, see: Two Little Girls in Blue *under Vincent Youmans;* Park Avenue *under Arthur Schwartz;* Ziegfeld Follies of 1936 *under Vernon Duke;* Life Begins at 8:40 *under Harold Arlen;* Lady in the Dark & The Firebrand of Florence *under Kurt Weill.*

LA LA LUCILLE

Opened: May 26, 1919, Henry Miller Th.
104 *performances.*
Book by Fred Jackson; lyrics by Arthur Jackson & B. G. DeSylva.

Produced by Alfred E. Aarons; directed by Herbert Gresham; dances by Julian Alfred.
Cast included: Janet Velie, John E. Hazzard, Helen Clark, Eleanor Daniels, Marjorie Bentley, J. Clarence Harvey.
Principal songs: Tee-Oodle-Um-Bum-Bo; There's More to a Kiss than the Sound; Nobody but You.

GEORGE WHITE'S SCANDALS
(2nd Edition)

Opened: June 7, 1920, Globe Th.
134 *performances.*
Sketches by Andy Rice & George White; lyrics by Arthur Jackson.
Produced by White; directed by White & William Collier.
Cast included: Ann Pennington, Lou Holtz, La Sylphe, Lester Allen, George "Doc" Rockwell, Ethel Delmar, George Bickel, George White.
Principal songs: On My Mind the Whole Night Long; Scandal Walk; Idle Dreams; Tum on and Tiss Me.

GEORGE WHITE'S SCANDALS
(3rd Edition)

Opened: July 11, 1921, Liberty Th.
97 *performances.*
Sketches by Bugs Baer & George White; Lyrics by Arthur Jackson.
Produced by White; directed by White & John Meehan.
Cast included: Ann Pennnigton, George White, Aunt Jemima (Tess Gardella), George LeMaire, Olive Vaughn, Lou Holtz, Victoria Herbert, Lester Allen, Gene Ford, Charles King, George Bickel, Bert Gordon.
Principal songs: South Sea Isles; Drifting Along with the Tide; She's Just a Baby.

GEORGE WHITE'S SCANDALS
(4th Edition)

Opened: Aug. 28, 1922, Globe Th.
88 *performances.*
Sketches by W. C. Fields, Andy Rice & George White; lyrics by B. G. DeSylva & E. Ray Goetz.

Produced & directed by White.

Cast included: Jack McGowan, Winnie Lightner, George White, W. C. Fields, Lester Allen, Pearl Regay, Ed Wynn, Franklyn Ardell, Olive Vaughn, Jay Velie, Janet Velie, Ralph Riggs, Shaw & Lee, Dolores Costello, Paul Whiteman Orchestra.

Principal songs: Cinderelatives (DeSylva); Where Is the Man of My Dreams? (DeSylva-Goetz); I Found a Four-Leaf Clover (DeSylva); I'll Build a Stairway to Paradise (DeSylva-Arthur Francis (Ira Gershwin)); Argentina (DeSylva).

OUR NELL

Opened: Dec. 4, 1922, Nora Bayes Th.
40 *performances.*
Book by A. E. Thomas & Brian Hooker; lyrics by Hooker; music also by William Daly.
Produced by Hayseed Productions (Ed. Davidow & Rufus LeMaire); directed by W. H. Gilmore & Edgar MacGregor; dances by Julian Mitchell.
Cast included: Mr. & Mrs. Jimmie Barry, Emma Haig, Olin Howland, John Merkyl, Thomas Conkey.
Principal songs: Innocent Ingenue Baby; Walking Home With Angeline; By and By.

GEORGE WHITE'S SCANDALS
(5th Edition)

Opened: June 18, 1923, Globe Th.
168 *performances.*
Sketches by George White & William K. Wells; lyrics by B. G. DeSylva, E. Ray Goetz, Ballard Macdonald.
Cast included: Johnny Dooley, Winnie Lightner, Margaret Breen, Lester Allen, Tom Patricola, Delyle Alda, Helen Hudson, George White, Charles Dornberger Orchestra.
Principal songs: The Life of a Rose (DeSylva); Let's Be Lonesome Together (DeSylva-Goetz); There Is Nothing Too Good for You (DeSylva-Goetz); You and I (DeSylva-Goetz-Macdonald).

SWEET LITTLE DEVIL

Opened: Jan. 21, 1924, Astor Th.
120 *performances.*
Book by Frank Mandel & Laurence Schwab; lyrics by B. G. DeSylva.
Produced by Schwab; directed by Edgar MacGregor; dances by Sammy Lee & Michel Fokine.
Cast included: Constance Binney, Irving Beebe, Marjorie, Gateson, Franklyn Ardell, William Holbrook.
Principal songs: Virginia; Someone Believes in You; The Jijibo; Under a One-Man Top; Mah-Jongg.

GEORGE WHITE'S SCANDALS
(6th Edition)

Opened: June 30, 1924, Apollo Th.
192 *performances.*
Sketches by William K. Wells & George White; lyrics by B. G. DeSylva.
Produced & directed by White.
Cast included: Will Mahoney, Winnie Lightner, Lester Allen, Tom Patricola, Helen Hudson, Elm City 4, The DeMarcos, Olive Vaughn, Dolores & Helene Costello, George White.
Principal songs: Somebody Loves Me (lyric by DeSylva & Ballard Macdonald); Night Time in Araby; Tune in to Station J.O.Y.; Rose of Madrid.

BE YOURSELF!

Opened: Sept. 3, 1924, Sam H. Harris Th.
93 *performances.*
Book by George S. Kaufman & Marc Connelly; lyrics with Kaufman & Connelly; music by Lewis Gensler & Milton Schwarzwald.
Produced by Wilmer & Vincent; directed by William Collier; dances by Vaughn Godfrey & Jack Mason.
Cast included: Queenie Smith, Jack Donahue, G. P. Huntley, Georgia Caine, Dorothy Whitmore, Barrett Greenwood.
Principal songs: I Came Here (Gensler); Uh-Uh! (Schwarzwald); The Wrong Thing at the Right Time (Schwarzwald).

LADY, BE GOOD!

Opened: Dec. 1, 1924, Liberty Th.
330 *performances.*
Book by Guy Bolton & Fred Thompson.
Produced by Alex A. Aarons & Vinton Freedley; directed by Felix Edwardes; dances by Sammy Lee.
Cast included: Fred & Adele Astaire, Walter Catlett, Cliff Edwards, Alan Edwards, Gerald Oliver Smith, Phil Ohman & Vic Arden (duo-pianists).
Principal songs: Hang on to Me; So Am I; Fascinating Rhythm; Oh, Lady Be Good!; "The Half of It, Dearie" Blues; Little Jazz Bird; Swiss Miss.

TELL ME MORE!

Opened: Apr. 13, 1925, Gaiety Th.
100 *performances.*
Book by Fred Thompson & William K. Wells, lyrics with B. G. DeSylva.
Produced by Alex A. Aarons; directed by John Harwood; dances by Sammy Lee.
Cast included: Alexander Gray, Phyllis Cleveland, Andrew Tombes, Lou Holtz, Emma Haig, Portland Hoffa.
Principal songs: Tell Me More!; Three Times a Day; Kickin' the Clouds Away; My Fair Lady; Why Do I Love You?

TIP-TOES

Opened: Dec. 28, 1925, Liberty Th.
194 *performances.*
Book by Guy Bolton & Fred Thompson.
Produced by Alex A. Aarons & Vinton Freedley; directed by John Harwood; dances by Sammy Lee.
Cast included: Queenie Smith, Jeanette MacDonald, Robert Halliday, Allen Kearns, Andrew Tombes, Harry Watson, Jr., Amy Revere, Phil Ohman & Vic Arden (duo-pianists).
Principal songs: Looking for a Boy; When Do We Dance?; These Charming People; That Certain Feeling; Sweet and Low-Down; Nightie-Night; Nice Baby!

SONG OF THE FLAME

Opened: Dec. 30, 1925, 44th St. Th.
219 *performances.*
Book & lyrics by Otto Harbach & Oscar Hammerstein II; music also by Herbert Stothart.
Produced by Arthur Hammerstein; directed by Frank Reicher; dances by Jack Haskell.
Cast included: Tessa Kosta, Guy Robertson, Greek Evans, Dorothy Mackaye, Hugh Cameron, Bernard Gorcey, Ula Sharon, Russian Art Choir.
Principal songs: Cossack Love Song; Song of the Flame; Midnight Bells (music by Gershwin alone).

OH, KAY!

Opened: Nov. 8, 1926, Imperial Th.
256 *performances.*
Book by Guy Bolton & P. G. Wodehouse.
Produced by Alex A. Aarons & Vinton Freedley; directed by John Harwood; dances by Sammy Lee.
Cast included: Gertrude Lawrence, Oscar Shaw, Victor Moore, Betty Compton, Gerald Oliver Smith, Fairbanks Twins, Constance Carpenter, Harland Dixon, Phil Ohman & Vic Arden (duo-pianists).
Principal songs: Dear Little Girl; Maybe; Clap Yo' Hands; Do Do Do; Someone to Watch Over Me; Fidgety Feet; Heaven on Earth (lyric by Howard Dietz).
Recorded Versions
Columbia OL 7050/OS 2550 (S.C.).
20th Fox (S) 4003 (O.C.) (1960) X.
   The only complete recording of a Gershwin score of the 20's. Jack Cassidy & Barbara Ruick head the fine cast on Columbia; David Daniels & Marti Stevens are the leads on the 20th Fox disc. This off-Broadway revival dropped two numbers from the original score, changed the lyrics of "Don't Ask" and "Dear Little Girl," & added 4 other Gershwin tunes.

FUNNY FACE

Opened: Nov. 22, 1927, Alvin Th.

250 *performances.*
Book by Fred Thompson & Paul Gerard Smith.
Produced by Alex A. Aarons & Vinton Freedley; directed by Edgar MacGregor; dances by Bobby Connolly.
Cast included: Fred & Adele Astaire, Victor Moore, William Kent, Allen Kearns, Betty Compton, Phil Ohman & Vic Arden (duo-pianists).
Principal songs: 'S Wonderful; Funny Face; High Hat; Let's Kiss and Make Up; He Loves and She Loves; Tell the Doc; My One and Only; The Babbitt and the Bromide.
Recorded Version
Verve MG V 15001 (F.V.) (1957) X.

The film soundtrack, starring Fred Astaire & Audrey Hepburn, retains 4 songs from the original, plus one that had been cut ("How Long Has This Been Going On?"), one from another Gershwin show ("Clap Yo' Hands"), and two new ones by Roger Edens & Leonard Gershe.

ROSALIE

Opened: Jan. 10, 1928, New Amsterdam Th.
327 *performances.*
Book by Wiliam Anthony McGuire & Guy Bolton; music & lyrics also by Sigmund Romberg & P. G. Wodehouse.
Produced by Florenz Ziegfeld; directed by McGuire; dances by Seymour Felix.
Cast included: Marilyn Miller, Jack Donahue, Frank Morgan, Bobbe Arnst, Margaret Dale, Oliver McLennan, Clay Clement, Gladys Glad, Hazel Forbes.
Principal Gershwin - Gershwin songs: How Long Has This Been Going On?; Say So! (lyric with Wodehouse); Oh, Gee! Oh, Joy! (lyric with Wodehouse).

TREASURE GIRL

Opened: Nov. 8, 1928, Alvin Th.
68 *performances.*
Book by Fred Thompson & Vincent Lawrence.
Produced by Alex A. Aarons & Vinton

Freedley; directed by Bertram Harrison; dances by Bobby Connolly.
Cast included: Gertrude Lawrence, Clifton Webb, Walter Catlett, Mary Hay, Paul Frawley, Constance Cummings, Peggy Conklin, Phil Ohman & Vic Arden (duo-pianists).
Principal songs: I've Got a Crush on You; Oh, So Nice; I Don't Think I'll Fall in Love Today; Feeling I'm Falling; Got a Rainbow; Where's the Boy? Here's the Girl!; K-ra-zy for You.

SHOW GIRL

Opened: July 2, 1929, Ziegfeld Th.
111 *performances.*
Book by William Anthony McGuire & J. P. McEvoy; lyrics with Gus Kahn.
Produced by Florenz Ziegfeld; directed by McGuire; dances by Bobby Connolly & Albertina Rasch.
Cast included: Ruby Keeler Jolson, Lew Clayton, Eddie Jackson, Jimmie Durante, Eddie Foy, Jr., Barbara Newberry, Harriet Hoctor, Frank McHugh, Doris Carson, Joseph Macaulay, Nick Lucas, Duke Ellington Orchestra.
Principal songs: Do What You Do!; So Are You!; Liza; An American in Paris (ballet).

STRIKE UP THE BAND

Opened: Jan. 14, 1930, Times Square Th.
191 *performances.*
Book by Morrie Ryskind, based on book by George S. Kaufman.
Produced by Edgar Selwyn; directed by Alexander Leftwich; dances by George Hale.
Cast included: Bobby Clark & Paul McCullough, Blanche Ring, Jerry Goff, Doris Carson, Dudley Clements, Gordon Smith, Margaret Schilling, Red Nichols Orchestra (incl. Benny Goodman, Gene Krupa, Glenn Miller, Jimmy Dorsey, Jack Teagarden).
Principal songs: I Mean to Say; A Typical Self-Made American; Soon; Hangin' Around With You; Strike Up the Band!; Mademoiselle in New Rochelle; I've Got

a Crush on You.

GIRL CRAZY

Opened: Oct. 14, 1930, Alvin Th.
272 performances.
Book by Guy Bolton & John McGowan.
Produced by Alex A. Aarons & Vinton
Freedley; directed by Alexander Left-
wich; dances by George Hale.
Cast included: Ginger Rogers, Willie
Howard, Ethel Merman, Allen Kearns,
Eunice Healey, William Kent, Antonio
& Renée DeMarco, Lew Parker, Roger
Edens (pianist), Red Nichols Orches-
tra (incl. Benny Goodman, Gene Krupa,
Glenn Miller, Jimmy Dorsey, Jack Tea-
garden).
Principal songs: Bidin' My Time; Could
You Use Me?; Sam and Delilah; Em-
braceable You; I Got Rhythm; But Not
for Me; Treat Me Rough; Boy! What
Love Has Done to Me!
Recorded Version
Columbia OL 7060/OS 2560 (S.C.).

Gershwin's hit-studded score is sung
by Mary Martin, Louise Carlyle & Eddie Chappell.

OF THEE I SING

Opened: Dec. 26, 1931, Music Box Th.
441 perfromances.
Book by George S. Kaufman & Morrie
Ryskind.
Produced by Sam Harris; directed by
Kaufman; dances by George Hale.
Cast included: William Gaxton, Victor
Moore, Lois Moran, George Murphy,
Dudley Clements, Edward H. Robins,
Ralph Riggs, Florenz Ames, Grace
Brinkley, June O'Dea.
Principal songs: Wintergreen for Presi-
dent; Love Is Sweeping the Country;
Of Thee I Sing (Baby); Who Cares?;
Hello, Good Morning; The Illegitimate
Daughter; Because, Because.
Recorded Version
Capitol S 350 (O.C.) (1952) X.

With a cast headed by Jack Carson
& Paul Hartman, the score has been
well preserved by the revival. Also included is "Mine" from *Let 'Em Eat
Cake.*

PARDON MY ENGLISH

Opened: Jan. 20, 1933, Majestic Th.
46 performances.
Book by Herbert Fields.
Produced by Alex A. Aarons & Vinton
Freedley; directed by John McGowan;
dances by George Hale.
Cast included: Jack Pearl, George Givot,
Lyda Roberti, Carl Randall, Barbara
Newberry, Harry T. Shannon, Gerald
Oliver Smith, Cliff Hall, Josephine Hou-
ston.
Principal songs: Lorelei; Isn't It a Pity?;
My Cousin in Milwaukee.

LET 'EM EAT CAKE

Opened: Oct. 21, 1933, Imperial Th.
90 performances.
Book by George S. Kaufman & Morrie
Ryskind.
Produced by Sam H. Harris; directed
by Kaufman; dances by Ned McGurn
& Eugene Van Grona.
Cast included: William Gaxton, Victor
Moore, Lois Moran, Dudley Clements,
Edward H. Robins, Philip Loeb, Ralph
Riggs, Florenz Ames, Consuelo Flower-
ton.
Principal songs: Wintergreen for Presi-
dent; Mine; Down With Ev'rything
that's Up; Let 'Em Eat Cake; On and
On and On; Blue, Blue, Blue.

PORGY AND BESS

Opened: Oct. 10, 1935, Alvin Th.
124 performances.
Book by DuBose Heyward; lyrics also
by Heyward.
Produced by The Theatre Guild; di-
rected by Rouben Mamoulian.
Cast included: Todd Duncan, Anne
Wiggins Brown, John W. Bubbles, Geor-
gette Harvey, Edward Matthews, Helen
Dowdy, Ruby Elzy, Warren Coleman,
Ford L. Buck, J. Rosamond Johnson,
Eva Jessye Choir.
Principal songs: Summertime (Hey-

ward); A Woman Is a Sometime Thing (Heyward); Gone, Gone, Gone (Heyward); My Man's Gone Now (Heyward); It Takes a Long Pull to Get There (Heyward); I Got Plenty o' Nothin' (lyric with Heyward); What You Want wid Bess? (Heyward); Bess, You Is My Woman Now; Oh, I Cain't Sit Down; It Ain't Necessarily So; I Loves You Porgy; A Red Headed Woman; There's a Boat dat's Leavin' Soon for New York; Bess, Oh Where's My Bess?; I'm on My Way (lyric with Heyward).

Recorded Versions
Odyssey 32360018 (S.C.).
Bethlehem EXPL 1 (S.C.) X.
RCA Camden CAL 500 X.
Decca DL (7)9024 (O.C.) (1942).
RCA Victor LM/LSC 2679 (S.C.).
Columbia OL 5410/OS 2016 (F.V.) (1959).
Verve (6)4068.
RCA Victor LOP/LSO 1507.
Decca DL (7)8854 X.

Both Columbia's low-priced Odyssey label reissue & the Bethlehem are 3-record sets, though the former (with Lawrence Winters & Camilla Williams) is far superior to the latter (Mel Tormé & Frances Faye), & still remains the definitive version. The Camden entry is a Gershwin-supervised classic, starring Helen Jepson & Lawrence Tibbett. The first Decca dates from the 1942 revival and features the original leads, Todd Duncan & Anne Brown; the first RCA Victor features the leads of the 1952 tour, Leontyne Price & William Warfield. The soundtrack LP, with Robert McFerrin & Adele Addison, is exceptionally well done. It was the film version that spawned the Verve (Ella Fitzgerald & Louis Armstrong), the second Victor (Lena Horne & Harry Belafonte), and the second Decca (Carmen McRae & Sammy Davis, Jr.).

VINCENT YOUMANS
composer

TWO LITTLE GIRLS IN BLUE
Opened: May 3, 1921, George M. Cohan Th.
135 *performances.*
Book by Fred Jackson; lyrics by Arthur Francis (Ira Gershwin); music also by Paul Lannin.
Produced by A. L. Erlanger; directed by Ned Wayburn.
Cast included: Madeline & Marion Fairbanks, Oscar Shaw, Fred Santley, Olin Howland, Evelyn Law, Julia Kelety, Emma Janvier.
Principal Youmans songs: Oh Me! Oh My!; Dolly (lyric with Schuyler Greene); Who's Who with You?

WILDFLOWER
Opened: Feb. 7, 1923, Casino Th.
477 *performances.*
Book & lyrics by Otto Harbach & Oscar Hammerstein II; music also by Herbert Stothart.
Produced by Arthur Hammerstein; directed by Oscar Eagle; dances by David Bennett.
Cast included: Edith Day, Guy Robertson, Olin Howland, Esther Howard, Charles Judels, James Doyle, Evelyn Cavanaugh.
Principal songs: Wild-Flower; Bambalina; April Blossoms; I Love You, I Love You, I Love You.

MARY JANE McKANE
Opened: Dec. 25, 1923, Imperial Th.
151 *performances.*
Book & lyrics by William Cary Duncan & Oscar Hammerstein II; music also by Herbert Stothart.
Produced by Arthur Hammerstein; directed by Alonzo Price; dances by Sammy Lee.
Cast included: Mary Hay, Hal Skelly,

Stanley Ridges, Kitty Kelly, Margaret & Elizabeth Keene, Dallas Welford.
Principal Youmans songs: My Boy and I; Toodle-oo; Flannel Petticoat Gal.

LOLLIPOP
Opened: Jan. 21, 1924, Knickerbocker Th. 152 *performances.*
Book & lyrics by Zelda Sears; additional lyrics by Walter DeLeon.
Produced by H. W. Savage; directed by Ira Hards; dances by Bert French, John Tiller & Mary Read.
Cast included: Ada May, Zelda Sears, Irene Dunne, Leonard Ceeley, Nick Long, Jr., Gus Shy, Harry Puck.
Principal songs: Tie a String Around Your Finger; Take a Little One-Step; Going Rowing; Deep in My Heart.

NO, NO, NANETTE
Opened: Sept. 16, 1925, Globe Th. 321 *performances.*
Book by Otto Harbach & Frank Mandel; lyrics by Irving Caesar.
Produced & directed by H. H. Frazee; dances by Sammy Lee.
Cast included: Louise Groody, Charles Winninger, Georgia O'Ramey. Wellington Cross, Josephine Whittell, Mary Lawlor, Jack (John) Barker, Frank Parker.
Principal songs: No, No, Nanette (lyric by Harbach); Too Many Rings Around Rosie; I Want to Be Happy; Tea for Two; You Can Dance with Any Girl at All; Where Has My Hubby Gone Blues.
Recorded Versions
Epic LN 3512 (S.C.) X.
Pathé 30146 (French S.C.) X.
Both "highlights" recordings are on one side of their respective LPs. Doreen Hume & Bruce Trent are on the Epic, with *Show Boat* on the reverse; the French cast of 5 principals shares the record with songs from *Rose-Marie*.

OH, PLEASE!
Opened: Dec. 17, 1926, Fulton Th.

75 *performances.*
Book by Otto Harbach & Anne Caldwell; lyrics by Caldwell.
Produced by Charles Dillingham; directed by Hassard Short; dances by David Bennett.
Cast included: Beatrice Lillie, Charles Winninger, Charles Purcell, Helen Broderick, Kitty Kelly, Charles Columbus, Nick Long, Jr.
Principal songs: Nicodemus; I Know that You Know; Like He Loves Me; I'm Waiting for a Wonderful Girl.

HIT THE DECK
Opened: Apr. 25, 1927, Belasco Th. 352 *performances.*
Book by Herbert Fields; lyrics by Clifford Grey & Leo Robin.
Produced by Lew Fields & Youmans; directed by Alexander Leftwich; dances by Seymour Felix.
Cast included: Louise Groody, Charles King, Stella Mayhew, Madeline Cameron, Bobbie Perkins, Brian Donlevy.
Principal songs: Join the Navy; Harbor of My Heart; Why, Oh Why; Sometimes I'm Happy (lyric by Irving Caesar); Hallelujah; Loo-Loo.
Recorded Versions
MGM E 3163 (F.V.) (1955).
Epic LN 3569 (S.C.) X.
Seven of the 12 songs on the soundtrack LP (with Tony Martin, Jane Powell, Debbie Reynolds) were in the original score, & one, "Keeping Myself for You," was from the first film version. Doreen Hume & Denis Quilley sing excerpts on one side of the Epic.

RAINBOW
Opened: Nov. 21, 1928, Gallo Th. 29 *performances.*
Book by Laurence Stallings & Oscar Hammerstein II; lyrics by Hammerstein.
Produced by Philip Goodman; directed by Hammerstein; dances by Busby Berkeley.
Cast included: Allan Prior, Louise Brown, Libby Holman, Charles Rug-

gles, Brian Donlevy, May Barnes, Harland Dixon, Helen Lynd, Ned McGurn.
Principal songs: I Want a Man; The One Girl; I Like You as You Are; Hay, Straw; The Bride Was Dressed in White.

GREAT DAY!

Opened: Oct. 17, 1929, Cosmopolitan Th.
36 performances.
Book by William Cary Duncan & John Wells; lyrics by William (Billy) Rose & Edward Eliscu.
Produced by Youmans; directed by R. H. Burnside & Frank M. Gillespie; dances by LeRoy Prinz.
Cast included: Mayo Methot, John Haynes, Allan Prior, Walter C. Kelly, Miller & Lyles, Maude Eburne, Ethel Norris, Lois Deppe, Vanessi.
Principal songs: Happy Because I'm in Love; Great Day; More than You Know; Without a Song.

SMILES

Opened: Nov. 18, 1930, Ziegfeld Th.
63 performances.
Book by William Anthony McGuire; lyrics by Harold Adamson, Clifford Grey, Ring Lardner.
Produced by Florenz Ziegfeld; directed by McGuire; dances by Ned Wayburn.
Cast included: Marilyn Miller, Fred & Adele Astaire, Tom Howard, Paul Gregory, Eddie Foy, Jr., Larry Adler, Clare Dodd, Georgia Caine, Bob Hope, Virginia Bruce.
Principal songs: Time on My Hands (lyric by Adamson & Mack Gordon); Carry on, Keep Smiling (Adamson); I'm Glad I Waited (Adamson-Grey); If I Were You, Love (Lardner).

THROUGH THE YEARS

Opened: Jan. 28, 1932, Manhattan Th.
20 performances.
Book by Brian Hooker; lyrics by Edward Heyman.
Produced by Youmans; directed by Edgar MacGregor; dances by Jack Haskell & Max Scheck.

Cast included: Natalie Hall, Michael Bartlett, Charles Winninger, Reginald Owen, Nick Long, Jr.
Principal songs: Kinda Like You; Through the Years; You're Everywhere; Drums in My Heart; Kathleen Mine.

TAKE A CHANCE

Opened: Nov. 26, 1932, Apollo Th.
243 performances.
Book by B. G. DeSylva & Laurence Schwab with Sid Silvers; lyrics by DeSylva; music also by Richard A. Whiting & Herb Brown Nacio (Nacio Herb Brown).
Produced by Schwab & DeSylva; directed by Edgar MacGregor; dances by Bobby Connolly.
Cast included: Jack Haley, Ethel Merman, Jack Whiting, June Knight, Sid Silvers, Robert Gleckler, Mitzi Mayfair, Oscar ("Rags") Ragland.
Principal Youmans songs: Should I Be Sweet?; Rise 'n' Shine; Oh, How I Long to Belong to You; My Lover.

CHAPTER TEN
RICHARD RODGERS
composer

LORENZ HART
lyricist

POOR LITTLE RITZ GIRL

Opened: July 28, 1920, Central Th.
119 performances.
Book by George Campbell & Lew Fields; music & lyrics also by Sigmund Romberg & Alex Gerber.
Produced by Lew Fields: directed by Ned Wayburn.
Cast included: Charles Purcell, Eleanor Griffith, Lulu McConnell, Andrew Tombes, Aileen Poe, Grant Simpson.
Principal Rodgers-Hart songs: You Can't Fool Your Dreams; What Happened Nobody Knows; Mary, Queen of Scots (lyric by Herbert Fields).

THE GARRICK GAIETIES

Opened: May 17, 1925, Garrick Th.
211 *performances.*
Sketches by Benjamin M. Kaye, Edith Meiser, Arthur Sullivan & Morrie Ryskind, Howard Green.
Produced by The Theatre Guild; directed by Philip Loeb; dances by Herbert Fields.
Cast included: Sterling Holloway, Romney Brent, James Norris, June Cochrane, Betty Starbuck, Edith Meiser, Philip Loeb, House Jamieson, Hildegarde Halliday, Lee Strasberg, Rose Rolando, Alvah Bessie, Elizabeth (Libby) Holman, Sanford Meisner, Eleanor Shaler.
Principal songs: Manhattan; April Fool; Sentimental Me; On with the Dance; An Old-Fashioned Girl (lyric by Edith Meiser).

DEAREST ENEMY

Opened: Sept. 18, 1925, Knickerbocker Th.
286 *performances.*
Book by Herbert Fields.
Produced by George Ford; directed by John Murray Anderson; dances by Carl Hemmer.
Cast included: Helen Ford, Charles Purcell, Flavia Arcaro, Harold Crane, Detmar Poppen, Helen Spring.
Principal songs: War Is War; Cheerio; I Beg Your Pardon; Here in My Arms; Where the Hudson River Flows; Bye and Bye; Old Enough to Love; Sweet Peter; Here's a Kiss.

THE GIRL FRIEND

Opened: Mar. 17, 1926, Vanderbilt Th.
301 *performances.*
Book by Herbert Fields.
Produced by Lew Fields; directed by John Harwood; dances by Jack Haskell.
Cast included: Sam White, Eva Puck, June Cochrane, Frank Doane, John Hundley, Evelyn Cavanaugh, Francis X. Donegan.
Principal songs: The Girl Friend; The Blue Room; Why Do I?; Good Fellow Mine.

THE GARRICK GAIETIES

Opened: May 10, 1926, Garrick Th.
174 *performances.*
Sketches by Benjamin M. Kaye, Newman Levy, Marion Page Johnson, Chester Heywood, Edward Hope.
Produced by The Theatre Guild; directed by Philip Loeb; dances by Herbert Fields.
Cast included: Sterling Holloway, Romney Brent, Betty Starbuck, Edith Meiser, Philip Loeb, Bobbie Perkins, Hildegarde Halliday, Eleanor Shaler.
Principal songs: Keys to Heaven; Mountain Greenery; What's the Use of Talking?; Sleepyhead.

PEGGY-ANN

Opened: Dec. 27, 1926, Vanderbilt Th.
333 *performances.*
Book by Herbert Fields.
Produced by Lew Fields & Lyle D. Andrews; directed by Robert Milton; dances by Seymour Felix.
Cast included: Helen Ford, Lulu McConnell, Betty Starbuck, Lester Cole, Edith Meiser, Jack Thompson, Margaret Breen, Grant Simpson, Fuller Mellish, Jr.
Principal songs: A Tree in the Park; A Little Birdie Told Me So; Where's That Rainbow?; Maybe It's Me.

BETSY

Opened: Dec. 28, 1926, New Amsterdam Th.
39 *performances.*
Book by Irving Caesar & David Freedman, revised by William Anthony McGuire.
Produced by Florenz Ziegfeld; directed by McGuire; dances by Sammy Lee.
Cast included: Belle Baker, Al Shean, Jimmy Hussey, Bobbie Perkins, Dan Healy, Allen Kearns, Madeleine Cameron, Barbara Newberry, Evelyn Law, Borrah Minevitch Harmonica Orchestra.

Principal songs: In Our Parlor on the Third Floor Back; If I Were You; This Funny World; Sing; Come and Tell Me; Blue Skies (music & lyrics by Irving Berlin).

A CONNECTICUT YANKEE

Opened: Nov. 3, 1927, Vanderbilt Th.
418 *performances.*
Book by Herbert Fields.
Produced by Lew Fields & Lyle D. Andrews; directed by Alexander Leftwich; dances by Busby Berkeley.
Cast included: William Gaxton, Constance Carpenter, William Norris, June Cochrane, Jack Thompson, Nana Bryant, Paul Everton.
Principal songs: My Heart Stood Still; Thou Swell; On a Desert Island With Thee; I Feel at Home With You.

SHE'S MY BABY

Opened: Jan. 3, 1928, Globe Th.
71 *performances.*
Book by Guy Bolton, Bert Kalmar, Harry Ruby.
Produced by Charles Dillingham; directed by Edward Royce; dances by Mary Read.
Cast included: Beatrice Lillie, Clifton Webb, Jack Whiting, Irene Dunne, Nick Long, Jr., William Frawley, Ula Sharon, Frank Doane.
Principal songs: You're What I Need; A Little House in Soho; A Baby's Best Friend; Try Again Tomorrow.

PRESENT ARMS

Opened: Apr. 26, 1928, Mansfield Th.
155 *performances.*
Book by Herbert Fields.
Produced by Lew Fields; directed by Alexander Leftwich; dances by Busby Berkeley.
Cast included: Charles King, Flora Le-Breton, Busby Berkeley, Joyce Barbour, Franker Woods, Fuller Mellish, Jr., Gaile Beverley.
Principal songs: You Took Advantage of Me; Do I Hear You Saying "I Love You"?; A Kiss for Cinderella; Blue Ocean Blues.

CHEE-CHEE

Opened: Sept. 25, 1928, Mansfield Th.
31 *performances.*
Book by Herbert Fields.
Produced by Lew Fields; directed by Alexander Leftwich; dances by Jack Haskell.
Cast included: Helen Ford, William Williams, Betty Starbuck, George Hassell, Philip Loeb, George Houston, Stark Patterson.
Principal songs: I Must Love You; Moon of My Delight; Dear, Oh Dear; Singing a Love Song.

SPRING IS HERE

Opened: Mar. 11, 1929, Alvin Th.
104 *performances.*
Book by Owen Davis.
Produced by Alex A. Aarons & Vinton Freedley; directed by Alexander Leftwich; dances by Bobby Connolly.
Cast included: Glenn Hunter, Lillian Taiz, John Hundley, Charles Ruggles, Inez Courtney, Joyce Barbour, Dick Keene, Lew Parker, Phil Ohman & Vic Arden (duo-pianists).
Principal songs: Yours Sincerely; With a Song in My Heart; Baby's Awake Now; Red Hot Trumpet; Why Can't I?

HEADS UP!

Opened: Nov. 11, 1929, Alvin Th.
144 *performances.*
Book by John McGowan & Paul Gerard Smith.
Produced by Alex A. Aarons & Vinton Freedley; director uncredited; dances by George Hale.
Cast included: Barbara Newberry, Jack Whiting, Victor Moore, Betty Starbuck, John Hundley, Ray Bolger, Janet Velie, Robert Gleckler, Lew Parker, Atlas & LaMarr, Phil Ohman (pianist).
Principal songs: Why Do You Suppose?; It Must Be Heaven; My Man Is on the Make; A Ship Without a Sail.

SIMPLE SIMON

Opened: Feb. 18, 1930, Ziegfeld Th.
135 *performances.*
Book by Ed Wynn & Guy Bolton.
Produced by Florenz Ziegfeld; directed by Zeke Colvan; dances by Seymour Felix.
Cast includeds Ed Wynn, Ruth Etting, Bobbe Arnst, Will Ahearn, Alan Edwards, Harriet Hoctor, Lennox Pawle, Hazel Forbes.
Principal songs: Send for Me; I Can Do Wonders with You; Ten Cents a Dance; I Still Believe in You; Don't Tell Your Folks.

AMERICA'S SWEETHEART

Opened: Feb. 10, 1931, Broadhurst Th.
135 *performances.*
Book by Herbert Fields.
Produced by Laurence Schwab & Frank Mandel; directed by Bobby Connolly & Monty Woolley.
Cast included: Harriette Lake (Ann Sothern), Jack Whiting, Gus Shy, John Sheehan, Inez Courtney, Jeanne Aubert, Dorothy Dare, Virginia Bruce, Jack Donohue.
Principal songs: I've Got Five Dollars; There's So Much More; We'll Be the Same; How About It?; Sweet Geraldine; Innocent Chorus Girls of Yesterday; A Lady Must Live.

JUMBO

Opened: Nov. 16, 1935, Hippodrome.
233 *performances.*
Book by Ben Hecht & Charles MacArthur.
Produced by Billy Rose; directed by John Murray Anderson & George Abbott; dances by Allan K. Foster.
Cast included: Jimmy Durante, Gloria Grafton, Donald Novis, Poodles Hanneford, Bob Lawrence, Arthur Sinclair, Lipman Duckat (Larry Douglas), Paul Whiteman Orchestra.
Principal songs: Over and Over Again; The Circus Is on Parade; The Most Beautiful Girl in the World; My Romance; Little Girl Blue.
Recorded Version
Columbia OL 5860/ OS 2260 (F.V.) (1962)
The M-G-M soundtrack (featuring Doris Day, Martha Raye & Jimmy Durante) contains the above five songs plus "Why Can't I?" & "This Can't Be Love."

ON YOUR TOES

Opened: Apr. 11, 1936, Imperial Th.
315 *performances.*
Book by Rodgers & Hart & George Abbott.
Produced by Dwight Deere Wiman; directed by Worthington Miner; dances by George Balanchine.
Cast included: Ray Bolger, Tamara Geva, Monty Woolley, Doris Carson, David Morris, Luella Gear, Robert Sidney, Demetrios Vilan, George Church, Earle MacVeigh.
Principal songs: It's Got to be Love; Too Good for the Average Man; There's a Small Hotel; The Heart Is Quicker than the Eye; Quiet Night; Glad to Be Unhappy; On Your Toes; Slaughter on Tenth Avenue (ballet).
Recorded Versions
Decca DL 9015 (O.C.) (1954)
Columbia OL 7090: OS 2590 (S.C.).
Columbia's LP, with Portia Nelson & Jack Cassidy, was issued just before the 1954 revival. Decca's recording of that production, featuring Bobby Van, Kay Coulter & Elaine Stritch, includes the interpolated "You Took Advantage of Me."

BABES IN ARMS

Opened: Apr. 14, 1937, Shubert Th.
289 *performances.*
Book by Rodgers & Hart.
Produced by Dwight Deere Wiman; directed by Robert Sinclair; dances by George Balanchine.
Cast included: Mitzi Green, Wynn Murray, Ray Heatherton, Duke McHale, Alfred Drake, Ray McDonald, Grace McDonald, Harold & Fayard Nicholas,

Robert Rounseville, Rolly Pickert, Aileen Poe, Dan Dailey.
Principal songs: Where or When; Babes in Arms; I Wish I Were in Love Again; Way Out West; My Funny Valentine; Johnny One Note; All at Once; The Lady Is a Tramp; Imagine.
Recorded Version
Columbia OL 7070/OS 2570 (S.C.).

There are probably more hit songs in this score than in any other by Rodgers & Hart. With Mary Martin starred, the recording does them full justice.

I'D RATHER BE RIGHT

Opened: Nov. 2, 1937, Alvin Th.
290 *performances.*
Book by George S. Kaufman & Moss Hart.
Produced by Sam H. Harris; directed by Kaufman; dances by Charles Weidman & Ned McGurn.
Cast included: George M. Cohan, Joy Hodges, Austin Marshall, Taylor Holmes, Marion Green, Florenz Ames, Joseph Macaulay, Georgie Tapps, Mary Jane Walsh, Marie Nash, Paul Parks.
Principal songs: Have You Met Miss Jones?; A Little Bit of Constitutional Fun; Sweet Sixty-Five; I'd Rather Be Right; Off the Record.

I MARRIED AN ANGEL

Opened: May 11, 1938, Shubert Th.
338 *performances.*
Book by Rodgers & Hart.
Produced by Dwight Deere Wiman; directed by Joshua Logan; dances by George Balanchine.
Cast included: Dennis King, Vera Zorina, Vivienne Segal, Walter Slezak, Charles Walters, Audrey Christie, Charles Laskey, Morton L. Stevens, Casper Reardon (harpist).
Principal songs: Did You Ever Get Stung?; I Married an Angel; I'll Tell the Man in the Street; How to Win Friends and Influence People; Spring Is Here; A Twinkle in Your Eye; At the Roxy Music Hall.

THE BOYS FROM SYRACUSE

Opened: Nov. 23, 1938, Alvin Th.
235 *performances.*
Book by George Abbott.
Produced & directed by Abbott; dances by George Balanchine.
Cast included: Jimmy Savo, Teddy Hart, Eddie Albert, Ronald Graham, Wynn Murray, Muriel Angelus, Marcy Westcott, Bob Lawrence, Robert Sidney, Burl Ives, George Church, Betty Bruce.
Principal songs: What Can You Do With a Man?; Falling in Love with Love; The Shortest Day of the Year; This Can't Be Love; He and She; You Have Cast Your Shadow on the Sea; Sing for Your Supper; Oh, Diogenes.
Recorded Versions
Columbia OL 7080/ OS 2580 (S.C.).
Capitol (S)TAO 1933 (O.C.) (1963).

Jack Cassidy, Portia Nelson & Bibi Osterwald are heard in a spirited rendering of the score on Columbia. The successful off-Broadway revival, on Capitol, features Ellen Hanley, Stuart Damon, Julienne Marie & Karen Morrow.

TOO MANY GIRLS

Opened: Oct. 18, 1939, Imperial Th.
249 *performances.*
Book by George Marion, Jr.
Produced & directed by George Abbott; dances by Robert Alton.
Cast included: Richard Kollmar, Eddie Bracken, Marcy Westcott, Desi Arnaz, Hal LeRoy, Mary Jane Walsh, Leila Ernst, Ivy Scott, Diosa Costello, Van Johnson, James MacColl.
Principal songs: Love Never Went to College; Spic and Spanish; I Like to Recognize the Tune; I Didn't Know What Time It Was; Give It Back to the Indians; She Could Shake the Maracas.

HIGHER AND HIGHER

Opened: Apr. 4, 1940, Shubert Th.
104 *performances.*
Book by Gladys Hurlbut & Joshua Logan.

Produced by Dwight Deere Wiman; directed by Logan; dances by Robert Alton.

Cast included: Jack Haley, Marta Eggert, Shirley Ross, Leif Erickson, Lee Dixon, Robert Chisholm, Billie Worth, Hollace Shaw, Robert Rounseville, Janet Fox, Jane Ball, Marie Nash, June Allyson, Vera Ellen.

Principal songs: From Another World; Nothing but You; Disgustingly Rich; Ev'ry Sunday Afternoon; It Never Entered My Mind.

PAL JOEY

Opened: Dec. 25, 1940, Ethel Barrymore Th.

374 *performances.*

Book by John O'Hara.

Produced & directed by George Abbott; dances by Robert Alton.

Cast included: Vivienne Segal, Gene Kelly, June Havoc, Jack Durant, Leila Ernst, Stanley Donen, Jean Casto, Van Johnson, Jerome Whyte.

Principal songs: You Mustn't Kick It Around; I Could Write a Book; That Terrific Rainbow; Happy Hunting Horn; Bewitched, Bothered and Bewildered; The Flower Garden of My Heart; Zip; Den of Iniquity; Take Him.

Recorded Versions

Columbia OL 4364 (S.C.).

Capitol S 310 (O.C.) (1952) X.

Capitol (D)W 912 (F.V.) (1957).

The success of the Columbia LP helped spark the 1952 revival, with the album's leads, Vivienne Segal & Harold Lang, going into the new production. Capitol's original cast version has everyone else in the cast, with Jane Froman & Dick Beavers substituting for the leads. The soundtrack release is recommended to Sinatra fans.

BY JUPITER

Opened: June 2, 1942, Shubert Th.

427 *performances.*

Book by Rodgers & Hart.

Produced by Dwight Deere Wiman &
Rodgers; directed by Joshua Logan; dances by Robert Alton.

Cast included: Ray Bolger, Constance Moore, Benay Venuta, Ronald Graham, Bertha Belmore, Margaret Bannerman, Mark Dawson, Ralph Dumke, Berni Gould, Vera-Ellen.

Principal songs: Jupiter Forbid; Life with Father; Nobody's Heart; Ev'rything I've Got; Careless Rhapsody; Wait till You See Her; Here's a Hand.

Recorded Version

RCA Victor LOC/LSO 1137 (O.C.) (1967).

The off-Broadway cast, headed by Bob Dishy, does exceptionally well by this *Boys from Syracuse*-inspired score.

A CONNECTICUT YANKEE
(*revised version*)

Opened: Nov. 17, 1943, Martin Beck Th.

135 *performances.*

Book by Herbert Fields.

Produced by Rodgers; directed by John C. Wilson; dances by William Holbrook & Al White, Jr.

Cast included: Dick Foran, Vivienne Segal, Julie Warren, Chester Stratton, Jere McMahon, Robert Chisholm.

Principal songs: My Heart Stood Still; Thou Swell; On a Desert Island with Thee; To Keep My Love Alive; Can't You Do a Friend a Favor?; I Feel at Home with You; You Always Love the Same Girl.

CHAPTER ELEVEN
B. G. DESYLVA
lyricist

LEW BROWN
lyricist

RAY HENDERSON
composer

This list contains all musicals by Messrs. DeSylva, Brown & Henderson including those written as a team & also those written with other collaborators. For other musicals with books co-authored by Mr. DeSylva, See DuBarry Was a Lady *&* Panama Hattie *under Cole Porter.*

SINBAD
Opened: Feb. 14, 1918, Winter Garden
164 performances.
Book & most lyrics by Harold Atteridge; music mostly by Sigmund Romberg; music & lyrics also by DeSylva, George Gershwin & Irving Caesar, Jean Schwartz, Joe Young & Sam Lewis.
Produced by Messrs. Shubert; directed by J. C. Huffman; dances by Jack Mason & Alexis Kosloff.
Cast included: Al Jolson, Kitty Doner, Forrest Huff, Mabel Withee, Hazell Cox, Grace Washburn, Edgar Atchison-Ely.
Principal DeSylva songs: 'N Everything; I'll Say She Does; I Gave Her That; Chloe.

LA LA LUCILLE (DeSylva)
(*See* George Gershwin).

BOMBO
Opened: Oct. 6, 1921, Al Jolson Th.
219 performances.
Book & most lyrics by Harold Atteridge; music mostly by Sigmund Romberg; music & lyrics also by DeSylva, Con Conrad, Cliff Friend, Walter Donaldson, Sam Lewis & Joe Young.
Produced by Messrs. Shubert; directed by J. C. Huffman; dances by Allan K. Foster.
Cast included: Al Jolson, Janet Adair, Forrest Huff, Vivien Oakland, Russell Mack, Portland Hoffa.
Principal DeSylva songs: Avalon (music by Vincent Rose); April Showers (music by Louis Silvers); Arcady (music by Conrad); Yoo-Hoo.

GEORGE WHITE'S SCANDALS
(4th Edition) (DeSylva)
(*See* George Gershwin).

ORANGE BLOSSOMS (DeSylva)
(*See* Victor Herbert).

THE YANKEE PRINCESS
Opened: Oct. 2, 1922, Knickerbocker Th.
80 performances.
Book by William LeBaron; lyrics by DeSylva; music by Emmerich Kalman.
Produced by A. L. Erlanger; directed by Julian Mitchell & Fred G. Latham.
Cast included: Vivienne Segal, John T. Murray, Frank Doane, Colin Campbell, Thorpe Bates, Vivien Oakland.
Principal songs: Roses, Lovely Roses; In the Starlight; I Still Can Dream.

GEORGE WHITE'S SCANDALS
(5th Edition) (DeSylva)
(*See* George Gershwin).

SWEET LITTLE DEVIL (DeSylva)
(*See* George Gershwin).

GEORGE WHITE'S SCANDALS
(6th Edition) (DeSylva)
(*See* George Gershwin).

BIG BOY
Opened: Jan. 7, 1925, Winter Garden
176 performances.
Book by Harold Atteridge; lyrics by DeSylva; music mostly by Joseph Meyer & James Hanley.
Produced by Messrs. Shubert; directed by J. C. Huffman & Alexander Leftwich; dances by Seymour Felix & Larry Ceballos.
Cast included: Al Jolson, Edythe Baker, Colin Campbell, Flo Lewis, Ralph Whitehead, Nancy Carroll.
Principal DeSylva songs: It All Depends on You (Brown-Henderson); Hello, 'Tucky (Meyer-Hanley); As Long as I've Got My Mammy (Meyer-Hanley); If You Knew Susie (Meyer); Keep Smiling at Trouble (Jolson-Lewis Gensler).

TELL ME MORE! (DeSylva)
(*See* George Gershwin).

GEORGE WHITE'S SCANDALS
(7th Edition)

Opened: June 22, 1925, Apollo Th.
171 *performances.*
Sketches by William K. Wells & Georg White; lyrics by DeSylva & Brown; music by Henderson.
Produced & directed by White; dances by Albertina Rasch.
Cast included: Harry Fox, Tom Patricola, Helen Morgan, McCarthy Sisters, Gordon Dooley, Miller & Lyles, Arthur Ball, Helen Hudson, Martha Morton, Elm City 4.
Principal songs: Fly Butterfly; Give Us the Charleston; I Want a Lovable Baby; The Whosis-Whatsis; What a World This Would Be.

CAPTAIN JINKS

Opened: Sept. 8, 1925, Music Box Th.
167 *performances.*
Book by Frank Mandel & Laurence Schwab; lyrics by DeSylva; music by Lewis Gensler.
Produced by Schwab & Mandel; directed by Edgar MacGregor; dances by Sammy Lee.
Cast included: Joe E. Brown, Louise Brown, J. Harold Murray, Max Hoffman, Jr., Marion Sunshine, Nina Olivette.
Principal songs: Sea Legs; Fond of You; I Do; Kiki.

GEORGE WHITE'S SCANDALS
(8th Edition)
Opened: June 14, 1926, Apollo Th.
424 *performances.*
Sketches by George White & William K. Wells; lyrics by DeSylva & Brown; music by Henderson.
Produced & directed by White.
Cast included: Ann Pennington, Willie & Eugene Howard, Tom Patricola, Harry Richman, Buster West, Frances Williams, McCarthy Sisters, Rose Perfect, John Wells, Fairbanks Twins, Portland Hoffa.
Principal songs: Lucky Day; The Birth of the Blues; Black Bottom; The Girl Is You and the Boy Is Me; Rhapsody in Blue (music by George Gershwin).

QUEEN HIGH
Opened: Sept. 8, 1926, Ambassador Th.
378 *performances.*
Book by Laurence Schwab & DeSylva; lyrics by DeSylva; music by Lewis Gensler.
Produced by Schwab; directed by Edgar MacGregor; dances by Sammy Lee.
Cast included: Mary Lawlor, Charles Ruggles, Frank McIntyre, Clarence Nordstrom, Luella Gear, June O'Dea, Gaile Beverley, Edgar Fairchild & Ralph Rainger (duo-pianists).
Principal songs: Cross Your Heart; Gentlemen Prefer Blondes; You'll Never Know; Everything Will Happen for the Best.

PIGGY
(Title changed during run to *I Told You So*)
Opened: Jan. 11, 1927, Royale Th.
83 *performances.*
Book by Daniel Kussell & Alfred Jackson; lyrics by Brown; music by Cliff Friend.
Produced & directed by William B. Friedlander; dances by John Boyle.
Cast included: Sam Bernard, Harry McNaughton, Brooke Johns, Paul Frawley, Wanda Lyons.
Principal songs: Ding Dong Dell; I Need a Little Bit; Let's Stroll Along and Sing a Song of Love; Oh, Baby!

GOOD NEWS!
Opened: Sept. 6, 1927, 46th St. Th.
557 *performances.*
Book by Laurence Schwab & DeSylva; lyrics by DeSylva & Brown; music by Henderson.
Produced by Schwab & Frank Mandel; directed by Edgar MacGregor; dances by Bobby Connolly.
Cast included: Mary Lawlor, John Price Jones, Gus Shy, Inez Courtney, Shirley Vernon, Zelma O'Neal, George Olsen Orchestra.
Principal songs: The Best Things in Life Are Free; Good News; The Varsity Drag;

Just Imagine; Lucky in Love; He's a Ladies' Man.
Recorded Version
MGM E 3771 ST (F.V.) (1947) X.

Six songs were retained, two others added (by Roger Edens, Comden & Green) for the film version featuring June Allyson, Peter Lawford, & Joan McCracken.

MANHATTAN MARY

Opened: Sept. 26, 1927, Apollo Th.
264 performances.
Book by George White & Billy K. Wells; lyrics by DeSylva & Brown; music by Henderson.
Produced & directed by White.
Cast included: Ed Wynn, George White, Ona Munson, Lou Holtz, Harland Dixon, McCarthy Sisters, Paul Frawley, Paul Stanton, Dorothy Walters, Susan Fleming, Mae Clarke.
Principal songs: Manhattan Mary; The Five-Step; It Won't Be Long Now; I'd Like You to Love Me.

GEORGE WHITE'S SCANDALS
(9th Edition)

Opened: July 2, 1928, Apollo Th.
240 performances.
Sketches by William K. Wells & George White; lyrics by DeSylva & Brown; music by Henderson.
Produced & directed by White; dances also by Russell Markert.
Cast included: Ann Pennington, Willie & Eugene Howard, Frances Williams, Harry Richman, Tom Patricola, Rose Perfect, Elm City 4, Arnold Johnson Orchestra (incl. Harold Arlen).
Principal songs: Pickin' Cotton; What D'Ya Say?; I'm on the Crest of a Wave; A Real American Tune.

HOLD EVERYTHING!

Opened: Oct. 10, 1928, Broadhurst Th.
413 performances.
Book by DeSylva & John McGowan; lyrics by DeSylva & Brown; music by Henderson.

Produced by Alex A. Aarons & Vinton Freedley; director uncredited; dances by Sam Rose & Jack Haskell.
Cast included: Jack Whiting, Ona Munson, Bert Lahr, Betty Compton, Victor Moore, Nina Olivette, Gus Schilling.
Principal songs: Don't Hold Everything; You're the Cream in My Coffee; To Know You Is to Love You; Too Good to Be True.

THREE CHEERS

Opened: Oct. 15, 1928, Globe Th.
210 performances.
Book by Anne Caldwell & R. H. Burnside; lyrics mostly by Caldwell; music mostly by Raymond Hubbell; additional lyrics by DeSylva & Brown; additional music by Henderson.
Produced by Charles Dillingham; directed by Burnside; dances by David Bennett & Mary Read.
Cast included: Will Rogers, Dorothy Stone, Alan Edwards, Oscar Ragland, Patsy Kelly, Janet Velie, Maude Eburne, Andrew Tombes, Edward Allan.
Principal DeSylva - Brown - Henderson songs: Because You're Beautiful; Maybe This Is Love; Pompanola.

FOLLOW THRU

Opened: Jan. 9, 1929, 46th St. Th.
403 performances.
Book by Laurence Schwab & DeSylva; lyrics by DeSylva & Brown; music by Henderson.
Produced by Schwab & Frank Mandel; directed by Edgar MacGregor; dances by Bobby Connolly.
Cast included: Irene Delroy, John Barker, Zelma O'Neal, Jack Haley, John Sheehan, Madeline Cameron, Eleanor Powell.
Principal songs: Button Up Your Overcoat; I Want to Be Bad; You Wouldn't Fool Me, Would You?; My Lucky Star.

FLYING HIGH

Opened: Mar. 3, 1930, Apollo Th.
357 performances.

Book by Jack McGowan, DeSylva & Brown; lyrics by DeSylva & Brown; music by Henderson.
Produced by George White; directed by Edward Clark Lilley; dances by Bobby Connolly.
Cast included: Bert Lahr, Oscar Shaw, Grace Brinkley, Russ Brown, Kate Smith, Pearl Osgood, Dorothy Hall, Gale Quadruplets, Gus Schilling.
Principal songs: Thank Your Father; Good for You, Bad for Me; Red Hot Chicago; Without Love; Wasn't It Beautiful?

GEORGE WHITE'S SCANDALS
(11th Edition)
Opened: Sept. 14, 1931, Apollo Th.
202 performances.
Sketches by George White, Irving Caesar, Harry Conn & Brown; lyrics by Brown; music by Henderson.
Produced & directed by White.
Cast included: Rudy Vallee, Ethel Merman, Willie & Eugene Howard, Everett Marshall, Ray Bolger, Gale Quadruplets, Ethel Barrymore Colt, Loomis Sisters, Barbara Blair, Alice Faye.
Principal songs: Life Is Just a Bowl of Cherries; This Is the Missus; The Thrill Is Gone; That's Why Darkies Were Born; My Song; Ladies and Gentlemen, That's Love.

HOT-CHA!
Opened: Mar. 8, 1932, Ziegfeld Th.
119 performances.
Book by Brown & Henderson, Mark Hellinger, Hy Kraft; lyrics by Brown; music by Henderson.
Produced by Florenz Ziegfeld; directed by Edgar MacGregor & Edward Clark Lilley; dances by Bobby Connolly.
Cast included: Bert Lahr, Lupe Velez, Buddy Rogers, Marjorie White, Lynn Overman, June Knight, June MacCloy, Velez & Yolanda, Antonio & Renée DeMarco, Revva Reyes, Tito Coral, Robert Gleckler, Eleanor Powell, Miriam Battista, Iris Adrian.

Principal songs: You Can Make My Life a Bed of Roses; Conchita; There I Go Dreaming Again; It's Great to Be Alive!

TAKE A CHANCE
Opened: Nov. 26, 1932, Apollo Th.
243 performances.
Book by DeSylva & Laurence Schwab with Sid Silvers; lyrics by DeSylva; music by Richard A. Whiting & Herb Brown Nacio (Nacio Herb Brown), Vincent Youmans.

Produced by Schwab & DeSylva; directed by Edgar MacGregor; dances by Bobby Connolly.
Cast included: Jack Haley, Ethel Merman, Jack Whiting, June Knight, Sid Silvers, Robert Gleckler, Mitzi Mayfair, Oscar ("Rags") Ragland.
Principal songs: Whiting-Brown: You're an Old Smoothie; Turn Out the Light; Eadie Was a Lady; Youmans: Should I Be Sweet? Rise 'n' Shine; Oh, How I Long to Belong to You; My Lover.

STRIKE ME PINK
Opened: Mar. 4, 1933, Majestic Th.
105 performances.
Sketches by Brown & Henderson, Jack McGowan, Mack Gordon; lyrics by Brown; music by Henderson.
Produced by Brown & Henderson; directed by Brown, Henderson & McGowan; dances by Seymour Felix.
Cast included: Lupe Velez, Jimmy Durante, Hope Williams, Hal LeRoy, Roy Atwell, Eddie Garr, George Dewey Washington, Ruth Harrison & Alex Fisher, Johnny Downs, Gracie Barrie, Milton Watson, Dorothy Dare, Carolyn Nolte.
Principal songs: Strike Me Pink; It's Great to Be Alive; Love and Rhythm; Let's Call It a Day; Home to Harlem.

SAY WHEN
Opened: Nov. 8, 1934, Imperial Th.
76 performances.
Book by Jack MacGowan; lyrics by Ted Koehler; music by Henderson.
Produced by Henderson & McGowan;

469

directed by Bertram Harrison; dances by Russell Markert.

Cast included: Harry Richman, Bob Hope, Linda Watkins, Taylor Holmes, Cora Witherspoon, Dennie Moore, Nick Long, Jr., Charles Collins, Michael Romanoff.

Principal songs: When Love Comes Swinging Along; Say When; It Must Have Been the Night; Let's Take Advantage of Now.

CALLING ALL STARS

Opened: Dec. 13, 1934, Hollywood Th.
36 *performances.*
Sketches by Brown, A. Dorian Otvos, Alan Baxter; lyrics by Brown; music by Harry Akst.
Produced by Brown; directed by Brown & Thomas Mitchell; dances by Sara Mildred Strauss.
Cast included: Lou Holtz, Phil Baker, Everett Marshall, Jack Whiting, Gertrude Niesen, Patricia Bowman, Harry ("Bottle") McNaughton, Al Bernie, Mitzi Mayfair, Judy Canova, Martha Raye, Ella Logan.
Principal songs: If It's Love; Stepping Out of the Picture; Straw Hat in the Rain.

GEORGE WHITE'S SCANDALS

Opened: Dec. 25, 1935, New Amsterdam Th.
110 *performances.*
Sketches by George White, Billy K. Wells, Howard Shiebler, A. Dorian Otvos; lyrics by Jack Yellen; music by Henderson.
Produced & directed by White; dances by Russell Markert.
Cast included: Rudy Vallee, Bert Lahr, Willie & Eugene Howard, Gracie Barrie, Cliff Edwards, Jane Cooper, Hal Forde, Sam, Ted & Ray.
Principal songs: Cigarette; I've Got to Get Hot; I'm the Fellow who Loves You; Life Begins at Sweet Sixteen.

YOKEL BOY

Opened: July 6, 1939, Majestic Th.
208 *performances.*
Book by Brown; lyrics by Brown & Charles Tobias; music by Sam Stept.
Produced & directed by Brown; dances by Gene Snyder.
Cast included: Phil Silvers, Judy Canova, Buddy Ebsen, Dixie Dunbar, Ralph Riggs, Mark Plant, Lew Hearn, Lois January.
Principal songs: Comes Love; A Boy Named Lem; I Can't Afford to Dream.

ZIEGFELD FOLLIES

Opened: Apr. 14, 1943, Winter Garden
553 *performances.*
Sketches by Bud Pearson & Les White, Charles Sherman & Harry Young, Lester Lawrence, Joseph Erens; lyrics by Jack Yellen; music by Henderson.
Produced by Messrs. Shubert, Alfred Blomingdale & Lou Walters; directed by John Murray Anderson, Arthur Pierson & Fred De Cordova; dances by Robert Alton.
Cast included: Milton Berle, Ilona Massey, Arthur Treacher, Jack Cole, Sue Ryan, Nadine Gae, Tommy Wonder, Dean Murphy, Christine Ayres, The Rhythmaires, Jack McCauley, Imogen Carpenter, Jay Martin, Katherine Meskill, Bil & Cora Baird, Arthur Maxwell, Ben Yost's Vi-Kings, Penny Edwards.
Principal songs: Love Songs Are Made in the Night; Come Up and Have a Cup of Coffee; Hold that Smile.

CHAPTER TWELVE
COLE PORTER
composer-lyricist

SEE AMERICA FIRST

Opened: Mar. 28, 1916, Maxine Elliott Th.
15 *performances.*
Book by T. Lawrason Riggs; lyrics also by Riggs.

Produced by Elisabeth Marbury; directed by J. H. Benrimo; dances by Ed Hutchinson.
Cast included: Clifton Webb, Clara Palmer, Felix Adler, Jeanne Cartier, Red Eagle.
Principal songs: I've a Shooting Box in Scotland; Buy Her a Box at the Opera; Ever and Ever Yours; See America First.

HITCHY-KOO 1919
Opened: Oct. 6, 1919, Liberty Th.
56 *performances.*
Sketches by George V. Hobart.
Produced by Raymond Hitchcock; directed by Julian Alfred.
Cast included: Raymond Hitchcock, Florence O'Denishawn, Joe Cook, Lillian Kemble Cooper, Billy Holbrook.
Principal songs: When I Had a Uniform on; My Cozy Little Corner in the Ritz; Old-Fashioned Garden; I Introduced; Another Sentimental Song.

GREENWICH VILLAGE FOLLIES
(6th Edition)
Opened: Sept. 16, 1924, Shubert Th.
127 *performances.*
Sketches by John Murray Anderson.
Produced by The Bohemians, Inc.; directed by Anderson & Lew Fields; dances by Larry Ceballos.
Cast included: Dolly Sisters, Moran & Mack, Bobby Arnst, George Rasely, Georgie Hale, Robert Alton, Don Barclay, Vincent Lopez Orchestra.
Principal songs: I'm in Love Again; Two Little Babes in the Wood; Brittany; Make Every Day a Holiday.

PARIS
Opened: Oct. 8, 1928, Music Box Th.
195 *performances.*
Book by Martin Brown; music & lyrics also by Walter Kollo & E. Ray Goetz.
Produced by Gilbert Miller with Goetz; directed by W. H. Gilmore.
Cast included: Irene Bordoni, Arthur Margetson, Louise Closser Hale, Erik Kalkhurst, Irving Aaronson's Com-

manders.
Principal Porter songs: Let's Do It; Two Little Babes in the Wood; Don't Look at Me that Way.

FIFTY MILLION FRENCHMEN
Opened: Nov. 27, 1929, Lyric Th.
254 *performances.*
Book by Herbert Fields.
Produced by E. Ray Goetz; directed by Monty Woolley; dances by Larry Ceballos.
Cast included: William Gaxton, Genevieve Tobin, Helen Broderick, Jack Thompson, Betty Compton, Thurston Hall, Evelyn Hoey, Marie Valli (June Knight), Ignacio Martinetti.
Principal songs: You Do Something to Me; You've Got that Thing; Find Me a Primitive Man; You Don't Know Paree; The Tale of an Oyster; Paree, What Did You Do to Me?

WAKE UP AND DREAM!
Opened: Dec. 30, 1929, Selwyn Th.
136 *performances.*
Sketches by John Hastings Turner, Ronald Jeans, Douglas Furber; music & lyrics also by Ivor Novello & Desmond Carter, Arthur Schwartz, Donovan Parsons & Furber, Phil Charig & Joseph Meyer.
Produced by Arch Selwyn with C. B. Cochran; directed by Frank Collins; dances by Tilly Losch, Jack Buchanan, Max Rivers.
Cast included: Jack Buchanan, Jessie Matthews, Tilly Losch, Dave Fitzgibbon, Frances Shelley, William Stephens, Toni Birkmayer, Lance Lister, Marjorie Robertson (Anna Neagle).
Principal songs: I Loved Him but He Didn't Love Me; What Is This Thing Called Love?; Which?; I'm a Gigolo; Looking at You.

THE NEW YORKERS
Opened: Dec. 8, 1930, Broadway Th.
168 *performances.*
Book by Herbert Fields.

Produced by E. Ray Goetz; directed by Monty Woolley; dances by George Hale. *Cast included:* Hope Williams, Jimmy Durante, Lew Clayton, Eddie Jackson, Ann Pennington, Frances Williams, Charles King, Richard Carle, Marie Cahill, Oscar ("Rags") Ragland, Kathryn Crawford, Paul Huber, Tammany Young, Fred Waring Pennsylvanians.

Principal songs: Where Have You Been?; I'm Getting Myself Ready for You; Love for Sale; The Great Indoors; Let's Fly Away; Take Me Back to Manhattan; I Happen to Like New York.

GAY DIVORCE

Opened: Nov. 29, 1932, Ethel Barrymore Th.

248 *performances.*

Book by Dwight Taylor with Kenneth Webb & Samuel Hoffenstein.

Produced by Dwight Deere Wiman & Tom Weatherly; directed by Howard Lindsay; dances by Carl Randall & Barbara Newberry.

Cast included: Fred Astaire, Claire Luce, Luella Gear, Eric Blore, Erik Rhodes, Roland Bottomley, G. P. Huntley, Jr., Betty Starbuck.

Principal songs: After You; Night and Day; How's Your Romance?; I've Got You on My Mind; Mister and Missus Fitch.

ANYTHING GOES

Opened: Nov. 21, 1934, Alvin Th.

420 *performances.*

Book by Guy Bolton & P. G. Wodehouse, revised by Howard Lindsay & Russel Crouse.

Produced by Vinton Freedley; directed by Lindsay; dances by Robert Alton.

Cast included: William Gaxton, Ethel Merman, Victor Moore, Bettina Hall, Vivian Vance, Helen Raymond, Paul Everton, Leslie Barrie.

Principal songs: All Through the Night; I Get a Kick Out of You; You're the Top; Anything Goes; Blow, Gabriel, Blow; Be

Like the Bluebird; The Gypsy in Me.

Recorded Versions

Epic FLM 13100/ FLS 15100 (O.C.) (1962).

Decca DL 8318 (F.V.) (1955).

Columbia ML 4751 X.

Eileen Rodgers heads the spirited revival cast on Epic; Bing Crosby, Donald O'Connor, Mitzi Gaynor & Jeanmaire do 6 Porter tunes on the Decca soundtrack, plus 3 new ones by Cahn & Van Heusen; Mary Martin (plus chorus) glides through 6 songs from the show on the Columbia, backed by *Band Wagon* selections.

JUBILEE

Opened: Oct. 12, 1935, Imperial Th.

169 *performances.*

Book by Moss Hart.

Produced by Sam H. Harris & Max Gordon; directed by Hassard Short & Monty Woolley; dances by Albertina Rasch.

Cast included: Mary Boland, June Knight, Melville Cooper, Derek Williams, May Boley, Charles Walters, Margaret Adams, Mark Plant, Richie Ling, Dorothy Fox, Olive Reeves-Smith, Jackie Kelk, Montgomery Clift, Leo Chalzell, Ted Fetter, Wyn Cahoon, Adele Jergens.

Principal songs: Why Shouldn't I?; The Kling-Kling Bird on the Divi-Divi Tree; When Love Comes Your Way; Me and Marie; Just One of Those Things; A Picture of Me Without You; Begin the Beguine.

RED, HOT AND BLUE!

Opened: Oct. 29, 1936, Alvin Th.

183 *performances.*

Book by Howard Lindsay & Russel Crouse.

Produced by Vinton Freedley; directed by Howard Lindsay; dances by George Hale.

Cast included: Jimmy Durante, Ethel Merman, Bob Hope, Polly Walters, Paul & Grace Hartman, Forrest Orr, Dorothy Vernon, Thurston Crane, Vivian Vance,

Lew Parker.

Principal songs: Ours; Down in the Depths; You've Got Something; It's De-Lovely; Ridin' High; The Ozarks Are Calling Me Home; Red, Hot and Blue; You're a Bad Influence on Me; Goodbye, Little Dream, Goodbye.

YOU NEVER KNOW

Opened: Sept. 21, 1938, Winter Garden 78 *performances.*

Book by Rowland Leigh; music & lyrics also by Dana Suesse, Robert Katscher & Leigh, Alex Fogarty & Edwin Gilbert. Produced by Messrs. Shubert with John Shubert; directed by Leigh & George Abbott (uncredited); dances by Robert Alton.

Cast included: Clifton Webb, Lupe Velez, Libby Holman, Paul & Grace Hartman, Toby Wing, Rex O'Malley, June Preisser, Roger Stearns, Charles Kemper, Truman Gaige.

Principal songs: You Never Know; At Long Last Love; For No Rhyme or Reason; From Alpha to Omega; What Shall I Do? (lyric by Leigh).

LEAVE IT TO ME!

Opened: Nov. 9, 1938, Imperial Th. 291 *performances.*

Book by Bella & Samuel Spewack. Produced by Vinton Freedley; directed by Samuel Spewack; dances by Robert Alton.

Cast included: William Gaxton, Victor Moore, Sophie Tucker, Tamara, Mary Martin, Edward H. Robins, George Tobias, Gene Kelly, Adele Jergens.

Principal songs: Get Out of Town; Most Gentlemen Don't Like Love; From Now On; My Heart Belongs to Daddy.

DUBARRY WAS A LADY

Opened: Dec. 6, 1939, 46th St. Th. 408 *performances.*

Book by Herbert Fields & B. G. DeSylva. Produced by DeSylva; directed by Edgar MacGregor; dances by Robert Alton. *Cast included:* Bert Lahr, Ethel Mer-

man, Betty Grable, Charles Walters, Benny Baker, Ronald Graham, Janis Carter, Adele Jergens.

Principal songs: When Love Beckoned in Fifty-Second Street; Do I Love You?; But in the Morning, No!; Give Him the Oo-La-La; Katie Went to Haiti; Well, Did You Evah!; It Was Written in the Stars; Friendship.

PANAMA HATTIE

Opened: Oct. 30, 1940, 46th St. Th. 501 *performances.*

Book by Herbert Fields & B. G. DeSylva. Produced by DeSylva; directed by Edgar MacGregor; dances by Robert Alton. *Cast included:* Ethel Merman, Arthur Treacher, James Dunn, Rags Ragland, Pat Harrington, Frank Hyers, Phyllis Brooks, Betty Hutton, Joan Carroll, Nadine Gae, Lipman Duckat (Larry Douglas), Janis Carter, June Allyson, Jane Ball, Betsy Blair, Lucille Bremer, Vera Ellen, Doris Dowling.

Principal songs: My Mother Would Love You; I've Still Got My Health; Fresh as a Daisy; Let's Be Buddies; Make It Another Old-Fashioned, Please; Visit Panama; All I've Got to Get Now Is My Man; I'm Throwing a Ball Tonight.

LET'S FACE IT!

Opened: Oct. 29, 1941, Imperial Th. 547 *performances.*

Book by Herbert & Dorothy Fields. Produced by Vinton Freedley; directed by Edgar MacGregor; dances by Charles Walters.

Cast included: Danny Kaye, Eve Arden, Benny Baker, Mary Jane Walsh, Edith Meiser, Vivian Vance, Mary Parker & Billy Daniel, Sunnie O'Dea, Jack Williams, Nanette Fabray, Joseph Macaulay, Jane Ball, Helene Bliss, Garry Davis.

Principal songs: Let's Face It; Farming; Ev'rything I Love; Ace in the Hole; You Irritate Me So; A Little Rumba Numba; I Hate You, Darling; Let's Not Talk About Love.

SOMETHING FOR THE BOYS

Opened: Jan. 7, 1943, Alvin Th.
422 performances.
Book by Herbert & Dorothy Fields.
Produced by Michael Todd; directed by Hassard Short & Herbert Fields; dances by Jack Cole.
Cast included: Ethel Merman, Bill Johnson, Betty Garrett, Paula Laurence, Allen Jenkins, Betty Bruce, Anita Alvarez, Jed Prouty, William Lynn, Frances Mercer, Bill Callahan, Murvyn Vye, Dolores (Dody) Goodman.
Principal songs: Something for the Boys; Hey, Good Lookin'; He's a Right Guy; Could It Be You; I'm in Love with a Soldier Boy; By the Mississinewah; The Leader of a Big Time Band.

MEXICAN HAYRIDE

Opened: Jan. 28, 1944, Winter Garden
481 performances.
Book by Herbert & Dorothy Fields.
Produced by Michael Todd; directed by Hassard Short & John Kennedy; dances by Paul Haakon.
Cast included: Bobby Clark, June Havoc, George Givot, Wilbur Evans, Luba Malina, Corinna Mura, Paul Haakon, Edith Meiser, Bill Callahan, Candy Jones.
Principal songs: Sing to Me, Guitar; I Love You; There Must Be Someone for Me; Abracadabra; Girls, Girls, Girls; Carlotta; Count Your Blessings.

SEVEN LIVELY ARTS

Opened: Dec. 7, 1944, Ziegfeld Th.
183 performances.
Sketches by Moss Hart, George S. Kaufman, Robert Pirosh, Joseph Schrank, Charles Sherman, Ben Hecht; music also by Igor Stravinsky.
Produced by Billy Rose; directed by Hassard Short & Philip Loeb; dances by Jack Donohue & Anton Dolin.
Cast included: Beatrice Lillie, Bert Lahr, Benny Goodman, Alicia Markova, Anton Dolin, Doc Rockwell, Dolores Gray, Nan Wynn, Mary Roche, Albert Carroll, Dennie Moore, Jere MacMahon, Paula Bane, Bill Tabbert, Billie Worth, Red Norvo, Teddy Wilson, Helen Gallagher, Temple Texas.
Principal songs: Ev'rytime We Say Goodbye; Only Another Boy and Girl; When I Was a Little Cuckoo; Hence, It Don't Make Sense.

AROUND THE WORLD IN EIGHTY DAYS

Opened: May 31, 1946, Adelphi Th.
75 performances.
Book by Orson Welles.
Produced by Mercury Productions; directed by Welles; dances by Nelson Barclift.
Cast included: Orson Welles, Arthur Margetson, Mary Healy, Julie Warren, Larry Laurence, Victoria Cordova, Stefan Schnabel, Guy Spaull, Jack Cassidy.
Principal songs: Look What I Found; There He Goes, Mr. Phileas Fogg; Should I Tell You I Love You?; Pipe Dreaming; If You Smile at Me; Wherever They Fly the Flag of Old England.

KISS ME, KATE

Opened: Dec. 30, 1948, New Century Th.
1,077 performances.
Book by Samuel & Bella Spewack.
Produced by Saint Subber & Lemuel Ayers; directed by John C. Wilson; dances by Hanya Holm.
Cast included: Alfred Drake, Patricia Morison, Harold Lang, Lisa Kirk, Harry Clark, Jack Diamond, Denis Green, Annabelle Hill, Lorenzo Fuller, Marc Breaux, Rudy Tone.
Principal songs: Another Op'nin', Another Show; Why Can't You Behave?; Wunderbar; So in Love; We Open in Venice; Tom, Dick or Harry; I've Come to Wive It Wealthily in Padua; I Hate Men; Were Thine that Special Face; Too Darn Hot; Where Is the Life that Late I Led?; Always True to You in My Fashion; Bianca; Brush Up Your Shakespeare.
Recorded Versions

Columbia OL 4140/ OS 2300 (O.C.).
MGM E 3077 (F.V.) (1953).
RCA Victor LPM/ LSP 1984 (S.C.) X.
Capitol (S)TAO 1267 (O.C.).

Porter's masterpiece is still best served by the original cast on Columbia; Capitol's with the show's leads is almost too aggressively stereophonic. The film soundtrack features Howard Keel, Kathryn Grayson & laundered lyrics. Keel is also on the imaginatively staged RCA release with Anne Jeffreys & Gogi Grant.

OUT OF THIS WORLD

Opened: Dec. 21, 1950, New Century Th.
157 *performances.*
Book by Dwight Taylor & Reginald Lawrence.
Produced by Saint Subber & Lemuel Ayers; directed by Agnes de Mille; dances by Hanya Holm.
Cast included: Charlotte Greenwood, William Eythe, David Burns, Priscilla Gillette, William Redfield, Barbara Ashley, Janet Collins, George Jongeyans (George Gaynes), Maria Karnilova, Erik Kristen.
Principal songs: Use Your Imagination; Where, Oh Where?; I Am Loved; Climb Up the Mountain; No Lover; Cherry Pies Ought to Be You; Nobody's Chasing Me; They Couldn't Compare to You; I Sleep Easier Now.
Recorded Version
Columbia OL 4390 (O.C.).

This is a sadly unappreciated score with a rich variety of rhymes & rhythms.

CAN-CAN

Opened: May 7, 1953, Shubert Th.
892 *performances.*
Book by Abe Burrows.
Produced by Cy Feuer & Ernest H. Martin; directed by Burrows; dances by Michael Kidd.
Cast included: Lilo, Peter Cookson, Hans Conried, Gwen Verdon, Erik Rhodes, Dania Krupska, Richard Purdy, Phil Leeds, Eddie Phillips, Ralph Beaumont, DeeDee Wood.

Principal songs: Never Give Anything Away; C'est Magnifique; I Am in Love; Allez-vous-en; It's All Right with Me; I Love Paris.
Recorded Versions
Capitol W 452 (O.C.).
Capitol (S)W 1301 (F.V. (1960) X.

Far from Porter's best, the score is enlivened by some spirited performances on the original cast disc. Six songs were cut for the soundtrack, featuring Frank Sinatra, Shirley MacLaine & Maurice Chevalier, with three other Porter songs added.

SILK STOCKINGS

Opened: Feb. 24, 1955, Imperial Th.
478 *performances.*
Book by George S. Kaufman, Leueen McGrath & Abe Burrows.
Produced by Cy Feuer & Ernest H. Martin; directed by Feuer; dances by Eugene Loring.
Cast included: Hildegarde Neff, Don Ameche, Gretchen Wyler, George Tobias, Leon Belasco, Henry Lascoe, David Opatoshu, Philip Sterling, Julie Newmar, Onna White.
Principal songs: Paris Loves Lovers; It's a Chemical Reaction, That's All; All of You; Siberia; Without Love; Satin and Silk.
Recorded Versions
RCA Victor LOC/ LSO 1102 (O.C.).
MGM E 3542 ST (F.V.) (1957) X.

Two songs, "Fated to Be Mated" & "The Ritz Roll and Rock" were added to the film score, & "As on Through the Seasons We Sail" was cut. Otherwise, choice rests with your preference for the stage leads or the movie leads (Fred Astaire & Cyd Charisse's "voice," Carole Richards).

CHAPTER THIRTEEN
HOWARD DIETZ
lyricist
ARTHUR SCHWARTZ
composer

All lyrics by Mr. Dietz unless otherwise noted. For other musicals with Dietz lyrics, see Dear Sir *under Jerome Kern;* Jackpot & Sadie Thompson *under Vernon Duke.*

THE GRAND STREET FOLLIES
(4th Edition)
Opened: June 15, 1926, Neighborhood Playhouse.
55 *performances.*
Sketches & lyrics by Agnes Morgan; music also by Randall Thompson, Lily Hyland, Walter Haenschen.
Produced by the Neighborhood Playhouse; directed by Miss Morgan.
Cast included: Albert Carroll, Agnes Morgan, Dorothy Sands, Paula Trueman, Vera Allen, Jessica Dragonette, Blanche Talmud.
Principal Schwartz songs: Little Igloo for Two; Polar Bear Strut (lyric by Theodore Goodwin).

THE NEW YORKERS
Opened: Mar. 10, 1927, Edyth Totten Th.
52 *performances.*
Sketches by Jo Swerling; lyrics by Henry Myers; music also by Edgar Fairchild, Charles Schwab.
Produced by Milton Bender & Myers; directed by Bender.
Cast included: Chester Clute, Tamara Drasin (later known as Tamara), Mona Sorel, Reina Swan.
Principal Schwartz songs: A Song About Love; Floating Thru the Air.

THE LITTLE SHOW
Opened: Apr. 30, 1929, Music Box Th.
321 *performances.*
Sketches by Dietz, Fred Allen, Newman

Levy, Marya Mannes, George S. Kaufman; music & lyrics also by Henry Myers, Morris Hamilton & Grace Henry, Kay Swift & Paul James (James P. Warburg), Herman Hupfeld, Charlotte Kent, Ralph Rainger, Henry Sullivan.
Produced by William A. Brady, Jr., Dwight Deere Wiman & Tom Weatherly; directed by Wiman & Alexander Leftwich; dances by Danny Dare.
Cast included: Clifton Webb, Libby Holman, Fred Allen, Romney Brent, Bettina Hall, Helen Lynd, Portland Hoffa, John (Jack) McCauley, Peggy Conklin, Constance Cummings, Adam Carroll & Ralph Rainger (duo-pianists).
Principal Dietz songs: I Guess I'll Have to Change My Plan (Schwartz); I've Made a Habit of You (Schwartz); Hammacher-Schlemmer, I Love You (Schwartz); Moanin' Low (Rainger); Caught in the Rain (Sullivan).

THE GRAND STREET FOLLIES
(7th Edition)
Opened: May 1, 1929, Booth Th.
93 *performances.*
Sketches & most lyrics by Agnes Morgan; music & lyrics also by Max Ewing, Max & Nathaniel Lief.
Produced by Actor-Managers, Inc. & Paul Moss; directed by Miss Morgan; dances by Dave Gould.
Cast included: Albert Carroll, Paula Trueman, Dorothy Sands, James Cagney, Otto Hulett.
Principal Schwartz songs: I Need You So (Dietz); I Love You and I Like You (M. & N. Lief); What Did Della Wear? (Morgan).

THE SECOND LITTLE SHOW
Opened: Sept. 2, 1930, Royale Th.
63 *performances.*
Sketches by Norman Clark, Bert Hanlon, Marc Connelly, William B. Miles, Donald Blackwell, James J. Coghlan; music & lyrics also by Del Cleveland & Ted Fetter, Herman Hupfeld.
Produced by William A. Brady, Jr.,

Dwight Deere Wiman & Tom Weatherly; directed by Wiman & Monty Woolley; dances by Dave Gould.
Cast included: J. C. Flippen, Al Trahan, Gloria Grafton, Ruth Tester, Tashamira, Joey Ray, Arline Judge.
Principal Dietz-Schwartz songs: Lucky Seven; What a Case I've Got on You; I Like Your Face; You're the Sunrise.

PRINCESS CHARMING
Opened: Oct. 13, 1930, Imperial Th.
56 *performances.*
Book by Jack Donahue; lyrics by Arthur Swanstrom; music also by Albert Sirmay.
Produced by Bobby Connolly & Swanstrom; directed by Connolly & Edward Clark Lilley; dances by Albertina Rasch.
Cast included: Evelyn Herbert, Robert Halliday, George Grossmith, Victor Moore, Jeanne Aubert, Douglass Dumbrille, Howard St. John, Duke McHale, Paul Huber.
Principal songs: You; I'll Never Leave You; Trailing a Shooting Star.

THREE'S A CROWD
Opened: Oct. 15, 1930, Selwyn Th.
271 *performances.*
Sketches by Dietz, Groucho Marx, Laurence Schwab, Corey Ford, William B. Miles & Donald Blackwell, Fred Allen, Arthur Sheekman & Hazel Flynn; music & lyrics also by Alec Wilder & Edward Brandt, Johnny Green & Edward Heyman, Burton Lane, Phil Charig, Charles Schwab & Richard Myers.
Produced by Max Gordon; directed by Hassard Short; dances by Albertina Rasch.
Cast included: Clifton Webb, Libby Holman, Fred Allen, Tamara Geva, Earl Oxford, Portland Hoffa, Margaret Lee, California Collegians (incl. Fred MacMurray).
Principal Dietz songs: The Moment I Saw You (Schwartz); Right at the Start of It (Schwartz); Something to Remember You By (Schwartz); All the King's Horses (Brandt-Wilder); Forget All Your Books (Lane); Practising Up on You (Charig).

THE BAND WAGON
Opened: June 3, 1931, New Amsterdam Th.
260 *performances.*
Sketches by George S. Kaufman & Dietz.
Produced by Max Gordon; directed by Hassard Short; dances by Albertina Rasch.
Cast included: Fred & Adele Astaire, Frank Morgan, Helen Broderick, Tilly Losch, Philip Loeb, John Barker.
Principal songs: Dancing in the Dark; New Sun in the Sky; Hoops; I Love Louisa; High and Low; Miserable with You; Where Can He Be?; White Heat; The Beggar Waltz; Confession; Sweet Music.
Recorded Versions
"X" LVA 1001 (O.C.) X.
MGM E 3051 (F.V.) (1953) X.
Columbia ML 4751 (S.C.) X.
The "X" release, featuring the Astaires, is a repressing of the first original cast long playing record ever made. Only 3 songs from the original were retained for the MGM film version, with 7 other Dietz-Schwartz numbers added. Fred Astaire, Jack Buchanan & Nanette Fabray are heard. The Columbia LP, backed by selections from *Anything Goes*, offers Mary Martin & chorus doing 8 songs from the show.

FLYING COLORS
Opened: Sept. 15, 1932, Imperial Th.
188 *performances.*
Sketches by Dietz.
Produced by Max Gordon; directed by Dietz; dances by Albertina Rasch.
Cast included: Clifton Webb, Tamara Geva, Charles Butterworth, Buddy & Vilma Ebsen, Patsy Kelly, Larry Adler, Philip Loeb, Imogene Coca.
Principal songs: Two-Faced Woman; A Rainy Day; Mother Told Me So; A Shine

on Your Shoes; Alone Together; Louisiana Hayride; Fatal Fascination.

REVENGE WITH MUSIC

Opened: Nov. 28, 1934, New Amsterdam Th.

158 *performances.*

Book by Dietz.

Produced by Arch Selwyn & Harold Franklin; directed by (Theodore) Komisarjevsky, Dietz (uncredited), Worthington Miner (uncredited), Marc Connelly (uncredited); dances by Michael Mordkin.

Cast included: Libby Holman, Charles Winninger, Georges Metaxa, Ilka Chase, Ivy Scott, Rex O'Mally, Joseph Macaulay.

Principal songs: You and the Night and the Music; If There Is Someone Lovelier than You; That Fellow Manuelo; When You Love Only One; Maria; Wand'ring Heart.

AT HOME ABROAD

Opened: Sept. 19, 1935, Winter Garden

198 *performances.*

Sketches by Dietz, Dion Titheridge, Raymond Knight, Marc Connelly.

Produced by Messrs. Shubert; directed by Vincente Minnelli & Thomas Mitchell; dances by Gene Snyder & Harry Losee.

Cast included: Beatrice Lillie, Ethel Waters, Herb Williams, Eleanor Powell, Reginald Gardiner, Eddie Foy, Jr., Paul Haakon, James MacColl, Vera Allen, André Charise.

Principal songs: That's Not Cricket; Hottentot Potentate; Paree; Farewell, My Lovely; Thief in the Night; Love Is a Dancing Thing; What a Wonderful World; Loadin' Time; Get Yourself a Geisha; Got a Bran' New Suit.

VIRGINIA

Opened: Sept. 2, 1937, Center Th.

60 *performances.*

Book by Laurence Stallings & Owen Davis; lyrics by Albert Stillman.

Produced by the Center Th.; directed by Leon Leonidoff & Edward Clark Lilley; dances by Florence Rogge.

Cast included: Gene Lockhart, Ronald Graham, Anne Booth, Mona Barrie, Ford Buck & John Bubbles, Dennis Hoey, Avis Andrews, Nigel Bruce, Patricia Bowman, Nora Kaye, Bertha Belmore, Lansing Hatfield.

Principal songs: Goodbye, Jonah; If You Were Someone Else; An Old Flame Never Dies (Stillman-Stallings); You and I Know (Stillman-Stallings); My Heart Is Dancing.

BETWEEN THE DEVIL

Opened: Dec. 22, 1937, Imperial Th.

93 *performances.*

Book by Dietz.

Produced by Messrs. Shubert; directed by Hassard Short & John Hayden; dances by Robert Alton.

Cast included: Jack Buchanan, Evelyn Laye, Adele Dixon, Vilma Ebsen, Charles Walters, Eric Brotherson, Tune Twisters.

Principal songs: I See Your Face Before Me; Triplets; By Myself; I'm Against Rhythm; You Have Everything.

STARS IN YOUR EYES

Opened: Feb. 9, 1939, Majestic Th.

127 *performances.*

Book by J. P. McEvoy; lyrics by Dorothy Fields.

Produced by Dwight Deere Wiman; directed by Joshua Logan; dances by Carl Randall.

Cast included: Ethel Merman, Jimmy Durante, Tamara Toumanova, Richard Carlson, Mildred Natwick, Dan Dailey, Jr., Robert Shanley, Roger Stearns, Nancy Wiman, Clinton Sundberg, Mary Wickes, Walter Cassel, Nora Kaye, Alicia Alonzo, Jerome Robbins.

Principal songs: This Is It; A Lady Needs a Change; Terribly Attractive; Just a Little Bit More; I'll Pay the Check; It's All Yours.

PARK AVENUE

Opened: Nov. 4, 1946, Shubert Th.
72 performances.
Book by Nunnally Johnson & George S. Kaufman; lyrics by Ira Gershwin.
Produced by Max Gordon; directed by Kaufman; dances by Helen Tamiris.
Cast included: Leonora Corbett, Arthur Margetson, Ray McDonald, Martha Stewart, Robert Chisholm, Marthe Errolle, Charles Purcell, Ruth Matteson, Raymond Walburn, Mary Wickes, David Wayne, Kyle McDonnell.
Principal songs: Don't Be a Woman If You Can; Land of Opportunitee; Sweet Nevada; For the Life of Me; There's No Holding Me; Goodbye to All That.

INSIDE U.S.A.

Opened: Apr. 30, 1948, New Century Th.
399 performances.
Sketches by Arnold Auerbach, Moss Hart, Arnold Horwitt.
Produced by Schwartz; directed by Robert H. Gordon; dances by Helen Tamiris.
Cast included: Beatrice Lillie, Jack Haley, John Tyers, Herb Shriner, Valerie Bettis, Eric Victor, Lewis Nye, Carl Reiner, Thelma Carpenter, Estelle Loring, Beverly Bozeman, J. C. McCord, Rod Alexander, Boris Runanin, Jack Cassidy, Tally Beatty.
Principal songs: Inside U.S.A.; Blue Grass; Rhode Island Is Famous for You; Haunted Heart; My Gal Is Mine Once More; At the Mardi Gras; First Prize at the Fair.

A TREE GROWS IN BROOKLYN

Opened: Apr. 19, 1951, Alvin Th.
270 performances.
Book by Betty Smith & George Abbott; lyrics by Dorothy Fields.
Produced by Abbott & Robert Fryer; directed by Abbott; dances by Herbert Ross.
Cast included: Shirley Booth, Johnny Johnston, Marcia Van Dyke, Nomi Mitty, Lou Wills, Jr., Nathaniel Frey, Harland Dixon, Jordan Bentley, James McCracken, Donn Driver.
Principal songs: Mine Till Monday; Make the Man Love Me; I'm Like a New Broom; Look Who's Dancing; Love Is the Reason; If You Haven't Got a Sweetheart; I'll Buy You a Star; Growing Pains.
Recorded Version
Columbia OL 4405 (O.C.).
   An inspired collection of songs.

BY THE BEAUTIFUL SEA

Opened: Apr. 8, 1954, Majestic Th.
270 performances.
Book by Herbert & Dorothy Fields; lyrics by Miss Fields.
Produced by Robert Fryer & Lawrence Carr; directed by Marshall Jamison; dances by Helen Tamiris.
Cast included: Shirley Booth, Wilbur Evans, Mae Barnes, Cameron Prud'homme, Richard France, Warde Donovan, Lola Fisher, Cathryn Damon, Libi Staiger, Larry Laurence, Reid Shelton.
Principal songs: Alone Too Long; Happy Habit; I'd Rather Wake Up by Myself; Hooray for George the Third; Hang Up!; More Love than Your Love.
Recorded Version
Capitol S 531 (O.C.) X.
   Another period piece for Shirley Booth, but the score has less appeal than that of *A Tree Grows in Brooklyn*.

THE GAY LIFE

Opened: Nov. 18, 1961, Shubert Th.
114 performances.
Book by Fay & Michael Kanin.
Produced by Kermit Bloomgarden; directed by Gerald Freedman; dances by Herbert Ross.
Cast included: Walter Chiari, Barbara Cook, Jules Munshin, Loring Smith, Elizabeth Allen, Jeanne Bal, Yvonne Constant, Leonard Elliott, Lu Leonard.
Principal songs: Why Go Anywhere at All?; Magic Moment; Who Can? You Can!; Oh, Mein Liebchen; Something

You Never Had Before; Come A-Wandering With Me; You're Not the Type.
Recorded Version
Capitol (S)WAO 1560 (O.C.) X.

A gay and lilting collection of songs that deserves to be better known.

JENNIE

Opened: Oct. 17, 1963, Majestic Th.
82 *performances.*
Book by Arnold Schulman.
Produced by Cheryl Crawford & Richard Halliday; directed by Vincent J. Donehue; dances by Carol Haney & Matt Mattox.
Cast included: Mary Martin, George Wallace, Robin Bailey, Ethel Shutta, Jack DeLon, Imelda DeMartin.
Principal songs: Waitin' for the Evening Train; When You're Far Away from New York Town; I Still Look at You that Way; Before I Kiss the World Goodbye; Where You Are.
Recorded Version
RCA Victor LOC/LSO 1083 (O.C.).

Not off the top shelf.

DOROTHY FIELDS
lyricist

For other musicals with books co-authored by Miss Fields, see Let's Face It!, Something for the Boys, Mexican Hayride *under Cole Porter;* Annie Get Your Gun *under Irving Berlin.*

BLACKBIRDS OF 1928

Opened: May 9, 1928, Liberty Th.
518 *performances.*
Sketches uncredited; music by Jimmy McHugh.
Produced & directed by Lew Leslie.
Cast included: Adelaide Hall, Bill Robinson, Aida Ward, Tim Moore, Elisabeth Welch, Mantan Moreland, Lois Deppe, Cecil Mack Choir.
Principal songs: Diga Diga Doo; Doin' the New Low-Down; I Can't Give You

Anything but Love; I Must Have that Man; Porgy.
Recorded Version
Columbia OL 6770 (O.C.).

Original cast stars Bill Robinson & Adelaide Hall are joined by Ethel Waters, the Mills Brothers, & the orchestras of Duke Ellington, Cab Calloway & Don Redman. An indispensable reissue.

HELLO, DADDY

Opened: Dec. 26, 1928, Mansfield Th.
198 *performances.*
Book by Herbert Fields; music by Jimmy McHugh.
Produced by Lew Fields; directed by John Murray Anderson & Alexander Leftwich; dances by Busby Berkeley & Buddy Bradley.
Cast included: Lew Fields, Betty Starbuck, Allen Kearns, Mary Lawlor, George Hassell, Wilfred Clark.
Principal songs: As Long as We're in Love; Futuristic Rhythm; Let's Sit and Talk About You.

INTERNATIONAL REVUE

Opened: Feb. 25, 1930, Majestic Th.
95 *performances.*
Sketches by Nat Dorfman, Lew Leslie; music by Jimmy McHugh.
Produced by Leslie; directed by Leslie & Edward Clark Lilley; dances by Busby Berkeley & Harry Crosley.
Cast included: Gertrude Lawrence, Harry Richman, Jack Pearl, Argentinita, Anton Dolin, Moss & Fontana, Florence Moore.
Principal songs: Exactly Like You; On The Sunny Side of the Street; I'm Feelin' Blue.

THE VANDERBILT REVUE

Opened: Nov. 5, 1930, Vanderbilt Th.
13 *performances.*
Sketches by Kenyon Nicholson, Ellis Jones, Sig Herzig, Edwin Gilbert & Arthur Burns, James Coghlan; Fields music by Jimmy McHugh; music & lyrics also by Jacques Fray & Edward Eliscu,

Mario Braggiotti & E. Y. Harburg, Cole Porter, Ned Washington, Michael Cleary & Herb Magidson.

Produced by Lew Fields & Lyle D. Andrews; directed by Fields & Theodore Hammerstein; dances by John Lonergan & Jack Haskell.

Cast included: Lulu McConnell, Joe Penner, Evelyn Hoey, Richard Lane, Fray & Braggiotti, Franker Woods, Francesca Braggiotti, Gus Schilling, Olga Markoff, Dorothy Dixon, Teddy Walters.

Principal Fields-McHugh songs: Blue Again; Button Up Your Heart.

STARS IN YOUR EYES
(*See* Arthur Schwartz)

UP IN CENTRAL PARK
(*See* Sigmund Romberg)

ARMS AND THE GIRL
Opened: Feb. 2, 1950, 46th St. Th.
134 performances.
Book with Herbert Fields; music by Morton Gould.

Produced by The Theatre Guild & Anthony Brady Farrell; directed by Rouben Mamoulian; dances by Michael Kidd.

Cast included: Nanette Fabray, Georges Guetary, Pearl Bailey, John Conte, Florenz Ames, Seth Arnold, Onna White, Peter Gennaro.

Principal songs: That's What I Told Him Last Night; A Cow and a Plow and a Frau; Nothin' for Nothin'; There Must Be Something Better than Love; You Kissed Me.

A TREE GROWS IN BROOKLYN
(*See* Arthur Schwartz).

BY THE BEAUTIFUL SEA
(*See* Arthur Schwartz).

REDHEAD
Opened: Feb. 5, 1959, 46th St. Th.
452 performances.
Book with Herbert Fields, Sidney Shel-

don, David Shaw; music by Albert Hague.

Produced by Robert Fryer & Lawrence Carr; directed by Bob Fosse.

Cast included: Gwen Verdon, Richard Kiley, Leonard Stone, Doris Rich, Cynthia Latham, William LeMassena, Buzz Miller.

Principal songs: Just for Once; Merely Marvelous; The Uncle Sam Rag; 'Erbie Fitch's Twitch; My Girl Is Just Enough Woman for Me; Look Who's in Love; The Right Finger of My Left Hand.

Recorded Version
RCA Victor LOC/LSO 1104 (O.C.).

A worthy addition to anyone's original cast LP library.

SWEET CHARITY
(*See* Cy Coleman).

CHAPTER FOURTEEN
VERNON DUKE
composer

THE GARRICK GAIETIES
Opened: June 4, 1930, Guild Th.
170 performances (for 2 editions).
Sketches by Carroll Carroll, Sally Humason, Benjamin M. Kaye, Newman Levy, Gretchen Damrosch Finletter, Leo Poldine, Landon Herrick, Louis M. Simon & Sterling Holloway; Duke lyrics by E. Y. Harburg, Ira Gershwin, Newman Levy; music & lyrics also by Richard Myers & Edward Eliscu, Charles M. Schwab & Henry Myers, Ned Lehak & Allen Boretz; Willard Robison, Thomas McKnight, Kay Swift & Paul James (James P. Warburg), Marc Blitzstein, Everett Miller & John Mercer, Peter Nolan & Josiah Titzell, Harold Goldman.

Produced by The Theatre Guild; directed by Philip Loeb; dances by Olin Howard.

Cast included: Albert Carroll, Edith Meiser, Philip Loeb, Sterling Holloway,

Nan Blackstone, Ruth Chorpenning, Hildegarde Halliday, William Tannen, Roger Stearns, James Norris, Imogene Coca, Ray Heatherton, Ted Fetter, Otto Hulett. (For 2nd edition, which opened Oct. 16, 1930, following added: Rosalind Russell, Katherine Carrington, Donald Burr, Edgar Stehli.)
Principal Duke-Harburg songs: I Am Only Human After All (lyric with Ira Gershwin); Too Too Divine.

WALK A LITTLE FASTER

Opened: Dec. 7, 1932, St. James Th.
119 *performances.*
Sketches by S. J. Perelman, Robert Mac-Gunigle; lyrics by E. Y. Harburg.
Produced by Courtney Burr; directed by Monty Woolley; dances by Albertina Rasch.
Cast included: Beatrice Lillie, Bobby Clark & Paul McCullough, Dave & Dorothy Fitzgibbon, Evelyn Hoey, Donald Burr, John Hundley, Edgar Fairchild & Ralph Rainger (duo-pianists).
Principal songs: That's Life; April in Paris; So Nonchalant; Speaking of Love; Where Have We Met Before?; A Penny for Your Thoughts.

ZIEGFELD FOLLIES

Opened: Jan. 4, 1934, Winter Garden
182 *performances.*
Sketches by H. I. Phillips, David Freedman, David Turgend, Fred Allen; Duke lyrics by E. Y. Harburg; music & lyrics also by Peter DeRose & Billy Hill, Joe Meyer, Billy Rose & Ballard Macdonald, Dana Suesse, Richard Myers, Sam Pokrass.
Produced by Mrs. Florenz Ziegfeld (Billie Burke); directed by Bobby Connolly & Edward Clark Lilley; dances by Robert Alton.
Cast included: Fannie Brice, Willie & Eugene Howard, Jane Froman, Everett Marshall, Vilma & Buddy Ebsen, Eve Arden, Cherry & June Preisser, Patricia Bowman, Victor Morley, Vivian Janis, Don Ross, Oliver Wakefield.

Principal Duke-Harburg songs: Water Under the Bridge; I Like the Likes of You; Suddenly; What Is There to Say?

ZIEGFELD FOLLIES

Opened: Jan. 30, 1936, Winter Garden
115 *performances.*
Reopened: Sept. 14, 1936, Winter Garden.
112 *performances.*
Sketches by David Freedman; lyrics by Ira Gershwin.
Produced by Lee Shubert; directed by John Murray Anderson & Edward Clark Lilley; dances by Robert Alton & George Balanchine.
Cast included: Fannie Brice, Josephine Baker, Bob Hope, Gertrude Niesen, Hugh O'Connell, Harriet Hoctor, Eve Arden, Judy Canova, Cherry & June Preisser, John Hoysradt (John Hoyt), Nicholas Brothers, Duke McHale, Stan Kavanaugh, Ben Yost Varsity 8.
Reopened cast included: Fannie Brice, Bobby Clark, Jane Pickens, Ruth Harrison & Alex Fisher, Cherry & June Preisser, Stan Kavanaugh, Gypsy Rose Lee, Cass Daley, Hugh Cameron, Ben Yost Varsity 8.
Principal songs: Island in the West Indies; Words Without Music; That Moment of Moments; I Can't Get Started.

THE SHOW IS ON

Opened: Dec. 25, 1936, Winter Garden
237 *performances.*
Sketches by David Freedman, Moss Hart; Duke lyrics by Ted Fetter; music & lyrics also by Hoagy Carmichael & Stanley Adams, Arthur Schwartz & Howard Dietz, George & Ira Gershwin, Harold Arlen & E. Y. Harburg, Herman Hupfeld, Will Irwin & Norman Zeno, Richard Rodgers & Lorenz Hart.
Produced by Messrs. Shubert; directed by Vincente Minnelli & Edward Clark Lilley; dances by Harry Losee.
Cast included: Beatrice Lillie, Bert Lahr, Reginald Gardiner, Mitzi Mayfair, Paul Haakon, Gracie Barrie, Charles Walters,

Vera Allen, Robert Shafer, Jack Mc-Cauley, Evelyn Thawl, Ralph Riggs.
Principal Duke-Fetter songs: Now; Casanova.

CABIN IN THE SKY

Opened: Oct. 25, 1940, Martin Beck Th.
156 *performances.*
Book by Lynn Root; lyrics by John Latouche.
Produced by Albert Lewis & Vinton Freedley; directed by George Balanchine & Lewis.
Cast included: Ethel Waters, Todd Duncan, Dooley Wilson, Rex Ingram, Katherine Dunham, J. Rosamond Johnson, Helen Dowdy, Talley Beatty.
Principal songs: Taking a Chance on Love (lyric with Ted Fetter); Cabin in the Sky; Do What You Wanna Do; In My Old Virginia Home (on the River Nile); Love Turned the Light Out; Honey in the Honeycomb.
Recorded Version
Capitol (S)W 2073 (O.C.) (1964) X.
Four songs not part of the original Broadway score were added for the 1964 off-Broadway revival. Rosetta LeNoire and Ketty Lester headed the cast.

BANJO EYES

Opened: Dec. 25, 1941, Hollywood Th.
126 *performances.*
Book by Joe Quillan & Izzy Elinson; lyrics by John Latouche, additional lyrics by Harold Adamson.
Produced by Albert Lewis; directed by Hassard Short & Lewis; dances by Charles Walters.
Cast included: Eddie Cantor, Tony & Sally DeMarco, Lionel Stander, Audrey Christie, June Clyde, Ray Mayer, Morton & Virginia Mayo, Bill Johnson, Richard Rober, Jacqueline Susann, Adele Jergens, Shirl Thomas (Shirl Conway), Doris Dowling, Tommy Wonder.
Principal songs: A Nickel to My Name; Not a Care in the World; I'll Take the City; We're Having a Baby (Adamson).

THE LADY COMES ACROSS

Opened: Jan. 9, 1942, 44th St. Th.
3 *performances.*
Book by Fred Thompson & Dawn Powell; lyrics by John Latouche.
Produced by George Hale; directed by Romney Brent; dances by George Balanchine.
Cast included: Evelyn Wyckoff, Joe E. Lewis, Ronald Graham, Stiano Braggiotti, Gower Champion & Jeanne Tyler, Mischa Auer, Ruth Weston, Wynn Murray, Marc Platt, Morton L. Stevens, Hugh Martin, Ralph Blane, Lubov Rostova.
Principal songs: Summer Is A-Comin' In; You Took Me by Surprise; This Is Where I Came In.

JACKPOT

Opened: Jan. 13, 1944, Alvin Th.
69 *performances.*
Book by Guy Bolton, Sidney Sheldon, Ben Roberts; lyrics by Howard Dietz.
Produced by Vinton Freedley; directed by Roy Hargrave; dances by Lauretta Jefferson & Charles Weidman.
Cast included: Nanette Fabray, Allan Jones, Betty Garrett, Jerry Lester, Benny Baker, Mary Wickes, Wendell Corey, Billie Worth, Morton L. Stevens, Jacqueline Susann.
Principal songs: What Happened?; Sugarfoot; I've Got a One-Track Mind; There Are Yanks (from the Banks of the Wabash).

SADIE THOMPSON

Opened: Nov. 16, 1944, Alvin Th.
60 *performances.*
Book by Howard Dietz & Rouben Mamoulian; lyrics by Dietz.
Produced by A. P. Waxman; directed by Mamoulian; dances by Edward Caton.
Cast included: June Havoc, Lansing Hatfield, Ralph Dumke, Beatrice Kraft, Doris Patston, Milada Mladova.
Principal songs: The Love I Long For;

Poor as a Church Mouse; When You Live on an Island.

TWO'S COMPANY

Opened: Dec. 15, 1952, Alvin Th.
90 *performances.*
Sketches mostly by Charles Sherman & Peter DeVries; lyrics by Ogden Nash, additional lyrics by Sammy Cahn.
Produced by James Russo & Michael Ellis; directed by John Murray Anderson & Jules Dassin; dances by Jerome Robbins.
Cast included: Bette Davis, Hiram Sherman, David Burns, Nora Kaye, Ellen Hanley, Oliver Wakefield, Bill Callahan, Stanley Prager, George S. Irving, Maria Karnilova, Buzz Miller, Peter Kelley, Tina Louise, Ralph Linn.
Principal songs: It Just Occurred to Me (Cahn); Roundabout; Out of the Clear Blue Sky; Haunted Hot Spot; Just Like a Man.
Recorded Version
RCA Victor LOC 1009 (O.C.) X.
Bette Davis' foghorn tends to obscure the attractiveness of the words and music.

THE LITTLEST REVUE

Opened: May 22, 1956, Phoenix Th.
32 *performances.*
Sketches by Nat Hiken & Billy Friedberg, Mike Stewart, Bud McCreery, George Baxt, Allan Manings & Bob Van Scoyk, Eudora Welty; Duke lyrics by Ogden Nash; music & lyrics also by John Strauss, John Latouche & Kenward Elmslie, Sheldon Harnick, Charles Strouse & Lee Adams, Sol Berkowitz, Michael Brown.
Produced by T. Edward Hambleton & Norris Houghton with Ben Bagley; directed by Paul Lammers; dances by Charles Weidman.
Cast included: Joel Grey, Tammy Grimes, Charlotte Rae, Larry Storch, Beverly Bozeman, Dorothy Jarnac.
Principal Duke-Nash songs: Madly in Love; I Want to Fly Now and Pay Later; You're Far from Wonderful; Love Is Still in Town; Good Little Girls (lyric by Sammy Cahn); Summer Is A-Comin' In (lyric by Latouche).
Recorded Version
Epic LN 3275 (O.C.) X.
An especially bright, inventive revue score.

HAROLD ARLEN
composer

EARL CARROLL VANITIES
(8th Edition)

Opened: July 1, 1930, New Amsterdam Th.
215 *performances.*
Sketches by Eddie Welch & Eugene Conrad; Arlen lyrics by Ted Koehler; music & lyrics also by Jay Gorney & E. Y. Harburg.
Produced by Carroll; directed by Carroll & Priestley Morrison; dances by LeRoy Prinz.
Cast included: Jimmy Savo, Jack Benny, Herb Williams, Harry Stockwell, Patsy Kelly, John Hale, Thelma White, Colette Sisters, Faith Bacon.
Principal Arlen-Koehler songs: Out of a Clear Blue Sky; Hittin' the Bottle; The March of Time.

YOU SAID IT

Opened: Jan. 19, 1931, 46th St. Th.
192 *performances.*
Book by Jack Yellen & Sid Silvers; lyrics by Yellen.
Produced by Yellen & Lou Holtz; directed by John Harwood; dances by Danny Dare.
Cast included: Lou Holtz, Mary Lawlor, Stanley Smith, Lyda Roberti, Benny Baker.
Principal songs: Sweet and Hot; You Said It; Learn to Croon; If He Really Loves Me; While You Are Young; It's Different With Me.

LIFE BEGINS AT 8:40

Opened: Aug. 27, 1934, Winter Garden
237 *performances.*
Sketches by David Freedman, H. I. Phillips, Alan Baxter, Henry Clapp Smith, Ira Gershwin & E. Y. Harburg, Frank Gabrielson; lyrics by Gershwin & Harburg.
Produced by Messrs. Shubert; directed by John Murray Anderson & Philip Loeb; dances by Robert Alton & Charles Weidman.
Cast included: Bert Lahr, Ray Bolger, Luella Gear, Frances Williams, Dixie Dunbar, Earl Oxford, Brian Donlevy, Robert Wildhack, Josephine Houston, James MacColl.
Principal songs: Shoein' the Mare; You're a Builder-Upper; Things; Fun to Be Fooled; What Can You Say in a Love Song?; Let's Take a Walk Around the Block; I Couldn't Hold My Man.

HOORAY FOR WHAT!

Opened: Dec. 1, 1937, Winter Garden
200 *performances.*
Book by Howard Lindsay & Russel Crouse; lyrics by E. Y. Harburg.
Produced by Messrs. Shubert; directed by Vincente Minnelli & Lindsay; dances by Robert Alton & Agnes de Mille.
Cast included: Ed Wynn, Jack Whiting, June Clyde, Vivian Vance, Paul Haakon, Leo Chalzel, Ruthanna Boris, Meg Mundy.
Principal songs: I've Gone Romantic on You; God's Country; Moanin' in the Mornin'; Down with Love; In the Shade of the New Apple Tree.

BLOOMER GIRL

Opened: Oct. 5, 1944, Shubert Th.
654 *performances.*
Book by Sig Herzig & Fred Saidy; lyrics by E. Y. Harburg.
Produced by John C. Wilson with Nat Goldstone; directed by E. Y. Harburg & William Schorr; dances by Agnes de Mille.
Cast included: Celeste Holm, David Brooks, Dooley Wilson, Joan McCracken, Mabel Taliaferro, Richard Huey, Toni Hart, Matt Briggs, Joe E. Marks, Margaret Douglass.
Principal songs: When the Boys Come Home; The Eagle and Me; Right as the Rain; Sunday in Cicero Falls; Evelina; It was Good Enough for Grandma; The Rakish Young Man with the Whiskers; I Got a Song; T'morra, T'morra.
Recorded Version
Decca DL (7)9126 (O.C.).
   The Civil War, slavery and women's rights are all dealt with in this attractive period score.

ST. LOUIS WOMAN

Opened: Mar. 30, 1946, Martin Beck Th.
113 *performances.*
Book by Arna Bontemps & Countee Cullen; lyrics by Johnny Mercer.
Produced by Edward Gross; directed by Rouben Mamoulian; dances by Charles Walters.
Cast included: Harold & Fayard Nicholas, Pearl Bailey, Rex Ingram, Ruby Hill, June Hawkins, Juanita Hall, Lorenzo Fuller, Herbert Coleman.
Principal songs: Come Rain or Come Shine; Legalize My Name; Any Place I Hang My Hat Is Home; Cakewalk Your Lady; Sleep Peaceful, Mr. Used-to-Be; Leavin' Time; A Woman's Prerogative; I Had Myself a True Love; Ridin' on the Moon.
Recorded Version
Capitol DW 2742 (O.C.).
   A recognized classic in the field.

HOUSE OF FLOWERS

Opened: Dec. 30, 1954, Alvin Th.
165 *performances.*
Book by Truman Capote; lyrics by Capote & Arlen.
Produced by Saint Subber; directed by Peter Brook; dances by Herbert Ross.
Cast included: Pearl Bailey, Diahann Carroll, Juanita Hall, Ray Walston, Dino DiLuca, Rawn Spearman, Geoffrey Holder, Ada Moore, Enid Mosier, Dolores

Harper, Frederick O'Neal, Don Redman, Carmen DeLavallade.
Principal songs: A Sleepin' Bee; Bamboo Cage; Two Ladies in de Shade of de Banana Tree; I'm Gonna Leave Off Wearin' My Shoes; Has I Let You Down?; I Never Has Seen Snow; House of Flowers.
Recorded Versions
Columbia OL 4969/OS 2320 (O.C.).
United Artists 5180 (O.C.) (1968).
Possibly Arlen's supreme achievement for the theatre. The U.A. album of the 1968 version is worth getting just to hear Josephine Premice sing "Somethin' Cold to Drink."

JAMAICA

Opened: Oct. 31, 1957, Imperial Th.
558 performances.
Book by E. Y. Harburg & Fred Saidy; lyrics by Harburg.
Produced by David Merrick; directed by Robert Lewis; dances by Jack Cole.
Cast included: Lena Horne, Ricardo Montalban, Josephine Premice, Adelaide Hall, Joe Adams, Ossie Davis, Erik Rhodes, Augustine Rios, Ethel Ayler, Hugh Bryant.
Principal songs: Savannah; Pretty to Walk With; Push de Button; Cocoanut Sweet; Pity the Sunset; Take It Slow, Joe; Ain't It de Truth?; Leave the Atom Alone; Napoleon; I Don't Think I'll End It All Today; Little Biscuit.
Recorded Version
RCA Victor LOC/LSO 1103 (O.C.).
Arlen's melodic & rhythmic gifts are amply displayed here.

SARATOGA

Opened: Dec. 7, 1959, Winter Garden
80 performances.
Book by Morton DaCosta; lyrics by Johnny Mercer.
Produced by Robert Fryer; directed by DaCosta; dances by Ralph Beaumont.
Cast included: Howard Keel, Carol Lawrence, Odette Myrtil, Edith King, Warde Donovan, Carol Brice, Tun Tun, Tru-

man Gaige, Augie Rios.
Principal songs: Petticoat High; A Game of Poker; Love Held Lightly; You or No One; The Man in My Life; Saratoga; Why Fight This? (music & lyric by Mercer).
Recorded Version
RCA Victor LOC/LSO 1051 (O.C.) X.
Though not a major work, the score ably captures the florid atmosphere of the story.

BURTON LANE
composer

EARL CARROLL VANITIES
(9th Edition)

Opened: Aug. 27, 1931, Earl Carroll Th.
278 performances.
Sketches by Ralph Spence & Eddie Welch; Lane lyrics by Harold Adamson; music & lyrics also by Cliff Friend, Ray Klages, Jack Meskill & Vincent Rose, Charlotte Kent, Max & Nathaniel Lief & Michael Cleary.
Produced by Earl Carroll; directed by Edgar MacGregor; dances by George Hale & Gluck Sandor.
Cast included: Will Mahoney, Lillian Roth, Mitchell & Durant, William Demarest, Milton Watson, Helen Lynd, Lucille Page, Slate Brothers.
Principal Lane-Adamson songs: Have a Heart; Heigh-Ho, the Gang's All Here.

HOLD ON TO YOUR HATS

Opened: Sept. 11, 1940, Shubert Th.
158 performances.
Book by Guy Bolton, Matt Brooks, Eddie Davis; lyrics by E. Y. Harburg.
Produced by Al Jolson & George Hale; directed by Edgar MacGregor; dances by Catherine Littlefield.
Cast included: Al Jolson, Martha Raye, Jack Whiting, Bert Gordon, Arnold Moss, Gil Lamb, Joseph Vitale, Russ Brown, Jinx Falkenburg, Eunice Healey, Margaret Irving, Joanne Marshall (Jo-

anne Dru), Constance Dowling, Joyce Matthews.

Principal songs: The World Is in My Arms; Would You Be So Kindly?; Don't Let It Get You Down; There's a Great Day Coming Manana.

LAFFING ROOM ONLY

Opened: Dec. 23, 1944, Winter Garden

233 *performances.*

Sketches by Ole Olsen & Chic Johnson, Eugene Conrad; lyrics by Lane.

Produced by Messrs. Shubert & Olsen & Johnson; directed by John Murray Anderson & Edward Cline; dances by Robert Alton.

Cast included: Olsen & Johnson, Betty Garrett, Frank Libuse, Mata & Hari, J. C. McCord, Lou Wills, Jr., William Archibald, Willie West & McGinty; Fred Waring Glee Club, Kathryn Lee.

Principal songs: Feudin' and Fightin' (lyric with Al Dubin); This Is as Far as I Go.

FINIAN'S RAINBOW

Opened: Jan. 10, 1947, 46th St. Th.

725 *performances.*

Book by E. Y. Harburg & Fred Saidy; lyrics by Harburg.

Produced by Lee Sabinson & William R. Katzell; directed by Bretaigne Windust; dances by Michael Kidd.

Cast included: Ella Logan, Albert Sharpe, Donald Richards, David Wayne, Anita Alvarez, Robert Pitkin, Lorenzo Fuller, J. C. McCord, Lyn Murray Singers.

Principal songs: This Time of the Year; How Are Things in Glocca Morra?; If This Isn't Love; Look to the Rainbow; Old Devil Moon; Something Sort of Grandish; Necessity; When the Idle Poor Become the Idle Rich; When I'm Not Near the Girl I Love; That Great Come-and-Get-It Day.

Recorded Versions

Columbia OL 4062/OS 2080 (O.C.).

RCA Victor LOC/LSO 1057 (O.C.) (1960).

One of Broadway's memorable scores has been well served on both original cast LPs. In addition to better sound, the RCA release offers Jeannie Carson, Howard Morris and Biff McGuire.

ON A CLEAR DAY YOU CAN SEE FOREVER

Opened: Oct. 17, 1965, Mark Hellinger Th.

280 *performances.*

Book & lyrics by Alan Jay Lerner.

Produced by Lerner; directed by Robert Lewis; dances by Herbert Ross.

Cast included: Barbara Harris, John Cullum, Titos Vandis, William Daniels, Clifford David, Rae Allen, Michael Lewis, Gerry Matthews, Byron Webster.

Principal songs: On a Clear Day (You Can See Forever); On the S. S. Bernard Cohn; She Wasn't You; Melinda; What Did I Have that I Don't Have; Come Back to Me.

Recorded Version

RCA Victor LOCD/LSOD 2006 (O.C.).

A score of consistently high quality.

E. Y. HARBURG
lyricist

EARL CARROLL'S SKETCHBOOK

Opened: July 1, 1929, Earl Carroll Th.

400 *performances.*

Sketches by Earl Carroll, Eddie Cantor, Sidney Skolsky, Eddie Welch; Harburg music by Jay Gorney; music & lyrics also by Vincent Rose, Charles & Harry Tobias, Ted Snyder & Benny Davis, Arnold Johnson & Irving Kahal, Abner Silver.

Produced by Carroll; directed by Carroll & Edgar MacGregor; dances by LeRoy Prinz.

Cast included: Will Mahoney, William Demarest, The Three Sailors, Patsy Kelly, George Givot, Dorothy Britton, Don Howard, Faith Bacon.

Principal Harburg-Gorney songs: Kinda

Cute; Like Me Less, Love Me More; Crashing the Golden Gate.

THE GARRICK GAIETIES
(*See* Vernon Duke)

EARL CARROLL VANITIES
(8th Edition)

Opened: July 1, 1930, New Amsterdam Th.

215 *performances.*

Sketches by Eddie Welch & Eugene Conrad; Harburg music by Jay Gorney; music & lyrics also by Harold Arlen & Ted Koehler.

Produced by Carroll; directed by Carroll & Priestley Morrison; dances by LeRoy Prinz.

Cast included: Jimmy Savo, Jack Benny, Herb Williams, Harry Stockwell, Patsy Kelly, John Hale, Thelma White, Colette Sisters, Faith Bacon.

Principal Harburg-Gorney songs: I Came to Life; Ring Out the Blues.

BALLYHOO OF 1932

Opened: Sept. 6, 1932, 44th St. Th.

95 *performances.*

Sketches by Norman Anthony; music by Lewis Gensler.

Produced by Anthony, Gensler, Bobby Connolly, Russell Patterson; directed by Anthony & Gensler; dances by Connolly.

Cast included: Willie & Eugene Howard, Jeanne Aubert, Lulu McConnell, Bob Hope, Paul Hartman, Donald Stewart, Vera Marche.

Principal songs: Riddle Me This; Falling Off the Wagon; How Do You Do It?; Thrill Me.

AMERICANA

Opened: Oct. 5, 1932, Shubert Th.

77 *performances.*

Sketches by J. P. McEvoy; Harburg music by Jay Gorney, Richard Myers, Harold Arlen, Burton Lane, Vernon Duke; music & lyrics also by Henry Souvaine & Johnny Mercer.

Produced by Lee Shubert; directed by Harold Johnsrud; dances by John Boyle & Charles Weidman.

Cast included: George Givot, Albert Carroll, Lloyd Nolan, Georgie Tapps, Charles Weidman Dancers (incl. José Limon, Letitia Ide), Doris Humphrey Group, Rex Weber, Francetta Malloy, Peggy Cartwright.

Principal Harburg songs: Brother, Can You Spare a Dime? (Gorney); Let Me Match My Private Life with Yours (Duke); Whistling for a Kiss (Mercer-Myers); You're Not Pretty but You're Mine (Lane); Satan's Li'l Lamb (Mercer-Arlen).

WALK A LITTLE FASTER
(*See* Vernon Duke).

ZIEGFELD FOLLIES (1934)
(*See* Vernon Duke)

LIFE BEGINS AT 8:40
(*See* Harold Arlen).

HOORAY FOR WHAT!
(*See* Harold Arlen).

HOLD ON TO YOUR HATS
(*See* Burton Lane).

BLOOMER GIRL
(*See* Harold Arlen).

FINIAN'S RAINBOW
(*See* Burton Lane).

FLAHOOLEY

Opened: May 14, 1951, Broadhurst Th.

40 *performances.*

Book by Harburg & Fred Saidy; music by Sammy Fain.

Produced by Cheryl Crawford, Harburg & Saidy; directed by Harburg & Saidy; dances by Helen Tamiris.

Cast included: Yma Sumac, Ernest Truex, Irwin Corey, Jerome Courtland, Edith Atwater, Barbara Cook, Bil & Cora Baird, Lulu Bates, Fay DeWitt, Marilyn Ross, Louis Nye, Nehemiah Persoff, Laurel Shelby.

Principal songs: You Too Can Be a Puppet; Here's to Your Illusions; Who Says There Ain't No Santa Claus?; The World Is Your Balloon; He's Only Wonderful; Jump, Li'l Chillun; The Springtime Cometh.

Recorded Version

Capitol S 284 (O.C.) X.

An unappreciated score of great charm.

JAMAICA

(*See* Harold Arlen).

THE HAPPIEST GIRL IN THE WORLD

Opened: Apr. 3, 1961, Martin Beck Th. 96 *performances.*

Book by Fred Saidy & Henry Myers; music by Jacques Offenbach.

Produced by Lee Guber; directed by Cyril Ritchard; dances by Dania Krupska.

Cast included: Cyril Ritchard, Janice Rule, Dran Seitz, Bruce Yarnell, Ted Thurston, Michael Kermoyan, Lu Leonard, Lainie Kazan, Maura K. Wedge.

Principal songs: The Happiest Girl in the World; Shall We Say Farewell?; Vive la Virtue; Adrift on a Star; Five Minutes of Spring.

Recorded Version

Columbia KOL 5650/KOS 2050 (O.C.).

The familiar Offenbach melodies seem strangely out of place in this musical approach to the *Lysistrata* legend.

DARLING OF THE DAY

(*See* Jule Styne).

CHAPTER FIFTEEN
HAROLD ROME
composer-lyricist

PINS AND NEEDLES

Opened: Nov. 27, 1937, Labor Stage. 1,108 *performances.*

Sketches by Charles Friedman, Arthur Arent, Marc Blitzstein, Emanuel Eisenberg, David Gregory.

Produced by the I. L. G. W. U.; directed by Friedman; dances by Gluck Sandor.

Cast included: Members of the I.L.G.-W.U.

Principal songs: Sing Me a Song with Social Significance; Sunday in the Park; One Big Union for Two; Chain Store Daisy; Nobody Makes a Pass at Me; It's Better with a Union Man; Doin' the Reactionary.

Recorded Version

Columbia OL 5810/OS 2210 (S.C.).

The best-remembered songs from all editions have been preserved by Barbra Streisand, Rose Marie Jun, Jack Carroll & Mr. Rome himself.

SING OUT THE NEWS

Opened: Sept. 24, 1938, Music Box Th. 105 *performances.*

Sketches by Charles Friedman.

Produced by Max Gordon, George S. Kaufman & Moss Hart; directed by Friedman; dances by Ned McGurn, Dave Gould, Charles Walters.

Cast included: Philip Loeb, Hiram Sherman, Mary Jane Walsh, Will Geer, Dorothy Fox, Michael Loring, Joey Faye, Hazel Scott, Richard Huey, Rex Ingram, June Allyson.

Principal songs: F.D.R. Jones; My Heart Is Unemployed; How Long Can Love Keep Laughing?; Yip-Ahoy; Plaza 6-9423.

LET FREEDOM SING

Opened: Oct. 5, 1942, Longacre Th. 8 *performances.*

Sketches by Sam Locke; lyrics & music also by Marc Blitzstein, Henry Myers, Edward Eliscu & Jay Gorney, Hy Zarat & Walter Kent, Roslyn Harvey & Lou Cooper, Lewis Allan & Earl Robinson.

Produced by Youth Theatre; directed by Joseph Pevney & Robert H. Gordon; dances by Dan Eckley.

Cast included: Mitzi Green, Berni Gould, Lee Sullivan, Betty Garrett, Mordecai Bauman, Phil Leeds.

Principal Rome songs: It's Fun to Be Free; Little Miss Victory Jones.

CALL ME MISTER
Opened: Apr. 18, 1946, National Th.
734 *performances.*
Sketches by Arnold Auerbach, Arnold Horwitt.
Produced by Melvyn Douglas & Herman Levin; directed by Robert H. Gordon; dances by John Wray.
Cast included: Betty Garrett, Jules Munshin, Bill Callahan, Lawrence Winters, George Hall, Harry Clark, Paula Bane, Maria Karnilova, Alan Manson, Danny Scholl, Betty Lou Holland, Chandler Cowles, George S. Irving.
Principal songs: Goin' Home Train; Little Surplus Me; The Red Ball Express; Military Life; The Face on the Dime; Yuletide Park Avenue; South America, Take It Away; Along with Me.

ALIVE AND KICKING
Opened: Jan. 17, 1950, Winter Garden
46 *performances.*
Sketches by Ray Golden, Henry Morgan, Jerome Chodorov, Joseph Stein & Will Glickman, Mort Stuart, I.A.L. Diamond; lyrics & music also by Paul Francis Webster, Ray Golden, Hoagy Carmichael, Sonny Burke, Sammy Fain, Irma Jurist & Leonard Gershe.
Produced by William R. Katzell & Ray Golden; directed by Robert H. Gordon; dances by Jack Cole.
Cast included: David Burns, Lenore Lonergan, Jack Gilford, Carl Reiner, Bobby Van, Jack Cole, Gwen Verdon, Fay DeWitt, Jack Cassidy, Jean Bal, Laurel Shelby.
Principal Rome songs: Love, It Hurts So Good; Cry Baby Cry; French with Tears.

MICHAEL TODD'S PEEP SHOW
Opened: June 28, 1950, Winter Garden
278 *performances.*
Sketches by Bobby Clark, H. I. Phillips, William Roos, Billy K. Wells; lyrics & music also by Chakraband & Bhumibol, Herb Magidson & Sammy Fain, Raymond Scott, Dan Shapiro & Sammy Stept, Bob Hilliard & Jule Styne.
Produced by Michael Todd; directed by Hassard Short & Bobby Clark; dances by James Starbuck.
Cast included: Lina Romay, Lilly Christine, Clifford Guest, "Bozo" Snyder, "Hi Wilberforce" Conley, Peiro Brothers, Corrine & Tito Valdez, "Red" Marshall, "Peanuts" Mann, Art Carroll.
Principal Rome songs: Gimme the Shimmy; Pocketful of Dreams; I Hate a Parade.

BLESS YOU ALL
Opened: Dec. 14, 1950, Mark Hellinger Th.
84 *performances.*
Sketches by Arnold Auerbach.
Produced by Herman Levin & Oliver Smith; directed by John C. Wilson; dances by Helen Tamiris.
Cast included: Mary McCarty, Jules Munshin, Pearl Bailey, Valerie Bettis, Donald Saddler, Robert Chisholm, Byron Palmer, Jane Harvey, Donald McKayle, Swen Swenson, Gene Barry, Garry Davis.
Principal songs: I Can Hear It Now; Little Things Mean So Much to Me; A Rose Is a Rose; Summer Dresses; You Never Know What Hit You.

WISH YOU WERE HERE
Opened: June 25, 1952, Imperial Th.
598 *performances.*
Book by Arthur Kober & Joshua Logan.
Produced by Leland Hayward & Logan; directed by Logan.
Cast included: Sheila Bond, Jack Cassidy, Patricia Marand, Sidney Armus, Paul Valentine, Harry Clark, Richard France, Florence Henderson, Tom Tryon, Larry Blyden, Frank Aletter, Mardi Bayne, Phyllis Newman, Stanley Grover, Reid Shelton, John Perkins, Sammy Smith.
Principal songs: Wish You Were Here;

Shopping Around; Could Be; Summer Afternoon; Where Did the Night Go?; Don José of Far Rockaway; Goodbye Love.
Recorded Version
RCA Victor LOC/LSO 1108 (O.C.).
A light, lyrical score that ably catches the flavor of vacationing middle-class New Yorkers.

FANNY
Opened: Nov. 4, 1954, Majestic Th.
888 *performances.*
Book by S. N. Behrman & Joshua Logan. Produced by David Merrick & Logan; directed by Logan; dances by Helen Tamiris.
Cast included: Ezio Pinza, Walter Slezak, Florence Henderson, William Tabbert, Gerald Price, Nejla Ates, Alan Carney, Tani & Dran Seitz, Herbert Banke, Mohammed el Bakkar.
Principal songs: Never Too Late for Love; Octopus Song; Restless Heart; Why Be Afraid to Dance?; Welcome Home; I Have to Tell You; Fanny; To My Wife; Love Is a Very Light Thing; I Like You.
Recorded Version
RCA Victor LOC/LSO 1015 (O.C.).
An ambitious, often moving work.

DESTRY RIDES AGAIN
Opened: Apr. 23, 1959, Imperial Th.
473 *performances.*
Book by Leonard Gershe.
Produced by David Merrick; directed by Michael Kidd.
Cast included: Andy Griffith, Dolores Gray, Scott Brady, Jack Prince, Libi Staiger, Swen Swenson, Marc Breaux, Don Crabtree, Rosetta LeNoire.
Principal songs: Hoop-de-Dingle; Ballad of the Gun; I Know Your Kind; Anyone Would Love You; Are You Ready, Gyp Watson?; That Ring on the Finger.
Recorded Version
Decca DL (7)9075 (O.C.).
Rome on the range.

I CAN GET IT FOR YOU WHOLESALE
Opened: Mar. 22, 1962, Shubert Th.
300 *performances.*
Book by Jerome Weidman.
Produced by David Merrick; directed by Arthur Laurents; dances by Herbert Ross.
Cast included: Lillian Roth, Elliott Gould, Sheree North, Harold Lang, Jack Kruschen, Ken LeRoy, Marilyn Cooper, Barbra Streisand, Bambi Linn, Luba Lisa.
Principal songs: When Gemini Meets Capricorn; The Sound of Money; Too Soon; Who Knows?; Have I Told You Lately?; Miss Marmelstein; A Funny Thing Happened.
Recorded Version
Columbia KOL 5780/KOS 2180 (O.C.).
The alternately tough and tender songs ably evoke the flavor of New York's Garment District in the 1930s.

THE ZULU AND THE ZAYDA
Opened: Nov. 10, 1965, Cort Th.
179 *performances.*
Play by Howard DaSilva & Felix Leon. Produced by Theodore Mann & Dore Schary; directed by Schary.
Cast included: Menasha Skulnik, Ossie Davis, Louis Gossett, Joe Silver, Sarah Cunningham.
Principal songs: It's Good to Be Alive; Rivers of Tears; Zulu Love Song; Oisgetzaichnet.
Recorded Version
Columbia KOL 6480/KOS 2880 (O.C.).
This "Play with Music" contains a dozen fine Harold Rome songs indigenous to both Zulu and Zayda.

CHAPTER SIXTEEN
KURT WEILL
composer

THE THREEPENNY OPERA
Opened: Apr. 13, 1933, Empire Th.

12 *performances.*
Book & lyrics by Gifford Cochran & Jerrold Krimsky, adapted from the original by Bertolt Brecht.
Produced by John Krimsky & Cochran; directed by Francesco Von Mendelssohn.
Cast included: Steffi Duna, Robert Chisholm, Rex Weber, Rex Evans, Herbert Rudley, Burgess Meredith, George Heller, Harry Bellaver.
Principal songs: Legend of Mackie Messer; Wedding Song; Pirate Jenny; Soldier Song; Love Duet; Ballad of the Easy Life; Jealousy Duet; Song of the Aimlessness of Life.

JOHNNY JOHNSON

Opened: Nov. 19, 1936, 44th St. Th.
68 *performances.*
Play and lyrics by Paul Green.
Produced by the Group Theatre; directed by Lee Strasburg.
Cast included: Russell Collins, Roman Bohnen, Phoebe Brand, Sanford Meisner, Robert Lewis, Lee J. Cobb, Art Smith, Albert Van Dekker, Elia Kazan, Luther Adler, Jules (John) Garfield, Morris Carnovsky, Joseph Pevney, Will Lee.
Principal songs: Johnny's Song; O Heart of Love; Song of the Goddess; On the Rio Grande; Song of the Guns; Mon Ami, My Friend; Psychiatry Song.
Recorded Version
Heliodor (S) 25024 (S.C.).

Headed by Burgess Meredith, Lotte Lenya, Hiram Sherman & Evelyn Lear, a fine group of singers ably preserves the power of Weill's first American score.

KNICKERBOCKER HOLIDAY

Opened: Oct. 19, 1938, Ethel Barrymore Th.
168 *performances.*
Book & lyrics by Maxwell Anderson.
Produced by The Playwrights' Co.; directed by Joshua Logan; dances by Carl Randall & Edwin Denby.

Cast included: Walter Huston, Jeanne Madden, Ray Middleton, Richard Kollmar, Mark Smith, Clarence Nordstrom, Howard Freeman, Robert Rounseville.
Principal songs: There's Nowhere to Go but Up; How Can You Tell an American?; September Song; It Never Was You; The Scars.

LADY IN THE DARK

Opened: Jan. 23, 1941, Alvin Th.
467 *performances.*
Book by Moss Hart; lyrics by Ira Gershwin.
Produced by Sam H. Harris; directed by Hassard Short & Hart; dances by Albertina Rasch.
Cast included: Gertrude Lawrence, Victor Mature, Macdonald Carey, Danny Kaye, Bert Lytell, Evelyn Wyckoff, Donald Randolph, Margaret Dale, Natalie Schafer, Virginia Peine, Nelson Barclift, Manfred Hecht.
Principal songs: Oh, Fabulous One; One Life to Live; Girl of the Moment; This Is New; The Princess of Pure Delight; My Ship; The Saga of Jenny; Tschaikowsky.
Recorded Versions
RCA Victor LPV 503.
RCA Victor LM 1882 (TV) (1954) X.
Columbia OL 5990/OS 2390 (S.C.).

The inimitable Miss Lawrence is heard on one side of the first album listed above. The television adaptation features Ann Sothern & Carleton Carpenter; the Columbia studio version—the most complete—is headed by Risë Stevens, Adolph Green & John Reardon.

ONE TOUCH OF VENUS

Opened: Oct. 7, 1943, Imperial Th.
567 *performances.*
Book by S. J. Perelman & Ogden Nash; lyrics by Nash.
Produced by Cheryl Crawford & John Wildberg; directed by Elia Kazan; dances by Agnes de Mille.
Cast included: Mary Martin, Kenny Baker, John Boles, Paula Laurence, Ted-

dy Hart, Sono Osato, Harry Clark, Lou Wills, Jr., Helen Raymond, Allyn Ann McLerie, Pearl Lang, Nelle Fisher, Jeff Warren.
Principal songs: One Touch of Venus; How Much I Love You; I'm a Stranger Here Myself; Speak Low; West Wind; Foolish Heart; The Trouble with Women; That's Him; Wooden Wedding.
Recorded Version
Decca DL (7)9122 (O.C.).
Bright, breezy, and well worth having.

THE FIREBRAND OF FLORENCE
Opened: Mar. 22, 1945, Alvin Th.
43 *performances.*
Book by Edwin Justus Mayer; lyrics by Ira Gershwin.
Produced by Max Gordon; directed by John Murray Anderson & John Haggott; dances by Catherine Littlefield.
Cast included: Earl Wrightson, Lotte Lenya, Melville Cooper, Marion Green, Bert Freed, Beverly Tyler, John (Jack) Cassidy, Ferdi Hoffman.
Principal songs: Sing Me Not a Ballad; A Rhyme for Angela; The Cozy Nook Trio; You're Far Too Near Me.

STREET SCENE
Opened: Jan. 9, 1947, Adelphi Th.
148 *performances.*
Book by Elmer Rice; lyrics by Langston Hughes.
Produced by Dwight Deere Wiman & The Playwrights' Co.; directed by Charles Friedman; dances by Anna Sokolow.
Cast included: Norman Cordon, Anne Jeffreys, Polyna Stoska, Brian Sullivan, Hope Emerson, Irving Kaufman, Don Saxon, Sheila Bond, Danny Daniels, Juanita Hall.
Principal songs: I Got a Marble and a Star; Somehow I Never Could Believe; Ice Cream; Wrapped in a Ribbon and Tied in a Bow; Lonely House; Wouldn't You Like to Be on Broadway?; What Good Would the Moon Be?; Moon-Faced, Starry-Eyed; Remember that I

Care; A Boy Like You; We'll Go Away Together.
Recorded Version
Columbia OL 4139 (O.C.).
Weill's most operatic American score is a notable and moving achievement.

LOVE LIFE
Opened: Oct. 7, 1948, 46th St. Th.
252 *performances.*
Book & lyrics by Alan Jay Lerner.
Produced by Cheryl Crawford; directed by Elia Kazan; dances by Michael Kidd.
Cast included: Nanette Fabray, Ray Middleton, Johnny Stewart, Jay Marshall, Lyle Bettger, Cheryl Archer.
Principal songs: Here I'll Stay; Progress; Green-Up Time; Economics; Susan's Dream; Mr. Right.

LOST IN THE STARS
Opened: Oct. 30, 1949, Music Box Th.
273 *performances.*
Book & lyrics by Maxwell Anderson.
Produced by The Playwrights' Co.; directed by Rouben Mamoulian.
Cast included: Todd Duncan, Leslie Banks, Inez Matthews, Warren Coleman, Shelia Guyse, Frank Roane, Herbert Coleman, Georgette Harvey, Robert McFerrin, Guy Spaull, William C. Smith.
Principal songs: The Hills of Ixipo; Thousands of Miles; Train to Johannesburg; The Little Grey House; Trouble Man; Lost in the Stars; Stay Well; Cry, the Beloved Country; Big Mole; A Bird of Paradise.
Recorded Version
Decca DL 8028 (O.C.).
A frequently impressive work, with dialogue included on the record to bridge the musical selections.

THE THREEPENNY OPERA
Opened: Mar. 10, 1954, Theatre de Lys.
95 *performances.*
Reopened: Sept. 20, 1955, Theatre de Lys.
2,611 *performances.*

493

Book & lyrics by Marc Blitzstein, adapted from the original by Bertolt Brecht.
Produced by Carmen Capalbo & Stanley Chase; *directed by* Capalbo.
Cast included: Lotte Lenya, Scott Merrill, Leon Lishner, Jo Sullivan, Charlotte Rae, Gerald Price, Beatrice Arthur.
Principal songs: The Ballad of Mack the Knife; Wedding Song; Pirate Jenny; Army Song; Love Song; Ballad of the Easy Life; Barbara Song; Jealousy Duet; Useless Song; Solomon Song.
Recorded Version
MGM (S) 3121 (O.C.).

In addition to this excellent English adaptation, there are also available excerpts from the 1928 Berlin production (Telefunken 66053) & the 1958 complete German version on two records (Columbia O2L 257/O2S 201). Lotte Lenya can be heard on all of them.

CHAPTER SEVENTEEN
RICHARD RODGERS
composer

OSCAR HAMMERSTEIN II
lyricist

All books by Mr. Hammerstein unless otherwise noted. See separate lists for all musicals by Mr. Hammerstein prior to his association with Mr. Rodgers & those by Mr. Rodgers after the death of Mr. Hammerstein.

OKLAHOMA!
Opened: Mar. 31, 1943, St. James Th.
2,212 *performances.*
Produced by The Theatre Guild; directed by Rouben Mamoulian; dances by Agnes de Mille.
Cast included: Betty Garde, Alfred Drake, Joan Roberts, Howard da Silva, Joseph Buloff, Celeste Holm, Lee Dixon, Katherine Sergava, Joan McCracken, Bambi Linn, George Church, Marc

Platt, Ralph Riggs, Diana Adams, George S. Irving, Hayes Gordon.
Principal songs: Oh, What a Beautiful Mornin'; The Surrey with the Fringe on Top; Kansas City; I Cain't Say No; Many a New Day; People Will Say We're in Love; Pore Jud; Out of My Dreams; All er Nothin'; The Farmer and the Cowman; Oklahoma.
Recorded Versions
Decca DL (7)9017 (O.C.).
Capitol (S)WAO 595 (F.V.) (1955).
Harmony 7364/11164 (S.C.).
Columbia OL 8010/OS 2610 (S.C.).

Decca's 78 rpm album started the original cast album trend. On LP, it's still worth owning, though it is not as complete or well recorded as the Capitol soundtrack (Gordon MacRae, Shirley Jones, Gloria Grahame), or Columbia's studio production (John Raitt, Florence Henderson, Phyllis Newman). The low-priced Harmony, featuring Nelson Eddy, is a good buy.

CAROUSEL
Opened: Apr. 19, 1945, Majestic Th.
890 *performances.*
Produced by The Theatre Guild; directed by Rouben Mamoulian; dances by Agnes de Mille.
Cast included: John Raitt, Jan Clayton, Jean Darling, Christine Johnson, Jean Casto, Murvyn Vye, Eric Mattson, Bambi Linn, Peter Birch, Pearl Lang, Russell Collins, Robert Pagent, Iva Withers, Jay Velie.
Principal songs: Carousel Waltz; You're a Queer One, Julie Jordan; Mr. Snow; If I Loved You; June Is Bustin' Out All Over; Blow High Blow Low; When the Chidren Are Asleep; Soliloquy; A Real Nice Clambake; What's the Use of Wond'rin'; You'll Never Walk Alone.
Recorded Versions
Decca DL (7)9020 (O.C.).
Capitol (S)W 694 (F.V.) (1956).
RCA Victor LOC/LSO 1114 (O.C.) (1965).

Columbia CSM 479 (TV) (1967).
RCA Victor LPM 1048 (S.C.) X.
Command 843 (SD) (S.C.).

Possibly the greatest of all R&H scores. The Decca original cast version has been sonically superseded by all the others, which are also more complete. Gordon MacRae and Shirley Jones are on the Capitol soundtrack, John Raitt and Eileen Christy on the RCA Lincoln Center revival, and Robert Goulet and Mary Grover on Columbia's specially-made set of the Armstrong TV production. Both the Victor (Robert Merrill, Patrice Munsel) and the Command (Alfred Drake, Roberta Peters) studio versions are particularly well sung.

ALLEGRO

Opened: Oct. 10, 1947, Majestic Th.
315 *performances.*
Produced by The Theatre Guild; directed by Agnes de Mille.
Cast included: John Battles, Annamary Dickey, William Ching, John Conte, Muriel O'Malley, Roberta Jonay, Lisa Kirk, Kathryn Lee, Harrison Muller, Edward Platt, Gloria Wills.
Principal songs: I Know It Can Happen Again; One Foot, Other Foot; A Fellow Needs a Girl; You Are Never Away; So Far; Money Isn't Everything; The Gentleman Is a Dope; Allegro.
Recorded Version
RCA Victor LOC/LSO 1099e (O.C.).

One of the team's least appreciated efforts, the score is still a must for show music buffs.

SOUTH PACIFIC

Opened: Apr. 7, 1949, Majestic Th.
1,925 *performances.*
Book with Joshua Logan.
Produced by Rodgers & Hammerstein, Leland Hayward & Logan; directed by Logan.
Cast included: Ezio Pinza, Mary Martin, Myron McCormick, William Tabbert, Juanita Hall, Betta St. John, Martin Wolfson, Harvey Stephens, Dickinson

(Richard) Eastham, Biff McGuire, Sandra Deel, Mardi Bayne, Alex Nicol.
Principal songs: Dites-moi; A Cockeyed Optimist; Some Enchanted Evening; Bloody Mary; There Is Nothin' Like a Dame; Bali Ha'i; I'm Gonna Wash that Man Right Outa My Hair; A Wonderful Guy; Younger than Springtime; Happy Talk; Honey Bun; You've Got to Be Carefully Taught; This Nearly Was Mine.
Recorded Versions
Columbia OL 4180/OS 2040 (O.C.).
RCA Victor LOC/LSO 1032 (F.V.) (1958).
Columbia OL 6700/OS 3100 (O.C.) (1967).

Rodgers and Hammerstein's most popular work is still heard at its best on the original cast recording. Columbia's 1967 edition (Florence Henderson, Giorgio Tozzi) is a much closer competitor than the RCA soundtrack (Mitzi Gaynor, Giorgio Tozzi).

THE KING AND I

Opened: Mar. 29, 1951, St. James Th.
1,246 *performances.*
Produced by Rodgers & Hammerstein; directed by John van Druten; dances by Jerome Robbins.
Cast included: Gertrude Lawrence, Yul Brynner, Dorothy Sarnoff, Doretta Morrow, Larry Douglas, Johnny Stewart, John Juliano, Gemze de Lappe, Michiko, Yuriko, Gloria Marlowe, Leonard Graves, Stephanie Augustine.
Principal songs: I Whistle a Happy Tune; My Lord and Master; Hello, Young Lovers; March of the Siamese Children; A Puzzlement; Getting to Know You; We Kiss in a Shadow; Something Wonderful; I Have Dreamed; Shall We Dance?
Recorded Versions
Decca DL (7)9008 (O.C.).
Capitol (S)W 740 (F.V.) (1957).
RCA Victor LOC/LSO 1092 (O.C.) (1964).

Columbia OL 8040/OS 2640 (S.C.).

Yul Brynner is heard on both the Decca and the Capitol versions of this lovely score. But the former does have Gertrude Lawrence, while the latter offers Deborah Kerr's voice, Marni Nixon. The 1964 revival (Risë Stevens, Darren McGavin) is vocally unsteady, but the Columbia studio cast (Barbara Cook, Theodore Bikel) is well worth investigating.

ME AND JULIET

Opened: May 28, 1953, Majestic Th.
358 *performances.*
Produced by Rodgers & Hammerstein; directed by George Abbott; dances by Robert Alton.
Cast included: Isabel Bigley, Bill Hayes, Joan McCracken, Ray Walston, Mark Dawson, Jackie Kelk, Arthur Maxwell, George S. Irving, Helena Scott, Bob Fortier, Shirley MacLaine, Michael King, Barbara Carroll (pianist), Buzz Miller.
Principal songs: That's the Way It Happens; Marriage Type Love; Keep It Gay; The Big Black Giant; No Other Love; It's Me; We Deserve Each Other; I'm Your Girl.
Recorded Version
RCA Victor LOC/LSO 1098e (O.C.).
A light, attractive collection of songs.

PIPE DREAM

Opened: Nov. 30, 1955, Shubert Th.
246 *performances.*
Produced by Rodgers & Hammerstein; directed by Harold Clurman; dances by Boris Runanin.
Cast included: Helen Traubel, William Johnson, Judy Tyler, G. D. (George) Wallace, Mike Kellin, Ruby Braff (trumpeter), Patricia Wilson, Steve Roland, Temple Texas, Mildred Slavin, Louise Troy, Ruth Kobart.
Principal songs: All Kinds of People; Ev'rybody's Got a Home but Me; A Lopsided Bus; Sweet Thursday; Suzy Is

a Good Thing; All at Once You Love Her; Will You Marry Me?; The Next Time It Happens.
Recorded Version
RCA Victor LOC/LSO 1097e (O.C.).
The cast performs well, but this is one of the least impressive of the masters' achievements.

FLOWER DRUM SONG

Opened: Dec. 1, 1958, St. James Th.
601 *performances.*
Book with Joseph Fields.
Produced by Rodgers, Hammerstein & Fields; directed by Gene Kelly; dances by Carol Haney.
Cast included: Miyoshi Umeki, Pat Suzuki, Larry Blyden, Juanita Hall, Ed Kenney, Keye Luke, Arabella Hong, Jack Soo, Anita Ellis.
Principal songs: You Are Beautiful; A Hundred Million Miracles; I Enjoy Being a Girl; Like a God; Chop Suey; Don't Marry Me; Grant Avenue; Love, Look Away; Sunday.
Recorded Versions
Columbia OL 5350/OS 2009 (O.C.).
Angel (S)35886 (London O.C.)(1960)
Decca DL (7)9098 (F.V.) (1961).
Some charming music, well sung and orchestrated. The English cast, headed by Yau Shan Tung and Yama Saki, and the film cast, headed by Miyoshi Umeki and Nancy Kwan, have much to recommend.

THE SOUND OF MUSIC

Opened: Nov. 16, 1959, Lunt-Fontanne Th.
1,443 *performances.*
Book by Howard Lindsay & Russel Crouse.
Produced by Leland Hayward, Richard Halliday, Rodgers & Hammerstein; directed by Vincent J. Donehue; dances by Joe Layton.
Cast included: Mary Martin, Theodore Bikel, Patricia Neway, Kurt Kasznar, Marion Marlowe, Lauri Peters, Muriel O'Malley, Karen Shepard, Brian Davies,

496

Joey Heatherton.

Principal songs: The Sound of Music; Maria; My Favorite Things; Do-Re-Mi; Sixteen Going on Seventeen; The Lonely Goatherd; So Long, Farewell; How Can Love Survive?; Climb Ev'ry Mountain; Edelweiss.

Recorded Versions

Columbia KOL 5450/KOS 2020 (O.C.). RCA Victor LOCD/LSOD 2005 (F.V.) (1965).

Warner Bros. W(S) 1377.

The sugary score is well sung by both the original cast and film versions, with the latter dropping three minor songs and adding two new ones by Rodgers alone, "I Have Confidence" and "Something Good." That Julie Andrews starrer is now the best selling album of all times. Better voices, however, may be heard on the Warner disc, which features members of the Trapp family.

OSCAR HAMMERSTEIN II
lyricist

This list contains all Broadway musicals by Mr. Hammerstein not written in collaboration with Richard Rodgers. All books & lyrics are by Mr. Hammerstein unless otherwise noted.

ALWAYS YOU

Opened: Jan. 5, 1920, Central Th.

66 performances.

Music by Herbert Stothart.

Produced & directed by Arthur Hammerstein; dances by Robert Marks.

Cast included: Helen Ford, Walter Scanlan, Ralph Herz, Edouardo Ciannelli, Julia Kelety, Bernard Gorcey, Anna Seymour, Cortez & Peggy, Russell Mack.

Principal songs: Always You; Syncopated Heart; My Pousse-Café; The Tired Business Man.

TICKLE ME

Opened: Aug. 17, 1920, Selwyn Th.

207 performances.

Book with Otto Harbach & Frank Mandel; lyrics with Harbach; music by Herbert Stothart.

Produced by Arthur Hammerstein; directed by William Collier; dances by Bert French.

Cast included: Frank Tinney, Vic Casmore, Allen Kearns, Marguerite Zender, Louise Allen, Frances Grant & Ted Wing.

Principal songs: Until You Say Goodbye; Tickle Me; If a Wish Could Make It So; Broadway Swell and Bowery Bum.

JIMMIE

Opened: Nov. 17, 1920, Apollo Th.

71 performances.

Book with Otto Harbach & Frank Mandel; lyrics with Harbach; music by Herbert Stothart.

Produced by Arthur Hammerstein; directed by Oscar Eagle; dances by Bert French.

Cast included: Frances White, Ben Welch, Paul Porcasi, Harry Delf, Hattie Burks, Don Burroughs.

Principal songs: Cute Little Two by Four; Baby Dreams; Jimmie; Rickety Crickety.

DAFFY DILL

Opened: Aug. 22, 1922, Apollo Th.

71 performances.

Book with Guy Bolton; music by Herbert Stothart.

Produced by Arthur Hammerstein; directed by Julian Mitchell.

Cast included: Frank Tinney, Guy Robertson, Marion Sunshine, Georgia O'-Ramey, Irene Olsen, Frances Grant & Ted Wing, Margaret & Elizabeth Keene.

Principal songs: I'll Build a Bungalow; Two Little Ruby Rings; A Coachman's Heart.

QUEEN O' HEARTS

Opened: Oct. 10, 1922, George M. Cohan Th.

39 *performances.*
Book with Frank Mandel; music by
Lewis Gensler & Dudley Wilkinson; ad-
ditional lyrics by Sidney Mitchell.
Produced by Max Spiegel; directed by
Ira Hards; dances by David Bennett.
Cast included: Nora Bayes, Harry Rich-
man, Norma Terris, Max Hoffman, Jr.,
Arthur Uttry, Franker Woods, Georgia
Brown, Edna Hibbard, Dudley Wilkin-
son, Consuelo Flowerton.
Principal Hammerstein songs: Dream-
ing Alone (Wilkinson); You Need
Someone (Gensler); Tom-Tom (Gens-
ler).

WILDFLOWER
(*See* Vincent Youmans).

MARY JANE McKANE
(*See* Vincent Youmans).

ROSE-MARIE
(*See* Rudolf Friml).

SUNNY
(*See* Jerome Kern).

SONG OF THE FLAME
(*See* George Gershwin).

THE WILD ROSE
(*See* Rudolf Friml).

THE DESERT SONG
(*See* Sigmund Romberg).

GOLDEN DAWN
Opened: Nov. 30, 1927, Hammerstein Th.
184 *performances.*
Book & lyrics with Otto Harbach; music
by Emmerich Kalman & Herbert Stot-
hart.
Produced by Arthur Hammerstein; di-
rected by Reginald Hammerstein; dances
by David Bennett.
Cast included: Louise Hunter, Paul
Gregory, Marguerita Sylva, Robert
Chisholm, Olin Howland, Barbara New-
berry, Gil Squires, Hazel Drury, Archie
Leach (Cary Grant), Russian Art Choir.
Principal songs: When I Crack My

Whip; We Two; Dawn (music by Robert Stolz & Stothart).

SHOW BOAT
(*See* Jerome Kern).

GOOD BOY
Opened: Sept. 25, 1928, Hammerstein Th.
253 *performances.*
Book with Otto Harbach & Henry
Myers; lyrics by Bert Kalmar; music by
Harry Ruby & Herbert Stothart.
Produced by Arthur Hammerstein; di-
rected by Reginald Hammerstein; dances
by Busby Berkeley.
Cast included: Eddie Buzzell, Helen
Kane, Barbara Newberry, Charles But-
terworth, Sam Hearn, Effie Shannon,
Dan Healy, Borrah Minevitch, Evelyn
Bennett.

THE NEW MOON
(*See* Sigmund Romberg).

RAINBOW
(*See* Vincent Youmans).

SWEET ADELINE
(*See* Jerome Kern).

FREE FOR ALL
Opened: Sept. 8, 1931, Manhattan Th.
15 *performances.*
Book with Laurence Schwab; music by
Richard A. Whiting.
Produced by Schwab & Frank Mandel;
directed by Hammerstein; dances by
Bobby Connolly.
Cast included: Jack Haley, Tamara, Lil-
lian Bond, Vera Marsh, Peter Higgins,
David Hutcheson, Philip Lord, Seth
Arnold, Benny Goodman Orchestra.
Principal songs: I Love Him, the Rat;
The Girl Next Door; Not that I Care;
When Your Boy Becomes a Man.

EAST WIND
(*See* Sigmund Romberg).

MUSIC IN THE AIR
(*See* Jerome Kern).

MAY WINE
(*See* Sigmund Romberg).

VERY WARM FOR MAY
(*See* Jerome Kern).

SUNNY RIVER
(*See* Sigmund Romberg).

CARMEN JONES
Opened: Dec. 2, 1943, Broadway Th.
502 *performances.*
Music by Georges Bizet.
Produced by Billy Rose; directed by
Hassard Short & Charles Friedman;
dances by Eugene Loring.
Cast included: Muriel Smith (alternating with Muriel Rahn), Luther Saxon
(with Napoleon Reed), Carlotta Franzell (with Elton J. Warren), June Hawkins, Cozy Cole, Glenn Bryant, Inez
Matthews.
Recorded Versions
Decca DL 9021 (O.C.).
RCA Victor LM 1881 (F.V.) (1954).
Heliodor (S) 25046 (S.C.).
There's much excitement in Hammerstein's resetting of Bizet's *Carmen.* The
soundtrack voices on RCA Victor are
Marilyn Horne, LeVern Hutcherson,
Olga James, Pearl Bailey & Diahann
Carroll. The imported Heliodor features
Grace Bumbry.

Don Chastain, Alvin Epstein, Mitchell
Gregg, Polly Rowles.
Principal songs: The Sweetest Sounds;
Loads of Love; La, La, La; Nobody
Told Me; Look No Further; No Strings.
Recorded Version
Capitol (S)WAO 1695 (O.C.).
A glossy collection of songs enhanced
by Miss Carroll's vocal sheen.

DO I HEAR A WALTZ?
Opened: Mar. 18, 1965, 46th St. Th.
220 *performances.*
Book by Arthur Laurents; lyrics by
Stephen Sondheim.
Produced by Rodgers; directed by John
Dexter; dances by Herbert Ross.
Cast included: Elizabeth Allen, Sergio
Franchi, Carol Bruce, Madeleine Sherwood, Julienne Marie, Stuart Damon,
Fleury D'Antonakis, Jack Manning.
Principal songs: Someone Woke Up;
This Week Americans; What Do We
Do? We Fly!; Someone Like You; Here
We Are Again; Take the Moment; Moon
in My Window; Do I Hear a Waltz?;
We're Gonna Be All Right.
Recorded Version
Columbia KOL 6370/KOS 2770 (O.C.).
The short-lived team of Rodgers &
Sondheim turned out a rueful, deftly
crafted score.

RICHARD RODGERS
composer

*This list contains the Broadway musicals
by Mr. Rodgers written after the death
of Oscar Hammerstein II.*

NO STRINGS
Opened: Mar. 15, 1962, 54th St. Th.
580 *performances.*
Book by Samuel Taylor; lyrics by Rodgers.
Produced by Rodgers; directed by Joe
Layton.
Cast included: Richard Kiley, Diahann
Carroll, Noelle Adam, Bernice Massi,

CHAPTER EIGHTEEN
LEONARD BERNSTEIN
composer

ON THE TOWN
Opened: Dec. 28, 1944, Adelphi Th.
463 *performances.*
Book & lyrics by Betty Comden &
Adolph Green.
Produced by Oliver Smith & Paul Feigay; directed by George Abbott; dances
by Jerome Robbins.
Cast included: Nancy Walker, Sono
Osato, John Battles, Betty Comden,
Adolph Green, Cris Alexander, Alice

Pearce, Robert Chisholm, Herbert Greene, Allyn Ann McLerie, Ben Piazza, Nelle Fisher.

Principal songs: New York, New York; I Can Cook, Too; Some Other Time; I Get Carried Away; Lonely Town; Ya Got Me; Lucky to Be Me.

Recorded Versions

Columbia OL 5540/OS 2028 (S.C.).

Decca DL 8030 (S.C.).

With Bernstein conducting, Nancy Walker, Betty Comden & Adolph Green head the cast on Columbia's nearly complete album. Walker, Comden & Green —plus Mary Martin—do 7 numbers on one side of the Decca.

WONDERFUL TOWN

Opened: Feb. 25, 1953, Winter Garden 559 *performances.*

Book by Joseph Fields & Jerome Chodorov; lyrics by Betty Comden & Adolph Green.

Produced by Robert Fryer; directed by George Abbott; dances by Donald Saddler.

Cast included: Rosalind Russell, George Gaynes, Edith Adams, Henry Lascoe, Dort Clark, Jordan Bentley, Cris Alexander, Ted Beniades, Nathaniel Frey, Dody Goodman, Warren Galjour, Libi Staiger, Joe Layton.

Principal songs: Christopher Street; Ohio; What a Waste; A Quiet Girl; A Little Bit in Love; Conversation Piece; Conga!; My Darlin' Eileen; Swing!; It's Love; Wrong Note Rag.

Recorded Versions

Decca DL (7)9010 (O.C.).

Columbia OL 5360/OS 2008 (TV) (1958).

Miss Russell is on both versions, but the cast is better on the Decca.

CANDIDE

Opened: Dec. 1, 1956, Martin Beck Th. 73 *performances.*

Book by Lillian Hellman; lyrics by Richard Wilbur.

Produced by Ethel Linder Reiner with Lester Osterman, Jr.; directed by Tyrone Guthrie.

Cast included: Max Adrian, Robert Rounseville, Barbara Cook, Irra Petina, William Olvis, Boris Aplon, William Chapman, Louis Edmonds, Joseph Bernard, Margot Moser, Conrad Bain, Stanley Grover, Jack DeLon.

Principal songs: The Best of All Possible Worlds; Oh, Happy We; It Must Be So; Glitter and Be Gay; You Were Dead, You Know (lyric with John Latouche); I Am Easily Assimilated (lyric by Bernstein); Eldorado (lyric by Miss Hellman); What's the Use?; Gavotte (lyric by Dorothy Parker); Make Our Garden Grow.

Recorded Version

Columbia OL 5180/OS 2350 (O.C.).

A score that has easily outlived its source.

WEST SIDE STORY

Opened: Sept. 26, 1957, Winter Garden 734 *performances.*

Book by Arthur Laurents; lyrics by Stephen Sondheim.

Produced by Robert E. Griffith & Harold S. Prince; directed by Jerome Robbins.

Cast included: Carol Lawrence, Larry Kert, Chita Rivera, Art Smith, Mickey Calin, Ken LeRoy, Lee Becker (Theodore), David Winters, Grover Dale, Martin Charnin, Marilyn Cooper, Reri Grist.

Principal songs: Jet Song; Something's Coming; Maria; Tonight; America; Cool; I Feel Pretty; Somewhere; Gee, Officer Krupke!

Recorded Versions

Columbia OL 5230/OS 2001 (O.C.).

Columbia OL 5670/OS 2070 (F.V.) (1961).

There's better placement of songs on the film soundtrack, and the lyric to "America" has been greatly sharpened. The movie voices (Marni Nixon, Jim Bryant, Betty Wand) are at least equal to those in the original cast. Bernstein has conducted the ballet music on one side of Columbia ML 5651/MS 6251.

CHAPTER NINETEEN
ALAN JAY LERNER
lyricist

FREDERICK LOEWE
composer

All books & lyrics by Mr. Lerner unless otherwise noted. For other musicals with Lerner lyrics, see Love Life *under Kurt Weill;* On a Clear Day You Can See Forever *under Burton Lane.*

GREAT LADY
Opened: Dec. 1, 1938, Majestic Th.
20 *performances.*
Book by Earle Crooker & Lowell Brentano; lyrics by Crooker.
Produced by Dwight Deere Wiman & J. H. DelBondio; directed by Bretaigne Windust; dances by William Dollar.
Cast included: Norma Terris, Tullio Carminati, Irene Bordoni, Helen Ford, Joseph Macaulay, Shepperd Strudwick, Annabelle Lyon, Leda Anchutina, André Eglevsky, Robert Shanley, Christine Johnson, Walter Cassel, Dorothy Kirsten, Alicia Alonzo, Nora Kaye, Jerome Robbins, Paul Godkin.
Principal songs: I Have Room in My Heart; There Had to Be the Waltz; May I Suggest Romance?

WHAT'S UP
Opened: Nov. 11, 1943, National Th.
63 *performances.*
Book by Lerner & Arthur Pierson.
Produced by Mark Warnow; directed by George Balanchine & Robert H. Gordon.
Cast included: Jimmy Savo, Gloria Warren, Johnny Morgan, Sondra Barrett, Pat Marshall, Phyllis Hill, William Tabbert, Larry Douglas.
Principal songs: Joshua; You've Got a Hold on Me; You Wash and I'll Dry; My Last Love.

THE DAY BEFORE SPRING
Opened: Nov. 22, 1945, National Th.
165 *performances.*
Produced by John C. Wilson; directed by Wilson & Edward Padula; dances by Antony Tudor.
Cast included: Bill Johnson, Irene Manning, John Archer, Tom Helmore, Pat Marshall, Estelle Loring, Hugh Laing, Mary Ellen Moylan, Bert Freed.
Principal songs: A Jug of Wine; My Love Is a Married Man; I Love You This Morning; The Day Before Spring; You Haven't Changed at All; God's Green World.

BRIGADOON
Opened: Mar. 13, 1947, Ziegfeld Th.
581 *performances.*
Produced by Cheryl Crawford; directed by Robert Lewis; dances by Agnes de Mille.
Cast included: David Brooks, Marion Bell, Pamela Britton, Lee Sullivan, George Keane, William Hansen, James Mitchell, Elliott Sullivan, Hayes Gordon, Helen Gallagher.
Principal songs: Brigadoon; Waitin' for My Dearie; I'll Go Home with Bonnie Jean; The Heather on the Hill; Come to Me, Bend to Me; Almost Like Being in Love; There but for You Go I; My Mother's Wedding Day; From This Day On.
Recorded Versions
RCA Victor LOC/LSO 1001 (O.C.).
MGM E 3135 (F.V.) (1954).
Columbia CSM 385 (TV) (1966).
Columbia OL 7040/OS 2540 (S.C.).
RCA Victor LPM/LSP 2275 (S.C.).

The most complete, best sung, and best recorded version is the Columbia studio cast LP headed by Shirley Jones and Jack Cassidy. Gene Kelly does most of the singing on the MGM soundtrack, while the TV production—available only from Armstrong dealers—spotlights Robert Goulet and Sally Ann Howes. The unlikely trio of Jane Powell, Robert Merrill and Jan Peerce are heard on the second RCA recording.

PAINT YOUR WAGON
Opened: Nov. 12, 1951, Shubert Th.
289 performances.
Produced by Cheryl Crawford; directed by Daniel Mann; dances by Agnes de Mille.
Cast included: James Barton, Olga San Juan, Tony Bavaar, Gemze de Lappe, James Mitchell, Kay Medford, Marijane Maricle.
Principal songs: I'm on My Way; I Talk to the Trees; They Call the Wind Maria; I Still See Elisa; In Between; Carino Mio; There's a Coach Comin' In Hand Me Down that Can o' Beans; Another Autumn; Wand'rin' Star.
Recorded Versions
RCA Victor LOC/LSO 1006 (O.C.).
RCA Victor LPM/LSP 2274 (S.C.).

The lusty, flavorsome score is far better served by the original cast than by the Jane Powell-Robert Merrill-Jan Peerce combination on the second Victor album.

MY FAIR LADY
Opened: Mar. 15, 1956, Mark Hellinger Th.
2,717 performances.
Produced by Herman Levin; directed by Moss Hart; dances by Hanya Holm.
Cast included: Rex Harrison, Julie Andrews, Stanley Holloway, Cathleen Nesbitt, Robert Coote, John Michael King, Viola Roache, Olive Reeves Smith, Christopher Hewett, Lola Fisher, Margot Moser.
Principal songs: Why Can't the English?; Wouldn't It Be Loverly?; With a Little Bit of Luck; I'm an Ordinary Man; Just You Wait; The Rain in Spain; I Could Have Danced All Night; On the Street Where You Live; Show Me; Get Me to the Church on Time; A Hymn to Him;

Without You; I've Grown Accustomed to Her Face.
Recorded Versions
Columbia OL 5090/OS 2015 (O.C.).
Columbia OL 6580/OS 2980 (Mexican O.C.) (1959).
Columbia OL 8060/OS 2660 (Italian O.C.) (1963).
Columbia OL 8050 (Israeli O.C.) (1964).
Columbia KOL 8000/KOS 2600 (F.V.) (1964).
RCA Victor LPM/LSP 2274 (S.C.).

The most successful original cast LP of all time is now surrounded by a fine group of satelite albums, including the film version starring Rex Harrison and the voice of Marni Nixon, plus a variety of foreign language interpretations. It should be noted, too, that Columbia OS 2015 is the stereo version of the London, not the Broadway cast. With so much to choose from, the purchaser can easily bypass the RCA lineup of Jane Powell, Robert Merrill, Jan Peerce & Phil Harris.

CAMELOT
Opened: Dec. 3, 1960, Majestic Th.
873 performances.
Produced by Lerner, Loewe & Moss Hart; directed by Hart; dances by Hanya Holm.
Cast included: Richard Burton, Julie Andrews, Robert Goulet, Roddy McDowall, Robert Coote, M'el Dowd, Bruce Yarnell, John Cullum, David Hurst, Marjorie Smith, Michael Kermoyan.
Principal songs: Camelot; C'est Moi; The Lusty Month of May; If Ever I Would Leave You; What Do the Simple Folk Do?; I Loved You Once in Silence; Guenevere; Follow Me; How to Handle a Woman.
Recorded Versions
Columbia KOL 5620/KOS 2031 (O.C.).
Warner Bros. B(S) 1712 (F.V.) (1967).

A richly melodic score. The acceptable

soundtrack LP does not indicate whether all the singing is done by stars Vanessa Redgrave, Richard Harris, and Franco Nero.

CHAPTER TWENTY
JULE STYNE
composer

BETTY COMDEN
ADOLPH GREEN
co-lyricists

All music & lyrics by Styne, Comden & Green unless otherwise noted. For other musicals with Comden & Green lyrics, see On the Town *&* Wonderful Town *under Leonard Bernstein.*

BILLION DOLLAR BABY
Opened: Dec. 21, 1945, Alvin Th.
219 *performances.*
Book by Comden & Green; music by Morton Gould.
Produced by Paul Feigay & Oliver Smith; directed by George Abbott; dances by Jerome Robbins.
Cast included: Mitzi Green, Joan McCracken, William Tabbert, Harold Gary, Robert Chisholm, Danny Daniels, James Mitchell, Helen Gallagher.
Principal songs: Broadway Blossom; Bad Timing; I Got a One Track Mind; I'm Sure of Your Love.

HIGH BUTTON SHOES
Opened: Oct. 9, 1947, New Century Th.
727 *performances.*
Book by Stephen Longstreet; lyrics by Sammy Cahn.
Produced by Monte Proser & Joseph Kipness; directed by George Abbott; dances by Jerome Robbins.
Cast included: Phil Silvers, Nanette Fabray, Jack McCauley, Sondra Lee, Joey Faye, Johnny Stewart, Helen Gallagher, Paul Godkin, Mark Dawson, Lois Lee, Clay Clement, Nathaniel Frey.

Principal songs: Can't You Just See Yourself?; There's Nothing Like a Model "T"; You're My Girl; Papa, Won't You Dance with Me?; On a Sunday by the Sea; I Still Get Jealous.
Recorded Version
RCA Victor LOC/LSO 1107 (O.C.).
Appealing Styne songs.

GENTLEMEN PREFER BLONDES
Opened: Dec. 8, 1949, Ziegfeld Th.
740 *performances.*
Book by Joseph Fields & Anita Loos; lyrics by Leo Robin.
Produced by Herman Levin & Oliver Smith; directed by John C. Wilson; dances by Agnes de Mille.
Cast included: Carol Channing, Yvonne Adair, Jack McCauley, Eric Brotherson, Alice Pearce, Rex Evans, Anita Alvarez, George S. Irving, Reta Shaw, Howard Morris, Mort Marshall, Peter Birch, Helen Wood.
Principal songs: Bye Bye Baby; A Little Girl from Little Rock; Just a Kiss Apart; You Say You Care; Diamonds Are a Girl's Best Friend; Homesick Blues.
Recorded Versions
Columbia OL 4290/OS 2310 (O.C.).
MGM 3231 (F.V.) (1953) X.
A good old-fashioned musical comedy score. The MGM soundtrack, backed by selections from Kern's *Till the Clouds Roll By*, offers some interpolated numbers and the purring of Marilyn Monroe and Jane Russell.

TWO ON THE AISLE
Opened: July 19, 1951, Mark Hellinger Th.
281 *performances.*
Sketches by Comden & Green.
Produced by Arthur Lesser; directed by Abe Burrows; dances by Ted Cappy.
Cast included: Bert Lahr, Dolores Gray, Colette Marchand, Elliott Reid, Stanley Prager, J. C. McCord, Larry Laurence.
Principal songs: Hold Me, Hold Me, Hold Me; There Never Was a Baby Like My Baby; Catch Our Act at the

Met; If You Hadn't but You Did; How Will He Know?
Recorded Version
Decca DL 8040 (O.C.).

One of the few revue scores recorded, and the only Broadway original cast L.P. featuring the great Bert Lahr.

HAZEL FLAGG

Opened: Feb. 11, 1953, Mark Hellinger Th.
190 *performances.*
Book by Ben Hecht; lyrics by Bob Hilliard.
Produced by Styne & Anthony Brady Farrell; directed by David Alexander; dances by Robert Alton.
Cast included: Helen Gallagher, Thomas Mitchell, Benay Venuta, John Howard, Jack Whiting, Sheree North, Jonathan Harris, John Brascia, Hugh Lambert.
Principal songs: I'm Glad I'm Leaving; Every Street's a Boulevard in Old New York; How Do You Speak to an Angel; Everybody Loves to Take a Bow; I Feel Like I'm Gonna Live Forever.
Recorded Version
RCA Victor LOC 1010 (O.C.) X.

Apart from "Every Street's a Boulevard," there's little to recommend here.

PETER PAN

Opened: Oct. 20, 1954, Winter Garden
152 *performances.*
Play by James M. Barrie; music & lyrics also by Mark Charlap & Carolyn Leigh.
Produced by Richard Halliday; directed by Jerome Robbins.
Cast included: Mary Martin, Cyril Ritchard, Margalo Gilmore, Kathy Nolan, Heller Halliday, Sondra Lee, Norman Shelly, Joe E. Marks.
Principal Styne-Comden-Green songs: Never Never Land; Wendy; Distant Melody; Captain Hook's Waltz.
Recorded Version
RCA Victor LOC/LSO 1019 (O.C.).

The songs for this charming album were divided about evenly between the two teams.

BELLS ARE RINGING

Opened: Nov. 29, 1956, Shubert Th.
924 *performances.*
Book by Comden & Green.
Produced by The Theatre Guild; directed by Jerome Robbins; dances by Robbins & Bob Fosse.
Cast included: Judy Holliday, Sydney Chaplin, Eddie Lawrence, Jean Stapleton, George S. Irving, Peter Gennaro, Bernie West, Frank Aletter, Steve Roland, Donna Sanders.
Principal songs: It's a Perfect Relationship; On My Own; It's a Simple Little System; Is It a Crime?; Just in Time; Long Before I Knew You; The Party's Over; I'm Going Back.
Recorded Versions
Columbia OL 5170/OS 2006 (O.C.).
Capitol (S)W 1435 (F.V.) (1960) X.

A spirited, melodious collection of songs. Miss Holliday & Dean Martin are on the Capitol soundtrack.

SAY, DARLING

Opened: Apr. 3, 1958, Anta Th.
332 *performances.*
Play by Richard Bissell, Abe Burrows, Marian Bissell.
Produced by Styne & Lester Osterman; directed by Burrows; dances by Matt Mattox.
Cast included: David Wayne, Vivian Blaine, Johnny Desmond, Jerome Cowan, Constance Ford, Horace McMahon, Robert Morse, Matt Mattox, Mitchell Gregg, Colin Romoff, Elliott Gould, Virginia Martin, Steve Condos, Richard Tone, Robert Downing.
Principal songs: It's the Second Time You Meet that Matters; Say, Darling; Dance Only with Me; Something's Always Happening on the River.
Recorded Version
RCA Victor LOC/LSO 1045 (O.C.) X.

Pleasant, though hardly memorable music & lyrics.

GYPSY

Opened: May 21, 1959, Broadway Th.

702 *performances.*
Book by Arthur Laurents; lyrics by Stephen Sondheim.
Produced by David Merrick & Leland Hayward; directed by Jerome Robbins.
Cast included: Ethel Merman, Jack Klugman, Sandra Church, Maria Karnilova, Paul Wallace, Lane Bradbury, Faith Dane, Chotzi Foley, Mort Marshall, Jacqueline Mayro, Joe Silver, Michael Parks, Loney Lewis, Peg Murray.
Principal songs: Let Me Entertain You; Some People; Small World; Little Lamb; You'll Never Get Away from Me; All I Need Is the Girl; Everything's Coming Up Roses; Together; You Gotta Have a Gimmick; Rose's Turn.
Recorded Versions
Columbia OL 5420/OS 2017 (O.C.).
Warner Bros. B(S) 1480 (F.V.) (1962).
One of the greatest show albums ever made. The soundtrack version, starring Rosalind Russell's voice, Lisa Kirk, is completely outclassed.

DO RE MI

Opened: Dec. 26, 1960, St. James Th.
400 *performances.*
Book by Garson Kanin.
Produced by David Merrick; directed by Kanin; dances by Marc Breaux & Deedee Wood.
Cast included: Phil Silvers, Nancy Walker, John Reardon, David Burns, George Mathews, George Givot, Nancy Dussault, Dawn Nickerson, Steve Roland, Donna Sanders.
Principal songs: I Know About Love; Cry Like the Wind; What's New at the Zoo?; Adventure; Make Someone Happy.
Recorded Version
RCA Victor LOC/LSO 1105 (O.C.).
An average score that is worth the price just to hear Miss Walker describe her life of "Adventure."

SUBWAYS ARE FOR SLEEPING

Opened: Dec. 27, 1961, St. James Th.

205 *performances.*
Book by Comden & Green.
Produced by David Merrick; directed by Michael Kidd.
Cast included: Sydney Chaplin, Carol Lawrence, Orson Bean, Phyllis Newman, Cy Young, Gordon Connell.
Principal songs: Girls Like Me; I'm Just Taking my Time; Ride Through the Night; Be a Santa; Comes Once in a Lifetime.
Recorded Version
Columbia KOL 5730/KOS 2130 (O.C.).
An attractive collection of songs, somewhat marred by Mr. Chaplin's vocal inadequacies.

FUNNY GIRL

Opened: Mar. 26, 1964, Winter Garden
1,348 *performances.*
Book by Isobel Lennart; lyrics by Bob Merrill.
Produced by Ray Stark; directed by Garson Kanin & Jerome Robbins; dances by Carol Haney.
Cast included: Barbra Streisand, Sydney Chaplin, Danny Meehan, Kay Medford, Jean Stapleton, Roger DeKoven, Joseph Macaulay, Buzz Miller, Lainie Kazan.
Principal songs: I'm the Greatest Star; Cornet Man; People; You Are Woman; Don't Rain on My Parade; Sadie, Sadie; Who Are You Now?; The Music that Makes Me Dance.
Recorded Versions
Capitol (S)VAS 2059 (O.C.).
Columbia BOS 3220 (F.V.) (1968).
Styne & Merrill have given Miss Streisand a remarkably rich and varied musical assortment which she interprets superbly. Some musical changes on the soundtrack, including addition of "My Man."

FADE OUT – FADE IN

Opened: May 26, 1964, Mark Hellinger Th.
271 *performances.*
Book by Comden & Green.
Produced by Lester Osterman & Styne;

directed by George Abbott; dances by Ernest Flatt.
Cast included: Carol Burnett, Jack Cassidy, Lou Jacobi, Tina Louise, Dick Patterson, Mitchell Jason, Reuben Singer, Virginia Payne, Tiger Haynes, Aileen Poe, Trish Dwelley.
Principal songs: Call Me Savage; The Usher from the Mezzanine; You Mustn't Be Discouraged; Fade Out—Fade In; Close Harmony.
Recorded Version
ABC Paramount (S)OC 3 (O.C.).

Not consistently inspired but entertaining enough.

HALLELUJAH, BABY!

Opened: Apr. 26, 1967, Martin Beck Th.
293 *performances.*
Book by Arthur Laurents.
Produced by Albert W. Selden & Hal James, Jane Nusbaum & Harry Rigby; directed by Burt Shevelove; dances by Kevin Carlisle.
Cast included: Leslie Uggams, Robert Hooks, Allen Case, Lillian Hayman, Barbara Sharma.
Principal songs: My Own Morning; Not Mine; Being Good Isn't Good Enough; Talking to Yourself; I Don't Know Where She Got It; Hallelujah, Baby!
Recorded Version
Columbia KOL 6690/KOS 3090 (O.C.).
Hallelujah, Leslie Uggams.

DARLING OF THE DAY

Opened: Jan. 27, 1968, George Abbott Th.
32 *performances.*
Book uncredited; lyrics by E. Y. Harburg.
Produced by The Theatre Guild & Joel Schenker; directed by Noel Willman; dances by Lee Theodore.
Cast included: Vincent Price, Patricia Routledge, Brenda Forbes, Peter Woodthorpe, Teddy Green.
Principal songs: To Get Out of This World Alive; It's Enough to Make a

Lady Fall in Love; Let's See What Happens; That Something Extra Special; Not on Your Nellie.
Recorded Version
RCA Victor LOC/LSO 1149 (O.C.).

The musical deserved a better fate, but we can still enjoy the singing of Miss Routledge and the delights of the score.

CHAPTER TWENTY-ONE
FRANK LOESSER
composer-lyricist

All music & lyrics by Mr. Loesser unless otherwise noted.

THE ILLUSTRATORS' SHOW

Opened: Jan. 22, 1936, 48th St. Th.
5 *performances.*
Sketches by Max Liebman, Hi Alexander, Kenneth Webb, Otto Soglow, Donald Blackwell, Harry Evans, Frank Gabrielson; Loesser music by Irving Actman; music & lyrics also by Edgar Fairchild & Milton Pascal, Charlotte Kent, Frederick Loewe & Earle Crooker, Michael Cleary & Max & Nathaniel Lief.
Produced by Soc. of Illustrators & Tom Weatherly; directed by Weatherly & Allen Delano; dances by Carl Randall.
Principal Loesser-Actman songs: Bang—the Bell Rang!; If You Didn't Love Me.

WHERE'S CHARLEY?

Opened: Oct. 11, 1948, St. James Th.
792 *performances.*
Book by George Abbott.
Produced by Cy Feuer & Ernest Martin with Gwen Rickard; directed by George Abbott; dances by George Balanchine.
Cast included: Ray Bolger, Allyn McLerie, Byron Palmer, Doretta Morrow, Horace Cooper, Jane Lawrence, Paul England, Cornell MacNeil.
Principal songs: The New Ashmoleon Marching Society and Student Conserva-

tory Band; My Darling, My Darling; Make a Miracle; Lovelier than Ever; Pernambuco; Once in Love with Amy; At the Red Rose Cotillion.

Recorded Version

English Columbia 33SX 1085 (London O.C.) (1958) X.

The only complete recording of the fondly-remembered score is that of the English company headed by Norman Wisdom.

GUYS AND DOLLS

Opened: Nov. 24, 1950, 46th St. Th.
1,200 *performances.*

Book by Abe Burrows & Jo Swerling.

Produced by Cy Feuer & Ernest Martin; directed by George S. Kaufman; dances by Michael Kidd.

Cast included: Robert Alda, Vivian Blaine, Sam Levene, Isabel Bigley, Pat Rooney, B. S. Pully, Stubby Kaye, Tom Pedi, Johnny Silver, Peter Gennaro, Scott Merrill, Onna White, Eddie Phillips.

Principal songs: Fugue for Tinhorns; The Oldest Established; I'll Know; A Bushel and a Peck; Adelaide's Lament; Guys and Dolls; If I Were a Bell; My Time of Day; I've Never Been in Love Before; Take Back Your Mink; More I Cannot Wish You; Luck Be a Lady; Sue Me; Sit Down, You're Rockin' the Boat; Marry the Man Today.

Recorded Version

Decca DL (7) 9023 (O.C.).

Still a classic in its field.

THE MOST HAPPY FELLA

Opened: May 3, 1956, Imperial Th.
676 *performances.*

Book by Loesser.

Produced by Kermit Bloomgarden & Lynn Loesser; directed by Joseph Anthony; dances by Dania Krupska.

Cast included: Robert Weede, Jo Sullivan, Art Lund, Susan Johnson, Shorty Long, Mona Paulee, Lee Cass, Zina Bethune.

Principal songs: Somebody Somewhere;

The Most Happy Fella; Standing on the Corner; Joey, Joey, Joey; Rosabella; Abbondanza; Sposalizio; Happy to Make Your Acquaintance; Big "D"; Warm All Over; My Heart Is So Full of You; How Beautiful the Days.

Recorded Version

Columbia O3L 240 (O.C.).

The 3-record set of the entire score reveals many facets of a distinguished musical talent. Highlights are on the single record, Columbia OL 5118/OS 2330.

GREENWILLOW

Opened: Mar. 8, 1960, Alvin Th.
95 *performances.*

Book by Loesser & Lesser Samuels.

Produced by Robert A. Willey with Frank Productions; directed by George Roy Hill; dances by Joe Layton.

Cast included: Anthony Perkins, Cecil Kellaway, Pert Kelton, Ellen McCown, William Chapman, Lee Cass, Grover Dale, Marion Mercer, Margery Gray.

Principal songs: The Music of Home; Gideon Briggs, I Love You; Summertime Love; Walking Away Whistling; Never Will I Marry; Faraway Boy; Clang Dang the Bell.

Recorded Version

RCA Victor LOC/LSO 2001 (O.C.) X.

Loesser in a bucolic, lyrical, frequently whimsical mood.

HOW TO SUCCEED IN BUSINESS WITHOUT REALLY TRYING

Opened: Oct. 14, 1961, 46th St. Th.
1,417 *performances.*

Book by Abe Burrows, Jack Weinstock, Willie Gilbert.

Produced by Cy Feuer & Ernest Martin with Frank Productions; directed by Burrows & Bob Fosse; dances by Hugh Lambert.

Cast included: Robert Morse, Rudy Vallee, Bonnie Scott, Virginia Martin, Charles Nelson Reilly, Claudette Sutherland, Ruth Kobart, Sammy Smith.

Principal songs: The Company Way; A

Secretary Is Not a Toy; Grand Old Ivy; Been a Long Day; Paris Original; Rosemary; I Believe in You; Brotherhood of Man.
Recorded Versions
RCA Victor LOC/LSO 1066 (O.C.).
United Artists 4151/5151 (F.V.) (1967).

With Michele Lee added to original stars Morse & Vallee, the soundtrack LP is a faithful, though decimated version of the long-on-comedy score.

RICHARD ADLER
composer-lyricist

JERRY ROSS
composer-lyricist

All music & lyrics by both Messrs. Adler & Ross unless otherwise noted.

JOHN MURRAY ANDERSON'S ALMANAC
Opened: Dec. 10, 1953, Imperial Th.
229 *performances.*
Sketches by Jean Kerr, Sumner Locke-Elliot, Arthur Macrae, Billy K. Wells, Herbert Farjeon, Lauri Wylie; music & lyrics also by Cy Coleman & Joseph McCarthy, Sheldon Harnick, Henry Sullivan & John Murray Anderson, Charles Zwar, Michael Grace & Sammy Gallop, John Rox, Harry Belafonte.
Produced by Grace, Stanley Gilkey & Harry Rigby; directed by Anderson & Cyril Ritchard; dances by Donald Saddler.
Cast included: Hermione Gingold, Billy DeWolfe, Harry Belafonte, Orson Bean, Polly Bergen, Nanci Crompton, Carleton Carpenter, Alice Pearce, Elaine Dunn, Celia Lipton, Kay Medford, Monique Van Vooren, Lee Becker (Theodore), Tina Louise, Larry Kert.
Principal Adler-Ross songs: You're So Much a Part of Me; When Am I Going to Meet Your Mother?; Acorn in the Meadow; Fini.

THE PAJAMA GAME
Opened: May 13, 1954, St. James Th.
1,063 *performances.*
Book by George Abbott & Richard Bissell.
Produced by Frederick Brisson, Robert E. Griffith & Harold Prince; directed by Abbott & Jerome Robbins; dances by Bob Fosse.
Cast included: John Raitt, Janis Paige, Eddie Foy, Jr., Carol Haney, Reta Shaw, Stanley Prager, Thelma Pelish, Jack Waldron, Peter Gennaro, Rae Allen, Shirley MacLaine, Buzz Miller, Carmen Alvarez, Virginia Martin.
Principal songs: I'm Not at All in Love; I'll Never Be Jealous Again; Hey, There; Her Is; Once a Year Day; Small Talk; There Once Was a Man; Steam Heat; Hernando's Hideaway; 7½ Cents.
Recorded Versions
Columbia OL 4840 (O.C.).
Columbia OL 5210 (F.V.) (1957).

Both releases have the same material and almost the same cast. The major change is Doris Day for Janis Paige on the soundtrack.

DAMN YANKEES
Opened: May 5, 1955, 46th St. Th.
1,019 *performances.*
Book by George Abbott & Douglass Wallop.
Produced by Frederick Brisson, Robert E. Griffith & Harold Prince; directed by Abbott; dances by Bob Fosse.
Cast included: Gwen Verdon, Stephen Douglass, Ray Walston, Russ Brown, Shannon Bolin, Jimmy Komack, Robert Shafer, Jean Stapleton, Nathaniel Frey, Eddie Phillips, Rae Allen.
Principal songs: Goodbye, Old Girl; Heart; A Little Brains, a Little Talent; A Man Doesn't Know; Whatever Lola Wants; Who's Got the Pain?; Near to You; Two Lost Souls.
Recorded Versions
RCA Victor LOC/LSO 1021 (O.C.).
RCA Victor LOC/LSO 1047 (F.V.)

(1958).

There are a few minor changes in the song lineup on the soundtrack, plus the regrettable substitution of Tab Hunter for Stephen Douglass.

KWAMINA

Opened: Oct. 23, 1961, 54th St. Th.
32 performances.
Book by Robert Alan Aurthur; music & lyrics by Adler.
Produced by Alfred de Liagre; directed by Robert Lewis; dances by Agnes de Mille.
Cast included: Sally Ann Howes, Terry Carter, Brock Peters, Robert Guillaume, Ethel Ayler, Joseph Attles, Norman Barrs, Rex Ingram, Rawn Spearman.
Principal songs: Cocoa Bean Song; Welcome Home; Nothing More to Look Forward To; Ordinary People; What's Wrong with Me?; What Happened to Me Tonight?; Another Time, Another Place.
Recorded Version
Capitol (S)W 1645 (O.C.) X.

A richly colorful score that makes excellent use of native rhythms.

MEREDITH WILLSON
composer-lyricist

All books by Mr. Willson unless otherwise noted.

THE MUSIC MAN

Opened: Dec. 19, 1957, Majestic Th.
1,375 performances.
Produced by Kermit Bloomgarden with Herbert Greene & Frank Productions; directed by Morton DaCosta; dances by Onna White.
Cast included: Robert Preston, Barbara Cook, David Burns, Pert Kelton, The Buffalo Bills, Iggie Wolfington, Helen Raymond, Paul Reed, Eddie Hodges, Danny Carroll.
Principal songs: Rock Island; Trouble;

Piano Lesson; Goodnight, My Someone; Seventy-Six Trombones; The Sadder-but-Wiser Girl; Marian the Librarian; My White Knight; Wells Fargo Wagon; Shipoopi; Lida Rose; Will I Ever Tell You?; Gary, Indiana; Till There Was You.
Recorded Versions
Capitol (S)WAO 990 (O.C.).
Warner Bros. B(S) 1459 (F.V.) (1962).
Capitol (S)T 1320.

Willson's skillful blending of corn and cacophony gets a remarkably fine aural production, particularly on the original recording. The composer-lyricist & wife, Rini, are heard on the second Capitol set.

THE UNSINKABLE MOLLY BROWN

Opened: Nov. 3, 1960, Winter Garden
532 performances.
Book by Richard Morris.
Produced by The Theatre Guild & Dore Schary; directed by Schary; dances by Peter Gennaro.
Cast included: Tammy Grimes, Harve Presnell, Cameron Prud'homme, Mony Dalmes, Edith Meiser, Mitchell Gregg, Christopher Hewett.
Principal songs: I Ain't Down Yet; Belly Up to the Bar, Boys; If I Knew; My Own Brass Bed; Dolce Far Niente.
Recorded Versions
Capitol (S)W 2152 (O.C.).
MGM (S) 4232 ST (F.V.) (1964).

A routine score, badly truncated on the Debbie Reynolds-Harve Presnell soundtrack album.

HERE'S LOVE

Opened: Oct. 3, 1963, Shubert Th.
334 performances.
Produced & directed by Stuart Ostrow; dances by Michael Kidd.
Cast included: Janis Paige, Craig Stevens, Laurence Naismith, Fred Gwynne, Paul Reed, Cliff Hall, David Doyle, Larry Douglas, Valerie Lee.
Principal songs: The Big Clown Balloons; Arm in Arm; You Don't Know; Here's Love; Pine Cones and Holly Ber-

ries; That Man Over There.
Recorded Version
Columbia KOL 6000/KOS 2400 (O.C.).

Some lively moments, though much of the score—and most of the voices—are undistinguished.

CHAPTER TWENTY-TWO
BOB MERRILL
composer-lyricist

For another musical with Merrill lyrics, see Funny Girl *under Jule Styne.*

NEW GIRL IN TOWN
Opened: May 14, 1957, 46th St. Th.
431 *performances.*
Book by George Abbott.
Produced by Frederick Brisson, Robert E. Griffith & Harold S. Prince; directed by Abbott; dances by Bob Fosse.
Cast included: Gwen Verdon, Thelma Ritter, George Wallace, Cameron Prud'homme, Mark Dawson, Lulu Bates, Eddie Phillips.
Principal songs: Anna Lilla; Sunshine Girl; Flings; It's Good to Be Alive; Look at 'Er; Did You Close Your Eyes?
Recorded Version
RCA Victor LOC/LSO 1106 (O.C.).

The atmospheric numbers capture the spirit of the tale better than the romantic pieces.

TAKE ME ALONG
Opened: Oct. 22, 1959, Shubert Th.
448 *performances.*
Book by Joseph Stein & Robert Russell.
Produced by David Merrick; directed by Peter Glenville; dances by Onna White.
Cast included: Jackie Gleason, Walter Pidgeon, Eileen Herlie, Robert Morse, Una Merkel, Susan Luckey, Peter Conlow.
Principal songs: I Would Die; Sid Ol' Kid; Staying Young; I Get Embarrassed; We're Home; Take Me Along; Promise

Me a Rose; Nine O'Clock; But Yours.
Recorded Version
RCA Victor LOC/LSO 1050 (O.C.).

There is much period charm and dramatic appeal in this somewhat neglected score.

CARNIVAL
Opened: Apr. 13, 1961, Imperial Th.
719 *performances.*
Book by Michael Stewart.
Produced by David Merrick; directed by Gower Champion.
Cast included: Anna Maria Alberghetti, James Mitchell, Kaye Ballard, Pierre Olaf, Jerry Orbach, Henry Lascoe, Anita Gillette, Luba Lisa, Will Lee, George Marcy, Paul Sydell, Igors Gavon.
Principal songs: Direct from Vienna; Yes, My Heart; Love Makes the World Go Round; Mira; Beautiful Candy; Always Always You; The Grand Imperial Cirque de Paris.
Recorded Version
MGM (S) 3946 (O.C.).

A tender, evocative score.

HENRY, SWEET HENRY
Opened: Oct. 23, 1967, Palace Th.
Book by Nunnally Johnson.
Produced by Edward Spector & Norman Twain; directed by George Roy Hill; dances by Michael Bennett.
Cast included: Don Ameche, Carol Bruce, Robin Wilson, Neva Small, Louise Lasser, Alice Playten, Milo Boulton, K. C. Townsend.
Principal songs: In Some Little World; I Wonder How It Is; Nobody Steps on Kafritz; Henry, Sweet Henry; Do You Ever Go to Boston?
Recorded Version
ABC (S) OC-4 (O.C.).

Little to recommend.

STEPHEN SONDHEIM
composer-lyricist

For other musicals with Sondheim lyrics, see West Side Story *under Leonard Bernstein;* Gypsy *under Jule Styne;* Do I Hear a Waltz? *under Richard Rodgers.*

A FUNNY THING HAPPENED ON THE WAY TO THE FORUM
Opened: May 8, 1962, Alvin Th.
964 *performances.*
Book by Burt Shevelove & Larry Gelbart.
Produced by Harold Prince; directed by George Abbott & Jerome Robbins (uncredited); dances by Jack Cole.
Cast included: Zero Mostel, Jack Gilford, David Burns, Raymond Walburn, John Carradine, Ruth Kobart, Brian Davies, Preshy Marker, Ronald Holgate, Eddie Phillips.
Principal songs: Comedy Tonight; Love, I Hear; Free; Lovely; Everybody Ought to Have a Maid; Pretty Little Picture.
Recorded Versions
Capitol (S)WAO 1717 (O.C.).
United Artists 4144/5144 (F.V.) (1966).
Sondheim's delectable score is all but smothered on the soundtrack release.

ANYONE CAN WHISTLE
Opened: Apr. 4, 1964, Majestic Th.
9 *performances.*
Book by Arthur Laurents.
Produced by Kermit Bloomgarden & Diana Krasny; directed by Laurents; dances by Herbert Ross.
Cast included: Lee Remick, Angela Lansbury, Harry Guardino, Gabriel Dell, Arnold Soboloff, James Frawley, Peg Murray.
Principal songs: Miracle Song; Anyone Can Whistle; A Parade in Town; Everybody Says Don't; See What It Gets You; With So Little to Be Sure Of.
Recorded Version
Columbia KOL 6080/KOS 2480 (O.C.).
The merits of the score were so apparent that Columbia recorded it even after the show had closed.

JERRY BOCK
composer

SHELDON HARNICK
lyricist

All music by Mr. Bock & lyrics by Mr. Harnick unless otherwise noted.

MR. WONDERFUL
Opened: Mar. 22, 1956, Broadway Th.
383 *performances.*
Book by Joseph Stein & Will Glickman; lyrics by Larry Holofcener & George Weiss.
Produced by Jule Styne & George Gilbert with Lester Osterman; directed by Jack Donohue.
Cast included: Sammy Davis, Jr., Jack Carter, Pat Marshall, Olga James, Chita Rivera, Hal Loman, Will Mastin, Sammy Davis, Sr., Karen Shepard.
Principal songs: Without You I'm Nothing; Mr. Wonderful; Ethel Baby; Too Close for Comfort.
Recorded Version
Decca DL 9032 (O.C.).
Sammy Davis belts out the breezy score with an exuberance not always warranted by the material.

THE BODY BEAUTIFUL
Opened: Jan. 23, 1958, Broadway Th.
60 *performances.*
Book by Joseph Stein & Will Glickman.
Produced by Richard Kollmar & Albert W. Selden; directed by George Schaefer; dances by Herbert Ross.
Cast included: Mindy Carson, Steve Forrest, Jack Warden, Lonnie Sattin, Barbara McNair, Brock Peters, William Hickey, Jack DeLon.
Principal songs: Leave Well Enough Alone; Uh-Huh, Oh Yeah!; All of These and More; Summer Is; Just My Luck; A Relatively Simple Affair.

FIORELLO!
Opened: Nov. 23, 1959, Broadhurst Th.

511

795 *performances.*
Book by Jerome Weidman & George Abbott.
Produced by Robert Griffith & Harold Prince; directed by Abbott; dances by Peter Gennaro.
Cast included: Tom Bosley, Patricia Wilson, Ellen Hanley, Howard DaSilva, Mark Dawson, Nathaniel Frey, Pat Stanley, Eileen Rodgers, Bob Holiday, Ron Husmann, Patricia Harty.
Principal songs: On the Side of the Angels; Politics and Poker; The Name's LaGuardia; I Love a Cop; 'Til Tomorrow; When Did I Fall in Love?; Gentleman Jimmy; Little Tin Box; The Very Next Man.
Recorded Version
Capitol (S)WAO 1321 (O.C.).
New York's beloved Little Flower gets an affectionate and witty tribute.

TENDERLOIN
Opened: Oct. 17, 1960, 46th St. Th.
216 *performances.*
Book by George Abbott & Jerome Weidman.
Produced by Robert Griffith & Harold Prince; directed by Abbott; dances by Joe Layton.
Cast included: Maurice Evans, Ron Husmann, Wynne Miller, Eileen Rodgers, Ralph Dunn, Irene Kane, Lee Becker (Theodore), Rex Everhart, Eddie Phillips, Margery Gray.
Principal songs: Little Old New York; Artificial Flowers; The Picture of Happiness; Tommy, Tommy; How the Money Changes Hands; Good Clean Fun; My Miss Mary; My Gentle Young Johnny.
Recorded Version
Capitol (S)WAO 1492 (O.C.) X.
Ron Husmann wins vocal honors in this delightfully flavorsome collection of songs.

SMILING THE BOY FELL DEAD
Opened: Apr. 19, 1961, Cherry Lane Th.
22 *performances.*
Book by Ira Wallach; music by David Baker.
Produced by Theodore Mann & George Kogel; directed by Word Baker (uncredited) & Mann.
Cast included: Danny Meehan, Phil Leeds, Joseph Macaulay, Claiborne Cary, Louise Larrabee.
Principal songs: Wonderful Future; World to Win; Wonderful Machine; Dear Old Dad.

SHE LOVES ME
Opened: Apr. 23, 1963, Eugene O'Neill Th.
301 *performances.*
Book by Joe Masteroff.
Produced by Harold Prince with Lawrence J. Kasha & Philip C. McKenna; directed by Prince; dances by Carol Haney.
Cast included: Barbara Cook, Daniel Massey, Barbara Baxley, Jack Cassidy, Ludwig Donath, Nathaniel Frey, Ralph Williams, Jo Wilder, Wood Romoff, Gino Conforti, Peg Murray.
Principal songs: Days Gone By; Tonight at Eight; Will He Like Me?; Ilona; A Romantic Atmosphere; Dear Friend; Ice Cream; She Loves Me; Grand Knowing You.
Recorded Version
MGM (S)E 4118 OC-2 (O.C.).
This remarkably tasty musical confection has been granted the deserved luxury of a two-record set.

FIDDLER ON THE ROOF
Opened: Sept. 22, 1964, Imperial Th.
(*Still running as of Sept. 1, 1968*)
Book by Joseph Stein.
Produced by Harold Prince; directed by Jerome Robbins.
Cast included: Zero Mostel, Maria Karnilova, Beatrice Arthur, Joanna Merlin, Austin Pendleton, Bert Convy, Julia Migenes, Tanya Everett, Gino Conforti.
Principal songs: Tradition; Matchmaker, Matchmaker; If I Were a Rich Man; To Life; Sunrise, Sunset; Do You Love

Me?; Miracle of Miracles; Anatevka.

Recorded Versions

RCA Victor LOC/LSO 1093 (O.C.).

Columbia OL 6490 (Israeli O.C., Hebrew) (1965).

Columbia OL 6650/OS 3050 (Israeli O.C., Yiddish) (1966).

Columbia OL 6610/OS 3010.

An eloquent score that may be savored in English, Hebrew and Yiddish. Herschel Bernardi, who succeeded Zero Mostel, has the last record all to himself.

THE APPLE TREE

Opened: Oct. 18, 1966, Shubert Th.

463 performances.

Book by Bock & Harnick, additional material by Jerome Coopersmith.

Produced by Stuart Ostrow; directed by Mike Nichols; dances by Lee Theodore & Herbert Ross.

Cast included: Barbara Harris, Alan Alda, Larry Blyden, Carmen Alvarez, Marc Jordan.

Principal songs: What Makes Me Love Him?; The Apple Tree; Go to Sleep, Whatever You Are; I've Got What You Want; Eve.

Recorded Version

Columbia KOL 6620/KOS 3020 (O.C.).

Barbara Harris shines in this collection of bright musical pieces culled from three separate one-act musicals.

CHARLES STROUSE
composer

LEE ADAMS
lyricist

BYE BYE BIRDIE

Opened: Apr. 14, 1960, Martin Beck Th.

607 performances.

Book by Michael Stewart.

Produced by Edward Padula; directed by Gower Champion.

Cast included: Chita Rivera, Dick Van Dyke, Kay Medford, Paul Lynde, Dick Gautier, Michael J. Pollard, Susan Watson, Marijane Maricle, Jerry Dodge, Kenny Burrell, Charles Nelson Reilly.

Principal songs: One Last Kiss; One Boy; An English Teacher; Baby, Talk to Me; A Lot of Livin' to Do; Rosie; Put on a Happy Face; Kids.

Recorded Versions

Columbia KOL 5510/KOS 2025 (O.C.).

RCA Victor LOC/LSO 1081 (F.V.) (1963).

The bright, youthful score is better served by the Broadway cast than by the Hollywood group headed by Ann-Margret, Janet Leigh & Mr. Van Dyke.

ALL AMERICAN

Opened: Mar. 19, 1962, Winter Garden

80 performances.

Book by Mel Brooks.

Produced by Edward Padula; directed by Joshua Logan; dances by Danny Daniels.

Cast included: Ray Bolger, Eileen Herlie, Ron Husmann, Anita Gillette, Fritz Weaver, Bernie West, Betty Oakes, Mort Marshall, Will B. Able.

Principal songs: We Speak the Same Language; Once Upon a Time; The Real Me; What a Country!; Nightlife; I've Just Seen Her.

Recorded Version

Columbia KOL 5760/KOS 2160 (O.C.).

Not one of the team's better efforts.

GOLDEN BOY

Opened: Oct. 20, 1964, Majestic Th.

569 performances.

Book by Clifford Odets & William Gibson.

Produced by Hillard Elkins; directed by Arthur Penn; dances by Donald McKayle.

Cast included: Sammy Davis, Billy Daniels, Paula Wayne, Kenneth Tobey, Ted Beniades, Roy Glenn, Jeanette DuBois, Johnny Brown, Jaime Rogers, Louis Gossett, Lola Falana.

Principal songs: Night Song; Gimme Some; Don't Forget 127th Street; Lorna's Here; This Is the Life; Golden Boy; While the City Sleeps; I Want to Be with You.

Recorded Version

Capitol (S)VAS 2124 (O.C.).

A lively pulsating reincarnation of the Odets play, with a score that represents Strouse & Adams' most solid achievement to date.

IT'S A BIRD   IT'S A PLANE IT'S SUPERMAN

Opened: Mar. 29, 1966, Alvin Th.
129 *performances.*
Book by David Newman & Robert Benton.
Produced & directed by Harold Prince; dances by Ernest Flatt.
Cast included: Jack Cassidy, Michael O'Sullivan, Patricia Marand, Bob Holiday, Don Chastain, Linda Lavin.
Principal songs: It's Superman; We Don't Matter at All; The Woman for the Man; You've Got Possibilities; What I've Always Wanted; Ooh, Do You Love You!; You've Got What I Need.

Recorded Version

Columbia KOL 6570/KOS 2970 (O.C.).

Broadway's first excursion into the "camp" camp, abetted by songs that ably reflect the innocence of the terrain.

TOM JONES
lyricist

HARVEY SCHMIDT
composer

All books by Mr. Jones unless otherwise noted.

THE FANTASTICKS

Opened: May 3, 1960, Sullivan St. Playhouse.
(*Still running as of Sept. 1, 1968*)
Produced by Lore Noto; directed by

Word Baker.
Cast included: Jerry Orbach, Rita Gardner, Kenneth Nelson, Richard Stauffer, Thomas Bruce (Tom Jones).
Principal songs: Try to Remember; It Depends on What You Pay; Much More; Soon It's Gonna Rain; Round and Round; Plant a Radish; They Were You.

Recorded Version

MGM (S) 3872 (O.C.).

A score rich in imagery and lyrical appeal.

110 IN THE SHADE

Opened: Oct. 24, 1963, Broadhurst Th.
330 *performances.*
Book by N. Richard Nash.
Produced by David Merrick; directed by Joseph Anthony; dances by Agnes de Mille.
Cast included: Robert Horton, Inga Swensen, Stephen Douglass, Will Geer, Steve Roland, Scooter (Anthony) Teague, Lesley Ann Warren, George Church, Jerry Dodge.
Principal songs: Another Hot Day; Love, Don't Turn Away; The Rain Song; A Man and a Woman; Old Maid; Everything Beautiful Happens at Night; Melisande; Simple Little Things; Is It Really Me?; Wonderful Music.

Recorded Version

RCA Victor LOC/LSO 1085 (O.C.).

A dramatic, flavorful—though strangely unappreciated—score.

I DO!   I DO!

Opened: Dec. 5, 1966, 46th St. Th.
584 *performances.*
Produced by David Merrick; directed by Gower Champion.
Cast: Mary Martin, Robert Preston.
Principal songs: I Love My Wife; My Cup Runneth Over; Nobody's Perfect; A Well Known Fact; The Honeymoon Is Over; Where Are the Snows; When the Kids Get Married; What Is a Woman?

Recorded Version

RCA Victor LOC/LSO 1128 (O.C.).

For the Sweete Shoppe crowd.

CHAPTER TWENTY-THREE
CY COLEMAN
composer

WILDCAT
Opened: Dec. 16, 1960, Alvin Th.
171 *performances.*
Book by N. Richard Nash; lyrics by Carolyn Leigh.
Produced by Michael Kidd & Nash; directed by Kidd.
Cast included: Lucille Ball, Keith Andes, Paula Stewart, Edith King, Don Tomkins, Charles Braswell, Swen Swenson.
Principal songs: Hey, Look Me Over; You've Come Home; What Takes My Fancy; One Day We Dance; Give a Little Whistle; El Sombrero; Corduroy Road.
Recorded Version
RCA Victor LOC/LSO 1060 (O.C.).
The "Hey, Look Me Over" score has a few other goodies, too.

LITTLE ME
Opened: Nov. 17, 1962, Lunt-Fontanne Th.
257 *performances.*
Book by Neil Simon; lyrics by Carolyn Leigh.
Produced by Cy Feuer & Ernest Martin; directed by Feuer & Bob Fosse.
Cast included: Sid Caesar, Virginia Martin, Nancy Andrews, Mort Marshall, Joey Faye, Swen Swenson, Nancy Cushman, Peter Turgeon, Mickey Deems.
Principal songs: The Other Side of the Tracks; Deep Down Inside; Boom-Boom; I've Got Your Number; I Love You; Real Live Girl; Here's to Us.
Recorded Version
RCA Victor LOC/LSO 1078 (O.C.).
Much far-out hilarity, abetted by the wit of Miss Leigh's lyrics and the rhythmic freshness of Mr. Coleman's music.

SWEET CHARITY
Opened: Jan. 30, 1966, Palace Th.
608 *performances.*
Book by Neil Simon; lyrics by Dorothy Fields.
Produced by Fryer, Carr & Harris; directed by Bob Fosse.
Cast included: Gwen Verdon, John McMartin, Helen Gallagher, Thelma Oliver, James Luisi, Arnold Soboloff, Ruth Buzzi.
Principal songs: Big Spender; If My Friends Could See Me Now; Too Many Tomorrows; There's Gotta Be Something Better than This; Baby, Dream Your Dream; Sweet Charity; Where Am I Going?; I'm a Brass Band; Rich Man's Frug.
Recorded Version
Columbia KOL 6500/KOS 2900 (O.C.).
A sassy, infectious score.

CAROLYN LEIGH
lyricist

For other musicals with Carolyn Leigh lyrics, see Wildcat & Little Me *under Cy Coleman.*

PETER PAN
Opened: Oct. 20, 1954, Winter Garden
152 *performances.*
Play by James M. Barrie; Leigh music by Mark Charlap; music & lyrics also by Jule Styne, Betty Comden & Adolph Green.
Produced by Richard Halliday; directed by Jerome Robbins.
Cast included: Mary Martin, Cyril Ritchard, Margalo Gilmore, Kathy Nolan, Heller Halliday, Sondra Lee, Norman Shelly, Joe E. Marks.
Principal Leigh-Charlap songs: Tender Shepherd; I've Gotta Crow; I'm Flying; I Won't Grow Up.
Recorded Version
RCA Victor LOC/LSO 1019 (O.C.).

The songs for this charming album were divided about evenly between the two teams.

HOW NOW, DOW JONES
Opened: Dec. 7, 1967, Lunt-Fontanne Th.
213 *performances.*
Book by Max Shulman; music by Elmer Bernstein.
Produced by David Merrick; directed by George Abbott; dances by Gillian Lynne.
Cast included: Anthony Roberts, Marlyn Mason, Brenda Vaccaro, Hiram Sherman, James Congdon, Sammy Smith, Charlotte Jones, Rex Everhart.
Principal songs: Live a Little; Walk Away; He's Here!; Step to the Rear.
Recorded Version
RCA Victor LOC/LSO 1142 (O.C.).
The averages are off.

JERRY HERMAN
composer-lyricist

I FEEL WONDERFUL
Opened: Oct. 18, 1954, Theatre de Lys.
48 *performances.*
Sketches by Barry Alan Grael.
Produced by Sidney S. Oshrin; directed by Herman; dances by Frank Wagner.
Cast included: Nina Dova, Albie Gaye, Janie Janvier, John Bartis, Phyllis Newman, Richard Tone, Barry Alan Grael.
Principal songs: I Feel Wonderful; When I Love Again; It's Christmas Today; Lonesome in New York.

PARADE
Opened: Jan. 20, 1960, Players Th.
95 *performances.*
Produced by Lawrence Kasha; directed by Herman; dances by Richard Tone.
Cast included: Dody Goodman, Richard Tone, Fia Karin, Charles Nelson Reilly, Lester James.
Principal songs: There's No Tune Like

a Show Tune; Your Hand in My Hand; Your Good Morning; Another Candle; Jolly Theatrical Season.
Recorded Version
Kapp 7005(S) (O.C.) X.
A bright, engaging introduction to the talents of Jerry Herman.

MILK AND HONEY
Opened: Oct. 10, 1961, Martin Beck Th.
543 *performances.*
Book by Don Appell.
Produced by Gerard Oestreicher; directed by Albert Marre; dances by Donald Saddler.
Cast included: Robert Weede, Mimi Benzell, Molly Picon, Tommy Rall, Thelma Pelish, Lanna Saunders, Juki Arkin, Ellen Madison, Ronald Holgate.
Principal songs: Shalom; Milk and Honey; There's No Reason in the World; That Was Yesterday; I Will Follow You; Hymn to Hymie; It's as Simple as That.
Recorded Version
RCA Victor LOC/LSO 1065 (O.C.).
An appealing score full of atmosphere and warmth.

MADAME APHRODITE
Opened: Dec. 29, 1961, Orpheum Th.
13 *performances.*
Book by Tad Mosel.
Produced by Howard Barker, Cynthia Baer, Robert Chambers; directed by Robert Turoff.
Cast included: Nancy Andrews, Cherry Davis, Jack Drummond, Mona Paulee, Rod Colbin.
Principal songs: Beat the World; You I Like; The Girls who Sit and Wait.

HELLO, DOLLY!
Opened: Jan. 16, 1964, St. James Th.
(Still running as of Sept. 1, 1968)
Book by Michael Stewart.
Produced by David Merrick; directed by Gower Champion.
Cast included: Carol Channing, David Burns, Eileen Brennan, Sondra Lee, Charles Nelson Reilly, Jerry Dodge,

Gordon Connell, Igors Gavon, Alice Playten.

Principal songs: It Takes a Woman; Put on Your Sunday Clothes; Ribbons Down My Back; Before the Parade Passes By; Elegance; Dancing; Motherhood; Hello Dolly!; It Only Takes a Moment; So Long, Dearie.

Recorded Versions

RCA Victor LOCD/LSOD 1087 (O.C.).

RCA Victor LOCD/LSOD 2007 (London O.C.) (1965).

Columbia OL 6710/OS 3110 (German O.C.).

RCA Victor LOC/LSO 1147 (O.C.) (1967).

Herman's exuberant score gets a much better workout from the New York company than from its somewhat pale London carbon—even with Mary Martin. The German version seems excessively Teutonic. The third RCA is the spirited Negro company headed by Pearl Bailey & Cab Calloway.

MAME

Opened: May 24, 1966, Winter Garden *(Still running as of Sept. 1, 1968)*

Book by Jerome Lawrence & Robert E. Lee.

Produced by Fryer, Carr & Harris; directed by Gene Saks; dances by Onna White.

Cast included: Angela Lansbury, Beatrice Arthur, Jane Connell, Willard Waterman, Frankie Michaels, Charles Braswell, Jerry Lanning, Margaret Hall.

Recorded Version

Columbia KOL 6600/KOS 3000 (O.C.).

Auntie Mame with songs—or a perfect specimen of the commercial Broadway musical at its highly-polished best.

MITCH LEIGH
composer

JOE DARION
lyricist

Music by Mr. Leigh unless otherwise noted.

SHINBONE ALLEY

Opened: Apr. 13, 1957, Broadway Th. *49 performances.*

Book by Darion & Mel Brooks; music by George Kleinsinger.

Produced by Peter Lawrence; director uncredited; dances by Rod Alexander.

Cast included: Eartha Kitt, Eddie Bracken, Erik Rhodes, Ross Martin, Jacques d'Amboise, Allegra Kent, Gwen Harmon, George S. Irving, Reri Grist, Lillian Hayman, Elmarie Wendel, Cathryn Damon.

Principal songs: Toujours gai; A Woman Wouldn't Be a Woman; Flotsam and Jetsam; Cheerio My Deario.

Recorded Version

Columbia OL 4963 (S.C.).

Titled *archie and mehitabel,* this imaginative aural version preceded the stage adaptation. Carol Channing, Eddie Bracken & David Wayne were featured.

MAN OF LA MANCHA

Opened: Nov. 22, 1965, ANTA Washington Sq. Th.

(Still running as of Sept. 1, 1968)

Book by Dale Wasserman.

Produced by Albert W. Selden & Hal James; directed by Albert Marre; dances by Jack Cole.

Cast included: Richard Kiley, Irving Jacobson, Ray Middleton, Robert Rounseville, Joan Diener, Jon Cypher, Gerrianne Raphael.

Principal songs: Man of La Mancha (I, Don Quixote); It's All the Same; Dulcinea; I Really Like Him; Little Bird, Little Bird; To Each His Dulcinea; The Quest (The Impossible Dream).

Recorded Version

Kapp (S) 4505 (O.C.).

An affecting, evocative work.

ILLYA DARLING

Opened: Apr. 11, 1967, Mark Hellinger

Th.
319 *performances.*
Book by Jules Dassin; music by Manos Hadjidakis.
Produced by Kermit Bloomgarden; directed by Dassin; dances by Onna White.
Cast included: Melina Mercouri, Orson Bean, Titos Vandis, Nikos Kourkoulos, Despo, Rudy Bond, Hal Linden, Harold Gary, Joe E. Marks.
Principal songs: Piraeus, My Love; Illya Darling; Never on Sunday; Love, Love, Love; After Love.
Recorded Version
United Artists 8901/9901 (O.C.).
  A spirited, bouzouki-flavored score, abetted by the exuberant Miss Mercouri.

JOHN KANDER
composer

FRED EBB
lyricist

All music by Mr. Kander & lyrics by Mr. Ebb unless otherwise noted.

FROM A TO Z
Opened: Apr. 20, 1960, Plymouth Th.
21 *performances.*
Sketches by Woody Allen, Herbert Farjeon, Nina Warner Hook; Ebb music by Paul Klein & Norman Martin; music & lyrics also by Jerry Herman, Jay Thompson, Dickson Hughes & Everett Sloane, Jack Holmes, William Dyer & Don Parks, Mary Rodgers & Marshall Barer, Charles Zwar & Alan Melville.
Produced by Carroll & Harris Masterson; directed by Christopher Hewett; dances by Ray Harrison.
Cast included: Hermione Gingold, Elliott Reid, Alvin Epstein, Louise Hoff, Stuart Damon, Bob Dishy, Nora Kovach, Kelly Brown, Paula Stewart, Beryl Towbin, Virginia Vestoff.
Principal Ebb songs: I Said to Love

(Klein); Charlie (Martin); Time Step (Klein).

A FAMILY AFFAIR
Opened: Jan. 27, 1962, Billy Rose Th.
65 *performances.*
Book & lyrics by James Goldman & William Goldman.
Produced by Andrew Siff; directed by Harold Prince; dances by John Butler.
Cast included: Shelly Berman, Eileen Heckart, Morris Carnovsky, Larry Kert, Rita Gardner, Bibi Osterwald, Lulu Bates, Jack DeLon, Paula Trueman, Beryl Towbin, Linda Lavin, Cathryn Damon.
Principal songs: Anything for You; My Son, the Lawyer; Every Girl Wants to Get Married; There's a Room in My House; Harmony; Revenge.
Recorded Version
United Artists A(S) 5099 (O.C.) X.
  "Promising" is as good a word as any.

PUT IT IN WRITING
Opened: May 13, 1963, Theatre de Lys.
24 *performances.*
Sketches by David Panich, Steven Vinaver, Jay Thompson; Ebb music by Norman Martin; music & lyrics also by Bud McCreery, C. Wood, Jay Thompson, Robert Kessler & Martin Charnin, Alan Kohan.
Produced by Lucille Lortel & Arthur Cantor; directed by Bill Penn; dances by Joyce Trisler.
Cast included: Jane Connell, Buzz Halliday, Bill Hinnant, Jack Blackton, Will Mackenzie.
Principal Ebb-Martin songs: I Hope You're Happy; What's Cooking?; Emmy Lou; Stock Report.

MORNING SUN
Opened: Oct. 6, 1963, Phoenix Th.
9 *performances.*
Book by Ebb; music by Paul Klein.
Produced by T. Edward Hambleton & Martin Tahse; directed by Daniel Petrie; dances by Donald Saddler.

Cast included: Patricia Neway, Bert Convy, Will Mackenzie, Danny Lockin, Carole Demas, David Thomas.
Principal songs: Morning Sun; Tell Me Goodbye; Good as Anybody; Seventeen Summers.

FLORA, THE RED MENACE
Opened: May 11, 1965, Alvin Th.
87 performances.
Book by George Abbott & Robert Russell.
Produced by Harold Prince; directed by Abbott; dances by Lee Theodore.
Cast included: Liza Minnelli, Bob Dishy, Cathryn Damon, Mary Louise Wilson, Daniel P. Hannafin, Danny Carroll, Joe E. Marks.
Principal songs: A Quiet Thing; Hello Waves; Dear Love; Knock Knock; Sing Happy; You Are You.
Recorded Version
RCA Victor LOC/LSO 1111 (O.C.).

A deftly constructed score that shows off the talents of Liza Minnelli in her first Broadway role.

CABARET
Opened: Nov. 20, 1966, Broadhurst Th.
(Still running as of Sept. 1, 1968)
Book by Joe Masteroff.
Produced & directed by Harold Prince; dances by Ronald Field.
Cast included: Jill Haworth, Jack Gilford, Bert Convy, Lotte Lenya, Joel Grey, Peg Murray, Edward Winter.
Principal songs: Willkommen; Don't Tell Mama; Perfectly Marvelous; It Couldn't Please Me More; Tomorrow Belongs to Me; Why Should I Wake Up?; Married; Meeskite; Cabaret.
Recorded Version
Columbia KOL 6640/KOS 3040 (O.C.).

The decadence and menace of pre-Hitler Berlin are strikingly caught in this chillingly atmospheric score.

THE HAPPY TIME
Opened: Jan. 18, 1968, Broadway Th.
(Still running as of Sept. 1, 1968)
Book by N. Richard Nash.
Produced by David Merrick; directed by Gower Champion.
Cast included: Robert Goulet, David Wayne, Julie Gregg, Mike Rupert, George S. Irving.
Principal songs: The Happy Time; Tomorrow Morning; The Life of the Party; Seeing Things; A Certain Girl.
Recorded Version
RCA Victor LOC/LSO 1144 (O.C.).

A pleasant, though hardly memorable collection.

519

Index

To help in identification, musicals (in italics) and songs (with quotation marks) are followed by the names of their composers. Page numbers in italics refer to Appendix listing of musicals and their writers.

Aarons, Alex A., 112, 114–119, 130–132, 151
Aaronson, Irving, 184, 185
"Abbondanza" (Loesser), 334
Abbott, George, 3, 35, 104, 153, 154, 158, 162, 216, 279, 290, 292, 317, 330, 331, 332, 340–342, 351, 352, 357, 363
Abravanel, Maurice, 256
"Absinthe Frappé" (Herbert), 16
Actman, Irving, 331
Adams, Lee, 370–375, 513
Adams, Margaret, 189
Adams, Stanley, 223
Adamson, Harold, 235
"Adelaide's Lament" (Loesser), 333
Adler, Larry, 209
Adler, Luther, 253, 368
Adler, Richard, 3, 317, 329, 330, 339–342, 508
Adrian, 308
"Adventure" (Styne), 321, 322
"Ah, Sweet Mystery of Life" (Herbert), 20
Akst, Harry, 177
"Al Fresco" (Herbert), 16
"Alabamy Bound" (Henderson), 169
Alberghetti, Anna Maria, 353
Albert, Eddie, 159
Alda, Alan, 369
Alda, Robert, 333

Alexander, Cris, 291
"Alexander's Ragtime Band" (Berlin), 86, 89
Algeria (Herbert), 415
"Alibi Baby" (Samuels), 205
Alive and Kicking (Rome), 490
"All Alone" (Berlin), 86, 94
All American (Strouse), 370, 372–373, 513
"All I Need Is the Girl" (Styne), 321
"All of These and More" (Bock), 362
"All of You" (Porter), 200
"All the Things You Are" (Kern), 83
"All Through the Night" (Porter), 188
"Allah's Holiday" (Friml), 40
Allegro (Rodgers), 274, 495
Allen, Fred, 206–208
Allers, Franz, 301, 304
"Allez-vous-en" (Porter), 200
"Almost Like Being in Love" (Loewe), 301
"Alone Together" (Schwartz), 210
Alonso, Alicia, 298
Alton, Robert, 184
"Always" (Berlin), 86, 96
"Always Do as People Say You Should" (Herbert), 13
"Always True to You in My Fashion" (Porter), 197

Always You (Stothart), 129, 270, 497
Ameche, Don, 200, 201
Ameer, The (Herbert), 12, 414
American Idea, The (Cohan), 421
Americana, 220, 488
America's Sweetheart (Rodgers), 151–153, 463
"And I Am All Alone" (Kern), 70
"And Love Was Born" (Kern), 81
Anderson, John, 99, 126, 155, 169, 195
Anderson, John Murray, 95, 153, 184
Anderson, Maxwell, 254, 259
Andrews, Julie, 304–306, 307, 308
Angel Face (Herbert), 21, 419
"Angelus" (Herbert), 20
Angelus, Muriel, 159
Animal Crackers (Ruby), 166
Annie Dear (Romberg), 436
Annie Get Your Gun (Berlin), 3, 6, 86, 101–103, 276, 452
"Another Autumn" (Loewe), 302
"Another Op'nin', Another Show" (Porter), 197
"Any Old Place With You" (Rodgers), 143

Anyone Can Whistle (Sondheim), 358–359, *511*
Anything Goes (Porter), 187–188, *472*
Apolinar, Danny, 411
Appell, Don, 392
Apple Tree, The (Bock), 369, *513*
"April in Paris" (Duke), 222
"April Showers" (Silvers), 55, 167
"April Snow" (Romberg), 61
Arden, Eve, 83, 195
"Are You Sure?" (Willson), 347
Arlen, Harold, 14, 110, 138, 219, 220, 223, 227–233, 238, *484*
Arms and the Girl (Gould), *481*
Arnaz, Desi, 159–160
Aronson, Boris, 321, 368, 402
Around the World in Eighty Days (Porter), 197, *474*
"Artificial Flowers" (Bock), 363
Artists and Models of 1924 (Romberg), *436*
As Thousands Cheer (Berlin), 96, 97–98, *451*
Astaire, Adele, 54, 114–119, 138, 208–209
Astaire, Fred, 54, 114–119, 138, 186, 208–209
At Home Abroad (Schwartz), 210, *478*
"At the Check Apron Ball" (Merrill), 352
Atkinson, Brooks, 126, 152, 153, 161, 188, 195, 199, 217, 225, 256, 257, 274, 281, 284, 300, 313, 401
Atteridge, Harold, 50
Atwell, Roy, 39
Auerbach, Arnold, 244
"Auf Wiedersehn" (Romberg), 52
Aumont, Jean Pierre, 407
"Auto Show Girl" (Rodgers), 142
"Avalon" (Rose), 167
Ayers, Lemuel, 198, 199, 216, 229, 230, 231, 266, 267, 356

"Babbitt and the Bromide, The" (Gershwin), 118
Babes in Arms (Rodgers), 155, *463*
"Babes in the Wood" (Kern), 69
Babes in Toyland (Herbert), 14–15, *414*

Babette (Herbert), 16, *414*
Bagley, Ben, 5, 226, 371
Bailey, Pearl, 230, 231, 395
Bajour (Marks), 409
Baker, Benny, 195, 196
Baker, Josephine, 223
Baker Street (Jessel), 409
Baker, Word, 377
Balaban, Bob, 410
Balanchine, George, 4, 154, 155, 223, 224, 300
"Bali Ha'i" (Rodgers), 277
Ball, Lucille, 386–387
Ballard, Lucinda, 101, 103, 201, 258, 274, 283, 284
Ballyhoo of 1932 (Gensler), 220, *488*
"Baltimore, Md., You're the Only Doctor for Me" (Schwartz), 204
"Bambalina" (Youmans), 133
Band Wagon, The (Schwartz), 208–209, 217, *477*
Banjo Eyes (Duke), 226, *483*
Barer, Marshall, 3, 318, 407
Barker, Howard, 408
Barker, John, 209
Barnes, Howard, 268, 274, 332
Barnes, Mae, 138
Barrison, Mabel, 14
Bartholomae, Philip, 68
Barton, James, 54, 301
Battles, John, 274, 291
Baum, L. Frank, 14
Bay, Howard, 60, 258, 399
Bayes, Nora, 111
"Be a Santa" (Styne), 322
Be Yourself! (Gensler), *454*
Bean, Orson, 362
"Beat Out dat Rhythm on a Drum" (Bizet), 271
Beaton, Cecil, 232, 233, 304–306, 364
"Before I Met You" (Kern), 71
"Begin the Beguine" (Porter), 189
Behrman, S. N., 247
"Being Good Isn't Good Enough" (Styne), 327
Belafonte, Harry, 340
Bell, Marion, 301
Bells Are Ringing (Styne), 4, 312, 316, 317, *504*
"Belly Up to the Bar, Boys" (Willson), 347
Ben Franklin in Paris (Sandrich), 409
Benchley, Robert, 43, 59, 94, 118, 133, 147, 254
Bennett, Robert Russell, 229
Bennett, Wilda, 93

Bentley, Marjorie, 112
Benton, Robert, 375, 377
"Benvenuta" (Loesser), 334
Benzell, Mimi, 392
Berlin, Irving, 3, 15, 22, 33, 84–107, 111, 232, 271, 312, *448*
Bernard, Sam, 93
Bernardi, Herschel, 368
Bernstein, Leonard, 3, 13, 288–295, 315–317, 339, 356, *499*
Besoyan, Rick, 147, 407
Best Foot Forward (Martin), 3, *162*
"Best of Friends Must Part, The" (Berlin), 88
"Best Things in Life Are Free, The" (Henderson), 174
Betsy (Rodgers), *461*
Betty Lee (Hirsch), *429*
Between the Devil (Schwartz), 211, *478*
"Between the Devil and the Deep Blue Sea" (Arlen), 228
Berle, Milton, 179
Bevan, Frank, 254
"Bewitched" (Rodgers), 161
"Big Back Yard, The" (Romberg), 61
Big Boy (Meyer), *466*
"Big Calown Balloons, The" (Willson), 347
"Big 'D'" (Loesser), 334, 335
"Big Spender" (Coleman), 389
Biggers, Earl Derr, 19
Bigley, Isabel, 279
Bikel, Theodore, 284
"Bill" (Kern), 72, 78
Billie (Cohan), 35, *423*
Billion Dollar Baby (Gould), 315, *503*
Billy Barnes Revue, The (Barnes), 5
"Bingo Eli Yale" (Porter), 183
"Birth of the Blues, The" (Henderson), 169
Bissell, Richard, 317, 341
"Black Bottom, The" (Henderson), 169, 170
Black Crook, The, 1, 61
Blackbirds of 1928 (McHugh), 213, *480*
Blackton, Jay S., 265
Blaine, Vivian, 317, 318, 333
Blane, Ralph, 3, 162
Bledsoe, Jules, 78, 79
Bless You All (Rome), *490*
Blitzstein, Marc, 261
Bloomer Girl (Arlen), 3, 219, 229–230, *485*
Bloomgarden, Kermit, 330, 344
Blossom, Henry, 17, 18

Blossom Time (Romberg), 54–55, *434*

Blore, Eric, 186

"Blow, Gabriel, Blow" (Porter), 188

"Blue Grass" (Schwartz), 215

Blue Kitten, The (Friml), 41, *425*

Blue Monday (Gershwin), 113

"Blue Monday Blues" (Gershwin), 114

Blue Paradise, The (Romberg), 52, *431*

"Blue Room" (Rodgers), 149

Blushing Bride, The (Romberg), *435*

Blyden, Larry, 369

"Bobolink Waltz, The" (Porter), 182

Bock, Jerry, 3, 61, 359–369, *511*

"Body and Soul" (Green), 207

Body Beautiful, The (Bock), 362, *511*

Boland, Mary, 96, 189, 190

Bolger, Ray, 151, 154, 162, 177, 331, 332, 373

Bolitho, William, 121

Bolton, Guy, 2, 67–73, 115, 117, 187

Bombo (Romberg-DeSylva), 55, *434, 466*

Bonanza Bound (Chaplin), 315

Bond, Sheila, 246, 259

Booth, Shirley, 215, 217

Bordoni, Irene, 99, 184, 185, 298

Bosley, Tom, 361, 363

"Boston Beguine, The" (Harnick), 360, 362

Boy Friend, The (Wilson), 304

"Boy! What Love Has Done to Me!" (Gershwin), 119

Boys from Syracuse, The (Rodgers), 158–159, *464*

Bracken, Eddie, 159

Brady, Scott, 248

Breakfast at Tiffany's (Merrill), 354

Breen, Robert, 127

Brennan, Eileen, 408

Brenner, Ruth, 207

Brent, Romney, 146, 147

Brian, Donald, 29, 33, 67

Brice, Carol, 233

Brice, Fanny, 68, 94, 223, 323, 324

"Bridget" (Porter), 182

Brigadoon (Loewe), 3, 300–301, *501*

"Brigadoon" (Loewe), 300

Bright Eyes (Hoschna), *427*

"Bring Me My Bride" (Sondheim), 357

Brinkley, Grace, 173, 175

Brisson, Frederick, 341

"Britannia Waives the Rules" (Rome), 244

Broderick, Helen, 97, 185, 209

Brooks, David, 301

Brooks, Donald, 286, 326

Brooks, Mel, 373

"Brother, Can You Spare a Dime?" (Gorney), 220

Broun, Heywood, 113, 145

Brown, Anne, 125

Brown, John Mason, 126, 158, 193, 195, 210, 278

Brown, Johnny, 373

Brown, Lew, 151, 164–179, *465*

Brown, Louise, 138

Brown, Nacio Herb, 138

Brox Sisters, 93, 94

Bruce, Carol, 79, 99

"Brush Up Your Shakespeare" (Porter), 5

Bryant, Nana, 150

Brynner, Yul, 277, 278

Bubbles, John W., 125

Buchanan, Jack, 186, 211

Buloff, Joseph, 267

"Bums' Opera, The" (Rodgers), 280

Bunch and Judy, The (Kern), *445*

Burghoff, Gary, 410

Burnett, Carol, 312, 325, 408

Burns, David, 357, 358, 394

Burns, Ralph, 286

Burr, Courtney, 222

Burrows, Abe, 3, 200, 318, 332, 337

Burton, Richard, 307, 308

"Bushel and a Peck, A" (Loesser), 333

"But Not for Me" (Gershwin), 119

Butterworth, Charles, 209

"Button Up Your Overcoat" (Henderson), 175

Buzzell, Eddie, 57

By Jupiter (Rodgers), 162, *465*

"By Myself" (Schwartz), 211

"By Strauss" (Gershwin), 223

By the Beautiful Sea (Schwartz), 215–217, *479*

"By the Mississississinewah" (Porter), 196

"Bye and Bye" (Rodgers), 148

Bye Bye Birdie (Strouse), 4, 370, 371–372, *513*

"Bye Bye Blackbird" (Henderson), 169

Cabaret (Kander), 4, 5, 402–406, *519*

Cabin in the Sky (Duke), 3, 219, 224–226, *483*

"Cabin in the Sky" (Duke), 225

Caesar, Irving, 113, 134, 137

Caesar, Sid, 387, 388

Cahill, Marie, 15

Cahn, Sammy, 3, 313

"California, Here I Come" (Meyer), 168

Call Me Madam (Berlin), 15, 104, 105, *452*

Call Me Mister (Rome), 244–245, *490*

"Call Me Savage" (Styne), 327

Calling All Stars (Akst), 177, *470*

Calloway, Cab, 395

Camelot (Loewe), 4, 307–309, *502*

"Camelot" (Loewe), 308

"Campfire Days" (Rodgers), 142

Campbell, Patten, 399

Can-Can (Porter), 3, 199–200, *475*

Canary, The (Berlin), *449*

Candide (Bernstein), 293, *500*

"Can't Help Lovin' dat Man" (Kern), 78

"Can't We Be Friends?" (Swift), 206

Cantor, Eddie, 92, 95, 166, 169, 214, 226

Capalbo, Carmen, 261

Capote, Truman, 230

Captain Jinks (Gensler), *467*

"Carlotta" (Porter), 196

"Carmen in Zoot" (Henderson), 178

Carmen Jones (Bizet), 271, *499*

Carmichael, Hoagy, 223

Carnival (Merrill), 4, 353–354, *510*

Carnovsky, Morris, 253

Carousel (Rodgers), 5, 7, 271–273, *494*

"Carousel in the Park" (Romberg), 61

Carpenter, Constance, 277

Carradine, John, 357

Carrington, Katherine, 81

Carroll, Albert, 147

Carroll, Diahann, 231, 232, 286

Carroll, Joan, 195

Carroll, Marie, 70

Cassell, Walter, 298

Cassidy, Jack, 216, 246

Castillo, 216

Castle, Vernon & Irene, 90, 91

Castle, William, 185
Casto, Jean, 272
Cat and the Fiddle, The (Kern), 2, 5, 41, 79–81, *447*
Catch a Star (Bock), 362
Catlett, Walter, 74, 75
Cawthorn, Joseph, 41, 67, 76
Century Girl, The (Herbert-Berlin), 90, *418, 448*
"C'est Magnifique" (Porter), 200
Champion, Gower, 4, 353–354, 372, 379–380, 392–393
"Chance to Dream" (Lerner), 299
Channing, Carol, 195, 312, 314, 392–394
Chaplin, Saul, 315
Chaplin, Sydney, 316, 323
Chapman, John, 249, 308, 314, 401
Charig, Phil, 134, 207
Charlap, Mark, 316, 385
Chase, Stanley, 261
Chee-Chee (Rodgers), 150, *462*
Cherry Blossoms (Romberg), *437*
"Cherry Pies Ought to Be You" (Porter), 199
Chiari, Walter, 217
Chodorov, Jerome, 292
Chodosh, Richard, 409
Chotzinoff, Samuel, 126
Christie, Audrey, 156
Church, George, 154, 267
"Church 'Round the Corner, The" (Kern), 75
"Cinderelatives" (Gershwin), 113
Cinders (Friml), *425*
City Chap, The (Kern), *446*
"Clap Yo' Hands" (Gershwin), 118
Clark, Bobby, 21, 94, 95, 120, 121, 166, 196, 222
Clark, Harry, 243, 245
Clayton, Jan, 79, 272, 273
"Cleopatterer" (Kern), 70
Clift, Montgomery, 189
Clifton, John, 410
"Climb Ev'ry Mountain" (Rodgers), 284
"Climb Up the Mountain" (Porter), 199
"Close as Pages in a Book" (Romberg), 61
Clowns in Clover (McHugh), 214
Clurman, Harold, 146, 245, 246, 277

Coca, Imogene, 147
"Cockeyed Optimist, A" (Rodgers), 276
Cocoanuts, The (Berlin), 95, *450*
"Coffee Break" (Loesser), 338
Cohan, George M., 2, 24–35, 73, 89, 157–158, 183, 345, 346, *420*
Cohan, Jerry, 26–27, 31, 33
Cohan, Josie, 27, 33
Cohan, Nellie, 26–27, 33
Cohan Revue, The (1916) (Cohan), 33, *422*
Cohan Revue, The (1918) (Cohan-Berlin), 33, *422, 449*
Coleman, Cy, 318, 382–390, *515*
Coleman, Robert, 281
Coleman, Warren, 260
Collier, William, 33
Collins, Charles, 299
Collins, Russell, 253
Colt, Alvin, 248, 280, 291, 333, 336, 386
Colt, Ethel Barrymore, 177
Comden, Betty, 3, 290–292, 310, 314–317, 322, 325–327, *503*
"Come, O Come to Pittsburgh" (Schwartz), 215
"Come on and Pet Me" (Youmans), 137
"Come to Me, Bend to Me" (Loewe), 300
"Comedy Tonight" (Sondheim), 356
"Comes Love" (Stept), 177
"Comes Once in a Lifetime" (Styne), 322
"Company Way, The" (Loesser), 336
Compton, Betty, 119
Comstock, F. Ray, 68, 73
"Conga!" (Bernstein), 292
Conkey, Thomas, 20
Connecticut Yankee, A (Rodgers), 149–150, 163, *462, 465*
Conried, Hans, 200
Conte, John, 274
"Conversation Piece" (Bernstein), 292
Cook, Barbara, 217, 345, 365
Cook, Joe, 112, 184
Cook, Olga, 54
Cooper, Melville, 189, 190
Coote, Robert, 305–307
Cordon, Norman, 258
Costello, Diosa, 159, 160
"Cotton Blossom" (Kern), 78
"Country Cousin, The" (Youmans), 131

"Couple of Senseless Censors, A" (Berlin), 95
Cowan, Jerome, 317
Coward, Noel, 138, 157, 222
Cowles, Chandler, 245
Cowles, Eugene, 12
Cradle Will Rock, The (Blitzstein), 241
Crawford, Cheryl, 127, 301
Crawford, Kathryn, 186
Crazy with the Heat, 178
"Crinoline Days" (Berlin), 93
Crinoline Girl, The (Wenrich), *428*
Criss-Cross (Kern), 41, *446*
Crooker, Earle, 298
Croswell, Anne, 407
Crouse, Russel, 104, 105, 188, 191, 229, 282
"Cry Like the Wind" (Styne), 322
"Cuddle Up a Little Closer, Lovey Mine" (Hoschna), 41
Cullum, John, 237
Cyrano de Bergerac (Herbert), 12, *413*

Da Costa, Morton, 232, 345
Daffy Dill (Stothart), *497*
Dailey, Dan, 155
Dairymaids, The (Kern), 66, *440*
Dale, Alan, 51, 66, 71, 113
Damn Yankees (Adler), 3, 341–342, *508*
Dance and Grow Thin (Berlin), 90
Dancing Around (Romberg), 52, *430*
Dancing Girl, The (Romberg), *435*
"Dancing in the Dark" (Schwartz), 209
"Dancing on the Ceiling" (Rodgers), 151
Dangerous Maid, A (Gershwin), 114
Daniels, Danny, 259
Daniels, Frank, 11, 12, 26
Darion, Joe, 396–401, *517*
Darling, Jean, 272, 273
Darling of the Day (Styne), *506*
Darnton, Charles, 114
Davenport, Marcia, 127
Davies, Marion, 70
Davis, Bette, 227
Davis, Blevins, 127
Davis, Sammy, 362, 373–374
Dawson, Mark, 279

Day Before Spring, The (Loewe), 300, *501*
Day, Edith, 132, 133
Dear Sir (Kern), 130, 205, *445*
Dearest Enemy (Rodgers), 45, 147–148, *461*
Débutante, The (Herbert), *417*
"Deep in My Heart, Dear" (Romberg), 56
DeGresac, Fred, 20
DeKoven, Reginald, 21
deMille, Agnes, 4, 210, 229, 230, 266, 269, 273, 274, 300, 301, 302
"Den of Iniquity" (Rodgers), 161
dePaul, Gene, 303
DePinna, Connie, 190
Desert Song, The (Romberg), 41, 56–58, *437*
"Desert Song, The" (Romberg), 57
Desmond, Johnny, 317, 318
Destry Rides Again (Rome), 4, 248, *491*
DeSylva, B. G., 75, 113, 138, 151, 164–179, *465*
DeWolfe, Billy, 340
"Diamonds Are a Girl's Best Friend" (Styne), 314
"Did You Ever Get Stung?" (Rodgers), 157
Diener, Joan, 400
Dietz, Howard, 4, 5, 103, 130, 202–217, 226, 235, *476*
"Diga Diga Doo" (McHugh), 213
Dillingham, Charles, 4, 16, 17, 75, 90
Dixon, Adele, 211
Dixon, Lee, 267
Do I Hear a Waltz? (Rodgers), 287, 359, *499*
"Do I Love You?" (Porter), 195, 196, 200
"Do It the Hard Way" (Rodgers), 161
"Do Look at Him" (Kern), 72
Do Re Mi (Styne), 321–322, *505*
"Do-Re-Mi" (Rodgers), 284
"Do What You Wanna Do" (Duke), 226
"Doin' What Comes Natur'lly" (Berlin), 101, 102
"Doing Good" (Strouse), 375
Doing Our Bit (Romberg), 54, *433*
Doll Girl, The (Kern), *441*
"Dolly" (Youmans), 132
Dolly Sisters, 51, 184

Donahue, Jack, 58, 75
Donaldson, Walter, 85, 138
Donehue, Vincent J., 281
"Donkey Serenade, The" (Friml), 39
Donnelly, Dorothy, 54, 205
Donner, Vyvyan, 57
"Don't Blame Me" (McHugh), 214
"Don't Ever Leave Me" (Kern), 79
"Don't Hold Everything" (Henderson), 174
"Don't Rain on My Parade" (Styne), 325, 354
"Don't Send Me Back to Petrograd" (Berlin), 94
"Doo-Dah-Dey" (Youmans), 138, 228
Dooley, Ray, 91
"Door of Her Dreams, The" (Friml), 43–45
"Dorando" (Berlin), 88
Douglas, Melvyn, 244
Dovey, Alice, 69
"Down in the Depths" (Porter), 191
Down in the Valley (Weill), 261
Downes, Olin, 127, 208, 259
Dr. DeLuxe (Hoschna), *427*
Drake, Alfred, 155, 197–199, 265, 267, 268
Drake, Ervin, 85, 409
Dream City or the Magic Knight (Herbert), *415*
Dream Girl, The (Herbert), 21, *420*
Dresser, Louise, 33
Dressler, Marie, 149
Dreyfus, Max, 38, 111, 130, 131
Dreyfus, Henry, 80, 172
"Drifting Along with the Tide" (Gershwin), 113
"Drinking Song, The" (Romberg), 56
DuBarry Was a Lady (Porter), 178, 193–195, *473*
duBois, Raoul Pène, 104, 153, 160, 192, 193, 194, 319, 320, 345
Duchess, The (Herbert), 18, *416*
Dudley, Bide, 118
Duffy, Henry, 299
Duke, Vernon, 109, 110, 163, 207, 219, 220, 221–226, 405, *481*
"Dulcinea" (Leigh), 400
Dumbrille, Douglass, 46
Dumke, Ralph, 79

Duncan Sisters, 54
Duncan, Todd, 125, 260
Duncan, William Cary, 137
Dunham, Katherine, 226
Dunne, Irene, 79, 150
Duquette, Tony, 308
Durant, Jack, 161
Durante, Jimmy, 153, 177, 186, 190, 191, 213, 214
Dussault, Nancy, 322
"D'Ye Love Me?" (Kern), 76

"Eadie Was a Lady" (Whiting), 139
"Eagle and Me, The" (Arlen), 230
Earl and the Girl, The (Kern), 66
Earl Carroll Vanities (1930) (Arlen-Gorney), 220, *484*, *488*
Earl Carroll Vanities (1931) (Lane), 235, *486*
Earl Carroll's Sketchbook (Gorney), 220, *487*
East Wind (Romberg), *438*
Ebb, Fred, 85, 402–406, *518*
Ebsen, Buddy, 79, 210
Eckart, William & Jean, 361, 395, 408
Edens, Roger, 139
Edwards, Cliff, 76
Egan, Leo, 73
Eglevsky, André, 298
Eileen (Herbert), 21, *418*
"El Sombrero" (Coleman), 386
Elkins, Hillard, 373
Ellington, Duke, 213
Ellis, Mary, 43, 44
Eltinge, Julian, 65
Elton, Edmund, 57
"Embraceable You" (Gershwin), 119
Emens, Homer, 17
Enchantress, The (Herbert), *417*
Engel, Lehman, 253
Erlanger, A. L., 28, 132
Ernest in Love (Pockriss), 407
Errol, Leon, 56, 75
Etting, Ruth, 151
Evans, Maurice, 363, 364
"Evelina" (Arlen), 230
Ever Green (Rodgers), 151
"Every Day is Ladies Day with Me" (Herbert), 18
"Every Little Movement" (Hoschna), 41
"Every Street's a Boulevard in Old New York" (Styne), 316

"Everybody Ought to Have a Maid" (Sondheim), 357

"Everybody Step" (Berlin), 93

"Ev'rything I Love" (Porter), 196

"Ev'rything's Coming Up Roses" (Styne), 320, 325

"Exactly Like You" (McHugh), 214

"F.D.R. Jones" (Rome), 244

Fabray, Nanette, 105, 106, 196, 312, 313, 314

"Face on the Dime, The" (Rome), 244

Face the Music (Berlin), 96–97, *451*

Fade Out—Fade In (Styne), 312, 325–326, *505*

Fairbanks Twins, 131

"Falling in Love with Love" (Rodgers), 159

Family Affair, A (Kander), 364, 405, *518*

Fanny (Rome), 3, 245, 247, *491*

Fantasticks, The (Schmidt), 375, 377–378, *514*

"Faraway Boy" (Loesser), 335

"Farmer and the Cowman, The" (Rodgers), 267

"Farming" (Porter), 196

Fascinating Flora (Kern), 66, *440*

"Fascinating Rhythm" (Gershwin), 116

Fascinating Widow, The (Hoschna), *428*

Faye, Alice, 176

"Feeling I'm Falling" (Gershwin), 118

Feigay, Paul, 290

"Fellow Needs a Girl, A" (Rodgers), 274

Fetter, Ted, 223, 226

"Feudin' and Fightin'" (Lane), 235

Feuer, Cy, 199, 330, 331, 337, 344

Ffolkes, David, 301

Fiddler on the Roof (Bock), 4, 7, 366–368, *512*

"Fidgety Feet" (Gershwin), 118

Fields, Dorothy, 60, 211–217, 388–390, *480*

Fields, Herbert, 60, 135, 145, 147, 148–151, 178, 185, 186, 193, 211, 212, 214

Fields, Joseph, 211, 280, 292

Fields, Lew, 15, 16, 54, 135,

143, 144, 145, 148, 149, 151, 211, 214

Fields, W. C., 205

Fifty Miles from Boston (Cohan), 30, 33, *421*

Fifty Million Frenchmen (Porter), 185–186, *471*

"Find Me a Primitive Man" (Porter), 185

Finian's Rainbow (Lane), 3, 219, 234–236, *487*

Fiorello! (Bock), 3, 360, 361, 363, *512*

Firebrand of Florence, The (Weill), 257, *493*

Firefly, The (Friml), 6, 37–39, *423*

"Firefly" (Coleman), 385

Fisher, Irving, 105

"Five Foot Two, Eyes of Blue" (Henderson), 169

Five O'Clock Girl, The (Ruby), 166, 317

"Five Step, The" (Henderson), 171

Flahooley (Fain), *488*

"Flaming Youth" (Henderson), 174

Flora, the Red Menace (Kander), 405, *519*

Flower Drum Song (Rodgers), 280, *496*

"Flower Garden of My Heart, The" (Rodgers), 161

Fluffy Ruffles (Kern), 66, *440*

Flying Colors (Schwartz), 209–210, *477*

Flying High (Henderson), 173, 175–176, *468*

Follow Me (Romberg), *432*

"Follow Me" (Loewe), 308

Follow Thru (Henderson), 172, 175, *468*

"Fodbidden Fruit" (Bock), 369

Forbidden Melody (Romberg), *439*

Ford, Helen, 148, 149, 298

Forde, Hal, 70

"Forget All Your Books" (Lane), 235

Fortune Teller, The (Herbert), 12–13, *413*

Forty-Five Minutes from Broadway (Cohan), 26, 29, 30, *420*

Fosse, Bob, 4, 161, 324, 337, 341, 388, 390

"Four Little Angels of Peace" (Rome), 243

Foy, Eddie, Jr., 154, 340, 341

Frank, Melvin, 303

Frawley, Paul, 93

Frazee, H. H., 134

Frederick, Pauline, 16

"Free" (Sondheim), 356

Free and Easy (Arlen), 230

Free for All (Whiting), *498*

"Free Trade and a Misty Moon" (Herbert), 21

Freedley, Vinton, 114, 117–119, 151, 186, 189–191, 193

"Friendship" (Porter), 195

Friml, Rudolf, 16, 22, 36–47, 270, *423*

Frohman, Charles, 65, 67

From A to Z, 405, *518*

"From Me to You" (Lerner), 299

"From This Moment On" (Porter), 199

Fryer, Robert, 292

"Fugue for Tinhorns" (Loesser), 333

Funny Face (Gershwin), 114, 118, 119, *455*

"Funny Face" (Gershwin), 118

Funny Girl (Styne), 5, 6, 312, 322–325, 354, *505*

Funny Thing Happened on the Way to the Forum, A (Sondheim), 356–358, *511*

Gabriel, Gilbert, 81, 124, 126, 137, 149, 173, 175

Gallagher, Helen, 389

"Game of Love" (Herbert), 20

Garde, Betty, 267

Gardiner, Reginald, 210

Gardner, Rita, 377

Garfield, John, 253

Garland, Robert, 82, 126

Garrett, Betty, 244, 245

Garrick Gaieties, The (1925) (Rodgers), 145–147, *461*

Garrick Gaieties, The (1926) (Rodgers), 145–147, *461*

Garrick Gaieties, The (1930) (Duke), 220, 222, *481*

Gautier, Dick, 372

Gaxton, William, 99, 122, 123, 150, 178, 185, 186, 187, 191, 192

Gay Divorce (Porter), 186, 187, *472*

Gay Life, The (Schwartz), 217, *479*

Gaynor, Charles, 5, 314

Gear, Luella, 186, 187, 205

Gelbart, Larry, 357

"Gentleman Is a Dope, The" (Rodgers), 274

"Gentleman Jimmy" (Bock), 363

Gentlemen Prefer Blondes (Styne), 312, 314, *503*

George M! (Cohan), 4, 34, 35, *423*

George Washington, Jr. (Cohan), 29, 31, 183, *420*

George White's Scandals (1920) (Gershwin), 113, *453*

George White's Scandals (1921) (Gershwin), 113, *453*

George White's Scandals (1922) (Gershwin), 113–114, 168, *453*

George White's Scandals (1923) (Gershwin), 113, *454*

George White's Scandals (1924) (Gershwin), 113, *454*

George White's Scandals (1925) (Henderson), 169, *466*

George White's Scandals (1926) (Henderson), 169–170, *467*

George White's Scandals (1928) (Henderson), 171, 227, *468*

George White's Scandals (1931) (Henderson), 176, 177, *469*

George White's Scandals (1935) (Henderson), 177, *470*

"Georgette" (Henderson), 168

Gershwin, George, 2, 41, 58, 64, 85, 108–127, 129, 130, 163, 168, 219, 221, 223, 232, 312, 359, *453*

Gershwin, Ira, 2, 85, 108, 111, 114–127, 129, 130, 131–132, 163, 215, 219, 220, 222, 223, 255, 256, 257, 359, *453*

Gesner, Clark, 410

"Get Happy" (Arlen), 228

"Get Me to the Church on Time" (Loewe), 307

"Get Yourself a Geisha" (Schwartz), 210

"Getting to Know You" (Rodgers), 279

Geva, Tamara, 154, 209

"Giannina Mia" (Friml), 39

Gibbs, Wolcott, 101, 161, 268, 274, 300, 305, 352

Gibson, William, 374

Gilford, Jack, 357, 358, 404, 405

Gillingwater, Claude, 17

Gingold, Hermione, 340, 405

Girl Crazy (Gershwin), 114, 119, 120, *457*

Girl Friend, The (Rodgers), 147–149, *461*

Girl from Brazil, The (Romberg), *431*

Girl from Montmartre, The (Kern), *441*

Girl from Utah, The (Kern), 67, *441*

Girl in Pink Tights, The (Romberg), 49, 61, *439*

Girl in the Spotlight, The (Herbert), *419*

"Girl Is You and the Boy Is Me, The" (Henderson), 169

Girl of My Dreams, The (Hoschna), *428*

"Girls Like Me" (Styne), 322

"Give Me Your Tired, Your Poor" (Berlin), 104

"Give My Regards to Broadway" (Cohan), 28

Ghostley, Alice, 362

"Glad to Be Home Again" (Berlin), 105

Glad to See You (Styne), 313

Gleason, Jackie, 352, 353

"Glitter and Be Gay" (Bernstein), 293

"Go to Sleep Whatever You Are" (Bock), 369

"God Bless America" (Berlin), 91

Godkin, Paul, 298

"God's Country" (Arlen), 229

Goetz, E. Ray, 184–186

Going Up (Hirsch), 41, *428*

Gold Bug, The (Herbert), *413*

Golden Boy (Strouse), 370, 373–374, *513*

Golden Dawn (Kalman), *498*

"Golden Days" (Romberg), 56

Golden Rainbow (Marks), 409

Goldman, James & William, 405

Goldsmith, Eleanor, 216, 236

Good Boy (Ruby), 166, *498*

"Good Clean Fun" (Bock), 364

"Good for You—Bad for Me" (Henderson), 175

Good Morning Dearie (Kern), *445*

Good News! (Henderson), 151, 171, 173–174, *467*

"Good News" (Henderson), 174

Goodman, Philip, 137

"Goodnight, My Someone" (Willson), 345

Gordon, Kitty, 66

Gordon, Max, 207–209, 244

Gorney, Jay, 205, 220

Gould, Berni, 243

Gould, Morton, 315

Governor's Son, The (Cohan), 26, 27–28, *420*

Goz, Harry, 368

Grable, Betty, 194, 195, 395

Grael, Barry Alan, 409

Grafton, Gloria, 153

Graham, Ronald, 159

Graham, William, 408

"Grand Imperial Cirque de Paris" (Merrill), 354

"Grand Old Ivy" (Loesser), 336, 337

Grand Street Follies (1926) (Schwartz), 130, 204, *476*

Grand Street Follies (Schwartz) (1929), *476*

Grant, Mary, 196

Granville, Bernard, 51

Gray, Dolores, 248, 312, 315

Gray, Timothy, 409

Great Day! (Youmans), 138, 228, *460*

"Great Day" (Youmans), 138

"Great Indoors, The" (Porter), 186

Great Lady (Loewe), 298, *501*

Green, Abel, 148

Green, Adolph, 3, 290, 292, 310, 314–317, 322, 325–327, *503*

Green, Johnny, 207

Green, Mitzi, 155

Green, Paul, 253

Greene, Herbert, 345

Greenstreet, Sydney, 82

Greenwich Village Follies (1922), 168

Greenwich Village Follies (1924) (Porter), 130, 184, *471*

Greenwich Village Follies (1925), 95

"Greenwich Village" (Kern), 72

Greenwillow (Loesser), 335–336, *507*

"Greenwillow Christmas" (Loesser), 336

Greenwood, Charlotte, 93, 199

Grey, Clifford, 75, 137

Grey, Joel, 34, 35, 402, 405

Griffies, Ethel, 104

Griffith, Andy, 248

Griffith, Robert, 341, 351, 363

Grimes, Tammy, 346, 409

Groody, Louise, 133–135

Grudeff, Marion, 409

Guerra, Robert, 411

Gussow, Melvin, 324

Guys and Dolls (Loesser), 4, 332–333, *507*

Gypsy (Styne), 4, 5, 6, 312, 318, 322, 356, *504*

"Gypsy Love Song" (Herbert), 12

Hadjidakis, Manos, 399

Hair (MacDermot), 410
Hajos, Mitzi, 66
Haley, Jack, 172, 215
"Half of It Dearie Blues, The" (Gershwin), 116
Half-Past Eight (Gershwin), 112
Hall, Adelaide, 213
Hall, Bettina, 80
Hall, George, 245
"Hallelujah!" (Youmans), 137
Hallelujah, Baby! (Styne), 312, 326–327, *506*
"Hallelujah, Baby!" (Styne), 327
Halliday, Richard, 282, 385
Halliday, Robert, 57, 59, 116
Hambleton, John, 156, 213
Hamlin, Fred, 14
"Hammacher Schlemmer, I Love You" (Schwartz), 206
Hammerstein, Arthur, 38–41, 133, 269, 270
Hammerstein, Oscar I, 19, 22
Hammerstein, Oscar II, 2, 3, 26, 40–43, 56, 58, 59, 76, 77, 79, 80, 82, 83, 85, 101–102, 124, 129, 132–133, 137, 141, 144, 145, 162–163, 264–287, 303, 319, 355–356, 359, *494, 497*
Hammond, Percy, 46, 59, 93, 117, 135, 139, 147, 148, 153, 174
Hancock, Carolyn, 147
"Hand Me Down that Can o' Beans" (Loewe), 302
Hands Up (Romberg), *431*
Haney, Carol, 341
"Hang on to Me" (Gershwin), 117
Happiest Girl in the World, The (Offenbach), 238, *489*
"Happy Because I'm in Love" (Youmans), 138
"Happy Hunting Horn" (Rodgers), 161
Happy Time, The (Kander), 4, 406, *519*
"Happy to Make Your Acquaintance" (Loesser), 334
Harbach, Otto, 2, 35, 38–45, 46, 56, 79, 81, 132–133, 134, 270, *427*
Harburg, E. Y., 14, 218–220, 222–223, 225, 228–230, 231, 232, 234–239, 303, 362, *487*
Harkrider, John, 46, 76, 77, 81, 195
"Harlem on My Mind" (Berlin), 97

Harnick, Sheldon, 3, 61, 359–369, *511*
Harrigan & Hart, 2, 11
Harris, Barbara, 237, 309, 369
Harris, Sam H., 28, 92, 98, 122, 158
Harrison, Jay, 262
Harrison, Rex, 304–307
Harrold, Orville, 19
Hart, Lorenz, 2, 35, 85, 129, 140–163, 204, 207, 223, 254, 270–271, 287, 312, *460*
Hart, Moss, 4, 96, 103–104, 157, 158, 189, 244, 255, 304, 307
Hart, Teddy, 159
Hartman, Grace, 190
Hastings, Hal, 342
"Haunted Heart" (Schwartz), 215
Have a Heart (Kern), 69, *442*
"Have You Met Miss Jones?" (Rodgers), 158
Havoc, June, 196, 226
Hawkins, John, Jr., 150
Haworth, Jill, 402
Hay, Mary, 74, 76
Hayes, Bill, 279
Hayes, Helen, 16
Haynes, Tiger, 326
Hays, David, 286
Hayward, Leland, 104, 275, 282
Hazel Flagg (Styne), 316, *504*
"He Loves and She Loves" (Gershwin), 118
Head Over Heels (Kern), *444*
Heads Up! (Rodgers), 151, *462*
"Heart" (Adler), 342
"Heat Wave" (Berlin), 98
"Heather on the Hill, The" (Loewe), 301
Heatherton, Ray, 155
Hecht, Ben, 316
Helburn, Theresa, 146, 163, 265, 271
Hello, Broadway! (Cohan), 33, 422
Hello, Daddy (McHugh), 214, *480*
Hello, Dolly! (Herman), 4, 390, 392–395, *516*
"Hello, Dolly!" (Herman), 7, 393–394
"Hello, Young Lovers" (Rodgers), 279
Hellzapoppin, 4, 6
Henderson, Ray, 151, 164–179, *465*
Henry, Sweet Henry (Merrill), 354, *510*
Her Regiment (Herbert), *418*

Her Soldier Boy (Romberg), *432*
Herbert, Evelyn, 59
Herbert, Victor, 2, 8–23, 25, 29, 35, 37, 38, 69, 75, 90, 111, 131, 168, *413*
"Here in My Arms" (Rodgers), 148
"Here's a Kiss" (Rodgers), 148
Here's Love (Willson), 346–347, *509*
Herlie, Eileen, 353, 373
Herman, Jerry, 390–396, *516*
"Hernando's Hideaway" (Adler), 342
Herzig, Sig, 229
"He's a Ladies Man" (Henderson), 173
Hester, Hal, 411
Hewes, Henry, 284, 361, 378, 393
"Hey, Look Me Over" (Coleman), 387
"Hey, There" (Adler), 342
Heyman, Edward, 208
Heyward, DuBose, 124–125, 127
"High and Low" (Schwartz), 209
High Button Shoes (Styne), 3, 312–314, *503*
"High Hat" (Gershwin), 118
High Jinks (Friml), 39, 40, *423*
High Spirits (Martin), 409
Higher and Higher (Rodgers), 162, *464*
Hilliard, Bob, 316
Hines, Elizabeth, 78
Hinnant, Bill, 410
Hinnant, Skip, 410
Hirsch, Louis, 21, 22, 35, 41, 50, 73
Hit the Deck (Youmans), 130, 135–137, 151, *459*
Hitchcock, Raymond, 4, 78, 184
Hitchy-Koo 1917, 168
Hitchy-Koo 1919 (Porter), 184, *471*
Hitchy-Koo 1920 (Kern), *444*
Hoey, Evelyn, 222
Hold Everything! (Henderson), 172, 174, *468*
Hold on to Your Hats (Lane), 235, *486*
Holgate, Ronald, 358
Holliday, Judy, 290, 312, 315–317
Holloway, Stanley, 304, 305
Holloway, Sterling, 146, 147
Holm, Celeste, 229, 265, 267
Holm, Hanya, 304

Holman, Libby, 78, 136, 138, 146, 206–208, 210, 211
Holofcener, Larry, 362
"Honestly Sincere "(Strouse), 372
"Honey in the Honeycomb" (Duke), 226
Honeymooners, The (Cohan), 30, 421
"Hoops" (Schwartz), 209
Hooker, Brian, 45
✗Hooray for What (Arlen), 228–229, 485
Hope, Bob, 82, 190, 191, 223
Hopkins, Miriam, 92
Hot-Cha! (Henderson), 177, 469
Hornblow, Arthur, 44, 45, 148
Horne, Lena, 214, 231–232
Horner, Harry, 195
Horwitt, Arnold, 4
Hoschna, Karl, 41
House of Flowers (Arlen), 230, 232, 485
Houston, Grace, 60
"How Are Things in Glocca Morra?" (Lane), 236
"How Beautiful the Days" (Loesser), 334
"How Can You Tell an American?" (Weill), 255
"How Much Is That Doggie in the Window?" (Merrill), 350
How Now, Dow Jones (E. Bernstein), 390, 516
"How to Handle a Woman" (Loewe), 308
How to Succeed in Business Without Really Trying (Loesser), 4, 336–338, 360, 507
Howard, Eugene, 51, 54, 169, 177
Howard, Willie, 51, 54, 114, 119, 169, 177
"How'd You Like to Spoon with Me?" (Kern), 66
Howland, Olin, 71
Hoyt, Charles, 2, 11
Hubbell, Raymond, 22
Huff, Forrest, 167
Hughes, Langston, 257
Hundley, John, 151
Hunter, Glenn, 151
Huston, Walter, 254–255
"Hymn to Him, A" (Loewe), 306

"I Ain't Down Yet" (Willson), 346
"I Am Ashamed that Women Are So Simple" (Porter), 199

"I Am in Love" (Porter), 200
"I Am Loved" (Porter), 199, 200
"I Am Only Human After All" (Duke), 222
"I Believe in You" (Loesser), 336, 337
"I Can Cook, Too" (Bernstein), 292
I Can Get It for You Wholesale (Rome), 249, 491
"I Can't Do the Sum" (Herbert), 14, 15
"I Can't Give you Anything but Love, Baby" (McHugh), 213
"I Could Have Danced All Night" (Loewe), 306
"I Could Write a Book" (Rodgers), 159
I Do! I Do! (Schmidt), 4, 375, 379–381, 514
"I, Don Quixote" (Leigh), 399, 400
"I Don't Think I'll Fall in Love Today" (Gershwin), 118
"I Enjoy Being a Girl (Rodgers), 281
I Feel Wonderful (Herman), 391, 516
"I Found a Four-Leaf Clover" (Gershwin), 113
"I Get a Kick Out of You" (Porter), 188
"I Get Carried Away" (Bernstein), 292
"I Get Embarrassed" (Merrill), 353
"I Got a Song" (Arlen), 230
"I Got Lost in His Arms" (Berlin), 102
"I Got Rhythm" (Gershwin), 119
"I Got the Sun in the Morning" (Berlin), 102
"I Guess I'll Have to Change My Plan" (Schwartz), 207
"I Hate Men" (Porter), 199
"I Have No Words" (Schwartz), 208
"I Jupiter, I Rex" (Porter), 199
"I Love a Parade" (Arlen), 228
"I Love Louisa" (Schwartz), 209
"I Love My Wife" (Schmidt), 380
"I Love Paris" (Porter), 200
"I Love You" (Coleman), 388
"I Love You" (Porter), 196, 199, 200
I Married an Angel (Rodgers), 155–157, 464

"I Married an Angel" (Rodgers), 157
"I Mean to Say" (Gershwin), 121
While" (Herbert), 21
"I Might Be Your Once-in-a-
"I Might Fall Back on You" (Kern), 78
"I Must Have that Man" (McHugh), 213
"I Must Love You" (Rodgers), 151
"I Say It's Spinach" (Berlin), 97
"I Sleep Easier Now" (Porter), 199
"I Still Get Jealous" (Styne), 314
"I Still See Elisa" (Loewe), 301
"I Walk a Little Faster" (Coleman), 385
"I Want a Man" (Youmans), 136, 138
"I Want to Be a Ballet Dancer" (Berlin), 94
"I Want to Be Bad" (Henderson), 175
"I Want to Be Happy" (Youmans), 133, 134
"I Want to Be With You" (Strouse), 374
"I Watch the Love Parade" (Kern), 81
"I Will Follow You" (Herman), 392
"I Wish I Were in Love Again" (Rodgers), 155
"I Wonder What the King Is Doing Tonight" (Loewe), 308
"I Worship You" (Porter), 185
"I Would Die" (Merrill), 353
"I'd Like to Poison Ivy" (Rodgers), 145
I'd Rather Be Right (Rodgers), 35, 157, 241, 464
Idol's Eye, The (Herbert), 12, 413
"If Ever I Would Leave You" (Loewe), 308
"If He Walked into My Life" (Herman), 396
"If I Loved You" (Rodgers), 272
"If I Were a Rich Man" (Bock), 367
"If I Were on the Stage" (Herbert), 17
"If My Friends Could See Me Now" (Coleman), 389

"If There Is Someone Lovelier than You" (Schwartz), 210
"If You Hadn't but You Did" (Styne), 315
"I'll Build a Stairway to Paradise" (Gershwin), 168
"I'll Know Him" (Henderson), 175
"I'll Tell the Man in the Street" (Rodgers), 157
"Ill Wind" (Arlen), 228
Illustrators' Show, The (Actman), 298, 331, 506
Illya Darling (Hadjidakis), 399, 517
"I'm an Ordinary Man" (Loewe), 306
"I'm Falling in Love with Someone" (Herbert), 20
"I'm Flying" (Charlap), 386
"I'm Going Back" (Styne), 317
"I'm Gonna Wash that Man Right Outa My Hair" (Rodgers), 276
"I'm in Love Again" (Porter), 184
"I'm on My Way" (Loewe), 301
"I'm on the Crest of a Wave" (Henderson), 171, 228
"I'm in Love with a Memory of You" (Schuman), 331
"I'm Looking for a Daddy Long Legs" (Berlin), 93
"I'm Not at All in Love" (Adler), 342
"I'm Sitting on Top of the World" (Arlen), 169
"I'm the Greatest Star" (Styne), 325
"I'm to Marry a Nobleman" (Cohan), 33
"Impossible Dream, The" (Leigh), 401
"In Egern on the Tegern See" (Kern), 81
"In Old New York" (Herbert), 19
"In Our Hideaway" (Berlin), 106
"Indian Love Call" (Friml), 43
Ingram, Rex, 244
Innocent Eyes (Romberg), 435
Inside U.S.A. (Schwartz), 4, 215, 216, 479
International Revue (McHugh), 214, 480
Irene (Tierney), 6, 75, 133, 166
"Is It a Crime?" (Styne), 317
"Is It Really Me?" (Schmidt), 378

"It" (Romberg), 57
"It Ain't Necessarily So" (Gershwin), 126
"It Amazes Me" (Coleman), 385
"It Couldn't Please Me More" (Kander), 404
It Happened in Nordland (Herbert), 15–16, 414
"It May Rain when the Sun Stops Shining" (Rodgers), 147
"It Was Good Enough for Grandma" (Arlen), 230
"Italian Street Song" (Herbert), 20, 38
It's a Bird It's a Plane It's Superman (Strouse), 370, 375, 514
"It's a Chemical Reaction" (Porter), 200
"It's a Lovely Day Tomorrow" (Berlin), 99
"It's All Right With Me" (Porter), 200
"It's All the Same" (Leigh), 401
"It's All Yours" (Schwartz), 213
"It's Better with a Union Man" (Rome), 243
"It's De-Lovely" (Porter), 191
"It's Good to Be Alive" (Merrill), 351
"It's Love" (Bernstein), 292
"It's Today" (Herman), 395, 396
"I've Come to Wive It Wealthily in Padua" (Porter), 197
"I've Got a Crush on You" (Gershwin), 118, 121
"I've Got the World on a String" (Arlen), 228
"I've Got Your Number" (Coleman), 388
"I've Gotta Crow" (Charlap), 386
"I've Grown Accustomed to Your Face" (Loewe), 306
"I've Still Got My Health" (Porter), 195
"I've Told Every Little Star" (Kern), 81

Jack and Jill (Newman),429
Jackpot (Duke), 483
Jackson, Fred, 130
Jacobson, Irving, 399, 400
Jamaica (Arlen), 231–232, 486
James, Hal, 398
James, Paul, 206

Janis, Elsie, 69
Jeanmaire, 61
"Jeannette and Her Little Wooden Shoes" (Herbert), 20
Jeffreys, Anne, 61, 258, 259
Jenkins, George, 260
Jennie (Schwartz), 217, 480
Jennings, John, 407
Jerome, Ben, 134
Jessel, Raymond, 409
Jimmie (Stothart), 133, 497
John Murray Anderson's Almanac (Adler), 340, 362, 385, 508
John, Tom, 34
Johnny Johnson (Weill), 253–254, 492
"Johnny One Note" (Rodgers), 155
Johnson, Albert, 96, 123, 153, 192, 208, 209
Johnson, Karen, 410
Johnson, Nunnally, 215
Johnson, Susan, 335
Johnson, Van, 159, 160
Johnston, Johnny, 217
Johnstone, Justine, 70
Jolson, Al, 51, 54, 55, 66, 113, 124, 167, 169, 235
Jones, John Price, 171, 173
Jones, Tom, 375–381, 514
Jornay, Roberta, 274
"Josephine" (Porter), 200
Jubilee (Porter), 188, 190, 472
Jumbo (Rodgers), 153, 463
"June Is Bustin' Out All Over" (Rodgers), 272
June Love (Friml), 425
"Just One of Those Things" (Porter), 189
"Just You Wait" (Loewe), 306
"Just You Watch My Step" (Kern), 71

Kahn, Gus, 85, 137
Kalem, Ted, 237, 325, 393
Kalmar, Bert, 94, 166, 317
Kander, John, 85, 402–406, 518
Kanin, Garson, 322, 324
Kasha, Lawrence, 364, 391
"Katie Went to Haiti" (Porter), 178, 195
Katinka (Friml), 39, 40, 424
"Katrina" (Loewe), 297
Kaufman, George S., 4, 110, 121, 122, 157, 158, 200, 208, 215, 244, 332
Kaufman, S. Jay, 144
Kaye, Benjamin, 145
Kaye, Nora, 298

Kaye, Danny, 195, 255, 257
Kaye, Stubby, 333
Kazan, Elia, 253
Kearns, Allen, 114, 116
Keel, Howard, 233
"Keep a-Hoppin' " (Willson), 347
"Keep Smiling and Carry On" (Donaldson), 138
Kellin, Mike, 280
Kelly, Gene, 159, 160, 192
Kelly, Patsy, 209
Kelly, Walter C., 51
Kelton, Pert, 76, 345
Kent, William, 43
Kerker, Gustave, 22
Kern, Jerome, 2, 22, 41, 52, 62–83, 85, 105, 111, 124, 130, 142, 163, 168, 205, 214, 270, 439
Kerr, Walter, 283, 284, 293, 302, 307, 321, 325, 326, 335, 338, 358, 365, 367, 374, 378, 394, 406
Kert, Larry, 294, 295
"Kickin' the Gong Around" (Arlen), 228
Kid Boots (Tierney), 166, 429
Kidd, Michael, 4, 200, 248, 303, 332, 386
"Kids" (Strouse), 372
Kiley, Richard, 286, 398–400
King, Charles, 135, 186
King, Dennis, 43, 45, 46, 79, 155, 156
King and I, The (Rodgers), 277–279, 495
King, John Michael, 306, 307
King of Cadonia, The (Kern), 66, 440
Kiralfy Brothers, 2
Kirk, Lisa, 198, 199
Kirsten, Dorothy, 298
"Kiss in the Dark, A" (Herbert), 21, 168
"Kiss Me Again" (Herbert), 17
Kiss Me, Kate (Porter), 3, 5, 197–199, 474
Kiss Waltz, The (Kern), 66, 440
"Kitchen Police" (Berlin), 91
Kitty Darlin' (Friml), 16, 424
Kitty's Kisses (Conrad), 429
Kiviette, 82, 96, 139, 171, 172, 209
Klein, Paul, 405
Kleinsinger, George, 399
"Kling-Kling Bird on the Divi-Divi Tree, The" (Porter), 189

Knickerbocker Holiday (Weill), 3, 254, 492
Knight, June, 139
Kober, Arthur, 245
Koehler, Ted, 177, 228
Koenig, John, 160
Kollmar, Richard, 159, 162, 254, 362
Kolodin, Irving, 7
Kronenberger, Louis, 391
Krutch, Joseph Wood, 126
Kuhner, John, 411
Kwamina (Adler), 342, 509

La Belle Paree (Kern), 66, 440
La La Lucille (Gershwin), 112, 129, 130, 168, 453
La Plume de Ma Tante, 5
La Vivandière (Herbert), 11
Lacey, Franklin, 344
Ladies First, 111
Lady, Be Good! (Gershwin), 114–118, 455
Lady Comes Across, The (Duke), 483
Lady Fair (Romberg), 57
"Lady Fair" (Henderson), 169
Lady in the Dark (Weill), 3, 6, 255–257, 492
"Lady Is a Tramp, The" (Rodgers), 155
"Lady of the Evening" (Berlin), 93
Lady of the Slipper, The (Herbert), 417
Laffing Room Only (Lane), 235, 487
Lahr, Bert, 119, 172–175, 177, 178, 193–195, 223, 312, 315
Lamour, Dorothy, 395
Lane, Burton, 207, 219, 220, 234–238, 309, 486
Lang, Harold, 161, 198
Langner, Lawrence, 146, 265
Lannin, Paul, 131
Lansbury, Angela, 395, 396
Larrimore, Francine, 41
LaRue, Grace, 93, 168
Laska, Edward, 66
Latouche, John, 225–226
Laughing Husband, The (Kern), 64, 441
Laurence, Paula, 196
Laurents, Arthur, 287, 293, 318–320, 326, 356, 358, 359
"Laurey Makes Up Her Mind" (Rodgers), 266
Lawlor, Mary, 174
Lawrence, Carol, 233, 294
Lawrence, Gertrude, 114, 117, 118, 214, 255–257, 277, 278

Lawrence, Jerome, 395
Lawrence, Steve, 409
Laye, Evelyn, 211
Layton, Joe, 4, 286
"Lazy" (Berlin), 86
"Learn to Do the Strut" (Berlin), 94
Leave It to Jane (Kern), 69–71, 443
"Leave It to Jane" (Kern), 71
Leave It to Me! (Porter), 192, 473
Lederer, George, 4
Lee, Robert E., 395
Lee, Sammy, 95
Lee, Tom, 99
"Leg of Mutton" (Romberg), 50
"Legalize My Name" (Arlen), 230, 231
Lehar, Franz, 2, 33, 63
Leigh, Carolyn, 316, 318, 384, 385–390, 515
Leigh, Mitch, 396–401, 517
Leigh, Vivien, 407
LeMaire, Charles, 43, 59, 132, 136, 139, 152, 173, 176
Lend an Ear (Gaynor), 5, 314
Lennart, Isobel, 323
Lenya, Lotte, 261, 262, 404, 405
Lerner, Alan Jay, 236, 259, 286, 296–309, 326, 501
LeRoy, Hal, 159
Leslie, Lew, 213
Let 'Em Eat Cake (Gershwin), 123, 457
"Let 'Em Eat Cake" (Gershwin), 123
Let Freedom Sing (Rome), 489
"Let Me Entertain You" (Styne), 320
"Let Me Match My Private Life with Yours" (Duke), 220
"Let's Be Buddies" (Porter), 195
"Let's Do It" (Porter), 182, 184
Let's Face It! (Porter), 193, 195, 314, 473
"Let's Fly Away" (Porter), 186
"Let's Have Another Cup o' Coffee" (Berlin), 97
"Let's Misbehave" (Porter), 184
Levant, Oscar, 109, 123
Levene, Sam, 333
Levey, Ethel, 27–30
Levin, Herman, 244, 304
Lewine, Richard, 4
Lewis, Robert, 253, 300
Liebling, Leonard, 126

Life Begins at 8:40 (Arlen), 485

"Life Is Just a Bowl of Cherries" (Henderson), 177

Life of the Party (Loewe), 299

"Life Upon the Wicked Stage" (Kern), 78

Li'l Abner (dePaul), 4, 303

Lillie, Beatrice, 150, 210, 215, 216, 222–224, 409

Lilo, 200

Lindsay, Howard, 104, 105, 188, 191, 229, 282

Linn, Bambi, 273

"Little Bit in Love, A" (Bernstein), 292

"Little Girl from Little Rock, A" (Styne), 314

"Little Green Snakes" (Merrill), 353

Little Johnny Jones (Cohan), 26, 28, 29, 34, 420

Little Mary Sunshine (Besoyan), 147, 407, 408

Little Me (Coleman), 387, 515

Little Millionaire, The (Cohan), 31, 33, 421

Little Nellie Kelly (Cohan), 422

Little Nemo (Herbert), 416

"Little Old Lady" (Carmichael), 223

Little Show, The (Schwartz), 203, 206–207, 476

"Little Surplus Me" (Rome), 244

"Little Tin Box" (Bock), 363

Little Tommy Tucker (Schwartz), 208

Little Whopper, The (Friml), 41, 424

Littlest Revue, The (Duke), 226, 371, 484

Lockridge, Richard, 157, 207

Loeb, Philip, 146, 147

Loesser, Frank, 3, 142, 313, 328–338, 339, 343, 360, 506

Loewe, Frederick, 296–309, 501

Logan, Ella, 236

Logan, Joshua, 3, 157, 214, 245–247, 255, 275

Lollipop (Youmans), 459

Long, Shorty, 335

"Lonely Goatherd, The" (Rodgers), 283

Lonely Romeo, A, 143

"Lonely Town" (Bernstein), 292

Longstreet, Stephen, 314

"Look for the Silver Lining" (Kern), 75, 168

"Look to the Rainbow" (Lane), 236

"Look Who's Dancing" (Schwartz), 217

"Looking at You" (Porter), 186

"Looking for a Boy" (Gershwin), 117

Loos, Anita, 314

"Lord Done Fixed Up My Soul" (Berlin), 99

"Lorna's Here" (Strouse), 374

Lorraine, Lillian, 51

Lorraine, Ted, 52

Losch, Tilly, 186, 209

Lost in the Stars (Weill), 259, 260, 493

"Lot of Livin' to Do, A" (Strouse), 372

Louie the 14th (Romberg), 56, 436

"Louisiana Hayride" (Schwartz), 210

Louisiana Purchase (Berlin), 99, 178, 451

Love Birds (Romberg), 54, 434

Love Call, The (Romberg), 437

"Love Don't Turn Away" (Schmidt), 378

"Love for Sale" (Porter), 186

"Love I Hear" (Sondheim), 357

"Love Is Like a Firefly" (Friml), 39

Love Life (Weill), 259, 326, 493

"Love, Look Away" (Rodgers), 281

"Love Makes the World Go Round" (Merrill), 353

Love o' Mike (Kern), 443

"Love Tiptoed Through My Heart" (Loewe), 298

"Love Will Call" (Rodgers), 144

"Lovely" (Sondheim), 357

"Lover, Come Back to Me" (Romberg), 59

"Love's Own Kiss" (Friml), 39

"Love's Intense in Tents" (Rodgers), 144

Lowell, Helen, 66

Luana (Friml), 46, 427

Lucky (Ruby-Kern), 430, 446

"Lucky Day" (Henderson), 169

Lukas, Paul, 104

"Lusty Month of May, The" (Loewe), 308

Macaulay, Joseph, 45

MacDermot, Galt, 410

MacDonald, Christie, 20

MacDonald, Jeanette, 114, 116

MacDonough, Glen, 14, 15, 21

Macgowan, Kenneth, 114, 145

Mackintosh, Robert, 246, 395

MacLaine, Shirley, 341

MacMurray, Fred, 82, 208

Mad Show, The (M. Rodgers), 5, 407

Madame Aphrodite (Herman), 390, 516

Madame Sherry (Hoschna), 41, 427

Madcap Duchess, The (Herbert), 21, 417

Magic Melody, The (Romberg), 54, 434

"Magic Moment" (Schwartz), 217

Maid in America (Romberg), 431

Mainbocher, 258

"Make a Miracle" (Loesser), 332

"Make Believe" (Kern), 78

"Make It Another Old Fashioned, Please" (Porter), 195

Make Mine Manhattan (Lewine), 4

"Make Someone Happy" (Styne), 322

Mame (Herman), 390, 395, 517

"Mame" (Herman), 396

Mamoulian, Rouben, 125, 226, 265, 273

"Man I Love, The" (Gershwin), 85, 117

Man of La Mancha (Leigh), 398–401, 517

Man Who Owns Broadway, The (Cohan), 421

Man with a Load of Mischief (Clifton), 410

Mandel, Frank, 35, 56–59, 134

"Mandy" (Berlin), 91

Maney, Richard, 6

"Manhattan" (Rodgers), 146

Manhattan Mary (Henderson), 171, 468

Mann, Daniel, 301

Manson, Alan, 245

Mantle, Burns, 125, 133, 174, 268

Maple, Audrey, 39

Marand, Patricia, 246

Marbury, Elisabeth, 68, 183

March, Fredric, 145

"March of the Toys" (Herbert), 15

"Maria" (Rodgers), 283

"Marie from Sunny Italy" (Berlin), 87

Marks, Walter, 409

Marre, Albert, 398, 400

Marsh, Howard, 56, 78, 79
Marshall, Everett, 177
Marshall, Mort, 314
Martin, Ernest, 199, 330–332, 337, 344
Martin, Hugh, 3, 162, 409
Martin, Mary, 192, 217, 257, 258, 275–277, 282–284, 304, 312, 316, 379, 380, 385
Martin, Norman, 405
Martin, Owen, 267
Martin, Virginia, 387
Marvenga, Ilse, 56
Marx Brothers, 95, 166
"Mary" (Cohan), 29
Mary (Hirsch), 35, 41, 75, 458
Mary Jane McKane (Youmans), 134, 137, 458
"Mary, Queen of Scots" (Rodgers), 145
Massey, Daniel, 365
Massey, Ilona, 179
Masteroff, Joe, 366, 402, 404
"Matchmaker, Matchmaker" (Bock), 368
Matthews, Jessie, 150, 151, 186
Mature, Victor, 255
Matz, Peter, 286
Maxwell, Arthur, 279
"May Party, The" (Loesser), 330
May Wine (Romberg), 59, 438
"Maybe" (Gershwin), 118
Mayer, Edwin Justus, 257
Mayhew, Stella, 66, 135
Mayro, Jacqueline, 319
Maytime (Romberg), 53, 432
McCarthy, Joseph, 78, 133, 166
McCarthy, Joseph Allan, 385
McCarthy, Justin, 45
McCarthy Sisters, 94, 169
McCauley, Jack, 314
McConnell, Lulu, 144
McCormick, Myron, 276
McCracken, Joan, 229, 230, 266, 279
McCullough, Paul, 95, 120, 121, 166, 222
McDonald, Grace, 83
McEvoy, J. P., 214
McGrath, Leueen, 200
McHale, Duke, 155
McHugh, Jimmy, 212–214
McKayle, Donald, 374
McLerie, Allyn Ann, 291
Me and Juliet (Rodgers), 279, 496
"Meine Kleine Akrobat" (Schwartz), 210
Meiser, Edith, 146, 147, 195
Meisner, Sanford, 146

"Melisande" (Schmidt), 379
Melody (Romberg), 438
Melody Man, The (Rodgers), 145
Melting of Molly, The (Romberg), 433
Mercer, Johnny, 220, 230–232, 303
Merman, Ethel, 101–105, 114, 119, 120, 138, 139, 177, 178, 187–188, 190, 191, 193–195, 196, 213, 214, 226, 312, 318–321
Merrick, David, 231, 245, 247–249, 354, 378, 279, 392
Merrill, Bob, 3, 85, 223, 224, 323, 325, 348–353, 510
Merry Malones, The (Cohan), 423
"Merry Minuet, The" (Harnick), 362
Merry Widow, The (Lehar), 2, 33, 63
Merry-Go-Round, 205
Messel, Oliver, 231, 232
Metaxa, Georges, 80, 210, 211
Mexican Hayride (Porter), 193, 196, 474
Michael Todd's Peep Show (Rome), 490
Middleton, Ray, 82, 103
Michaels, Sidney, 409
Mielziner, Jo, 103, 122, 154, 156, 157, 160, 187, 190, 200, 246, 254, 258, 272, 273, 276, 278, 280, 333
"Military Life" (Rome), 244
Milk and Honey (Herman), 390, 392, 516
"Milk and Honey" (Herman), 392
Miller, Marilyn, 51, 58, 73, 74, 75, 91, 97, 99, 138
Mills, Florence, 214
"Mine" (Gershwin), 123
Minevitch, Borrah, 76
Minnelli, Vincente, 83
"Mira" (Merrill), 353
"Mis'ry's Comin' 'Round" (Kern), 78
Miss Dolly Dollars (Herbert), 414
Miss Information (Kern), 69, 442
Miss Liberty (Berlin), 103, 452
"Miss Marmelstein" (Rome), 249
Miss 1917 (Herbert-Kern), 69, 111, 418, 443
"Mister and Missus Fitch" (Porter), 186
"Mister Snow" (Rodgers), 272

Mitchell, James, 301
Mitchell, Julian, 14
Mlle. Modiste (Herbert), 6, 17, 29, 415
"Moanin' Low" (Rainger), 206, 207
Molly Darling (Johnstone), 429
"Moment of Madness, A" (Coleman), 385
Monk, Julius, 5
Montalban, Ricardo, 231, 232
Monte Cristo, Jr. (Romberg), 433
Montgomery, David, 18, 26
"Montmart'" (Porter), 200
"Moon of My Delight" (Rodgers), 151
"Moon-Faced, Starry-Eyed" (Weill), 259
"Moonbeams" (Herbert), 18
"Moonlight Mama" (Rodgers), 145
Moore, Grace, 94, 95
Moore, Karen, 319
Moore, Monette, 210
Moore, Victor, 29, 30, 99, 114, 122, 123, 172, 178, 187, 192
Mooring, Mark, 57, 135
Moran, Lois, 122, 123
"More Than You Know" (Youmans), 138
Morehouse, Ward, 26
Morgan, Frank, 209
Morgan, Helen, 73, 76, 78, 79, 169, 214
Morison, Patricia, 197–199
Morning Sun (Klein), 518
Morris, Howard, 314
Morris, Richard, 346
Morrison, Hobe, 359
Morse, Lee, 151
Morse, Robert, 317, 337, 338, 353
Most Happy Fella, The (Loesser), 7, 334–335, 507
Mostel, Zero, 7, 357, 367
Motley, 200, 302, 335
"Mountain Greenery" (Rodgers), 146
Mr. President (Berlin), 105, 106, 453
Mr. Wix of Wickham (Kern), 65, 439
Mr. Wonderful (Bock), 362, 511
"Mr. Wonderful" (Bock), 362
Munson, Ona, 171
Murphy, George, 82
Murray, Wynn, 155, 159
Music Box Revue (4 editions) (Berlin), 4, 86, 92–95, 450

Music Hath Charms (Friml), 46, *427*
Music in the Air (Kern), 2, 79–81, *447*
Music Man, The (Willson), 5, 35, 330, 343–347, *509*
"My Boy and I" (Youmans), 134
"My Coloring Book" (Kander), 405
"My Darling, My Darling" (Loesser), 332
My Fair Lady (Gershwin), 117
My Fair Lady (Loewe), 4, 5, 6, 7, 35, 302–307, *502*
"My Favorite Things" (Rodgers), 284
"My Funny Valentine" (Rodgers), 118, 155
"My Gal Is Mine Once More" (Schwartz), 215
My Golden Girl (Herbert), *419*
"My Heart Belongs to Daddy" (Porter), 192, 197
"My Heart Is So Full of You" (Loesser), 334
"My Heart Stood Still" (Rodgers), 150
My Lady's Glove (Romberg), *432*
"My Lord and Master" (Rodgers), 279
"My Lucky Star" (Henderson), 175
"My Mammy" (Donaldson), 55
My Maryland (Romberg), 58, *437*
"My One and Only" (Gershwin), 118
"My Own Morning" (Styne), 327
My Princess (Romberg), *437*
My Romance (Romberg), 61, *439*
"My Song" (Henderson), 177
Myrtil, Odette, 233

"'N Everything" (DeSylva), 167
Naldi, Nita, 54
"Name's LaGuardia, The" (Bock), 363
Nash, N. Richard, 378, 386
Nash, Ogden, 226, 257
Nathan, George Jean, 60, 126, 157, 186, 274
Naughty Marietta (Herbert), 19, 38, *416*
"Neapolitan Love Song" (Herbert), 21

"'Neath the Southern Moon" (Herbert), 20
Neff, Hildegarde, 200, 201
Nelson, Kenneth, 377
Nesbitt, Cathleen, 306
"Never Will I Marry" (Loesser), 336
"New Ashmoleon Marching Society" (Loesser), 332
New Faces of 1952, 362
New Girl in Town (Merrill), 3, 7, 351, *510*
New Moon, The (Romberg), 58–59, *438*
"New Sun in the Sky" (Schwartz), 209
"New York, New York" (Bernstein), 292
New Yorkers, The (Porter), 186, *471*
New Yorkers, The (Schwartz), 204, *476*
Newman, David, 375
Nicholas, Fayard & Harold, 155, 231
Nichols, Lewis, 268
Nichols, Mike, 369
Nielsen, Alice, 12, 13, 16
Night Boat, The (Kern), *444*
Night Out, A (Youmans), 137
"Night Was Made for Love, The" (Kern), 80, 81
"Night and Day" (Porter), 186
"Night Song" (Strouse), 374
Nightcap (Herman), 391
Nina Rosa (Romberg), *438*
9:15 Revue, 222, 228
"Nine O'Clock" (Merrill), 353
90 in the Shade (Kern), 67, *442*
No Foolin' (Friml), *426*
"No Lover" (Porter), 199
"No Other Love" (Rodgers), 280
No, No, Nanette (Youmans), 41, 45, 130, 133, *459*
"No, No, Nanette" (Youmans), 59, 134
No Strings (Rodgers), 4, 286, *499*
Nobody Home (Kern), 68, *442*
"Nobody Makes a Pass at Me" (Rome), 243
Norris, William, 14
"Not Now but Later" (Friml), 39
"Not Yet" (Kern), 72
Noto, Lore, 378
Novis, Donald, 153
"Now" (Duke), 223

"Now Generation, The" (Apolinar), 411

O'Brien Girl, The (Hirsch), 35, 41, *429*
Odets, Clifford, 373–374
Oenslager, Donald, 152, 171, 172, 190, 253
Oestreicher, Gerard, 392
Of Thee I Sing (Gershwin), 121–123, 158, 359, *457*
"Of Thee I Sing (Baby)" (Gershwin), 123
"Off the Record" (Rodgers), 157
Oh, Boy! (Kern), 69, 70, *443*
Oh Captain! (Livingston), 211
"Oh, How I Hate to Get Up in the Morning" (Berlin), 91, 99, 100
"Oh, How I Long to Belong to You" (Youmans), 139
Oh, I Say! (Kern), *441*
Oh, Kay! (Gershwin), 114, 117–118, *455*
"Oh, Lady Be Good!" (Gershwin), 116
Oh, Lady! Lady!! (Kern), 71–73, 78, *443*
"Oh, Me! Oh, My!" (Youmans), 132
Oh, My Dear (Hirsch), 73
Oh, Please! (Youmans), *459*
"Oh So Nice" (Gershwin), 118
"Oh, What a Beautiful Morning" (Rodgers), 266, 268
O'Hara, John, 159
Oklahoma! (Rodgers), 3, 5, 6, 163, 229, 265–269, *494*
"Oklahoma" (Rodgers), 269
"Ol' Man River" (Kern), 78
Olaf Pierre, 354
Old Dutch (Herbert), 16, *416*
"Old Enough to Love" (Rodgers), 148
"Old-Fashioned Garden" (Porter), 184
"Oldest Established, The" (Loesser), 333
Oliver, Edna May, 70, 76
Oliver, Thelma, 389
Olsen and Johnson, 4, 235
Olsen, George, 76, 173
"Omar Khayyam" (Romberg), 51
On a Clear Day You Can See Forever (Lane), 236, 309, 487
"On the Street Where You Live" (Loewe), 307
"On the Sunny Side of the

Street" (McHugh), 214

On the Town (Bernstein), 3, 290, 315, *499*

On Your Toes (Rodgers), 3, 154, *463*

"Once in Love with Amy" (Loesser), 332

Once Upon a Mattress (M. Rodgers), 3, 407, 408

"Once Upon a Time" (Strouse), 373

"One Alone" (Romberg), 57

"One Big Union for Two" (Rome), 243

"One Boy" (Strouse), 372

One Dam Thing After Another (Rodgers), 150

110 in the Shade (Schmidt), 375, 378, *514*

"127th Street" (Strouse), 373

"One Kiss" (Romberg), 59

"One Last Kiss" (Strouse), 372

"One Moment Alone" (Kern), 81

One Touch of Venus (Weill), 257, 258, *492*

O'Neal, William, 59, 103

"Only a Rose" (Friml), 45

"Only for Americans" (Berlin), 104

Only Girl, The (Herbert), 21, *417*

"Only Music that Makes Me Dance, The" (Styne), 325

"Open a New Window" (Herman), 396

Orange Blossoms (Herbert), 21, 168, *419*

"Orange Grove in California, An" (Berlin), 94

Orbach, Jerry, 377

"On the Other Side of the Tracks" (Coleman), 388

Our Nell (Gershwin), *454*

"Out in the Open Air" (Lane), 235

"Out of the Clear Blue Sky" (Duke), 226

Out of This World (Porter), 199, *475*

Over the Top (Romberg), 54, *433*

"Over There" (Cohan), 33

"Pack Up Your Sins and Go to the Devil" (Berlin), 94

Padula, Edward, 371

Paige, Janis, 340, 341

Paint Your Wagon (Loewe), 301–302, *502*

Pajama Game, The (Adler), 3, 317, 330, 340–341, *508*

Pal Joey (Rodgers), 3, 5, 158–162, *465*

Palmer, Leland, 411

Panama Hattie (Porter), 178, 193–195, *473*

Panama, Norman, 303

"Papa, Won't You Dance with Me?" (Styne), 314

Parade (Herman), 392, 396, *516*

Parade (Moross), 241

"Parade in Town, A" (Sondheim), 359

Pardon My English (Gershwin), 115, *457*

"Paree" (Schwartz), 210

Paris (Porter), 184–185, *471*

"Paris Original" (Loesser), 338

Park Avenue (Schwartz), 215, *479*

Parker, Dorothy, 153, 222

Parker, H. T., 38

"Party's Over, The" (Styne), 317

Pascal, Gabriel, 302–303

"Pass that Football" (Bernstein), 292

Passing Show, The (1894), 4

Passing Show of 1914, The (Romberg), 51, *430*

Passing Show of 1915, The, 51

Passing Show of 1916, The (Romberg), *431*

Passing Show of 1917, The (Romberg), *432*

Passing Show of 1918, The (Romberg), 54, *433*

Passing Show of 1919, The (Romberg), 54, *434*

Passing Show of 1923, The (Romberg), *435*

Passing Show of 1924, The (Romberg), *435*

Patricola, Tom, 170

Peacock, Bertram, 54

Pearl, Jack, 115, 214

Peasant Girl, The (Friml), *423*

Peggy-Ann (Rodgers), 6, 149, *461*

Pember, Clifford, 72

Penn, Arthur, 374

Pennington, Ann, 169, 170

"People" (Styne), 325, 354

"People Will Say We're in Love" (Rodgers), 268

Percival, Walter, 17

Perelman, S. J., 257

Perkins, Anthony, 335–336

Peter Pan (Styne-Charlap), 316, 385, *504, 515*

"Piano Lesson" (Willson), 345

Pickert, Rolly, 155

Picon, Molly, 392

"Picture of Happiness, The" (Bock), 363

"Picture of Me Without You, A" (Porter), 189

Pidgeon, Walter, 352, 353

Piggy (Friend), *467*

Pins and Needles (Rome), 4, 6, 73, 241–244, *489*

Pinza, Ezio, 247, 275, 276

Pipe Dream (Rodgers), 280, *496*

Platt, Marc, 267

"Play a Simple Melody" (Berlin), 90

Pleasures and Palaces (Loesser), 338

Pockriss, Lee, 407

Poe, Aileen, 144

"Politics and Poker" (Bock), 363

Pollard, Michael J., 372

Pond, James, 206

Pons, Helene, 155

Poor Little Ritz Girl (Romberg-Rodgers), 54, 129, 144, *435, 460*

Poppy (Samuels), 205

"Pore Jud" (Rodgers), 268

"Porgy" (McHugh), 213

Porgy and Bess (Gershwin), 2, 5, 79, 124–127, *457*

Porter, Cole, 2, 3, 129, 178, 180–201, 285, *470*

Post, W. H., 45

Powell, Eleanor, 210

Powers, Tom, 70

"Praise the Lord and Pass the Ammunition" (Loesser), 331

Present Arms (Rodgers), 150, *462*

Presnell, Harve, 346

Preston, Robert, 345, 379, 380, 409

"Pretty Girl Is Like a Melody, A" (Berlin), 92

"Pretty Little Picture" (Sondheim), 356

Prideaux, Tom, 41

Prima Donna, The (Herbert), 18, *416*

Prince Ananias (Herbert), 11, *413*

Prince Harold, 4, 317, 341, 351, 363, 364, 366, 402, 404–406

Princess Charming (Schwartz), *477*

Princess Flavia (Romberg), *436*
Princess Pat, The (Herbert), 21, *418*
Princess Theatre, 2, 68–73, 242
Prior, Allan, 138
"Promise Me a Rose" (Merrill), 353
Pruette, William, 17
Puck, Eva, 26, 78, 148
Pully, B. S., 333
Purcell, Charles, 53, 148
Put It in Writing (Martin), *518*
"Puzzlement, A" (Rodgers), 279

Queen High (Gensler), *467*
Queen o' Hearts (Gensler), *497*
"Quiet Girl, A" (Bernstein), 292
Quine, Richard, 83

"Rackety-Coo" (Friml), 40
Rado, James, 410
Ragland, Rags, 194
Ragni, Gerome, 410
"Rags to Riches" (Adler), 340
"Rain in Spain, The" (Loewe), 5, 305, 307
Rainbow (Youmans), 136–138, *459*
Rainger, Ralph, 206
Raitt, John, 272, 273, 340, 341
Ramblers, The (Ruby), 166
Randall, Carl, 71, 72
Randolph, Robert, 324
Rasch, Albertina, 210
Rascoe, Burton, 268
Rathbun, Stephen, 114
Raye, Martha, 394
"Real American Folk Song, The" (Gershwin), 111
"Real Live Girl" (Coleman), 388
Reardon, John, 322
"Red Ball Express" (Rome), 245
"Red Blues, The" (Porter), 200
Red, Hot and Blue! (Porter), 190, 191, *472*
"Red Hot Chicago" (Henderson), 175
"Red Mikado, The" (Rome), 244
Red Mill, The (Herbert), 18, *415*
Red Petticoat, The (Kern), 66, *441*
"Red Rose Cotillion, The" (Loesser), 332
Redhead (Hague), 4, *481*
Regay, Pearl, 57
"Remember" (Berlin), 86, 96
"Remember That I Care"

(Weill), 259
Revenge with Music (Schwartz), 210, 211, *478*
Reynolds, Herbert, 52, 67
Reynolds, James, 45, 75, 76, 94, 148, 186
"Rhode Island Is Famous for You" (Schwartz), 215
Rhodes, Erik, 187
"Rhythm" (Rodgers), 223
Rice, Edward E., 2, 87
Rice, Elmer, 257
Rich, Helen, 71
Rich Mr. Hoggenheimer, The (Kern), 66
Richman, Harry, 169–171, 177, 214
"Ride Through the Night" (Styne), 322
"Ridin' High" (Porter), 191
"Riff Song" (Romberg), 57
Riggs, T. Lawrason, 183
"Right as the Rain" (Arlen), 230
Ring, Blanche, 16
Rio Rita (Tierney), 78, 166
Ripley, Constance, 190, 211
"Rise 'n' Shine" (Youmans), 139
Rise of Rosie O'Reilly, The (Cohan), *422*
Ritchard, Cyril, 316
Ritter, Thelma, 352
Rivera, Chita, 372
Riverwind (Jennings), 407
"Road that Lies Before, The" (Kern), 70
"Road to Paradise" (Romberg), 53
Robbins, Jerome, 4, 104, 245, 290, 291, 293, 298, 314, 316–319, 324, 341, 357, 366, 385
Roberta (Kern), 41, 81–82, *447*
Roberti, Lyda, 82, 115
Roberts, Joan, 265, 267
Robertson, Guy, 78
Robeson, Paul, 78, 79
Robin, Leo, 314
Robinson, Bill, 213
Robinson Crusoe, Jr. (Romberg), *431*
Robinson, Clark, 82, 148
"Rock Island" (Willson), 345
Rock-a-bye Baby (Kern), *444*
Rodgers, Mary, 3, 407
Rodgers, Richard, 2, 3, 35, 64, 85, 101–103, 129, 140–163, 223, 264–287, 309, 312, 359, *460*, *494*, *499*
Rogers, Ginger, 114, 119, 394
Rogers, Jaime, 374

"Roll Yer Socks Up" (Merrill), 352
"Romany Life" (Herbert), 13
Romberg, Sigmund, 37, 41, 47, 48–61, 88, 144, *430*
Rome, Harold, 240–249, *489*
"Rose's Turn" (Styne), 320
"Room for One More" (Rodgers), 144, 270
Root, Lynn, 224
Root, Wells, 146, 169
"Rosabella" (Loesser), 334
Rosalie (Romberg-Gershwin), 58, *437*, *456*
Rose, Billy, 153, 169, 197
Rose of Algeria, The (Herbert), *416*
Rose of Stamboul, The (Romberg), *435*
Rose, Reva, 410
Rose, Vincent, 167
Rose-Marie (Friml), 41–45, 147, *425*
"Rose-Marie" (Friml), 43
Rosenfeld, Paul, 127
Rosenthal, Jean, 379
"Roundabout" (Duke), 226
Ross, Jerry, 3, 317, 329, 330, 339–342, *508*
Rowland, Adele, 68
"Roxy Music Hall, The" (Rodgers), 157
Royal, Ted, 301
Royal Vagabond, The (Cohan), 34, *422*
Ruby, Harry, 94, 166, 317
Ruggles, Charles, 138
Running for Office (Cohan), 26, 28, 30, *420*
Russell, Lillian, 11
Russell, Rosalind, 147, 292–293
Ryan, Robert, 106
Ryskind, Morrie, 121, 122, 158, 178, 205

"Sadie, Sadie" (Styne), 324
"Sadie Salome, Go Home" (Berlin), 89
Sadie Thompson (Duke), 226, *483*
"Saga of Jenny" (Weill), 257
Saidy, Fred, 229, 234
St. Louis Woman (Arlen), 230, 231, *485*
Saint Subber, Arnold, 199
Sally (Kern), 6, 73–76, 168, *444*
Salute to Spring (Loewe), 298, 299
"Sam and Delilah" (Gershwin), 119
Samuels, Lesser, 334

San Juan, Olga, 301
Sanborn, Pitts, 126
Sanderson, Julia, 67
Sandrich, Mark, Jr., 409
Saratoga (Arlen), 232, 233, *486*
Sergeant, Winthrop, 126
Sarnoff, Dorothy, 278
"Satan's Li'l Lamb" (Arlen), 220
Savage, Henry W., 69
Savo, Jimmy, 159, 300
Sawyer, Charles Pike, 114
"Say a Prayer" (Loewe), 306
Say, Darling (Styne), 3, 317, 341, *504*
"Say It with Music" (Berlin), 93
Say When (Henderson), 177, *469*
"Say, Young Man of Manhattan" (Youmans), 138
Schaffer, Louis, 242
Scheff, Fritzi, 12, 16–18
Schmidt, Harvey, 375–381, *514*
Schraps, Ernest, 60
Schuman, William, 331
Schwab, Laurence, 56, 58
Schwartz, Arthur, 4, 5, 83, 110, 130, 202–217, *476*
Schwartz, Jean, 50
Second Little Show (Schwartz), 207, *476*
"Secretary Is Not a Toy, A" (Loesser), 336, 337
See America First (Porter), 181, 183, *470*
Segal, Vivienne, 41, 52, 57, 71, 72, 111, 150, 155, 156, 159–161
Selden, Albert, 398
Seldes, Gilbert, 146
Selwyn, Ruth, 222, 228
"Sentimental Me" (Rodgers), 146
"September Song" (Weill), 148, 255
Serenade, The (Herbert), 12, *413*
"Serenade" (Romberg), 56
Sergava, Katharine, 267
"7½ Cents" (Adler), 342
Seven Lively Arts (Porter), 197, *474*
"Seventy-Six Trombones" (Willson), 345
"Shall We Dance?" (Rodgers). 278
"Shalom" (Herman), 392
Shannon, Harry T., 172
Sharaff, Irene, 97, 154, 159, 162, 190, 217, 256, 278, 279,

282, 294, 295, 321, 324, 389
Shaw, Oscar, 71, 94, 114, 175
Shean, Al, 81
"She Didn't Say Yes" (Kern), 81
She Loves Me (Bock), 4, 364–366, *512*
Sherwood, Robert E., 103
She's a Good Fellow (Kern), *444*
She's My Baby (Rodgers), 150, *462*
Shevelove, Burt, 356–357
Shinbone Alley (Kleinsinger), 399, *517*
"Shine on Your Shoes, A" (Schwartz), 210
"Ship Without a Sail, A" (Rodgers), 151
"Shipoopi" (Willson), 5
"Shoeless Joe from Hannibal, Mo." (Adler), 342
Shoestring '57, 371
Shoestring Revue, 5, 371
Shoot the Works, 220
Short, Hassard, 93, 95
"Shortest Day of the Year, The" (Rodgers), 159
"Should I Be Sweet?" (Youmans), 139
Show Boat (Kern), 2, 73, 74, 75, 77–79, 83, 137, *446*
Show Girl (Gershwin), *456*
Show Is On, The (Duke), 223, 224, *482*
"Show Me" (Loewe), 306
Show of Wonders, The (Romberg), *432*
Shubert, Lee & J. J., 4, 50, 51, 54, 55, 58, 61, 192, 223, 235
"Shy" (M. Rodgers), 408
Shy, Gus, 171
"Siberia" (Porter), 200
"Sid Ol' Kid" (Merrill), 353
Siff, Andrew, 364
Silk Stockings (Porter), 6, 199–201, *475*
Silvers, Louis, 167
Silvers, Phil, 177, 312–314, 321, 322
Simon, Neil, 388, 390
Simon, Robert, 126
Simple Simon (Rodgers), 151, 152, *463*
Simpson, Grant, 144
Sinbad (Romberg-DeSylva), 54, 113, 167, *433*, *466*
"Sing for Your Supper" (Rodgers), 159
"Sing Me a Song with Social Significance" (Rome), 243

Sing Out the News (Rome), 244, *489*
"Sing to Me, Guitar" (Porter), 196
Singing Girl, The (Herbert), 12, *413*
"Sir Galahad" (Kern), 70
"Sirens' Song, The" (Kern), 70
Sitting Pretty (Kern), 445
Slaughter on Tenth Avenue (Rodgers), 154
Slezak, Walter, 81, 155, 156, 247
Sloane, A. Baldwin, 14, 22
Smallens, Alexander, 125
"Smile and Show Your Dimple" (Berlin), 99
Smiles (Youmans), 153, *460*
Smiling the Boy Fell Dead (Baker), *512*
Smith, Betty, 216
Smith, Harry B., 11, 12, 20, 67, 90
Smith, Kate, 91, 173
Smith, Oliver, 161, 282, 283, 290, 291, 294, 295, 300, 301, 302, 304, 318, 346, 379, 393
Smith, Paul Gerard, 118
Smith, Queenie, 114
Smith, Robert B., 20, 21
"Smoke Gets in Your Eyes" (Kern), 82
Snyder, Ted, 88, 89
"So Am I" (Gershwin), 116
"So Do I" (Youmans), 139
"So Far" (Rodgers), 274
"So in Love" (Porter), 197, 200
"Soft Lights and Sweet Music" (Berlin), 97
"Softly, as in a Morning Sunrise" (Romberg), 59
"Soliloquy" (Rodgers), 5, 273
"Some Day" (Friml), 45
"Some Enchanted Evening" (Rodgers), 275, 277
"Some People" (Styne), 320, 325
"Some Sort of Somebody" (Kern), 69
"Somebody Loves Me" (Gershwin), 168
"Somehow I Never Could Believe" (Weill), 259
"Someone to Watch Over Me" (Gershwin), 118
Something for the Boys (Porter), 193, 196, *474*
"Something Seems Tingle-ingleing" (Friml), 40
"Something Sort of Grandish" (Lane), 236

"Something to Remember You By" (Schwartz), 208
"Something Wonderful" (Rodgers), 279
Sometime (Friml), 40, 41, 269, *424*
"Sometimes I'm Happy" (Youmans), 137
Sondheim, Stephen, 287, 294, 318–320, 354–359, *510*
"Song Is You, The" (Kern), 81
"Song of Love" (Romberg), 54
Song of the Flame (Gershwin), 41, *455*
"Song of the Vagabonds" (Friml), 45
"Song of the Woodman" (Arlen), 223
"Soon" (Gershwin), 121
Sothern, Ann, 152, 153
Soudekine, Sergei, 125, 126
Sound of Music, The (Rodgers), 281–284, *496*
"Sound of Music, The" (Rodgers), 283
Sousa, John Philip, 22
"South America, Take It Away" (Rome), 245
South Pacific (Rodgers), 3, 79, 275–277, 306, 359, *495*
"South Sea Isles" (Gershwin), 113
Sovey, Raymond, 155
"Speak Low" (Weill), 257
Spearman, Rawn, 232
Spencer, Kenneth, 79
Spewack, San & Bella, 192, 197
"Spic and Spanish" (Rodgers), 160
Spring Is Here (Rodgers), 151, *462*
"Spring Is Here" (Rodgers), 157
Spring Maid, The (Reinhardt), 20, 63
Springtime of Youth (Romberg), *435*
"Stairway to Paradise" (Gershwin), 113
Stallings, Laurence, 137, 211
"Standing on the Corner" (Loesser), 334
"Star Light, Star Bright" (Herbert), 11
Stark, Ray, 323
Stars in Your Eyes (Schwartz), 211, 213, 214, *478*
"Staying Young" (Merrill), 353
"Steam Heat" (Adler), 342
Steel, John, 93, 94
Stepping Stones (Kern), *445*

Stept, Sam, 177
"Stereophonic Sound" (Porter), 200
Stewart, Michael, 353, 371, 392
Stillman, Albert, 211
Stone, Dorothy, 299
Stone, Fred, 18, 26
Stop! Look! Listen! (Berlin), 90, *448*
"Stormy Weather" (Arlen), 228
Stoska, Polyna, 258, 259
Stothart, Herbert, 133, 270
"Southearted Men" (Romberg), 59
Strasberg, Lee, 146, 253
Street Scene (Weill), 3, 257–259, *493*
Streets of New York, The (Chodosh), 409
Streisand, Barbra, 249, 312, 322–325
Strike Me Pink (Henderson), 177, *469*
Strike Up the Band (Gershwin), 2, 117, 119–122, *456*
Strouse, Charles, 370–375, *513*
Student Prince in Heidelberg (Romberg), 56, *436*
Styne, Jule, 3, 161, 201, 310–327, 356, 362, *503*
Subways Are for Sleeping (Styne), 321–322, *505*
"Sue Me" (Loesser), 333
Sullivan, Brian, 259
Sullivan, Jo, 334
"Summer Is" (Bock), 61, 362
"Summertime" (Gershwin), 5
"Summertime Love" (Loesser), 336
"Sunday" (Styne), 313
"Sunday in Cicero Falls" (Arlen), 230
"Sunday in the Park" (Rome), 243
Sunny (Kern), 41, 45, 74–76, *445*
"Sunny" (Kern), 76
Sunny River (Romberg), *439*
"Sunrise, Sunset" (Bock), 368
"Sunshine Girl, The" (Merrill), 352
"Supper Time" (Berlin), 98
"Surrey with the Fringe on Top, The" (Rodgers), 268
Suzi (Renyi), *428*
Suzuki, Pat, 281, 282
"Swanee" (Gershwin), 113
Sweet Adeline (Kern), 79, *447*
"Sweet and Low Down" (Gershwin), 117

Sweet Charity (Coleman), 4, 388–390, *515*
Sweet Little Devil (Gershwin), *454*
"Sweet Peter" (Rodgers), 148
Sweetheart Time (Donaldson), 85
Sweethearts (Herbert), 20–21, *417*
"Sweethearts" (Herbert), 20–21
Swenson, Swen, 386, 388
Swift, Kay, 206
"Swing!" (Bernstein), 292
"Swiss Miss" (Gershwin), 115
"Sympathy" (Friml), 39
Syrjala, S., 243

Take a Chance (Youmans-Whiting), 138–139, 176, *460, 469*
"Take Back Your Mink" (Loesser), 333
"Take Him" (Rodgers), 161
Take Me Along (Merrill), 352, *510*
"Takin' a Chance on Love" (Duke), 226
"Taking My Time" (Styne), 322
Talk of New York, The (Cohan), 30, *421*
"Talking to You" (Martin), 409
Taylor, Samuel, 286
Tamara, 82, 192
Tamiris, Helen, 60
Tarver, Ben, 410
Tattooed Man, The (Herbert), 12, *415*
"Tattooed Man, The" (Herbert), 12
Taubman, Howard, 236, 287, 338, 354, 359, 392, 393
"Tea for Two" (Youmans), 134
"Tee-Oodle-Um-Bum-Bo" (Gershwin), 113
"Telephone Hour, The" (Strouse), 371, 372
"Tell Her in the Springtime" (Berlin), 95
Tell Me More! (Gershwin), 114, 117, *455*
Templeton, Fay, 28–30, 82
"Ten Cents a Dance" (Rodgers), 151
Tenderloin (Bock), 363–364, *512*
Ter Arutunian, Rouben, 351
Terris, Norma, 76, 78, 298
"Thank Your Father" (Henderson), 175

"That Certain Feeling" (Gershwin), 117
"That Great Come-and-Get-It Day" (Lane), 236
"That Old Gang of Mine" (Henderson), 169
"That Terrific Rainbow" (Rodgers), 161
"That Was Yesterday" (Herman), 392
"That's Him" (Weill), 257, 258
"That's Why Darkies Were Born" (Henderson), 177
Theatre Guild, 124, 146, 147, 163, 241, 265, 271, 273, 274
"Then I'll Have Time for You" (Henderson), 175
"There Ain't No Flies on Me" (Merrill), 352
"There Is Nothin' Like a Dame" (Rodgers), 276, 277
"There Once Was a Man" (Adler), 342
"There's Gotta Be Something Better than This" (Coleman), 389
"There's More to the Kiss than the XXX" (Gershwin), 111
"There's No Business Like Show Business" (Berlin), 101, 103
"There's No Tune Like a Show Tune" (Herman), 396
"These Charming People" (Gershwin), 117
"They Always Follow Me Around" (Berlin), 90
"They Call It Dancing" (Berlin), 93
"They Call the Wind Maria" (Loewe), 301
"They Couldn't Compare to You" (Porter), 199
"They Didn't Believe Me" (Kern), 52, 67
"They Like Ike" (Berlin), 105
"They Love Me" (Berlin), 105
"They Say It's Wonderful" (Berlin), 101, 102
"Thine Alone" (Herbert), 21
"Thirteen Collar" (Kern), 69
"This Can't Be Love" (Rodgers), 159
This Is the Army (Berlin), 99, 100, 451
"This Is the Missus" (Henderson), 176, 177
"This Nearly Was Mine" (Rodgers), 277
Thompson, Fred, 118
Thompson, Thomas, 358

Thompson, Woodman, 57
Thomson, Virgil, 127
"Those Were the Good Old Days" (Adler), 342
"Thou Swell" (Rodgers), 150
Three Cheers (Henderson), 468
Three Musketeers, The (Friml), 37, 46, 426
"Three Musketeers, The" (Rodgers), 147
Three Twins (Hoschna), 41, 427
Threepenny Opera, The (Weill), 251, 261, 262, 491, 493
Three's a Crowd (Schwartz), 207–208, 235, 477
"Thrill Is Gone, The" (Henderson), 177
Throckmorton, Cleon, 139
Through the Years (Youmans), 138, 460
"Through the Years" (Youmans), 138
Tickle Me (Stothart), 133, 270, 497
Tierney, Harry, 22, 78, 133, 166
"Till Good Luck Comes My Way" (Kern), 78
"Till the Clouds Roll By" (Kern), 70
"Time on My Hands" (Youmans), 138
Tinney, Frank, 54, 133, 270
"Tin Pan Alley" (Coleman), 385
Tip-Toes (Gershwin), 114, 116, 117, 455
" 'Tis the End, So Farewell" (Friml), 40
"To Keep My Love Alive" (Rodgers), 150
"To Know You Is to Love You" (Henderson), 175
"To Life" (Bock), 367
"To the Inn We're Marching" (Romberg), 56
Tobias, Charles, 177
Tobin, Genevieve, 185
Todd, Michael, 60, 196
"Tom, Dick and Harry" (Porter), 199
"Too Bad" (Porter), 200
"Too Close for Comfort" (Bock), 362
"Too Darn Hot" (Porter), 197
"Too Good to Be True" (Henderson), 175
Too Many Girls (Rodgers), 159, 160, 464

"Too Many Rings Around Rosie" (Youmans), 134
Toot-Sweet (Whiting), 73
Toot-Toot! (Kern), 444
"Toot Toot, Tootsie" (Erdman), 55
Torrence, David, 41
"Totem Tom-Tom" (Friml), 43
Tovarich (Pockriss), 407
"Tradition" (Bock), 367
"Tramp, Tramp, Tramp" (Herbert), 20
Traubel, Helen, 280
Treacher, Arthur, 179
Treasure Girl (Gershwin), 114, 115, 118, 456
Tree Grows in Brooklyn, A (Schwartz), 215–216, 217, 479
Trentini, Emma, 12, 19, 38, 39
Trip to Chinatown, A (Hoyt), 2
"Trouble" (Willson), 345, 347
Truex, Ernest, 69
"Try to Forget" (Kern), 81
"Tschaikowsky" (Weill), 257
Tucker, Sophie, 192
Tumble In (Friml), 41, 269
Tun Tun, 233
"Twinkle in Your Eye, A" (Rodgers), 157
"Two Little Babes in the Wood" (Porter), 182
"Two Little Bluebirds" (Kern), 76
Two Little Girls in Blue (Youmans), 129, 130, 131, 458
Two on the Aisle (Styne), 312, 315, 503
Two's Company (Duke), 226, 484
Tynan, Kenneth, 281, 372
"Typical Self-Made Man, A" (Gershwin), 121

Uggams, Leslie, 312, 326
Umeki, Miyoshi, 281
"Unofficial Spokesman, The" (Gershwin), 121
Unsinkable Molly Brown, The (Willson), 346–347, 509
Up and Down Broadway, 89
Up in Central Park (Romberg), 37, 60, 439
Urban, Joseph, 46, 74, 76, 77, 81, 176
"Usher from the Mezzanine, The" (Styne), 326

Vagabond King, The (Friml), 45, 426
Valando, Tommy, 362

Valenti, Michael, 411

Vallee, Rudy, 176, 177, 337, 338

Van & Schenck, 91

Vance, Vivian, 190, 195, 196

Vanderbilt Revue, The (Mc-Hugh), *480*

VanDyke, Marcia, 217

"Varsity Drag" (Henderson), 174

Velez, Lupe, 177

Velvet Lady, The (Herbert), *418*

"Venus, My Shining Love" (Cohan), 27

Venuta, Benay, 162

Verdon, Gwen, 200, 342, 351, 352, 388–389

Very Good Eddie (Kern), 64, 68–69, *442*

Very Warm for May (Kern), 83, *448*

Viceroy, The (Herbert), 12, *414*

Virginia (Schwartz), 211, *478*

Voelpel, Fred, 286

Voice of McConnell, The (Cohan), *422*

VonTilzer, Albert, 168

VonTilzer, Harry, 87, 111

Vreeland, Frank, 148

Vye, Murvyn, 273

Wake Up and Dream! (Porter), 186, *471*

Walburn, Raymond, 358

Walk a Little Faster (Duke), 222, *482*

Walker, Don, 61, 335, 342

Walker, Nancy, 291, 292, 321, 322

"Walking Away Whistling" (Loesser), 335

Wallace, George, 280

Wallop, Douglass, 342

Walsh, Mary Jane, 159, 195, 196

Walston, Ray, 342

Walters, Charles, 189, 194, 195

Walton, Tony, 357, 358, 369, 373

"Waltz Huguette" (Friml), 45

"Waltz Was Born in Vienna, A" (Loewe), 298

"Wand'rin' Star" (Loewe), 301

"Wanting You" (Romberg), 59

"War Is War" (Rodgers), 148

Waring, Fred, 186

Wasserman, Dale, 398–400

Watch Your Step (Berlin), 86, 90, 91, *448*

Waters, Ethel, 97–98, 210, 225

Watson, Susan, 372

Watt, Douglas, 129

Watts, Richard, Jr., 57, 126, 158, 192, 225, 233, 284, 352, 359, 378, 393, 401

Wayburn, Ned, 132

Wayne, David, 236, 317, 318

"We Open in Venice" (Porter), 198, 199

Weatherly, Tom, 206, 207

Webb, Clifton, 76, 97, 99, 114, 150, 183, 206–209

Weede, Robert, 334, 392

Weidman, Jerome, 249, 363

Weill, Kurt, 148, 161, 250–263, 326, *491*

Weiss, George, 362

"Well, Did You Evah?" (Porter), 195

"We'll Go Away Together" (Weill), 259

Welles, Orson, 197

"We're Home" (Merrill), 353

"Were Thine that Special Face" (Porter), 198

Werrenrath, Reinald, 81

West, Mae, 41

West Side Story (Bernstein), 4, 5, 7, 293–295, 356, *500*

Westcott, Marcy, 159

"What a Waste" (Bernstein), 292

"What Chance Have I?" (Berlin), 99

"What Do the Simple Folk Do?" (Loewe), 308

"What D'Ya Say?" (Henderson), 171

"What Happened Nobody Knows" (Rodgers), 145

"What Is This Thing Called Love?" (Porter), 182, 186

What Makes Sammy Run? (Drake), 409

"Whatever Lola Wants" (Adler), 342

"What'll I Do?" (Berlin), 86, 94

What's Up (Loewe), 299, 300, *501*

Wheaton, Anna, 70

"When a Fellow's on the Level with a Girl that's on the Square" (Cohan), 30

"When a Maid Comes Knocking at Your Heart" (Friml), 39

"When I Had a Uniform On" (Porter), 184

"When I Lost You" (Berlin), 90

"When I'm Not Near the Girl I Love" (Lane), 236

When Sweet Sixteen (Herbert), *416*

"When the Idle Poor Become the Idle Rich" (Lane), 236

"When the Kids Get Married" (Schmidt), 380

"When We Are M-A-Double R-I-E-D" (Cohan), 30

"When We Get Our Divorce" (Kern), 76

"When You Come Back" (Cohan), 34

"When You Want 'Em, You Can't Have 'Em" (Gershwin) 111

"When You're Away" (Herbert), 21

"When You're Pretty and the World Is Fair" (Herbert), 18

"Where Am I Going?" (Coleman), 389

"Where Have You Been?" (Porter), 186

"Where Is the Life that Late I Led?" (Porter), 198

"Where, Oh Where?" (Porter), 199

"Where or When" (Rodgers), 155

Where's Charley? (Loesser), 3, 331–332, *506*

"Where's the Boy?" (Gershwin), 118

"Where's the Mate for Me?" (Kern), 78

"Which?" (Porter), 186

"Whip-poor-will" (Kern), 75

Whirl of the World, The (Romberg), 50, 51, *430*

White Eagle, The (Friml), *426*

White, George, 113, 168–171

White, Miles, 161, 179, 229, 230, 232, 266, 267, 272, 273, 313, 346, 372

White, Sammy, 78, 148

Whiting, Jack, 139, 152, 174, 316

Whiting, Richard A., 73, 138

"Who?" (Kern), 76

"Who Am I that You Should Care for Me?" (Youmans), 137

"Who Can? You Can!" (Schwartz), 217

"Whoop-Ti-Ay" (Loewe), 302

Whoopee (Donaldson), 85

"Who's Got the Pain?" (Adler), 342

"Who's Who With You?" (Youmans), 132

"Why Can't the English?" (Loewe), 306

"Why Can't You Behave?" (Porter), 197

"Why Did Nellie Leave Her Home?" (Cohan), 27

"Why Do I Love You" (Kern), 78

"Why Shouldn't I?" (Porter), 189

"Why Shouldn't We?" (Stothart), 43

"Why Try to Change Me Now?" (Coleman), 385

"Why Was I Born?" (Kern), 79

Wild Rose, The (Friml), 426

Wildcat (Coleman), 386, 515

Wildflower (Youmans), 41, 130, 132–133, 458

"Will You Remember?" (Romberg), 53

Williams, Bert, 92

Williams, Frances, 169, 171

Williams, Herb, 210

Williams, Hope, 177, 186

Williams, Jack, 195, 196

"Willkommen" (Kander), 402–403

Willson, Meredith, 329, 330, 343–347, 509

Wilner, Max, 54

Wilson, Dooley, 225

Wilson, Francis, 26

Wilson, Sandy, 304

Wiman, Dwight Deere, 154, 158, 162, 206, 207, 214, 298

Winchell, Walter, 126, 174

Winninger, Charles, 54, 76, 77, 78, 133, 134

"Wintergreen for President" (Gershwin), 123

Winters, Lawrence, 244

Wish You Were Here (Rome), 3, 245, 246, 490

"Witchcraft" (Coleman), 385

"Witches Brew" (Styne), 327

"With a Little Bit of Luck" (Loewe), 305, 307

"With a Song in My Heart" (Rodgers), 151

"Without a Song" (Youmans), 138

"Without Love" (Henderson), 175

"Without Love" (Porter), 200

"Without You" (Loewe), 306

Wittop, Freddy, 34, 379, 393

Wizard of Oz, The (Sloane), 14, 18

Wizard of the Nile, The (Herbert), 11, 413

Wodehouse, P. G., 2, 69–73, 75, 115, 117, 187–188

Wolsky, Albert, 411

"Woman's Prerogative, A" (Arlen), 230

"Wonderful Guy, A" (Rodgers), 276

Wonderful Town (Bernstein), 292–293, 316, 500

Wonderland (Herbert), 415

Wood, Peggy, 33, 53

Woodward, Edward, 409

Woollcott, Alexander, 46, 75, 81, 89, 93

Woolley, Monty, 185, 186

World of Pleasure, A (Romberg), 431

"Wouldn't It Be Loverly?" (Loewe), 306

"Wunderbar" (Porter), 199

Wyler, Gretchen, 200

Wynn, Ed, 40, 41, 54, 151, 152, 171, 228–229

"Yale Bulldog Song" (Porter), 182

"Yankee Doodle Boy, The" (Cohan), 26, 28, 34

Yankee Prince, The (Cohan), 33, 421

Yankee Princess, The (Kalman), 466

"Yatata Yatata Yatata" (Rodgers), 274

Yellen, Jack, 177, 179

"Yes, My Heart" (Merrill), 353

Yes, Yes, Yvette (Charig), 134

Yip, Yip, Yaphank (Berlin), 90, 449

Yokel Boy (Stept), 177, 470

"You and I" (Willson), 344

"You and the Night and the Music" (Schwartz), 210

"You Are Beautiful" (Rodgers), 281

"You Are Love" (Kern), 78

"You Can Dance with Any Girl at All" (Youmans), 134

"You Cannot Make Your Shimmy Shake on Tea" (Berlin), 92

"You Can't Brush Me Off" (Berlin), 99

"You Can't Fool Your Dreams" (Rodgers), 144

"You Can't Get a Man with a Gun" (Berlin), 101, 102

"You Do Something to Me" (Porter), 185

"You Fascinate Me So" (Coleman), 385

"You Gotta Have a Gimmick" (Styne), 321

"You Have Cast Your Shadow on the Sea" (Rodgers), 159

"You Irritate Me So" (Porter), 196

"You Mustn't Be Discouraged" (Styne), 326

You Never Know (Porter), 192, 473

You Said It (Arlen), 484

"You Took Advantage of Me" (Rodgers), 151

"You Wouldn't Fool Me, Would You?" (Henderson), 175

"You'd Be Surprised" (Berlin), 92

"You'll Never Walk Alone" (Rodgers), 273

Youmans, Vincent, 2, 41, 59, 110, 128–139, 228, 311, 458

"Young at Heart" (Richards), 385

Young, John, 14, 15, 31

Young, Rida Johnson, 53, 66

Young, Stark, 79, 126

"Younger than Springtime" (Rodgers), 277

"You-oo, Just You" (Gershwin), 111

Your Own Thing (Apolinar), 410–411

You're a Good Man, Charlie Brown (Gesner), 410

"You're a Queer One, Julie Jordan" (Rodgers), 272

"You're Driving Me Crazy" (Donaldson), 138

"You're Here and I'm Here" (Kern), 64

You're in Love (Friml), 39, 40, 269, 424

"You're Just in Love" (Berlin), 105

"You're Lonely and I'm Lonely" (Berlin), 99

"You're Not Pretty but You're Mine" (Lane), 220

"You're the Cream in My Coffee" (Henderson), 175

"You're the Fairest Flower" (Besoyan), 408

"You're the Top" (Porter), 188, 199

"You've Got that Thing" (Porter), 185

"You've Got to Be Carefully Taught" (Rodgers), 277

Ziegfeld, Florenz, 4, 46, 56, 58, 74, 77, 78, 95, 138, 151, 178, 214
Ziegfeld Follies (1907), 4
Ziegfeld Follies (1911) (Berlin), *448*
Ziegfeld Follies (1916) (Kern), *442*
Ziegfeld Follies (1919) (Berlin), 91–92, *449*
Ziegfeld Follies (1920) (Berlin), *449*
Ziegfeld Follies (1921) (Herbert-Friml), *419, 425*
Ziegfeld Follies (1923) (Herbert), *419*
Ziegfeld Follies (1927) (Berlin), 95, *451*
Ziegfeld Follies (1934) (Duke), 223, *482*
Ziegfeld Follies (1936) (Duke), 154, 223, *482*
Ziegfeld Follies (1943) (Henderson), 179, *470*
Ziegfeld's Midnight Frolic (McHugh), 214
"Zip" (Rodgers), 161
Zipprodt, Patricia, 368, 402
Zorina, Vera, 99, 155–157, 178
Zulu and the Zayda, The (Rome), *491*